Gender History Across Epistemologies

T0326904

Gender and History Special Issue Book Series

Gender and History, an international, interdisciplinary journal on the history of femininity, masculinity, and gender relations, publishes annual special issues which are now available in book form.

Bringing together path-breaking feminist scholarship with assessments of the field, each volume focuses on a specific subject, question or theme. These books are suitable for undergraduate and postgraduate courses in history, sociology, politics, cultural studies, and gender and women's studies.

Titles in the series include:

Gender History Across Epistemologies
Edited by Donna R. Gabaccia and Mary Jo Maynes

Gender and the City before Modernity
Edited by Lin Foxhall and Gabriele Neher

Historicising Gender and Sexuality
Edited by Kevin P. Murphy and Jennifer M. Spear

Homes and Homecomings: Gendered Histories of Domesticity and Return
Edited by K. H. Adler and Carrie Hamilton

Gender and Change: Agency, Chronology and Periodisation
Edited by Alexandra Shepard and Garthine Walker

Translating Feminisms in China
Edited by Dorothy Ko and Wang Zheng

Visual Genders, Visual Histories: A special Issue of Gender & History
Edited by Patricia Hayes

Violence, Vulnerability and Embodiment: Gender and History
Edited by Shani D'Cruze and Anupama Rao

Dialogues of Dispersal: Gender, Sexuality and African Diasporas
Edited by Sandra Gunning, Tera Hunter and Michele Mitchell

Material Strategies: Dress and Gender in Historial Perspective
Edited by Barbara Burman and Carole Turbin

Gender, Citizenships and Subjectivities
Edited by Kathleen Canning and Sonya Rose

Gendering the Middle Ages: A Gender and History Special Issue
Edited by Pauline Stafford and Anneke B. Mulder-Bakker

Gender and History: Retrospect and Prospect
Edited by Leonore Davidoff, Keith McClelland and Eleni Varikas

Feminisms and Internationalism
Edited by Mrinalini Sinha, Donna Guy and Angela Woollacott

Gender and the Body in the Ancient Mediterranean
Edited by Maria Wyke

Gendered Colonialisms in African History
Edited by Nancy Rose Hunt, Tessie P. Liu and Jean Quataert

Gender History Across Epistemologies

EDITED BY

DONNA R. GABACCIA
AND
MARY JO MAYNES

A John Wiley & Sons, Ltd., Publication

This edition first published 2013

Originally published as Volume 24, Issue 3 of *Gender & History*

Blackwell Publishing was acquired by John Wiley & Sons in February 2007. Blackwell's publishing program has been merged with Wiley's global Scientific, Technical, and Medical business to form Wiley-Blackwell.

Registered Office

John Wiley & Sons Ltd, The Atrium, Southern Gate, Chichester, West Sussex, PO19 8SQ, United Kingdom

Editorial Offices

350 Main Street, Malden, MA 02148-5020, USA

9600 Garsington Road, Oxford, OX4 2DQ, UK

The Atrium, Southern Gate, Chichester, West Sussex, PO19 8SQ, UK

For details of our global editorial offices, for customer services, and for information about how to apply for permission to reuse the copyright material in this book please see our website at www.wiley.com/wiley-blackwell.

Library of Congress Cataloging-in-Publication Data

Gender history across epistemologies / edited by Donna R. Gabaccia and Mary Jo Maynes.
   pages cm
  "Originally published as Volume 24, Issue 3 of Gender & History."
  Includes bibliographical references and index.
  ISBN 978-1-118-50824-4 (pbk.)
 1. Sex role–History.   2. Gender identity–History.   3. Women–Identity–History.   4. Women–History.   I. Gabaccia, Donna R., 1949–   II. Maynes, Mary Jo.   III. Gender & history
  HQ1075.G4632 2013
  305.309–dc23

                                                                        2012048065

A catalogue record for this book is available from the British Library.

Cover image: Postcard (At the Golden Gate) 2009

Cover design by: Nicki Averill Design

Set in 11/12.5pt Times by Aptara Inc., New Delhi, India

Printed in Malaysia by Ho Printing (M) Sdn Bhd

1   2013

CONTENTS

Notes on Contributors   vii

Introduction: Gender History Across Epistemologies   1
DONNA R. GABACCIA AND MARY JO MAYNES

1 Master Narratives and the Wall Painting of the House of the Vettii, Pompeii   20
   BETH SEVERY-HOVEN

2 'More Beautiful than Words & Pencil Can Express': Barbara Bodichon's
   Artistic Career at the Interface of her Epistolary and Visual Self Projections   61
   MERITXELL SIMON-MARTIN

3 Public Motherhood in West Africa as Theory and Practice   80
   LORELLE SEMLEY

4 Profiling the Female Emigrant: A Method of Linguistic Inquiry for
   Examining Correspondence Collections   97
   EMMA MORETON

5 Beyond Constructivism?: Gender, Medicine and the Early History of Sperm
   Analysis, Germany 1870–1900   127
   CHRISTINA BENNINGHAUS

6 'I Just Express My Views & Leave Them to Work': Olive Schreiner as a
   Feminist Protagonist in a Masculine Political Landscape with Figures   157
   LIZ STANLEY AND HELEN DAMPIER

7 Gender without Groups: Confession, Resistance and Selfhood in the
   Colonial Archive   181
   CHRISTOPHER J. LEE

8 The Power of Renewable Resources: *Orlando*'s Tactical Engagement with the
   Law of Intestacy   198
   JAMIE L. McDANIEL

9 The Politics of Gender Concepts in Genetics and Hormone Research in
   Germany, 1900–1940   215
   HELGA SATZINGER

10 The Language of Gender in Lovers' Correspondence, 1946–1949   235
   SONIA CANCIAN

11 Gender-Bending in El Teatro Campesino (1968–1980): A *Mestiza*
   Epistemology of Performance   246
   MEREDITH HELLER

12 Changing Paradigms in Migration Studies: From Men to Women to Gender   262
   NANCY L. GREEN

13 Reconsidering Categories of Analysis: Possibilities for Feminist Studies
   of Conflict   279
   SHIRIN SAEIDI

14 An Epistemology of Collusion: *Hijras*, *Kothis* and the Historical
   (Dis)continuity of Gender/Sexual Identities in Eastern India   305
   ANIRUDDHA DUTTA

Index   331

NOTES ON CONTRIBUTORS

Christina Benninghaus is an Affiliated Research Scholar at the Department of History and Philosophy of Science at Cambridge University, where she conducts research on the history of infertility. Since receiving her PhD from the European University Institute in Florence in 1994, she has taught German and European history at Halle, Bielefeld and Bochum. Her areas of specialisation include gender history and the history of youth. A social and cultural historian by training, she has become increasingly interested in the history of science and medicine.

Sonia Cancian is lead scholar of the Digitising Immigrant Letters project at the University of Minnesota's Immigration History Research Center. In Montreal, she is affiliated with Concordia University's History Department and the Simone de Beauvoir Institute. Dr Cancian is the author of *Families, Lovers, and their Letters: Italian Postwar Migration to Canada* (Winnipeg: University of Manitoba Press, 2010). She is currently editing a collection of love letters written by migrants and non-migrants to be published by McGill-Queen's University Press.

Helen Dampier studied at Rhodes University in South Africa and obtained her doctorate from the University of Newcastle, UK. Her research interests focus on life writing and also historiography and its claims, and she is currently a Senior Lecturer in History at the School of Cultural Studies, Leeds Metropolitan University.

Aniruddha Dutta is a PhD candidate in Feminist Studies and Development Studies at the University of Minnesota, with research interests in globalisation, social movements and media studies. Dutta's dissertation, 'Globalizing through the Vernacular: The Making of Indian Sexual Minorities within Gender/Sexual Transnationalism', studies gender/sexual identity and rights-based politics at the interface of subaltern queer subcultures and the transnational development industry.

Donna R. Gabaccia is Professor of History at the University of Minnesota. She is author of many books and articles on immigrant life in the US, on gender, class and labour (*Foreign Relations: Global Perspectives on U.S. Immigration*, Princeton: Princeton University Press 2012), on food studies (*We Are what Eat: Ethnic Food and the Making of Americans*, Cambridge: Harvard University Press, 1998) and on Italian migration around the world (*Italy's Many Diasporas*, Seattle: University of Washington Press, 2000). Gabaccia also teaches and publishes about migration in world history, has longstanding interests in interdisciplinary methodologies and served as president of the Social Science History Association in 2008. Her ongoing research includes an interdisciplinary collaboration that seeks to explain the so-called 'feminisation' of international migration and an individual research project that asks why the United States, almost alone among the many countries formed through international migration, labels itself proudly as a nation of immigrants.

Nancy L. Green is Professor (*directrice d'études*) of History at the École des Hautes Études en Sciences Sociales (Paris) and a specialist of migration history, comparative methods and French and American social history. Her most recent book (edited with Marie Poinsot) was *Histoire de l'immigration et question coloniale en France* (Paris: Documentation franchiaise, 2008).

Meredith Heller is a doctoral candidate in theatre and feminist studies at the University of California, Santa Barbara. Her dissertation focuses on the signification of gender, sex and identity in US gender-bending stage acts. Her research interests are feminist performance, gender and body theory, queer, transgender and sexuality studies and drag.

Christopher J. Lee is an Assistant Professor of History at the University of North Carolina at Chapel Hill. He is the editor of *Making a World After Empire: The Bandung Moment and Its Political Afterlives* (Athens: Ohio University Press, 2010). He is currently completing a book on British-ruled Central Africa that is under contract with Duke University Press.

Mary Jo Maynes is a Professor in the Department of History at the University of Minnesota. She is a historian of modern Europe with interests in comparative and world history. Her specialities include: European social and cultural history, history of the family, history of women and gender and personal narratives as historical sources. Her recent books include: *The Family: A World History* (Oxford: Oxford University Press, 2012), *Telling Stories: The Use of Personal Narratives in the Social Sciences and History* (Ithaca: Cornell University Press, 2008) and *Secret Gardens, Satanic Mills: Placing Girls in European History* (Bloomington: Indiana University Press, 2004).

Jamie L. McDaniel is Assistant Professor of English at Pittsburg State University in Kansas. His research focuses on cultural constructions of gender normativity and propriety in legal, economic, political, cinematic and literary discourses. He has an article on property and economic recognition in Jean Rhys's novels forthcoming in the *Journal of Liberal Arts and Sciences*, as well as an examination of the connections among disability, trauma and gendered deviance in Italian horror films forthcoming in *Culture, Medicine, and Psychiatry*. He is currently preparing a biography of the contemporary British writer, Penelope Fitzgerald.

Emma Moreton is a Senior Lecturer in the Department of English and Languages at Coventry University, where she teaches undergraduate and postgraduate modules in literary stylistics and corpus linguistics. She is currently in the fourth year of a PhD at the University of Birmingham. Her research interests include Text Encoding Initiative (TEI) markup as a means of digitally representing historical documents and using corpus methods to investigate immigrant letter collections.

Shirin Saeidi's research concentrates on gender, conflict and the state in the Middle East. Her doctoral thesis, entitled 'Hero of Her Own Story: Gender and State Formation in Contemporary Iran', was recently defended at the University of Cambridge. Saeidi's 2010 article ' Creating the Islamic Republic of Iran: Wives and Daughters of Martyrs, and Acts of Citizenship', *Citizenship Studies* 14 (2010) was selected as the editor's choice article of the edition. She is currently conducting archival and ethnographic research on the experiences of Afghan refugees in Iran.

Dr Helga Satzinger is a biologist, historian of science and Reader in the Department of History at University College London (UCL). She was previously an Assistant Professor at the Centre for Interdisciplinary Women and Gender Studies (ZIFG) at Technical University Berlin (1997–2004) and a reader at the Wellcome Trust Centre for the History of Medicine at UCL (2005–2011).

Lorelle Semley is the author of *Mother Is Gold, Father Is Glass: Gender and Colonialism in a Yoruba Town* (Bloomington: Indiana University Press, 2011). She is Assistant Professor of History at the College of the Holy Cross where she teaches African, African diaspora and gender history. Her current book examines black citizenship during the French colonial empire.

Beth Severy-Hoven received her PhD in Ancient History and Mediterranean Archaeology from Berkeley, CA, and teaches Classics at Macalester College. Following her 2003 book, *Augustus and the Family at the Birth of the Roman Empire* (New York and London: Routledge, 2003), she has begun to focus her research on slavery and Petronius' *Satyrica*.

Meritxell Simon-Martin is a PhD candidate at the Centre for the History of Women's Education, University of Winchester. She is the author of 'Letter Exchange in the Life of Barbara Leigh Smith Bodichon: the First Female Suffrage Campaign in Britain Seen through her Correspondence' in Claudette Fillard and Françoise Orazi (eds), *Exchanges and Correspondence: The Construction of Feminism* (Newcastle: Cambridge Scholars Publishing, 2010).

Liz Stanley is Chair of Sociology at the University of Edinburgh, Director of the University's Centre for Narrative and Auto/Biographical Research (NABS) and Principal Investigator of the Olive Schreiner Letters Project (www.oliveschreinerletters. ed.ac.uk and www.oliveschreiner.org). Recent research has focused on aspects of memory-making, with her most recent book *Mourning Becomes... Post/Memory and Commemoration of the South African War* published in the UK and USA by Manchester University Press and in South African by Wits University Press. A feminist theorist who engages with lots of practical action, her work more generally has theorised the auto/biographical genre and been concerned with operationalising a feminist epistemology.

Introduction: Gender History Across Epistemologies

Donna R. Gabaccia and Mary Jo Maynes

The cover image, *Postcard (At the Golden Gate) 2009*, is Ruth Claxton's re-working of a Victorian oil painting by Valentine Cameron Prinsep. Prinsep's original evokes orientalist fantasies of the languorous, passive and submissive woman of the East and embodies the masculine gaze so pervasive in western art. Claxton's pointed slashing gives the formerly passive subject a gaze of her own, and a sharp one at that. She still looks downward, but the passivity suggested by her stance is contested by the potential for her instantly to turn her gaze toward the viewer; with beams emanating from her eyes, she has become the gazer, the seer. At the same time, Claxton's alteration draws critical attention to the embodied stereotype of the eastern female. It leads us to notice the performance of gender: underneath the lush exterior, the hyper-feminine draperies and bracelets, who is actually there? Viewed this way, the image provokes epistemological insights even as it re-represents gender stereotypes. The familiar gendered image becomes ambiguous and indeterminate. The once passive object of scrutiny, in becoming the viewer, focuses our attention on the relationship between knowledge and perspective that has long held a central place in feminist epistemology. Thus *Postcard (At the Golden Gate) 2009* provides a perfect point of entry into a special issue of *Gender & History* devoted to the theme of 'Gender History across Epistemologies'.

Epistemological critiques – questions about how we know what we know – are intrinsic to gender history. Indeed, the claim that all knowledges are views from somewhere has been a core insight of modern western feminist theory since its emergence in the 1960s. This claim, in sum, has insisted that the perspective of the knower shapes what he or she looks at, sees and ultimately can know. Questioning the claim to objective truth prevalent in many disciplines, feminists undertook analyses of masculinist biases inherent in theory and practice in many fields of knowledge. Parallel critiques that subsequently emerged within disciplinary fields leapt over their borders and thus contributed to a wider awareness of perspectivity as a key element of feminist epistemology.

Feminist historians, in bringing a gendered perspective into history, in deploying gender as an analytic category and in studying it as an historical construct, have nevertheless proceeded from a variety of epistemological frameworks and used a correspondingly wide range of methods, developed through debate as well as through interdisciplinary borrowing.[1] Among these debates, the most pervasive and epistemologically profound is undoubtedly the one, dating to the mid-1980s, that posited 'gender history' as a non-essentialist alternative to 'women's history'. This debate, which in turn reflected the wider postmodern critique of the practices of social history, continued into the 1990s, when cultural and social historians' research practices and ways of knowing seemed starkly different and when the interdisciplinary alliances of the two groups of historians seemed to diverge particularly sharply.

These disputes began with calls for deconstructing the category of 'woman', based on the assertion that the category 'woman' does not exist pre-discursively – that is, 'woman' is not an objective, trans-historical category rooted in biology, but rather that categories like 'woman' are constructed in and through human culture and especially language.[2] Drawing on and pushing beyond post-structuralist philosophers, historian Joan Scott's enormously influential work initiated an ongoing historiographical interest in gender as a pervasive signifier of power relations; indeed, in the eyes of many subsequent historians of gender, the history of sexual difference came to centre on the cultural processes, especially as manifest in language and systems of representation, whereby meaning is created and power legitimised.[3] Implicit in much of this work was a critique of prior feminist historical scholarship that had instead sought to limn dimensions of female experience and trace women's exercise of historical agency even under changing and diverse conditions of male domination. Cultural historians argued that such histories naturalised rather than challenged sexual difference, especially when sexual difference was in effect reduced to a biological category.

Throughout the 1990s, the shift to discourse analysis was welcomed and practiced in some circles, but also resisted and analysed.[4] Treating gender and sex primarily as cultural constructions inspired many new approaches to historical scholarship; however, many feminist historians continued to insist on the importance of analysing how gender related to a material world they posited as existing independently of language, and others worried about the potential for the turn to gender history to undermine feminist political efforts built around the political identity 'women'. In the eyes of some feminist historians, furthermore, making women's experiences more visible seemed quite compatible with the cultural project of examining '[t]he process whereby . . . difference was constituted'.[5] Perhaps, as Scott later concluded, gender history seemed so exciting in the 1990s precisely because of 'its radical refusal to settle down, to call even a comfortable lodging a "home"'.[6]

This refusal to settle down, we would suggest, still describes the varied epistemological premises of scholars in gender history. However, except when making programmatic statements or engaging directly in debate, historians of gender often leave their epistemological groundings implicit rather than explicit. Ignoring these differences does not make them go away, and the aim of this special issue is to examine how various ways of knowing operate in current historical research on gender and, through specific examples, to draw to the surface lurking questions of epistemological clash, convergence or, perhaps, reconciliation.

Since epistemological disputes have been an ongoing feature of gender history, why do we offer a special issue on 'Gender Histories across Epistemologies' at this particular moment? This special issue reflects our conviction that recent approaches to gender history suggest surprising crossovers and even common grounds that debaters of the 1990s did not imagine. Indeed, most of the authors in this special issue, while referring to earlier controversies, do not feel obliged to position themselves exclusively within them. Most, instead, chip passages through or detour around older impasses. Often they incorporate into their analyses insights seemingly based on multiple ways of knowing, including some – for example quantitative data analysis generally associated with positivist approaches – that were once viewed as incompatible or irreconcilable with the premises of gender history.

This is not to say that differing ways of knowing, differing methods and differing disciplinary instincts have lost their power. For example, some of the cross-epistemological conversations we were looking to encourage did not materialise. In particular, and despite the invitation in this issue's call for papers for work employing quantitative methods, we received only two submissions centring on the use of quantitative data: Nancy Green's discussion of gender in migration history in the United States and France and Emma Moreton's linguistic analysis of a corpus of migrant letters. While these two authors demonstrate how they reconcile gender analysis and quantitative methods, the larger project of bringing empiricist epistemologies into conversation with gender history still appears to be daunting, though not impossible.

Moreover, we saw evidence of the continuing power of disciplinary frames, for example, throughout the complex editorial process that created this special issue. The authors whose work is included come from a wide range of disciplinary or inter-disciplinary locations including, in addition to history: classics, gender/sexuality studies, education, English literature, history of science and medicine, linguistics, sociology and theatre studies. Each submission was sent to outside reviewers, and in the vast majority of cases the topics addressed made it necessary to engage reviewers from at least two different disciplines. As we soon discovered, however, reviewers offered more than usually divergent evaluations of the paper they had been asked to review. A typical outcome was trenchant critique from one reader and enthusiastic encouragement from the other. As editors, we insisted that authors respond to the whole range of comments which, in turn, posed challenges for almost all authors in revising their articles for publication. Although we are pleased with the generosity of the authors in responding so positively to radically different readings and evaluations of their work, we cannot help but observe that powerful scepticism is still likely to be expressed when scholars cross boundaries or attempt to bridge or complement theories, methods or assumptions that still define the disciplines, whether or not the underlying issue is epistemological.

Collectively the essays in this special issue suggest how, and with what consequences, historians of gender are crossing disciplinary, methodological, national, linguistic, historiographical, temporal and generational divides; in doing so they are building on past debates while exploring new opportunities for resolving them. They do this, first, by reminding feminist historians to query gender as a category of analysis, just as much as they do other categories, as Jeanne Boydston advocated in her influential 2008 essay published in this journal.[7] For example, Beth Severy-Hoven, in her analysis of wall art in ancient Pompeii, reminds us not only that we should avoid undue assumptions about what gender means transhistorically, but also to be cautious about the place of gender – vis-á-vis other – dynamics at work in a particular situation. Similarly, Shirin Saeidi's research on nationalism and gender in recent Iranian history has led her to rethink her presumptions and the analytic role of gender: 'gender and sexuality can simultaneously be categories, questions and tools', she argues. This messiness and interdependence marks as 'methodologically impractical any prescription for prioritising or de-prioritising gender as a category'.[8]

They do this, too, by engaging with and historicising earlier debates and moments of gender scholarship, by mobilising their acknowledgment of epistemological difference to understand better the intellectual and political genealogies of gender history and by recognising the dialectical processes that mark the evolution of fields of scholarship, while also questioning what is possible or constructive in terms of cross-epistemological conversations at the current moment of gender history. Readers can thus draw on the collected articles to ponder epistemological questions in a range of ways. Several articles can be usefully read for their explicit focus on knowledge production as a gendered historical process. The related articles by Helga Satzinger and Christina Benninghaus, for example, speak closely to each other on the theme of scientific research on sex, gender and reproduction. Helga Satzinger's article about research on genetics and hormones in Germany in the early twentieth century explores the gendered character of the 'scientific method' at multiple levels: by documenting the gender order that scientists observed at the cellular level; by examining the research lab as a gendered workplace and by noting ideological debates about gender that infused the scientists' social and political worlds. Satzinger, in turn, sees her investigation as contributing to epistemology in the realm of historiography as well as that of science: '[b]y unravelling the politics of multiple gender concepts in the sciences of the early twentieth century', Satzinger writes, 'I hope to link the history of the scientific study of sex difference with gender historians' work on multiplicities of genders and their continuous renegotiation'.[9]

Christina Benninghaus, who focuses her contribution on a related problem in the history of science and medicine – namely, research on infertility in late-nineteenth and early-twentieth-century Germany – takes a quite different approach. While cognisant of the interplay among cultural presumptions that shaped knowledge production, such as the role of male doctors' expectations in their interactions with patients or questions of propriety surrounding the collection of sperm samples, Benninghaus draws on evidence of medical research practices in the framework of Bruno Latour's actor-network theory (ANT) to question prevailing grand narratives that chart the triumph of a 'two-sex model' and emphasise the historical pathologisation of the female body. Following Latour's suggestions, Benninghaus connects the history of the instruments and procedures used in science and medicine with a wide range of actors interested in questions of infertility. She includes not only medical doctors and researchers, but also patients and their spouses, media and the wider public, and examines the various 'loops' that build the large network in which the understanding of, and practices around, infertility evolved. Gender still plays a large role in this analysis, but not the same role that has heretofore prevailed. According to Benninghaus, gender provided 'a contemporary set of ideas about masculinity, femininity and sex difference' that was 'used as a resource, explanation and argument by those negotiating infertility'.[10] For all of their differences, both authors problematise in provocative ways the relationship between scientific knowers constructing knowledge about sex and gender and their objects of study; the articles' purview includes scientific instruments and microscopic entities along with the human actors who more commonly populate historical narratives.

In a very different realm – a study of nationalism, citizenship and gendered violence in Iran in the 1980s – Shirin Saeidi also calls for explicit attention to processes of knowledge production in her contribution. She does so both by developing a critique of the overly generalised conceptions – such as the gendered nature of nationalism and nation building projects – that circulate in the field of feminist conflict studies, and also by problematising her own relationship to the women she interviewed in her research process. Probing that relationship can reorient the researcher. On another front, Saeidi calls attention to aspects of the interviews and memoirs she discusses that resonate through a surprisingly large number of other articles in this issue: in her analysis, words are not 'mere words' but also performances, actions in their own right 'used to express interviewees' disapproval of, or allegiance to, reformist or conservative political movements in Iran. At the same time, and perhaps outside of their intentions, they were also displaying how state-sponsored associations between gender, sexuality and the nation during war might be acted upon on the ground'.[11]

Pursuing this theme of words as performances, we are struck by authors' recurrent questioning of what counts as action and how to read and interpret words as forms of action. While obviously echoing the call for attention to language at the core of earlier epistemological debates, these newer approaches proceed from quite distinct ways of reading words and texts. Benninghaus, for example, describes three different types of readings she deploys when approaching the sources: 'using texts, statistics and published cases to grasp a "reality" otherwise not accessible, understanding them as communication at least partly structured by intentions and reading them as representations, as texts reflecting contemporary ways of thinking'.[12] However, the articles based on research on letters (the process involved in producing this issue yielded four such studies) perhaps provide the most pointed illustration of different ways of reading. They can productively be read in juxtaposition with one another to explore the kind of knowledge that letters can yield; by reading across these articles, we can literally read across epistemologies.

Liz Stanley and Helen Dampier use the letters of the white South African writer Olive Schreiner to assess her political influence. They begin their inquiry with large epistemological questions that might pertain to any historical inquiry: '[w]ith what certainty can knowledge claims about the past be advanced? Can cause and effect links be demonstrated . . . And if . . . [they] . . . can, then what is appropriate and sufficient evidence to convincingly show this?' To make claims about cause and effect in the question of Schreiner's political influence, Stanley and Dampier reconstruct and then analyse what they term 'the Schreiner epistolarium' – a corpus of extant letters that 'has interesting characteristic features, presences and absences'.[13] They depart from the ways that historians have often read letters – that is, within an epistemological framework in which letters are largely understood in terms of their reference to events in the author's life. When historians read letters this way, they tend to see them as problematic sources because of their perspectivity and their embeddedness in very particular relationships. Instead, Stanley and Dampier emphasise the 'performative character' of Schreiner's letters by demonstrating through their examples how 'these letters in and of themselves changed things'. The supposed deficiencies of letters when viewed as representations of past events, through this new way of reading, are transformed into strengths 'because they provide an analytical purchase on understanding context and its dynamics'.[14] The new way of approaching these particular documents, the authors suggest, opens up new possibilities for observing the operation of agency on the margins – in this case, marginality defined by gender and imperial power.

Emma Moreton starts her analysis of a large corpus of Irish emigrant letters with a critique that echoes that of Stanley and Dampier in some respects. She points to the usual way of analysing such letters primarily as representational and based upon reading the words to interpret the author's meaning with reference to its broader social or cultural context. Some scholars, Moreton notes, have looked at linguistic patterns in letters, focusing for example on exemplary linguistic strategies or word patterns. Moreton makes a distinction between this type of approach and her own approach – corpus linguistics. Her more systematic linguistic analysis of a corpus of letters, a quantitatively large though necessarily partial subset of an unspecifiable universe of letters (here echoing in some respects Stanley and Dampier's 'epistolarium'), reminds us that studies that employ other methods of reading letters often rest on unexamined assumptions about the place of a given letter in the social, cultural or epistolary context in which it is embedded. Although we can know many things from the careful reading of single letters, we cannot know how representative they are of 'letters' more generally, or even of a particular correspondence.

Therefore, Moreton argues, to make strong knowledge claims about gendered language based on a huge body of sources such as emigrant letters, an alternative approach is necessary, one that, like Stanley and Dampier's, treats letters as 'acts' rather than as representations. However, in contrast to Stanley and Dampier's approach, Moreton 'decontextualises the components of language'. The 'way of knowing' that Moreton describes and employs – corpus linguistics – offers an alternative way of reading letters based on data collection from large numbers of texts. Her analysis assesses frequencies of usages of words or terms and distributional patterns, and moves back and forth between the individual letter and the group of letters, 'noticing what is typical or unusual about one text when compared with many texts'. The point of this way of reading is not to capture lived experience. It aims, rather, to distance the analyst from lived experience, 'taking language out of its flow and reality, freezing it and rearranging it to give "new perspectives on the familiar"'.[15] Moreton matches her methodology closely to the types of knowledge claims she seeks to make and prove based on the body of letters. Claims about how we know what we know are thus central to both of these articles; each presents and defends a distinctive epistemology for reading gender history in/into letters.

For Sonia Cancian letters also perform actions; in the particular case of the migrant letters she examines, they are exercises in identity building and in maintaining a human relationship. The letter writers create and sustain a long-distance relationship through letters that draw upon, work with and sometimes reformulate specific cultural models. Their gender ideologies are drawn variously from opera, the folk conventions of their Italian villages or new behaviours they encounter (for example, hunting in Canada). But Cancian reads them not merely for how they reveal the operation of gender ideology, but also as evidence of 'the myriad ways in which the writers push these ideologies in one way or another'.[16] The letters are doing important work that constructs gender in a particular social relationship.

The fourth contributor who works with letters, Meritxell Simon-Martin, tacks back and forth between letters and paintings in her analysis of British feminist Barbara Bodichon's self-construction as a female artist. Like the other authors we have discussed, Simon-Martin conceives of her approach to both types of sources as an alternative to a simply empirical reading. She does not treat the letters as an archive from which knowledge about Bodichon can be plucked. Parallel to the ways of reading presented by Cancian and Stanley and Dampier, Simon-Martin emphasises the performative dimensions of the Bodichon letters and their usefulness as a point of entry, not into Bodichon's authentic self, but rather into her ongoing project of self presentation – and specifically of her self-presentation as a female artist. Bodichon's letter writing 'is not an expression of the self', Simon-Martin argues, but '[r]ather the self-narrating subject is an effect of the autobiographical act; [Bodichon] is partially constituted through the act of letter writing'. Additionally, we should add, Simon-Martin interprets even Bodichon's self-categorisation in sources such as the 1880 census and her marriage certificate – sources that are so often treated as repositories of facts – as acts of self-construction. She points to such declarations as especially important for women 'afflicted with the curse of amateurism' that was a component of nineteenth-century bourgeois femininity.[17] By declaring her profession as artist in official records, Bodichon challenged the limits of this gender ideology.

Simon-Martin views Bodichon's paintings as another site of the same project of self-construction, a site marked by distinctive generic characteristics. Bodichon at times uncritically adopts the conventions of these artistic genres. For example, her picture *Sisters Working in our Fields* is 'embedded in the systems of signification on which Bodichon drew to produce it. Most notably, Bodichon's public self-projection as a landscapist specialised in Algeria is complicit with discourses on orientalism'. Nevertheless, as in her writings, Bodichon was also capable of re-appropriating discourse. Her choice to create landscape paintings 'permitted Bodichon to redefine the category of female artist: she claimed landscapes as a legitimate theme for a woman painter and asserted her right to paint *en plein air*'.[18]

Simon-Martin's article is not the only one here that moves away from epistemological terrains of relative familiarity to historians accustomed to working with written records, in order to explore ways of knowing that instead – as with the woman lounging at the Golden Gate – require them to turn their gaze upon images. Beth Severy-Hoven's analysis of the wall paintings of an ancient home in Pompeii offers, literally, a new way of seeing the apparently gendered perspectivity operating in this particular historical context. As she argues, '[i]n this ancient Italian home – and I suggest in many others – a master gaze significantly inflects the male one'. Rather than reading the images separately and in a straightforward fashion as 'masculine', Severy-Hoven looks at 'the comparisons and contrasts called for by the formal compositions and juxtapositions of the paintings themselves' to read out of them 'the status of the owners as masters'. While she notes the 'vast cultural and epistemological gap between twentieth-century Euro-American psychoanalytic theory and ancient Italian concepts and experiences of gender and sexuality', identifying that gap allows her to see in images of torture, suffering and sexual submission resonances of the slave/master relationship rather than a straightforward mechanism of gender differentiation.[19]

To mention one final example of experimentation with knowing based on attentiveness to the visual, Meredith Heller's analysis of the Teatro Campesino between 1968 and 1980 draws upon a range of sources including written texts, but important aspects of her argument rest on exploring what she calls '*mestiza* performance practices'. This takes her into the realm of reading photographs, fliers and other visual media to illustrate 'instances of male/female, non-female, androgynous, sexless and otherworldly genderbending performance by Chicanas'.[20] By 'gazing', Heller is able to 'see' the agency and resistance of the female performers in a theatre group that has frequently been studied as an example of how gendered relationships of power remained peripheral to the group's effort to tackle and challenge racial and ethnic hierarchies and inequities.

Besides offering creative epistemological approaches to textual and visual sources, this special issue also highlights the extent to which, in the decades since gender history's emergence, it has moved from being a largely western project to becoming a global project. Many of the articles here point strongly to the complexities of grappling with global geopolitical dimensions of 'how we know what we know', once again echoing the revisionism we can see in the *Postcard (At the Golden Gate) 2009*.

Within history, historiographical knowledge has tended to develop within frameworks designated by time (such as 'ancient' or 'medieval' or 'modern') and space (ranging from the scale of village micro-histories to world histories). Arguably, the nation-state has because of its ideological and institutional clout been a strong influence on the historiography of the modern world, but it is not the only such organising principle of historiography even if it is probably the most familiar one. Within national historiographies, particular research traditions, sources, languages and theoretical orientations have shaped what has been considered knowable about the past. Comparing across national or temporally-defined historiographies thus calls attention to each field's peculiarities. The intellectual ferment characteristic of the late-imperial and postcolonial era has brought an explicit geopolitical critique to national historiographies, as well as to many other ways of knowing about the past. It has pushed historians to be more alert to the global geopolitical and extra-national influences on historical ways of knowing, even regarding such seemingly local, intimate or subjective arenas as gender relations or gender identity formation. This critique has been a defining element in some subfields, such as postcolonial African history. More recently it has begun to inform metropolitan historiographies as well.

It is noteworthy that we find relatively little evidence in these articles of projects defined by national historiographies of the traditional sort. To some extent this reflects the fact that many of the authors are not, by disciplinary training, historians; but even those authors who are trained as historians more often cross than respect historiographical boundaries. Lorelle Semley's contribution presents an argument about 'public mothering' that explicitly calls attention to distinctive conceptualisations of gender and mothering that operate in western feminist theory and historiography as opposed to West African history and historiography. As a North American doing research in Africa she struggles to develop a gender analysis that does not force the lives of individual African women into categories developed by North American or European historians of gender or empire. To explore what she sees as distinctive ways of conceptualising relations between gender and power that do not presume a 'public/private' divide as conceptualised in the west, Semley must in turn defy geographically defined borders of investigation. Her article first takes up questions of African historiography through a conceptual lens developed in North America before again circling back to Africa and then returning to Semley's North American classrooms.

For Nancy L. Green, focusing on migration, the transnational has also always been an important terrain of analysis. Her article poses the problem of the nation state in a way that highlights questions of epistemology through comparative historiography. Certainly she cites differences in national trends in migration, but closer to the heart of her claims are provocative comparisons about the questions upon which historians have focused in two different national-historiographic contexts and how these questions in turn have structured understandings of the role of gender in migration history. To offer one example of her thinking along these lines, Green notes that '[a]s assumptions about assimilation (through the 1960s in the United States, through the 1970s in France) gave way to enquiries about ethnicity in the United States and the "droit à la différence" (the right to be different) in France, researchers asked few questions about the gendered meanings of those terms'.[21] Concepts embedded in historiography, in other words, followed temporal shifts in nationally specific political debates. The place of gender in these historiographies also resonated at times with the transnational flow of ideas and at times with national-historiographic peculiarities. Comparative convergences and divergences of this sort call to our attention both general and nationally specific political projects that have shaped how we know what we know about migration history.

Modern nation states have – as Green notes – routinely tracked and counted mobile people, creating an archive from which historians in France and the United States are only now beginning to produce gendered knowledge (about states, labour markets, communities and individuals). Green's discussion of feminist historians who work quantitatively with this archive suggests how empirically-oriented social historians attempt to come to terms with the binary of 'male' and 'female' which is constitutive of the data they use. Green suggests how we can know gender even when presented with fixed binaries, for example by paying attention to variations in the numbers of male and female migrants. To explain these variations one must explore the gendering of state policies, educational and family systems and labour markets in both sending and receiving societies. It is not, then, the sex of migrants that explains variations in their numbers relative to each other, but rather gender relations deduced in part from those numbers.

A significant cluster of essays in this collection point to paths scholars take as they attempt to escape the 'gaze' of nation-states, their archive-building bureaucracies and the national historiographies they have shaped. One provocative approach is to seek out or to construct archives that document the perspectives of border-crossers, including but not limited to the type of migration history that Green describes. Viewing gender history from the perspective of migrants and other travellers allows scholars to challenge the 'nationality' of their subjects, their analytic categories and their ideas, as well as to problematise their own relations to their research subjects. We would like to note three different types of 'border crossing' that come into focus in several of the articles: first, research projects that track the movements of historical actors across borders; second, research that brings the researchers themselves into cross-border relationships with research subjects and third, and closely related to the second, research situations that problematise the practice of carrying analytic concepts of gender across borders.

People who cross borders are complicated subjects of historical study. Nation-states have created most of the main categories through which their mobility has been documented historically. They have usually distinguished emigrants sharply from immigrants (categories that are important not only to Green but also, for example, to Moreton's analysis of the letter-writing Lough sisters) as well as from refugees or exiles (including, for example, several of the Jewish scientists studied by Satzinger). For modern states, the categories of emigrants, immigrants and refugees/exiles are salient and consequential in their implications for biopolitical projects of nation building (with desirable immigrants viewed as potential additions and emigrants as potential losses to the 'body politic'). As politically salient categories, border-crossers' movements have, in turn, been subject to state construction and scrutiny, creating massive archives which incorporate the gaze of the nation state.

On the other hand, upper-class 'travellers' – such as Barbara Bodichon, as analysed by Meritxell Simon-Martin – have not always been scrutinised by border police or documented in the same category as 'migrants'. Yet they too crossed borders – not only national boundaries, but also the borders of metropole/colony, race and culture. By reflecting on the historical experiences of various types of travellers – including those who cycled repeatedly through the same places or those who left home again and again, only to return, sometimes multiple times – the epistemological and historiographical consequences of border crossing can be more fully explored. As historians examine gender history from the perspective of border crossing they begin to see how nation states, their archives and their historiographies render the mobile as interesting but also often threatening aberrations from an imagined and sedentary human 'normalcy'. Male mobility typically has provoked different official concerns than female mobility. Even more deeply, crossing political boundaries often entails crossing gender systems as well, thus calling attention to their instability, their cultural specificity and their malleability. Alertness to the ideological filters inherent in state archives documenting mobility is critical to using them to study gender; moreover, the use and sometimes even the scholarly assemblage of novel types of archives can produce knowledge that is less moulded by states, and that therefore sheds new light on the relationship between mobility and gender.

The usual categories deployed by the nation state – notably the distinction between the sedentary and the mobile, the emigrant and the immigrant – disappear almost entirely in Sonia Cancian's analysis of letters exchanged between two lovers from north-eastern Italy, Loris Palma and Antonietta Petris. Both lovers moved over the course of their relationship and both were undoubtedly 'counted' by one set of authorities or another as emigrants and as immigrants, but these categories were not the operative ones for them. Both certainly felt consequences when one moved and the other remained temporarily in place. Their communication through an unfolding epistolary relationship (first, within Italy, and then across the ocean separating Canada and Italy) continually repositioned them metaphorically in time and space; in their communication with each other, they sometimes looked temporally forward (into the future) and sometimes temporally backwards (towards the past), sometimes (spatially) away from their current location and sometimes (spatially) towards it.

Letter writing mediated – or perhaps, as Cancian suggests, even constructed – their personal relationship, allowing each correspondent to experience their communication as a continuation or unfolding of their earlier, brief, face-to-face contacts. Cancian's careful reading of the emotionally charged and, despite the distance, intimate world created through the letters demonstrates an epistemological paradox: the dynamic construction of gender ideologies apparent here is knowable only because of the mobility and separation of the two lovers. They wrote, as Cancian says, only when 'intimate face-to-face conversations, and ordinary, world-making discourse were no longer possible'.[22] Had their face-to-face relationship continued, in fact, their subjectivities, their use of language and the gendering of their communication about emotions, dreams, memories and imagined futures would have been subsequently knowable – if at all – only in a very different way, through retrospection, for example, as captured through oral histories. But, as Cancian's analysis makes clear, neither the original relationship nor the historian's reconstruction of it would have been the same. If corpus linguistics, which Emma Moreton employs in her study of the Irish immigrant letter writers, is always 'about making comparisons', Cancian's exploration of gendered intimacy and emotion is possible only because an implied comparison (in this case with the face-to-face relationships of sedentary people who need no letters in order to construct meaning and intimacy) is impossible.[23] As Cancian's work suggests, border crossings and the separation of persons involved in intimate relationships that they sometimes demand offer particularly fruitful sites for seeing the dynamics of gender relations; intimacy across separation sets the context for putting thoughts down on paper that otherwise would not have taken this more permanent form. Moreover, border-crossers inevitably confront multiple ideologies of gender, thus pushing them to 'see' gender more explicitly than they might have, had they stayed home, and challenging a prior understanding of sex or gender that might have just seemed 'natural'.

In Jamie McDaniel's analysis of Virginia Woolf's *Orlando*, border crossing plays a central, if metaphoric, role. The article focuses on a well-known feminist classic's main character, who crossed borders of time, gender and sex. Read in juxtaposition with Stanley and Dampier, Green or Cancian, McDaniel's article reveals how border crossings facilitated Orlando's adoption of a new epistemology of property and propriety. Writing as a literary scholar, McDaniel calls attention to his decision to reconsider what he considers 'the value that literary scholarship places on a kind of critical detachment from its objects of inquiry'. Rejecting that stance, McDaniel views Virginia Woolf's extensively analysed text through immersion in the epistemologies that Woolf herself mobilised in writing *Orlando*. McDaniel calls his choice 'epistemological doubling'.[24] By epistemological doubling, McDaniel intends more than the mere blending or juxtaposition of differing ways of knowing; here, epistemological doubling means self-consciously adopting and mimicking the ways of knowing adopted by Woolf herself – e.g. literary analysis, a gendered legal history of property and biographies of both an individual (Orlando) and the British nation.

In adopting multiple and shifting epistemological stances, McDaniel becomes a biographer of Woolf – one who can see linkages among Woolf's personal biography, her intellectual positions and British national history more broadly. Woolf's engagement with the writer Vita Sackville-West's loss of her house and lands and her corresponding interest in women's property rights (which were under debate at the time she wrote) interact with Orlando's biography and developing thoughts about property as the fictional character lives and travels with the 'gipsies'. In adopting Woolf's 'preoccupation with looking back' through time, through Orlando's long and complex biography and through the history of property relations, McDaniel is able to 'revisit narratives of national and gender identity' – narratives that excluded women and the propertyless – and to redefine what marked Woolf and Orlando as British women.[25] *Orlando* itself becomes a work of fiction that tells a history of the British nation and not just a biography of its main character. Woolf's most important work of fiction tells this story in a way that reveals Woolf's dawning realisation that women's writings themselves constitute valuable property, and once again, we note, calling attention to words as actions.

Olive Schreiner also moved across borders – both those between the colony of South Africa and the metropole and those defined by race and gender within South Africa. As a border crosser privileged by reason of her race and status as a writer, Schreiner was able to 'translate' developments in colonial South Africa for British citizens in the metropole. But she could do this so effectively, Stanley and Dampier suggest, in part because she had left South Africa to live in Britain and had then experienced the shock of viewing her own society – 'the slow pace of life in the white enclave and the narrowness of white people's lives and opinions', a nation of 'Philistines' – from new perspectives as an outsider after her return from Britain.[26] Conversely, her fame in the metropole gave her credibility in the colony that would otherwise have been unlikely.

Crossing borders in the research process can also have profound epistemological implications. Sometimes this can result from as common a practice as translation. For example, historian of science Helga Satzinger points to the challenge of translation across languages most forcefully when she writes about the problematic use in the English language of the term 'gender' when writing the history of biological sex difference in Germany. Satzinger notes that 'in the German-language "Geschlechterforschung" (gender studies) there is no need for the explicit sex-gender distinction in order to indicate the realm of socially-constructed "gender"'.[27] As a native-speaker of German, Satzinger is able not only to see how the term 'gender' carries a distinctive relationship to biological sex difference in English and in German, she is able to mobilise the linguistic difference between German and English languages in order to probe the history of scientific research on gender and sex at the turn of the twentieth century. The problem that Satzinger points to – that is, the particularity of the sex/gender distinction as it has come to operate in English is not just a problem for German speakers but indeed for speakers of a large number of languages. Furthermore, precisely because the meaning and resonance of the word 'gender' differs across languages, gender history itself has, at times, become associated with historical practice in the Anglo-American scholarly world, and resisted as such elsewhere, another very important reminder of the power of words and the geopolitical dimensions of border crossing.

Border crossing also raises the important issue of when and how the scholar's relationship to his or her subject shapes the knowledge created. Whether or not insider and outsider researchers produce distinctive knowledges is an issue that has long engaged researchers who study colonised peoples, migrants and racial minorities, where it has been understood both as defining the politics (and identity politics) implicit in scholarship and as a very broad epistemological question. Shirin Saeidi reports that the informants she interviewed for her study of the lives of non-elite Iranians during the Iraq/Iran war of the 1980s expected her to cultivate an emotional understanding of them in order to bridge the gap between her assumptions and categories of analysis and their ways of narrating their own memories of life in war-torn Iran. Her informants' sharp emotional reactions to some of her questions and observations revealed her 'unconscious perspectives, as respondents demanded recognition of their emotional positionality towards me'. Her border crossing into Iran and other places where Iranians lived in exile, and also into the personal realm of her interviewees' lives, challenged the analytic categories she took with her to the field. 'I became accustomed to continually moving', she writes, 'between people, feelings, claims and ideas during interviews and archival work until the specific complexities at issue became apparent– not depictions of gender and sexual categories as I understood them through my own history, solidarities and education'.[28] Although Cancian does not explicitly address this issue in her essay, she also describes a research process in which she is both an insider and an outsider to the Italian migrant letter writers who are the object of her investigation. Cancian's endnotes indicate how crucial her relationship to the female letter writer, Antonietta Petris, has been to the development of this scholarly project. As a tri-lingual Canadian of recent Italian origin, living in Montreal, Cancian can claim status as an insider but is simultaneously someone who through her education has travelled outside that community, only to return to it as a researcher. This process was critical to Cancian's acquiring access to the letters and even to her ability to read and understand them – distinguishing, for example, standard Italian from the dialects of north-eastern Italy. Without establishing a personal and ongoing trusting relationship with Petris, Cancian could not have made visible to others the struggles over gender and intimacy between the two young, letter writing lovers of the post-war period.

Scholars who venture across borders carry with them their own ideas of gender. Essays focused on Iran, India, Malawi and Benin all raise questions about how well concepts of gender and methods of gender analysis travel. 'North-South' border crossings are particularly charged in a postcolonial context where the hierarchically organised global systems of power of the nineteenth and twentieth centuries still live on in contemporary ways of knowing. As already noted, Shirin Saeidi documents her rethinking of concepts of gender she carried into the field. Christopher Lee's investigation led him to doubt the utility of the usual categories of social historical and gender analysis in his efforts to make sense of an incident he discovered in the National Archives of Malawi. Working from an archived text from the early twentieth century, Lee's close reading of the violent conflict documented within it between an unidentified European man and an African woman called Adaima, while seemingly highly idiosyncratic, nevertheless allowed him to see with vivid clarity the personal experiences of inter-racial sexual relations that often occurred under colonial rule. At the same time, western (or northern) analytic categories, including gender, possess limitations for explaining the meaning or significance of Adaima's violent outbursts. They do not reveal her motivations nor, as Lee argues, should her experience be read as representative of the lives of other women. The European man's fear of Adaima and his recourse to colonial authorities also remain somewhat puzzling. What is the gendering of power revealed in this idiosyncratic story? In short, the 'vast cultural and epistemological gaps' that Severy-Hoven sees separating modern western readers from ancient Pompeii also continue to complicate conversations across modern geopolitical and cultural borders as well.[29] At present, satisfactory 'translation' across the north/south divide remains elusive.

The essays by Stanley and Dampier on the writer Olive Schreiner and by Lorelle Semley on the seemingly enigmatic West African women, Alaba Ida and Yá Shègén, reveal a somewhat different cluster of epistemological challenges raised by the global mobility of a key, if much debated, concept of European and American gender ideology – the notion of 'separate spheres' or the division between public and private. Stanley and Dampier note the paradox of separate spheres in a South African setting: the narrow 'private sphere' within which middle-class white women in South Africa believed themselves to be confined could scarcely have existed without the constant entries and exits of black South African service workers. Schreiner's 'political letters' constituted a breach of the boundary that supposedly excluded women such as herself from political activity; indeed, much of Stanley and Dampier's essay focuses on the possibility of knowing from existing sources whether or not (and how) her 'exhortatory' letters influenced the political decisions and behaviour of her brother and several other men in power to whom she 'expressed her views' and 'left them to work'. As they conclude, the result is an 'alternate history of a momentous period in the South African past', one in which the female, Olive Schreiner, comes into focus as 'a shrewd and effective political strategist' but also one for whom the binary of public and private loses much of its power to organise our ways of knowing about the past.[30]

The conceptual framework of separate spheres is the same in both articles, but it still remains difficult to imagine the 'public mothers' explored by Lorelle Semley in her account of influential African women under French colonial rule as falling within the same category of boundary-breaching female political strategists to which Stanley and Dampier assign Schreiner. Semley explores a complex genealogy for 'public motherhood' – an understanding that mothers can and should in particular circumstances exercise legitimate societal power, which connects contested African practices to political theorisation by African American and white European and American feminists. Semley's portrait of the African public/private divide and the space for public motherhood is a complex and critical one, however. She notes how differently African and western scholars interpret the collective action of a group of elderly women who, during the 1929 'Women's War', exposed their naked bodies in order to shame and challenge local African leaders. But at the same time, the fate of the two 'public mothers' that Semley discusses in some detail – Alaba Ida and Yá Shègén (Akanké Owebeyi Aduké) – points toward the limits of West African maternalism and not toward celebration of a distinctively African model of 'othermother'. Semley suggests that Alaba Ida and Yá Shègén lived in an African society and culture that also constrained how mothers could exercise public authority and power; those limits were not only impositions of the French colonial state, although in the stories of both women they were thoroughly entwined in France's exercise of colonial power in the region. Rather than posing these female figures as alternatives to those models possible within a western ideology of separate spheres, then, Semley asks whether scholars should instead consider a different and more radical perspective of 'black women and public mothers as modern, and, dare one say, universal?'[31]

Aniruddha Dutta's investigation of gender/sexual identity formation in eastern India also raises questions about the relationship between 'indigenous' categories and those imported through transnational scholarship. He starts by questioning categories of gender/sexual identity, in particular the often-articulated contrast between a historically grounded category of transgender identity – the *hijra* – with the more recently emergent (politically activist and thus supposedly less 'authentic') transgender identity – *kothi*. Dutta poses the history he recounts in explicitly epistemological terms. His analysis tracks the British colonial categorisation of the *hijras* in the context of attempts to 'describe, classify and control them' in a manner similar to colonial authorities' controlling classifications of other practices such as 'widow-burning' and 'child marriage' in the service of justifying imperialist rule. Even though postcolonial anthropology has overturned these colonial views, the categories still trouble western epistemologies: 'the *hijra* has functioned as a quintessential marker of Indic gender/sexual difference... As colonial depictions were superseded in the twentieth century, the *hijra* was reclaimed as a prominent non-western "third gender" or transgender group resisting the western schema of sexual dimorphism'.[32] Using ethnography and interviews to supplement the written record, Dutta argues against seeing the *hijra* as a single, persistent and monolithic category; he terms the *hijra* as 'an active epistemological project' rather than one rooted in an unchanging past. In this respect, *hijra* have more in common with *kothi* than is usually recognised. Dutta, in effect, historicises the *kothi* to point to similarities between the two groups: 'both the *hijra* and the *kothi* . . . emerge as (seemingly) coherent identities through the collusion of multiple subcultural and governmental processes'.[33] In order to see these identities in a new light, Dutta calls for and demonstrates an epistemology that can bridge various sites and methods of inquiry, ranging from the colonial archive to ethnographies of kinship, the politics of non-governmental organisations and contemporary media analyses.

As Dutta's analysis makes clear, the archive remains central to almost all ways of knowing and different types of archives and different understandings of 'the archive' offer different perspectives on the past. That relationships of power constitute every archive, that they create archival silences and that they necessitate new methodologies for interpreting the silences, constituted, for historians, some of the most important insights of the post-structural philosophers. In the words of Deborah Cherry archives are 'shaped in and by historically specific relations between power and knowledge which have determined who is recorded, when, where and how'.[34] In the case of the Schreiner epistolarium, and other studies of letter writers, we see additional sources of silence that are less the direct product of unequal power relations than of the ways in which communication is mediated. Because Schreiner more frequently met face-to-face with her political allies in the feminist and nascent multi-racial human rights movements of South Africa, she produced an archive where scholars can better see and know her strategies for educating those who disagreed with her than they can know and see the political dynamics of her collaborations and alliances.

Christopher Lee directly and creatively addresses the issue of archival silences as he seeks to understand and to translate the meaning of the violent (and apparently threatening) behaviour of the woman Adaima and the father of her child, whose complaint survives – however oddly situated – in the colonial archive. According to Lee, the archive within which Adaima's story is embedded makes its meaning elusive, just as the concepts and language structuring the colonial archive 'shape our conditions of knowledge and analysis of the past'. But while Lee acknowledges that the archival placement of this document would make it 'easy to pass over this archived story, to consider it exceptional and therefore disregard it', he asserts that the document reflects not the perspective of the colonial state alone but also (in Antoinette Burton's terms) 'fugitive traces of historical subjectivity'. Lee makes a powerful argument for attending to such archival remnants of marginal lives, however fragmentary, and the 'idiosyncrasies of individual experience', more generally. Must this individual's life be 'scaled up to represent a form of group politics', he asks pointedly, before it acquires meaning?[35] Or are there forms of knowledge that can only emerge from single cases just as there are other understandings of gender that emerge only through systematic analysis of large numbers of cases, as Emma Moreton's analysis of gendered language illustrates?

Historians have also always been involved in the creation of archives as part of their research, raising issues concerning what about the past can be knowable and how it can be known. For example, the archive of letters created by Professor Kerby Miller and utilised by Emma Moreton for her research was photocopied and then transcribed (and used for traditional publications in some cases) long before it was digitised in order to facilitate the software-enhanced quantitative methods of corpus linguistics. Sonia Cancian digitised rather than photocopied the letters she collected but has not attempted the type of analysis (illustrated by Moreton's article) that digitisation facilitates. Neither have the scholarly creators of the 'Olive Schreiner Epistolarium', directed by Liz Stanley; for them digitisation was merely a convenient mechanism for compiling and linking the thousands of letters which Schreiner, in the course of her transnational life and political work, scattered across the private collections (of recipients) and archives in several nations. The essence of their archive building entailed the global search for and compilation of the scattered letters so as to make the epistolarium fuller, if still by nature partial. All these examples call attention to how archives raise epistemological issues, including that of the scholar as curator and archivist. Which 'new' archives attract the financial and temporal resources required for their collection and maintenance? If scholars are unable to 'curate' the archives they create over the long term, do they arguably create new silences, or – to use another metaphor – render their archives and their perspectival sources as invisible to future scholars as Adaima is in the context of colonial Malawi? While gender historians have excelled in revealing how gendered relations of power in the creation of archives can render powerless people invisible and silent, we now need to attend to the possibility that scholarly curation of emergent archives may also be a gendered process that will shape future knowledge production.

The letters analysed by Cancian raise a further question about archival dimensions of epistemology, since these letters have been preserved and curated privately, and only Cancian's carefully cultivated relationship to the family curators of the letters 'opens them' and their perspectival knowledge to the view of public scholarship. Here, in the world of archives, preservation and access, we see replicated the kinds of 'separate spheres' explored in so many of the essays collected in this special issue. Because the transnational social field and intimate private world created in these letters 'made meaning' for the letter writers, and because that meaning has to some degree been passed on orally and emotionally to the descendants of the letter writers, the letters survive as a kind of family archive or 'shrine' to memory and family history. No scholar curator, and even no archive (such as the University of Minnesota's Immigration History Research Center, which digitises such letters in the hopes of generating publicly accessible knowledge through them), can promise private or family curators that scholars will produce the same meaning or knowledge from the letters that the family may hope to preserve and even to control. These issues do not differ too significantly from those raised by the creation of significant scholarly collections of interviews and oral histories: for example, those created and used by Saeidi in her work on war-torn Iran in the 1980s. Ownership of and access to 'private archives' shapes the kind of knowledge that scholars committed to publication (i.e. making public) can create from them. In this context, even the willingness of scholars to accommodate and respond to private, familial or community concerns – for example about the use of private letters – may be gendered and certainly has special implications for historians of gender.

The joining of scattered and diverse archives – which, as Simon-Martin reminds us, is especially typical of the practices of biographers and historians of individual lives – points toward the mixed methodologies and multi-sited (transnational or multi-national) research that is increasingly characteristic of the human, social and natural sciences in our own times. Indeed, it is the kind of knowledge that can be created from diverse archives and from eclectic methodologies that seems most characteristic of the essays collected here. While it is possible to think of the use by historians of photographs (Heller), works of art (Simon-Martin and Severy-Hoven), interviews (Dutta and Saeidi), letters (Stanley and Dampier, Cancian, Simon-Martin and Moreton), fiction (McDaniel) and 'things' (Benninghaus) as characteristic mainly of 'interdisciplinary' or 'mixed methodologies', we follow Simon-Martin in believing these sources raise some of the same questions about the production of knowledge as traditional archives, with their silences. As Simon-Martin observes, '[e]ach of these types of primary source is a genre, with its own regulatory codes and conditions of production that determine the perspectival information conveyed'.[36] Each type of source, each archive, is thus mediated in ways that scholars can acknowledge, while creating knowledge from multiple perspectives rather than reading single archives and their silences. Variations within a single genre – different sets of works on letters, for example – reveal how they were produced, preserved (or not), and redeployed by people other than their original recipients. Thinking of various types of archive and the sources they preserve in terms of their qualities as 'genres' and what they contain, disclose or hide, calls our attention back to the large problem of what is knowable about gender in the past.

In nearly all of these articles, there is attention to the ongoing and active process of subject construction that produces and is produced by categories and sources. There are individuals in virtually all of these papers – individuals who are mysterious and knowable in a variety of ways and to varying degrees. The papers are filled with biographies or partial biographies, life-story interviews, correspondences whose exchanges disclose authors who, in the course of the analysis, often become more recognisable as persons.

The better-documented lives (for example, Olive Schreiner's or Barbara Bodichon's) yield more clues for the gender historian. But even these do not lead to preordained interpretations or completely coherent subjects who, as one might expect from older models of biography, act straightforwardly as agents in their own lives and those of others, with aims and consequences knowable to the historian. Simon-Martin, writing about Bodichon, distances herself from such a claim: 'I argue that we do not have direct information about how Bodichon "lived" as a female artist'.[37] Similarly, the German scientists and doctors whom Helga Satzinger and Christina Benninghaus investigate, even as they emerge as individuals with distinctive political and scientific agendas, are as much products of their labs and their milieus as they are their creators.

Even in the cases of more obscure and less well-documented lives, we can see the ongoing negotiation between the individual and the social, the never definitive process of self-construction that takes various forms, unevenly recorded. According to Cancian, letter writing created an opportunity and a need for a person 'to construct, articulate and deliberate their knowledge of the world'.[38] But in so doing, the correspondence she analyses demonstrates they were also constructing central elements of their own identities. Sometimes these new elements of identity emerged through criticism of gendered expectations they felt had been imposed on them. 'To write and exchange intimate letters usually permitted correspondents to seek solace and "spiritual communion" in a separate space in which the outside world was excluded . . . the writers exchanged letters indicating they were each other's intimate confidents – the only persons [they inferred] with whom they shared a world that was separate from the one they shared with others'.[39]

Subjects on the margins of literate cultures or archival projects remain more elusive. Semley's 'public mothers' come across as fascinating, but not-quite-knowable. Part of Christopher Lee's fascination with Adaima's case was its anomalous character, that it went against the grain of his categorical expectations: 'I realised that what was holding me back was not the content of the document, which remained invaluable, but established techniques of social history that emphasised common patterns of experience through aggregate data, the collection of multiple life histories, and, in sum, the privileging of groups over individuals'. Here, this social historian's will to see history from below combines with awareness of how any individual story resists mere categorisation. So Lee presents an analysis that 'position[s] Adaima's story somewhere between the genres of biography and social history, since it speaks to broader patterns of historical experience as well as the unique significance of individual lives'.[40] The surprisingly large number of individuals whose stories, or partial stories, emerge in the articles in this issue attest to historians' ongoing concern with 'broader patterns of historical experience as well as the unique significance of individual lives'. Many of the insights about gender history that this issue yields derive from research that focuses precisely on the points of intersection between identifiable individual projects of self-construction and the social networks, cultural forms and political systems that inform them.

Notes

1. At the Minnesota Workshop on 'Gender History across Epistemologies' where many of the papers published here were first presented, Meritxell Simon-Martin provided a useful discussion of some of the epistemological debates summarised here. Her discussion was very helpful to us as we wrote our introduction.
2. Denise Riley, *'Am I That Name? Feminism and the Category of 'Women' in History* (London: Macmillan, 1988), pp. 1–2.
3. Joan Wallach Scott, 'Gender: A Useful Category of Historical Analysis', *The American Historical Review* 91 (1986), pp. 1053–75; Joan Wallach Scott, 'The Evidence of Experience', *Critical Inquiry* 17 (1991), pp. 773–97; Joan Wallach Scott, *Gender and the Politics of History* (New York: Columbia University Press, 1988). See also the forum, 'Revisiting "Gender: A Useful Category of Historical Analysis"', *American Historical Review* 113 (2008), pp. 1344–430.
4. Kathleen Canning, 'Feminist History after the Linguistic Turn: Historicizing Discourse and Experience', *Signs* 19 (1994), pp. 368–404; Catherine Hall, 'Politics, Post-structuralism and Feminist History', *Gender and History* 3 (1991), pp. 204–10; Linda Gordon, 'Review of *Gender and the Politics of History*', *Signs* 15 (1990), pp. 853–8; Mary Maynard, 'Beyond the "Big Three": the Development of Feminist Theory into the 1990s', *Women's History Review* 4 (1995), pp. 259–81; Joan Hoff, 'Gender as a Postmodern Category of Paralysis', *Women's History Review* 3 (1994), pp. 149–68; Laura Lee Downs, 'If "Woman" is Just an Empty Category, Then Why Am I Afraid to Walk Alone at Night? Identity Politics Meets the Postmodern Subject', *Comparative Studies in Society and History* 35 (1993), pp. 414–37, here p. 424.
5. Downs, 'If "Woman" is Just an Empty Category', p. 415.
6. Joan Wallach Scott, 'Feminism's History', *Journal of Women's History* 16 (2004), pp. 10–29, here p. 21.
7. Jeanne Boydston, 'Gender as a Question of Historical Analysis', *Gender & History* 20 (2008), pp. 558–83.
8. Shirin Saeidi, 'Reconsidering Categories of Analysis: Possibilities for Feminist Studies of Conflict', *Gender & History* 24 (2012), pp. 799–824, here pp. 802.
9. Helga Satzinger, 'The Politics of Gender Concepts in Genetics and Hormone Research in Germany, 1900–1940', *Gender & History* 24 (2012), pp. 735–54, here p. 736.
10. Christina Benninghaus, 'Beyond Constructivism?: Gender, Medicine and the Early History of Sperm Analysis, Germany 1870–1900', *Gender & History* 24 (2012), pp. 647–76, here p. 669.
11. Saeidi, 'Reconsidering Categories of Analysis', p. 806.
12. Benninghaus, 'Beyond Constructivism?', p. 656.

13. Liz Stanley and Helen Dampier, '"I Just Express My Views & Leave Them to Work": Olive Schreiner as a Feminist Protagonist in a Masculine Political Landscape with Figures', *Gender & History* 24 (2012), pp. 677–700, here pp. 678, 694.
14. Stanley and Dampier, 'I Just Express My Views & Leave Them to Work', pp. 690–93, 693, 694.
15. Emma Moreton, 'Profiling the Female Emigrant: A Method of Linguistic Inquiry for Examining Correspondence Collections', *Gender & History* 24 (2012), pp. 617–46, here p. 620.
16. Sonia Cancian, 'The Language of Gender in Lovers' Correspondence, 1946–1949', *Gender & History* 24 (2012), pp. 755–64, here p. 755.
17. Meritxell Simon-Martin, '"More Beautiful than Words & Pencil Can Express": Barbara Bodichon's Artistic Career at the Interface of her Epistolary and Visual Self Projections', *Gender & History* 24 (2012), pp. 581–99, here p. 584.
18. Simon-Martin, 'More Beautiful than Words & Pencil Can Express', p. 592.
19. Beth Severy-Hoven, 'Master Narratives and the Wall Painting of the House of the Vettii, Pompeii', *Gender & History* 24 (2012), pp. 540–80, here pp. 542, 556, 541.
20. Meredith Heller, 'Gender-Bending in El Teatro Campesino (1968–1980): A *Mestiza* Epistemology of Performance', *Gender & History* 24 (2012), pp. 766–81, here pp. 767, 768.
21. Nancy L. Green, 'Changing Paradigms in Migration Studies, From Men to Women to Gender', *Gender & History* 24 (2012), pp. 782–98, here p. 793.
22. Cancian, 'The Language of Gender', p. 757.
23. Moreton, 'Profiling the Female Emigrant', p. 539; Cancian, 'The Language of Gender'.
24. Jamie McDaniel, 'The Power of Renewable Resources: *Orlando*'s Tactical Engagement with the Law of Intestacy', *Gender & History* 24 (2012), pp. 718–34, here p. 720.
25. McDaniel, 'The Power of Renewable Resources', p. 720.
26. Stanley and Dampier, 'I Just Express My Views & Leave Them to Work', p. 680.
27. Satzinger, 'The Politics of Gender Concepts, p. 736.
28. Saeidi, 'Reconsidering Categories of Analysis', p. 805.
29. Severy-Hoven, 'Master Narratives and the Wall Painting of the House of the Vettii, Pompeii', p. 541.
30. Stanley and Dampier, 'I Just Express My Views & Leave Them to Work', pp. 693, 694.
31. Lorelle Semley, 'Public Motherhood in West Africa as Theory and Practice', *Gender & History* 24 (2012), pp. 600–16, here p. 612.
32. Aniruddha Dutta, 'An Epistemology of Collusion: *Hijras*, *Kothis* and the Historical (Dis)continuity of Gender/sexual Identities in Eastern India', *Gender & History* 24 (2012), pp. 825–49, here p. 826. For *hijras* as a 'third sex' or 'third gender', see Serena Nanda, *Neither Man nor Woman: The Hijras of India* (Belmont: Wadsworth Publishing, 1990); Gil Herdt, *Third Sex, Third Gender* (New York: Zone Books, 1994).
33. Dutta, 'An Epistemology of Collusion', p. 844.
34. As quoted in Meritxell Simon-Martin, p. 584.
35. Christopher J. Lee, 'Gender without Groups: Confession, Resistance and Selfhood in the Colonial Archive', *Gender & History* 24 (2012), pp. 701–17, here pp. 702, 713, 709 Antoinette Burton, *Archive Stories: Facts, Fictions and the Writing of History* (Durham: Duke University Press, 2005), p. 14.
36. Simon-Martin, 'More Beautiful than Words & Pencil Can Express', pp. 581–2.
37. Simon-Martin, 'More Beautiful than Words & Pencil Can Express', p. 584.
38. Kathleen A. DeHaan, 'Negotiating the Transnational Moment: Immigrant Letters as Performance of a Diasporic Identity', *National Identities* 12 (2010), pp. 107–31, here p. 108 quoted in Cancian, 'The Language of Gender', p. 757.
39. Cancian, 'The Language of Gender', pp. 757–8.
40. Lee, 'Gender without Groups', p. 702.

1 Master Narratives and the Wall Painting of the House of the Vettii, Pompeii

Beth Severy-Hoven

From the god in the doorway who pulls aside his clothing to weigh his exposed penis against a bag of money on a set of scales, to the reception room scene of a stripped king being torn apart by his crazed female relatives (Figure 7), the paintings in the House of the Vettii have titillated tourists and intrigued scholars since they were first uncovered in Pompeii in the 1890s. What questions about ancient Italian society can we productively bring to bear on these images, and how should we formulate them?

Two studies from the 1990s point to some intriguing avenues of approach to these old walls. David Fredrick and Ann Olga Koloski-Ostrow use feminist film theory, particularly Laura Mulvey's pioneering work on the male gaze in twentieth-century cinema, to reveal some of the work done by mythological paintings in Pompeii in encoding social hierarchies.[1] In her 1975 formulation, Mulvey theorises how the patriarchal conditions of early Hollywood produced a cinematic language which was male. In particular, she applies psychoanalytic theory to film and the way it 'structures ways of seeing and pleasure in looking' by highlighting two features of the gaze which please the male viewer by protecting him from symbolic 'castration', a loss of power or privilege.[2] One of these features is embedded in the way images are presented visually: parts of the female body are focalised, exaggerated or beautified, which distracts the viewer from that body's lack of a penis and the implied threat to the male viewer's own. The second means is via narrative; Mulvey argues 'the male figure cannot bear the burden of sexual objectification' and so enjoys the active role of moving the story along.[3] The arc of many of these male-driven stories also ultimately condemns those who are female, providing entertainment through either their punishment or forgiveness for their lack of a penis.[4]

Although Mulvey specifically addresses film, particularly 'illusionistic narrative film' from mainstream Hollywood in the 1930s, 1940s and 1950s, scholars have applied her perspective to numerous other forms of imagery to understand how they encode patriarchy.[5] Using film theory to understand mythological panels is particularly compelling because these still paintings allude to well-known stories. This type of art, thus, both focuses the viewer's eye and presents a full story arc, much like film, particularly the way Mulvey approaches film. Moreover, as Katharina Lorenz has recently emphasised, images in houses tend to be juxtaposed within rooms in unique ways – that is, although the same scene from a myth might be repeated within a house

Gender History Across Epistemologies, First Edition. Edited by Donna R. Gabaccia and Mary Jo Maynes.
Chapters © 2013 The Authors. Book compilation © 2013 Blackwell Publishing Ltd.

or across different houses, only rarely do different rooms or houses combine a similar set of mythological scenes.[6] In the way its paintings compositionally and thematically correspond and contrast, each room and each house thus tells its own story using both image and narrative. Finally, ancient Pompeii was a male-dominated society, and it is well worth considering how the paintings in houses inscribed local power structures and pleased patrons.

Fredrick and Koloski-Ostrow, the classical scholars who bring Mulvey's cinematic perspectives to bear on ancient Italian painting, indeed bring forth important insights; however, both authors also come across imagery which contradicts Mulvey's patterns. As Fredrick observes,

> [T]he erotic object is not only female in wall painting: it can be anatomically female or male, or both – Narcissus, Endymion and Hermaphroditus are all popular. Moreover, a significant number of the victims of sexual violence in the paintings are male (e.g., Actaeon and Hylas); their symbolic castration is also on display. What might these passive or feminized male forms contribute to the grammar of erotic bodies on Pompeian walls?[7]

Koloski-Ostrow comes to a strikingly similar question in analysing the paintings of the *Casa del Menandro* and *Casa degli Amorini dorati* using the same theoretical framework to understand what she rightly sees as the 'strongly erotic and violent content of this mythological repertoire'.[8] After using an image of Actaeon to explore the workings of Mulvey's gaze, she observes that this male figure, physically torn apart by his own hunting dogs after catching sight of a bathing goddess, Diana, suffers the very 'castration' which Mulvey argues men fear and from which early- to mid-twentieth-century cinema provides pleasing avenues of escape.[9]

My goal is to work on these questions posed by Fredrick and Koloski-Ostrow, to pick up again this conversation across epistemologies and to interrogate both bodies of knowledge – studies of ancient wall painting and psychoanalytically-based feminist film analysis. How do Pompeian wall paintings contradict the patterns articulated by Mulvey? What are some ancient sources of these contradictions? How do the 'camera angle', the internal gazers and the narrative presented in paintings position and please the viewer? What are some modern sources of these contradictions, that is, how have subsequent film theorists responded to Mulvey and what do they bring to the question of how 'passive or feminized male forms contribute to the grammar of erotic bodies on Pompeian walls?'[10]

My answers will proceed along two vectors. In one, I point to the vast cultural and epistemological gap between twentieth-century Euro-American psychoanalytic theory and ancient Italian concepts and experiences of gender and sexuality. Mulvey, drawing upon Sigmund Freud and Jacques Lacan, gives primary, perhaps even exclusive weight to the differences between male and female bodies. I will argue that it is productive to contrast this focus on gender with ancient Italian practices of slavery, in which what we conceive of as gender, if used in isolation, might have done a poor job of articulating relationships of power. A case study of the decoration of a house in Pompeii potentially owned by a former slave helps explore this contrast. In two paired receiving rooms of the House of the Vettii, the formal compositions of the paintings deliberately call our attention to possible comparisons and contrasts. The imagery resonates with Roman slave practices; paired scenes of corporal punishment and sexualised violence negate the difference between male and female and focus on other means of articulating status hierarchies, particularly the dominion of gods over mortals. In several paintings the Vettii and the artists they commissioned combine stories from Greek mythology in unique ways to assert the status of the owners as masters. In this ancient Italian home – and I suggest in many others – a master gaze significantly inflects the male one.[11]

Although this first vector reclassifies some imagery in the context of ancient slavery as not gender inversion or instability, but as a pleasurable visual mastery over both male and female bodies, other paintings in the house do encourage the viewer's identification with, rather than avoidance of, suffering. For example, these same rooms juxtapose a painting of a visually objectified princess, Ariadne, who later wins immortality, with an image of the male hero Hercules, who also became a god, shown as a child being attacked by snakes. The scenes again equate a male and female body, but now they are the protagonists, divinised at the end of the 'film', so they also encourage the viewer to identify with the suffering Ariadne and Hercules. In Mulvey's terms, the viewer bears the burden of sexual objectification in these images, and 'castration' is not avoided. How should we understand the appeal of these images? What can they tell us about Pompeian society?

Scholarly reaction to Mulvey's work in the field of film studies proves useful, particularly Carol Clover's 1992 analysis of a different violent art, American and British horror films of the 1970s and 1980s.[12] In *Men, Women, and Chainsaws*, Clover explores multiple examples of cross-gender viewer identification and the pleasures of pain. Clover also sees this phenomenon as able to be explained only partially via psychoanalytic theory because of a cultural distance: 'many horror scenarios have a pre-Freudian and premodern cast'.[13] In considering the popularity of violent, gender-bending films, however, Clover also draws attention to Mulvey's blind spot on masochism, the pleasures viewers feel when they are scared or sympathise with characters in pain. Fredrick also points to the potential in analysing how some ancient paintings explore alternative, subordinate subject positions via mythological or fictional characters, although his explanations for this move tend to focus on the anxieties of elite Roman males.[14] Given the broad popularity of such images in Pompeian homes, and their prominence in the case study house (which certainly was not owned by a member of the elite from the capital), I will deploy some of Clover's conceptions of the 'masochistic aesthetic' to explore 'that particular audience's stake in that particular nightmare'.[15] Again the crux of my answer will come from cultural particularities of ancient Italy, in which all boys were potential objects of the erotic gaze and thus experienced a period of objectification and subordination. In such a society, cross-gender identification and Freud's 'female masochism' are surprisingly promising notions to consider.

In this paper, I will first present an overview of the House of the Vettii and its likely owners. Next I will explore in more depth how modern scholars have engaged with ancient Italian painting in studying social history, and in particular how gender has been used as a focal point in this analysis. Finally, we will walk through the House of the Vettii, analysing its surviving paintings using both techniques from film theory and information on ancient Italian culture, from slavery to sexual categories. My main goal is to demonstrate that in reading imagery from ancient Italy, gender cannot be viewed productively when separated from a master/slave dichotomy and from ancient Italian conceptions of sexuality, an argument made easier to perceive by looking for where a theory imported from another place and time slips in its explanatory power.

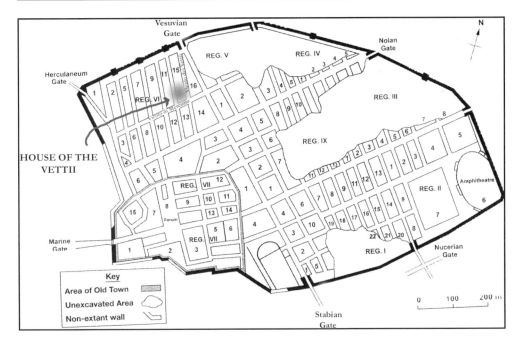

Figure 1: Map of walled part of Pompeii (adapted from Alison E. Cooley and M. G. L. Cooley, *Pompeii: A Sourcebook* [London: Routledge, 2004], Figure 1.1, p. 6).

The house and its owners

Pompeii – a small to medium-sized town on the south-west coast of Italy – was famously buried during the eruption of Mount Vesuvius in 79 CE. The House of the Vettii is located in what is now known as Region VI, a neighbourhood in the north-west corner of the walled part of town and to the north and east of the forum area (Figure 1).

This region has a concentration of large-sized homes leading into the forum, but otherwise contains what Andrew Wallace-Hadrill identifies as a characteristic mix of small to large houses and shops.[16] Block 15 is on the northeastern end of the region, near the Vesuvian Gate; the House of the Vettii occupies the entire southern end of the block. The main entrance (into room *a* on Figure 2) is from the Vicolo dei Vettii into the main reception room or *atrium*, but a side service entrance from the Vicolo di Mercurio also exists (into room 2). The size of the ground floor of the house is approximately 1100m[2], placing it among the large houses in Pompeii.[17]

The house was discovered during excavations in the years 1894–95 and was carefully documented in publications by August Mau and later Antonio Sogliano.[18] As a result, we know the arrangement of marble furniture in the garden, locations of pottery finds and the like. In addition, within a few years of excavation the roofing of much of the house was reconstructed, which contributed to the remarkable preservation of the *in situ* painted decoration, although the house has recently fallen into disrepair and has been closed to visitors.

Scholars such as Willem Peters, Arnold de Vos and Mariette de Vos concur that the house was extensively renovated between the earthquake of 62 CE and the destruction

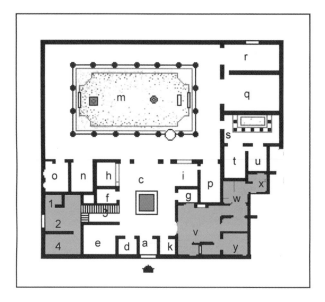

Figure 2: Floor plan of the House of the Vettii (VI 15, 1), Pompeii, (heavily adapted from August Mau, *Pompeji in Leben und Kunst* [Leipzig: Wilhelm Engelmann, 1900], p. 311, Figure 159).

of the town by the eruption of Vesuvius in 79 CE.[19] I shall be focusing upon this last ancient phase of the home's history. Figure 2 shows the general layout in plan.

On the whole, the House of the Vettii is a large but not unusual *atrium*-style Italian house. Looking through the main doorway into *a*, the visitor would enjoy a framed and symmetrical sight-line through the entryway, *atrium* or front hallway (*c*) and colonnaded rear garden (*m*), even though the house itself is not symmetrical. For the most part, individual rooms open onto the front hall or rear garden, which were open to the sky and thus provided air and light to all rooms of the house. An astonishing number of the rooms opening onto these are richly decorated with wall paintings generally agreed to have been carried out by a single workshop as part of the renovations following the earthquake of 62 CE.[20] Many large houses in Pompeii offered rooms decorated with expensive panels of mythological scenes; the House of the Vettii has six.[21] The large garden was also richly ornamented with bronze and marble sculpture and fountains – as much luxurious display was packed into the space as possible.[22]

Two small service areas are also evident (*v*–*y* and 1–4, shaded in Figure 2). The first consists of a set of rooms around a small central *atrium* (*v*) with stairs to the lost second floor and a small central pool to capture rainwater from a presumed opening in the roof. This section's plain decor, inclusion of a kitchen (*w*) and architectural segregation from the rest of the house suggest this area was reserved for the labour of the servants of the household and was not meant to be visited by the public or invited guests. The second service area is also utilitarian. Although this section could be entered through a long, narrow corridor (room 3) from the main *atrium* of the house, it was also accessible from the street through the doorway into room 2. This entrance was a gate large enough to allow the passage of draft animals, which were stabled in room 4. To the left of this entrance was a latrine (room 1). In the corridor to the *atrium*, remains are visible of a stairway to the second floor, but again none of the upper part of the house survives.

Evidence suggests the house may have been owned by former slaves, or freedmen. Scholars from de Vos and de Vos to John Clarke generally agree that Aulus Vettius Conviva and Aulus Vettius Restitutus were owners of the aptly named House of the Vettii.[23] These names appear on two bronze seals found inside the front hall close to the remains of a large chest on the south wall; 'A. Vetti Restituti', or 'of Aulus Vettius Restitutus' and the image of an amphora were engraved into one, 'A. Vetti Convivaes [*sic*]', or 'of Aulus Vettius Conviva' and a caduceus were carved into the other.[24] A ring was also found with the initials AVC.[25] Although Henrik Mouritsen casts reasonable doubt on the reliability of seal stamps in identifying the owner(s) of Pompeian homes, even he agrees that the ring and seals help confirm the identification of Conviva and Restitutus as owners in this particular instance.[26] In addition, in a slogan painted onto the outer east wall of the house, Restitutus asks voters to support a certain Sabinus in his run for political office.[27] Such programmata are well-known in Pompeii. Although scholars disagree on whether or not the supporter named in them must be the owner or intimate associate of the owner of the house whose facade is so painted, the seals, ring and programmata in this instance work together to show that Conviva and Restitutus were likely residents of the house and socially prominent.[28]

Similar evidence points to the status of these men as freed. First, Vettius Conviva seems to be identified in another graffito on the southern facade of the house as an *Augustalis*, a type of priest.[29] Fragments of a seal ring may also have had the abbreviation *Aug* following his name.[30] Scholars such as Steven Ostrow and Andrik Abramenko have shown that this local priesthood was largely held by former slaves, and that this office would indicate Conviva possessed some wealth and standing in the community, since candidates for the sacred college donated costly gifts of public benefaction and were chosen by the town council.[31] 'Restitutus' was commonly, if not exclusively, a slave name.[32] When he was freed, the *praenomen* (first name) and *nomen* (family name) of his former master would have been added, and thus A. Vettius Restitutus was in all likelihood also a freedman.

A. Vettius Conviva appears as a witness in a famous preserved set of business tablets owned by one Q. Caecilius Iucundus.[33] The tablets were buried in the earthquake of 62 CE; by this time, Conviva was a free man, since he is identified in them with the *praenomen*, *nomen* and *cognomen* characteristic of free males. Altogether the evidence is convincing that he was a freedman and an owner of this large house during its final phase. But who was A. Vettius Restitutus, and what was his relationship to Conviva? Scholars traditionally call the men 'brothers', which is possible but far from provable.[34] Their shared *praenomen* and *nomen* indicate that they may have been owned by the same person and subsequently freed – any familial relationship they would have had is obscured by their freedman nomenclature, which privileges their relationship to their former master.[35] They may have been brothers, or they may have been fellow slaves (*colliberti*), who, as Sandra Joshel has demonstrated, often formed economic and social partnerships,[36] or they may have been father and son.[37] Another alternative is that Restitutus was Conviva's ex-slave – his name would be the same whether he was freed by Conviva himself or by Conviva's former master. Given Conviva's more established status, I might suggest that he was an owner of the house, and that Restitutus was an important member of his household – a son, brother or freedman – to whom the property perhaps passed upon Conviva's death. Two branches of the *gens Vettia* are known in Pompeii; both families produced several candidates for local offices in the early empire and thus could have had former slaves of the wealth and status of the owners of the House of the Vettii.[38]

What are the implications if this house was owned by former slaves? First, we will need to think about ancient Italian notions of slavery and the dynamics through which some slaves became free. Then I shall review how earlier scholars have seen freedmen in the decoration of the House of the Vettii. Finally, I articulate how I will interpret the imagery with their status in mind.

Slavery and freedom

Keith Bradley and Richard Saller, among others, have explored extensively what the jurist Gaius referred to as the 'primary distinction in the law of persons', demonstrating how slave was distinguished from free in terms of law, labour, discipline, religion and sexuality.[39] Slave-owning Romans considered their slaves to be part of their *familia*. A legal family unit was defined as the eldest free male (*paterfamilias*) and those subject to his authority, including his free and legitimate children, his slaves and potentially his wife.[40] Within a large urban household, slaves had specialised jobs organised into a social hierarchy. Work performed for the free members of the family would have included food storage, preparation and service, textile production and cleaning, house maintenance and childcare; depending upon the house, services might also entail work for the family shop or business, secretarial and accounting tasks, management, work as an artisan, valet or dresser, messenger, entertainer, tutor, guard and the like.[41]

Legally, slaves were considered a particular type of property, and they were not allowed to own capital of their own. Even so, many owners allowed their slaves to keep a small private fund, from which some slaves eventually bought their freedom. Slaves had even less control over their human offspring than the products of their labour. The children of a slave woman had the same status as their mother; they were the property of her owner, liable to be exposed at birth or sold, lent, given or willed out of the household at his or her whim. Although slaves sometimes took spouses, these bonds created no legal ties between the couple or between slave fathers and children. In fact, all the slave's familial relationships outside of that to the owner went formally unacknowledged in the broader community.[42] Finally, as will be discussed in greater detail below, slaves had no control over their own bodies. The elite, male authors of our surviving literature assume that male and female slaves were available to their masters for sexual use, and they consider corporal punishment appropriate for slaves, but not for freeborn members of a household.

The transition out of slavery into freedom was predictably complex. Among slaves with specialised and marketable skills, manumission was not uncommon; slaves either saved the money to purchase themselves or were freed by their owner in a will or for varied purposes during the owner's lifetime.[43] Within the Roman legal system, someone freed by a citizen became a citizen.[44] Freedmen were thereby able to marry and produce legitimate children, make contracts and wills, vote, take legal action and own property. As has been recently and carefully documented by Mouritsen, two factors continued to shape the lives of a freedman or freedwoman throughout their lives, however: stigmas attached to having been a slave and continuing obligations to one's former owner.[45] Patrons retained a claim on their former slave's labour, estate, public obedience and sexual services. Formal restrictions on the activities of freedmen seem to stem from their onetime lack of bodily integrity: ex-slaves were forbidden from joining the Roman military and holding most political and religious offices. An important exception was two cults created by the first emperor Augustus, including the priesthood of the *Augustales* which we have noted A. Vettius Conviva held. Many freedmen also invested energies in the success of their legitimate children, since once adults they would have the opportunities of the freeborn open to them.[46]

The House of the Vettii in scholarship

Previous scholars have approached the House of the Vettii and other art commissioned by freedmen with the status of ex-slaves in mind. Lauren Hackworth Petersen has argued well, however, that they tend to draw heavily on impressions of the concerns and predicaments of wealthy freedmen gleaned from the way they are mocked for comic effect by elite writers such as Juvenal, Martial and Petronius.[47] For example, Petronius composed a fictional banquet given by an ex-slave Trimalchio in which he depicts the host as overly material and crass, lacking sophistication and education in myth or history. The fictional freedman also makes critical social errors in the way he presents his own masculinity and sexual history, and he fails to distinguish himself from and control his slaves, among many other faults. Although some of these echo aspects of the transition from slavery to freedom which I have outlined, Petersen rightly emphasises the irresponsibility of using this stereotyped caricature as evidence for the concerns and interests of real people of a different class from the powerful elite author.[48] We must remember that the freed were part of a subculture largely lost to us but in which, as Joshel and Petersen have shown, labour was a source of pride and identity, rather than shame, as it was among the elite.[49]

In characterising the House of the Vettii, some scholars have succumbed to this tendency to draw on literary caricatures of freedmen, a tendency Petersen calls 'Trimalchio vision'.[50] Petronius presents his character as wildly overcompensating in behaviour and material display for the education and refinement which he lacks.[51] The decoration of the House of the Vettii has similarly been called 'overburdened' and 'outlandish'.[52] Special emphasis in this type of reading is placed on the painting of Priapus in the doorway, weighing his mighty member on a set of scales, an image echoed in a marble statue of Priapus found elsewhere in the house.[53] Clarke emphasises that this god was associated with fertility and averting the evil eye through laughter, but it is difficult not to see these aggressively male images as overcompensation.[54] Economic historian Michael Rostovtzeff also reads the famous painted frieze, in room *q*, of miniature Cupids and Psyches busy at a wide range of labours as biographical information about how the Vettii earned their wealth.[55]

A theoretical apparatus imported from outside the field of classics is one way to evade Trimalchio vision. Mulvey's work from 1975 provides tools for decoding an image's expression of power relations. These methods are both visual – in terms of costuming, body position, focalisation, the way characters view others inside the frame and how that encourages an external viewer to look – and narrative – in terms of who acts, who is acted upon and who is punished. This is the draw of Mulvey's approach, even though her ideas have been challenged on many fronts, including her own critique in subsequent work.[56]

In addition to such theoretical tools, another tack I intend to take is to consider persistently whether or not it matters if the owners of the house were freeborn or freed. A significant body of recent scholarship, including the work of Maud Gleason, Erik Gunderson, Anthony Corbeill and Amy Richlin, has analysed the literary production and artistic commissions of elite Roman men for the ways they define and defend their privileged status as men or attack the legitimacy of rivals based on questionable masculinity.[57] Freedmen and other men had just as much, if not more motivation to assert their status as men and masters for themselves, for their peers, for their fellow citizens and for their own slaves and ex-slaves. In the end, the fact that this house may have been owned by former slaves only serves as a useful prompt to consider the question whether or not gender alone encodes social hierarchies in its mythological paintings.

I hope to demonstrate that considering the stories told by the images of this house from a freed rather than a freeborn male's point of view – or just from a master's rather than a male's point of view – reveals much, regardless of the owner's actual status. As we have seen, Pompeian households had a slave/free dynamic as much as a male/female one, and behaviours, institutions, ideas and objects helped hold both hierarchies in place. Joshel and Sheila Murnaghan note in the introduction to their 1998 book, *Women and Slaves in Greco-Roman Culture*, that 'material culture had a role in structuring the relations of men and women, masters and slaves, and functioned to uphold citizen discourses of gender and social status'.[58] How material culture structured both social hierarchies at the same time, however, has been underexplored: 'scholars of antiquity overlook gender when talking about status or overlook status when talking about gender'.[59] Thinking about the transition from an objectified slave to an objectifying master can help us unsettle more broadly our notion of what it meant to be male in this slave-owning society and to consider its effects on the potential of psychoanalytic interpretation.

Houses, painting, myth and gender

Scholars such as Andrew Wallace-Hadrill, Eleanor Windsor Leach, Katharina Lorenz, John Clarke and Shelley Hales have studied broadly the work done by the wall painting of ancient Italian houses to create and project the identity of the owner, their role in the home and in the wider community.[60] The mythological panel has provided particularly rich fodder for analysis. Wallace-Hadrill defines it as 'a formally constructed scene, in a Hellenizing idiom, of a subject from Greek mythology'.[61] Particularly prevalent in later styles of Pompeian wall painting, such scenes are usually set into privileged sections in the centre of a decorated wall, rather like a framed painting in a modern home, but here painted into a fresco which covers the entire wall (Figure 7).[62]

Daniela Corlàita Scagliarini, John Clarke and others have argued that such paintings tend to be absent from spaces through which people moved, where the decoration was not designed to encourage lingering study or promote conversation.[63] As we have briefly seen, in terms of basic architectural structure, large Italian houses of the early imperial period consisted of two primary features, the main hall or *atrium* and a colonnaded garden, often but not always aligned on a central access and with smaller rooms opening off from each.[64] In homes decorated with wall painting, mythological scenes tend to be presented in the reception rooms, including rooms designed for the dinner party. Such paintings are usually elaborate and engaging, calling for explanation and thus prompting conversation, as is evinced not just by the decoration of such rooms across Pompeii and beyond, but in some literary accounts analysing similar mythological art.[65] The mythological panels of a home displayed the owner as Hellenised, cultured, wealthy and urbane; as we shall now investigate further, they have also been read as a complex discourse about relationships of power. [66]

In a compelling example, Fredrick uses the work of Mulvey to analyse Pompeian paintings of the mythical figure, Ariadne.[67] This princess helped the hero Theseus escape the labyrinth on Crete, only to be abandoned by him on a different island; she was later discovered there by her future husband, the god Dionysus. The three extremely common scenes of Ariadne's abandonment by Theseus while she sleeps, of her realisation of her abandonment upon awakening and of the discovery of her by Dionysus while she again sleeps make her 'the single most popular individual subject in Pompeii'.[68] Ariadne's storyline fits Mulvey's concept of sadistic voyeurism well. In Fredrick's words:

> The paintings voyeuristically insist on sexual difference in the absolute division of mobility and power between Ariadne on the one hand and Theseus and Dionysus on the other. Theseus's departure and Dionysus's arrival are sadistic in Mulvey's terms in that they emphasise the movement of the narrative around the static figure of Ariadne, whose fate is determined by the males: punishment by exposure on a desolate island, or the 'reward' of union with Dionysus, a 'marriage' which Ovid, in *Ars Amatoria* 1.527–64, presents as a rape.[69]

In turn, the panel on the south wall of room *p* in the House of the Vettii provides an excellent illustration of Mulvey's 'fetishistic scopophilia' in the paintings of Ariadne (Figure 3). A satyr lifts clothing off the reclining Ariadne so that the approaching Dionysus can gaze at the front of her naked body. We as viewers are guided by his example to view her erotically, as well as by the way her drapery falls to reveal to us her bare backside.[70] Fredrick provides critical insight in finding an expression of power tied up with the pleasure and privilege of looking, and he identifies as a major theme of images throughout this house the concealing or revealing of bodies using drapery, veils or disguises.[71]

What then catches Fredrick's attention, however, are the many scenes also popular in Pompeian homes in which male bodies are exposed to the viewer or punished by the storyline. Examples include Actaeon and his hunting dogs, described above; Hylas, the young lover of Hercules pulled to his watery destruction by a lust-filled nymph and Endymion, the mortal youth loved by the moon goddess Selene and usually depicted reclining nude beneath the night sky. Fredrick interprets these scenes as 'men playing the feminine' and relates them to similar examples found in elite literature in the capital, such as in elegy and satire.[72] Maria Wyke, Marilyn Skinner and others have explained those inversions as expressions of political alienation and a loss of power among elite men in Rome as they adapted to life under autocratic rule.[73] Fredrick also usefully explores the cultural associations of the Roman banquet as a source for these 'gender inversions.' He argues that anxieties arose in elite males over the vulnerabilities they perceived to be inherent in the banquet – a time and space when the body became

Figure 3: Artist unknown, 'Ariadne', south wall of room *p,* House of the Vettii (VI 15, 1), Pompeii, 62–79 CE (photograph by Michael Larvey, Austin, Texas, with permission of the Ministry for Cultural Heritage and the Environment, Special Superintendent of Naples and Pompeii).

susceptible to, even penetrable by, various pleasures, including food, drink and sex.[74] Both of these phenomena may help explain how and why such images became a feature of pattern books, or at least common in the repertoire of images from which patrons chose.[75] Trends may have originated in Rome, and as Wallace-Hadrill and Clarke suggest, among the owner's motivations in selecting art in this house was to display the luxury characteristic of the upper classes. But alienation due to the increasing concentration of political power into fewer and fewer hands at the top level in Rome would have held little meaning in Pompeii.[76] And even if 'mythological paintings … articulated … a space where Romans could contemplate – and insert themselves into – scenes of erotic fascination, passivity, bodily dissolution and mutilation', into which roles did home owners insert themselves?[77]

I put forward two approaches to these fundamental questions. For some of the images which seem to invert gender hierarchy and which certainly do not provide escape from 'castration' for the male viewer, I suggest that by focusing on gender we are misunderstanding the viewer and the nature of his pleasure. Koloski-Ostrow points toward this viewer:

As a spectator of these scenes, the viewer sees not just anatomical differences between men and women, but social difference as well. The men (or gods) who control the women or men of suffering possess more than the penis. They wield the phallus, the ultimate symbol of the male Roman social order. The house owners who commissioned such scenes for their own domestic stages thereby created a painted script with subtle, and not so subtle, messages of control easily legible to visitors and members of their own households. Such mythological images strongly suggest that an inherent 'language of power' is painted symbolically in these houses, mainly for the pleasure of male viewers presumably, which emphasises anew the authority of the *dominus*. Distinctive gender differences are depicted in a visual 'language of power' for the pleasure and use of the *dominus* in these houses.[78]

I propose that we take Koloski-Ostrow's cue further and focus more on the viewer's status as a *dominus*, or master, and less on his maleness.

Gender can be extremely useful in signifying, and therefore studying, relationships of power, many of which have little or nothing to do with the relationship between actual men and women, as Joan Scott so well articulated in 1986.[79] But if gender is culturally constructed, it is constructed differently by each culture, and similarly the degree to which gender is used to signify other relationships of power has the potential to vary over time and space, as well. Mulvey's 1975 spin on European psychoanalytic theory, with its notions of castration and the phallus, insists on the primacy of gender, and on a gender which is closely tied to anatomical sex. Our use of these terms can obscure cultural difference, and an exclusive focus on gender can cause status categories not particularly active or resonant for us, such as slave and master, to fade from our view.[80] In the case study, we shall see that some images which torture and eroticise male bodies should not be read as gender inversions, but as ancient Italian expressions of the privilege of a master to enjoy female *and* male bodies.

In turn, some of the paintings in both narrative and visual focus do encourage the viewer to sympathise with a suffering body. These images imply that escape from 'castration' is not the only interest of the male viewer, which challenges Mulvey's notion of the male gaze in a different way. As noted above, Fredrick pursues intriguing reasons for at least elite men to have desired temporarily to explore subordinate subject positions. I will expand the conversation by using reactions to Mulvey among feminist film theorists, particularly the work of Clover, who in analysing twentieth-century British and American horror film finds similarly problematic gender slippage and visual pleasure from pain.

Case study: ancient slavery, sexuality and the House of the Vettii

Among the rooms of the House of the Vettii endowed with mythological paintings, two apparently paired receiving rooms opening into the east wall of the rear garden will command most of our attention. The northern of the two (*p*) has walls elaborately painted as an imitation picture gallery (Figure 4). Faux marbles in the lower zone support an intricate theatrical facade in the middle and upper registers. In the centre of all three walls, imitation masterpiece paintings are set into a dark red background. To the longer walls, the north and south, are added images of white faux tapestries to either side of the myth scenes. On the north wall, the mythological panel features Pasiphae, wife of Minos, the king of Crete, who was punished by the gods with lust for a bull (Figure 5). The famed Athenian craftsman Daedalus, visible in the foreground with his back to the viewer, points to the wooden cow he has constructed for her to conceal

Figure 4: Room *p*, north and east walls, House of the Vettii (VI 15, 1), Pompeii (photograph by author, with permission of the Ministry for Cultural Heritage and the Environment, Special Superintendent of Naples and Pompeii).

herself and consummate her desire. The Minotaur who lived within the labyrinth (later defeated by Theseus) resulted from their union.

Ariadne, Theseus's helper and Pasiphae's daughter, is shown on the opposing south wall being discovered by Dionysus (Figure 3). Between these two scenes, on the east wall, are presented Juno and Ixion (Figure 6). Ixion was a mortal man who lusted after Juno, Jupiter's wife; Jupiter substituted a cloud-figure, Nephele, for his wife during the rape and then caught the blasphemer. Ixion was scourged and bound to a fiery wheel, part of which is visible to the viewer's left in the painting while a seated Juno looks on from the right. The nude male figure of Mercury, the messenger of the gods, stands between Ixion and Juno, as though he is explaining to her what has occurred. Nephele, the crouching female figure in the foreground, subsequently bore Centaurus, the father of the breed of half-horse, half-human centaurs.

In the parallel room to the south (*n*), at the other end of the peristyle garden, the upper register of the decoration has been lost. Above a red socle appears a

Figure 5: Artist unknown, 'Punishment of Pasiphae', north wall of room *p*, House of the Vettii (VI 15, 1), Pompeii, 62–79 CE (photograph by Michael Larvey, Austin, Texas, with permission of the Ministry for Cultural Heritage and the Environment, Special Superintendent of Naples and Pompeii).

middle zone separated into bright yellow gold central spaces for mythological paintings and flanking faux 'windows' into an illusionary cityscape beyond the wall (Figure 7). The myth scenes in this room present Pentheus being killed by female followers of Dionysus on the east wall (Figure 7), the punishment of Dirce on the south (Figure 8) and an infant Hercules battling snakes on the north (Figure 9). Pentheus was a king of Thebes who denied that his cousin Dionysus was a son of Jupiter. Dionysus punished him by driving their female relatives mad and having them physically tear Pentheus apart during a religious ritual. The mortal woman Dirce was punished by the twin sons Antiope bore for Jupiter; Dirce had long imprisoned and then attempted to kill Antiope, either her sister or the first wife of her own husband in Thebes. When Hercules was a baby, his stepmother Juno sent snakes to kill him in his bed. His defeat of the serpents constituted his first heroic feat and proved that Jupiter was his father rather than Amphitryon, an exile of Tiryns living in Thebes who was married to his mother.

As Clarke has noted, the 'decoration of the Vettii's house, perhaps the finest of Pompeii's last two decades, is both rich and iconographically bewildering. Much ink ... has flowed in attempting to explain its various – and variously linked – iconographical programs'.[81] Mary Lee Thompson argues that both rooms programmatically

Figure 6: Artist unknown, 'Punishment of Ixion', east wall of room
p, House of the Vettii (VI 15, 1), Pompeii, 62–79 CE (photograph
by Michael Larvey, Austin, Texas, with permission of the Ministry
for Cultural Heritage and the Environment, Special Superintendent
of Naples and Pompeii).

contrast divine reward and punishment.[82] Karl Schefold elaborates upon this, noting,
for example, that room *p* contrasts two divinely associated sexual offences – those of
Pasiphae and Ixion which resulted respectively in the birth of the monstrous Minotaur
and centaurs – with the happy union of the god Dionysus and mortal Ariadne.[83] But
to date Theo Wirth has done the most substantive work on the purposeful comparisons
and contrasts set up by the paintings in these rooms, and his suggestions have largely
been followed by later scholars, such as Richard Brilliant and Clarke.[84] Overall, Wirth
sees a story about the power of the gods, particularly Jupiter and his sons as guarantors
of world order. This general theme is articulated by pairings across the two rooms, such
as a guilty woman in each (Dirce and Pasiphae), a guilty man (Pentheus and Ixion) –
all four punished by gods or their supporters – and a boy or woman saved by a god
(Hercules and Ariadne, respectively).

   In parallel with these thematic similarities across paintings and across the rooms,
Wirth identifies visual similarities as well. For example, he notes that the scene of
Pasiphae features a (wooden) cow, that of Dirce a bull. He identifies the Pentheus and
Dirce scenes as pendants, with a matching colour scheme and composition, in which
a male and a female are punished by figures of the opposite gender in the setting
of Mount Cithaeron near Thebes. In room *p*, the pendants are Ixion and Pasiphae,
which both offer scenes of illicit, cross-status love (a human desiring a god and a

Figure 7: East wall of room *n*, featuring 'Punishment of Pentheus', House of the Vettii (VI, 15, 1), Pompeii, 62–79 CE (photograph by Michael Larvey, Austin, Texas, with permission of the Ministry for Cultural Heritage and the Environment, Special Superintendent of Naples and Pompeii).

human desiring an animal). Wirth finds deliberate contrasts between the rooms, such as the quiet moments depicted in *p* and the highly dramatic presentations in room *n*. In room *p* he finds a set of stories about relations between the sexes, with examples both blissful and unfortunate, taken largely from myths associated with Crete, while room *n* draws out a narrative about family relationships, particularly parents and children, as Jupiter saves his son Hercules, Pentheus is torn to pieces by his maenadic mother and Dirce is killed by sons avenging their mother, all stories about the Greek city of Thebes.

These briefly described pages of thick scholarly interpretation attest that the decoration achieved the goal noted earlier of creating lively discussion, and I do not particularly disagree with any of my fellow interpreters. I would not be surprised to learn that many of their suggestions had already occurred to ancient viewers over the course of multiple dinner conversations in this home. Like Fredrick and Koloski-Ostrow, however, I suggest we should also look in these images for how they inscribe key power structures of the household and the community.

The master gaze

As explored earlier, this home may have been owned by ex-slaves when it was extensively repainted following the earthquake of 62 CE, and it is worth considering the implications of this possibility. If we assume, even just for the moment of this article, that the paintings of the house were commissioned by former slaves, we are

Figure 8: Artist unknown, 'Punishment of Dirce', south wall of room *n*, House of the Vettii (VI 15, 1), Pompeii, 62–79 CE (photograph by Michael Larvey, Austin, Texas, with permission of the Ministry for Cultural Heritage and the Environment, Special Superintendent of Naples and Pompeii).

encouraged to interpret these mythological scenes within the context of Roman slavery. I will argue that much of the extensive programme of wall paintings in rooms *n* and *p* of the House of the Vettii create and project the status of the owners as masters. To find these messages, I will be looking at the comparisons and contrasts called for by the formal compositions and juxtapositions of the paintings themselves. This method of analysing the images and their compositional similarities with nearby images first, and myth or narrative second, was first called for in the House of the Vettii by Wirth, but has been asserted as the most appropriate approach to Pompeian mythological paintings by Bettina Bergmann and Lorenz, as well as in approaching Roman mosaics by Susanne Muth.[85]

For example, although scholars from Thompson to Wirth have noted the focus on punishment in the scenes in these rooms, the relationship between punishment and

Figure 9: Artist unknown, 'Hercules', north wall of room *n*, House of the Vettii (VI 15, 1), Pompeii, 62–79 CE (photograph provided by Superstock.com, with permission of the Ministry for Cultural Heritage and the Environment, Special Superintendent of Naples and Pompeii).

slavery has not been part of the analysis. At least four of the six mythological panels display torture: Dirce is being pulled apart by a bull, Pentheus by his maenadic female relatives, Ixion is on a rack in the form of a wheel and Daedalus is presenting Pasiphae with the cow costume she will use to satisfy her divinely imposed lust for a bull. This focus on punishment is no accident. As noted earlier, Lorenz has demonstrated that although many individual paintings recur across Pompeii, they are grouped together within rooms in unique ways to create new meanings.[86] In these rooms in this particular house and as outlined by Wirth, two of the scenes are crafted as pendants of each other. In room *p*, the scenes of Pasiphae and Ixion (Figures 5 and 6), juxtaposed on the north and east walls respectively (Figure 10), each feature a seated female figure, Pasiphae on the far left and Juno on the far right, facing each other across the corner of the room.

N ⬅

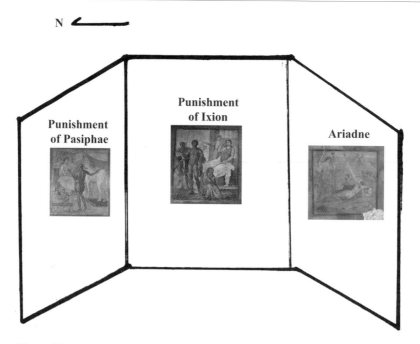

Figure 10: Arrangement of mythological panels in room *p*, House of the Vettii (VI 15, 1), Pompeii (created by author, photographs used with permission of the Ministry for Cultural Heritage and the Environment, Special Superintendent of Naples and Pompeii).

A standing male figure occupies the centre of each composition (Daedalus and Mercury), and on the far side rests the instrument of torture, a heifer suit for Pasiphae and a wheel to which Ixion is bound. In room *n*, Dirce and Pentheus are similarly paired, as will be explored further below. One painting from each set – Ixion in *p* and Pentheus in *n* – is unique in surviving ancient Italian painting, and details of the compositions of their pendants were changed from iconographic models to make them parallel their partners more closely.[87]

Certainly, this concerted focus on punishment may be a message about divine wrath and retribution. What has been missed, however, is the significance of corporal punishment and torture in distinguishing slave from free in ancient Italy. Saller has demonstrated convincingly that Roman authors considered physical abuse in the form of beatings or whippings appropriate for slaves but not for freeborn children.[88] The Roman state administered punishment in a variety of ways scaled from most to least degrading and painful depending upon social status; the worst was reserved for slaves and lower-class foreigners, including crucifixion and burning alive.[89] Most stark, however, is the fact that a slave's testimony was admissible in a Roman court *only* if it had been obtained under torture.[90] Thus, corporal punishment – strongly and purposefully present in these rooms – had a cultural association with slavery as well as with mythological figures who offended the divine.

In the House of the Vettii's scenes of Dirce, Pentheus, Ixion and Pasiphae, note that we are not seeing sympathy for the punished or identification with the tortured in these paintings commissioned by masters. These punishments are instead eroticised;

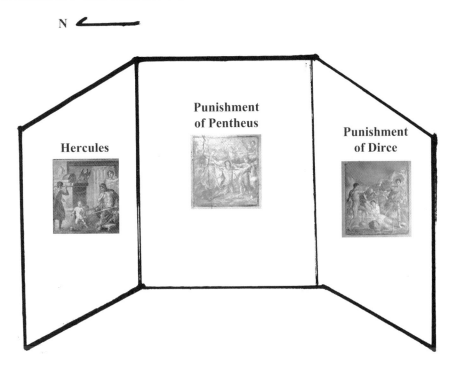

Figure 11: Arrangement of mythological panels in room *n*, House of the Vettii (VI 15, 1), Pompeii (created by author, photographs used with permission of the Ministry for Cultural Heritage and the Environment, Special Superintendent of Naples and Pompeii).

the bodies of those being punished are presented for the viewer's pleasure. This is particularly clear in the paintings of Dirce and Pentheus in room *n* (Figures 8 and 7). Just like the Pasiphae and Ixion images, the compositions of these paintings cry out for comparison (Figure 11). They each feature a central, tortured figure, kneeling, with arms outstretched to expose the naked upper body to the view of the spectator.

Mulvey's notion of the way that the camera fetishises body parts is helpful in unpacking this image, but a focus on gender misleads. One might read the Dirce scene as a fetishising of the female torso, but it is critical to keep in mind that Pentheus is presented in an identical pose on the adjoining wall.[91] Each is flanked and held in place primarily by two figures of the opposite sex, their tormentors, in an outdoor setting.

The assaulting figures in *both* scenes also look at the vulnerable, nude victims, directing our view. Clover usefully questions Mulvey's proposition that the only gaze presented in cinema is that of the sadistic voyeur. She explores instead two types of viewing internal to horror – the 'assaultive gaze', masculine, predatory and often the first person view of the camera, and the 'reactive gaze', usually coded as feminine, the spectator who is assaulted, harmed or frightened by seeing something horrific.[92] Given that in the Vettii paintings those who look at the central, tortured figures are the torturers, it seems fair to call this an 'assaultive gaze,', and the external viewer of the painting is invited to share it. A similar display of pain for the pleasure of others is explicit in a mythological panel from room *e* in the house. On the south wall, a seated

Dionysus and a female figure, probably his wife Ariadne, occupy the centre of the scene, while a small winged cupid and goat-god Pan fight in the foreground, hurting each other for the entertainment of the spectators.[93]

Within room *n*, Pentheus and Dirce actually lean toward each other, which, as noted above, required a reversal of Dirce's position from the iconographic model reconstructed from images of this story in other paintings and media.[94] Both a man and a woman are thus shown tortured in an eroticised manner on adjacent walls in this room, in mirror image to the man and woman punished on adjoining walls in room *p*. The paired paintings purposefully undermine any hierarchy between the genders and instead subordinate both a male and female body to the gaze of the viewer. I argue this viewer is the patron, a patron positioned by this gaze as master, that is, one who orders, observes and even enjoys the punishment of both males and females.

The way Roman notions of sexuality intersect with slavery reinforces this positioning of the viewer as master. In the same way that a male or female slave's body was treated as penetrable by stick or lash, it was considered open to the master for sexual use as well.[95] Slave boys were kept in part as sexual pets.[96] The law did not allow a woman dressed as a slave to be considered a rape victim, while a freeborn male citizen was able to sue someone for outrage if that person treated him like a slave in any way, including striking or flogging him, invading his home, preventing him from enjoying public amenities such as baths and theatres, dishonouring his wife, children or slaves or sexually penetrating his person.[97] Freeborn citizen children wore a protective amulet, called a *bulla*, which among other things helped visibly mark them as sexually off-limits, unlike slave children.[98]

This assumed sexual use of male and female slaves by their master put slaves into a specific sexual category in Roman society, and masters in another, regardless of the slave's gender. Holt Parker and Skinner have articulated how the Romans who left our surviving literature understood sexuality in ways that do not involve our contemporary notions of heterosexual and homosexual, or attraction to the same or opposite sex. In dominant Roman ideology, sexual activity was considered someone penetrating someone else, and the operative categories which arose from this were active and passive, penetrator and penetrated.[99] This was a hierarchical distinction which intersected with other statuses, including gender and age. 'Doers' tended to be adult, freeborn citizen men; 'does' were women, but also male slaves, children and non-citizens. To 'be done' carried some degree of shame. As Ellen Oliensis writes, 'Penetration is the prerogative of free men, penetrability the characteristic condition of slaves and women; sexual intercourse is an enactment and reflection of social hierarchy, and conversely, social subordination always implies the possibility of sexual submission'.[100] Moses Finley first noted the implications of the Roman habit of referring to even an adult male slave as a *puer*, 'boy'; it reinforces on many levels a male slave's lack of manhood, bodily integrity and independent standing in the community.[101] In turn, to be a master was to be a doer, to have the capacity to penetrate male and female bodies at will.

I suggest that the insistence on the irrelevance of gender in these paired scenes of torture arises from this relationship between sexuality and power that is not well articulated by what we think of as gender. Interestingly, in looking at British and American horror, Clover sees similar patterns and provides similar explanations. She remarks that horror knows full well that male does not equal female, and yet 'repeatedly contemplates mutations and slidings whereby women begin to look a lot like men (slasher films), men are pressured to become like women (possession films), and some people are impossible to tell apart'.[102] To understand this slippery presentation of gender, Clover explores Thomas Laqueur's notion that the pre-modern world exhibited one-sex cultural reasoning and that two-sex cultural reasoning developed in the modern era.[103] That is, in the ancient Mediterranean, according to Laqueur, bodies were understood as falling along a sliding scale of sexual difference, rather than being either one or the other in a binary male/female system. Clover suggests that 'horror may in fact be the premier repository of one-sex reasoning in our time'.[104] In particular, she argues that rape revenge films equate entry points into the male and female body, marking all bodies as penetrable and suggesting 'a universe in which vagina and anus are indeed for all practical purposes the same thing'.[105]

Although some substitute other forms of torture for rape, the paired paintings of Pentheus and Dirce, Ixion and Pasiphae in the House of the Vettii imply a similar universe in which the category 'penetrable' counts at least as much as the categories of 'male' and 'female'. I would add that an important structural element in the dynamic of one-sex thinking in Roman Italy was slavery. A freedman in particular – but all males raised in a slave-owning household – knew that being male was no guarantee of a dominant status; all children, male and female, slave and free, began life in some sense at one end of the gender/sexuality scale, and then some males moved to the other end over their lifetimes. If we look at these images with Roman slavery and sexuality in mind, that there should be male and female objects of the viewer's penetrating gaze is in no way surprising. Slave and master were crucial categories, and sex and corporal punishment were activities through which those categories were negotiated and defined. When the owner selected these images of eroticised torture, he was inscribing his own power to punish or to enjoy onto his very walls.

It is worth pausing here to consider the likely function of rooms *p* and *n* as dining rooms (*triclinia*), because the banquet was a place and time of intense contact between slave and free.[106] As is well explored by scholars such as John D'Arms, Katharine Dunbabin and Lisa Bek, the banquet (*convivium*) was a prominent part of Pompeian life and accommodated architecturally throughout the town.[107] Hosting a banquet advertised social status in terms of the luxury of its provision, its decoration and the way it was enacted. Custom prescribed arrangement of up to three couches, for up to a dozen persons to dine, and assigned positions on the couches delimited social hierarchy. The host literally controlled the pecking order.[108] Guests might include social superiors, who would be given the best seats, peers, on down to the host's own former slaves.[109] The pleasures of food, drink, sex, conversation and other diversions and entertainments are commonly associated with the *convivium* in surviving literature and imagery.[110] The banquet was a key locus for a host's performance of his role in the community as someone with a specific position in the social hierarchy, taste, real estate and other privileges of power.

Reclining on the left arm to dine, as was the fashion for banquets, also required the presence of many slaves to place food and drink close to each effectively one-handed guest, not to mention the slaves or other workers who might be present to perform various types of entertainment.[111] The banquet was thus a place where the service of the enslaved was immediate, physical and ubiquitous. For masters, these slaves would have also been an important audience for the art and performance of the *convivium*.

Elite Roman authors thought that reclining to dine distinguished the gentleman from the slave and the child.[112] D'Arms, in looking at the banquet from the slaves' point of view, asks 'how far did proximity to the tables of the powerful increase their sense of superiority over fellow slaves, and how far did it serve merely to accentuate the distance between their own condition and that of their owners, the privileged consumers of the luxuries and comforts that the slaves dispensed?'[113]

If he was the owner and if he had been a slave, the dining room may also have been particularly important to Vettius Conviva, whose unusual name, Conviva, is related to the Latin term for a banquet, *convivium*.[114] We have no way of knowing if he indeed was once assigned tasks at his master's table, or if he just had a name that denoted characteristic slave labour. The five rooms of this home suitable for banqueting (*e*, *p*, *n*, *q* and *t*) show great interest on his part, and may even reflect an attempt to subvert his former master's interest in naming him and create a positive spin on his identification with the banquet; Conviva transformed himself from 'serving wench' to 'host extraordinaire'.

I would argue, at any rate, that the dining room was a place where the distinction between slave and free was highly activated, rather than blurred. As noted earlier, Fredrick interprets what he sees as the destabilising of gender hierarchy in the Vettii's and other dining room paintings as a banqueting viewer's temporary assumption of an alternative subject position, an indulgence in passivity or admission of a less than confident social superiority.[115] Looking from the perspective of slavery, the paintings we have seen in these two rooms – with images depicting or alluding to the torture of men and women eroticised for the viewer's pleasure – instead reinforce the powerful position of the owner over his domain. The images provided a constant (if mythologically cloaked) reminder to himself, his guests and his slaves of the power of the owner to torture, a concrete illustration of Paul Zanker's summative evaluation of Pompeian painting: 'the society of the early empire projects its fantasies of a happy life onto the mythical figures and then enjoys these projections of the image'.[116] Of course, during a banquet a master actually could perform his privilege in the flesh by punishing any misbehaving slaves or fondling others.[117]

Moreover, if we look for a power hierarchy besides gender which can be represented in mythological paintings – that of human and divine – we see in these images a strict maintenance of power relations. Pentheus, Ixion and Pasiphae all failed to respect someone's divinity; Pentheus and Ixion tried to subject a deity to imprisonment or sex, only to be tortured themselves as a result.[118] That human/divine might sometimes work as an analogy for slave/free is perhaps clinched by the fourth scene in the series, that of Dirce, who is punished not for disrespecting divinity, but for enslaving a respectable fellow mortal. Such story lines of vengeance for inappropriate enslaving, imprisoning or desiring may have held particular appeal for an ex-slave, but a narrative enforcing a line between slave and free would please any master.

To reinforce the notion of a master gaze in the House of the Vettii, I would like to look briefly at images addressed specifically to the audience of slaves within the house. We have already seen how the mythological scenes of punishment and torture in reception rooms *p* and *n* might be interpreted as emphasising the owners' ability to dispense corporal punishment on or sexually enjoy their slaves. In the service quarters we find more images reinforcing the master's ability to control the bodies of human property, albeit in different modes.

Figure 12: Artist unknown, 'Erotic Scene', room x^1, House of the Vettii (VI 15, 1), Pompeii, 62–79 CE (photograph by author, with permission of the Ministry for Cultural Heritage and the Environment, Special Superintendent of Naples and Pompeii).

As mentioned, two small service areas (*v-y* and 1–4, shaded in Figure 2) are evident in what survives of the house. The one which concerns us consists of a set of rooms around a small central *atrium (v)*. A built-in hearth, found covered with pots and pans in adjacent room *w*, reveals its role as a kitchen. As one can see from the plan, the whole section is closed off architecturally from the rest of the house, being accessible only through one doorway from the main *atrium*. Its decor is quite plain. The differentiation of this area from the rest of the house in architecture and decoration clearly marks its position on the grand/humble axis defined by Wallace-Hadrill in his study of Pompeian houses; guests entering the home would know from these markers that this space was for slaves and other workers.[119] As noted, most of the service area has only the sparsest decoration of plain white or yellow paint. However, in the tiny room to the north of the kitchen (x^1), far into the utilitarian part of the house, are found three large scenes of male-female couples engaged in sexual activities (Figure 12).

The walls are divided into the traditional three horizontal and vertical zones by simple, wide red lines; an owl is depicted on the short south wall.[120] The erotic paintings are simply rendered on a pale background, one each in the centre of the other three walls and framed by cursorily decorated thin red lines. They strongly resemble those from the famous brothel farther south near the forum in Pompeii.[121] Although the brothel paintings are crudely executed, they allude to the erotic art found in elite homes that idealise lovemaking and are thus designed to 'class up the joint'.[122] What are they doing in the service area of this wealthy home?

Clarke suggests that images were painted here as a favour for a master's favourite, and that the male servant who lived here shared in his master's view of women as sexual objects.[123] But again I would argue that focusing on gender to the exclusion of other critical and intersecting social statuses can mislead us. Given the nature of the sexual dynamic between a slave and master regardless of sex or gender, of which an ex-slave was certainly aware if not intimately experienced, I suspect there may be something else going on here. For an audience of male and female slaves, who would certainly spend the most time around these images, they may have served as a reminder of one of their servile tasks. Other evidence of slave sexuality and anxiety about the sexual category of enslaved men has been found in this part of the house. An informal inscription tells us of a slave named Eros, 'Desire', a not uncommon name for male slaves. Inside the service *atrium* (*v*) on the wall near the doorway was carved 'Eros cinedae', 'Eros is a *cinaedus*' or 'Eros likes to be sexually passive'.[124] The note had subsequently been scratched out.

Control over the household staff is expressed in paint in a very different way in the service area. I am speaking of the *lararium* (Figure 13), located in the small *atrium* (*v*). Many homes contained such shrines to household divinities, usually including deities of place, such as the *lares*, as well as the divine twin of the head of the household, referred to as his *genius*. At meals and holidays, members of the free family, their slaves and freedpersons made offerings at these shrines, called *lararia*.[125] Thus slaves and others enacted their dependency upon the master of the house every day by expressing adoration of his *genius*. In the Vettii shrine, typical images of the Lares and the Genius of the Paterfamilias are depicted. The *genius* figure in the centre is particularly expressive, included as an object of cult devotion, but depicted in the process of conducting an offering. The image defined the master as one who was worshiped within his house, but who in a larger sense communicated with the gods on behalf of his house.[126] In the Vettii household, the shrine is located explicitly in the area where slave work was performed, a not uncommon yet far from standardised location.[127] I think of it as a similar representation and enactment of dominance as in the erotic scenes, here using religious rather than sexual imagery and practice. The erotic paintings and this image on the *lararium* shrine are the only figural scenes in the whole of the surviving utilitarian area.

I also want to pause to emphasise that gender is used elsewhere in the house to encode social hierarchies, such as in reception room *t*, part of the master's suite off the tiny second peristyle and thus in the most intimate spaces of the house.[128] Much of the elegant decoration in this room has been lost. What survives shows a dark socle and middle zone separated into panels by delicate white lines and illusionary shutters painted as though open to allow a view of a *trompe l'oeil* garden beyond. Two of what were once three central mythological panels survive: on the south wall a drunken Hercules assaults Auge, a priestess of Athena, and on the east wall Achilles's disguise as a maiden on Skyros is revealed.[129] (Since Achilles knew he would die young if he fought at Troy, his mother encouraged him to hide from recruiters among the daughters of the king of Skyros. Two endings explain how he was discovered. In one, Odysseus tracks him to the palace and sets out gifts of jewellery and weapons; Achilles's interest in the male-gendered objects give him away. In the other version, Achilles reveals himself when he rapes the king's daughter, Deidameia.)

Figure 13: Household shrine, west wall of room *v*, House of the Vettii (VI 15, 1), Pompeii, 62–79 CE (photograph by author, with permission of the Ministry for Cultural Heritage and the Environment, Special Superintendent of Naples and Pompeii).

In what survives of the imagery in this room masculinity always wins out, and the male viewer is pleasured in just the ways outlined by Mulvey. Auge is presented much as the tortured figures in room *n*, kneeling, with her clothing falling off to expose her nude torso. She holds up a hand to ward off the approaching Hercules unsuccessfully. He comes from behind her, to the right of the viewer and helping to direct the viewer's gaze at her exposed body, as do two of the three other figures in the painting. Hercules holds his club between them; his needs clearly will not be denied. In turn, Achilles's masculinity is not threatened even in a dress. He stands in the middle of what survives of the painting, his clothing falling off to display his maleness. To be clear this does not make him vulnerable, one of the king's daughters runs from him, her clothing also falling to provide an erotic view of her exaggerated backside. Both stories result in heroic children: princess Deidameia bears Achilles Neoptolemus as a result of her rape by Achilles on Skyros, and Hercules's rape of Auge leads to the birth of Telephus. In birthing heroes instead of monsters, the scenes may contrast purposefully with the scenes in room *p* just around the corner of the peristyle. It is unfortunate that even less of the decoration from the adjoining room, *u*, including none of the mythological paintings, survive to tell us more.

To summarise, the paintings we have surveyed in this home present the owner as master on a number of grounds: not only does he own and display wealth, he maintains mastery over the rest of the household in terms of religion, sexuality and corporal punishment. The scenes of male bodies both tortured and eroticised need not reveal an exploration of alternative, subordinate subject positions, a destabilising of gender hierarchies. They need not be much about gender at all, although gender is used as a discursive hierarchy elsewhere in the house. These scenes are about a social status and lived experience in which being male did not guarantee, and thus could not signify, dominance: slavery. Mulvey's notions of fetishistic scopophilia and sadistic voyeurism work well on many of these images when they are not tied exclusively to a binary notion of gender: subordinate (slave) bodies are eroticised by the camera angle and costuming and punished by the storyline. These techniques of analysing the way visual narratives encode power are useful, but their theoretical basis in castration in some ways is not, because not all male viewers evade castration, even if masters do. But other images in the house, including ones that play with the boundary between mortals and gods, do not allow even a master who is a viewer to evade pain, objectification or 'castration'. Here we reach a different problem in Mulvey's approach from 1975, one also addressed by Clover in terms of twentieth-century horror films and by Fredrick in terms of ancient Italian painting.

Masochism

Indeed, what should we make of an image which encourages us to *identify* with a figure in pain? One panel in each of our receiving rooms does not depict violent punishment, but instead presents a character currently beset with challenges but who will ultimately triumph: the struggling infant Hercules on the north wall of room *n*, and the abandoned Ariadne on the south wall of room *p* (Figures 9 and 3). Each is a mortal later transformed into a god, whose divinity (and thus position in the social hierarchy) was at one time unrecognised. Again we have one male and one female, and their placement in the two rooms calls for comparison – they would be back to back save for the intervening spaces (Figures 10 and 11). Stories of heroic boundary-crossers might be particularly appealing to former slaves, but also to males born free but who still had to make the transition from objectified youth to penetrating adult man. What is problematic about this appeal, however, is its basis in identification with a character in pain or humiliation, sometimes across genders; the threat of 'castration' is on display, which Mulvey's scophophilia and sadistic voyeurism give us no means of understanding.

The Hercules scene (Figure 9) comes closest of all the mythological panels in these two rooms in the House of the Vettii to expressing sympathy and encouraging the viewer to identify outright with the main figure. Hercules is presented as a small child strangling two serpents sent by Juno to kill him. His pose echoes the other paintings in room *n* with his kneeling, triangular posture and frontal display of his tortured body (Figure 11). However, he leans away from the other paintings, and he holds the snakes, while no one holds him. The onlookers within his scene wonder at his success rather than orchestrate his demise, including a well-dressed woman and seated man, presumably his mother Alcmene and her husband Amphitryon. Above is positioned a sculpted eagle, part of a monument behind the struggling toddler demarcating his true father, Jupiter. Hercules's situation is dire, a vulnerable mortal child, but his innate status as hero and future god is also revealed and ultimately triumphant. Hercules is used elsewhere in Italian art and Mediterranean storytelling to celebrate social climbers; freedmen serving as priests in the imperial cult of Herculaneum decorated their central shrine 'with paintings of clear thematic import depicting events in the life of Hercules which showed the eponymous mythological founder of the town as an example of social mobility'.[130] The Vettii – as freedmen, or just as adult men – may have identified with the hero similarly.[131] Clover observes a similar pattern in twentieth-century action and war films, in which a male hero often suffers some form of humiliation which he then avenges through the bulk of the movie, although the focal point here is definitely on the moment of threat to the hero.[132]

The scene of Ariadne (Figure 3), which parallels that of Hercules, is much more problematic. On one level, it confirms again that gender as a social and discursive hierarchy is not absent in the house, even if it is not the only one. Although she is a successful, upwardly mobile boundary-crosser, Ariadne is quite subordinated by her femininity, as we have already seen. Two critical moments in Ariadne's life are condensed in the painting. Although Theseus's departing ship can be seen in the background in the central upper portion of the painting, Dionysus appears in the foreground on the left, approaching and gazing at her sleeping, nude form. Ariadne is thus both abandoned and about to be 'saved' and immortalised by active males. Here the hierarchy of gender is powerfully asserted. As explored earlier, the composition and narrative match Mulvey's notions of fetishistic scopophilia and sadistic voyeurism in the male gaze elegantly. The image of Ariadne faces that of her mother Pasiphae across room *p*, and in fact the viewer has same view of Pasiphae's cow suit as of Ariadne, which visually helps sexualise the Pasiphae scene (Figure 10). On one level this may be a witty if dirty joke about those oversexed Cretan women. On another, it shows that even the less overtly violent scenes in the house may be interpreted as part of a larger story about subjugation via sexuality. But Ariadne's pairing with Hercules as a mortal who became divine is troubling to Mulvey's paradigms: the pairing suggests identification with this female figure otherwise thoroughly subordinated.

This ambiguity in the image of Ariadne is pushed even further by another interesting visual effect. On the same wall and to the right of this panel of Ariadne in room *p*, above the small south doorway, appears an image of the half-goat divinity Pan discovering Hermaphroditus, the child of the gods Hermes and Aphrodite with both male and female anatomical traits (Figures 14 and 15). Ariadne's pose very much resembles that of the reclining Hermaphroditus, including the right arm raised up over the head in an iconographic gesture which Clarke has identified as signifying 'erotic repose'.[133] She provides the view from behind, Hermaphroditus the (surprising) view from the front. Each figure is also accompanied by a small satyr or Pan, with one arm raised in surprise or delight and positioned just behind the legs of the reclining figure. Note that the Pan who sees Hermaphroditus' male attribute provides us with a reactive gaze; he turns his head, covering his eyes as though they are being assaulted. We viewers are thereby directed not to objectify Hermaphroditus, and even perhaps to identify with him/her instead.

Figure 14: South wall of room *p*, featuring paintings 'Ariadne' and 'Hermaphroditus', House of the Vettii (VI 15, 1), Pompeii, 62–79 CE (photograph by Michael Larvey, Austin, Texas, with permission of the Ministry for Cultural Heritage and the Environment, Special Superintendent of Naples and Pompeii).

Another painting of a hermaphrodite is presented to the right of someone leaving room *q* on the north side of the peristyle (Figure 16). The revealed phalli of the hermaphrodites in these passageways in and out of important reception rooms probably generated apotropaic laughter the same way as the famous painting of the well-endowed Priapus found in the entryway to the house.[134] When this large room was used for dining, the image on the inside of the doorway of room *q* would have been visible to banqueters, including the guest of honour, and although the setting is clearly pastoral, the postures of Hermaphroditus and his admirer, the rustic god Silenus, here differ from the similar pair in room *p*. Silenus looks over the shoulder of the erotically reposed Hermaphroditus, gazing into his/her upturned face and appreciating what is revealed in his/her lap. The pair intriguingly mimics depictions of couples reclining at banquet.[135]

What are we to make of these comparisons between Ariadne and Hermaphroditus, Ariadne and Hercules and perhaps Hermaphroditus and dinner guests? Again on some level gender difference is being neutralised. In part we should see this as a further expression of the one-sex cultural reasoning described earlier. If ancient Italians considered humans not sexually dimorphic, but having bodies somewhere along a sliding scale between male and female extremes, the mythological figure of Hermaphroditus illustrates a midway point, a body with both male and female iconographic elements.[136] Within the framework of Roman ideologies and practices of sexuality and slavery, over

Figure 15: Artist unknown, 'Hermaphroditus', south wall of room *p*, House of the Vettii (VI 15, 1), Pompeii, 62–79 CE (photograph by Michael Larvey, Austin, Texas, with permission of the Ministry for Cultural Heritage and the Environment, Special Superintendent of Naples and Pompeii).

Figure 16: Artist unknown, 'Hermaphroditus and Silenus', south wall of room *q*, House of the Vettii (VI 15, 1), Pompeii, 62–79 CE (photograph by Sansaini, provided by Deutsches Archäologisches Institut Rom, Negative 1956.0460, with permission of the Ministry for Cultural Heritage and the Environment, Special Superintendent of Naples and Pompeii).

time it was possible for individuals to move along the scale, such as from slave to freed, or from boy to man. The stories told by Hermaphroditus's narrative vignettes in this house explore this possibility, since in each the character assumed to be a passive object of desire is discovered by a pursuer to be an active, desiring subject.

What differs in these scenes, however, as opposed to the torture scenes described above, is that the neutralising of gender difference does not subordinate male, female and hermaphroditic bodies, but instead encourages cross-gender identification. Clover also finds and investigates this phenomenon, particularly in her study of late twentieth-century British and American rape-revenge films. Although she notes that earlier cinematic rapes encouraged viewers to identify with the rapist to some extent, which fits well with Mulvey's paradigms, from the mid-1970s increasingly the cinematic view and the narrative of rape-revenge films sympathise with the victim/hero and separate the viewer from the rapist/villain. Since the audience for these films is overwhelmingly young men, Clover observes that 'the only way to account for the spectator's engagement in the revenge drive is to assume his engagement with the rape-avenging woman'.[137]

To explain this cross-gender identification and the pleasure it might provide, Clover returns to Freud for answers. She notes that he is not as focused on castration per se as is Mulvey, but rather 'the fear of standing in a passive or "feminine" relation to another man and the particular sort of "castration" that might proceed from that'.[138] Freud called a man's assumption of this 'feminine' position, masochism.[139]

In his article focusing on the imagery of Ariadne in Pompeii, Fredrick also calls this exploration of marginalised, subordinate subject positions, 'playing the female'. I'd like to bring into the conversation Clover's thoughts on its appeal to help expand on Fredrick's account. Like Fredrick, Clover emphasises the repetitiveness of these stories in horror, and she ties this to the psychological mechanism of 'repetition compulsion', 'whereby a person "deliberately places himself in distressing situations, thereby repeating an old [but unremembered] experience"'.[140] Through mediated repetition, the unpleasant experiences are converted to pleasant rehearsals, although the mechanism for how this is accomplished is disputed.[141] Clover points out that this common type of storyline – a pleasure in looking at and sympathising with those in fear and pain – is unaccounted for in Mulvey's analysis.[142]

Clover leaves open the nature of the past pain mediated by this process, simply generalising that 'the pleasure of looking at others in fear and pain has its origins in one's own past-but-not-finished fear and pain'.[143] She theorises that such pain does not necessarily imply trauma, but may be a feature of normal human development.[144] Freud's notion of masochism has certainly been challenged in its applicability to women, but this reading of how men might use a perception of femininity to express repressed desires and fears within a patriarchal system holds potential. I think we can at least ponder why the patrons of Pompeian wall painting might have been 'compulsively' drawn to such stories and images, and in fact we have already done so. Consider first the freedman, a boundary crosser, no longer owned but still owing allegiance and even sexual service to his master.[145] Gender-crossing or movement along a gender spectrum was a particularly apt representation of his experience, and for the freed slavery is an excellent example of 'past-but-not-finished fear and pain'.

But what if the paintings of the House of the Vettii were not selected by ex-slaves? Psychoanalytic theory, both Freudian and Lacanian, in part asks questions about the implications of the psychosexual development of a person raised in a household and in a society with sexual differentiation, and how we can see these effects in the products created by human beings. Our answers have to change if the men and women in question were also raised in a slave-owning society and household. Everyone – male or female, slave or free – witnessed a very real difference in status between males with no anatomical differences. It is one thing to say one has the phallus and one does not, but what does that mean, and how might it be represented?

Within the House of the Vettii, I would argue that this is reflected in the way that gender is at play. Male and female are being used to signify, but what they signify is that such signs may fail to categorise a body appropriately. The two hermaphrodites communicate in image and narrative that from one point of view a body may appear feminine (pale in colour, large buttocks, long hair, potential penetratee for male companion), but from another point of view a body may be something else entirely (phallus, potential penetrator of male companion). Both hermaphroditic scenes include onlookers in the process of discovering, physically uncovering and witnessing the hidden male characteristics of their intended objects of desire. As noted earlier, Fredrick observes that many of the mythological scenes in this house play with the process of concealing, hiding and then unveiling.[146] He relates this – quite appropriately – to the power and pleasure of looking, but I wonder if stories of unrecognised gods and of previously unappreciated and unrevealed masculine attributes were not particularly appealing stories to men in ancient Italy, who themselves had a subordinated period in their lives and then experienced a transformation into a new status. The images in the receiving rooms revel in the triumphs of boundary-crossers: the indeterminate Hermaphroditus, abandoned Ariadne, threatened boy Hercules and doubted new god Dionysus.

Conclusions and implications

Consider again Koloski-Ostrow and her Mulveyan analysis of a painting of Actaeon. It is hard to imagine what in that 'film' of a male mutilated for desiring a female is pleasurable to Mulvey's twentieth-century male viewer. Now look with the lens of an ancient Italian slave owner. What may have been pleasurable in that 'film' to a *dominus* – a master who sees a lovely young male torn limb from limb because he has merely glimpsed a female above his station? The master fetishistically enjoys the exposed, even dismembered young male body *and* enjoys the punishment of a subordinate acting out. Is gender destabilised here, or do we need to reconsider our understanding of gender and the gaze within ancient Italian culture?

In an intriguing 2008 article, Jeanne Boydston argues 'that the primaryness of gender in a given situation should be one of our questions, rather than one of our assumptions'.[147] In making her claim, she lays out both the necessity of and the limitations imposed by conceptual categories:

> Categories of analysis are not analytically neutral. They are not mere frameworks for organising ideas. They are frameworks that reflect and replicate our own understandings of the world. The moment we cease to acknowledge that aspect of their work and invest any particular category of analysis with the authority of permanence and universality, we cease to be historians and become propagandists of a particular epistemological order.[148]

The method Boydston describes for avoiding this trap is to look for anomalies which do not fit neatly into our conceptual categories because here cultural differences and historical processes lie.[149]

I submit that the wall paintings of the paired dining rooms *n* and *p* within the House of the Vettii provide a particularly useful anomaly that should encourage us to reconsider deploying gender, or rather gender alone, to analyse the power dynamics encoded in Pompeian wall painting. Paired scenes of eroticised torture pointedly put male and female bodies on display for the host, guests, family and slaves during the social ritual of the banquet. This apparent negation of gender hierarchy arises from the particular ways gender intersects with slavery and sexuality in this historical place and time. Due to the slaves housed within it, the very patriarchal Roman family resists analysis in traditional Freudian or even Lacanian terms; the phallus is a poor signifier in the context of this form of slavery and this form of family. To use Clover's terms, 'What film makers [and ancient Italians] seem to know better than film critics [and historians] is that gender is less a wall than a permeable membrane'.[150] Temporarily assuming a freedman's perspective helps us see how prioritising gender and pulling it out of its intersections with other important cultural frames can mislead.

In turn, Actaeon is not alone in being inexplicable through 'a classical psycho-analytic paradigm'.[151] Clover points out that such wounded male figures are also ubiquitous in late twentieth-century British and American horror films. She describes the 'extraordinarily popular theme of assaultive gazing that is foiled – thwarted, swallowed up, turned back on itself, and of assaultive gazers who end up blinded or dead or both'.[152] And she diagnoses the repetition of the theme as a compulsive 're-enactment of unremembered experience of unpleasure'.[153] We have seen how a set of paintings in this house utilises a similar masochistic aesthetic to celebrate, in terms humorous to heroic to grisly, figures whose positions in various social hierarchies were not always recognised or reverenced appropriately, precisely the pain the images may be rehearsing.

Although this would be exacerbated in the case of a slave child, it was a fact of life for all children of ancient Italy (male, female, slave and free) that they were perceived as possible objects of desire by adult men – all were at one time objects of the gaze. For the adult men who patronised and consumed art, to sympathise, however briefly, with a character like Ariadne, Actaeon or Hermaphroditus was to revisit – not imagine – the feeling of the assaultive gaze, and sometimes to foil it.

In analysing classic Hollywood film, Mulvey sets out to 'highlight the ways in which its formal preoccupations reflect the psychical obsessions of the society which produced it' and explore how 'mainstream film coded the erotic into the language of the dominant patriarchal order'.[154] These are compelling goals. Ancient Italian painting also coded the erotic into the language of the dominant patriarchal order. In that order, the *pater* subordinated women and some men, particularly slaves, and led a society in which slavery was a major psychical obsession; moreover, everyone, including these *patres*, began life as subordinated objects of adult male desire, even though some were more protected from that desire than others. Fredrick begins his analysis of house painting across Pompeii with the observation that as a group the mythological panels feature stories of gods and heroes, but that 'their content is usually not "heroic". It is erotic, and within the erotic context, frequently violent'.[155] This content speaks to the intersections of gender, sexuality and slavery in ancient Italian households. In the House of the Vettii, such images create a world in which Vettius Restitutus and Vettius Conviva were masters, with all the powers and privileges that implied in Pompeian society.

Notes

The author wishes to acknowledge gratefully the insightful suggestions of several anonymous readers of this article at various stages of its development. All translations are my own.

1. David Fredrick, 'Beyond the Atrium to Ariadne: Erotic Painting and Visual Pleasure in the Roman House', *Classical Antiquity* 14 (1995), pp. 266–87; Ann Olga Koloski-Ostrow, 'Violent Stages in Two Pompeian Houses: Imperial Taste, Aristocratic Response, and Messages of Male Control', in Ann Olga Koloski-Ostrow and Claire L. Lyons (eds), *Naked Truths: Women, Sexuality, and Gender in Classical Art and Archaeology* (London: Routledge, 1997), pp. 243–66; Laura Mulvey, 'Visual Pleasure and Narrative Cinema', *Screen* 16 (1975), pp. 6–18, republished in Laura Mulvey, *Visual and Other Pleasures* (Bloomington: University of Indiana Press, 1989), pp. 14–26.

2. Mulvey, 'Visual Pleasure', p. 7.

3. Mulvey, 'Visual Pleasure', p. 12.

4. Mulvey, 'Visual Pleasure', pp. 13–17.

5. Mulvey, 'Visual Pleasure', pp. 17, 7.

6. Katharina Lorenz, 'Die Quadratur des Sofabildes: Pompejanische Mythenbilder als Ausgangspunkt für eine Phänomenologie antiker Wahrnehmung', in P. Neudecker and P. Zanker (eds), *Palilia* 16: *Lebenswelten: Bilder und Raüme in der römischen Stadt der Kaiserzeit* (Wiesbaden: Ludwig Reichert, 2005), pp. 205-21, here p. 209.

7. Fredrick, 'Beyond the Atrium', p. 279.

8. Koloski-Ostrow, 'Violent Stages', p. 254.

9. Koloski-Ostrow, 'Violent Stages', p. 257.

10. Fredrick, 'Beyond the Atrium', p. 279.

11. For a critique of theories based on psychoanalysis as culturally and historically bounded, see Page duBois, *Sowing the Body: Psychoanalysis and Ancient Representations of Women* (Chicago: University of Chicago Press, 1988), especially pp. 7–17. See also Jeanne Boydston, 'Gender as a Question of Historical Analysis', *Gender & History* 20 (2008), pp. 558–83.

12. Carol Clover, *Men, Women, and Chainsaws: Gender and the Modern Horror Film* (Princeton: Princeton University Press, 1992).

13. Clover, *Men, Women, and Chainsaws*, p. 16.

14. David Fredrick, 'Mapping Penetrability in Late Republican and Early Imperial Rome', in David Fredrick (ed.), *The Roman Gaze: Vision, Power and the Body* (Baltimore: Johns Hopkins University Press, 2002), pp. 236–64, here pp. 253–8; David Fredrick, 'Grasping the Pangolin: Sensuous Ambiguity in Roman Dining', *Arethusa* 36 (2003), pp. 309–43.

15. Clover, *Men, Women, and Chainsaws*, pp. 222–3.

16. Andrew Wallace-Hadrill, *Houses and Society in Pompeii and Herculaneum* (Princeton: Princeton University Press, 1994), pp. 72–8.

17. Wallace-Hadrill, *Houses and Society*, p. 213. Out of the 234 houses Wallace-Hadrill sampled in Regions I and VI, only ten are larger than the House of the Vettii (*Houses and Society*, Table 4.1).

18. August Mau, 'Scavi di Pompei, 1894–5, Reg. VI, Isola ad E della 11', *Mitteilungen des Deutschen Archäologischen Instituts, Römische Abteilung* 11 (1896), pp. 3–97; Antonio Sogliano, 'La Casa dei Vettii in Pompei', *Monumenti antichi dell'Accademia dei Lincei* 8 (1898), cols. 233–416.

19. Willem J. Th. Peters, 'La composizione delle pareti dipinte nella Casa dei Vetti a Pompei', *Mededeelingen van het Nederlands Instituut te Rome* 39 (1977), pp. 102–23; Arnold and Mariette de Vos, *Pompei, Ercolano, Stabia* (Bari: Guide archeologiche Laterza, 1982), pp. 167–74.

20. The most extensive analysis is found in Peters, who excludes the small side rooms *h* and *i* and possibly rooms *d*, *u* and *x* from the attribution to a single workshop.

21. On paintings in inset panels, see Roger Ling, *Roman Painting* (Cambridge: Cambridge University Press, 1991), pp. 112–41; and Eleanor Winsor Leach, *The Social Life of Painting in Ancient Rome and on the Bay of Naples* (Cambridge: Cambridge University Press, 2004), pp. 132–55.

22. Giovanni Pugliese Carratelli (ed.), 'VI 15, 1. Casa dei Vettii', in *Pompei: Pitture e Mosaici* (Rome: Istituto della enciclopedia italiana, 1994), vol. 5: *Regio VI*, Part Two, pp. 46–572, here p. 470.

23. John Clarke, *The Houses of Roman Italy 100 BC–AD 250* (Berkeley: University of California Press, 1991), p. 208; de Vos and de Vos, *Pompei, Ercolano*, p. 167.

24. A short, winged wand entwined by two snakes, the caduceus is a staff carried by Hermes, messenger god and patron of merchants and travellers.

25. First reported in *Notizie degli scavi di antichità* 1895, p. 32; see also Sogliano col. 252.

26. Henrik Mouritsen, *Analecta Romana Instituti Danici* Supplementum 15: *Elections, Magistrates and Municipal Élite: Studies in Pompeian Epigraphy* (Rome: L'Erma, 1988), pp. 14–16, n. 40.

27. *CIL* IV.3522. The *Corpus Inscriptionum Latinarum*, the edition of classical Latin inscriptions conventionally referred to as *CIL*, began to be published in 1863 and is continuing. The fourth volume contains most of the materials from Pompeii: C. Zangemeister and R. Schoene (eds), *Inscriptiones parietariae Pompeianae Herculanenses Stabianae* (Berlin: Berlin Academy of Sciences, 1871).

28. M. Della Corte, *Case ed abitanti di Pompei* (Naples: Faustino Fiorentino, 3rd edn 1965), pp. 9–23; James L. Franklin, Jr, *Pompeii: the Electoral Programmata, Campaigns and Politics, AD 71–79* (Rome: American Academy in Rome, 1980), pp. 18–19, 87, *pace* Mouritsen, *Elections, Magistrates and Municipal Élite*, pp. 18–19.

29. *CIL* IV.3509.

30. *Notizie degli scavi di antichità* 1895, p. 32.

31. Steven E. Ostrow, '"Augustales" along the Bay of Naples: a Case for Their Early Growth', *Historia: Zeitschrift für Alte Geschichte* 34 (1985), pp. 64–101; Steven E. Ostrow 'The *Augustales* in the Augustan Scheme', in Kurt A. Raaflaub and Mark Toher (eds), *Between Republic and Empire: Interpretations of Augustus and His Principate* (Berkeley: University of California Press, 1990), pp. 364-79, here pp. 368–71; Andrik Abramenko, *Die munizipale Mittelschicht im kaiserzeitlichen Italien: Zu einem neuen Verständnis von Sevirat und Augustalität* (Frankfurt: P. Lang, 1993), pp. 127–92; Lauren Hackworth Petersen, *The Freedman in Roman Art and Art History* (Cambridge: Cambridge University Press, 2006), pp. 57–83.

32. Iiro Kajanto, 'The Latin Cognomina', *Commentationes Humanarum Litterarum, Societas Scientiarum Fennica* 36 (1965), pp. 2–428, here p. 356. We also know of an *Augustalis* in Pompeii with the third name Restitutus (M. Cerrinius Restitutus); *CIL* X.994. The graffito elsewhere in town *CIL* IV.4719, 'Restitutus servos bonus', 'Restitutus is a good slave', may be a derogatory metaphorical use of the term 'slave' rather than independent confirmation that Restitutus was a slave name.

33. Jean Andreau, *Les Affaires de Monsieur Jucundus* (Rome: L'Ecole française de Rome, 1974), p. 267 and Table 96.

34. For example, Della Corte, *Case ed abitanti di Pompei*, pp. 89–93, and Clarke, *Houses of Roman Italy*, p. 208.

35. On the way people name themselves in inscriptions, see Sandra Joshel, *Work, Identity and Legal Status at Rome* (Norman: University of Oklahoma Press, 1992), particularly pp. 35–7 on formal patterns of freed and slave nomenclature.

36. Joshel, *Work, Identity and Legal Status*, pp. 59–60, 128–60.

37. I would like to thank my student Dhruva Jaishankar for this last suggestion. In order to be father and son with these names, they would have to have both been slaves of Aulus Vettius; presumably the father Conviva emancipated himself then purchased freedom for his son as well.

38. Franklin, *Pompeii: the Electoral Programmata*, p. 122; Paavo Castrén, *Acta Instituti Romani Finlandiae* 8: *Ordo Populusque Pompeianus: Polity and Society in Roman Pompeii* (Rome: Bardi, 1975), pp. 239–40; James L. Franklin, Jr, *Pompeis Difficilis Est: Studies in the Political Life of Imperial Pompeii* (Ann Arbor: University of Michigan Press, 2001), pp. 181–3.

39. Gaius, *Institutes* 1.9–11. See especially Keith Bradley, *Slaves and Masters in the Roman Empire: A Study in Social Control* (Oxford: Oxford University Press, 1987) and Keith Bradley, *Slavery and Society at Rome* (Cambridge: Cambridge University Press, 1994); Richard P. Saller, *Patriarchy, Property and Death in the Roman Family* (Cambridge: Cambridge University Press, 1994).

40. On the *paterfamilias*, see Saller, *Patriarchy, Property and Death*, pp. 102–53. On the various potential legal relationships between husband and wife, see Susan Treggiari, *Roman Marriage: Iusti Coniuges from the Time of Cicero to the Time of Ulpian* (Oxford: Clarendon Press, 1991), pp. 13–36 and Jane F. Gardner, *Women in Roman Law and Society* (Bloomington: Indiana University Press, 1986), pp.11–14.

41. On the occupations of slaves and freedpersons, see Bradley, *Slavery and Society*, pp. 57–80; Joshel, *Work, Identity and Legal Status*, pp. 145–61 and Mouritsen, *Freedman*, pp. 206–47.

42. On the general status of slaves in Roman law, see especially Alan Watson, *Roman Slave Law* (Baltimore: Johns Hopkins University Press, 1987). On the precariousness of slave families, see Beryl Rawson, 'Family Life among the Lower Classes at Rome in the First Two Centuries of the Empire', *Classical Philology* 61 (1966), pp. 71–83; Keith R. Bradley, 'The Age at Time of Sale of Female Slaves', *Arethusa* 11 (1978), pp. 243–52 and Bradley, *Slaves and Masters*, pp. 47–80.

43. On the motives for manumitting slaves, see Bradley, *Slavery and Society*, pp.158–65 and on manumission as a phenomenon, see Bradley, *Slaves and Masters*, pp. 83–112. On freedpersons in general, see most recently Henrik Mouritsen, *The Freedman in the Roman World* (Cambridge: Cambridge University Press,

2011); but also Susan Treggiari, *Roman Freedmen during the Late Republic* (Oxford: Clarendon Press, 1969) and Joshel, *Work, Identity and Legal Status at Rome*, pp. 32–7.

44. By the imperial period, the conditions of the *lex Aelia Sentia* (4 CE) had to be met for an ex-slave to become a full citizen, including a minimum age of thirty years for slaves and twenty years for masters; see Bradley, *Slavery and Society*, p. 156. Exceptions were possible, such as when freeing someone for the sake of marrying them (Gaius, *Institutes*, 1.9).

45. Mouritsen, *Freedman*, especially pp. 36–119, 279–99.

46. Mouritsen, *Freedman*, pp. 248–78.

47. Petersen, *The Freedman in Roman Art*, especially pp. 1–12.

48. Petersen, *The Freedman in Roman Art*, pp. 6–10; for comparison see Amy Richlin, *The Garden of Priapus: Sexuality and Aggression in Roman Humor* (New Haven: Yale University Press, 1983), pp. 164–209.

49. Joshel, *Work, Identity and Legal Status*; Petersen, *The Freedman in Roman Art*, pp. 84–120.

50. Petersen, *The Freedman in Roman Art*, p. 6.

51. Petersen, *The Freedman in Roman Art*, p. 183.

52. John R. Clarke, *Looking at Lovemaking: Constructions of Sexuality in Roman Art, 100 BC–AD 250* (Berkeley: University of California Press, 1998), p. 177; for comparison see Clarke, *Houses of Roman Italy*, p. 234 and Paul Zanker, *Pompeii: Public and Private Life*, tr. Deborah Lucas Schneider (Cambridge: Harvard University Press, 1998), p. 202.

53. Clarke, *Looking at Lovemaking*, Figures 65 and 66.

54. Clarke, *Looking at Lovemaking*, pp. 174–7.

55. Michael Ivanovitch Rostovtzeff, *The Social and Economic History of the Roman Empire* (Oxford: Clarendon Press, 1957), p. 92.

56. See especially Laura Mulvey, 'Afterthoughts on "Visual Pleasure and Narrative Cinema" Inspired by *Duel in the Sun*', in T. Bennett (ed.), *Popular Fiction, Technology, Ideology, Production, Reading* (London: Routledge, 1990), pp. 139–51.

57. Maud W. Gleason, *Making Men: Sophists and Self-Presentation in Ancient Rome* (Princeton: Princeton University Press, 1995); Erik Gunderson, *Staging Masculinity: The Rhetoric of Performance in the Roman World* (Ann Arbor: University of Michigan Press, 2000); Anthony Corbeill, 'Political Movement: Walking and Ideology in Republican Rome', in Fredrick (ed.), *The Roman Gaze*, pp. 182–215; Richlin, *The Garden of Priapus*, pp. 164–209.

58. Sandra R. Joshel and Sheila Murnaghan (eds), *Women and Slaves in Greco-Roman Culture: Differential Equations* (London and New York: Routledge, 1998), p. 20.

59. Joshel and Murnaghan, *Women and Slaves*, p. 18.

60. For example, Wallace-Hadrill, *Houses and Society*; Leach, *Social Life of Painting*; Katharina Lorenz, *Bilder machen Räume: Mythenbilder in pompeianischen Häusern* (Berlin and New York: de Gruyter, 2008); Clarke, *Houses of Roman Italy* and Shelley Hales, *The Roman House and Social Identity* (Cambridge: Cambridge University Press, 2003).

61. Wallace-Hadrill, *Houses and Society*, p. 150.

62. For a recent and nuanced analysis of Pompeian painting styles, see Leach, *Social Life of Painting*. A more traditional account is provided in Roger Ling, *Roman Painting* (Cambridge: Cambridge University Press, 1991). The mythological panels may allude to even grander picture galleries in which portable canvases or boards were affixed to the wall. We only know of these through literary sources, for which see Leach, *Social Life of Painting*, pp. 132–52. The true fresco forms of this house are found even in what are taken to be imperial houses and villas, however, so interpreting them as lower-class imitations of the 'real thing' would be misleading.

63. Daniela Corlàita Scagliarini, 'Spazio e decorazione nella pittura pompeiana', *Palladio* 23–25 (1974–1976), pp. 3–44; Clarke, *Houses of Roman Italy*, pp. 32–77.

64. Many smaller houses in Pompeii do not have peristyles, even though some are elaborately painted; see Penelope M. Allison, *Pompeian Households: An Analysis of the Material Culture* (Los Angeles: Cotsen Institute of Archaeology, 2004).

65. These include Philostratus the Elder, *Imagines*; Achilles Tatius, *Leucippe and Clitophon*, 3.7; Lucian, *Essay on Images*; Petronius, *Satyrica*, 25, etc. In modern scholarship, see most recently Jaś Elsner, *Roman Eyes: Visuality and Subjectivity in Art and Text* (Princeton: Princeton University Press, 2007), especially pp. 67–109; Lorenz, 'Die Quadratur des Sofabildes', pp. 206–09; and Paul Zanker, 'Mythenbilder im Haus', in Roald F. Docter and Eric M. Moormann (eds), *Classical Archaeology Towards the Third Millenium: Reflections and Perspectives* (Amsterdam: Allard Pierson, 1999), pp. 40–48, here pp. 42–3.

66. Zanker argues that the mythological panels serve foremost as an 'educational icon', a sign of wealth and the respectable education which wealth could bring. Zanker, 'Mythenbilder im Haus', pp. 42-3.

67. Fredrick, 'Beyond the Atrium', pp. 266–87.

68. Fredrick, 'Beyond the Atrium', p. 272.

69. Fredrick, 'Beyond the Atrium', p. 273.

70. Fredrick, 'Beyond the Atrium', pp. 272–3.

71. Fredrick, 'Beyond the Atrium', p. 280.

72. Fredrick, 'Beyond the Atrium', pp. 279–80.

73. Maria Wyke, 'Written Women: Propertius' *Scripta Puella*', *Journal of Roman Studies* 77 (1987), pp. 47–61; Maria Wyke, 'Mistress and Metaphor in Augustan Elegy', *Helios* 16 (1989), pp. 25–47; Marilyn B. Skinner, '*Ego Mulier*: The Construction of Male Sexuality in Catullus', *Helios* 20 (1993), pp. 107–30.

74. Fredrick, 'Mapping Penetrability' and Fredrick, 'Grasping the Pangolin'.

75. For discussions of the possibility of pattern books and how painting workshops functioned, see Ling, *Roman Painting*, pp. 128–9, 212–13, 217–20; Eric M. Moormann (ed.), *Mededeelingen van het Nederlands Instituut te Rome* 54: *Mani di pittori e botteghe pittoriche nel mondo romano* (Assen: Van Gorcum, 1995), pp. 61–298 and Penelope N. Allison, '"Workshops" and "Patternbooks"', *Kölner Jarhbuch für Vor- und Frühgeschichte* 24 (1991), pp. 79–84.

76. Eleanor Winsor Leach, 'Reading Signs of Status: Recent Books on Roman Art in the Domestic Sphere', *American Journal of Archaeology* 96 (1992), pp. 551–7, here p. 556.

77. Fredrick, 'Beyond the Atrium', p. 284.

78. Koloski-Ostrow, 'Violent Stages', p. 257; for comparison see Fredrick, 'Beyond the Atrium', p. 278.

79. Joan W. Scott, 'Gender: A Useful Category of Historical Analysis', *The American Historical Review* 91 (1986), pp. 1053–75.

80. See duBois, *Sowing the Body*, pp. 7–17.

81. John Clarke, *Art in the Lives of Ordinary Romans* (Berkeley: University of California Press, 2003), p. 99.

82. Mary Lee Thompson, 'The Monumental and Literary Evidence of Programmatic Painting in Antiquity', *Marsyas* 9 (1960–1961), pp. 36–77, here p. 67.

83. Karl Schefold, *La peinture pompéienne: Essai sur l'evolution de sa signification* (Brussels: Latomus, 1972), pp. 208–09, 130–31.

84. Theo Wirth, 'Zum Bildprogramm in der Casa dei Vettii', *Römische Mitteilungen* 90 (1983), pp. 449–55; Richard Brilliant, *Visual Narratives: Storytelling in Etruscan and Roman Art* (Ithaca: Cornell University Press, 1984), pp. 71–80; Clarke, *Houses of Roman Italy*, pp. 221–7.

85. Wirth, 'Zum Bildprogramm'; Bettina A. Bergmann, 'The Roman House as Memory Theater: The House of the Tragic Poet in Pompeii', *Art Bulletin* 76 (1994), pp. 225–56; Bettina A. Bergmann, 'Pregnant Moment: Tragic Wives in the Roman Interior', in Natalie Boymel Kampen (ed.), *Sexuality in Ancient Art: Near East, Egypt, Greece and Italy* (Cambridge: Cambridge University Press, 1996), pp.199–218; Lorenz, *Bilder machen Räume* and Lorenz, 'Die Quadratur des Sofabildes', pp. 205–21; Susanne Muth, *Erleben von Raum – Leben in Raum: zur Funktion mythologischer Mosaikbilder in der römisch-kaiserzeitlichen Wohnarchitektur* (Heidelberg: Archäologie und Geschichte, 1998).

86. Lorenz, 'Die Quadratur des Sofabildes'.

87. William C. Archer, 'The Paintings of the Casa dei Vettii in Pompeii', (unpublished doctoral thesis, University of Virginia, 1981), pp. 404, 449; for Daedalus and Pasiphae, see pp. 416–17; on Dirce, see p. 471. For a detailed analysis of the iconography of Dirce, see Eleanor Winsor Leach, 'The Punishment of Dirce: A Newly Discovered Continuous Narrative in the Casa di Giulio Polibio and its Significance within the Visual Tradition', *Römische Mitteilungen* 93 (1986), pp. 118–38. For other examples of modifications to common scenes for the purposes of a programmatic ensemble, see Leach, *Social Life of Painting*, p. 151; and Lorenz, 'Die Quadratur des Sofabildes', pp. 209–20.

88. Saller, *Patriarchy, Property and Death*, pp. 142–53. On the punishment of slaves and the use of fear to control or degrade them, also see Bradley, *Slaves and Masters*, pp. 113–14, 121–3, 134–6; Moses I. Finley, *Ancient Slavery and Modern Ideology* (New York: Viking Press, 1980), pp. 95–8.

89. Peter Garnsey, *Social Status and Legal Privilege in the Roman Empire* (Oxford: Clarendon Press, 1970), pp. 123–31, 158–72.

90. Watson, *Roman Slave Law*, pp. 84–9; Gaius, *Institutes*, 9.41.12, 9.41.18; *Digest*, 22.5.22.1.

91. Allison R. Sharrock, 'Looking at Looking: Can You Resist a Reading?' in Fredrick, *The Roman Gaze*, pp. 265–95, worries over the potential gender and thus power inversion in the Pentheus scene. Strangely, however, she compares it to the gender dynamics of a scene next to it in a modern book on Roman painting

(The Sack of Troy from the House of Menander in Ling, *Roman Painting*, pl. XIC), rather than the scenes on the adjoining walls. The Dirce scene from this room is much closer in composition and directly inverts the gender of the characters in the Pentheus painting.

92. Clover, *Men, Women, and Chainsaws*, pp. 174–232.

93. See Carratelli, 'VI 15, 1. Casa dei Vettii', Figures 31 and 32, pp. 488–91. Helen Morales, 'The Torturer's Apprentice: Parrhasius and the Limits of Art', in Jaś Elsner (ed.), *Art and Text in Roman Culture* (Cambridge: Cambridge University Press, 1996), pp. 182–209, Morales explores first-century Roman ethical interpretations of assaultive and reactive gazes. I am grateful to the anonymous reviewer who brought both of these to my attention.

94. Archer, 'Paintings of the Casa dei Vettii', p. 471.

95. I use the gendered term 'master' here deliberately, since the sexual use of slaves by women owners is strongly condemned in the surviving literature; see Watson, *Roman Slave Law*, p. 15; and Joshel, *Work, Identity and Legal Status*, p. 30, n.17. Among other things, it upset the hierarchy between enslaved and free for a free woman to have sexual relations with a male slave, for reasons which will become clear shortly.

96. John Pollini, 'Slave-Boys for Sexual and Religious Service: Images of Pleasure and Devotion', in A. Boyle and W. Dominik (eds), *Flavian Rome: Culture, Image, Text* (Leiden and Boston: Brill, 2003), pp. 149–66; Richlin, *Garden of Priapus*, pp. 34–44.

97. *Digest* (of Justinian), 47.10.15.15. Joshel, *Work, Identity and Legal Status*, pp. 27–8. See for comparison Gaius, *Institutes*, 3.220–21; *Digest*, 47.10.1.3, 2, 5.pr, 5.9–10, 7.5, 13.7, 15.2, 15.15–23, 15.33 and 17.11–18.2. On the laws which prohibit the sexual use of freeborn males, see Elaine Fantham, '*Stuprum*: Public Attitudes and Penalties for Sexual Offences in Republican Rome', *Échos du Monde Classique/Classical Views* 35 (1991), pp. 267–91 and Craig A. Williams, *Roman Homosexuality: Ideologies of Masculinity in Classical Antiquity* (Oxford: Oxford University Press, 1999), pp. 96–124.

98. Plutarch, *Roman Questions*, 101. On the *bulla*, see H. R. Goette, 'Die Bulla', *Bonner Jahrbücher* 186 (1986), pp. 133–64; and Robert E. A. Palmer, 'Bullae insignia ingenuitatis', *American Journal of Ancient History* 14 (1989), pp. 1–69.

99. These are modern interpretive terms rather than translations of Roman vocabulary. For an analysis of the various Latin terms, see Holt N. Parker, 'The Teratogenic Grid', in Judith P. Hallett and Marilyn B. Skinner (eds), *Roman Sexualities* (Princeton: Princeton University Press, 1997), pp. 47–65. On Roman sexual ideologies, see the recent synthesis in Marilyn B. Skinner, *Sexuality in Greek and Roman Culture* (Malden: Blackwell, 2005), pp. 193–282; but also Jonathan Walters, 'Invading the Roman Body: Manliness and Impenetrability in Roman Thought', in Hallett and Skinner, *Roman Sexualities*, pp. 29–46. On evidence for challenges to the dominant ideology, see Amy Richlin, 'Not Before Homosexuality: The Materiality of the *Cinaedus* and the Roman Law against Love between Men', *Journal of the History of Sexuality* 3 (1993), pp. 523–73 and Pamela Gordon, 'Some Unseen Monster: Reading Lucretius on Sex', in Fredrick, *The Roman Gaze*, pp. 86–109.

100. Ellen Oliensis, 'The Erotics of *Amicitia*: Readings in Tibullus, Propertius, and Horace', in Hallett and Skinner, *Roman Sexualities*, pp. 151–71, here p. 154.

101. Finley, *Ancient Slavery*, pp. 95–8.

102. Clover, *Men, Women, and Chainsaws*, p. 15.

103. Thomas Laquer, *Making Sex: Body and Gender from the Greeks to Freud* (Cambridge: Harvard University Press, 1990).

104. Clover, *Men, Women, and Chainsaws*, p. 15.

105. Clover, *Men, Women, and Chainsaws*, p. 158.

106. In *Pompeian Households*, Allison cautions that rooms in Pompeian houses were used for multiple functions across the day and year and that Pompeian archaeological remains do not well match the room functions and names listed in our Roman literary sources. Nevertheless, that the finely appointed small to medium-sized rooms *n* and *p*, located off the peristyle garden and providing views of it, were not at least sometimes used for banquets would be difficult to believe.

107. Most *atrium*-style houses in Pompeii had more than one room which could be used for dining purposes; see Clarke, *Art in the Lives*, p. 224; Wallace-Hadrill, *Houses and Society*, p. 55; Katharine M. D. Dunbabin, 'Triclinium and Stibadium', in William J. Slater (ed.), *Dining in a Classical Context* (Ann Arbor: University of Michigan Press, 1991), pp. 121–48, here p. 124, n. 22; John H. D'Arms, 'The Roman *Convivium* and the Ideal of Equality', in Oswyn Murray (ed.), *Sympotica: A Symposium on the Symposium* (Oxford: Clarendon Press, 1990), pp. 308–20. On such spaces see Katharine M. D. Dunbabin, 'Convivial Spaces: Dining and Entertainment in the Roman Villa', *Journal of Roman Archaeology*

      9 (1996), pp. 66–80 and Lise Bek, '*Quaestiones Conviviales*: The Idea of the *Triclinium* and the Staging of the Convivial Ceremony from Rome to Byzantium', *Analecta Romana Instituti Danici* 12 (1983), pp. 81–107.

108. D'Arms, 'The Roman *Convivium*'.

109. D'Arms, 'The Roman *Convivium*'.

110. On the *convivium*, see the Roman articles in Slater, *Dining in a Classical Context*; Katherine M. D. Dunbabin, *The Roman Banquet: Images of Conviviality* (Cambridge: Cambridge University Press, 2003) and Matthew B. Roller, *Dining Posture in Ancient Rome: Bodies, Value and Status* (Princeton: Princeton University Press, 2006).

111. On the work and treatment of slaves at Roman *convivia*, see especially John H. D'Arms, 'Slaves at Roman *Convivia*', in Slater, *Dining in a Classical Context*, pp. 171–83; and on theatrical performances at banquets, Christopher P. Jones, 'Dinner Theater', in Slater, *Dining in a Classical Context*, pp. 185–98.

112. From slaves or those like slaves: Columella, *On Agriculture*, 11.1.10; Petronius, *Satyrica*, 64; Martial, *Epigrams*, 5.70; Plutarch, *Life of Pompey*, 40.7; from boys: Plutarch, *Roman Questions*, 33; Suetonius, *Life of Augustus*, 64.3; Suetonius, *Life of Claudius*, 32; Tacitus, *Annals*, 13.61.1. These and more are discussed in Alan Booth, 'The Age for Reclining and Its Attendant Perils,' in Slater, *Dining in a Classical Context*, pp. 105–20; see Roller, *Dining Posture*, for a rich recent analysis of the significance of reclining to dine.

113. D'Arms, 'Slaves at Roman *Convivia*', pp. 179–80. See for comparison Keith R. Bradley, 'The Roman Family at Dinner', in Enge Nielsen and Hanne Sigismund Nielsen (eds), *Meals in a Social Context: Aspects of the Communal Meal in the Hellenistic and Roman World* (Aarhus: Aarhus University Press, 1998), pp. 36–55.

114. This is the only instance of the name Conviva known to Kajanto in his extensive catalogue of Latin *cognomina* – it was an unusual name; 'The Latin Cognomina', p. 306.

115. Fredrick, 'Mapping Penetrability' and Fredrick, 'Grasping the Pangolin'.

116. Zanker, 'Mythenbilder im Haus', p. 47.

117. Fredrick, 'Mapping Penetrability', p. 256, D'Arms, 'Slaves at Roman *Convivia*', pp. 175–6.

118. Ancient storytellers disagree on how Pasiphae came to be punished with desire for a bull; some say her husband Minos offended Poseidon through incorrect sacrifice, others say he offended Jupiter, yet others say Pasiphae herself failed to cultivate Aphrodite; see Diodorus Siculus, *Library*, 4.77.2, 13.4; Hyginus, *Fabula*, 40; and First Vatican Mythographer, 47. For a modern account, see Robert Graves, *The Greek Myths*, vol. 1 (London: Penguin, 1955), pp. 293–4.

119. Wallace-Hadrill, *Houses and Society*, pp. 10–14, 38–61.

120. What the owl may signify is unclear. In classical Greek culture the owl was associated with Athena and thus with wisdom, but at least in elite Roman culture the owl was a bird of ill-omen, associated with death and foreboding; see Pliny, *Natural History*, 10.17; Vergil, *Aeneid*, 4.462 and Servius's commentary; Ovid, *Metamorphoses*, 5.546, 6.430, 10.452, 15.791; and Lucan, *Pharsalia*, 5.395, 6.688. Perhaps here it is just meant to indicate a nocturnal setting.

121. The brothel's erotic panels featuring male-female couples can be dated to around 72 CE based on the impression of a coin of that date found in the plaster of the brothel; see Clarke, *Looking at Lovemaking*, p. 199. The panels are visible above eye level along the main hallway in the spaces above the lintels of doorways to the many small bedrooms. All seven are of similar size and are painted on a pale background with a simple red frame.

122. Clarke, *Looking at Lovemaking*, pp. 145–69, 199–206.

123. Clarke, *Houses of Roman Italy*, pp. 220–21.

124. de Vos and de Vos, *Pompei, Ercolano, Stabia*, p. 170; Antonio Sogliano, 'La Casa dei Vettii in Pompei', col. 268.

125. On household cults, see especially Jan Theo Bakker, *Living and Working with the Gods* (Amsterdam: J. C. Gieben, 1994); but also Pedar Foss, 'Watchful *Lares*: Roman Household Organization and the Rituals of Cooking and Eating', in Ray Laurence and Andrew Wallace-Hadrill (eds), *Journal of Roman Archaeology*, supplement 22: *Domestic Space in the Roman World: Pompeii and Beyond* (1997), pp. 201–18; Thomas Fröhlich, *Lararien- und Fassadenbilder in den Vesuvstädten: Untersuchungen zur "volkstümlichen" pompejanischen Malerei* (Mainz: von Zabern, 1991) and Franz Bömer, *Untersuchungen über die Religion der Sklaven in Griechenland und Rom. I: Die wichtigsten Kulte und Religionen in Rom und im lateinischen Westen* (Wiesbaden: Steiner, 1981).

126. On the master's role in relations with the gods, see Cato, *On Agriculture*, 143 and Richard P. Saller, 'The Hierarchical Household in Roman Society: A Study of Domestic Slavery', in M. L. Bush (ed.), *Serfdom*

and Slavery: Studies in Legal Bondage (London and New York: Longman Press, 1996), pp. 112–29, here pp. 121–2.

127. See Foss, 'Watchful *Lares*', pp. 201–18. In his survey of 154 Pompeian buildings of diverse size, 36 per cent of the built-in household shrines were directly associated with the kitchen area, which in the larger homes was consistently part of the service quarters.

128. Some scholars refer to this architectural unit as a *gynaeceum*, or women's quarters; see Amedeo Maiuri, *Gineco e "Hospitium" nella casa pompeiana* (Rome: Accademia nazionale dei Lincei, 1954), pp. 456–7; de Vos and de Vos, *Pompei, Ercolano, Stabia*, p. 171; Carratelli, 'VI 15,1. Casa dei Vettii', Figure 160. I agree with Wallace-Hadrill, *Houses and Society*, p. 58, however, that there is no evidence or compelling reason to identify this as a secluded or privileged space for women. Roman authors thought of this as a distinctive feature of Greek houses (Vitruvius, *On Architecture*, 6.7; Cornelius Nepos, *Lives*, preface 6–7), although we have difficulty locating *gynaecea* in surviving houses of the Greek world; see Lisa C. Nevett, 'Separation or Seclusion?' in Michael Parker Pearson and Colin Richards (eds), *Architecture and Order: Approaches to Social Space* (London: Routledge, 1997), pp. 98–112. Leach, *Social Life of Painting*, p. 49, is much more correct to identify such a suite of rooms with the Roman term *diaeta*.

129. Illustrated in Fredrick, 'Beyond the Atrium', Figures 12 and 8.

130. Leach, *Social Life of Painting*, p. 6; E. M. Moormann, 'Sulle decorationze della Herculanensium Augustalium Aedes', *Croniche Ercolanese* 13 (1983), pp. 175–7. For a broader analysis of Hercules and social class, see Eric Csapo, *Theories of Mythology* (Malden: Blackwell, 2005), pp. 301–10.

131. For examples of historical or literary figures identifying with myths and using them to understand their own situations, see especially Zanker, 'Mythenbilder im Haus'.

132. Clover, *Men, Women, and Chainsaws*, pp. 17–18.

133. Clarke, *Looking at Lovemaking*, pp. 68–70.

134. On the locations of images of Priapus across Pompeii and in this home, see especially Pia Kastenmeier, 'Priap zum Gruße: der Hauseingang der Casa dei Vettii Pompeji', *Mitteilungen des Deutschen Archèalogischen Instituts* 108 (2001), pp. 301–11. On Hermaphroditus as a guardian figure, see Aileen Ajootian, 'The Only Happy Couple: Hermaphrodites and Gender', in Koloski-Ostrow and Lyons (eds), *Naked Truths*, pp. 220–42, here p. 230.

135. For images of banqueting couples, see for example the central paintings on the north and west walls of room *g* in the House of the Chaste Lovers in Pompeii (IX 12, 6–7), Roller, *Dining Posture*, plates VII and II; a panel taken from the Casa di Guiseppe II (VIII 2, 38/39, Museo Nazionale di Napoli 8968), Roller, *Dining Posture*, Figure 8; and an unprovenanced panel from Herculaneum (Museo Nazionale di Napoli 9024), Roller, *Dining Posture*, plate VI.

136. Fredrick, 'Beyond the Atrium', pp. 281–2.

137. Clover, *Men, Women, and Chainsaws*, p. 152.

138. Clover, *Men, Women, and Chainsaws*, p. 216.

139. See especially Sigmund Freud, 'Analysis Terminable and Interminable' in Sigmund Freud, *The Standard Edition of the Complete Psychological Works of Sigmund Freud*, vol. 23, James Strachey (ed.), tr. James Strachey (London: Hogarth Press, 1986), pp. 216–53, treated extensively by Clover, *Men, Women, and Chainsaws*, pp. 213–22.

140. Clover, *Men, Women, and Chainsaws*, p. 213, quoting Jean Laplanche and J. B. Pontalis, *The Language of Psycho-Analysis*, tr. Donald Nicholson-Smith (New York: Norton, 1973), p. 78.

141. Clover, *Men, Women, and Chainsaws*, p. 213, n. 104; and Edward Bibring, 'The Conception of the Repetition Compulsion', *The Psychoanalytic Quarterly* 12 (1943), pp. 468–519.

142. In 1988, Gaylyn Studlar also published a monograph challenging Mulvey on the question of masochism in film: *In the Realm of Pleasure: Von Sternberg, Dietrich and the Masochistic Aesthetic* (Urbana and Chicago: University of Illinois Press, 1988). Studlar's approach is nevertheless different. Working towards a notion of the gaze that is not exclusively male, she argues that all film spectatorship is masochistic and grounds masochism in the relationship with the mother during the infantile stage of human psychosexual development.

143. Clover, *Men, Women, and Chainsaws*, p. 230.

144. In *In the Realm of Pleasure*, Studlar works to locate the impulse toward masochism in the primal relationship with the mother.

145. Seneca the Elder wrote, 'lack of chastity is a crime in the freeborn, a necessity in a slave, a duty for the freedman', *Controversiae*, 4. preface 10.

146. Fredrick, 'Beyond the Atrium', pp. 281–3.

147. Boydston, 'Gender as a Question', p. 576.

148. Boydston, 'Gender as a Question', p. 560.

149.   Boydston, 'Gender as a Question', p. 560.
150.   Clover, *Men, Women, and Chainsaws*, p. 46.
151.   Clover, *Men, Women, and Chainsaws*, p. 209.
152.   Clover, *Men, Women, and Chainsaws*, p. 209.
153.   Clover, *Men, Women, and Chainsaws*, p. 213.
154.   Mulvey, 'Visual Pleasure', p. 8.
155.   Fredrick, 'Beyond the Atrium', p. 267.

2 'More Beautiful than Words & Pencil Can Express': Barbara Bodichon's Artistic Career at the Interface of her Epistolary and Visual Self Projections

Meritxell Simon-Martin

The climate is delicious the sea & distant mountains more beautiful than words & pencil can express ... the new vegetation & the new animals the wonderfully picturesque town & people ... I did not expect anything half so wonderfully beautiful as I find.

Letter from Bodichon to Marian Evans (novelist George Eliot), Algeria, 21 November–
8 December 1856[1]

Barbara Leigh Smith Bodichon (1827–1891) was a mid-Victorian watercolour painter and one of the leaders of the women's movement in England. This article problematises the construction of historical knowledge about Bodichon via an examination of her artistic career through her letters and paintings. Conceived as an alternative to empirical readings of primary sources, it teases out the mediated nature of epistolary and visual narratives. By focusing on two examples of first-person documentation, it addresses the epistemological question of what historical knowledge about Bodichon's artistic career we can gain through her letters and paintings. Ultimately, this article claims their significance as insightful sources of historical knowledge despite their partial, perspectival and mediated ontology.

In an attempt to make the most of the (very often scarce) primary sources available, biographers make use of a combination of records to provide the most comprehensive analysis of historical figures. Memoirs, personal correspondence, contemporary newspapers and official documents are among the most frequently used historical evidence. Bodichon's life is documented from first-, second- and third-person perspectival texts. Her letters, paintings and publications are articulations of her subjectivity. Letters written to her reveal how Bodichon was perceived and addressed by her correspondents and display a second-person dimension of her identity. Letters exchanged among acquaintances referring to her, newspaper reviews commenting on her feminist and artistic endeavours, as well as official records provide additional layers of information about her. Each of these types of primary source is a genre, with its own regulatory codes

Gender History Across Epistemologies, First Edition. Edited by Donna R. Gabaccia and Mary Jo Maynes.

and conditions of production that determine the perspectival information conveyed. Providing nuanced 'versions' of Bodichon, these sources complement, overlap and may contradict each other.

This article focuses on two first-person primary sources: letters and paintings. Traditionally, letters have been used as straightforward empirical data in historical investigation: as windows into the soul of letter writers. Artistic productions have also been read as transparent screens through which one can see a coherent artistic subject. Yet, as Liz Stanley and Helen Dampier remind us in their contribution to this collection, no written (and I would add, visual) sources escape their mediated ontological nature. Letters tend now to be conceived as autobiographical acts of self-projection where the subject constructs multiple personae determined by the person to whom s/he is writing.[2] In like manner, visual representations are now studied as actions with their own historically bound social conventions and generated within symbolic repertoires – both embedded in systems of signification.[3]

Moving away from an empirical reading of primary sources, in her book *Painting Women*, Deborah Cherry reads the autobiographical narratives and artistic productions of Victorian female artists as created in and by systems of signification ordered in sexual difference. She analyses the sign 'woman' that nineteenth-century female painters (including Bodichon) produced, redefined and circulated through their lifestyle as painters – documented in memoirs, letters and published autobiographies – and through their artwork. For example, she teases out 'the relations of class power which shaped the exchange of looks between artist and model' in Bodichon's 1854 pencil sketch of Elizabeth Siddall – a Pre-Raphaelite muse and artist, formerly a milliner and by then presenting symptoms of consumption. Cherry argues that in her visual representation Bodichon portrayed the sitter 'with massive forehead, columnar neck, large heavy lids and averted gaze' – her appearance 'reworked into a blank and passive mask of beauty'. As a result, the woman Siddall was transformed into the sign 'Siddall': an ideal of femininity codified by a bourgeois painter. Cherry supports her argument by referring to Bodichon's description of her relationship with Siddall in a letter sent to her best friend, Bessie Rayner Parkes (1829–1925). Distancing herself from this working-class woman Bodichon wrote: 'Miss S.[iddall] is a genius and very beautiful and although she is not a lady her mind is poetic'. Cherry concludes that, both in her sketch and letter, Bodichon treated Siddall 'as an object of philanthropic concern who needed hospitalisation as an invalid', not as a fellow-artist.[4] Accounting for their discursivity, Cherry reads Bodichon's sketch and letter not as 'transparent records' detailing her life and describing her work but as documents 'saturated in and structured by historical conditions and discourses'.[5]

Like Cherry, in my study of Bodichon's artistic career I analyse the bourgeois and, as we will see, colonial underpinnings of her feminist outlook. Cherry's work draws on Elizabeth Cowie's theoretical project, which conceptualises 'woman' not as a biological or psychological agent but as a 'sign' – that is, a category produced in signifying practices and a signifier of difference in relation to men.[6] Drawing on Judith Butler's concept of *performativity*, I read Bodichon's letters and paintings as autobiographical acts constitutive of the self. Understanding epistolary and visual narratives as parallel yet different sources of self-constitution, I also complement Cherry's analysis of Bodichon's artistic career by contrasting her artistic self-fashioning as distinctly articulated in her epistolary and visual self-projections. I unpack Bodichon's self-presentation as a female painter at the textual/visual interface as a way of discussing epistemo-logical questions about the production of historical knowledge. Reading letter writ-ing and painting as *performative* autobiographical acts of self-formation, I argue that Bodichon's letters and paintings unfold the making of a female artist through a hybrid mode of self-presentation. Bodichon carved out her identity as a female painter within a male-dominated artistic community throughout her life by innumerable daily habits and life choices – a phenomenon not directly accessible to us, as I will further explain. Simultaneously, she projected an articulation of her artistic selfhood in her letters and paintings – a verbal/visual presentation constitutive of her self. Bodichon forged her artistic identity through epistolary and visual narratives within norms of cultural intel-ligibility. In turn, she individuated her self-image as a female artist determined by the characteristics of each of these genres. That is, Bodichon's letters and paintings acted as parallel, yet different means through which she constituted her identity as a painter. As a result, her epistolary and visual self-projections reveal nuanced aspects of her artistic self-conception, which attests to Bodichon's multiple, fragmented and in the end, unresolved self. In my final remarks I discuss the significance of this unfolding self as a source of historical knowledge about Bodichon's artistic career. Before putting forward my *performative* reading of her letters and paintings, I first give a short account of Bodichon's life and briefly discuss the nature and state of her archive.

Bodichon's personal papers: archival contingencies

Barbara Bodichon was a 'mid-nineteenth century' English feminist, philanthropist and painter. Her father, Benjamin Smith, was a successful businessman and Liberal Member of Parliament.[7] She was the eldest of five illegitimate children. Her mother died when Bodichon was seven.[8] Born into a liberal Unitarian family, she received an unusually broad education and a progressive upbringing. When she turned twenty-one, her father endowed her with an independent yearly allowance that permitted her to pursue her feminist, philanthropic and artistic interests.[9] A committed feminist from an early age, she fought for women's rights on paper and in action, contributing to the launching of the women's movement in England and its earliest instrument of publicity: *The English Woman's Journal*. Her most well-known achievement was the foundation, together with Emily Davies, of the first college for women in Britain: Girton College, at Cambridge University. During her lifetime she was also known as a generous and enthusiastic philanthropist, giving time and money to emigration and education projects, such as Portman Hall, the infant school she established in London in 1854. Bodichon also built a quite distinguished career as a painter. She exhibited in England and in the United States, including several solo presentations. A lover of nature and outdoor activities, she mainly painted landscapes – inspired by the places she lived and visited. Bodichon led a rather nomadic lifestyle. Married at the age of thirty to a French doctor settled in Algiers, the couple lived six months in England and six months in Algeria. She also travelled frequently in Britain and abroad, including an eight-month honeymoon trip across North America. Sketching tours, convalescence stays and sightseeing trips formed an integral part of her active leisured lifestyle.

Bodichon has been the object of notable scholarly interest.[10] Her archive consists of personal correspondence, a short travel journal with sketches, family photographs, legal documents, pencil and ink drawings, watercolour paintings and personal artefacts such as a series of exhibition medals, books from her private library and a locket containing a strand of her hair. Most of these items are held at Girton College. The rest is scattered across other British and North-American institutions. Some of her letters have been edited and published and a selection of her feminist pamphlets reprinted. Cherry laments that nineteenth-century women's artwork has 'not always had the good fortune to survive, or even survive intact, into the twentieth century'. For archives are far from neutral. They are 'shaped in and by historically specific relations between power and knowledge which have determined who is recorded, when, where and how'.[11] Bodichon's paintings are dispersed. Some were donated to Girton College by Bodichon during her lifetime and bequeathed to the college in her will. Others are held in private collections and many others have been untraceable. Her personal correspondence is equally fragmented and incomplete. Many of her letters are lost (or purposely destroyed). Letters with date, heading and ending and without missing pages are the exception. Other letters are in a poor state – torn or stained with ink, which makes them partially unreadable. Reading her letters is additionally difficult due to her very often (seemingly) rushed handwriting and to the frequent absence of punctuation marks. Sometimes only early-twentieth-century typescript copies are available and the originals of some of the letters now in print are no longer extant. Notwithstanding, the determination to write women into history has led hosting institutions to acquire documentation related to Bodichon by gift and by purchase. Hence, regarded as a legitimate subject of history, Bodichon's archive is quite extensive.

Bodichon's letters and paintings: a hybrid *performative* self-constitution

Informed by post-structuralism and postmodernism, some scholars have cast doubt on the possibility of elucidating the essence of the self of a historical subject through autobiographical material. Distinguishing 'flesh-and-blood' subjects from their narrating 'I', autobiography theorists Sidonie Smith and Julia Watson argue that the historical 'I' is unknowable. We are certain of its existence because 'there are traces of this historical person in various kinds of records'. But this 'real' 'I' cannot be known through autobiographical writing. Instead, 'The "I" available to readers is the "I" who tells the autobiographical narrative' – the narrating 'I'.[12] Likewise, Smith and Watson argue against artwork becoming 'a body of mimetic evidence out of which the historian or critic forms a narrative for the artist'. For, 'In so doing, the historian/critic assumes knowledge of and access to the artist's "true self"'.[13]

Informed by these insights, I argue that we do not have direct information about how Bodichon 'lived' as a female artist. Yet, her epistolary 'I' and her visual 'I' – narrating 'I' in Smith and Watson's conceptual vocabulary – provide glimpses of how she carved out her career within the artistic establishment. As I have argued elsewhere, drawing on Judith Butler's theory of gender identity via Sidonie Smith's notion of *autobiographical performativity*, I conceptualise letter writing as a *performative* autobiographical act of identity formation constitutive of one's self. Hence, letter writing is not an expression of the self. Rather the self-narrating subject is an effect of the autobiographical act; she is partially constituted through the act of letter writing. Writing a letter is an autobiographical gesture that functions as a source of self-formation – operating simultaneously with countless other forms of self-production.[14] On that account, Bodichon carved out her identity as a female artist throughout her life by countless everyday gestures and life decisions, like arranging her activities in the day around her sketching sessions and training under the aegis of renowned masters at different stages of her career. Simultaneously, she acted out an epistolary articulation of her identity through the signifying practice of self-narrating by means of her epistolary 'I'. This epistolary re-enactment coexisted alongside other forms of self-constitution – for example, the visual self-projections captured in her paintings. Indeed, expanding this *performative* reading of autobiographical telling to include visual representation, I read Bodichon's paintings and informal drawings as a *performative* gesture that creates its maker. As sources of self-formation, letters and paintings are valuable, though not conclusive, sources of knowledge about Bodichon. As I will further explain, her epistolary and visual narratives provide partial yet plausible hints about how she lived her artistic career.

Letters and paintings acted as sites where Bodichon individuated her identity as a female artist. These visual and textual self-presentations involved agentic action in the form of discourse reappropriation. In Paul Smith's conceptual vocabulary, there is an ideological 'I' in each autobiographical act that occupies, contests and revises a range of subject positions.[15] As sites of agency, epistolary narratives and visual representations function as forums where historically bounded permeating discourses are reappropriated in the process of verbalising an epistolary/visual self-image. In her textual and visual narratives Bodichon individuated her identity as a female painter within norms of cultural intelligibility. Or, to put it differently, the autobiographical 'I' in her epistolary and visual self-projections is the locus of an agentic engagement with an intersectionality of discourses. In the process of fashioning her artistic identity, Bodichon engaged critically with discursive traditions, including prevailing notions of bourgeois femininity.

In turn, Bodichon individuated her narrative self-image as a female artist determined by the distinct features of these two genres: questions of audience, purpose, memory, letter writing codes, letter exchange conventions, the artistic canon and conditions of production and reception are some of the factors that delimited/enabled the articulation of her self-projection in each medium. That is, Bodichon's letters and paintings acted as parallel yet different means through which she constituted her identity as a painter. As a result, her epistolary and visual self-projections reveal nuanced aspects of her artistic self-conception. In Smith and Watson's theoretical vocabulary, Bodichon's hybrid self-representation is a *relational* interface: 'the visual and textual are set side by side, with neither subordinated to the other', but in dialogue where the two independent mediums complement and interrogate each other. Hence, in Bodichon's narrative self, 'the visual and textual are not iterations of the *same* but versions gesturing toward a subjectivity neither can exhaustively articulate'.[16] I now turn to examine Bodichon's multiple, fragmented and unresolved self as articulated through a *relational* hybrid self-representational mode.

Bodichon's artistic identity at the intersection of her epistolary and visual self-projections

During the preparations for the touring American Exhibition of British Art (1857–1858), critic William Rossetti wrote brief biographical sketches of the painters, referring to Bodichon as an 'amateur (I think) of great power'.[17] Rossetti's dubitative remark suggests that Bodichon had a rather ambiguous artistic status during her lifetime. The Victorian art world was inimical to women. It was structured in sexual difference, where masculine and feminine artistic identities developed within relations of power. Female painters were excluded from most art schools and from membership of artistic institutions. They encountered impediments to exhibiting their works in the most prestigious galleries, selling their paintings for high prices and receiving acclaim from the critical establishment. Hampered from pursuing their artistic ambitions through official channels, women were 'afflicted with the curse of amateurism' – a sign of bourgeois femininity and the antithesis of masculine professional practice.[18] Amateur female painters displayed their works in drawing-rooms or bound them in albums circulated among family and friends, and sold them for charitable purposes. Nonetheless, as biographer Pam Hirsch suggests, Bodichon regarded herself as an artist. She indicated 'artist' and 'painter' as her profession respectively in her marriage certificate and the 1881 census.[19] Her epistolary and visual narratives confirm this self-conception and are testimony as to how she carved out an artistic identity that challenged men's exclusive claims to professionalism.

Bodichon spent her childhood and teenage years between Hastings and London, where she received a home education monitored by a governess and a series of tutors and painting masters. In Hastings Bodichon met her lifelong friend Bessie Parkes, the daughter of a Birmingham lawyer settled in London. Letter exchange permitted them to be in contact with each other and provided them with the space for expressing friendship love, explaining anecdotes, giving personal opinions, talking about intimate feelings, offering advice as well as projecting life expectations. Indeed, sharing with a confidante her reflections on the dilemmas she confronted as a young woman, in her letters Bodichon worked out the choices that entailed becoming an adult – including the possibility of pursuing an artistic career.

Once Bodichon wrote to Parkes:

Dearest Bessie,
I have a quiat [*sic*] deal to say to you about work, & life, & the necessity of yr fixing early on a train of action, you I mean, what is so sad, so utterly black as a wasted life, & how common! – I believe there are thousands & tens of thousands who like you & I intend doing –, intend working – but live & die, only intending.
I know something lovely about two girls under 20 both, who being left with little money & no near relations, left England & established themselves in Edinbro' & kept a school in the worst part, & fed & still feed a light & a strong light in a place of utter moral darkness
They do it still & are both very lively & happy & are perfectly independent travelling when necessary by themselves & all that, they devote all their time to this object [and they] are quite rewarded by the good which is visible that they do, to their own eyes & every ones[']. Is not this very beautiful! I will tell you what I think about you when you come here
. . . I must explain what I have done, that is given up coloring (my dear color box is locked up for 6 months) 'some natural tears I shed' or very nearly but I was so convinced of my inability to draw that it was not so difficult as I expected.
It was wretched work! Coloring without forms & so see me sticking to outlines & light & shadow Mrs. Scharf Aunt Julia & some other artists said 'you may be an artist, for you love nature & color well, but you have never learnt to draw'
To be happy is to work, work – work – work – for ever [*sic*] But the soul must have some leisure, & that should be the [unreadable] with great souls, souls which can strengthen one an other [*sic*], Alas! . . .
Yrs affect
BLS[20]

I suggest that this excerpt – most probably written in the late 1840s – is testimony to Bodichon's early epistolary articulation of her artistic ambition. Drawing on the circulating narrative of the unfortunate genteel daughter who is forced to work on her father's death (or bankruptcy), Bodichon laments the lives of those middle-class women who are caught in a spiral of drawing-room conversation and family visiting. Instead, she urges her friend (and by extension, herself) to fix 'early on a train of action'. I interpret her claim, 'To be happy is to work', to mean an (un)paid purposeful occupation. Illustrative of this association between work and happiness is the example she gives of the two sisters who set up a school in Edinburgh.

Identifying herself, to a certain extent, with these two sisters and distancing herself from the 'wasted' lives of leisured bourgeois daughters, Bodichon is determined to unlock her artistic talent by training in drawing. Taking on board her friends' and relatives' criticism, she decides to focus on improving her drawing technique. As Stanley and Dampier write in their article, causality is difficult to prove through epistolary narratives. But since we know from the school minutes that Bodichon took drawing lessons with Francis Cary at Bedford College in 1849, this letter was likely written before or during that year. And it may be interpreted as a preliminary thought she shared with her friend before making the decision to improve her drawing techniques under the aegis of a professional teacher.

The ill-fortuned genteel girl was a circulating bourgeois discourse that the mid-Victorian 'women's rights women' reappropriated to justify more employment and education opportunities. In her publications, Bodichon herself intertwined the discourse with a call for expanding the number of jobs available for women on the grounds of self-fulfilment – a feminist approach that distinguished her from most of her co-workers. Nonetheless, like her colleagues, Bodichon's feminist stance is imbued with class tensions. Thus, in the above epistolary narrative, while Bodichon equates working with happiness, she also acknowledges the necessity for 'some leisure'. My interpretation is tentative because of an unreadable word (due to Bodichon's unclear handwriting) that precludes understanding of the whole sentence. However, I suggest that her claim for leisure has a bourgeois connotation that resonates with Bodichon's middle-class standpoint. Bodichon herself was able to write letters, not only by reason of her advantaged social position (which guaranteed her the literacy and financial resources required to engage in letter exchanges), but also due to the time she was granted to spend in self-development activities such as letter writing – an amount of free time unaffordable among the working classes. Eventually, Bodichon's middle-class standpoint resulted in a class-biased outlook that took for granted middle-class superiority vis-à-vis the lower ranks – another circulating discourse she shared with her social counterparts. A striking example is Bodichon's justification of the two sisters' lifestyle on the grounds that they enlightened the 'utter moral darkness' in which the people living 'in the worst part' of Edinburgh stood.

The excerpt quoted above is an early testimony to Bodichon's unfolding artistic becoming. It articulates her first steps towards becoming an artist: she claims her right to happiness through a self-fulfilling occupation, asserts her painting talent and expresses her determination to unlock her artistic potential by taking further training. In her epistolary narrative, she individuated her sense of self as a painter drawing on contemporary discourses. In other words, her epistolary 'I' is the locus of an agentic engagement with an intersectionality of discourses: Bodichon projected her self-image as a painter by challenging bourgeois domesticity, by reappropriating the 'unfortunate genteel woman' narrative, and by contributing to discourses on middle-class superiority.

In turn, Bodichon articulated this individuated self-conception conditioned by the distinct features of letter writing, namely, the presence of an addressee, letter writing conventions and letter exchange social codes. The intrinsic presence of the epistolary 'you' determines the narrative strategies adopted by the epistolary 'I': from type of paper, handwriting and overall neatness of the letter to the selection of content, tone and register of the narrative. Writing to a close friend meant that Bodichon followed informal letter writing codes: addressing Parkes as 'Bessie', writing her letter with crossed out words, not following a formulaic narrative and writing a rather unstructured text, seemingly without making a fresh copy of her letter. Likewise, unlike, say, her formal letters to acquaintances, it is to close friends such as Parkes that Bodichon confided her hopes and fears. Following the letter exchange code of reciprocity, Parkes replied by offering a personalised response to her friend's epistolary narrative. Sharing codes of cultural intelligibility as well as congenial stances, Parkes indeed approved of taking on 'a train of action' (a would-be poet, she published her first poems in 1852) and advised Bodichon to improve her drawing technique: 'I am glad you are going to study form because I always thought your colouring much the best of the two; but I know it must have been very hard to put the paints away!' she wrote sympathetically.[21] This interactive feedback with endless new beginnings extended along a chain of letters between the two friends. And it fuelled Bodichon's articulation of her artistic selfhood, which she reformulated according to her correspondent's responses. Each letter written by Bodichon in this chain offers a snapshot of her process of artistic self-fashioning.

Bodichon's professional artistic self-conception was confidently asserted in 'Ye Newe Generation', an ink drawing sketched for private circulation (Figure 1). The drawing, now in Girton College, is reprinted in *Barbara Bodichon, 1827–1891, Centenary Exhibition*.[22] The drawing is unsigned and undated but is attributed to Bodichon and is suggested to have been produced around 1850. The sketch illustrates four young women lined-up each firmly holding a different instrument: a spear, an umbrella, a piece of paper, brushes and a pallet. They are facing an unfinished sketch of a bull in a confident gesture of defiance. In the background, a woman at an angle hides her face in her hands as if crying. Assuming it is by Bodichon, I suggest that the drawing attests to her claim for women's professional self-realisation. Mobilising the ongoing discourse on dress reform publicised by contemporary feminist campaigners (including Bodichon in her publications), she depicts the four women in loose jackets and skirts, sturdy boots and wide-brimmed hats. This is the attire she wore during her outdoor sketching sessions to produce the paintings she exhibited and sold.

Seemingly created for fun, addressed to a like-minded spectatorship and exempt from 'the visual codes which regulated publicly exhibited paintings or published illus-trations', 'Ye Newe Generation' is a positive statement in favour of women's right to a professional identity – here as painters and writers.[23] Indeed, the conditions of production and consumption of this sketch created a favourable environment for Bodichon's overt subversion of the history of art's representation of women – rendered objects of masculine understandings of womanhood under the male gaze. The drawing captures a feminist politics of looking where female figures are represented as cultural producers. Circulated around family members (like 'Aunt Julia', who encouraged her

Figure 1: Barbara Bodichon, 'Ye Newe Generation' *c*.1850 (by permission of the Mistress and Fellows, Girton College, Cambridge).

artistic ambitions) and female friends (like Parkes, who herself aspired to be a poet and nurtured Bodichon's talent), the spectatorship of this drawing can be read as confirming Bodichon's intended signification and approving of the confident professional self-image she wished to circulate.

The caption 'Ye Newe Generation' suggests an inclusive understanding of professional self-realisation: the coming generation of female practitioners. Hirsch claims the four main figures in the drawing are Bodichon, would-be poet Bessie Rayner Parkes and fellow artists Anna Mary Howitt and Jane Benham.[24] Cherry names painter Eliza Fox as the fourth character instead.[25] Yet, as neither Bodichon nor her friends are easily recognisable, the drawing could be interpreted as Bodichon having in mind a collective understanding of the new generation of professional women. Notwithstanding, the apparent inclusive message of this visual self-projection stands in tension with Bodichon's self-projections otherwise articulated. Bodichon's feminist outlook may be interpreted as genuinely intended towards personal and social betterment: in favour of her own and, more generally, women's access to education, employment, legal and political rights. However, as in her pamphlets and articles, her epistolary and visual narratives remain unclear about whom she included as feminist subjects. I have already highlighted Bodichon's problematic bourgeois standpoint in the above letter excerpt. Her class bias is equally evident in the letter she wrote to Parkes referring to Siddall, quoted in the introduction. Likewise, Bodichon's letters written from Algeria leave native women out of the sort of autonomous subjectivity she claimed for herself and other feminist subjects. In the letter she sent to her friend Marian Evans during her first trip to the African continent (opening quotation), Bodichon wrote:

we went to see the women of an Arab Prince I can hardly bear to write about the visit – it was so painful to me – picturesque enough but what a life! I hope to God they have no souls or they must be more miserable than the miserablest thing thinking in the world.

Fatima or (Fatuma as they call it here) has a little daughter so pretty so graceful with such a power of undeveloped thought in her beautiful strait forehead that when I thought of her just 11 (the marriageable age) going probably to be tossed out of her home (so dreary little a home) into the house of some strange man whom she will never see before she becomes his property, the tears came [unreadable] into my eyes & I seized her suddenly with rather a rough grasp & as I kissed her, dear little gracious creature! with feelings mountains above her comprehension. I renewed every vow I ever made over wretched women to do all in my short life with all my small strength to help them. Believing that as water finds it[s] level & the smallest stream fr.[om] the High Reservoir mounts any where [*sic*] as high as that is a water so that freedom & justice we English women struggle for today will surely run someday into these low places.[26]

As this excerpt shows, Bodichon reconceptualised herself as a women's rights campaigner as a result of her encounter with the female Other. This reformulation delimited the boundaries of her feminism to the exclusion of native women as autonomous subjects. As in the case of working-class women, Bodichon included Other women not as feminist subjects but as 'needing' objects of her feminism. Indeed, as Cherry writes in *Beyond the Frame*, 'The forces that shaped the western [feminist] activist and her sense of herself as an autonomous subject simultaneously subjected the "native female" to the relays of colonial and imperial power'.[27] The feminist claim to liberal individualism (that underpins Bodichon's statement in favour of women's professional self-realisation, for example) went hand in hand with the exclusion of native women, whose condition was 'degraded', for example, by the sort of child marriage Bodichon describes in her letter. She condemned arranged marriages in favour of 'equal unions', which is what she considered her own to be. As Cherry argues, this companionate love (as opposed to polygamy and arranged marriages) was one of many imperialist markers of western feminism.[28] Against supposedly oppressed and inferior Algerian women, Bodichon reconceptualised herself as a feminist within a nationalist identity where English women struggled for (and eventually enjoyed) 'freedom & justice'. Consequently, native women (and working-class women like Elizabeth Siddall), excluded from autonomous subjectivity, became the object of philanthropic concern. In this second letter excerpt, Bodichon's epistolary narrative, though also addressed to a like-minded middle-class liberal audience, reveals a nuanced aspect of her artistic self that remains undisclosed in her ink drawing: a claim to professional self-realisation underpinned by a feminist approach that eventually ruled out equality between women.

Bodichon's landscapes provide additional snapshots of her professional artistic becoming. From an early age, Bodichon went on painting expeditions with a view to practising her drawing and colouring techniques. Later in life her sketching tours regularly took her to Wales, Cornwall, the Lake District and the Isle of Wight. During her nine-month honeymoon trip across North America, she also embarked on her outdoor painting sessions by herself while her husband went on long walks. Bodichon followed this outdoor painting pattern after her marriage. In Algeria she went off to sketch by the seashore, up the hill in Mustapha Supérieur and during her excursions around the country. Back at home, she finished off her sketches in her purposely-built studios in Champagne du Pavillon, Scalands Gate and The Poor House (respectively her Algerian, Sussex and Cornwall homes).

Figure 2: Barbara Bodichon, 'Sisters Working in our Fields', Algeria, *c*.1858–1860 (in the collection of Pam Hirsch, and reproduced with her permission).

Though she painted in oil sporadically, watercolours were Bodichon's preferred medium. The vast majority depicted the landscapes she captured during her sketching expeditions. Eventually, Bodichon became a watercolourist mostly associated with Algerian scenery. Drawing and sketching in watercolours was part and parcel of domestic accomplishments, 'the hallmarks of a "lady" whose gentility was confirmed by the non-commercial status of her work and its circulation to family and friends'.[29] I suggest that Bodichon's Algerian landscape *Sisters Working in our Fields* (Figure 2) stands as an example of her professional self-conception. Dated *c*.1858–1860, the painting is held in a private collection, and although it was not reprinted in *Barbara Bodichon, 1827–1891, Centenary Exhibition*, the image is available in several scholarly books.[30]

Sisters Working in our Fields depicts the Bay of Algiers from a hill, most probably around the area of Mustapha Supérieur, the smart neighbourhood where Bodichon lived. Two women are portrayed in close-up. They are in a bent forward, working on the field. Little is known about the conditions of production and reception of this landscape. Most probably painted with a view to exhibiting it, the watercolour is conceived for the English artistic community – the establishment that ultimately assessed its worth. Projecting an artistic persona for this audience, Bodichon produced a watercolour that conformed to the canon. She drew on western pictorial conventions and reproduced compositional formulae distinct from western landscape painting.[31] Most notably, Bodichon drew on codes of pictorial intelligibility: the 'rules of recognition' that 'allowed the strange to be presented within the familiar'; that is, to turn 'land into landscape, into a category of western art' intelligible to the English bourgeois consumer.[32]

This pictorial codification was mediated by memory, a meaning-creation mechanism that interpreted how Bodichon experienced viewing and sketching. An understanding (not a replica) of what Bodichon saw during her sketching sessions, *Sisters*

Working in our Fields is embedded in the systems of signification on which Bodichon drew to produce it. Most notably, Bodichon's public self-projection as a landscapist specialising in Algeria is complicit with discourses on orientalism. The scene attests to Bodichon turning 'Algeria's sites into sights' – what Cherry has termed 'pictorialising'.[33] Thus, like most orientalist paintings, Bodichon's Algerian landscapes do not depict the violent encounter between colonisers and colonised but portray the country as a seemingly uninhabited and uncultivated land, which in colonial discourse served to justify western intervention. Equally complicit with colonialism is *Sisters Working in our Fields*, where Bodichon depicts the aftermath of colonial policy: two members of the Order of Charity of St Vincent de Paul are portrayed cultivating what was very often expropriated land. Allocating movement and productive labour to Europeans, the native population was displaced and rendered invisible. Eventually, as a resident in Algeria painting for an English spectatorship, Bodichon contributed to presenting the country 'as a series of visually pleasurable scenes' that 'appealed to a metropolitan community for whom the "Orient" was entertainment'.[34] The epistolary drawing that accompanied the letter quoted in the opening to this paper (Figure 3) illustrates this process of 'pictorialising': surrounded by luxuriant vegetation and an oriental landscape, Bodichon portrays herself sitting on the sand, wearing an outdoor outfit, piece of paper in hand in a gesture of writing/painting, ready to put into words/forms the two Arabs she is attentively observing. The letter itself can be interpreted as an epistolary articulation of Bodichon's difficulties transforming the 'delicious' climate, 'the sea & distant mountains', 'the new vegetation & the new animals the wonderfully picturesque town & people' into texts intelligible to her audience in England.

Notwithstanding, Bodichon's conformity to the artistic canon is not complete. As we have already seen, the visual medium is the locus of agentic engagements with a matrix of circulating discourses. As such, Bodichon's public artistic image as captured in her paintings is also the result of her defiance of prescriptive notions of 'feminine' artistic production and, concomitantly, 'feminine' respectability and decorum. Bodichon took on this challenge by means of her viewing position. By depicting the Algerian bay in *Sisters Working in our Fields*, Bodichon was portraying a location 'already well known from guidebooks, tourist itineraries, antecedent imagery, colonial histories or archaeological reports', which demonstrates to what extent Bodichon's choice of theme was culturally determined.[35] Yet this choice also permitted Bodichon to redefine the category of female artist: she claimed landscapes as a legitimate theme for a woman painter and asserted her right to paint *en plein air*. The academic hierarchy privileged historical representations in oil, relegating female artists to household scenes and still-life. Inner settings were partly justified on the grounds of the presumed weak nature and systematic ill-health among middle-class women. These beliefs were used against them painting outdoors, making of physical frailty a sign of bourgeois femininity.[36] We have already seen how, inspired by her own sketching outfit and addressed to a like-minded familiar audience, Bodichon drew the new generation of professional women in appropriate outdoor clothing. The same self-image is displayed in her epistolary drawings. In the illustrations that accompanied the letter excerpted in the opening quotation, (Figure 4) Bodichon portrayed herself with an outfit for outdoor activities: an unsupported skirt, loose jacket and broad-brimmed hat. Dismissing the tight corseting and restrictive clothing that characterised the 'genteel' appearance of the three aristocratic ladies depicted in Figure 4, she contributed to redefining femininity

Figure 3: Barbara Bodichon, drawing included in a letter to Marian Evans, Algeria, 21 November–8 December 1856 (The George Eliot and George Henry Lewes collection, 1834–1981, Beinecke Rare Book and Manuscript Library, Yale University).

as 'active, strong, working and self-determined'.[37] Equally challenging to normativity, in *Sisters Working in our Fields* Bodichon indirectly claimed her right to sketch out of doors, with its concomitant 'unfeminine' outfit; that is, she claimed her right to adopt the sort of professional attitude required to produce a high standard landscape, worth exhibiting, selling and reviewing. With paintings such as *Sisters Working in our Fields*, most probably exhibited and sold, Bodichon turned amateur sketching in watercolours into a professional practice (a transformation that run parallel to the raising recognition of watercolours within the artistic establishment).[38]

Bodichon's refusal to conform entirely to the artistic canon is also evident in her epistolary narratives. Privately, while she confessed to rejoice at getting praise for her drawings and making money out of the paintings she sold, she also reasserted her artistic self-worth independently of the establishment. Writing from London in 1862 she confided to her close friend, Irish poet William Allingham:

Figure 4: Barbara Bodichon, drawing included in a letter to Marian Evans, Algeria, 21 November–8 December 1856 (The George Eliot and George Henry Lewes collection, 1834–1981, Beinecke Rare Book and Manuscript Library, Yale University).

I wish you could see my pictures. I have been ambitious and had a disappointment – refused at the R.[oyal] A.[cademy] – I sent a monster in oil. I am not disheartened at all and I love my art more than ever – in fact more in proportion to other loves than ever for I confess the enthusiasm with which I used to leave my easel and go to teach at the school [Portman Hall] or help Bessie in her affairs [as editor of the *English Woman's Journal*] is wearing off, and if it were not that at thirty-five one has acquired habits which happily cannot be broken I should not go on as I do; I could not *begin* as I used ten years ago at any of these dusty dirty attempts to help one's poor fellow creatures, and it is quite natural that my life abroad and out of doors should make me more enterprising for board-hunts or painting excursions, than for long sojourns in stifling rooms with miserable people.[39]

Bodichon privately articulated her artistic confidence within a tense juxtaposition of selves. In the letters and paintings mentioned so far, her feminism is embedded in her artistic self-image: it fuelled her career. This epistolary narrative reveals a colliding relation between her feminist and painting endeavours – a contention that ultimately made difficult her engagement with the London-based women's movement.

Finally, parallel to her artistic recognition, Bodichon challenged prejudices against women as valid sources of expertise by circulating both a public and private self-image as knowledgeable in art. Her artistic self-assertion is illustrated in a series of travel letters Bodichon sent to Marian Evans during her trip across France and Spain at the end of 1867. The original letters are no longer extant. What is available today is an eighteen-sheet compilation that looks like a manuscript edited for publication. Indeed, at the intersection of a public/private audience, Bodichon wrote her letters with a view to publishing them. A further edited version was finally published in *Temple Bar* as 'An Easy Railway Journey in Spain' in 1869.[40]

Inserting drawings into her epistolary narrative, Bodichon projects herself as an authority in Arab culture and art. Having visited the cathedral and the monasteries of Las Huelgas and La Cartuja de Miraflores in Burgos, Bodichon wrote:

> We saw Burgos very well but it is worth a month's study. Nothing can exceed the richness & picturesqueness of the cathedral. I wandered in on Sunday & I knelt down with 80 or 100 women all in black veils I had one or two & I found it quite natural no one took any notice of me & I liked the service as much as any of them – perhaps it impressed me more, at least I felt more impressed with the sentiment of the people. Some of the men's heads were so pious & noble it was like looking at a sacred picture to see them. But I have no intention of telling you anything which you could find in guide books. The next day I wandered about with Streets Gothic Architecture in Spain & saw everything he writes about. Two remarks I have to make he says there is no influence of the moors in the buildings. Here I think this is not true. the wooden doors of the Convent of Las Huelgas & of the Cathedral are of the exact panelling of the oldest doors in Algiers. There are also in the Convent of Miraflores in the sills of the arches which look out on that most dreary of monastic graveyards some tiles which I believe to be Moorish
> [detailed drawing of a tile with caption: 'All the colours outlined in chocolate colour & the pattern [slightly?] raised Bright blue]
> . . . It is really pitiful to see so much pure beauty unappreciated everywhere here in Spain. I really am quite reconciled to England buying up everything for the South Kensington Museum! That seemed to me wicked before I came & saw how utterly the best things are uncared for here.[41]

As Tim Young persuasively writes, 'Travellers do not simply record what they see . . . . They observe and write according to established models, having these in mind even when they wish to query or depart from them. No one who travels and writes of their experience can be said to be writing purely as an individual. Descriptions and judgements reveal the values of class, gender, and nationality'.[42] Accordingly, in the excerpt above, Bodichon is following an already established tradition of female travellers using the written medium to assert their expertise. In turn, her judgement of the value and state of Spanish art is the result of an agentic intersection of discourses. Adopting a 'masculine' omniscient and commanding subject position, she neutralises the assessment of an unnamed author on the influence of the Arabs in Spanish art by virtue of her expertise as an artist resident in Algeria and as an experienced traveller. And she resorts to a detailed drawing of a tile to support her claim – as if the visual provided her with a better medium to demonstrate her expertise. Likewise, drawing on the dominant bourgeois discourse of British economic, political and cultural superiority, Bodichon uses her authorial power to justify the appropriation of Spanish artwork with no sign of self-deprecation.

As these examples illustrate, Bodichon's letters and paintings unfold the making of a female artist through a hybrid mode of self-presentation. She projected her artistic ambition early in her letters and asserted her professional self-image both in her sketches and paintings. Individuating her artistic selfhood within norms of cultural intelligibility and determined by the features of each genre, her letters and paintings articulate nuanced aspects of her artistic self-conception. By reading Bodichon's epistolary and visual narratives against each other these tensions are unveiled – subtleties that would otherwise remain undisclosed. Hence, a discursive reading of Bodichon's letters and paintings permits pointing out her bourgeois and colonial standpoint – a problematic aspect of her feminism that Hirsch's assessment of Bodichon's career only briefly addresses. Thus, for example, in her biography she acknowledges that 'Perhaps her landscapes, celebrating the beauty of Algeria, could be seen as complicit in the production of an Orientalist Other for the consumption of Western purchasers'. But she concludes that 'this was certainly not her intention'. For 'Her own view of her role in Algeria was more curatorial, capturing a landscape, sometimes peopled, sometimes not, *before* it was overly Europeanised'.[43] Alternatively, reading her autobiographical material as produced in and by systems of signification, I suggest that Bodichon drew on dominant discourses of Otherness precisely to be in a position to make her words/landscapes intelligible to her audiences. Caught by cultural prejudices she did not challenge, I suggest she was accomplice to colonialism. Ultimately, Bodichon's epistolary and visual narratives attest to her multiple, fragmented and in the end unresolved self. The following section concludes this *performative* reading of Bodichon's letters and paintings by discussing what knowledge about Bodichon's artistic career is revealed through her letters and paintings.

Bodichon's unresolved artistic self and the production of historical knowledge

Implicit in empirical historical inquiry is the idea that Bodichon – the essence of her self, and by extension, her historical 'I' – is captured in and recoverable through her autobiographical material. Instead, my argument is that the unresolved self that emerges from her letters and paintings is not 'flesh-and-blood' Bodichon but the epistolary and visual self-image she chose to project. Understanding letter writing and painting as *performative* mechanisms, letters and paintings acted as sources of self-formation (which coexisted alongside countless others). Accordingly, Bodichon's circulating self-images disclose her self-constitution. Hence, her epistolary and visual 'I' reveals glimpses of how she carved out her artistic career within the artistic establishment – the subject positions she took agenticly within discursive fields by means of the enabling features of each medium.

But the knowledge we gather through her letters and paintings (her self-images) does not correspond to Bodichon's 'core self'. It is the partial knowledge of her self-formation to which we have access: Bodichon's self-constitution as enacted in her letters and paintings. This particular self-constitution may not fully correspond to the self-image she projected in the countless other forms through which she forged her artistic selfhood – in her publications or in daily habits, for example. As letter writing and painting form autobiographical acts constitutive of her self, we can presume a correlation between her epistolary and visual 'I' on the one hand and otherwise-articulated 'I's on the other. On that account, Bodichon's letters and paintings would offer plausible hints about how she 'lived' her artistic career – how she fashioned her identity in 'lived' gestures. At the same time, her epistolary and visual 'I' emerges as an unresolved artistic self, with complementing, overlapping and opposing aspects emerging from her letters and paintings. A comparable tension can be assumed to exist between her epistolary/visual self-image and her 'lived' artistic fashioning. Furthermore, as Bodichon expresses in the opening quotation, her difficulties in putting her 'experiences' into words/images can be interpreted as an allusion to the limits of letters and paintings as sources of self-formation and as a reminder of the impossibility of accounting for the richness of Bodichon's life through historical sources.

To conclude, this *performative* reading of Bodichon's artistic self-conception at the intersection of her epistolary and visual narratives aims to set the ground for further re-examinations of Bodichon's artistic career. Her letters and paintings show that, in the process of carving out her artistic identity as a landscapist within a male-dominated world, Bodichon challenged men's exclusive claims to professionalism and contributed to mobilising a revised category of woman artist. In this sense, the knowledge we gather through Bodichon's letters and paintings is valuable since it provides a partial yet insightful understanding of her agentic artistic becoming. The 'truthfulness' of her narratives cannot be easily claimed in referential terms; rather, hers is a perspectival and subjective construction of 'reality'. We can argue, however, that the artistic community's embrace of Bodichon's public image was indicative of her artistic achievement. For she succeeded not only in exhibiting and selling – markers of an artist's professional practice of art – but also in publishing articles as an expert on Algeria and art, including a piece on Kabyle pottery in the leading *Art Journal*.[44]

On the other hand, reviews of her artistic productions were not unanimously complimentary. In 1859, for example, the literary and art journal *The Athenaeum* judged her Algerian landscapes to be 'raw, rash and colourless'.[45] And her status as an artist seems to have remained ambiguous – as Rossetti's biographical note suggests. Her publications, engravings, journal illustrations and even personal artefacts and official records – other means through which Bodichon forged her artistic identity – would most likely confirm Bodichon's professional artistic identity (and unveil tensions). Her artistic career could be further assessed via an exploration of the multidimensional nature of her identity. An examination of how others responded to her projected self-image – in newspaper reviews commenting on her artwork and in letters written to/about her – would permit further evaluation of the position Bodichon gained within the artistic establishment. Alternatively, research could be directed towards studying the interaction between the different dimensions of Bodichon's artistic identity, focusing for instance on her intersubjective artistic making: how others' perception of her self-images fed her artistic becoming (as I briefly suggest in my analysis of Parkes's epistolary response to Bodichon's intention to improve her drawing technique). Reviewing Bodichon from fragmented and perspectival pieces of information neither reconstructs her as unified historical subject nor produces the definitive history of her life. Nonetheless, these other sources of knowledge (though equally partial, perspectival and mediated) would certainly complicate and enhance our understanding of Bodichon's artistic career.

Notes

The author would like to thank Donna Gabaccia, Mary Jo Maynes and the two anonymous reviewers for their comments on previous versions of this article, as well as Joyce Goodman and Stephanie Spencer from the University of Winchester for their help and support.

1. Algeria, 21 November–8 December 1856, Beinecke Library, Yale University, George Eliot and George Lewes Collection, Box 7.
2. See for example Rebecca Earle, *Epistolary Selves: Letters and Letter-Writers, 1600–1945* (Aldershot: Ashgate, 1999); Jan Montefiore and Nicky Hallett (eds), 'Lives and Letters', *Journal of European Studies* 32 (2002), pp. 97–318; Maire Fedelma Cross and Caroline Bland (eds), *Gender and Politics in the Age of Letter Writing* (Aldershot: Ashgate, 2004).
3. See for example Deborah Cherry, *Painting Women: Victorian Women Artists* (London and New York: Routledge, 1993); Sidonie Smith and Julia Watson (eds), *Interfaces: Women, Autobiography, Image, Performance* (Ann Arbor: University of Michigan Press, 2003).
4. Cherry, *Painting Women*, p. 189.
5. Cherry, *Painting Women*, p. 7.
6. Elizabeth Cowie, 'Woman as sign', *m/f* 1 (1978), pp. 49–63.
7. Pam Hirsch, *Barbara Leigh Smith Bodichon* (London: Chatto and Windus, 1998), pp. 2–8.
8. Hirsch, *Barbara Leigh Smith Bodichon*, pp. 9–15.
9. Hirsch, *Barbara Leigh Smith Bodichon*, p. 40, 187–94, 266–91, 71–83, 43, 109, 132, 159–60, 165–6, 291, 129, 149–63.
10. Most notably Sheila Herstein, *A Mid-Victorian Feminist, Barbara Leigh Smith Bodichon* (New Haven: Yale University Press, 1985); Pam Hirsch, 'Barbara Leigh Smith Bodichon, Artist and Activist', in Clarissa Campbell Orr (ed.), *Women in the Victorian Art World* (Manchester: Manchester University Press, 1995). pp. 167–86; Hirsch, *Barbara Leigh Smith Bodichon*; Pam Hirsch, 'Barbara Leigh Smith Bodichon: Feminist Leader and Founder of the First University College for Women', in Mary Hilton and Pam Hirsch (eds), *Practical Visionaries: Women, Education, and Social Process, 1790–1930* (New York: Longman, 2000), pp. 84–100; Pauline Nestor, 'Negotiating a Self: Barbara Bodichon in America and Algiers', *Postcolonial Studies: Culture, Politics, Economy* 8 (2005), pp. 155–64.
11. Cherry, *Painting Women*, pp. 3, 6.
12. Sidonie Smith and Julia Watson, *Reading Autobiography: A Guide for Interpreting Life Narratives* (Minneapolis: University of Minnesota Press, 2001), p. 59.
13. Sidonie Smith and Julia Watson (eds), *Interfaces: Women, Autobiography, Image, Performance* (Ann Arbor: University of Michigan Press, 2003), p. 11.
14. Judith Butler, *Gender Trouble: Feminism and the Subversion of Identity* (New York and London: Routledge, 1990); Sidonie Smith, 'Performativity, Autobiographical Practice, Resistance', *a/b: Auto/Biography Studies* 10 (1995), pp. 17–31; Meritxell Simon-Martin, 'Barbara Leigh Smith Bodichon's Travel Letters: Performative Self-Formation in Epistolary Narratives', *Women's History Review* 22 (forthcoming 2013).
15. Paul Smith, *Discerning the Subject* (Minneapolis: University of Minnesota Press, 1988) quoted in 'Smith and Watson', *Reading Autobiography*, p. 63.
16. Smith and Watson, *Interfaces*, p. 22.
17. Quoted in Hirsch, *Barbara Leigh Smith Bodichon*, p. 160.
18. Orr, *Women in the Victorian Art World*, p. 6.
19. Hirsch, *Barbara Leigh Smith Bodichon*, p. 129 and p. 303, respectively.
20. Undated, Cambridge University, Girton College Archives, Girton College Personal Papers (GCPP) Parkes 5/165.
21. Undated, GCPP Parkes 5/2.
22. Girton College, *Barbara Bodichon 1827–1891 Centenary Exhibition: An Exhibition of Watercolours, Oils, Sketches and Memorabilia Held in the Mistress's Flat Girton College, Cambridge, 22nd–30th June 1991* (Girton College, 1991).
23. Deborah Cherry, *Beyond the Frame: Feminism and Visual Culture, 1850–1900* (London and New York: Routledge, 2000), p. 46.
24. Hirsch, *Barbara Leigh Smith Bodichon*, p. 118.
25. Cherry, *Painting Women*, p. 47.
26. See endnote 1.
27. Cherry, *Beyond the Frame*, p. 60.
28. Cherry, *Beyond the Frame*, p. 62.
29. Cherry, *Painting Women*, p. 83.
30. For example Cherry, *Beyond the Frame*, p. 88.
31. Cherry, *Beyond the Frame*, p. 97.
32. Cherry, *Beyond the Frame*, p. 86.
33. Cherry, *Beyond the Frame*, pp. 79, 75.
34. Cherry, *Beyond the Frame*, p. 69.

35. Cherry, *Beyond the Frame*, pp. 88, 82.
36. Cherry, *Painting Women*, pp. 2–5.
37. Cherry, *Painting Women*, p. 170.
38. Cherry, *Painting Women*, p. 106.
39. Suggested date in reprint [July 1862], H. Allingham and Helen Baumer Williams (eds), *Letters to William Allingham* (London: Longmans, 1911), p. 77.
40. 'An Easy Railway Journey in Spain', *Temple Bar* 25 (January 1869), pp. 240–49.
41. [November–16 December] 1867, George Eliot and George Lewes Collection, Box 7.
42. Tim Youngs, *Travellers in Africa: British Travelogues, 1850–1900* (Manchester: Manchester University Press, 1994), p. 209.
43. Hirsch, *Barbara Leigh Smith Bodichon*, p. 139.
44. Information on her exhibitions and sold paintings can be found in journal articles and official records, for example. 'Kabyle Pottery', *Art Journal* (February 1865), pp. 45–6.
45. *The Athenaeum*, 19 February 1859, quoted in Cherry, *Beyond the Frame*, p. 95.

3 Public Motherhood in West Africa as Theory and Practice

Lorelle Semley

Several years ago, I was first seduced by the story of a West African woman named Alaba Ida. Born in the 1850s, she became an influential agent of the French colonial regime in the 1910s, in what is now the Republic of Benin. Taken captive when the neighbouring state of Dahomey destroyed Kétu in 1886, she was freed upon France's defeat of Dahomey seven years later and may have been among the first refugees to accompany French army officers into Kétu to begin the process of resettlement. By tradition, the new king, Alákétu (king; 'owner' of Kétu) Onyegen, inherited all of his predecessor's wives, and at that time Alaba took the prestigious title of *ida* (senior royal wife) and thus was known, thereafter, as Alaba Ida. She also allied herself with French colonial authorities by supporting the work of the 1906 Anglo-French Boundary Commission that made most of Kétu part of the French colony of Dahomey rather than part of neighbouring British-controlled Nigeria.[1] After 1908, she gained more influence as her husband became increasingly ill and blind and another man, appointed by French colonial authorities as a *sous-chef* (assistant chief), proved ineffective. One elderly Kétu man described her extraordinary rise to power after the king lost his sight and could not see a European extending his hand in greeting: 'Alaba Ida shook hands with the European', the man told me, 'and [she] became very powerful'.[2]

The true turning point in Alaba Ida's position came in 1911, when the French selected her and a second woman named Yá Shègén as colonial intermediaries to restore order in Kétu after the murder of a visiting African interpreter. The local French official explained that in the region 'women really matter[ed]'.[3] But the unprecedented move proved short-lived, and by 1917 both women had been deposed. Alaba Ida lived for another twenty years when, it is said, she died old, forgotten and disgraced, her final resting place a garbage heap. In many ways, Alaba Ida's dramatic rise and fall follows a not uncommon script about an influential woman spurned by society and, in this case, first recruited and then betrayed by European imperialism. When Alaba Ida is faulted or celebrated for appearing unique in the historical record, her story is too easily analysed in universalist, exceptionalist or romanticist ways. If Chandra Mohanty has chided scholars for making assumptions about the 'third world woman' as victim, Jeanne Boydston warned against seeing 'deviations' to gender norms only in histories of African, Asian, Latin American or Native American cultures.[4] Still, the allure and danger of remarkable examples like that of Alaba Ida relate precisely to the uniqueness

Gender History Across Epistemologies, First Edition. Edited by Donna R. Gabaccia and Mary Jo Maynes.
Chapters © 2013 The Authors. Book compilation © 2013 Blackwell Publishing Ltd.

of her individual narrative. Here, Alaba Ida should draw us in intellectually not only because of the details of her life and death, but also for what she demonstrates about gender, history and ways of knowing.

I analyse the historical personage of Alaba Ida as a 'public mother', because of the notorious position she achieved as an elderly woman in the Yoruba town of Kétu. In various West African communities such as Kétu, birthmothers of children and women of a certain age or stature could informally be known widely in their communities as 'Mother'. In the case of 'public mothers' in Yoruba societies, the local term for 'mother' often serves as part of the official title of women priests and royal ministers, and in the names of both 'witches' and divine or sacred women.[5] So, motherhood carries several extended and more public meanings. Indeed, part of the problem with Alaba Ida's influence related to the fact that it did not derive from her role as an appointed minister or as a priest, but rather from her position as a royal wife. Whereas motherhood can conjure real and mystical forms of power, the term 'wife' has been as much an expression of subordination to a superior as of some women's gender status. In fact, some men who are dependents, especially to a political or religious leader, may be referred to as 'wives'.[6] Thus, this article develops the concept of public motherhood, as understood in some West African cultures, as an epistemological challenge to the vast motherhood scholarship in the social sciences and literary studies that has been partly shaped by different assumptions about biology and the body.

I borrow the term 'public motherhood' from literary scholar Chikwenye Ogunwemi, who, like other scholars who have written on maternalism in African, Western and Latin American contexts, discusses how women exercise political influence by highlighting their role as biological mothers.[7] For Ogunyemi, women – especially elder women – operate as 'caretakers' in the public domain. Ogunyemi distinguishes astutely between the elder woman as public mother and the young woman as wife, but makes a casual jump from the elder woman's role in the household to a wider one in the community.[8] Nigerian sociologist Oyèrónké Oyěwùmí, author of *The Invention of Women: Making an African Sense of Western Gender Discourses*, similarly makes an important theoretical intervention by differentiating between wives and mothers in order to explain the peculiarity of elder women's power.[9] However, Oyěwùmí generalises broadly from specific social and historical contexts in West Africa in order to argue in very 'naturalising' terms for a fundamental difference between the ideal of the mother in African communities and what she sees as the problematic 'heart' of Western feminism: the wife.[10] While benefitting from their insights, my use of public motherhood avoids both Oyěwùmí's emphasis on the (perceived) 'naturalness' of African motherhood and Ogunyemi's singular focus on the nurturing work of public mothers by concentrating on the metaphor and symbolism of motherhood as the basis of elderly women's authority. After all, it is not the childbearing mother who personifies this power but the postmenopausal woman titled as 'Mother' and her power often exceeds the realm of 'nurturing'.

When I turned to theories of motherhood in feminist scholarship, I found that the women I saw as public mothers did not easily fit. Confronted with this discrepancy between my findings and the secondary literature, I turned to black feminist writings on motherhood as well as Africanist texts on women and gender that were attentive to race, class and imperialism. These analyses expand the scholarship on motherhood and resonate with my encounter with Alaba Ida in the archive and the field. However, much of the writing on motherhood falls into what I have come to see in terms of three, often overlapping, frameworks – biological, socio-historical and cultural/discursive. While most studies of motherhood address biological motherhood and mothering in the broadest terms, scholars often define maternalism as a specific sociohistorical phenomenon dating to the nineteenth century in which women used their status as mothers to influence politics and public debate.[11] Feminist scholars also examine how society and language contribute to the social construction of women and to the idea of women as 'Other'.[12] These perceptions remain compelling and useful, but elderly women like Alaba Ida embody a power that may conjure the deep symbolism of childbirth without requiring biological motherhood. Moreover, the social debates that involved Alaba Ida went beyond 'women's issues' to address the broader workings of imperial policy. To think of public mothers discursively also requires an understanding of changing local and colonial constructions of women's power and vulnerability.

With this in mind, the first part of this article contextualises Alaba Ida as a historical figure in French colonial Dahomey, showing how she evokes and complicates the concept of public motherhood. To demonstrate my own academic journey through the larger literature on motherhood defined by biological, sociohistorical and discursive approaches, I open with a discussion of the African-American scholar Anna Julia Cooper to foreground the contributions of black feminist and Africanist scholars to the field. I am not arguing that Cooper represents a facile continuity between African and African diaspora notions of motherhood, but rather that she demonstrates the intellectual intervention and innovation of black scholars in the study of motherhood, gender and history. Thus, engagement with all of this scholarship allows me to see Alaba Ida as part of a larger theoretical paradigm, rather than as a singular, exoticised example.

Indeed, I arrived at the concept of public motherhood through both the remarkable story of Alaba Ida and the general Africanist gender historiography, rather than through the vast body of feminist literature on motherhood. Scholars of West Africa have long differentiated between the multiple social positions of mothers, wives and sisters. West African mothers, as postmenopausal elders rather than as childbearing wives, could represent the pinnacle of power as 'public mothers'. However, they could remain socially vulnerable if they lacked resources or were perceived as exercising supernatural power or 'secret knowledge'.[13] Similarly sisters in a well-placed family, especially in certain royal ones, could enjoy certain political and social freedoms and even socially 'become men'.[14] By contrast, the wife, so often erroneously thought of synonymously as a mother, occupies an ultimate position of subordination, though the first wife could exercise some influence over subsequent brides. What made Alaba Ida unique was the way she occupied several of these social positions in problematic ways.

Alaba Ida 'practiced' public motherhood dangerously because she constantly engaged visibly with the local community and the French colonial administration, while her position in relation to both remained in question. As part of her duties for the French, Alaba Ida collected taxes, gathered military recruits and, generally, acted as an intermediary, undoubtedly making her unpopular with the local population.[15] Many elders in Kétu emphasised in conversations with me her position as a royal wife rather than her relationship with the French colonial administration and denied that wives of the king ever advised the king in any official or unofficial capacity. Those who say Alaba Ida 'governed' explain that she did so in place of her husband. (The term for 'govern', *joba*, has at its root the term *oba*, technically meaning 'ruler' but often translated as 'king'.) Some in Kétu do use the term 'queen', but one brusque man insisted to me that she was *not* a queen at all but an *aya oba* or royal wife who gave orders simply because her husband, the king of Kétu, was blind.[16] Others deny that Alaba Ida could ever have left the *àáfin*, the king's residence, since as a royal wife she was secluded so that men could not see her or relate to her freely. A man caught looking at the wife of the king was said to be subject to corporal punishment, even death; royal wives' shaven heads and plain clothes were intended to discourage the advances of other men.[17] In the past, even kings themselves had been shrouded in mystery and were rarely seen in public.[18] Alaba Ida disregarded these expectations of seclusion by frequently visiting the lone French officer and circulating in town. She may even have attempted to appropriate the hammock, shoes and drums associated with the office of the king, perhaps in an effort to usurp his cultural and symbolic power.[19]

Comparing Alaba Ida to Yá Shègén, the second woman intermediary appointed by the French, further highlights the tenuous line that Alaba Ida drew as a royal wife, colonial agent and public mother and better contextualises Alaba Ida's downfall. In fact, Akanké Owebeyi Aduké, with her priestly title 'Yá Shègén' (probably a shortened version of Ìyá Shègén or 'Mother Shègén'), was closer to a public mother with recognised official duties in the town.[20] As a priest, she was an *iyálorìshà* (mother-in-deity) of the *òrìshà* (deity) named Ondo. The *òrìshà* are believed to have been women or men worthy of praise and worship because of remarkable lives in earlier times. But Ondo and his wife Are, for example, are celebrated as founders of Pobé, a town outside the Kétu region and the original home of Yá Shègén and many of her original followers. As a result, Yá Shègén also operated from a marginal position because, in some ways, she was an outsider. Yá Shègén does not appear in the French colonial record until 1906, when the French colonial administrator speaks of her as 'almost a divinity'.[21] Indeed, her religious duties remained paramount even though she was filling a political role in working for the French. For example, because *òrìshà* dictate certain taboos for people initiated into the group and because followers of Ondo are forbidden to ride in a hammock, the elderly Yá Shègén could never journey by foot to meet French colonial administrators. Instead, French officials came to her village outside the town.[22] She was assigned specific responsibility for several eastern villages, some of them recalcitrant and troublesome ones, making her akin to an 'assistant district head'. But, as with Alaba Ida, her formal administrative title was never stated.[23] At first the French admired Yá Shègén's influence as a religious leader, but in the end, they were not impressed with her ability to carry out orders on their behalf. In fact, Yá Shègén faded from colonial reports and many people's memories, though her priestly title persisted after her death.

It is significant that Alaba Ida's official engagement with the French, like Yá Shègén's, not only eventually backfired but also exhibited the limits of French thinking on women's power. Though Alaba Ida took on most of the duties of the 'district chief', including military and labour recruitment, taxation and supervision of subordinate village heads, she was never formally given the title of *chef du canton*, the designation given to former African kings at the time.[24] The French instead referred to her by her title 'Ida', meaning senior wife, which they translated as 'queen', often rendering her name 'Queen Ida' in the colonial records. Though French administrators described Alaba Ida in the early 1910s as 'alert, despite her age, very authoritarian, with an intelligent and lively spirit...a precious resource for the administration', by 1915, following more unrest in the region, the outbreak of the First World War and a change in the French colonial leadership, local French administrators rejected the premise of rule by women, calling it 'untraditional' and unacceptable for Kétu.[25]

Indeed, Alaba Ida is immortalised, but in derisive songs. In the late 1960s, some fifty years after Alaba Ida's 'reign', Nigerian historian A. I. Asiwaju collected Gèlèdé songs about the colonial period. In Gèlèdé ceremonies, male dancers wearing elaborate sculpted masks on their heads don the shirt, skirt and head-tie of a woman, ostensibly to honour 'mothers' or to placate 'witches'. One song Asiwaju recorded portrayed Alaba Ida's leadership as disastrous, bringing death and disease. To associate Alaba Ida with death is to portray her as a 'witch', a common accusation against elderly women seen as 'public mothers' with some knowledge of religious ritual and other secrets. Some townspeople today scorn Alaba Ida's origins or her femininity; she was not really from Kétu, they say, or she was barren and childless. Some even hesitate to utter her name. History has been particularly harsh to Alaba Ida because of her final act as *ida* (senior wife). Upon Alákétu Onyegen's death in 1918, as the senior wife, she and the *ramu* (favourite wife) were expected to be buried with him to serve him in the afterlife.[26] It is unclear whether Alákétu Onyegen had named a 'favourite wife', but the French colonial administration refused to permit the sacrifice of anyone. Alaba Ida was eventually sent to Pobé, rumoured as the home of her son, a former *tirailleur* (African soldier), but fearing for her life she later escaped to a French military outpost.[27] She wandered for many days in the forest with nothing to eat but wild birds she had carried with her, and some said she emerged from the brush to take food from cast iron pots outside of people's homes. Her association with birds and the night connote witchcraft in Yoruba culture, especially when practiced by elderly women. Stories of wandering and paranoia allude to senility, a state Alaba Ida is said to have exhibited in the years leading up to her death. Such a disgraceful demise also appears to punish Alaba Ida for her multiple transgressions.[28]

The images of Alaba Ida and Yá Shègén – as 'queen', 'witch' or 'priest' – evoked the power of their womanhood, and yet both were severely constrained by their status as colonial intermediaries. Alaba Ida and Yá Shègén also were defined by their relationships to male figures: Alaba Ida to her husband the Alákétu, Yá Shègén to her *òrìshà*, Ondo. Although both tried to establish an independent base of power by retaining messengers, giving commands, advising and administering punishments, neither was able to build an autonomous base of wealth or support. One man maintained that the king's ministers and chiefs had become Alaba Ida's, but in fact as a royal wife, she had no personal wealth. Though royal wives sometimes conducted trade at the market, they could not set up the personal networks other established women traders could. Alaba Ida, without brothers, land or livestock, had to depend wholly on government subsidies and gifts. Yá Shègén, with access to some income and resources through a small piece of land cultivated by her followers, had more opportunity to generate wealth, but priests redistributed their wealth for ceremonies and dependents. Moreover, Yá Shègén's *òrìshà* probably was not popular throughout Kétu, linked as it was to the history and identity of a region beyond the kingdom.[29] Thus, as elderly women, both Alaba Ida and Yá Shègén evoked the image of the 'public mother', but they did not fulfil that role in similar ways.

One woman minister insisted to me, in defining her own political office in Kétu, that Alaba Ida was not charged with official duties but simply served as the wife of the king.[30] In fact, neither Alaba Ida nor Yá Shègén was an official titled minister of the kingdom, with recognised authority over the general population. The power delegated to them by the French colonial administration was easily called into question. Of the two, Alaba Ida was more vulnerable to criticism because her influence derived almost solely from her association with the king and the French colonial administration, while Yá Shègén commanded authority primarily from her religious role. Yá Shègén's religious office drew upon the concept of *ìyá* as a 'public mother', while the designation of *ida*, senior wife, emphasised Alaba Ida's ambivalent position in the palace and the community. I came to realise that as much as she inspired my theory of public motherhood, Alaba Ida's 'practice' of it exceeded my own definition because she operated as a public mother without an actual title or sanctioned authority. Alaba Ida may have enjoyed important standing in the king's household as the senior royal wife, but to Kétu residents she embodied the epitome of subordination, a wife of the king. As Alaba Ida appeared publicly and commanded people, she appeared to trounce 'tradition' while drawing upon existing avenues for women's power. The profound fragility of Alaba Ida's power also resonated with the realities of titled public mothers. The same powerful woman who noted that Alaba Ida was not an official minister, told me that had she been a man, she could have been king.

The simultaneous celebration and assumed vulnerability of mothers runs throughout the motherhood literature. To build a theory of public motherhood around Alaba Ida and Yá Shègén casts new light on questions of experience, institutions and cultural symbolism, especially in relation to power derived not from the physicality of motherhood but the mysticism of it. The powerful imagery associated with childbirth – an event at once awesome and mundane – is at the heart of the symbolism of the title 'mother' bestowed on elderly women, regardless of their status as biological mothers.[31] Local cultural ideas and practices occurred alongside newly imposed colonial hierarchies, exposing changing power relations among mothers, wives, fathers, kings, husbands and colonial officials. As much as the French saw the situation through their own eyes in terms of 'queens' and kings and questions of social order, they could not fully comprehend the symbolism associated with royal wives or public mothers. French administrators made assumptions about the nature of African women's authority when they appointed the two women as intermediaries and then evoked the trope of African women's powerlessness when the women no longer proved useful. These themes of womanhood, power and the metaphor of motherhood led me to the familiar vision of the black mother along with all of the reductive stereotypes and real and imagined connections between Africa and the African diaspora. But rather than limiting my options, the intersection of race, gender and empire embedded in the black feminist and Africanist literature opened a new broader vista on the motherhood literature and gender history in general.

To begin with Anna Julia Cooper reveals how motherhood, as a concept, operated rhetorically to denote multiple forms of power, especially within broader historical themes of race and empire. By analysing mothering as experience and institution, Cooper exposed these possibilities because womanhood, race and empire emerged in her writing in surprising ways, suggesting a roadmap for re-reading other authors. Cooper's long life from 1858 to 1964 spanned the end of slavery and the height of the Civil Rights Movement in the United States. As a foundational scholar in the interdisciplinary, theoretical style of feminist, African American and cultural studies scholarship, Cooper also experienced and theorised biological, sociohistorical and discursive approaches to motherhood.[32] She never remarried after being widowed in her early twenties but adopted several children of family and friends later in her life. Although able to pursue academic life more freely as a single woman, Cooper remained economically vulnerable. Her theories of womanhood and her allusions to motherhood reflected her hardships and triumphs. And her transnational vision of the world shaped by her studies of slave trades, imperialism and the Haitian Revolution, revealed the connections between the social and historical contexts of her life and her life work.[33]

Anna Julia Cooper's most famous speech, delivered in 1886 and entitled 'Womanhood: A Vital Element in the Regeneration and Progress of a Race', presented black women's education and social uplift as central to the advancement of the black community and related women's roles as mothers as crucial to the 'betterment of the world'. Cooper simultaneously projected women as citizens and symbols of humanity, not because of women's 'nature' but because of women's intellectual promise.[34] Indeed, in her 1893 speech at the Columbian Exposition in Chicago, Cooper applied this broader vision of womanhood to enslaved black women: 'full of heroic struggle . . . . The painful, patient, and silent toil of mothers to gain a fee simple title to the bodies of their daughters . . . to keep hallowed their own persons'. On one level, womanhood was about black women's freedom and control over their own and their children's own physical bodies which Cooper compares to the power of land ownership. Cooper also alluded to women's control over their metaphysical selves or broader sense of being. 'The white woman could at least plead for her own emancipation', Cooper remarked, 'the black woman, doubly enslaved, could but suffer and struggle'.[35] Yet with the opportunities emergent with emancipation, Cooper demanded more than biological and even social roles for mothers: 'Let woman's claim be as broad in the concrete as in the abstract . . . . We want . . . the universal triumph for justice and human rights . . . a gateway for ourselves, our race, our sex . . . a grand highway for humanity'.[36] As Cooper extended her role for women to the metaphorical and 'abstract', she placed woman at the centre of humanity, human rights and progress, suggesting that women, especially black women, historically had not been perceived as such, but as 'Other'. In these ways, her scholarship encompasses the biological, historical and discursive approaches to motherhood in the feminist scholarship. As Cooper described women playing simultaneous roles as parents, citizens and intellectual actors, she also moved toward some of the broader ideas underlying public motherhood.

To understand Anna Julia Cooper in this historically contextualised way allows for a reconceptualisation of many other feminist writers, beginning with those who particularly focused on motherhood in terms of childrearing. Even Betty Friedan's classic 1963 text can be analysed beyond critiques of her reification of motherhood and post-1960s 'second-wave' feminism from the perspective of white, suburban, middle-class and heterosexual American women. Many scholars have explored the different experiences of women of colour, working-class women and professionals and have demonstrated that popular culture projected multiple, even conflicting messages, celebrating and critiquing multiple identities for women.[37] Friedan herself could not escape the historical context of the early 1960s. She wrote during the rising tide of the Civil Rights Movement, the emergence of independent nations in Africa and the Caribbean and the intensification of cold war competition in Asia and Africa. White flight from the black city gave birth to the suburbs where the 'problem that has no name' emerged. This was the outside world from which white suburbia implicitly and explicitly sought refuge. Despite Friedan's silences or, better, embedded within them, the realities of race were scrawled across the pages of her book in black and white.

In fact, a short essay in Toni Cade Bambara's landmark 1970 edited volume, *The Black Woman: An Anthology*, offered an intellectual alternative that pre-dated much of the perceived 'classic' motherhood literature of the 1970s and 1980s, including Adrienne Rich's *Of Woman Born: Motherhood as Experience and Institution* (1976) or Nancy Chodorow's *The Reproduction of Mothering: Psychoanalysis and the Sociology of Gender* (1978).[38] Black, Latina, Asian-American and Native American women writers including Maxine Hong Kingston's *The Woman Warrior: Memoirs of a Girlhood Among Ghosts* (1976) and Cherríe Moraga and Gloria Anzaldúa's *A Bridge Called My Back: Writings by Radical Women of Color* (1981) also engaged in explorations of motherhood (and daughterhood) while celebrating their variable identities as women, people of colour, lesbians and/or artists.[39] Meanwhile, the essay 'Motherhood' written by City College of New York graduate and opera singer, Joanna Clark, opened with the birth of her son, about whom Clark said, 'I think I made a mistake'. But her critique was of the 'foolishness' and 'farce' of motherhood in a broader society. Judged in the hospital for nursing her son and refusing to circumcise him, Clark wrote: 'my first lesson in motherhood. You are everybody's whipping boy'.[40] She exposed the absurdities of a welfare system that preferred to pay her not to work rather than cover expenses for her transportation to school or for childcare, only to drop her from the rolls when her absent husband falsely claimed that he could provide child support. Driven by desperation and sheer exhaustion, Clark put her children in foster care, soon recognising that foster parents received more financial support than she did as the 'blood mother'.[41] Remarried and living with her children again, she referred to the infamous Moynihan Report of 1965 that blamed matriarchal black women for the 'tangle of pathology' crippling black families. Clark ended her essay with an incisive and political plea: a 'sit-down' for social security and unemployment insurance for mothers.[42] Spanning both the act (and art) of mothering and politics of maternalism, defined as political action by mothers, her story offered a different way to understand motherhood as experience and institution.

Clark explored the contradictory emotions of motherhood, from defending her choices about her son to placing her son and daughter in foster care. Hers was not a romanticisation of motherhood for its biological and mystical power.[43] Nor did she engage in black feminist theories about the universal valuation of the mother and grand-mother in African and diasporic societies. Patricia Hill Collins develops the concept of 'othermothers' as women who take on a powerful communal and political activist role beyond the physical role as biological mothers.[44] Such a concept appears to foreshadow the theory of public motherhood described here, but the idea of 'othermothers' builds upon certain assumptions about African and diasporic societies and presents them as specific to such communities. By contrast, Clark's portrait of motherhood provides a no-nonsense discussion of the politics of breastfeeding and circumcision and the faulty mechanics of strollers on city streets within a racist and sexist society.[45] Her experience is shaped by the realities of being a black woman but her reality is relatable: to married women; single, working women and women and men frustrated by government bureaucracies.[46] Clark's short essay exposed shared and disparate experiences of motherhood by neither universalising nor essentialising.

It is precisely that intersection between experience and political activism that links mothering literature and sociohistorical approaches like maternalism, as various feminist scholars sought to place the theme of motherhood within national and even imperial histories. Scholars and activists describe maternalism as political action by self-identified mothers concerned with diverse issues involving women and families. Maternalist activists range from conservative to radical and include single, lesbian, married and/or working-women of all races, ethnicities and nationalities. The term 'maternalism' also often captures the dialectical relationship between women's deployment of a 'politics of motherhood' and state and government policies that seek to control women's and children's lives.[47] Thus, the state and state violence, social and child welfare, and reproduction and sexuality have been salient themes in maternalist literature. Despite the many examples of activism by black, poor, right-wing, Latin American or lesbian women, elite and/or middle-class (often white) women working with and against the state often emerge within a normative (often Western) vision.[48] Discourses evoking womanhood, manhood, race, empire, class and sexuality also connected Africa, Europe, the Americas and Asia. To this end, maternalist frameworks, particularly when deployed by Africanist scholars, potentially offer insight into women's diverse and changing relationships with motherhood as part of other historical and political processes. Indeed, the two interrelated goals of this article are to outline a theory of public motherhood and to deploy black feminist and Africanist scholarship as a bridge between the image of the public mother and scholarship on motherhood. To re-interrogate maternalism here, a classic example from African history and historiography – the 1929 Women's War [*Ogu Umunwaanyi*] in southeastern Nigeria – addresses the tension between perspectives from the colony and metropole.

The 1929 Women's War suggests a new order of thinking that recognises local and changing concepts of womanhood and femininity in relation to socio-economic factors. During two months in 1929, on the eve of the worldwide depression, hundreds if not thousands of Igbo- and Ibibio-speaking women marched on the homes and offices of African agents of the British colonial administration to protest economic, political and religious changes occurring under the colonial regime in Nigeria. Fifty-one women and one man were killed during the protests. Their testimony, filtered through colonial documents, fragments of songs and historical fiction, showed their anger over taxation on women, changes to the market system, colonially-appointed local leaders and a host of sociocultural norms including bridewealth, gift exchange and morality. Although women appeared to be acting explicitly as mothers, scholars disagree about the relative importance of economic, political and cultural issues during the protests.[49] Ultimately women who participated in the Women's War employed a multi-sided approach evoking indigenous and British colonial sociocultural symbols that simultaneously called for the return of past practices and reform.

At the same time, participants in the Women's War expressed a broader, potentially transnational, vision of their maternalist activism. During her testimony before the British colonial Commission of Inquiry, a woman named Ahudi threatened, 'No doubt women like ourselves are in your own country. If need be we shall write to them to help us'.[50] Scholars of empire also have shown how maternalist policymakers in Europe looked to the colonies. However, British and French feminists often subscribed to imperial ideologies, sometimes promoting ideas of racial purity or engaging in forms of 'feminist imperialism' to serve women's interests in the metropole.[51] The women who acted during the Women's War also engaged in these languages of motherhood, fertility, purity and 'transnational feminism', but on their own terms, bringing the constructed and contextualised nature of motherhood and the politics of motherhood to the fore.[52]

Yet the relationship between women as mothers and political actors rarely escapes powerful assumptions about biology and the body; maternalist politics in the end depend on certain assumptions about the childbearing body of women. This image of women's bodies may vary across cultures. For example, integral to the account of the 1929 Women's War is the story that the elderly women protestors exposed their nude bodies to challenge and shame local African leaders. Temma Kaplan explores the uneasy reaction of Western feminists when they learn of the elderly women's display. But Africanist scholars recognise the cultural and political use of the elderly woman's body as evocative and provocative symbols of motherhood.[53] In the minds of the women protesters, such actions denoted their particular power as women and as mothers.[54] Thus, the material body of the mother could be defined in variable ways, suggesting the importance of understanding the cultural discourses that define mothers in different historical contexts.

Scholars have written critically about the ways that cultural discourses define women and motherhood since Simone de Beauvoir's 1949 declaration that 'one is not born, but rather becomes, woman'.[55] The work of African American scholar Evelyn Brooks Higginbotham and Africanist historian Nancy Rose Hunt recast Beauvoir's observations, especially given how Beauvoir's philosophical arguments related to her own anxieties about race and empire. Beauvoir wrote extensively of her own travels in Africa, Latin America and Asia, and two years before she wrote *The Second Sex* [*Le Deuxième sexe*], she completed a four-month tour of the United States, published as the memoir *America Day by Day* [*L'Amérique au jour le jour*]. Her attacks on American racism previewed her later comparisons between sexism and racial prejudice against black, Jewish and colonised populations.[56] For Beauvoir, the ultimate symbols of debasement were the black (male) slave and the 'unfree' white woman; the black woman was absent. In their analyses, Higginbotham and Hunt do not simply add black women in but, instead, demonstrate multiple nodes where race, gender, sexuality, nation and empire meet and influence one another.

In *The Second Sex*, often seen as a statement on the condition of women, Beauvoir also elaborates on the connections between race, sex, class and empire. Unlike blacks or workers who could rise up in protest at a historical moment, she portrayed women as dispersed and divided by race and class. Yet for women, she argued, difference has always been absolute: 'He is the Subject, he is the Absolute. She is the Other'. Viewing the category of the Other as a universal one, she wrote, 'Jews are the "others" for anti-Semites, blacks for racist Americans, indigenous people for colonists, proletarians for the propertied classes'.[57] In the end she found 'deep analogies' between blacks praised for being the 'good black' and women celebrated for representing the 'true woman' by the 'master class'.[58] Within Beauvoir's universalising language, she also continued to stress the historical construction of both race and gender, thus maintaining the possibilities for change. Yet, besides Richard Wright and Frantz Fanon, Beauvoir appeared to have had little interaction and conversation with blacks, especially women, even though her theories on women and gender were shaped profoundly by race.

In fact, Evelyn Brooks Higginbotham's definition of race as a 'metalanguage' reveals how Beauvoir's work and subsequent interpretations of it overlook the inter- play of race and empire in Beauvoir's theory. Also, because race operates in ways 'arbitrary and illusory' yet seemingly 'natural and fixed', it affects all types of social relationships, including class, gender and sexuality. Indeed, Higginbotham criticises scholars of gender and African American studies for ignoring the 'technologies' of race as a concept, in shaping historical processes and as having the power to liberate and oppress simultaneously. Her typology is not unlike the one used here to examine motherhood literature as concept, socio-historical force and as an ambivalent discourse that seemingly empowers and renders women vulnerable. Higginbotham's discussion of the power of discursive tools to silence difference also signals a way to think about the rhetorical power of motherhood. Despite the recognition of the constructedness of gender, race, sexuality, class, etc., a certain 'metalanguage' of motherhood and the woman's body remains under-examined. To quibble with the connection between motherhood and physical childbirth and the issue of childcare may seem displaced because much feminist scholarship has long analysed how 'woman' is not 'natural', a 'given' nor 'biological' but a 'social category' created by historical context, discourse and/or 'a stylised repetition of acts'.[59] Is it possible to think of motherhood in the same way, as created and performed through culture and language, rather than as a given shaped by government policies and media? And does the childbearing body still haunt the image of the mother, after all?

Nancy Rose Hunt's study of the medicalisation of childbirth in the Democratic Republic of the Congo, examines childbirth as a site of power struggle through a series of objects and processes that tell a larger story about colonialism, masculinity, religion and the interplay between past and present. Thus, the book begins with the story of an initiation ceremony for young men to prevent 'reduc[ing] the womb to a uterus'. Hunt also argues that in order to understand the full meaning of the medicalisation of childbirth – to take a multifaceted concept of birth, death, danger and confine it to a small, sterile space – it is necessary to incorporate men's activities as they, themselves, are associated with symbolic wombs.[60] Moreover, she demonstrates how Congolese 'middle figures', such as teachers, nurses and midwives, for example, mediated the colonising process, facilitating the birth of a colonial and postcolonial Congolese soci- ety.[61] Encompassing the range of physical, social and historical experiences, discourses about motherhood run through Hunt's text, along and beyond the real and imagined bodies of women.

This article has sought to reveal the crucial dialogue between all of these fields of scholarship on motherhood and to make the concept of public motherhood part of the conversation. The black feminist and Africanist scholarship does not chronicle a different history of motherhood but sheds light on the depth and breadth of motherhood as experience, institution and discourse. Similarly, this theory of public motherhood provides a new framework for thinking about women's power. West African practices and ideologies that conferred titles and authority on certain elderly women serve as a point of departure. Yet Alaba Ida pushed the boundaries of what was expected and acceptable in a historical context shaped by local and imperial forces because her actual position as a royal wife connoted subordination and seclusion rather than public authority. Her extraordinary story, thus, relates to the fundamental questions that gender scholars ask about historical interpretation and narrative. What makes the personage of Alaba Ida and the framework of public motherhood different is the way that Africa and Africans emerge at the centre of a re-ordering of epistemologies about gender and power.

* * *

Yet I am reminded of the difficulty of shifting Africa to the centre of theoretical frameworks whenever I conduct a class debate at the end of my Women's and Gender History course with the stated resolution, 'Africanists must develop their own theoretical frameworks to address gender in African history'. After a semester of reading classic theoretical pieces in Africanist and gender historiography alongside case studies, fiction and film, students read two overview pieces on gender frameworks in preparation for the final class debate. Those arguing for separate Africanist approaches use Amina Mama's introduction to *Engendering African Social Sciences* published in 1997 as a guide.[62] Most recently, instead of Joan Scott's revised essay 'Some More Reflections on Gender and Politics' from 1999, students arguing against separate Africanist theories read Jeanne Boydston's 'Gender as a Question of Historical Analysis', published in 2008.[63] To support their positions, students incorporate previous readings and even their own final projects for the course.

The last three times that I have taught the class in this format, the side arguing against separate Africanist frameworks has prevailed, often arguing from a position that theories derived from Western authors can work in African contexts because it is problematic to essentialise and thereby marginalise African communities and practices. Students arguing for specific Africanist approaches often wind up pointing out how Western approaches make assumptions about African women as victims and that Western ideologies cannot always appreciate African cultural practices. But those calling for the 'universality' of Western approaches are uncomfortable and those championing African 'peculiarities' do not seem convinced. Most appear deflated when the 'West' wins; one student admitted to me after class that she wished the 'African side' had won. It is near impossible for students to see the African approaches as recasting Western gender theories.[64]

In fact, Boydston's article uses Africanist, Iranian and Native American cases to call for a more nuanced approach to American gender history that does not assume the 'primary-ness' of gender.[65] But over a decade earlier, Amina Mama and other Africanists had been making similar observations that 'class, gender, race, imperialism are simultaneous social forces, both interwoven and recursive upon each other'. Using a woven cloth metaphor, Mama identifies common 'threads' such as class, gender and neo-colonialism that sometimes only appear on the underside of the material because of the need for attention to both subordinate and dominant discourses. Mama's observations could apply to any historical context, informing all types of historical study in the broadest sense, but even she potentially limits her own framework by characterising it as 'African-centred'.[66]

Certainly, I am not alone in being enticed by the idea of unique African stories like that of Alaba Ida. However, many Africanist and African American scholars have also recognised the broader implications of their work, combining ideas about human rights, women's rights, anti-imperialism and anti-racism. Some African scholars have posed new concepts to capture their complex feminisms. Molara Ogundipe-Leslie developed the term 'stiwanism' from her acronym STIWA (Social Transformation Including Women in Africa) to 'discuss the needs of African women today in the tradition of the spaces and strategies provided in our indigenous cultures…as co-partners in social transformation'. Literary scholar, Obioma Nnaemeka writes of her own term for African feminism as 'negofeminism', or 'feminism of negotiation' and 'no ego feminism' in contrast with 'the ego trip that engenders feminist arrogance, imperialism, and power struggles'.[67] At the same time, feminist scholars and activists of Africa, Asia and Latin America view access to clean water, housing, war, human rights and development policy as central to women's rights in order to reconfigure society itself, not just women's place within it.[68] Still, the ideas of African and African-American women and activists have often been portrayed as peripheral and particular rather than integral and applicable to a wider world. Indeed, is it possible to think of black women and public mothers as modern, and, dare one say, universal?

Notes

This article draws upon my book *Mother Is Gold, Father Is Glass: Gender and Colonialism in a Yoruba Town* (Bloomington: Indiana University Press, 2011), especially Chapter Four. I benefited from insightful comments at the *Gender & History* Workshop on 'Gender History across Epistemologies' 15 and 16 April 2011 at the University of Minnesota and suggestions by anonymous reviewers and co-editors Donna Gabaccia and Mary Jo Maynes.

1. Institut pour la Recherche Appliqué du Dahomey (IRAD), Document du Porto-Novo 20, Cercle de Pobé-Kétou. Anonymous and undated document. Archives Nationales du Bénin (ANB), 1E 11 3-1, Lieutenant H. Aubé, 'Rapport sur la mission accomplie dans la region Kétou-Savé du 18 janvier au 20 février 1894', 3 March 1894.
2. Babatunde Oroufila, interview with the author, 24 June 1997.
3. ANB, 1E 11 2-3, Bertheux, 'Rapport sur situation politique de la partie orientale Zagnanado, Kétou-Hollis-Adja-Ouéré', 22 May 1911.
4. Chandra Mohanty, 'Under Western Eyes: Feminist Scholarship and Colonial Discourses', *Feminist Review* 30 (1988), pp. 61–88; Jeanne Boydston, 'Gender as a Question of Historical Analysis', *Gender & History* 20 (2008), pp. 558–83, here pp. 561, 566.
5. In Yoruba communities, the term for 'mother' used in informal names and official titles is *ìyá*. On the complexity of 'witches', often referred to as 'our mothers' in Yoruba culture, see Teresa N. Washington, *Our Mothers, Our Powers, Our Texts: Manifestations of Àjé in Africana Literature* (Bloomington: Indiana University Press, 2005).
6. Ife Amadiume, *Male Daughters, Female Husbands: Gender and Sex in an African Society* (London: Zed Books, 1987); Niara Sudarkasa, *The Strength of Our Mothers: African and African American Women and Families: Essays and Speeches* (Trenton: Africa World Press, 1996), pp. 171–2; Oyèrónké Oyěwùmí, 'Introduction: Feminism, Sisterhood, and other Foreign Relations', in Oyèrónké Oyěwùmí (ed.), *African Women and Feminism: Reflecting on the Politics of Sisterhood* (Trenton: Africa World Press, 2003), pp. 1–24, here pp. 15–16; Edna Bay, *Wives of the Leopard: Gender, Politics, and Culture in the Kingdom of Dahomey* (Charlottesville: University of Virginia Press, 1998), p. 20. Some dependent men acted out their 'wifely' role by actually dressing as women. J. Lorand Matory, *Sex and the Empire That is No More: Gender and the Politics of Metaphor in Oyo Yoruba Religion*, 2nd edn (New York: Berghahn, 1997), p. 9.
7. Julia Wells, 'Maternal Politics in Organizing Black South African Women: The Historical Lessons', in Obioma Nnaemeka (ed.), *Sisterhood, Feminisms, and Power: From Africa to the Diaspora* (Trenton: Africa World Press, 1998), pp. 251–62, here p. 253; Cherryl Walker, 'Conceptualising Motherhood in Twentieth Century South Africa', *Journal of Southern African Studies* 21 (1995), pp. 417–37; Leslie R. Wolfe and Jennifer Tucker, 'Feminism Lives: Building a Multicultural Movement in the United States', in Amrita Basu (ed.), *The Challenge of Local Feminisms: Women's Movements in Global Perspective* (Boulder and Oxford: Westview Press, 1995), pp. 435–62, here p. 448; Seth Koven and Sonya Michel, 'Womanly Duties: Maternalist Politics and the Origins of Welfare States in France, Germany, Great

Britain, and the United States, 1880–1920', *American Historical Review* 95 (1990), pp. 1076–108, here p. 1079.

8. Chikwenye Okonjo Ogunyemi, *Africa Wo/Man Palava: The Nigerian Novel by Women* (Chicago: University of Chicago Press, 1996), pp. 10, 46.

9. For critiques see, J. Lorand Matory, 'Gendered Agendas: The Secrets Scholars Keep about Yorùbá-Atlantic Religion', *Gender and History* 15 (2003), pp. 409–39; Bibi Bakare-Yusuf, 'Yorubas Don't Do Gender: A Critical Review of Oyeronke Oyewumi's *The Invention of Women: Making an African Sense of Western Gender Discourses*', in Signe Arnfred (ed.), *African Gender Scholarship: Concepts, Methodologies, and Paradigms* (Dakar: CODESRIA, 2004), pp. 61–81.

10. Oyèrónkẹ́ Oyěwùmí, 'Family Bonds/Conceptual Binds: African Notes on Feminist Epistemologies', *Signs* 25 (2000), pp. 1093–8, here p. 1094.

11. Ann Snitow, 'Feminism and Motherhood: An American Reading', *Feminist Review* 40 (1992), pp. 33–51; Terry Arendell, 'Conceiving and Investigating Motherhood: The Decade's Scholarship', *Journal of Marriage and the Family* 62 (2000), pp. 1192–207. For examples of maternalist historiography in the United States and Europe, see Gisela Bock and Pat Thane (eds), *Maternity and Gender Policies: Women and the Rise of the European Welfare State, 1880s–1950s* (New York: Routledge, 1991); Seth Koven and Sonya Michel, 'Introduction: "Mother Worlds"', in Seth Koven and Sonya Michel (eds), *Mothers of a New World: Maternalist Politics and the Origins of Welfare States* (New York: Routledge, 1993), pp. 1–42; Elinor A. Accampo, Rachel G. Fuchs and Mary Lynn Stewart (eds), *Gender and the Politics of Social Reform in France, 1870–1914* (Baltimore: Johns Hopkins University Press, 1995); Molly Ladd-Taylor, *Mother-Work: Women, Child Welfare, and the State, 1890–1930* (Chicago: University of Ilinois Press, 1994); Ruth Feldstein, *Motherhood in Black and White: Race and Sex in American Liberalism, 1930–1965* (Ithaca: Cornell University Press, 2000); Rebecca Jo Plant, *Mom: The Transformation of Motherhood in Modern America* (Chicago: University of Chicago Press, 2010).

12. For example, see Simone de Beauvoir, *The Second Sex*, tr. Constance Borde and Sheila Malovany-Chevallier (1949, repr. London: Jonathan Cape, 2009).

13. Washington, *Our Mothers, Our Powers*, pp. 14–17; Pierre Verger, 'Grandeur et décadence du culte *Ìyámi Òsòròngà* (ma mère la sorcière) chez les Yoruba', *Journal de la Société des Africanistes* 35 (1965), pp. 141–243; Henry John Drewal and Margaret Thompson Drewal, *Gelede: Art and Female Power among the Yoruba* (Bloomington: Indiana University Press, 1983).

14. Amadiume, *Male Daughters, Female Husbands*; Karen Sacks, *Sisters and Wives: The Past and Future of Sexual Equality* (Chicago: University of Illinois Press, 1982).

15. Lorelle Semley, *Mother Is Gold, Father Is Glass: Gender and Colonialism in a Yoruba Town* (Bloomington: Indiana University Press, 2011), pp. 77–8.

16. Soule Brouaima, interview with the author, 10 December 1998.

17. Céline Idowu, Boyoko Iko and Sikiratou Idowu, interview with the author, 1 March 1999; Adebayo Adegbite and Adeniran Alabi Fagbohun, interview with the author, 7 March 1999.

18. P. C. Lloyd, 'Sacred Kingship and Government among the Yoruba', *Africa* 30 (1960), pp. 221–37.

19. Benjamin Oyewusi, interview with the author, 27 and 30 November 1998; A. I. Asiwaju, 'The Alaketu of Ketu and the Onimeko of Meko: The Changing Status of Two Yoruba Rulers under French and British Rule', in Michael Crowder and Obaro Ikime (eds), *West African Chiefs: Their Changing Status under Colonial Rule in Africa* (New York: Africana Publishing, 1970), pp. 134–60, here p. 146.

20. Bénin, Direction des Archives Nationales, 'Rapport du tournée dans le cercle de Zagnanado', *Mémoire du Bénin* 1(1993), pp. 82–87, here p. 86.

21. ANB, 1E 20 2-3, 'Rapport Mensuel, Cercle de Zagnanado', January 1906.

22. ANB, 1E 11 2-4, 'Rapport sur l'incident du village de Digne', 11 November 1912.

23. IRAD, Document of Porto-Novo 20. Several villages listed have other men who served as head or 'chief' of the village. Archives Nationales Outre-Mer (ANOM), 14 Mi 837, 'Rattachement du Canton de Kétou au Cercle de Pobé', 13 July 1915.

24. The unsigned and undated document from IRAD, Document du Porto-Novo 20, refers to her as *chef du canton* (head of district) and suggests that she oversaw village heads. Asiwaju writes that Alaba was head of the district, but based on interviews rather than on French colonial documents. A. I. Asiwaju, 'The Alaketu of Ketu', p. 145. Another document from 1915 states that Onyegen was *chef du canton*, ANOM, 14 Mi 837, 'Demande de rattachement du Canton de Kétou au Cercle Provisoire du Pobé', Lieutenant-Gouverneur du Dahomey à Gouverneur Général de l'Afrique Occidentale Française (AOF), 17 October 1915.

25. Alice L. Conklin, *A Mission to Civilize: The Republican Idea of Empire in France and West Africa, 1895–1930* (Stanford: Stanford University Press, 1997), p. 113; IRAD, Document of Porto-Novo 20; ANB,

1E 11 1-5, 'Transmission d'un rapport et d'un dossier annexe en Commission permanente du conseil de Gouvernement rélatifs au rattachement du canton de Kétou à la circonscription provisoire de Pobé', Lieutenant-Gouverneur du Dahomey à Gouverneur de l'AOF, 17 October 1915.

26. A. I. Asiwaju, *Western Yorubaland under European Rule 1889–1945: A Comparative Analysis of French and British Colonialism* (Atlantic Highlands: Humanities Press, 1976), pp. 271–2; Montserrat Palau Marti, *Le Roi-Dieu Au Bénin* (Paris: Berger-Levrault, 1964), p. 59.

27. ANB, 1E 11 1-5, 'Destitution de la Reine Ida de Kétou', Le Capitaine Commandant de Cercle de Holli-Kétou, 2 March 1918.

28. ANB, 1E 11 1-5, 'Retour de l' Ex-Queen Ida', Le Capitaine Malnous de l'Infanterie Commandant le Cercle à Gouverneur du Dahomey, 17 May 1918; Saoudatou Moussa, interview with the author, 19 February 1999. Parrinder reports that she died in 1938 in Irocogny, a village near Kétu, Edward Geoffrey Parrinder, *Story of Ketu, an Ancient Yoruba Kingdom* (Ibadan, Ibadan University Press, 1967), p. 66.

29. IRAD, Document du Porto-Novo 20. The *òrìshà* Ondo possesses or 'mounts' his priests, described as males in accounts from the 1950s and 1970s. The priesthood may have changed or Yá Shègén's title may have been unique to Obatedo. Pierre Verger, 'Trance and Convention in Nago-Yoruba Spirit Mediumship', in John Beattie and John Middleton (eds), *Spirit Mediumship and Society in Africa* (New York: Africana Publishing Corporation, 1969), pp. 50–66; Margaret Thompson Drewal, 'Symbols of Possession: A Study of Movement and Regalia in an Anago-Yoruba Ceremony', *Dance Research Journal* 7 (1975), pp. 15–24.

30. Ìyá Libara Catherine Oyewole Adebiyi, interview with the author, 15 July 1997.

31. Alaba Ida reportedly had a daughter and a son but sometimes people claimed she had been childless, as though it was proof of her malevolence. IRAD, Document du Porto-Novo 20.

32. On Cooper and her contemporaries, see Paula Giddings, *When and Where I Enter: The Impact of Black Women on Race and Sex in America* (New York: William Morrow, 1984); Hazel V. Carby, *Reconstructing Womanhood: The Emergence of the Afro-American Woman Novelist* (Oxford: Oxford University Press, 1987), pp. 95–120; Ann duCille, *The Coupling Convention: Sex, Text, and Tradition in Black Women's Fiction* (Oxford: Oxford University Press, 1993) and Deborah Gray White, *Too Heavy a Load: Black Women in Defense of Themselves, 1894–1994* (New York: W.W. Norton, 1999).

33. Vivian M. May, *Anna Julia Cooper, Visionary Black Feminist* (New York: Routledge, 2007), pp. 14–16, 23; Vivian M. May, '"It is Never a Question of the Slaves": Anna Julia Cooper's Challenge to History's Silences in her 1925 Sorbonne Thesis', *Callaloo* 31 (2008), pp. 903–18; Robin D. G. Kelley, '"But a Local Phase of a World Problem": Black History's Global Vision, 1883–1950', *The Journal of American History* 86 (1999), pp. 1045–77. To relate Cooper's life story to her writing need not diminish it as merely experiential. Carby, *Reconstructing Womanhood*, pp. 16–17; May, *Anna Julia Cooper*, pp. 40–43.

34. Anna Julia Cooper, 'Womanhood: A Vital Element in the Regeneration and Progress of the Race (1886)', in Charles Lemert and Esme Bhan (eds), *The Voice of Anna Julia Cooper: Including* A Voice from the South *and Other Important Essays, Letters, and Papers* (Oxford: Rowman and Littlefield), pp. 53–71, here pp. 59–60, 63.

35. Anna Julia Cooper, 'The Intellectual Progress of the Colored Women in the United States since the Emancipation Proclamation: A Response to Fannie Barrier Williams (1893)', in Lemert and Bhan (eds), *The Voice of Anna Julia Cooper*, pp. 201–05, here p. 202.

36. Cooper, 'The Intellectual Progress,' pp. 204–05.

37. bell hooks, *Feminist Theory: From Margin to Theory* (Boston: South End Press, 1984), pp. 1–3; Joanne Meyerowitz, 'Beyond the Feminine Mystique: A Reassessment of Postwar Mass Culture, 1946–1958', in Joanne Meyerowitz (ed.), *Not June Cleaver: Women and Gender in Postwar America, 1945–1960* (Philadelphia: Temple University Press, 1994), pp. 229–62; Plant, *Mom*, pp. 146–77. On reconciling what Gayatri Spivak called 'hegemonic feminist theory' and what Chela Sandoval calls 'U.S. Third World feminism', see Chela Sandoval, 'U.S. Third World Feminism: The Theory and Method of Oppositional Consciousness in the Postmodern World,' *Genders* 10 (1991), pp. 1–24.

38. Adrienne Rich, *Of Woman Born: Motherhood as Experience and Institution* (New York: Norton, 1976); Nancy Chodorow, *The Reproduction of Mothering: Psychoanalysis and the Sociology of Gender* (Berkeley: University of California Press, 1979).

39. Maxine Hong Kingston, *The Woman Warrior: Memoirs of a Girlhood among Ghosts* (1976; repr. New York: Vintage, 1989); Cherríe L. Moraga and Gloria E. Andalzúa (eds), *This Bridge Called My Back: Writings by Radical Women of Color* (Berkeley: Third Woman Press, 2002).

40. Joanna Clark, 'Motherhood', in Toni Cade Bambara (ed.), *The Black Woman: An Anthology*, (New York: New American Library, 1970), pp. 63–72, here pp. 63–4.

41. Clark, 'Motherhood', pp. 66, 70.

42. Clark, 'Motherhood', pp. 71–2; Patrick Moynihan, 'The Negro Family: The Case for National Action' (Washington: United States Department of Labor Office of Policy Planning and Research, March 1965), <http://www.dol.gov/oasam/programs/history/ webid-meynihan.htm>.

43. See Sara Ruddick, 'Maternal Thinking', *Feminist Studies* 6 (1980), pp. 342–67, here pp. 343–5.

44. Patricia Hill Collins, 'The Meaning of Motherhood in Black Culture and Black Mother/Daughter Relationships', *Sage: A Scholarly Journal on Black Women* 4 (1987), pp. 2–10, here p. 6; Stanlie M. James, 'Mothering: A Possible Black Feminist Link to Social Transformation?' in Stanlie M. James and Abena Busia (eds), *Theorizing Black Feminisms: The Visionary Pragmatism of Black Women* (London: Routledge, 1993), pp. 44–54.

45. Patricia Hill Collins, *Black Feminist Thought: Knowledge, Consciousness, and the Politics of Empowerment* (New York and London: Routledge, 1991), pp. 115–37; Clark, 'Motherhood', pp. 63–4.

46. Black feminists participated in civil rights organisations, white-dominated feminist groups and new autonomous groups. Combahee River Collective, 'A Black Feminist Statement', in Beverly Guy-Sheftall (ed.), *Words of Fire: An Anthology of African-American Feminist Thought* (New York: The New Press, 1995), pp. 232–40, here p. 233; Beverly Guy-Sheftall, 'Introduction: The Evolution of Feminist Consciousness among African American Women', in Beverly Guy-Sheftall (ed.), *Words of Fire,* pp. 1–22, here pp. 13–14; Becky Thompson, 'Multiracial Feminisim: Recasting the Chronology of Second Wave Feminism', *Feminist Studies* 28 (2002), pp. 336–60, here p. 338.

47. Lynn W. Weiner, 'Maternalism as a Paradigm: Defining the Issues', *Journal of Women's History* 5 (1993), pp. 96–8. Alexis Jetter, Annelise Orleck and Diana Taylor (eds), *The Politics of Motherhood: Activist Voices from Left to Right* (Hanover: University Press of New England, 1997), pp. 3–20.

48. Koven and Michel (eds), *Mothers of a New World*; Bock and Thane (eds), *Maternity and Gender Policies*; Sonia Alvarez, *Engendering Democracy in Brazil: Women's Movements in Politics* (Princeton: Princeton University Press, 1990); Maxine Molyneux and Elizabeth Dore (eds), *Hidden Histories of Gender and the State in Latin America* (Durham: Duke University Press, 2000); Jetter et al. (eds), *The Politics of Motherhood*; Donna Bassin, Margaret Honey and Meryle Marher Kaplan (eds), *Representations of Motherhood* (New Haven: Yale University Press, 1994).

49. Judith Van Allen, '"Aba Riots" or "Women's War": Ideology, Stratification, and the Invisibility of Women', in Nancy Hafkin and Edna Bay (eds), *Women in Africa: Studies in Social and Economic Change* (Stanford: Stanford University Press, 1976), pp. 59–85; Caroline Ifeka-Moller, 'Female Militancy and Colonial Revolt: The Women's War of 1929, Eastern Nigeria', in Shirley Ardener (ed.), *Perceiving Women* (London: Malaby Press, 1975), pp. 127–57; Misty Bastian, '"Vultures of the Marketplace": Southeastern Nigerian Women and Discourses of the Ogu Umunwaanyi (Women's War) of 1929', in Jean Allman, Susan Geiger and Nakanyike Musise (eds), *Women in African Colonial Histories* (Bloomington: Indiana University Press, 2002), pp. 260–81; T. Obinkaram Echewa, *I Saw the Sky Catch Fire* (New York: Dutton, 1992). The names of those killed are listed in Bastian, 'Vultures of the Marketplace', pp. 273–4.

50. The quote comes from Aba Commission of Inquiry, *Notes of Evidence Taken by the Commission of Inquiry Appointed to Inquire into the Disturbances in the Calabar and Owerri Provinces, December, 1929* (London: Waterlow, 1930), pp. 114–15 as quoted in Bastian, 'Vultures of the Marketplace', p. 275.

51. Anna Davin, 'Imperialism and Motherhood', in Frederick Cooper and Ann Laura Stoler (eds), *Tensions of Empire: Colonial Cultures in a Bourgeois World* (Berkeley: University of California Press, 1997), pp. 87–151, here pp. 87–8, 91; Antoinette M. Burton, 'The White Women's Burden: British Feminists and The "Indian Woman", 1865–1915', in Nupur Chaudhuri and Margaret Strobel (eds), *Western Women and Imperialism: Complicity and Resistance* (Bloomington: Indiana University Press, 1992), pp. 137–57, here pp. 137–9; Carolyn J. Eichner, '*La Citoyenne* in the World: Hubertine Auclert and Feminist Imperialism', *French Historical Studies* 32 (2009), pp. 63–84, here pp. 64–5.

52. Bastian, 'Vultures of the Marketplace', pp. 268–72.

53. Echewa, *I Saw the Sky Catch Fire*, pp. 145–6.

54. Temma Kaplan, 'Naked Mothers and Maternal Sexuality: Some Reactions to the Aba Women's War', in Jetter et al. (eds) *The Politics of Motherhood*, pp. 209–22.

55. Beauvoir, *The Second Sex*, p. 293.

56. For the effect of the Algerian War on Beauvoir, see Julien Murphy, 'Beauvoir and the Algerian War: Toward a Postcolonial Ethics', in Margaret A. Simons (ed.), *Feminist Interpretations of Simone de Beauvoir* (University Park: Pennsylvania State University Press, 1995), pp. 261–97. Beauvoir's iconoclastic statements about pregnancy and childbirth are less instructive even for analyses of motherhood literature. Yolanda Astarita Patterson, *Beauvoir and the Demystification of Motherhood* (Ann Arbor: UMI Research Press, 1989).

57. Beauvoir, *The Second Sex*, pp. 6–7.
58. Beauvoir, *The Second Sex*, pp. 8–9, 12–13.
59. Denise Riley, *'Am I That Name?': Feminism and the Category of 'Women' in History* (Minneapolis: University of Minnesota Press, 1988), pp. 1–2; Joan Wallach Scott, *Gender and the Politics of History*, revised edn (New York: Columbia University Press, 1999), pp. 2, 4; Judith Butler, *Gender Trouble*, (New York, London: Routledge, 1990), p. 179.
60. Nancy Rose Hunt, *A Colonial Lexicon: Of Birth Ritual, Medicalization, and Mobility in the Congo* (Durham: Duke University Press, 1999), p. 33.
61. Hunt, *A Colonial Lexicon*, pp. 2, 12.
62. Amina Mama, 'Engendering the African Social Sciences: An Introductory Essay', in Ayesha Imam, Fatou Sow and Amina Mama (eds), *Engendering the African Social Sciences* (Dakar, Senegal: CODESRIA, 1997), pp. 1–30.
63. Joan Wallach Scott, 'Some More Reflections on Gender and Politics' in Scott, *Gender and the Politics of History*, pp. 199–222; Boydston, 'Gender as a Question'.
64. I thank the Holy Cross students in my HIST299: Women's and Gender History in African History course in the fall of 2011 for their participation in the class and final debate.
65. Boydston, 'Gender as a Question', pp. 564–6, 572–3, 576.
66. Mama, 'Engendering the African Social Sciences', pp. 21–2, 25, 27.
67. Molara Ogundipe-Leslie, 'Stiwanism: Feminism in an African Context', in Molara Ogundipe-Leslie (ed.), *Recreating Ourselves: African Women and Critical Transformations* (Trenton: Africa World Press, 1994), pp. 207–41, here pp. 229–30; Obioma Nnaemeka, 'Foreword: Locating Feminisms/Feminists', in Susan Arndt, *The Dynamics of African Feminism: Defining and Classifying African Feminist Literatures* (Trenton: Africa World Press, 2002), pp. 9–15, here p. 12; Obioma Nnaemeka, 'Feminism, Rebellious Women, and Cultural Boundaries: Rereading Flora Nwapa and Her Compatriots', *Research in African Literatures* 26 (1995), pp. 80–113; Susan Arndt, *The Dynamics of African Feminism: Defining and Classifying African-Feminist Literatures* (Trenton: Africa World Press, 2002), pp. 27–70.
68. Amanda Kemp, Nozizwe Madlala, Asha Moodley and Elaine Salo, 'The Dawn of a New Day: Redefining South African Feminism', in Basu (ed.), *The Challenge of Local Feminisms*, pp. 131–62; Angela Miles, 'North American Feminisms/Global Feminisms – Contradictory or Complementary?' in Nnaemeka (ed.), *Sisterhood, Feminisms and Power*, p. 172.

4 Profiling the Female Emigrant: A Method of Linguistic Inquiry for Examining Correspondence Collections

Emma Moreton

Introduction

Mass emigration from Ireland to the United States in the nineteenth century has been examined in terms of its economic, political and social impact on both home and the New World. Drawing on a range of sources such as census information, shipping records and other public documentation, research suggests that during this period there was an increase in migration amongst females, mostly single women in their late teens and early twenties.[1] Knowing that it was unlikely they would ever return to Ireland, the letter was the main method through which these young women kept in touch with loved ones back home.

Over the past few decades there has been a growing interest in the emigrant letter and how this type of source might inform our understanding of social history during the postal era of globalisation. The sourcing, preservation and documentation of emigrant letter collections are growing, and whilst their value as sociohistorical artefacts is generally accepted, finding the best means to exploit such resources is yet to be agreed upon. For David Gerber, emigrant letters have generally been used in one of two ways: to 'provide color and drama in historical narratives, or to document societal-level and group-level generalizations', or as edited collections which 'let the letter-writers speak for themselves, while providing some background information that enables readers to place the [author] in the general societal framework of a certain place and time'.[2] Influential studies such as William I. Thomas and Florian Znaniecki's *The Polish Peasant in Europe and America*, Charlotte Erickson's *Invisible Immigrants: The Adaptation of English and Scottish Immigrants in Nineteenth-Century America*, Kerby Miller's *Emigrants and Exiles: Ireland and the Irish Exodus to North America* and Walter Kamphoefner, Wolfgang Helbich and Ulrike Sommer's *News from the Land of Freedom: German Immigrants Write Home*, have demonstrated the value in using personal letters to gain a fuller, multi-perspectival understanding of both the complex social processes of emigration (such as push/pull factors and the role of institutions and communities) and the conditions and daily lives of the emigrants themselves.[3] However, Gerber suggests that while ' . . . social historians have been especially skilled

Gender History Across Epistemologies, First Edition. Edited by Donna R. Gabaccia and Mary Jo Maynes.
Chapters © 2013 The Authors. Book compilation © 2013 Blackwell Publishing Ltd.

in understanding large categorical social groups – social classes, ethnic groups, religious denominations, and men and women' they have sometimes failed to understand 'the individual self, in relation to other individual selves, [in relation] to the world'.[4] Gerber's own study of British emigrants in America takes an approach that begins with the individual. Viewing the personal letter as an object of study in its own right, Gerber examines how such documents embody relationships, experiences and mental worlds; and more recent studies taking a similar (qualitative) approach, have examined how, through the emigrant letter (or in the case of Anna De Fina and Kendall A. King, the personal narrative), transatlantic relationships are changed and maintained, identities assimilated and narratives constructed and performed.[5]

Such studies, which place emphasis on the individual, seek to get as close as possible to the letter writers' lived experience. The reality of the authors' lives – or the way in which the authors construe their experiences – is revealed through the language contained within the letter. The analyst examines the content of the letter on a semantic level, making sense of its content by placing it within the context of situation (the circumstances in which the letter was produced) or broader still within the context of culture (the societal pressure for the author to perform in a particular way – by writing the letter in the first place and by respecting a particular culture of letter writing when doing so). In most cases the researcher is inferring outwards from the letter, taking the content of the letter to then make claims about what that content means or what it reveals about the context of situation and culture. Intuitively, the conclusions drawn make great sense; however, methodologically speaking, the conclusions are potentially open to criticism as there is a leap of faith and assumption leading from the analyst's intuition to his/her conclusion/point.

The work of Stephan Elspaß, Nicola McLelland, Marina Dossena and Arja Nurmi and Minna Palander-Collin goes some way to addressing this methodological issue by adopting a bottom-up, empirical approach to studying emigrant letters.[6] Taking as their starting point words and phrases, they then look at how these words and phrases typically behave in sentences, paragraphs and texts, before considering what these linguistic patterns or phraseology might reveal about the situational and cultural contexts in which the letters were produced.[7]

Marina Dossena, for example, examines the use of formulaic as well as dialectal features of language in a corpus of nineteenth-century Scottish emigrant letters to see how such linguistic strategies contribute to, and reinforce, social bonds between author and recipient.[8] (In its most general sense, a corpus is a collection of texts, designed to be representative of the way that language is used in a particular context.) To do this, Dossena looks at a subsection of letters from the Corpus of Nineteenth-Century Scottish Correspondence: forty-two letters (approximately 27,000 words), dating from 1815 to 1892, by thirteen male informants and two female informants.[9] A close qualitative study of the linguistic features characteristic of the letters teased out some interesting findings. Dossena observed that 'involvement strategies' in the openings and closings of the letters were 'mainly dependent on the conventions of formulaic usage' as set out in letter writing manuals of the time. However, she goes on to say that 'within the body of the letter . . . encoders express their psychological proximity to their recipients by means of other linguistic devices', such as the use of Scotticisms (dialect, which, as observed by Dossena, is often employed humorously to stress a 'common cultural background'); visualisations of context (descriptions of people, places and likenesses) and epistemic modality (words which express certainty/probability, such as *might* and *suppose*, which are used to 'predict the recipient's reactions or the encoder's suppositions about what is going on at home').[10] Although empirical in nature and taking a more bottom-up approach to identifying salient linguistic features across a range of texts, this study is still primarily qualitative and therefore open to the same criticisms previously mentioned. The conclusions resulting from (what are very interesting) observations would have greater strength if it were possible to test their significance reliably. Are these observations typical, unusual or evenly distributed across different authors, for example? Quantitative investigation and/or statistical tests would help to make claims about the relevance of these observations. Arguably, without quantitative support, it is difficult to appreciate fully the significance of the linguistic features being noticed.

To demonstrate the value in applying statistical measures to test, challenge or support qualitative observations, Nicola McLelland used quantitative methods of analysis to examine the language of nineteenth-century German emigrant men's and women's private correspondence.[11] Referring to twentieth-century studies in language and gender,[12] McLelland argues that research into gender differences has lacked clarity, in part, because it has been qualitative rather than quantitative: '[p]roblems arise when data that are essentially anecdotal in nature are treated as if indicative of general trends without appropriate statistical analysis'.[13] In her study, McLelland focuses on some of the linguistic strategies identified in recent scholarship as being more typical of women in conversation – such as the use of epistemic modality (as previously mentioned, words like *might* and *suppose*), hedging devices (words like *seem*, *believe* and *sometimes*) and question tags (such as *isn't it? shouldn't I?* and *don't they?*) – and then uses statistical methods to test whether such gender differences are evident in a corpus of nineteenth-century letters.

The analysis involved using two corpora: Corpus One (a pilot corpus) containing twenty-two letters by women and twenty-two by men (approximately 30,000 words), dating from 1850 to 1900 and representing seven female and eight male authors; Corpus Two (a much larger, more representative corpus) containing ninety-one letters by men and ninety-one by women (approximately 84,000 words), from the same time period and representing thirty-eight female and thirty-eight male authors.

Of the linguistic features investigated in Corpus One, only the discourse particle '*doch*' (often used as an intensifier or emphatic device) showed any significant difference between genders, being more frequently used by female authors in phrases such as '*ich denke*' (broadly translated as 'I think') to soften assertions. The data also gestured towards female authors being more likely to 'soften imperatives, express more wishes, and [be] more emphatic in their formulations than . . . men', although these findings were somewhat tentative.[14] However, when the same investigation was carried out using the larger corpus (Corpus Two), these findings received little statistical support. What the findings did show, however, was that the female authors used more intensifying adverbs (in English these would be words like 'very', 'really' and 'so'), they were more likely to address the recipient in the body of the letter and they referred to themselves using the first person (I) more frequently than their male counterparts. The data also showed that the female authors tended to adopt more politeness strategies ('*bitte(n)*' (a verb meaning to ask/request) and '*Bitte*' (similar to 'please' or 'you're welcome') when making requests; however, as McLelland points out, this finding could simply be a result of more requests being made by women than by men in the first place. McLelland hypothesises that the high frequency of '*doch*' in Corpus One may be explained in terms of educational background. It is one particular author who contributes over a third of all occurrences of '*doch*' in Corpus One and this author also adopts a more colloquial, speech-like style in her letters, indicative of a lower level of education.

The study by McLelland (as with similar quantitative studies by Elspaß, and Nurmi and Palander-Collin) demonstrates the possibilities and opportunities of using more quantitative methods of analysis both to examine letters and to understand gender; however, it is very difficult to achieve a balance between offering a rigorous, replicable and systematic quantitative approach and at the same time not losing sight of the very personal, idiosyncratic and subjective data at hand, that is, the author behind the letter.[15]

The current article builds on this body of quantitative research, proposing a complementary methodology which is based on the theories and techniques of corpus linguistics for examining emigrant letters – a methodology which attempts to bridge the gap between the content observed and the conclusions that are later drawn from that content, and one which moves constantly between the quantitative and the qualitative and back again. Whilst recognising that linguistic choices will reveal something about the context of situation, context of culture and how the author construes events and perceives the world, corpus linguistics decontextualises the components of language. Corpus linguistics does not look at language at the semantic level, but instead looks at language at the textual level. It is a mode of study that takes language out of its flow and reality, freezing it and rearranging it to give 'new perspectives on the familiar'.[16] It draws on what is known about language and how language is used to make conclusions about how the author is using language. The conclusions drawn are based on empirical data collection: frequencies, distributional patterns and proportions. Because of the design of the corpus, it is possible to move constantly between the individual and the group and back again, noticing what is typical or unusual about one text when compared with many texts. Corpus linguistics, as applied to the study of correspondence, takes language out of context, reorganises it to notice new things based on quantitative investigation, and then puts the findings back into context to try to build a picture of the life and experiences of the author. This approach makes it possible to investigate systematically the language used by different authors and then to notice what those authors each have in common. As such, it provides a multi-layered approach to examining language and gender, allowing the analyst to test whether linguistic observations are about gender alone or gender in combination with other social, cultural or economic factors (such as age, class, location or level of education, for instance).

What is a corpus?

A corpus can be defined as a 'bod[y] of naturally occurring language data stored on computers' and corpus techniques of analysis as the 'computational procedures which manipulate this data in various ways . . . to uncover linguistic patterns which can enable us to make sense of the ways that language is used'.[17] The 'body of naturally occurring language' can be anything from a few sentences to a large set of texts (the term 'texts' here refers to both written language and spoken transcriptions), but the main point to emphasise is that the data has been collected for a specific purpose, with the aim being something 'other than to preserve the texts themselves because they have intrinsic value', which is, as Susan Hunston explains, what distinguishes a corpus from a digital archive.[18] A corpus does not simply preserve and store texts so that they can be accessed more easily and by a wider number of people; rather, a corpus is designed with the intention of being representative of a particular type of text – newspapers, academic essays, letters, political speeches and so on, from a particular era, on a particular subject or by a particular socio-economic group and so on. Representativeness is usually achieved by 'breaking the whole down into component parts and aiming to include equal amounts of data from each of the parts'.[19] So, for example, a corpus of political speeches during the UK general election campaign of 2010 might include an equal weighting of speeches for the news media, TV debates and public addresses, by a range of politicians from the three major parties. What goes into the corpus, then, depends on what the corpus will be used for and what research questions it will seek to address. However, it will also depend on 'what [data] is available', and quite often the analyst is negotiating a fine balance between selecting texts that are representative and working with whatever texts are available.[20] This issue of representativeness is always problematic and arguably no more so than when working with letters. In the case of emigrant letters, the analyst is always working with what is available – designing a representative corpus of personal letters is simply not achievable as there is no way of accounting for the experiences of those emigrants who chose not to write, who could not write or whose letters were lost, destroyed or, years later, for various reasons, not donated.

The second thing that distinguishes a corpus from a digital archive is the way in which data content is explored and analysed. Although the data in a digital archive may be accessed online, without the need physically to visit a library or an archive, the content is generally studied linearly (as one would do with an original manuscript) Digitisation alone (and by that I mean optical character recognition [OCR] scanning or transcribing the letters and saving them in an electronic format) makes a document more accessible and to a certain extent more searchable (in a very limited sense of the term); however, it does not allow the collection to be explored in depth, or in creative ways. With a corpus, the data is stored in such a way that 'it can be studied non-linearly, and both quantitatively and qualitatively', using computer software.[21] The data (in this case the emigrant letter) can be marked-up in various ways – for contextual information such as gender, age, date of correspondence, socio-economic status, religious denomination, location (home and New World); for key themes such as homesickness, money, work, family, health, American life or for pragmatic features such as apologising, making requests, humour and so on. The data can also be annotated for parts of speech (word classification) and semantic categorisation. This markup and annotation allows individual letters and subgroups to be easily searched and compared in relation to one another and in relation to the whole. Additionally, computer software allows the content of the corpus, or subsections of the corpus (known as subcorpora) to be explored in ways that would be difficult, and in many cases impossible (depending on the amount of data being examined and the type of search being carried out), using more traditional methods of content analysis. Computer software allows the analyst to observe recurrent patterns, distributional trends and other statistical features, which would be hard to notice through reading alone. For this reason, it is often the data that will lead the investigation, pointing the analyst to features of the texts which s/he may not have noticed otherwise.

Background remarks

The letters used in this study are borrowed from Kerby Miller (Curator's Professor, Department of History at the University of Missouri), who has created an archive of Irish emigrant correspondence. The collection contains well over 5,000 Irish emigrant letters of which the Lough family correspondence are a small but significant part, having been referred to in several publications.[22] In the early 1950s, a few of the Lough letters were donated initially to Arnold Schrier, an American graduate student, by Canice and Eilish O'Mahony of Dundalk, Co. Louth. Schrier, now Professor Emeritus at the University of Cincinnati, employed these and other letters in his book, *Ireland and the Irish Emigration, 1850–1900.*[23] In the 1970s and 1980s, the rest of the Lough letters were donated to Miller by the O'Mahonys and by Edward Dunne and Mrs Kate Tynan of Portlaoise, County Laois. Both Miller and Schrier, who subsequently collaborated on Irish migration research, made transcriptions of the letters and Miller returned the original manuscripts to the donors. In most cases, Miller's collection contains photocopies of the original manuscripts together with the typed transcripts.

The complete letter collection is described as the LOUGH Corpus. The individual letter series (subcorpora) of each sister are described as: LIZZIE Corpus (which contains letters written by Elizabeth Lough), ANNIE Corpus, ALICE Corpus and JULIA Corpus. All italicised words and phrases are examples taken from the letters. Words in capitals represent the lemma (that is all variations of a particular word form, so BE would represent all forms of the verb to be: is, am, are, was, were etc.). Raw frequencies are presented in angle brackets.

The following is a summary of the background research carried out by Professor Miller, relating to the Lough family. The Lough (pronounced Locke) sisters came from a Roman Catholic family in Meelick, Queen's County, Ireland. There were five sisters – Elizabeth, Alice, Julia, Annie and Mary. Four of the sisters – Elizabeth, Alice, Julia and Annie – emigrated to America between 1870 and 1884, while Mary, the youngest sister, remained in Ireland with her mother and father. Elizabeth (or Lizzie) Lough (later Elizabeth Walsh) emigrated circa 1870–1871 to Winsted, Litchfield County, Connecticut. She worked as a seamstress and housewife, having five children – three boys (Tom, John William and James) and two girls (Alice and Catherine Elizabeth). Her husband, Dan Walsh, appears to have died in the early twentieth century, before Lizzie; there is no mention of Lizzie in letters written by her sisters from 1912 onwards, so it is suspected that she died not long after her husband. Alice (or Alisha) Lough (later Alice Elliott) also emigrated circa 1870. She too lived in Winsted between 1876 and 1880, but then moved to Westfield, Hampden County, Massachusetts in 1881 where she remained, as a housewife, until she died sometime between 1918 and 1928. Alice married Edward Elliott and had seven children – five boys (Edward, James, William, John and Phillip) and two girls (Mary Elizabeth and Alice). Annie (or Nan) Lough (later Annie McMahon) emigrated circa 1878. She lived in Winsted from 1884 to 1928 (when her letters stop), working mainly as a servant and housewife. She married John McMahon; she did not have any children. Julia Lough (later Julia McCarthy) was the last sister to emigrate – in late September 1884. She lived with her sister Lizzie (and husband Dan) in Winsted between 1884 and 1895. She then moved in 1895 to Torrington, Litchfield County, Connecticut, where she remained until 1928 (when her letters stop). Julia was something of a success story, working as a seamstress to begin with, then an apprentice dressmaker, before becoming a professional dressmaker and opening up her own shop that employed several members of staff. She married Thomas McCarthy and had several children although only Elise is named in the letters.

The LOUGH corpus

The starting point for a corpus investigation is quantitative. What is unusual, interesting or typical about a text can only be explained by comparing it against other texts. It is this 'comparative information that quantitative corpus data can provide'.[24] By constantly moving between the cohort and the individual it is possible to notice both what is typical and distinguishing about a text or texts. In this study I will investigate the letters of the four Lough sisters who emigrated from Ireland to the US in the mid to late nineteenth century. I will examine the collection (or corpus) as a whole to see if there are any recurring patterns or phraseology, and what these might reveal; I will also compare the letter series (or subcorpora) of each individual sister to see how their language differs, and what this might reveal. I will, where relevant, use two reference corpora of emigrant correspondence from around the same period: twenty-one randomly selected letters by male Irish authors from a range of socio-economic backgrounds and twenty-one letters by female Irish authors. Letters for the reference corpora were also borrowed (and transcribed) from Professor Miller's archive. These two corpora (although very small for the purpose of this study) will allow me to test whether the findings from the LOUGH Corpus are representative of female emigrant correspondence more generally as well as the extent to which the language of male and female authors differs.

There are a total of ninety nine letters in the Lough collection held at the University of Missouri; however ten of these were excluded from this study as they did not contain sender information, making it difficult to assign these letters confidently to one of the four subcorpora. As I will be comparing the letter series of each individual sister it is important that each correspondence is correctly assigned to a subcorpus – a wrongly assigned letter could affect the results. Another three letters were discounted, as these – although part of the Lough collection – were not written by any of the four sisters. Although the corpus is relatively small (compared with many corpora, for example, the British National Corpus or the Bank of English, which reach into millions of words), it will nonetheless provide a good foundation on which later studies, looking at larger bodies of data, can build. Corpus linguistics is about making comparisons by looking at what happens in one text and then seeing if this is typical of many texts, and vice versa. The same statistical measures are used when looking at a small amount of data as when looking at a large amount, thereby making it possible to compare corpora or subcorpora of different sizes.

To prepare the letters for corpus analysis they first needed to be digitised and then saved in plain text format (a format which is compatible with most corpus software programmes). The digitised letters are an exact copy of Professor Miller's original transcriptions with all spelling variations, punctuation, omissions, deletions and insertions in keeping with the original manuscript. The process of digitisation and markup, and the issues and challenges of working with original manuscripts and various versions

Table 1: The LOUGH Corpus.

LOUGH Sisters	Number of letters	Number of tokens
Annie	38	18933
Julia	33	12269
Alice	10	3587
Elizabeth (Lizzie)	5	3488
TOTAL	86	38277

of transcription, is a topic for discussion in its own right, but these issues, although very relevant, are not within the scope of this article. It was not necessary to markup the letters for contextual information (date, location, gender, etc.) for the purpose of this study; nor was it necessary to annotate the letters for parts of speech as this study is intended to be data-led (i.e. basic frequency information will lead the investigation; I will not be approaching the corpus with specific, predetermined grammatical/structural searches in mind). All quantitative findings will need to be examined qualitatively (using concordance lines, which display the words in context) to establish how a word or phrase is functioning – whether as a noun, verb, adjective, etc.

As shown in Table 1, (after removing those letters which cannot be assigned to one of the Lough sisters) the LOUGH Corpus contains eighty-six letters – a total of 38,277 words. Annie Lough, the third sister to emigrate in 1878, appears to have written the most letters of the four sisters – a total of thirty-eight letters (18,933 words) between 1890 and 1928, nine of which were to her mother and twenty-six to her sister Mary (see Table 2), both of whom remained in the Loughs' home town – Meelick, Queen's County, Ireland – until their deaths. Julia Lough, the last sister to emigrate in 1884, also wrote regularly – mainly to her mother (twenty-three letters) and also her sister (ten letters) – a total of thirty-three letters (12,269 words) between 1884 and 1927. Elizabeth and Alice were the first sisters to emigrate between 1870 and 1871, yet they wrote the smallest number of letters. Elizabeth wrote five letters (3,488 words) to her mother, father and sisters between 1876 and 1877, when she first emigrated to the US and Alice wrote ten letters (3,587 words) to her sister and mother between 1888 and 1914 (two when she first emigrated and then another three at roughly five-year intervals – five of

Table 2: Breakdown of senders/recipients.

	No. of letters sent			
Addressee	Annie	Julia	Lizzie	Alice
Mother	9	23	1	3
Sister (Mary Lough, later Fitzpatrick)	26	10	0	7
Mother and Sister	1	0	0	0
Nephew – James	1	0	0	0
Niece – Alice	1	0	0	0
Father, Mother and Sisters	0	0	2	0
Father and Mother	0	0	2	0

Table 3: Type/token ratios for the LOUGH Corpus.

	Annie	Julia	Lizzie	Alice	Total
Type	1718	1463	654	597	2681
Token	18933	12269	3488	3587	38277
Type/Token Ratio	9.07%	11.92%	18.75%	16.64%	7.00%

the letters are not dated, but the content would suggest they were written several years after emigrating). It should be pointed out, however, that this information is based on the number of letters held in Professor Miller's archive (in other words, the number of letters which were donated). As mentioned previously, when discussing the issue of representativeness, there is no way to know how many letters were actually sent or how many were lost or destroyed.

Having grouped the Lough data, it is now possible to explore the content of the letters using computer software. There are a number of useful corpus analysis programmes available, some of which are web-based – Antconc,[25] Wmatrix[26] and Sketch Engine[27] – while others are computer-based – WordSmith[28] and ConcGram.[29] I have chosen to use Antconc for two reasons: first, it is freely available online and second, it has certain functionalities which I am interested in using for this investigation – specifically, the n-gram procedure which will be discussed later in the article.

The starting point – simple frequency data

The first calculation that Antonc can provide is something called a type/token ratio, which can be obtained for the corpus as a whole and for each subcorpus. The term 'token' refers to the total number of words in a corpus. The term 'type' refers to the number of original (or different) words in the corpus. So, for example, the word HOME occurs 193 times in the LOUGH Corpus, which would equal 193 tokens, but would only count as one type.[30] The type/token ratio is calculated by dividing the number of types by the number of tokens – this figure is then expressed as a percentage. A low type/token ratio (tending towards 0%) suggests that certain words are being used over and over again. A high type/token ratio (tending towards 100%) suggests a more diverse range of language is being utilised, with fewer words being repeated. Looking at Table 3, the data shows that the LOUGH Corpus has an overall type/token ratio of 7%. Breaking this down by subcorpora, the data shows that Annie has the lowest type/token ratio (9.07%), followed by Julia (11.92%). The type/token ratios for Alice and Lizzie are slightly higher, 16.64% and 18.75% respectively.

On the surface, this might suggest that Annie's and Julia's letters are more formulaic and repetitive, whereas Alice's and Lizzie's letters contain greater lexical variety and complexity. However, it is more likely that this difference in percentages reflects the size of the corpora. The larger the corpus the more likely some words, particularly grammar words, are repeated, which in turn will reduce the type/token ratio. To demonstrate this, Table 4 and Figure 1 show the accumulative type/token ratios, year after year, for each sister (note that only the letters containing a date are included in this investigation). Taking Julia as an example, the data shows that her first letter in 1884

Table 4: Accumulative type/token ratios for each subcorpus.

JULIA

Letter No.	5	6	8	9	10	13	15	17	18	19	20	21	23	26	27	77	30	28	29	32	58
Date	1884	1884	1888	1889	1889	1890	1890	1890	1891	1891	1891	1891	1892	1893	1893	1893	1893	1894	1894	1895	1927
Accumulative Type	46	250	335	458	530	592	641	674	724	768	791	823	878	914	942	983	1001	1083	1121	1160	1198
Accumulative Token	61	600	977	1430	1933	2429	2814	3188	3550	3907	4243	4562	5004	5356	5828	6192	6545	7310	7810	8251	8622
Ratio%	75.41	41.67	34.29	32.03	27.42	24.37	22.78	21.14	20.39	19.66	18.64	18.04	17.55	17.06	16.16	15.88	15.29	14.82	14.35	14.06	13.89

ANNIE

Letter No.	12	70	22	25	31	33	34	37	38	40	42	43	44	36	46	48	49	52	53	55	56	57	59	60
Date	1890	1891	1891	1893	1895	1898	1899	1901	1901	1902	1906	1906	1906	1910	1912	1913	1914	1918	1918	1919	1919	1925	1928	1928
Accumulative Type	205	417	477	611	653	653	721	753	792	817	848	870	891	975	1039	1065	1087	1149	1251	1326	1396	1380	1389	1424
Accumulative Token	491	1532	2027	2965	3580	4621	5168	5571	6019	6393	6833	7174	7479	8005	8651	9158	9565	10224	11104	11932	12444	12688	12901	13536
Ratio%	41.75	27.22	23.53	20.61	18.24	14.13	13.95	13.52	13.16	12.78	12.41	12.13	11.91	12.18	12.01	11.63	11.36	11.24	11.27	11.11	11.22	10.88	10.77	10.52

ALICE

Letter No.	7	11	41	45	50
Date	1888	1889	1904	1910	1914
Accumulative Type	170	305	392	436	464
Accumulative Token	395	928	1380	1756	2042
Ratio%	43.04	32.87	28.41	24.83	22.72

LIZZIE

Letter No.	1	2	3	4
Date	1876	1876	1876	1877
Accumulative Type	409	502	543	631
Accumulative Token	1450	2033	2390	2939
Ratio%	28.21	24.69	22.72	21.47

contains sixty-one tokens (or words) and forty-six types, giving an overall type/token ratio of 75.41%, suggesting that the letter contains a good amount of linguistic diversity with relatively little repetition (although not surprisingly since this is a very short letter). However, looking at the accumulative figures for letters sent between 1884 and 1889 (1,933 tokens and 530 types), there is a much lower type/token ratio (27.42%), which would suggest that some repetition is occurring in the five letters sent during this period. This is to be expected: as mentioned earlier, the larger the corpus the more likely it is that words will be repeated; however, the formulaic nature of letter writing perhaps also goes some way to explaining the dramatic drop in type/token ratio from Julia's first letter sent in 1884, which has a type/token ratio of 75.41%, to her last letter sent in 1927, which has a type/token ratio of 13.89%. The extent of the formulaic writing would require further investigation. Certainly, the openings and closing are likely to follow a standard format, but it would be interesting to examine the body of the letters to see whether they too adopt a set pattern, with less new information being presented over time.

Michael Toolan suggests that what is potentially very interesting when examining accumulative type/token ratios are any sharp 'spikes' or 'dips' in the predictable decline in type/token ratios.[31] In the Lough data there is a sharp decline, or dip, between Julia's first letter sent in 1884 (75.4%) and her second letter sent later that year (41.7%) – a difference of 33.7%. Similarly for Annie, there is a noticeable difference of 14.6% between her first letter sent in 1890 (41.8%) and her second letter sent in 1891 (27.2%), after which the decline is much less pronounced. These dips could be explained, in part, by the length of the letters: in both cases the first letter is quite short whereas the second letter is much longer; however, it could also be indicative of a more formulaic writing style adopted by the two younger sisters, possibly indicative of differences in education between the Lough sisters, although further analysis would be needed to test this hypothesis.

An average type/token ratio can also be calculated. This goes some way to resolving the problem of type/token ratios being lower for larger corpora and higher for smaller corpora, and allows data sets of different sizes to be compared. This is done by calculating the type/token ratio for the first 1,000 words of a corpus, then the next 1,000 words, then the next, and so on. Finally, an average is calculated based on these figures. Table 5 shows the average type/token ratio for the LOUGH Corpus and the two reference corpora (FEMALE Ref. and MALE Ref.). The data shows that female authors have a slightly lower type/token ratio (39.97%) compared with male authors (44.86%). The average type/token ratio for the LOUGH Corpus is slightly lower than both reference corpora at 34.02%, which might support earlier observations that the Lough letters (particularly in the case of Julia Lough and Annie Lough) are perhaps more formulaic than one might expect – an observation that is certainly worth further investigation: what is being repeated and what function does this repetition serve?

Words and frequencies

Having established the lexical density of the letters, the next stage is to look at which words are being repeated (or not, as the case may be). Using Antconc it is possible to create wordlists for the whole corpus and each subcorpus. Table 6 shows the twenty most frequently occurring words in the LOUGH Corpus.

Table 5: Average type/token ratios across three corpora.

	Average Type/Token
FEMALE Ref Corpus	39.97
MALE Ref Corpus	44.86
LOUGH Corpus	34.02

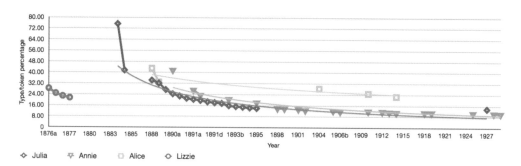

Figure 1: Accumulative type/token ratios for each subcorpus presented visually.

The left column ('Word') shows the words listed in order of frequency with the right column (Raw freq.) providing the actual number of occurrences. Table 6 shows that grammar words are most common: *I* <freq. 1,807>, *you* <freq. 1,324>, *to* <freq. 1,313>, *and* <freq. 1,296>, *the* <freq. 909>. Grammar words are the glue that holds the content together – so it is perhaps not surprising that these words occur more frequently. However, the propensity for certain grammar words over others can be equally revealing. Table 6, for example, shows that the pronouns *I* and *you* are the most frequently occurring words in the LOUGH Corpus with *I* scoring slightly higher than *you*: <freq. 1,807> versus <freq. 1,324> (a ratio of 4:3). One might expect the first person singular pronoun *I* to score high in ego-documents such as letters; however, previous studies have identified gendered variations in terms of pronoun usage. Nicola McLelland, for example, found that female authors tended to refer to themselves using the first person singular pronoun *I* more than male authors; and a study by Arja Nurmi and Minna Palander-Collin found that pronoun usage reflected the power relations between author and recipient – when the relationship was equal (letters between siblings, for example) the first person pronoun usage was high; when the relationship was unequal (letters between children and parents, for example) the first person pronoun usage was low.[32] Their study also found that the sex of the recipient had an effect on pronoun usage, with authors referring to themselves more frequently using *I* when the recipient was female. The current study supports some of these findings with *I* occurring more frequently in the LOUGH Corpus (an average of 47.21 occurrences per 1,000 words) and the FEMALE Corpus (an average of 41.90) than in the MALE Corpus (an average of just 32.94) – see Table 7. The findings did not, however, support Nurmi's and Palander-Collins's observation that first person pronoun usage tends to be greater in letters between authors and recipients of equal status (such as siblings); instead, in the Lough letters, the data showed that *I* occurs slightly more frequently in

Table 6: Wordlist for the LOUGH Corpus.

Word	Raw freq.
I	1807
you	1324
to	1313
and	1296
the	909
a	652
is	673
all	586
of	544
it	432
she	418
for	414
her	413
will	411
very	400
in	391
was	385
are	325
have	306
hope	304

Table 7: Occurrence of *I* in each corpus.

	I (Raw freq.)	*I* (Normalised)	*You* (Raw freq.)	*You* (Normalised)
LOUGH Corpus	1807	47.21	1324	34.59
FEMALE Ref.	693	41.90	353	21.34
MALE Ref.	681	32.94	291	14.07

Table 8: Occurrences of *I* in letters sent to parents/siblings.[33]

No. of letters to:	*I* (Raw freq.)	*I* (Normalised)	*You* (Raw freq.)	*You* (Normalised)
Sister (48)	919	45.29	772	38.04
Parents (43)	957	50.37	592	31.16

letters addressed to the mother (an average of 50.37 occurrences per 1,000 words) than in those addressed to the sister (an average of 45.29 occurrences) – see Table 8. Note that the 'normalised' figures in Table 7 and Table 8 allow meaningful comparisons to be made across data sets of different sizes. It is calculated by dividing the raw frequency by the number of tokens x 1,000. This gives an average frequency (of a particular word or phrase) per 1,000 words.

The pronoun *you* is also potentially very interesting as it has the ability to occupy two grammatical positions (Subject and Object), so its usage might reveal something

Table 9: Position of *I* in projection clauses.

No. of words to the left	L7	L6	L5	L4	L3	L2	L1	**NODE**
Freq. of 'I'	0	3	4	6	27	147	0	**YOU**

about the author/recipient relationship: how the authors are positioning themselves and how they are positioning the recipient. Analysis of the concordance lines for *you* shows that it frequently occurs in the position of Subject of what can be described as a projected clause, where the projecting clause contains the pronoun *I*, as in *I hope you will write soon* (*I hope* being the projecting clause: the part which projects an idea, fact or proposition; and *you will write soon* being the projected clause: the idea, fact or proposition that is being projected). In short, *you*, in these occurrences, is the real or psychological Subject of these sentences.

Table 9 shows that the pronoun *I* (in these projection clauses) most commonly occurs either two words to the left (L2) <freq. 147> or three words to the left (L3) <freq. 27> of the search word *you*, with the most frequent structures being *I hope you* <freq. 95>, *I suppose you* <freq. 28>, *I am sure you* <freq. 15>, *I wish you* <freq. 11>, *I know/no you* <freq. 11>, *I think you* <freq. 7> and *I am glad you* <freq. 4>). In these instances, the projecting clause (i.e. the clause which introduces the projected clause – the main fact, idea or proposition) contains a mental verb or an adjective carrying epistemic modality (such as *suppose* or *sure* (expressing probability or certainty)), or a mental verb carrying boulemic modality (such as *hope* or *wish* (expressing desire or volition)). It is, arguably, at this point that a phraseological pattern begins to emerge: *I + Verb + You*; *I + BE + Adj + You*. In any case, the prominence of *you* as doer, agent or focalised, constructed centre of attention, is very striking. I will talk more about projection clauses later in the article.

Breaking the wordlist down further, Table 10 provides the word frequency lists for each subcorpus (as well as the corpus as a whole). The data shows that the grammar words *I* and *you* score high in all four subcorpora; however, although there are <759> occurrences of *I* in the ANNIE Corpus and only <236> occurrences in the LIZZIE Corpus, statistically Lizzie is using *I* much more frequently than the other sisters – on average 67.66 times per 1,000 words, compared with 40.09 for Annie, 50.53 for Julia and 53.53 for Alice. Annie appears to be using *I* (40.09) and *you* (38.66) almost on a 1:1 ratio, perhaps suggesting that she is often directly involving or addressing the recipient in her letters; whereas Lizzie is using *I* (67.66) approximately two and a half times more frequently than she is using *you* (22.94), perhaps suggesting that her letters are more author focused. In all subcorpora the same grammar words (*I, you, and, to, the*) are being repeated, which may indicate that certain grammatical structures are also being repeated; this, in turn, may go some way to explaining the low type/token ratio discussed earlier, although further exploration would be needed before any conclusions could be drawn.

Another possible avenue for investigation is the use of *will*, which ranks high across three of the subcorpora: <freq. 229> in the ANNIE Corpus, <freq. 123> in the JULIA Corpus, and <freq. 40> in the ALICE Corpus. The modal verb *will* is interesting as it has several different functions and can be used to express epistemic modality (i.e. certainty/probability), or boulemic modality (i.e. desire/volition). There

Table 10: Wordlist for each subcorpus.

	LOUGH Corpus			ANNIE Corpus			JULIA Corpus			LIZZIE Corpus			ALICE Corpus		
	Word	Raw freq.	Normalised	Word	Raw freq.	Normalised	Word	Raw freq.	Normalised	Word	Raw freq.	Normalised	Word	Raw freq.	Normalised
	I	1807	47.21	and	767	40.51	I	620	50.53	I	236	67.66	I	192	53.53
	you	1324	34.59	I	759	40.09	to	422	34.4	to	126	36.12	to	147	40.98
	to	1313	34.30	you	732	38.66	and	391	31.87	you	80	22.94	you	124	34.57
	and	1296	33.86	to	618	32.64	you	388	31.62	is	73	20.93	and	107	29.83
	the	909	23.75	the	508	26.83	the	249	20.3	the	71	20.36	the	81	22.58
	a	652	17.03	all	343	18.12	a	208	16.95	she	70	20.07	very	61	17.01
	is	673	17.58	a	339	17.91	is	201	16.38	it	50	14.33	all	56	15.61
	all	586	15.31	is	311	16.43	all	152	12.39	of	47	13.47	of	54	15.05
	of	544	14.21	of	292	15.42	of	151	12.31	an	42	12.04	is	52	14.50
	it	432	11.29	it	236	12.47	her	140	11.41	for	40	11.47	a	51	14.22
	she	418	10.92	will	229	12.1	am	137	11.17	not	40	11.47	me	43	11.99
	for	414	10.82	for	226	11.94	she	134	10.92	her	39	11.18	her	40	11.15
	her	413	10.79	very	218	11.51	in	127	10.35	my	38	10.89	will	40	11.15
	will	411	10.74	in	210	11.09	will	123	10.03	he	37	10.61	she	39	10.87
	very	400	10.45	hope	201	10.62	for	122	9.94	all	35	10.03	they	39	10.87
	in	391	10.22	was	201	10.62	not	116	9.45	was	35	10.03	was	38	10.59
	was	385	10.06	her	194	10.25	have	113	9.21	but	32	9.17	have	37	10.32
	are	325	8.49	are	184	9.72	it	113	9.21	have	32	9.17	in	34	9.48
	have	306	7.99	she	175	9.24	was	111	9.05	no	32	9.17	it	33	9.20
	hope	304	7.96	well	157	8.29	are	109	8.88	am	31	8.89	but	32	8.92

Table 11: Occurrences of WILL in the LOUGH Corpus.

WILL	Freq.
I will	88
You will	106
she will	30
Maggie, Mary, Lizzie etc. will	24
it will	23
God, heaven will	8
we will	12
lines will	12
they will	11
he will	5
letter will	3

```
ope they are well so Dear mother I will bring my letter to a close I hope you
I know they are but very few now I will close now dear Sister with best and kindest
very well with it so Der Mother  I will conclude with fondest and best love to youe
love to them and now dear Sister I will finish as I cannot wish you a merry Xma
ou know I am thinking of you and I will not forget you next year with Gods help. I
yo will write as soon as you do. I will not write again till I get an answer to
when the last one was not a girl I will not say any more now till I hear from you
isitor as you I dont ask for any I will say good by now with love to you and an
ry you will write soon again and I will send you a longer letter next time and thi
see their grandfather some times I will try and send you their pictures some ti
I was going to write to Mary but I will wait now till I get her next letter y all
t I will have it before Xmas and I will write to you again before Xmas With the
```

Figure 2: Sample Concordance Lines for 'I WILL'.

are <411> occurrences of *will* in the LOUGH Corpus. Six of these occurrences show *will* functioning as a noun (as in *God's will* and *holy will*), so these can be discounted, leaving <405> occurrences of *will* functioning as a modal verb. Of these <405> occurrences almost half come after the pronouns *I* <freq. 88> and *you* <freq. 106> (see Table 11).

Looking more closely at the concordance lines for *I will* the data shows that in most instances (<61> out of <88> occurrences) *will* is being used in 'signing off' structures to signal the close of the letter (see Fig. 2 for examples), with the meaning being one of intention. All of the instances below – *I **will** conclude*, *I **will** finish*, *I **will** bring my letter to a close* – could be substituted with *I intend to* and as such are expressing boulemic modality. As with '*I am writing to you because . . .*' and '*You ask me X, so I will tell you . . .*', these are meta-discursive phrases which help to structure the text as well as serving an interactive function.[34]

Concordance lines display the search term (in this case *I will*) in context. The concordance lines are presented this way (that is with the search term centrally aligned) so as to allow the analyst to notice linguistic patterns – words that typically appear to the right or left of the search term.

The concordance lines for *you will* show that what follows is a limited range of verbs. There are verbs to do with the act of sending/receiving letters (*write*, *send*, *receive*, *get*); and there are verbs to do with cognition (*like*, *forgive*, *excuse*). (See concordance lines above. Note that the verb *keep* is difficult to categorise as it functions in very

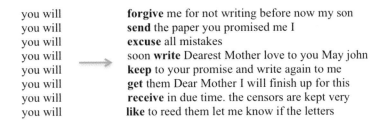

Figure 3: Sample Concordance Lines for 'YOU WLL'.

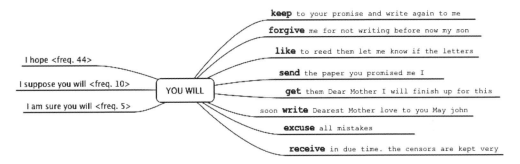

Figure 4: Patterns for 'you will'.

different ways and has different meanings depending on the context in which it is being used. In the concordance lines being examined here, *keep* is used in the context of *you will keep to your promise*, where *keep* is part of a fixed expression, meaning 'fulfil your agreement'). In all of these instances of *you will* it is difficult to know whether *will* is expressing epistemic or boulemic modality as there is not enough context for either function to predominate. When, for example, the author says, *you will forgive me for not writing before now*, it is not clear whether *will* is being used to express certainty (as in 'I am quite sure that you will forgive me'), or desire/volition (as in 'I want you to forgive me' or 'I hope you intend to forgive me').

An investigation of the wider context, however, reveals that in most cases (<90> out of <106> occurrences) *you* is the Subject and *will* is the auxiliary modal of a projected clause, preceded by a projecting clause (see Figure 4), with the most frequent patterns being *I hope you will*, *I suppose you will* and *I am sure you will*.

With this wider phraseological context it now becomes more possible to determine the function of *will* in these instances. The type of modality (whether epistemic or boulemic) is projected onto the recipient via the projecting clause, pushing a mild obligation, or placing social pressure onto the addressee to respond in a certain way. The concordance lines for *you will* seem to suggest that *will* is more frequently used to express boulemic modality, with the main pattern (*I hope you will* + V) being used to express the author's desire for the recipient's willingness to do something. Through these clauses the author's wants, needs, desires or intentions are transferred onto the recipient – they become the recipient's own and create a psychological bond between both participants.

Another observation which can be made from Table 10 is that across all four subcorpora the only lexical word which appears (in the top twenty) is the verb *hope* with a frequency of <201> in the ANNIE Corpus. However, moving further down the wordlists more content words begin to appear. Table 12 provides a list of the ten most frequent lexical verbs in each subcorpus (i.e. the first ten lexical verbs as they appear, in whatever form, in the wordlist). Note that I am looking at lexical verbs and not auxiliary verbs (HAVE, BE, DO), which tend to serve a grammatical function.

Looking at Table 12 there are two things that stand out. First, there are a high number of mental verbs of cognition, perception and desire (*hope, suppose, see, think, like, love, hear, know*), with certain verbs (*hope, love* and *think*) appearing across all four subcorpora. Second, nearly all of these verbs appear to be in their base form, with the following exceptions: Lizzie uses the past tense *got* and *thought*, the participle *seen* and *taken* and the continuous form *going*. The high frequency of base forms may in part be explained by the high frequency of *to* and *will* across all four subcorpora (as what tends to follow both *to* and *will* is the base form of the verb, as in *to hear, to think, will send, will go*). However, a closer look at the context surrounding these mental verbs in their base form (of which there are <1,115> occurrences) reveals that they are rarely used after *will* (just <25> instances); they are more frequently used after *to* (a total of <173> instances – the most common structures being *to see* <freq. 72> and *to hear* <freq. 75>); but they are most frequently used in the present tense after the first person singular pronoun *I* (a significant <453> instances).

The high frequency of these mental verbs of cognition, perception and desire is interesting for two main reasons. The first is that these verbs, as explained by Michael Halliday and Christian Matthiessen, 'relate to inner experience (what we experience as going on inside ourselves, in the world of consciousness)' and usually describe emotions, thoughts or perceptions, thereby providing insight into the psychological worldview of the author.[35] The second is that these verbs are special because they have the ability to project: that is they have the 'ability to set up another clause "outside" the "mental" clause as the representation of the "content" of consciousness'.[36] This latter point appears to support previous findings which show a high frequency of the projecting clause *I hope* (*hope* being a mental verb of desire).

Halliday and Matthiessen make a distinction between the projection of propositions and the projection of proposals, with each type of projection having its own lexicogrammar. 'Whereas propositions, which are exchanges of information [i.e. exchanges which require a verbal response], are projected mentally by processes [verbs] of cognition – thinking, knowing, understanding, wondering, etc. – proposals, which are exchanges of goods-&-services [i.e. exchanges which require a non-verbal response], are projected mentally by processes [verbs] of desire'.[37] Further, what is interesting about the lexicogrammar of proposals is that they can be followed by a future declarative (will + base form) or non-finite (including to-infinitive) dependent clause (as in *I hope you **will write** soon* or *I hope **to hear** from you soon*). So, when a verbal response is required the verb is likely to be one of cognition (as in *I know you are trying to do the best you can*). When a non-verbal response is required the verb is likely to be one of desire (as in *I hope you will write often*) – see Table 13. Projection clauses in the LOUGH Corpus will be examined in more detail later in the article.

Table 12: The most frequent lexical verbs in each subcorpus.

LOUGH Corpus			ANNIE Corpus			JULIA Corpus			LIZZIE Corpus			ALICE Corpus		
Verb	Freq.	Norm.	Verb	Freq.	Norm.	Verb	Freq.	Norm.	Verb	Freq.	Norm.	Verb	Freq.	Norm.
hope	304	7.94	hope	201	10.62	hope	74	6.03	think	31	8.89	see	23	6.41
write	197	5.15	write	120	6.34	get	66	5.38	get	18	5.16	hope	19	5.30
get	151	3.94	see	74	3.91	hear	65	5.30	write	22	6.31	send	18	5.02
see	143	3.74	love	69	3.64	write	52	4.24	got	11	3.15	get	15	4.18
think	140	3.66	suppose	64	3.38	think	49	3.99	seen	11	3.15	like	15	4.18
love	127	3.32	know	57	3.01	know	42	3.42	thought	11	3.15	love	15	4.18
hear	112	2.93	get	52	2.75	see	40	3.26	hope	10	2.87	know	13	3.62
know	112	2.93	work	48	2.54	love	35	2.85	going	9	2.58	live	13	3.62
suppose	103	2.69	hear	47	2.48	go	34	2.77	love	8	2.29	think	13	3.62
work	84	2.19	think	47	2.48	let	25	2.04	taken	8	2.29	write	13	3.62

Table 13: Examples of propositions and proposals.

Type of Exchange	
Proposition	Proposal
Exchange of information	Exchange of goods & services
Verbal response	Non-verbal response
Mental verbs of cognition (*know, think, suppose* etc.)	Mental verbs of desire (*hope, wish, want* etc.)
I know you are trying to do the best you can	*I wish you would write oftener*
I think you are growing smarter	*I hope you will send me the paper*
I suppose you are always busy	*I want you to give five shillings of mine to Mary*

Words in context: n-grams and clusters

Some of the observations above begin to piece together when the next test is carried out, by looking at n-grams. N-grams are: X number of words which appear consecutively Y number of times. The analyst can set the parameters, so, for example, using the n-gram function within Antconc the analyst could search for all 3-grams (three words appearing consecutively) which occur five times or more in the corpus. Table 14 gives a summary of the most frequently occurring 2, 3, 4, 5 and 6-grams.

Table 14 shows that the quantitative findings discussed in previous sections are partly realised in these n-grams, with the lexical verb *hope* followed by the modal auxiliary verb *will* ranking high across four of the five searches. However, this only reveals part of the picture – there are <274> instances of the 2-gram *I hope*, but only <58> instances of *I hope you will*. To get a fuller understanding of the phraseology surrounding a particular word or phrase Antconc has the capability to search for clusters. Figure 5 shows the three, four, five and six word clusters surrounding the phrase *I hope*.

The word tree presented in Figure 5 highlights the lexical and grammatical (lexicogrammatical) patterns surrounding *I hope*.[38] The diagram shows that not all options are equally probable. What most frequently follows *I hope*, in the Lough corpus, is the pronoun *you*; and what most frequently follows *I hope you* is the modal auxiliary *will*. As the tree branches out the lexicogrammatical choices become fewer, so *I hope you will not*, for example, occurs just twice in the corpus and in itself is not overly significant. Looking at the broader picture, however, through examining lots of evidence at the same time, a phraseological pattern for *I hope* begins to emerge. The question then would be whether this pattern is typical of this data set only, or typical of letters/personal narratives more generally? Is this phraseology used more by one author than another? Finally, what do these linguistic choices reveal about the author, their sex or their experiences?

The quantitative observations so far have teased out several possible lines of inquiry, which could be examined qualitatively. The analyst might, for example, investigate the low type/token ratio and whether or not the significant dip in ratio between Julia's and Annie's first and second letters (indicative of words and phrases being repeated) is typical or unusual amongst different authors (perhaps looking at female/male authors, or authors from different socioeconomic backgrounds). Are, for example, some

Table 14: Most frequent n-grams in the LOUGH Corpus.

2-gram	Freq.	3-gram	Freq.	4-gram	Freq.	5-gram	Freq.	6-gram	Freq.
I am	284	**I hope you**	95	**I hope you will**	58	few lines will find you	12	these few lines will find you	10
I hope	274	**hope you will**	61	love to you and	22	**I hope you will write**	11	**I hope you will write soon**	9
and I	149	I am sure	56	I am sending you	21	with love to you and	11	**hope you will write soon and**	8
to you	147	and I hope	45	**and I hope you**	19	**and I hope you will**	10	and let me know all the	7
you will	121	Dear Mother I	45	and let me know	17	these few lines will find	10	let me know all the newes	7
all the	120	love to you	42	give my love to	16	and let me know all	9	love to you and John and	7
hope you	114	I am glad	41	Dear Mother I am	15	**hope you will write soon**	9	few lines will find you all	6
I was	108	let me know	40	I am sure you	15	I am sending you some	8	**hope these few lines will find**	6
to her	108	are all well	35	to hear from you	15	let me know all the	8	**I hope these few lines will**	6

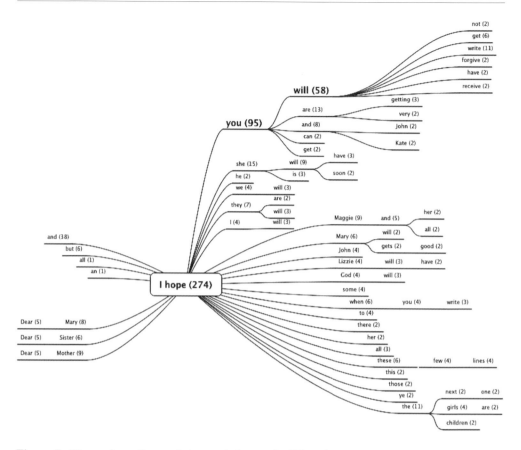

Figure 5: Three-, four-, five- and six-word clusters for 'I hope'.

authors more formulaic than others? To what extent is the main body of the letter formulaic? Which lexicogrammatical structures are being repeated and can any trends be
identified? Another line of inquiry might be to examine the high frequency of *I/you*
in the Lough letters and whether this is in some way genre indicative. Would a study
of other text types (narratives, diaries or spoken language) reveal similar findings? As
observed by Nicola McLelland, and supported in this study, *I* is more characteristic of
female authors; however, how is it being employed, in which context and when talking
about what?[39] Its use in projection clauses (as discussed in this article) is only part of
the picture. Alternatively, the analyst might choose to investigate the high frequency of
will and whether it is functioning in an epistemic or boulemic sense (to show probability or desire/volition). What other linguistic strategies are used to express modality?
Are there any gender or class differences in the use of modality? Arja Nurmi and
Minna Palander-Collins, for example, found little variation in modal usage according
to social differences; however, they did find some differences in usage between male
and female authors, with the modals *will* and *would* being more typical of female
writers.[40] Closer investigation showed, however, that these findings varied depending
on the author/recipient relationship.

For the present study, I am going to look in more detail at the high frequency
of mental verbs of cognition and desire, which occur after the pronoun *I* as part

```
ting you know all the News I think I keep  you Well posted. if I did not Write but
my love to them all when you write I mail  you some papers every week hope you get
for her is Kate with her in Galway I sent  you some Transcripts two weeks ago when
d] we are very well at present and I thank  you very much for them nice post cards
a letter from you in answer to one I wrote you the first week in September. I hope
```

Figure 6: Examples of Non-Projecting Structures.

of a projecting clause. I am especially interested in exploring the function of these clauses and what they might reveal about the author/recipient relationships in the Lough letters.

From quantitative to qualitative: concordance lines

I have chosen to explore projection clauses further as the quantitative findings so far appear to suggest that these structures (or phraseological patterns) are frequently used by the Lough sisters and may be indicative of a local grammar. The main pattern under investigation is: $I + V + you + (modal/aux) + V$ (as in *I hope you will write*). I have several questions to explore: which verbs (other than *hope*) most commonly occur in projecting clauses?; are there more projections of propositions (requiring a verbal response – typically expressed through a cognitive verb)? or are there more projections of proposals (requiring a non-verbal response – typically expressed through a verb of desire)?; which auxiliary verbs most commonly follow *you* in the projected clause?; does this pattern $(I + V + you + (modal/aux) + V)$ attract similar text types? – is it genre-indicative?; is this pattern used equally by all three sisters?, or does one sister use it more than the others? and finally, is this phraseology used as frequently by male and/or other female authors?

I began by carrying out a search on *I * you* ('*' is a wildcard meaning 'any word which appears in X position') in the LOUGH Corpus. As the findings in Table 15 illustrate, the search brought up <188> instances of this structure. There are three things to note at this stage. First, this search did not bring up all projection clauses, but only those where *I* occurs one word to the left of the wildcard '*'. As shown in Table 9, previously, *I* can sometimes occur several words to the left of the pronoun *you*, as in *I hope when you write again you* . . . ; however, for this investigation I focused only on those (most common) structures where *I* occurs directly to the left of the mental verb. Second, the search produced only those projection clauses containing the pronouns *I/you* (separate searches would need to be carried out to identify clauses containing *I + you/he/she/they*, etc.). Third, not all instances of *I * you* are projection clauses. In <41> out of the <188> occurrences *you* is the Object of the main clause (rather than the Subject of a projected clause).

After having removed the non-projecting structures, there are <147> occurrences of *I * you* functioning as projection clauses in the LOUGH Corpus.

The auxiliary modals that most frequently follow *you* are listed in Table 16. The data shows that *will* is by far the most common modal used in this structure.

The verbs in Table 15 can be categorised in terms of the experience they are construing. For example, *assure, tell, thank* and *told* could be described as communicating or saying verbs; *dream, hope, know, like, see, suppose, think, want, wish* and *wonder* could be described as mental verbs of cognition, perception or desire; and *keep, mail,*

Table 15: Search results for *I * you* in the LOUGH Corpus.

I * you	Freq.
assure	4
dreamed	1
hope	95
keep	1
knew	1
know / no	11
like	1
mail	1
received	4
see	2
send	1
sent	5
suppose	28
tell	1
thank	3
think	7
told	1
want	5
wish	11
wonder	1
write	1
wrote	3
TOTAL	**188**

Table 16: Auxiliary modals following *I * you* in the LOUGH Corpus.

	Modal V.	Raw freq.
I * You	can	3
	could	4
	must	1
	ought	1
	will	42

receive, send, sent, write, wrote could be categorised as verbs of action. The data shows that the pattern *I + Verb + You* seems to attract more mental verbs, with *hope, know/no, suppose* and *wish* being the most common.

Of the <147> occurrences of *I * you* functioning as a projection clause, the most common verb to occur in this pattern is *hope*. As shown in Figure 5 earlier, over half of all instances of *I hope you* (<58> out of <95>) are followed by *will*. In these instances the author is placing a mild obligation on the recipient to do something – usually write, or forgive for lack of communication. Of the remaining occurrences of *I hope you*, most are standard, formulaic phrases which one might expect in any letter (*I hope you are well, I hope you get good health, I hope you can read my writing*). These, very

```
pe you are getting along good and I Know you are trying to do the best you can I
pe you are very well yourself and I Know you are trying to do the best you can I
every as I would wish for you and I know you are doing the best you can in your
must try and keep well if you can I know you never can stop thinking of Dear Annie
haps sooner than you think [sic]  I know you would grow young again [Page Four]
not get this before Christmas and I know you would not be happy if you did not
I did not write till the last for I knew you would worry and I was sure you would
```

Figure 7: Sample Concordance Lines for 'I KNOW YOU'.

```
y glad I made the change although I think you and mother did not like it by your
r she is going to write this week I think you are growing smarter all the time to
er in your own dear hand writing. I think you done just splendid It was a very nice
r if those things of mine fit her I think you have been more than generous to give
I get her next letter [--damaged] I think you two ought to be very comfortable
y cold weather Julie wrote to you I think you will have hers first I suppose she
to see such style when I go home  I think it is nonsense I think you ought to burn
```

Figure 8: Sample Concordance Lines for 'I THINK YOU'.

```
ve some very hansom under clothes I wish you could see them evry stitch of clothes
ible cold and talk of snow drifts I wish you could see some of them this last week
und the skirt 20 yds all together I wish you could see it I think I will send you a
ie will come to see you often and I wish you could go see her sometimes give my
icture in my next letter if I can I Wish you would try an have some of your picturs
letter and glad you are all well  I wish you would write oftener but I suppose you
ve but I take pleasure in sewing. I wish you was near so I could help you   you
```

Figure 9: Sample Concordance Lines for 'I WISH YOU'.

```
s 16 years she has only two girls I suppose you all read about our presidents death
would wish so much to see you all I suppose you all felt bad for Parnell it was too
mas  how is the winter over there I suppose you are bussey getting ready for xmis
ends here are very well and Alice I suppose you are going to school and is at home
Mary gets good health Dear Mother I suppose you were worried some about that letter
that ye well spend a happy xmas   I suppose you will be getting good xmas presents
```

Figure 10: Sample Concordance Lines for 'I SUPPOSE YOU'.

formulaic, projection structures are commonly found in the openings and closings of letters (as also noted by Dossena) and are described by Mike Scott and Chris Tribble as channel maintainers, helping to sustain the lines of communication between author and recipient.[41]

The Figures above show sample concordance lines for the other main projection clauses.

Looking at the concordance lines for *I know you* and *I think you*, first of all, it appears that *know* and *think* in these clauses are being used as subjective modality markers, rather than true mental projection verbs. These phrases seem to be used when expressing sympathy, or as a way of showing solidarity. The author, in these lines, places themselves in the position of the recipient, imagining their behaviour, what they are doing and how they are feeling. In the case of *I wish* (specifically, *I wish you could see* <freq. 3>) this empathy is reversed and the recipient is invited to imagine something from the author's perspective. Other instances of *I wish* are used to admonish – *I wish you would write oftener* and *I wish you would try to have your photo taken*.

Whereas *wish* is being used to express boulemic modality (the author, in these instances, is expressing a desire for the recipient to do something (*write oftener*) or

Table 17: Frequency of I * you.

	Freq. of I * You	Normalised
Annie	104	5.49
Julia	57	4.65
Lizzie	10	2.87
Alice	17	4.74
LOUGH	188	**4.91**
FEMALE Ref.	35	**2.12**
MALE Ref.	23	**1.11**

experience something (*see her*)), *suppose*, on the other hand, is being used to express epistemic modality. With a degree of certainty, albeit hedged, the author is predicting what the recipient is thinking, feeling or doing. The use of epistemic modality, in these occurrences, emphasises, strengthens and reinforces familial bonds – bonds that are based on past, shared experiences between the two participants. In saying *I suppose you were worried some about that letter* the author is doing more than empathising – she is showing a connection with the recipient which is based on previous and exist-ing knowledge between the two correspondents, which transcends space and time – the message being: 'based on past experiences, and knowing you in the intimate way that I do, my guess is that you are feeling worried'.

The type of projection taking place in these concordance lines (except for instances of *wish*) is a proposition, where the mental verb is one of cognition (*know*, *think*, *suppose*). These projections of propositions require a verbal response, placing a mild obligation on the recipient to (verbally) acknowledge and address the points being raised. These clauses, then, help to facilitate the interactive nature of the letter – establishing and maintaining a dialogue between the two participants. However, as discussed earlier in this article, the most frequently occurring verb in the pattern *I * you* is *hope*, often used to project a proposal (i.e. something which requires a non-verbal response, as in *I hope you will try and be very happy and enjoy yourself*). A closer look at the distributional trends of these *I * you* structures shows that whereas *I hope you* more typically appears in the openings and closing of the letters, *I think/know/suppose you* tends to occur more frequently in the main body.

Having carried out a search on the projection clause *I * you* in the LOUGH Corpus I then carried out the same search, but this time looking at each subcorpus to see whether one sister uses this structure more than others. The same search was also carried out using the MALE and FEMALE reference corpora to see whether any gender differences (concerning the use of projection clauses) could be identified. The findings are shown in Table 17. Looking at the normalised figures, the data suggests that there is no significant difference in the usage of this structure between Annie, Julia and Alice, although Lizzie seems to use *I * you* much less than her siblings. The data also suggests that female authors use this structure more than male authors; however this is a very general and tentative finding as both reference corpora contain a mixture of authors from different socioeconomic backgrounds, making it difficult to draw any specific conclusions. Indeed, the same search, but this time using a much larger

Table 18: Frequency of I * You (+ Modal).

Corpus	I+1,2you+will	I+1,2you+can	I+1,2you+could
usephem	35.4	4	2.6
brephem	16.6	2.4	1.1
usspok	**13.3**	**58.3**	**18.8**
brbooks	7.4	7.5	4.8
brspok	**4.6**	**53.5**	**27.7**
usbooks	4.5	6.4	3.7
sunnow	3.8	4.1	2.9
strathy	3.1	3.8	2.6
brmags	2.4	4.7	2.2
indy	1.9	2.7	1.2
npr	1.7	11.3	6
usacad	1.6	1.6	0
guard	1.5	2.7	1.4
times	1.5	2.8	1.4
oznews	1.3	2.2	2.2
newsci	1	1.1	0.5
bbc	17	1.6	0.6
usnews	9	1	0.8
wbe	5	0.8	0.5
econ	5	0.3	0.1

(450 million word), contemporary reference corpus (the Bank of English),[42] showed that this structure most commonly occurs in spoken language (see Table 18 – 'brspok' refers to the British spoken language subsection of the corpus and 'usspok' refers to the US spoken language subsection), which could mean that the differences in usage of *I * you* are more indicative of differences in educational background, with letters that adopt a more colloquial, speech-like style making greater use of projection clauses.

Discussion and conclusions

At the beginning of this article I proposed a method of inquiry based on the theory and techniques of corpus linguistics. Taking simple frequency data as the starting point, I was alerted to certain linguistic patterns, which an ordinary reading of the letters may not have allowed. The language contained within the letters was first taken out of its context; it was reorganised to reveal recurring linguistic features worth further, more qualitative, investigation. The findings were then considered within the situational and cultural context of international migration to try and build a picture of how, through letters, family bonds were changed and maintained over space and time.

The approach this article adopts starts with individual words and then examines how those words behave in sentences. What emerges is a specific phraseological pattern (*I + V + you + (modal/aux) + V*), which, further comparative investigations seem to suggest, is used more by female authors than male authors. These projecting structures place the recipient (*you*) – in this case, usually the mother or sister, Mary – as the Subject of the projected clause. However, at the same time, they also place the author (or more specifically the author's expectations, needs or desires) in the sentence initial position. In other words, these structures lead with some expectation of the author that is highlighted before we reach the main point of the sentence, which requires action, whether verbal or non-verbal, on the part of the recipient. The function of these clauses is to project an imagined narrative onto those back home, arguably serving to maintain a psychological link between the emigrant and her family in Ireland. It is through these, somewhat mundane, repeated phraseological patterns that familial relationships are strengthened and reinforced.

The approach taken in this article is very selective. As mentioned earlier, the initial quantitative investigations highlighted several possible lines of inquiry; however, I chose to follow just one of those, while ignoring others. What this approach does offer, however, is a clear, data-led rationale for choosing to examine certain linguistic features in the first place. The numbers themselves are not problematic, nor, necessarily, are the statistical measures or tests that are applied. What, arguably, is problematic are the research questions that are asked in the first place, the data that is used to explore those questions, and/or the conclusions that are later inferred from the results. McLelland's study, discussed earlier, shows how statistics cannot be taken at face value, but should be tested, re-tested and tested again in different ways, against different data sets and by scholars from different disciplinary perspectives.[43] Each line of inquiry will provide different findings, but combined will allow for a fuller, more complete profiling of the female experience of migration. The present study found that a certain pattern appears to be used more by female authors; however until this finding is tested against other data sets (taking into account factors such as social class, educational background, frequency of writing and so on) it is difficult to speak conclusively about the results. Nevertheless, the methodology proposed here is transparent and replicable. The results can be tested, challenged, rejected or confirmed and it is through this process that nuances relating to gender history can begin to emerge.

In many ways this article has brought up more questions than it has provided answers, but one of its main aims was to demonstrate how quantitative methods of analysis might tease out interesting linguistic features for further (quantitative *and* qualitative) analysis. This article has put forward a complementary methodology for examining gender history. It has highlighted some of the possibilities and challenges of using quantitative methods to support, build-on or challenge more qualitative research. Equally, however, it is hoped that some of the quantitative findings discussed here will be taken up by scholars using more qualitative approaches, providing new layers of meaning to the quantitative findings, and, ultimately, the individual emigrants whom these numbers represent.

Notes

1. See Kerby A. Miller with David N. Doyle and Patricia Kelleher, 'For Love and Liberty: Irish Women, Migration and Domesticity in Ireland and America, 1815–1920', in P. O'Sullivan (ed.), *The Irish World Wide* (Leicester: Leicester University Press, 1995), pp. 54–61.
2. David A. Gerber, *Authors of Their Lives: The Personal Correspondence of British Immigrants to North America in the Nineteenth Century* (New York: New York University Press, 2006), p. 31.
3. William I. Thomas and Florian Znaniecki, *The Polish Peasant in America*, 5 vols, 1918-1920 (2 vols. Repr. New York: Dover Publications Inc., 1958). Charlotte Erickson, *Invisible Immigrants: The Adaptation of English and Scottish Immigrants in Nineteenth-Century America* (London: The London School of Economics and Political Sciences, 1972); Kerby A. Miller, *Emigrants and Exiles: Ireland and the Irish*

Exodus to North America (Oxford: Oxford University Press, 1985) and Walter D. Kamphoefner, Wolfgang Helbich and Ulrike Sommer (eds), *News from the Land of Freedom: German Immigrants Write Home* (Ithaca and London: Cornell University Press, 1988).

4. Gerber, *Authors of Their Lives*, p. 32.
5. Sonia Cancian, *Families, Lovers and their Letters: Italian Postwar Migration to Canada* (Manitoba: University of Manitoba Press, 2010); Kathleen A. DeHaan, 'Negotiating the Transnational Moment: Immigrant Letters as Performance of a Diasporic Identity', *National Identities* 12 (2010), pp. 107–31; Anna De Fina and Kendall A. King, 'Language Problem or Language Conflict? Narratives of Immigrant Women's Experiences in the US', *Discourse Studies* 13 (2011), pp. 163–88.
6. Stephan Elspaß, 'Standard German in the 19th-century? (Counter-) Evidence from the Private Correspondence of "Ordinary People"', in Andrew R. Linn and Nicola McLelland (eds), *Standardization: Studies from the Germanic Languages* (Amsterdam: Benjamins, 2002), pp. 43–65; Nicola McLelland, '"Doch mein Mann möchte doch mal wissen…" A Discourse Analysis of 19th-century Emigrant Men and Women's Private Correspondence', in Stephan Elspaß, Nils Langer, Joachim Scharloth and Wim Vandenbussche (eds), *Germanic Language Histories from Below (1700–2000)* (Berlin: De Gruyter, 2007), pp. 45–68; Marina Dossena, '"As This Leaves Me at Present" – Formulaic Usage, Politeness and Social Proximity in Nineteenth-Century Scottish Emigrants' Letters', in Elspaß, Langer, Scharloth and Vandenbussche (eds), *Germanic Language Histories from Below*, pp. 1–30; Marina Dossena, '"Many Strange and Peculiar Affairs": Description, Narration and Evaluation in Scottish Emigrants' Letters of the Nineteenth Century', *Scottish Language* 27 (2008), pp. 1–18; Arja Nurmi and Minna Palander-Collin, 'Letters as a Text Type: Interacting in Writing', in Marina Dossena and Ingrid Tieken-Boon van Ostade (eds), *Studies in Late Modern English Correspondence: Methodology and Data* (Bern: Peter Lang, 2008), pp. 21–50.
7. The term 'phraseology', in this article, refers to the way in which a word typically behaves in context – both the grammatical position it tends to adopt and the words it tends to collocate with. Phraseology and collocation are linked, but whereas collocation tends to refer to word pairings, phraseology refers to extended patterns, where meaning might be carried over several words. The regularities (or patterning) and subtleties in the usage of a word, Hunston argues, are 'difficult to intuit, and [are] observable only when a lot of evidence is seen together': Susan Hunston, *Corpora in Applied Linguistics* (Cambridge: Cambridge University Press, 2002), p. 12. Idioms are fixed expressions and linked to metaphor and figures of speech, but could also be described as phraseology – whereas idioms tend to fixed and self-contained, phraseology is more open to subtle variations.
8. Dossena 'As This Leaves Me at Present'.
9. For full details of the design and contents of the corpus see: Marina Dossena, 'Towards a Corpus of Nineteenth-century Scottish Correspondence', *Linguistica e Filologia* 18 (2004), pp. 195–214.
10. Dossena, 'As This Leaves Me at Present', p. 21.
11. McLelland, 'Doch mein Mann möchte doch mal wissen…'.
12. Studies include: Victoria L. Bergvall, Janet M. Bing, and Alice F. Freed (eds), *Rethinking Language and Gender Research* (London: Longman, 1996); Jennifer Cheshire and Peter Trudgill (eds), *The Sociolinguistics Reader, vol. 2: Gender and Discourse* (London: Arnold, 1998); Janet Holmes, *Women, Men and Politeness* (London: Longman, 1995); Helga Kotthoff and Ruth Wodak (eds), *Communicating Gender in Context* (Amsterdam: Benjamins, 1997); Mary M. Talbot, *Language and Gender: An Introduction* (Oxford: Blackwell, 1998); Ruth Wodak, *Gender and Discourse* (London: Sage Publications, 1997).
13. McLelland, 'Doch mein Mann möchte doch mal wissen…', p. 46.
14. McLelland, 'Doch mein Mann möchte doch mal wissen…', p. 55.
15. See studies by Elspaß, and Nurmi and Palander-Collin, previously mentioned. Elspaß, 'Standard German in the 19th-century?'; Nurmi and Palander-Collin 'Letters as a Text Type: Interacting in Writing'.
16. Hunston, *Corpora in Applied Linguistics*, p. 3. The epistemological assumptions that underpin corpus linguistics as a methodology were also discussed by Professor Guy Cook at the 2011 Sinclair Open Lecture at the University of Birmingham.
17. Paul Baker, *Using Corpora in Discourse Analysis* (London: Continuum, 2006).
18. Hunston, *Corpora in Applied Linguistics*, p. 2.
19. Hunston, *Corpora in Applied Linguistics*, p. 28.
20. Hunston, *Corpora in Applied Linguistics*, p. 26.
21. Hunston, *Corpora in Applied Linguistics*, p. 2.
22. See especially Miller, Doyle and Kelleher, 'For Love and Liberty and Miller, *Emigrants and Exiles*.
23. Arnold Schrier, *Ireland and the Irish Emigration, 1850–1900* (Minneapolis: University of Minnesota Press, 1958).

24. Michael Stubbs, 'Conrad in the computer: examples of quantitative stylistic methods', in Ronald Carter and Peter Stockwell (eds), *The Language and Literature Reader* (London: Routledge, 2008), pp. 230–43.

25. Laurence Anthony, 'AntConc Version 3.2.2' (Tokyo, Japan: Waseda University, 2011). <http://www.antlab.sci.waseda.ac.jp/>.

26. Paul Rayson, 'Wmatrix' (Lancaster University, 2009). <http://ucrel.lancs.ac.uk/wmatrix/>.

27. Adam Kilgarriff, Pavel Rychly, P. Smrz. and D. Tugwell, 'The Sketch Engine. Proc. EURALEX 2004', (Lorient, France), pp. 105–16. <http://www.sketchengine.co.uk>.

28. Mike Scott, *WordSmith Tools Version 4* (Oxford: Oxford University Press, 2004).

29. Chris Greaves, 'Concgram.' (John Benjamins Publishing Company, 2005). <http://benjamins.com/# catalog/softwares/cls.1>.

30. Note: Antconc does not distinguish between word class (unless the data is tagged for Parts of Speech), so HOME, whether it was used as a noun or an adjective, would be categorised as one 'type'.

31. Michael J. Toolan, *Narrative Progression in the Short Story* (Amsterdam: John Benjamins Publishing Company, 2009).

32. McLelland, 'Doch mein Mann möchte doch mal wissen . . .'; Nurmi and Palander-Collin 'Letters as a Text Type.

33. Note: all letters were included in this investigation (including letters where the authorship is unknown), provided the letter was specifically addressed to either 'mother', 'mother/father' or 'sister'.

34. For more information on metalanguage and metadiscursive phrases see: James Paul Gee, *Social Linguistics and Literacies: Ideology in Discourse* (London: Taylor & Francis, 2008); Annelie Ädel, *Metadiscourse in L1 and L2 English* (Amsterdam: John Benjamins Publishing Company, 2006).

35. Micheal A. K. Halliday and Christian Matthiessen, *An Introduction to Functional Grammar* (London: Arnold, 2004), p. 170.

36. Halliday and Matthiessen, *An Introduction to Functional Grammar*, p. 206.

37. Halliday and Matthiessen, *An Introduction to Functional Grammar*, p. 461.

38. The term lexicogrammar suggests that lexis and grammar cannot be separated, but are instead two ends of the same cline.

39. McLelland, 'Doch mein Mann möchte doch mal wissen . . .'.

40. Nurmi and Palander-Collin 'Letters as a Text Type'.

41. Dossena, 'As This Leaves Me at Present'; Mike Scott and Chris Tribble, *Textual Patterns: Key Words and Corpus Analysis in Language Education* (Amsterdam: John Benjamins Publishing Company, 2006).

42. Bank of English (COBUILD and The University of Birmingham, 1991 [2002]). <http://www.titania.bham.ac.uk/docs/svenguide.html>.

43. McLelland, 'Doch mein Mann möchte doch mal wissen . . .'.

5 Beyond Constructivism?: Gender, Medicine and the Early History of Sperm Analysis, Germany 1870–1900

Christina Benninghaus

Like any other kind of historiography, gender history has produced commonplaces and generalisations. Among these is the notion that, starting from the eighteenth century, the female body was pathologised and interpreted not only as a somewhat less perfect version of the human body but as fundamentally different from the male body, even as abnormal and deviant. In his groundbreaking study *Making Sex: Body and Gender from the Greeks to Freud*, Thomas Laqueur argues that this shift is to be understood as a reaction to broader political and cultural developments and does not primarily mirror changes in medical knowledge. According to his widely recognised interpretation, bourgeois society needed new reasons for the subordination of women.

The proposition that medical and scientific knowledge is produced within social settings and that it is profoundly affected by broader cultural changes and beliefs has proved immensely productive for the gender history of science and medicine. However, a constructivist perspective has not always encouraged historians to pay close attention to the scientific contexts, procedures and instruments, the history of which they were studying. 'Social essentialism' – here understood as a tendency to attribute historical change a priori to broader social or cultural, rather than internal scientific or medical developments, and to interpret innovations in science and medicine as a direct reflection of cultural demands or problems – has at times hampered advances in gender history. Likewise, the political aim of criticising the medical treatment of women has sometimes led to a certain indifference regarding the fate of male patients.

Over the last two decades, however, historical studies on the medicalisation of the male body, impotence and spermatorrhea, the climacterium virile and experiments with rejuvenation have challenged the familiar idea that it was predominantly the female body that was pathologised. I want to contribute to this research by looking at the ways in which male sterility developed into a medical object and into a self-evident part of popular knowledge. I am especially interested in the emergence of sperm analysis as a modern medical technology, which around 1890 came to be seen as an integral part of infertility diagnosis.

On a methodological level, my paper tries to avoid the pitfalls of social essentialism by drawing on Actor-Network-Theory (ANT). Developed in the 1980s in the field of

Gender History Across Epistemologies, First Edition. Edited by Donna R. Gabaccia and Mary Jo Maynes.
Chapters © 2013 The Authors. Book compilation © 2013 Blackwell Publishing Ltd.

science and technology studies, ANT is less a theory than a descriptive method.[1] It aims to understand events and processes of innovation by looking at the way in which humans and non-humans or objects interact and form associations. As my case study hopefully will demonstrate, and as I will discuss at the end of my paper, ANT allows for a more nuanced understanding of the processes that made 'male sterility' happen. It does so by encouraging us to look at the interplay between bodies and instruments, texts and disciplines, doctors and patients.

Within gender history, dichotomies between biology and culture, between the material and the discursive, between sex and gender have long been discussed. Likewise questions of agency have been on the agenda for decades, and the relationship between shifts in gender relations and broader cultural, social and economic changes has always troubled gender historians who wanted to integrate gender history into broader contexts or to write long-term histories of gender. While I do not see ANT as the perfect answer to all these problems – why, indeed, should such an answer exist? – there is a striking resemblance between the issues that drive ANT and the salient questions of gender history. Empirically, my case study is based on published medical and popular texts that were written for a German-speaking audience and reflect the medical practice of German physicians. However, as will become apparent, the concern for male sterility was an international phenomenon.

Before turning to my case study, I want to reflect on the importance of social constructivism for gender history. In my view, the situation is somewhat paradoxical. While social constructivism has been criticised, and while a certain weariness of constructivist views has existed for years, constructivism lingers. In what follows, I will use the well-known narrative of the one-sex/two-sex model to elaborate on the attractiveness and the problems of social constructivism.

Social constructivism, gender history and the one-sex/two-sex narrative

During the 1980s and 1990s, social constructivism held sway in history and the social sciences. Familiar topics of social and political history were cast in a new light as historians tried to capture the communicative and symbolic processes by which 'imagined communities' like nations, social classes or generations were formed. Cultural practices and institutions were analysed to understand how the 'invention of traditions' was used to legitimise hierarchies, not only, but predominantly, in times of rapid social change.[2] Historians and sociologists of science used constructivism to analyse science as social interaction. They looked at the practices by which knowledge was created and paid special attention to paradigmatic shifts and the emergence of new concepts. Their work of de-naturalisation or de-legitimisation was directed at the image of scientific knowledge as objective, universal and non-historical.[3] Important studies claimed that not only methodologies and technologies, but even the scientific knowledge they produced, had to be interpreted as socially constructed. Hence authors like Nelly Oudshoorn came to challenge 'the idea that there is such a thing as a "natural" body' and studied how the biological 'facts' about hormones came into existence.[4] 'The myth of scientific heroes discovering the secrets of nature needs to be replaced by another image of science, an image which enables us to study how scientific facts are deeply embedded in society and culture'.[5]

In the history of medicine, constructivism was used to look at the processes in which medical knowledge was produced. The 'invention' not only of new forms of medical treatment – like organ transplantation – but also of diseases or medical problems like infertility was analysed.[6] Studies asked how the labelling of certain physical or psychological conditions as illness occurred. Special attention was paid to local circumstances – e.g. the rather unusual possibilities provided by the Parisian hospitals – which enabled the production of specific kinds of medical knowledge. The role of patients in negotiating concepts of disease and technologies of treatment was taken into account.[7]

Whether in political history, social history or the history of science and medicine, constructivism went against the grain of everyday thinking. It aimed to show that identities, knowledge and scientific objects normally perceived as 'natural' and self-evident were in fact socially produced and that histories of their 'invention' could be written. Common to these endeavours was an iconoclastic attitude, a concentration on analysing processes and practices and a fascination with moments of rapid change and innovation.

This was also the case in gender studies. Sex difference, masculinity and femininity – usually perceived as just a natural given – were shown to be performed in interactions and stabilised by institutions. To think of sex (and not only of gender) not as 'real' but as a result of representations and performance was extremely attractive and at least for a younger generation of feminists it felt instantly liberating.[8] As in the other historical and social sciences, social constructivism proved immensely productive and inspiring. It was an invitation to see the world with different eyes and to rewrite whiggish histories of scientific discoveries and medical success and of women's liberation as a side effect of modernity.

For feminist purposes, research challenging biologistic accounts of sex difference was especially interesting. Alongside sociological research on the performance of sex and gender or anthropological research on societies said to know more than two sexes, historical studies on the emergence of medical and biological knowledge about the sexes were read with much interest.

Thomas Laqueur's book, *Making Sex*, was probably the single most influential historical contribution in this field.[9] Two years after its first publication in English in 1990, it was also available in German, French and Italian. The book offered its readers a long-term perspective rather uncommon for historical studies, spanning two thousand years of history, 'from the Greeks to Freud', in fewer than 300 pages. The visual evidence, on which much of Laqueur's argument rests, seemed especially convincing and comprehensible even for readers not familiar with history. The early modern prints Laqueur reproduced show female genitals that do, indeed, look like penises. These images stuck in the mind.

In the context of gender studies, Laqueur's book and comparable texts, like Claudia Honegger's *Die Ordnung der Geschlechter*, met with fascination. Like anthropological research they were read as examples of a foreign world in which different concepts of sex and gender existed. To claim that 'for almost 2000 years people in Europe only had one and not two types of genitals: the female sexual organs were regarded simply as a variant of the male genitals, turned inside out', suggested that societies without a strictly binary gender order were possible and that the body was nothing more than a surface to be inscribed with varying meanings.[10] The time of the one-sex model appeared like a lost utopia.

Furthermore, the political stance taken by these studies fitted well into a widespread criticism of medicine and gynaecology as ways of subordinating women. They resonated with the aims of the feminist health movement of the 1980s. The very existence of gynaecology was not explained within a framework of increasing specialisation or professionalisation but was interpreted as an indication of the increasing pathologisation of the female body, a pathologisation which had to be fought.[11]

Hence, it is perhaps not surprising that the interest in this narrative has survived remarkably well. Readers of overviews on gender history and the history of medicine will almost necessarily encounter Laqueur's study and its terminology. With little variation, the story of the one-sex model and its replacement and the permanent pathologisation of female bodies is told over and over again:

> Prior to the Enlightenment, women appear to have been considered 'inferior' versions of men in medical terms, with men and women widely believed to represent two different forms of one essential sex, as represented by Laqueur's 'one-sex' model. Women were understood to possess the same basic reproductive structures as men, with the genitalia instead placed inside the body and the vagina considered an internal penis and the ovaries as testicles. A fundamental change is seen to have occurred in European attitudes towards human sexual anatomy over the eighteenth century, or earlier, whereby the two sexes began to be seen as opposites. Nonetheless the female reproductive organs, concealed within the abdominal cavity, continued to present medical challenges. Such challenges encouraged the continued characterisation of female biology as somehow problematic long after the death of the one-sex model.[12]

The one-sex/two-sex-narrative is still used as an analytic framework in recent historical literature.[13] It continues to be a favourite with sociological introductions to gender studies,[14] and it is used as a backdrop by authors in the field of men's studies who wish to underline the newness of their research agenda and find it useful to claim that in the past 'assumptions of gender difference led medical scientists to focus almost exclusively on the female reproductive system as an object of study'.[15] The one-sex/two-sex narrative is even used to back feminist criticism of current medical practices like the introduction of an HPV vaccination by pointing to the supposedly long history of women's pathologisation.[16]

That the one-sex/two-sex narrative has survived so well cannot be attributed to a lack of criticism. Rather, there seems to be an intellectual barrier, which discourages historical findings and controversies not congruent with the grand narrative of the 'making' of sex in the eighteenth or nineteenth centuries and the accompanying social construction of the female body as especially pathological, from entering sociological research and historical overviews. I want to highlight five areas of contention.

First, already in an early review of Thomas Laqueur's *Making Sex*, Katherine Park and Robert Nye argued against the claim that 'male scientists have always constructed the signs of sexual difference on women's "unstable" bodies'. Instead, Park and Nye suggested that men's bodies were also unstable. 'Men have historically held themselves to ideals of masculinity as unrealistic and coercive as anything they have imposed on women'.[17] Over the last two decades, a whole array of studies has been published which have demonstrated that the male body has indeed been an object of intense medical concern. Historical work on neurasthenia and shell shock, on masturbation and impotence, on spermatorrhoea, sterility and the climacterium virile and the corresponding attempts to rejuvenate the male body with the help of hormones or sterilisation have demonstrated that earlier assumptions that it would be impossible to write the history of the male body were wrong.[18] The image of the male body, which the medical and biological knowledge produced by nineteenth century experts conveys, is much less favourable than the older narrative seems to suggest. I will come back to this point later.

Second, the identification of a pre-modern one-sex model, proposed by Laqueur, has been called into question by a number of experts in the early modern period. They have criticised Laqueur for misinterpreting early modern medical concepts, for concentrating too much on Latin texts and for decontextualising the materials used.[19] Several authors have criticised the idea that early modern medical texts presented the male and female genitals as similar. According to these authors, it would be misleading to take comparisons and analogies drawn by contemporary authors as proof for a belief in the similarity of female and male genitals.[20] Furthermore, the very attempt to uncover a dominant model might be somewhat anachronistic. Early modern thinking about sex might be better characterised as showing an 'enduring synchronic diversity' as it came from different traditions, was produced in a variety of contexts and was influenced by new religious, philosophical and scientific ideas. Hence, in a recent article, Bethan Hindson has pointed out that sixteenth- and seventeenth-century attitudes towards menstruation were neither uniform nor predominantly negative but rather remarkably ambivalent and context specific.[21]

Third, the identification of the two-sex model as the dominant mode of thinking in modern medicine is problematic, to say the least. In fact, Laqueur himself suggested that during the nineteenth century one- and two-sex-models existed simultaneously. That bourgeois society indulged in an ideology of separate spheres might be safely assumed. Whether this necessarily translated into a belief in profound sexual difference in medicine might need further exploration. Within Laqueur's argumentation, to give an example, female orgasm plays an important role. According to his interpretation, the rejection of the idea that both men and women produced semen put an end to the belief that female orgasm was necessary for conception. 'Near the end of the century of Enlightenment, medical science and those who relied upon it ceased to regard the female orgasm as relevant to generation'.[22] However, a closer look at materials dealing with the diagnosis and treatment of infertility in married couples shows that discussions about the relationship between conception and female orgasm carried on much longer. In 1856, to give an example, a paper presented to the Berlin society of obstetrics reported on an inquiry among married couples on this question.[23] While the inquiry found that female orgasm was not necessary for conception, the question continued to be discussed. The idea that women could ovulate spontaneously or the notion that the uterus had to suck in the semen were supported by experiments on animals and by observations during medical examinations. As medical case records from the early twentieth century show, doctors treating infertile couples inquired about the sexual sensations experienced by their female patients. And advice manuals continued to argue that female orgasm was important for conception.[24] To live in a culture of separate spheres did not stop scientists, doctors and ordinary people from inquiring about, assuming and detecting similarities and analogies between male and female bodies.[25]

While the three lines of criticism mentioned so far point to empirical inconsistencies regarding the one-sex/two-sex narrative, more general questions arise if we look at the theoretical foundation of the concept. As a prime example of social constructivism, it is often referred to when scholars want to counter essentialist beliefs in the naturalness of sex. While it certainly works very well in this respect and, hence, is very useful, for example, in teaching gender history, a closer look at the ways in which Laqueur links shifts in medical knowledge to broader social and cultural changes reveals problems inherent to social constructivism.

As has been mentioned above, the one-sex/two-sex narrative relies on the assumption that the shift in medical concepts of sex emerged due to a growing need for a new justification for gender hierarchies. In a very well researched article, Michael Stolberg has questioned the validity of this explanation by pointing to inconsistencies in the periodisation offered by Laqueur and Schiebinger. According to Stolberg, an analysis of the dominant medical discourse shows that 'the shift toward explicit, anatomically based sexual dimorphism took place some two hundred years earlier' than Laqueur has suggested.[26] If this was indeed the case, Laqueur's argument that the two-sex model was invented because it suited enlightened thinkers who wished to justify the subordination of women, cannot be sustained. Not politics but developments in science and medicine, in theology and in certain social conditions seem to be the reason why the 'two-sex-model' was regarded as increasingly convincing in the sixteenth and seventeenth centuries. Stolberg does not intend to question constructivism as a methodological approach, but his critique of Laqueur points to one of the major problems of social constructivism: because causal relations are often extremely difficult to establish, historians can easily be tempted to point to even larger processes or events ('enlightenment', 'industrialisation', the 'First World War') when looking for possible explanations. As Stolberg's contribution shows, careful attention to chronology and a balanced consideration of internal (scientific, medical) developments and of specific social contexts that can be shown to have impacted on historical actors, are central to avoiding such pitfalls.[27]

I would like to raise a fifth problem which, however, does not concern the historical correctness of the one-sex/two-sex narrative or the methodological problem of establishing causal relations in history, but the historical usefulness of social constructivism more generally. In his introduction, Laqueur stated that he had not written his 'book as an explicit attack on the current claims of sociobiology'. Instead, he wanted to 'offer material for how powerful prior notions of difference or sameness determine what one sees and reports about the body'.[28] That historical research is relevant to political discourses is a position shared by many gender historians. However, to stress that *all* medical knowledge reflects cultural beliefs and that 'political questions regarding the nature of women' were *always* at stake when biology was discussed, can easily lead not only to a rather dismissive attitude towards that knowledge, and the people who produced it, but to a reading of history that is ahistorical or 'flat'.

This problem has also concerned critics of constructivism working in the field of science and technology studies. They have identified a certain 'joy in repetition': 'Even today, much research . . . is designed to demonstrate that this scientific truth or that technology is constructed socially'.[29] Lorraine Daston, therefore, welcomes that the history of science has become more historically disciplined: 'To claim that science is socially constructed is to impugn both validity and honesty . . . In contrast, to historicise the category of the fact, objectivity, or proof is not thereby to debunk it, no more than to write the history of the special theory of relativity thereby undermines it'.[30]

It might be difficult to approach past knowledge about sex with an equally detached attitude. But if gender historians work from the assumption that biological or medical knowledge generally and predominantly reflected an attempt to justify the subordination of women, that 'it is *always* woman's sexuality that is being constituted', they might be reluctant to engage thoroughly with the history of this knowledge.[31] Already in 1993, Ludmilla Jordanova cautioned gender historians to distance themselves from their own ideas about gender:

> If this is not done, scholarly reaction is likely to be angry, even hostile to past ways of imagining gender. Thus some historians of science and medicine have construed the dichotomies around masculine and feminine as directly oppressive to women, it is as if they blame them for creating societies that think differently about gender from our own . . . If some illnesses, such as hysteria and chlorosis, were associated more with women than with men, more than labelling was involved. If differences between male and female bodies were elaborated to suit existing preconceptions, their plausibility still needs explanation.[32]

While the political agenda of social constructivism helped gender studies of science and medicine and gender history to gain momentum, the extent to which the historical analysis profits from social constructivism has been questioned. As Joan Scott has pointed out, the constructivist position which is at the heart of 'gender' as a category might not have served us very well in understanding how processes of knowledge production regarding sex have worked. According to Scott, the commitment of many gender historians to show that scientific knowledge was socially constructed almost necessarily meant that internal dynamics within the sciences were underestimated.[33]

In recent years, a more historically disciplined approach has proved to be very productive in furthering our understanding of the ways in which scientific knowledge and medical practices emerged and were stabilised and how, if at all, this was connected to changes in gender relations or concepts of sex difference. Only in recent years, to give an example, have we learnt more about the rather disturbing origins of the category of 'gender' as it was developed in the context of psychological and medical experiments on intersexuality.[34] It is a highly charged term originally invented by those who wanted to prove experimentally that sex was malleable. By historicising 'gender' we learn more about the biases and preconceptions that it entailed and that might shape and hamper research in gender history.

New historical studies on the body, to give another example, try to go beyond the familiar dichotomy of essentialism versus constructivism. They understand bodies as historically produced materialities which are shaped over the life course by a complex interplay of nature and culture. Following such an approach, a historical study of the body will not restrict itself to discourses, nor will it perceive of sex as a question of performance only. Rather, bodies will be understood as 'simultaneously composed of genes, hormones, cells and organs – all of which influence health and behaviour – and of culture and history'.[35] While the political stance associated with gender history is rarely openly criticised, there seems to be a quiet move towards post-constructivist approaches with their strong interest in reconstructing practices and processes and in paying attention to materialities, localities and internal dynamics.

'Cherchez l'homme' – male sterility and the making of sperm testing, 1860–1890

In 1891, Meyer's *Konversationslexikon*, one of the leading German encyclopaedias, published a supplement to its fourth edition. A year before, the fifteenth volume had included an article on infertility, which spoke only of women. The supplement, however, offered another entry 'Unfruchtbarkeit (Sterilität), männliche'. It stated that male infertility had recently received growing attention and that it could be caused by syphilis, tuberculosis or cancer but was mainly due to inflammations following an infection with gonorrhoea. Readers were informed that sterility was different from impotence and that it could be caused by aspermatism – the lack of semen – or by azoospermia – the lack of spermatozoa in the semen. The latter condition was said to be much more common and something that could be assessed only if the 'seemingly completely normal semen' was examined under a microscope.[36]

The article indicates that by the early 1890s, male infertility had become an element of public knowledge. In the decades before, a redefinition of the phenomenon of male sterility had taken place within the medical community. It had been dealt with both by gynaecologists writing on infertility and by venereologists, dermatologists and general practitioners who considered male sterility in the context of pathologies of the male genital system like spermatorrhea and impotence.[37]

Male sterility had become a subject of medical monographs, handbooks and dissertations, and it was also included in the general medical literature on infertility.[38] Hence, when Paul Müller – professor of obstetrics and gynaecology at Berne – published his medical compendium *Infertility in Marriage* in 1885, he included chapters on sperm production, and on impotence and male sterility and its diagnosis and treatment, devoting forty of his 200 pages explicitly to the study of the male reproductive body.[39] In the following years, the interest in male sterility increased even further. When Enoch Heinrich Kisch, professor at the University of Prague and practitioner at the famous spa of Marienbad, frequented by many childless women, published his handbook, *The Sterility of Women, Its Causes and Its Treatment* in 1886, he included eleven pages on azoospermia and a list of forty articles and books relevant to the problem. In the second edition of his book, published in 1895, Kisch devoted more space to the topic of male sterility and the list of relevant literature now comprised 158 titles. Obviously the topic had gained importance.[40]

Starting from the late 1880s, new ideas about male sterility also entered advice literature addressed to women or to infertile couples. The second edition of a medical handbook for women, *Die Frau als Gattin und Mutter*, published in 1889 stated explicitly that men were more often responsible for the childlessness of a marriage because they often had been infected with a venereal disease which caused their semen to become 'watery' and which reduced the number of spermatozoa.[41] In her *Frauenbuch*, a medical self-help book for women first published in 1896, Hope Bridget Adams estimated that in seven out of ten infertile marriages, the problem was caused by the husband either because he was sterile himself or because he had infected his wife with gonorrhoea.[42] Another manual specifically addressed to childless couples and published in 1891, contained a chapter entitled, 'The Sterility of the Husband and its Hygiene', in which the author repeated four times that 'impotentia generandi' (sterility) was nothing a man could feel: 'To know about this form of impotence is of greatest importance. Unfortunately, the person involved hardly ever knows about it. This is the case because any outward signs of a disease are missing and only the doctor using the microscope can detect the illness'.[43]

Towards the end of the nineteenth century, male sterility and its association with missing spermatozoa had clearly become part of the collective imagination. Doctors and patients were advised that sperm analysis was to be used in all cases of infertility in a marriage. As one practitioner put it in an article published in 1880: 'Truly, in contrast to the well-known criminological demand "cherchez la femme!", often it ought to be "cherchez l'homme" in pending cases of sterility'.[44]

The image of sperm cells frantically moving about slashing their tails is a familiar part of our visual universe. We are used to the association of motility and fecundity and take it for granted that sperm tests allow a good estimate of a man's reproductive abilities. Hence, it seems only logical that medical experts recommended sperm testing and believed in its ability to tell the 'truth' about the reproductive capacities of men. The introduction of sperm analysis could thus be told as a rather convincing example for the advances of modern medicine.

A more critical view could be developed by looking at the gender concepts presented in the texts just mentioned. A discourse analysis of these medical articles, talks and monographs would show that the texts construe male sterility as a hitherto neglected, but legitimate, object of medical practice. Claiming new territory for medical intervention, the male body is represented as a dangerous source of venereal disease, emitting poison instead of healthy seeds. The women, by contrast, are presented as innocent brides who are easily infected with, and rendered sterile by, gonorrhoea. They seem to be passive victims of the disease and of their husbands, but also of ruthless gynaecologists eager to perform unnecessary operations and of their own uncontrollable desire for children. Bourgeois gender concepts typical of the late nineteenth century are clearly evoked and an obvious interest in the forging of professional identities can be detected. Medical experts employing 'rational' forms of treatment are represented as impartial arbitrators using the microscope to detect the truth and acting in the best interests of science, their patients and a society dependent on smoothly functioning families and stable gender norms.

I will, however, develop a third approach here, more congruent with current approaches to the history of science and medicine, which aims at understanding how the new awareness and procedures came into being and how they developed into a seemingly unproblematic part of our world. Historians of science and medicine have shown that such self-evident understanding is a result of complex processes of negotiation and interaction – among experts, between doctors and patients but also between bodies, instruments and humans.[45] If it had not proved to be rather misleading, 'construction' would in fact be a very good word to capture the energy that went into the creation, circulation and stabilisation of facts and methods. In the history of medicine a number of attempts have been made to craft narratives that pay attention to practices, processes and networks. They share a fascination with dynamics and actors and refrain from reducing the past to discourses, despite their use of texts as their main source. It is beyond the scope of this article to do justice to the range of approaches or to discuss the potential of studies aiming for example, at writing the 'biographies of disease'.[46] Instead of launching into a theoretical or historiographical discussion of various approaches, I want to show how my own research developed as I began to approach it through Actor-Network-Theory.

In his chapter, 'Science's Blood Flow', published as part of *Pandora's Hope: Essays on the Reality of Science Studies*, Bruno Latour has suggested a kind of routine to reconstruct the ways in which scientific facts come into existence, gain stability and remain alive. He encourages us to look very closely at the networks which are formed as experts, things, collaborators and the wider public interact. For analytical purposes, these tightly knotted networks might be unravelled so that different 'loops' can be distinguished. Following Latour's suggestions, I will look at the instruments and concepts available to gynaecologists and venereologists and the methods of sperm collecting they developed (loop 1), at the ways in which colleagues could be persuaded to approve of the procedures (loop 2), at the intention and behaviour of patients who had to comply (loop 3) and at the popularisation of medical knowledge about infertility (loop 4). My aim is to reach a better understanding of the dynamics which led to the establishment of sperm analysis and, more generally, to an awareness of the possibility of male sterility in the years between 1860 and 1900.

My analysis is based on printed materials from the time period studied. These consist mainly of medical articles and monographs, but include advice literature and other forms of popular writings. Priority is given to texts available to the German-speaking medical community. This includes texts produced by emigrants but written in German, translations of English or French publications into German, as well as reports about foreign research published in German medical journals or included in overviews of the current literature. For a study using ANT, medical case records or private papers of individual experts would make the most obvious material. While the larger research project, in the context of which this article was written, also relies on hospital case records, in the German case such materials do not seem to exist for the late nineteenth century. At the time, infertility diagnoses and treatment took place within private medical practice. If materials have survived, I am not aware of them.

To reconstruct the procedures used and the interaction between doctors and patients, case studies which can often be found as part of the medical texts have proved especially valuable. They reveal important information on the way in which diagnosis and treatment were organised. They can also be understood as means of communication between physicians, and, hence, as part of network-building process, and they are analysed as forms of self-representation showing how their authors perceived of themselves, their work and their patients. My reading of the source materials has thus been threefold – using texts, statistics and published cases to grasp a 'reality' otherwise not accessible, understanding them as communication at least partly structured by intentions and reading them as representations, as texts reflecting contemporary ways of thinking. This threefold reading also explains why some materials are quoted more than once in this paper for rather different purposes.

Collecting sperm, compromising morals and compiling statistics (loop 1)

Latour suggests starting the historical investigation by looking at the way in which elements of the material world were mobilised by scientific processes. In the case of male sterility, sperm was indeed in for a new experience, finding itself in odd places sucked up in syringes, carried about in small glass receptacles and dripped on microscope slides. To put sperm under a microscope and to make the movement of spermatozoa visible was a practice which had been technically possible since the seventeenth century. It might therefore seem surprising that medical authors writing during the 1870s and 1880s invariably stated that male sterility had only recently become the object of medical research. In fact, experiments on semen had been undertaken much earlier, and there also had been a general awareness that infertility was not necessarily due to the female partner in a marriage. Readers of the Brockhaus's encyclopaedia edition of 1836, to give an example, were told that male sterility could not only stem from impotence but from the 'imperfect or abnormal condition of the semen'. The 1847 edition defined sterility explicitly as a condition which occurred 'in both sexes'.[47] Helen Berry and Elizabeth Foyster have pointed out that medical authors of the seventeenth and eighteenth century acknowledged 'that sexually functioning adult men could be infertile'.[48] And letters, autobiographies and novels show that, during the nineteenth century, couples did not necessarily assume that the woman was to blame if a marriage was childless.[49] But while people knew about the possibilities of male sterility, they would not have imagined a microscopic sperm test to be a simple way of diagnosing it. It was only during the 1850s that the concept of sperm analysis started to make sense and only during the following decades that increasing demand, changing styles of treatment and favourable material conditions combined to turn it into a common practice. The dynamics that fed into this process are complex.

During the first half of the nineteenth century, the process of generation continued to be an object of fierce scientific controversy. As research in the history of biology has shown, it was extremely difficult to develop the concept of two merging cells forming the beginning of a new embryo. The process of generation remained invisible and different hypotheses existed to explain as to how both sexes contributed. Sperm was believed to excite the egg into development or to leave an imprint on the material provided by the egg. The role of sperm cells in this process was completely unclear. Until the 1840s, they were usually classified as parasites of the male testes and therefore called 'spermatozoa' from the Greek words for 'sperm' and 'living beings'. This hypothesis explained why they looked rather similar in different species and why they seemed to have inner organs made visible by better microscopes. Even when it was suggested that they were of significance for the process of generation, as semen lacking spermatozoa was shown to be infertile, this did not explain what their function was. A widespread assumption was that they helped to keep the sperm in motion. It was only after the development of cell theory – that is, only from the 1840s onwards – that spermatozoa were believed to be cells. Searching for them, studying their appearance and their motility now took on a new meaning.[50]

Already in the 1850s, the first studies of the connection between the malposition of the testes and venereal disease, on the one hand, and male infertility, on the other, were published.[51] Their authors specialised in the treatment of men and presented case studies on patients who had suffered from double epididymitis after gonorrhoea or whose testicles had not passed into the scrotum. They showed that in such cases the semen was 'destitute of spermatozoa'. However, it took several years before a causal connection between a lack of spermatozoa and sterility became accepted. When J. B. Curling, surgeon at the London Hospital and specialist in diseases of the testes, published an important paper 'Sterility in Man' in 1864, he assumed that by then it was 'quite established' that to be fertile, 'the semen must contain zoosperms'. Curling still had to make it explicit that the presence of spermatozoa was 'admitted by the best physiologists to be essential' for the fertility of sperm.[52]

While sperm analysis was occasionally performed during the 1850s and early 1860s – Curling's cases stemmed from the years between 1859 and 1863 – it became more widespread in the following decade. This was in tune with general developments in medicine. The growing interest in cellular pathology – Virchow's ground-breaking book was published in 1858 – meant that the employment of microscopes as part of medical practice became increasingly common.[53] During the 1860s, students of medicine started to be trained in microscopy. Throughout medicine, laboratory methods gained importance. Though their impact on treatment was limited, they became the yardstick of scientific medicine.[54] Due to the introduction of meat inspection in the 1870s, microscopes were produced in ever larger numbers while their prices decreased. Hence, advocates of sperm testing could expect their colleagues to be familiar with using a microscope and to be able to afford one.[55]

With the enormous success of bacteriology and the hopes it inspired – especially exuberant in Germany – diagnostic methods which made use of the microscope became even more widespread during the 1880s and 1890s, a process which is likely to have increased the acceptance of sperm testing both among physicians and patients.[56] Fluids and tissue were examined, and it was generally accepted that the microscope would produce objective information about the condition of the body. This more general development in medicine provided a favourable situation for sperm testing to be introduced.

To illustrate this point, we might look at Alexander Peyer's *An Atlas of Clinical Microscopy*, which in German was called 'Microscopy at the Bedside'. First published in 1884, and translated into English and French in 1885 and 1887, it was addressed to ordinary physicians, encouraging them to undertake microscopic analyses as part of their daily practice 'at the bedside'. The first edition contained eighty drawings of microscopic views of urine, sputum and faeces. Hidden in the chapter on urine, there were also two drawings of sperm illustrating aspermatism and azoospermia. Apparently Peyer had analysed sperm himself and expected other physicians to be interested in the topic. But it was only in the fourth edition, published in 1897, that Peyer included a short chapter on 'abnormal sperm', presenting eight different drawings. By this time, Peyer encouraged his readers explicitly to undertake sperm testing, assuring them that it could be done easily by examining a drop of sperm under the microscope.[57] To sum up, sperm analysis made sense within the framework of scientific medicine for which the use of laboratory methods became more and more common and it rested on the availability of the necessary equipment and on the skills which a younger generation of doctors had acquired during their studies.

However, before sperm could be brought under the microscope, it had to be collected. While this might not appear as an important consideration today, it was a major problem for the establishment of sperm analysis in the late nineteenth century. Those interested in testing sperm devised different methods to get hold of the precious fluid. In 1868, James Marion Sims recommended seeing the wife of a husband whose sperm was to be analysed after the couple had sexual intercourse. 'Then some cervical mucus is removed with a syringe, and placed on an object-glass'. If no spermatozoa could be traced, Sims repeated the examination, eventually asking to be allowed to examine the woman while she was still in bed literally just minutes after intercourse. If still no spermatozoa could be detected, Sims advocated a method first described by the above-mentioned Curling. 'He directs the man, immediately after intercourse, to squeeze a drop of mucus from the urethra on the object-glass, and from this the examination is made'. Sims despised a third method: 'Gosselin and other French physicians direct the man to use one of the abominable things so common in France (and, I am sorry to say, now also in my own country), which are intended to protect the male against infection, and the female against both infection and conception. This, with its contents, is sent to the microscopist for the necessary investigation'.[58] Other physicians, however, did not agree. They preferred the use of condoms or asked husbands to have intercourse, withdraw and collect some sperm in little glass receptacles.[59] Sims was heavily criticised by some who thought his dealings rather inappropriate, but in the mid-1880s his procedure was presented as a standard way of collecting sperm in one of the first handbooks on sterility.[60] Other authors decided not to elaborate too much on the subject.[61] They simply asked their patients to get them a quantity of sperm without suggesting what they were to do. To my knowledge, nobody openly advocated masturbation as a way of collecting sperm during the 1870s or 1880s. Contemporary medical texts on impotence regarded masturbation as the prime cause for male sexual disorders.[62] Apparently, it was out of the question to recommend it for diagnostic purposes. Ejaculation was to take place where it belonged: in the context of sexual intercourse of a married couple.[63]

Moral concerns not only hampered the microscopic analysis of sperm, they also meant that epidemiological data about the frequency of male sterility was hard to collect. In her book, *Disciplining Reproduction*, Adele Clarke has pointed out that scientific research on reproduction lagged behind other areas of physiology. She argues that 'the reproductive sciences were and remain illegitimate science precisely because of their historical and specific relations to sexuality and sexology. The "immense will to knowledge" of Western science in terms of investigating reproduction was actually relatively quiescent until well into the twentieth century'.[64] Male sterility is a good example of the difficulties connected with collecting relevant information. To screen the sperm of a group of men, e.g. recruits or medical students, was apparently out of the question.[65] Hence, it was difficult to know how widespread male sterility was. The evidence presented in the literature on sperm usually relied on case studies which were accumulated by individual physicians. As a consequence, the number of cases presented was often rather small.[66]

Ferdinand Adolph Kehrer's publication of 1879 was usually quoted as the first study to offer an estimate of the frequency and, hence, the importance of male sterility.[67] Between 1876 and 1879, Kehrer, a gynaecologist from Gießen, had treated forty couples for infertility. He had been able to examine both partners, and he also analysed the sperm. In fourteen of these cases, he had diagnosed azoospermia as the major cause for infertility. While earlier publications had concentrated on men who had been infected by gonorrhoea and had experienced inflammations of the testes or on men whose testes had not descended, Kehrer's cases were not pre-selected. On this basis, Kehrer claimed that in about a third of all sterile marriages, the husband was to be blamed for the childlessness of the couple – an estimate that was accepted and repeated by many subsequent authors.[68]

Kehrer's study was persuasive because he combined different forms of obtaining and presenting evidence. He offered not only statistical information which he presented in detailed tables, he also included individual case reports.

Case No. 1. Man aged 35, manager of an estate, very tall, muscular, suffered from gonorrhoea for three weeks in 1866, also from orchitis sinistra. For a quarter of a year both testicles are said to have hurt when squeezed. – Large penis, middle-sized testicles, the left one somewhat smaller, of normal firmness, the pointed tail of the right epididymis is considerably larger, fairly tender, hard lump on the middle of the left cauda epididymis. Sperm analysed on 5 February 1878 after 11 days without intercourse and after three weeks without intercourse on the 27 February 1878, four hours post coitum. The sperm is viscous, ropy, yellowish, contains albumen crystals, many lymphocytes, larger granulocytes . . . – never could any spermatozoa be detected.[69]

Sterile men, the case histories showed, could be tall and of muscular build, they could look bright and beautiful but also seedy and pale. Most of them had been affected by gonorrhoea at least once. Some admitted to have been ardent masturbators. In social terms, almost all of the men presented in Kehrer's sample came from the lower middle classes or belonged to the bourgeoisie. By combining statistics and case records, Kehrer managed to show that male sterility was far more common than hitherto believed and that it could exist even if neither the case history, nor the genitals or the rest of the male body, nor even – at first glance – the semen, betrayed any abnormality. Kehrer concluded 'Here only the microscope decides'.[70]

During the 1870s and 1880s, spermatozoa (moving or absent or dead), 'sterile men' (with a sexual biography including gonorrhoea) and 'male sterility' (as a quantitative phenomenon) became objects of discourse. In Latour's diction: they became part of a collective composed of humans and nonhumans, part of networks, part of our world. Their mobilisation depended on different techniques and instruments: on microscopes, statistics and medical case histories and on the collaboration between husbands and wives, couples and doctors.

Gynaecologists as andrologists (loop 2)

Male sterility was a rewarding object for scientifically minded physicians as it offered the possibility to reach an 'objective' diagnosis by a comparatively easy but prestigious method. Kehrer's approach, which also included animal experiments, was certainly scientifically informed, but given the moral and aesthetic concerns sperm testing engendered, scientific curiosity did not suffice to turn it into a medical or scientific practice. Rather, it seems that the dynamic which drove the introduction of sperm analysis grew out of frustration with the diagnosis and treatment of female infertility. If we turn to Latour's second loop and ask how colleagues got involved and how their interest in male sterility and sperm analysis could be secured, we see that it was mainly gynaecologists who pushed for sperm analysis. They usually gave two kinds of reasons for their rather indelicate pursuit: the need to prevent women from unnecessary operations and unjust charges and, second, the wish to replace the puzzle about female infertility with a method which allowed some objectivity.

During the 1850s and 1860s, new ways of treating female infertility had been developed. I cannot go into detail, but made possible by anaesthetics and later by antisepsis and encouraged by a general interest in establishing the local causes of disease, surgical methods loomed large in the treatment of infertility.[71] According to contemporary theories, female infertility was often caused by mechanical obstructions; for example, a tight cervix was believed to stop sperm from entering the uterus. Correspondingly, gynaecologists used cervical incision as a method for widening the cervix. However, such operations were painful and dangerous. It took patients weeks to recover, if they recovered at all.[72]

James Marion Sims was probably the most vocal advocate of uterine surgery when he presented a lecture to the British Medical Association in 1868. The lecture was later published in the British Medical Journal and Sims's translator and friend Hermann Beigel introduced its content into the second German edition of Sims's book, *Uterine Surgery*.[73] In his lecture, Sims recommended the use of the microscope. Without it 'our treatment of the sterile state is simply blind empiricism. With it, our diagnosis becomes absolutely certain, and our treatment at least rational'. Sims castigated himself for treating women for infertility without ascertaining the fertility of their husbands beforehand.

> I am sorry to say that I have had the misfortune to incise the cervix in half a dozen cases of sterility, where I found afterwards, to my great mortification, that the husbands were incapable of procreation, because their semen had no spermatozoa.... I made the mistake of operating on these cases, because the social position, moral character, and appearance of health in the husband, conjoined with the excessive dysmenorrhoea and utter prostration of the wife, led me to operate without the preliminary step of ascertaining whether there were spermatozoa or not. I wish others to profit by my mistakes.[74]

Sims's dilemma was the direct result of his enthusiasm for the surgical treatment of female infertility. In Germany, the above mentioned Ferdinand Adolph Kehrer experienced much the same problem. Like Sims, Kehrer had turned to sperm analysis after performing surgery on infertile women. In his article on uterine surgery, published three years before his often quoted statistics on male sterility in 1876, Kehrer reported on eighty-six cases in which he had operated on the cervix of women suffering from painful menstruation or seeking help because of childlessness in their marriage. Kehrer was experienced at operating and had developed a specially designed instrument for incising the cervix. One of his patients, Frau Schmidt, lived in the village of Rechtenbach. She was thirty-one years old and had been married for six years without conceiving a child. According to Kehrer's diagnosis, her uterus was slightly bent forward. She suffered from a 'chronic catarrh' and the cervix was regarded as thick and the cervical canal as too tight. Kehrer decided to incise the cervical os. The operation took place on 31 October 1873. From 2 November, Frau Schmidt was plagued by pains in the abdomen, and on 3 November she was in agony. She had a very high temperature and died on 7 November.[75] Her death, which Kehrer did not attribute to the operation itself but to the material he used to keep the cervix open after the operation, must have come as a shock. It was abundantly clear that without the surgery she might have lived for decades to come. Her death was painful and unnecessary, a tragedy.

Kehrer lost one more patient and apparently got very concerned about the possible justification for this form of treatment. To see whether the operations had any merit at all, he compiled statistics on their results. It turned out that the operation seemed to lighten the troubles of those women who had very painful menstruations. Regarding the enhancement of the chances to conceive, however, the operation was of little use.

Kehrer therefore strongly recommended that in every case other possible causes of childlessness had to be investigated before an incision of the cervix was taken into consideration. Arguing that '[a]mong the injustice done to the female sex, the tendency to blame the woman for the childlessness of a marriage has the most far reaching consequences', Kehrer recommended that the husband be examined and his semen tested even before any examination of the wife.[76]

Sims, Kehrer and other gynaecologists were drawn to sperm analysis when hopes regarding the surgical treatment of female infertility were dashed. However, even for those physicians who did not support the contemporary craze for surgical treatments, male sterility was an attractive object. German-born Emil Noeggerath, who practiced in New York, arrived at sperm analysis after spending years unsuccessfully trying to isolate the pathogen which caused gonorrhoea. He suspected that many of the women who saw him because of their childlessness had been infected with gonorrhoea by their husbands and had, as a consequence, become infertile. However, a clear diagnosis could not be reached and the treatment remained one of trial and error.[77] 'Let us be candid', he wrote, 'and confess that the reason why the statistics of our treatment of sterility are not coming forth is simply due to the scarcity of results obtained by our present means'.[78]

Female infertility was difficult both to diagnose and to treat. In the 1870s and 1880s, the bimanual pelvic examination and the use of the speculum were becoming accepted. However, there were severe limitations on what could be diagnosed. The conditions of the fallopian tubes and the ovaries could only be judged by touch. It was only after the First World War that methods were developed that allowed doctors to test for tubal blockage. Likewise, hormonal deficiencies were not yet part of the diagnostic repertoire. It would take decades before the mechanism of the menstrual cycle was understood and before sex hormones developed into scientific objects and pharmaceutical products.[79]

Compared to the difficulties gynaecologists encountered when diagnosing female infertility, male sterility was a much more suitable object for modern concepts of medical diagnosis. As male sterility was regarded as predominantly acquired, a detailed inquiry into the sexual biography of the husband – who was suspected to be the source of venereal disease in a married couple – could lead to salient results. Women, by contrast, were dubious sources of information as they were perceived as innocent regarding sexual and biological matters. Talking to them about a possible infection of their husbands or overindulgence in masturbation not only had to be done more tactfully, it was also likely to be pointless. The examination of the male genitals could be done more easily as well. Doctors not only looked at male genitals but touched and squeezed them; they punctured testicles and used bougies to widen the urethra. They used catheters to deal with strictures and they applied electricity and hot and cold baths to the testicles in order to encourage sperm production. Palpable swelling of the testicles pointed to former inflammations. However, the chemical and microscopical analysis of urine and semen promised to be even more informative and relevant. As already described, it resonated with the prestige of bacteriology. This was especially attractive for gynaecologists, who worked in a field which was regarded as less prestigious than other areas of medicine. Hence, it is not surprising that medical experts publishing on male sterility chose to portray themselves as scientifically orientated physicians: 'Quite often, a single slide preparation excites our eye sight until late at night. It is necessary to search and to seek thoroughly and scrupulously before we come to a conclusion which might destroy long held hopes and most ardent wishes or which gives rise to "sweet expectations".[80]

It is hard to say how reliable semen analysis, as practiced in the 1870s and 1880s, really was. Systematic sperm counting was introduced only in 1891 and might not have been very widespread. Most experts probably relied on their experience and classified sperm according to the motility of the spermatozoa, their quantity and their shapes in categories like 'low quality', 'suspicious', 'valuable' and 'outstanding'. There is little evidence that doctors doubted the validity of their results. And it seems likely that the simplicity of the techniques employed in early sperm testing encouraged its spread. On the whole, the examination of the male body and of sperm was in tune with an understanding of modern medicine which was interested in diagnosing, not merely possible, but 'essential' causes for a certain medical problem.[81] While it remained very difficult to assess the causes of female sterility, male sterility could be diagnosed rather easily, and thus fit the bill.

The introduction of sperm analysis occurred at a historical moment when the medicalisation of the female body had reached a new stage. Surgical methods and the dangers they entailed suggested more caution, especially as infertility patients were not terribly ill and as they often came from the middle classes. Furthermore, the diagnosis of male sterility fitted well into the framework of scientific medicine. While the aetiology of male sterility was often unclear, sperm testing at least allowed for a comparatively clear-cut diagnosis and prognosis. Once the problem of collecting sperm in appropriate ways was solved, sperm testing must have been an attractive method for those physicians eager to use laboratory techniques. Apparently turning the male body and its reproductive capacities into an object of modern medicine did not require constituting a new area of specialisation. Gynaecologists were quite happy to examine both partners and experts in dermatology, venereology, psychology and sexology could be called upon if further examinations were deemed necessary.

Patients (loop 3)

The third loop Latour suggests studying concerns collaborators, that is people or institutions that supported the production of scientific knowledge but were not involved in it themselves. These can be individuals, foundations or states that financed research projects, provided opportunities for research or markets for new technologies. When thinking about medical practice, patients seem to be the most important collaborators. Hence, we might ask, how they were enlisted.

Unfortunately, the motives and experiences of childless couples are notoriously elusive. In the absence of case records and relevant documents, the interaction between patients and doctors cannot be reconstructed in a straightforward and comprehensive way. Published case histories occasionally allow glimpses at conflicts between doctors and patients; articles sometimes include advice on how to deal with certain problems – for example, the question of who should be informed about what or how bad news should be broken. But this evidence is patchy. Any attempt to write about doctor-patient interaction almost necessarily borders on speculation. At best, we might assume that the way in which physicians wrote about their patients and their interactions reveals certain general attitudes and ways of thinking that also influenced medical practice.

Sometime in the spring of 1881, Herr and Frau B. from Munich decided to go for sperm testing. They had been married for four years but did not have any children so far. We do not know how long Frau B. had already been undergoing treatment, but extrapolating from other comparable cases we might well assume that she had already been examined several times, possibly by different experts and had probably also gone through some minor treatment. Perhaps she had been to a spa the year before. The couple consulted Dr Josef Levy, a gynaecologist specialising in infertility treatment. Levy inquired in detail about Herr B.'s family, noting that his only brother was insane while his mother had been treated for hysteric fits. The physical examination found B.'s testicles to be rather small and saggy. However, his sexual capacities were not diminished, or so he said. In May 1881, Levy started a series of twelve pre-arranged visits to the couple's home. His aim was to determine B.'s fertility by analysing his sperm. Levy carried his microscope with him and arrived at the house shortly after intercourse had taken place to take sperm from the vagina and the cervix of Frau B. and to analyse it on the spot. The first three examinations showed negative results: no hint of spermatozoa could be detected. To Levy's dismay, the couple did not want to continue the procedure which, while it may not have been dangerous, must have violated their sense of propriety and decency. But as Levy subscribed to very high scientific standards, he wanted to continue, demanding a larger number of observations. Apparently he managed to urge the couple to carry on, pointing to their 'duty' to find out about the causes of their sterility. Using his authority, he managed to do four more tests, but five times he was sent away because no intercourse had taken place. In November 1881, after twelve attempts at sperm analysis, Levy gave in. He talked to Herr B. and signalled that he believed the azoospermia to be permanent. As B. did not show any signs of past infections with gonorrhoea, Levy conjectured some hereditary defect.

In the following year and a half, B. took up gymnastics and swimming and spent time in the mountains. At Levy's suggestion, B. also had his testicles faradised – a form of electrotherapy. However, all attempts to increase the fertility of B. were to no avail. New sperm tests showed that his semen still did not contain any spermatozoa. While the couple, who had wanted children very badly, remained childless, they were said to be 'content'. Having been married and trying to get pregnant for at least six years, they felt that they had 'fulfilled their duty in every possible direction'.[82]

For those desperate to have children, infertility treatment was often a long process. As in the case of Herr and Frau B., interrogations and examinations were usually repeated. Couples were required to report on their sexual habits:

> [H]ow were the sexual conditions at the beginning of marriage; timing and frequency of intercourse; how is the act performed; is manual stimulation used; does the penis penetrate the vagina completely or incompletely; sexual arousal; any painful sensations during coitus; is the sperm discharged; . . . how does the husband perform; strength and length of erection?[83]

To gain complete information, doctors were advised to speak to each spouse separately and to come back to sexual matters several times if patients were not forthcoming. Foucault has suggested that physicians were generally comparatively discreet when tackling marital sexuality. This, however, does not seem to have applied to infertility patients.

Middle-class women formed the majority of patients who actively sought medical treatment because of their childlessness.[84] They were used to consulting physicians; they could spare time to travel to spas or to recuperate from operations; they had the necessary economic resources and they regarded motherhood as a quintessential part of their lives. Gynaecologists complained frequently about their ferocious quests for treatment. They were said to visit expert after expert, to travel from town to town until they finally reached menopause after having been treated 'often completely in vain and more than useful', their genitals having been cauterised, their cervix dilated, their uterus abrased, the portio possibly amputated.[85] While we do not need to take this description at face value, case records show that treatment often continued for several years. From the point of view of women who either had gone through treatment or who were thinking of having an operation, sperm diagnosis was an attractive option even if it showed that they had to give up hope. To 'know' for sure that no children were to be expected, was valuable in itself.[86]

Men who feared a diagnosis of sterility had little to gain. Azoospermia was usually considered a permanent condition for which no effective treatment existed. Men like the above mentioned B. could try to alleviate the situation by doing sports or keeping a healthy diet. Other forms of treatment included the mechanical widening of the urethra, massages of the testicles and the etching of the glans. Attempts at operating on the spermatic duct were mentioned in the literature but do not seem to have been very common. On the whole, the effectiveness of available treatment was believed to be very limited. Sperm testing was usually not followed by treatment. It was only a diagnostic procedure. But to live with a negative result could be very challenging. Gynaecologists reported that it was hard for men who knew that they were sexually potent and who experienced ejaculation to accept a medical diagnosis according to which they were 'on par with eunuchs as far as reproduction' was concerned.[87] Not surprisingly, patients were not necessarily willing to believe the diagnosis right away. Fürbringer, one of the experts on male sterility, recalled a patient who 'knew that his sexual potency was quite exceptional. On hearing the verdict [that he was sterile], he was extremely annoyed, denied sneeringly the very possibility and finally threatened to file an action because of this outrageous accusation'.[88]

Gynaecologists were well aware that the diagnosis of sterility could pose a severe threat to the happiness of a marriage, sometimes causing couples to divorce. The knowledge offered was especially explosive if it was connected to gonorrhoea, that is if the husband had infected his wife or if he had become sterile himself due to an infection. When Emil Noeggerath presented his study on sterility and its connection to gonorrhoea at the very first meeting of the American Gynaecological Society in 1876, Dr Trenholme of Montreal was alarmed.

> On behalf of one half of this continent, at least as far as area is concerned, I feel that I should call for protection from the doctrines of this paper. We, upon our side of the line, look upon it as rather a reproach not to have a large family; and if our Canadian ladies found out that their sterility was dependent upon the former condition of their husbands, I do not know what would take place.[89]

Marital peace was at stake when husbands were diagnosed with gonorrhoea and sterility.

On the whole, men had good reasons to reject sperm analysis. However, its acceptance seems to have increased considerably during the 1870s and 1880s. While

Kehrer complained about the passive rejection of sperm testing among his patients in the 1870s, Lier and Ascher found that urban middle-class patients, treated during the 1880s, were normally quite cooperative. Since the late 1870s, authors dealing with infertility had advised their colleagues 'to inquire into the history of the husband of every woman that calls upon you to be treated; and if advice be asked for the cure of sterility, the semen of the husband must be examined first'.[90] Apparently, the public awareness of the possibility of male sterility and the usefulness of sperm testing increased, while individual resistance faltered.[91] Men still do not seem to have flocked to the consultation rooms of sterility experts but could often be persuaded to cooperate especially if their wife had already gone through treatment. By 1900, 'conscientious gynaecologists' were reported to refrain from the examination of women, 'before the husband's sperm had been analysed'.[92]

Judging from their publications, physicians used different lines of argumentation to make husbands comply. First and most importantly, they tried to compel husbands to have their sperm tested by denying any further treatment to their wives.[93] In this way, they used the wish for a child expressed by many women and the social pressure generated by their families and friends to force husbands to have their sperm tested. Second, gynaecologists appealed to the men's consciences and to ideals of fairness and justice. In their writings, they used a strikingly juridical vocabulary. They deplored the fact that women were taking 'the blame'; they proposed sperm analysis to see whether the man was 'guilty' or whether he could be freed from the 'suspicion' of infertility. Based on microscopic analysis, a 'final judgement' was to be reached and the 'amerceable' partner was to be identified. To clarify the 'question of guilt' a 'hearing' of the husband was necessary and so on. With this choice of language, physicians represented themselves not as healers – after all male sterility was usually seen as incurable – but as judges. They gave the impression that by using the microscope they were able to determine the truth. Rather than enlightening their patients about the uncertainties of their diagnosis, they presented it as clear-cut, obvious, just and reliable. If they were the source of infertility in a marriage, husbands were supposed to take the blame and to confront their guilt.

Third, gynaecologists offered ways of negotiating knowledge. As in the case of the above mentioned B., the negative diagnosis was revealed in a private communication between husband and doctor. Whether the wife was to be informed and to what extent, was often left to the husband to decide. As Fürbringer recorded in a case of male sterility caused by gonorrhoea, 'we told the wife that the childlessness of the marriage was definite. Yet that the question of whose fault it was could not be decided. The couple adopted and lived happily ever after'.[94]

On the whole, gynaecologists represented the experience of childlessness as fundamentally gendered. They portrayed their female patients as rather irrational in their demands, implying that they were fixated on becoming pregnant and accusing them of an illogical belief in the effectiveness of certain procedures.[95] Men, by contrast, were not expected to act out of a burning desire for a child. Rather, they were represented as open to rational arguments centred on questions of justice. They were expected to accept a scientifically sound diagnosis, even if it contradicted the bodily experience of potency. And they were trusted with the management of the couple's reproductive future, saving their wives from unnecessary operations and filtering information in a way that would allow them to save the marriage. In their writings and presumably also in their interaction with male patients, physicians counterbalanced the stroke against a man's masculinity that was entailed in sterility diagnosis by offering another form of male identity – one centred not on the reproductive abilities of the physical body but on honour, responsibility, rationality and a form of relating to the body which was mediated by scientific medicine.

The fourth loop suggested by Latour concerns the wider public. As already mentioned at the beginning of my case study, medical writings on infertility were soon taken up by encyclopedias, self-help manuals and advice literature. They helped to raise awareness and to increase the acceptance of sperm analysis. I do not want to go into detail, but it might be worth noting that the literature did not yet present infertility as a demographic problem, nor was the issue regarded as a concern for public hygiene. We do find these argumentations later – that is, at the beginning of the twentieth century, when concern about degeneration was taking hold and when venereal disease was recast as a public threat. However, in the time period that is the focus here, sterility was presented as a medical problem and a predominantly individual tragedy.

None of the four loops studied could in itself guarantee the stability of male sterility as a scientific fact and of sperm testing as a medical procedure. Theories of conception had to be developed, but they could only become relevant to infertility treatment when microscopes were readily available and when the problem of sperm collection was solved. Patients had to comply, but they did so not simply out of a 'natural' or spontaneous wish for a child but against the backdrop of the dangers of available treatment. Gynecologists were interested in sperm testing as it was perceived as a 'scientific' and respectable form of diagnosis. But without the demands of their female patients who believed in the possibilities of modern medicine, they might not have turned to the rather indelicate procedure of sperm collection. Men did not necessarily want to learn about their reproductive capacities (or incapacities), but the growing public awareness of the frequency of gonorrhoea and of male sterility made it increasingly difficult to reject a sperm test. And so on. It was the communication between the loops that made sterility real, the connections between bodies and microscopes, professional interests of doctors and demands made by patients, notions of respectability, guilt and gender. They formed what we might call a network, a network that was specific to the societies in which it developed, a network that had its own history, which unfolded over a period of some twenty years, a network about which a report can be written.

Conclusion

During the 1870s and 1880s, male sterility became a well-defined medical object. It was diagnosed using a quickly spreading microscopic technique, was attributed mainly, but not entirely, to gonorrhoea and was said to cause a third of all sterile marriages. Laboratory methods, statistics and case records were used to bring male sterility into focus, to turn it into a stable entity, something which could be discussed in academic papers or in advice literature, something the frequency of which could be counted, something that by using drawings of microscope slides could be visualised. Male patients were confronted with new information about their bodies that could confirm or question their experience and sense of potency. Female patients were often asked to collaborate and to let their vaginas be used as receptacles for sperm. Spermatozoa were offered a stage on which to demonstrate their motility (or lack thereof) – a show nobody had been particularly interested in before.

The network that comprised microscopes and statistics, doctors and patients and the wider public has survived until today, while spermatorrhea and neurasthenia, which around 1890 were just as 'real' as azoospermia, have disappeared. It would take another article (or possibly a book) to show how male sterility was reformulated and stabilised over the decades, when sophisticated methods of sperm testing were introduced, when sperm banking and artificial insemination were designed, when new theories about the spread of male sterility and its causes were developed. Male sterility did not disappear from encyclopaedias and advice literature, and it even developed into a public health issue in the 1910s and 1920s when political concerns about degeneration and a declining birth rate helped to keep the issue of sterility on the agenda. However, among gynaecologists, the interest in male sterility waned as new instruments to examine the female body became available.

In this article, I have traced the process through which male sterility developed into an object of medical concern. The article contributes to a growing body of literature on the male (reproductive) body. This literature contradicts the notion that pathologisation was a phenomenon predominantly directed towards female bodies. While a dichotomous gender order might have associated men with intellect, culture and mental productivity, while it might have imagined them as unsexed representatives of humanity, this did not prevent physicians from developing an interest in the male body and in sperm. Once laboratory methods were integrated into ordinary medical practice, sperm was analysed sometimes even 'at the bedside'. Notions of respectability had to be negotiated when sperm were to be turned into a medical object. However, once this was achieved, the medicalisation of the male body that went with it was profound. Statements like 'only the microscope decides' or 'the doctor using the microscope decides' meant that male patients lost any voice they might have had in the process of negotiating their sterility. Using the close association of science, rationality and masculinity, physicians forced men to accept a diagnosis that contradicted their bodily experiences.[96] How and if this 'truth' was to be broken to women was still another question.

As a topic of concern male sterility is not difficult to detect. By 1890, it was present as a well-defined object in medical handbooks, encyclopaedias and other popular texts. That it was not 'invisible' to medical experts but has been to gender historians, points to the importance of paradigms and narratives which shape our vision of the past. I have used the one-sex/two-sex narrative as an example to demonstrate the enormous stability such narratives can develop. Despite being much criticised, it continues to be reiterated. In a way, it is at the centre of its own network connecting ideas, people, institutions and the wider public. I am looking forward to reading more about the history of this network of social constructivism as it emerged during the 1970s and 1980s.

Among the concepts used for resisting social essentialism and going 'beyond constructivism', actor-network-theory has gained popularity. In this article, I have tried to show how it has inspired my own research. I would like to highlight three aspects: first, as a style of research, ANT proposes to adopt an ant-like movement, following connections between different actors and spheres. By forcing myself to look at material conditions and at interactions (between doctors and patients and within the scientific community), I learned that the process in which sperm testing developed and spread did not simply unfold but that it was driven and hampered by diverse dynamics. What seemed like a fairly obvious thing – that sperm can be analysed and male sterility diagnosed – appeared as a historically produced certainty, the making of which took more than ideas and clever doctors. Chronology proved to be very important for understanding this process, hence the large number of dates given in this article.

Second, with its interest in agency, things, connections and dynamics, ANT provokes heuristics and interpretations that are comparatively unorthodox. Rather than choosing a specific body of materials as a corpus, a researcher inspired by ANT will be forced to follow connections and directions which only become apparent during the process of research. I had, for example, not foreseen that I would need information on the prices of microscopes or on the curricula of students of medicine when I started my research on infertility. I was also surprised that the question of male sterility was primarily dealt with by gynaecologists.

Moreover, not only the choice of sources, but also their interpretation becomes more complex as it alternates between different perspectives. I was surprised to see that the material world and patients have left their traces in the medical texts as their authors described their practice and discussed the problems they encountered. The medical texts studied for this article cannot replace the fieldnotes of a participant observer or transcripts of interviews, however, they do allow insights into medical practice as they include descriptions, statistics of treatments and case histories which – even if they had been invented – would have seemed realistic to contemporary readers and, hence, reveal details about ordinary practice. Furthermore, each text was an individual element of a professional communication, speaking to other texts and to specific audiences. Close attention to the ways in which authors took up arguments and data, reviewed other works and replicated or criticised them, allowed me to reconstruct how the process of knowledge production among colleagues worked.

Third, ANT helped me to think about the place of sex and gender in this story. In his *Reassembling the Social*, Latour suggests thinking about processes of innovation not as consequences of a social world structured by gender, class, ethnicity and other social differences but as events in which associations (of humans and non-humans) are produced. This somewhat controverts the way of thinking cultivated within gender history. When I started my research on infertility and came to realise that male sterility was quite an issue, I immediately assumed that a crisis of masculinity must have been the reason for this somewhat astonishing development. It took me quite some time and a lot of reading to admit that the medical concern for male infertility predated the *fin-de-siècle* fears regarding degeneration and a dissolving of the gender order by at least a decade, if not two or three. Looking at the ways in which the authors framed their texts and paying attention to the communication process within the various disciplines involved made other explanations more plausible. Gender was important for the introduction of sperm testing. As a contemporary set of ideas about masculinity, femininity and sex difference gender was used as a resource, explanation and argument by those negotiating infertility. The whole endeavour of sperm testing was described as an exercise in restoring the gender order and in doing justice to women. Such a far-reaching goal was useful as doctors had no effective treatment to offer, and as they had to enlist male patients who had little to gain. Men were not keen to have their sperm analysed, but doctors could appeal to their responsibility to protect their (irrational, childish and superstitious) wives, to notions of honour that expected the wrongdoer to take the blame and to a male rationality that accepted the truth produced by modern science and medicine.

The masculinity of doctors, by contrast, was not spelled out. The authors, all of whom were men, presented themselves as scientists (staying up late at night, straining their eyes at the microscope) and as courageous practitioners dealing with difficult patients, organising sperm tests and producing sound diagnoses. They did not allude to their own masculinity. Perhaps this is simply a reflection of the fact that women had hardly even started to try to enter the profession. Perhaps it was a way of neutralising their own bodies. Gynaecologists might have been especially interested in denying the fact that they were men and in assuming a kind of gender-neutral expertise.

And sex? That sperm is emitted and therefore can more easily be turned into an object of medical investigation is an aspect of sex difference that was without much significance before the middle of the nineteenth century. It took a number of preconditions and circumstances to make sperm testing into a feasible procedure. Once this was achieved, male patients were confronted with the expectation that they would accept a medically produced truth that possibly contradicted their sense of potency. To understand why this profound medicalisation of the male body was possible requires taking both sex and gender into account. Semen played a role in this process. In the context of sperm testing, it was equipped with a new kind of agency. If it did not contain any spermatozoa or if these were not moving, sperm could cause grief and divorce. This agency depended, of course, on doctors who accepted certain hypotheses about reproduction, on the availability of microscopes and on willing male and female patients. But this dependency was mutual; it holds true the other way round as well: doctors could not invent sterility; they produced the diagnosis with the help of theories, microscopes, patients and the spermatozoa which appeared to be dead or alive. Sperm analysis worked because it assembled a collective of humans and non-humans. In this process, spermatozoa came to matter in a historically new way, familiar to us and still around.

Notes

This paper has profited immensely from comments by Dominque Tobell, Sandra Maß, Xenia von Tippelskirch, Nick Hopwood, the participants of the 'Gender History across Epistemologies' Workshop, the editors of this volume and two very generous anonymous reviewers. They have given me a lot to think about and made working on this paper an intellectually stimulating and challenging experience.

1. Jim S. Dolwick, '"The Social" and Beyond: Introducing Actor-Network Theory', *Journal of Maritime Archaeology* 4 (2009), pp. 21–49, here p. 36.
2. Benedict Anderson, *Imagined Communities: Reflections on the Origins and Spread of Nationalism* (London: Verso, 1983); Eric J. Hobsbawn and Terrence O. Ranger (eds), *The Invention of Tradition* (Cambridge: Cambridge University Press, 1983); Mark Roseman, 'Introduction: Generational Conflict and German History', in Mark Roseman (ed.), *Generations in Conflict: Youth Revolt and Generation Formation in Germany 1770–1968* (Cambridge: Cambridge University Press, 1995), pp. 1–46.
3. Lorraine Daston, 'Science Studies and the History of Science', *Critical Inquiry* 35 (2009), pp. 798–816.
4. Nelly Oudshoorn, *Beyond the Natural Body: An Archaeology of Sex Hormones* (London: Routledge, 1994), p. 9.
5. Oudshoorn, *Beyond the Natural Body*, p. 10.
6. Ludmilla Jordanova, 'The Social Construction of Medical Knowledge', *Social History of Medicine* 8 (1995), pp. 361–81; Thomas Schlich, *Die Erfindung der Organtransplantation: Erfolg und Scheitern des Chirurgischen Organersatzes (1880–1930)* (Frankfurt a. M.: Campus Verlag, 1998); Thomas Schlich,

'Wissenschaft: Die Herstellung wissenschaftlicher Fakten als Thema der Geschichtsforschung', in Norbert Paul and Thomas Schlich (eds), *Medizingeschichte: Aufgaben, Probleme, Perspektiven* (Frankfurt a. M.: Campus Verlag, 1998), pp. 107–29; Jens Lachmund and Gunnar Stollberg, *The Social Construction of Illness: Illness and Medical Knowledge in Past and Present* (Stuttgart: Franz Steiner Verlag, 1992); Eva Fleischer, 'Die Erfindung der Unfruchtbarkeit der Frau – Historische Voraussetzungen der heutigen "Sterilitätstherapien"', in Eva Fleischer and Ute Winkler (eds), *Die kontrollierte Fruchtbarkeit: neue Beiträge gegen die Reproduktionsmedizin* (Wien: Verlag für Gesellschaftskritik, 1993), pp. 23–48.

7.   Jens Lachmund, to give an example, compared the ways in which auscultation was developed as the most important form of physical diagnosis, both in Paris and in Vienna. Due to local circumstances, the methods of auscultation differed. To be used in the treatment of ordinary patients (outside the hospital) auscultation had to be performed in ways that promised to enhance the outcomes of therapy and that were acceptable to patients. For further details see Jens Lachmund, 'Between Scrutiny and Treatment: Physical Diagnosis and the Restructuring of 19th-century Medical Practice', *Sociology of Health & Illness* 20 (1998), pp. 779–801; Jens Lachmund, 'Making Sense of Sound: Auscultation and Lung Sound Codification in Nineteenth-Century French and German Medicine', *Science, Technology & Human Values* 24 (1999), pp. 419–50.

8.   Already in the early 1990s, the fascination of students with Judith Butler's early work and the rather hostile reactions of older feminists were understood as a generational conflict. Did social constructivists form an 'imagined community'? For generational differences in the reaction to constructivism see *Feministische Studien* 11 (1993), vol. 2: Kritik der Kategorie 'Geschlecht'.

9.   Thomas Laqueur, *Making Sex. Body and Gender from the Greeks to Freud* (Cambridge: Harvard University Press, 1990).

10.   Stefan Hirschauer, 'Praktiken und ihre Körper. Über materielle Partizipanden des Tuns', in Karl H. Hörning and Jutta Reuter (eds), *Doing Culture. Neue Positionen zum Verhältnis von Kultur und sozialer Praxis* (Bielefeld: transcript, 2004), pp. 73–91, here p. 76.

11.   For a later interpretation see George Weitz, *Divide and Conquer: A Comparative History of Medical Specialization* (Oxford: Oxford University Press, 2006).

12.   Gayle Davis, 'Health and Sexuality', in Mark Jackson (ed.), *The Oxford Handbook of the History of Medicine* (Oxford: Oxford University Press, 2011), pp. 503–23, here p. 506.

13.   Jennifer V. Evans, '"It is caused of the Womans part or of the Mans Part": The Role of Gender in the Diagnosis and Treatment of Sexual Dysfunction in Early Modern England', *Women's History Review* 20 (2011), pp. 439–57. This article is based on a thorough study of vernacular advice to infertile couples, adverts for medication and recipe books. It allows a glimpse at a rather confusing world in which different ways of thinking about the body and its reproductive capacities have existed simultaneously. Rather than accepting these inconsistencies as a feature of early modern medicine, Evans tries hard to establish some kind of chronology. 'The medical texts examined here date from the period between 1550 and 1780. Thus they provide a generous overview of the shifts and developments in early modern reproductive understanding. Within these sources it is clear that across the period many terms were used interchangeably to define sexual dysfunction, such as: sterility, barrenness, impotency, unfruitful, insufficient and imbecility. However, there was a shift in direction across the period which made gender a more central aspect in understanding these disorders. As will be shown, this shift created a general tendency for separating sexual disorders along gender-specific lines. However, this trend was not entirely clear-cut and regular', (p. 441). 'The transition towards a gender-specific terminology and understanding of infertility was neither consistent nor linear . . . The progression towards two separate, gendered, forms of sexual dysfunction was not cohesive or straightforward', (p. 443).

14.   See for example Angelika Wetterer, 'Konstruktion von Geschlecht: Reproduktionsweisen der Zweigeschlechtlichkeit', in Ruth Becker and Beate Kortendiek (eds), *Handbuch der Frauen- und Geschlechterforschung. Theorie, Methoden, Empirie.* (Wiesbaden: VS Verlag für Sozialwissenschaften, 2010), pp. 126–36.

15.   Cynthia R. Daniels and Janet Golden, 'Procreative Compounds: Popular Eugenics, Artificial Insemination and the Rise of the American Sperm Banking Industry', *Journal of Social History* 38 (2004), pp. 5–27, here p. 25. See also Michael Meuser, 'Frauenkörper – Männerkörper. Somatische Kulturen der Geschlechterdifferenz', in Markus Schroer (ed.), *Soziologie des Körpers* (Frankfurt a. M.: Suhrkamp, 2005), pp. 271–94; Michael Meuser, 'Der "kranke Mann" – wissenssoziologische Anmerkungen zur Pathologisierung des Mannes in der Männergesundheitsforschung', in Martin Dinges (ed.), *Männlichkeit und Gesundheit im historischen Wandel, ca. 1800 – ca. 2000* (Stuttgart: Franz Steiner Verlag, 2007), pp. 73–86; Torsten Wöllmann, 'Andrologie und Macht: Die medizinische Neuerfindung des Männerkörpers', in Ilse Lenz, Lisa Mense and Charlotte Ullrich (eds), *Reflexive Körper? Zur Modernisierung von Sexualität und*

Reproduktion (Opladen: Leske + Budrich, 2004), pp. 255–79; Nelly Oudshoorn, *The Male Pill: A Biography of a Technology in the Making* (Durham: Duke University Press, 2003), p. 3.

16. Katja Sabisch, '"Hoffnungslos durchseucht". Zur diskursiven Infektiosität des Humanen Papilloma Virus in den deutschen Medien, 2006–2009', *Gender: Zeitschrift für Geschlecht, Kultur und Gesellschaft* 1 (2009), pp. 107–24.

17. Katherine Park and Robert A. Nye, 'Destiny Is Anatomy [Review of: *Making Sex: Body and Gender from the Greeks to Freud*]', *The New Republic: A Journal of Politics and the Arts* 18 (1991), pp. 53–7, here p. 56.

18. On neurasthenia as a predominantly, though not exclusively, male condition see Marijke Gijswijt-Hofstra, 'Introduction: Cultures of Neurasthenia from Beard to the First World War', in Marijke Gijswijt-Hofstra and Roy Porter (eds), *Cultures of Neurasthenia from Beard to the First World War* (Amsterdam: Edition Rodopi B. V., 2001), pp. 1–30, here pp. 23–4; see also Joachim Radkau, *Das Zeitalter der Nervosität. Deutschland zwischen Bismarck und Hitler* (Munich: Carl Hanser Verlag, 1998); Hans-Georg Hofer, 'Nerven, Kultur und Geschlecht – Die Neurasthenie im Spannungsfeld von Medizin- und Körpergeschichte', in Frank Stahnisch and Florian Steger (eds), *Medizin, Geschichte und Geschlecht. Körperhistorische Rekonstruktionen von Identitäten und Differenzen* (Stuttgart: Franz Steiner Verlag, 2005), pp. 225–44. In societies subscribing to a 'spermatic economy', masturbation was very much conceived of as a male problem. On masturbation see Alan Hunt, 'The Great Masturbation Panic and the Discourses of Moral Regulation in Nineteenth- and Early Twentieth-Century Britain', *Journal of the History of Sexuality* 8 (1998), pp. 575–615; George L. Mosse, 'Masculinity and the Decadence', in Roy Porter and Mikulas Teich (eds), *Sexual Knowledge, Sexual Science: The History of Attitudes to Sexuality* (Cambridge: Cambridge University Press, 1994), pp. 251–66; Jean Stengers and Anne Van Neck, *Masturbation: The History of a Great Terror* (New York: Palgrave, 2001); Michael Stolberg, 'An Unmanly Vice: Self-Pollution, Anxiety, and the Body in the Eighteenth Century', *Social History of Medicine* 13 (2000), pp. 1–23; Thomas W. Laqueur, *Solitary Sex: A Cultural History of Masturbation* (New York: Zone Books, 2003). On spermatorrhea, a male condition leading to a permanent loss of sperm, see Ellen Bayuk Rosenman, 'Body Doubles: The Spermatorrhea Panic', *Journal of the History of Sexuality* 12 (2003), pp. 365–99; Robert Darby, 'Pathologizing Male Sexuality: Lallemand, Spermatorrhea, and the Rise of Circumcision', *Journal of the History of Medicine and Allied Sciences* 60 (2005), pp. 283–319. On the climacterium virile see Hans-Georg Hofer, 'Climacterium virile, Andropause, PADAM. Zur Geschichte der männlichen Wechseljahre im 20. Jahrhundert', in Dinges (ed.), *Männlichkeit und Gesundheit*, pp. 123–38; Michael Stolberg, 'Das männliche Klimakterium. Zur Vorgeschichte eines modernen Konzepts (1500–1900)', in Dinges (ed.), *Männlichkeit und Gesundheit*, pp. 105–22. On attempts at rejuvenation which originally clearly centred on the male body see Heiko Stoff, *Ewige Jugend. Konzepte der Verjüngung vom späten 19. Jahrhundert bis ins Dritte Reich* (Cologne: Böhlau Verlag, 2004). On male sterility see Florence Vienne, 'Die Geschichte der männlichen Sterilität schreiben – Das Beispiel der NS-Zeit', *Feministische Studien* 23 (2005), pp. 143–9; Florence Vienne, 'Der Mann als medizinisches Wissensobjekt. Ein blinder Fleck in der Wissenschaftsgeschichte', *N.T.M.* 12 (2006), pp. 222–30; Florence Vienne, 'Gestörtes Zeugungsvermögen. Samenzellen als neues humanmedizinisches Objekt, 1895–1945', in Florence Vienne and Christina Brandt (eds), *Wissensobjekt Mensch. Humanwissenschaftliche Praktiken im 20. Jahrhundert* (Berlin: Kulturverlag Kadmos, 2008), pp. 165–86; Christina Benninghaus, '"Leider hat der Beteiligte fast niemals eine Ahnung davon . . ." – Männliche Unfruchtbarkeit, 1870–1900', in Dinges (ed.), *Männlichkeit und Gesundheit*, pp. 139–55; Signe Nipper Nielsen, 'Da manden blev steril', *Fortid og Nutid* 3 (2006), pp. 163–82. On impotence see Angus McLaren, *Impotence: A Cultural History* (Chicago: University of Chicago Press, 2007); Christa Putz, *Verordnete Lust. Sexualmedizin, Psychoanalyse und die 'Krise der Ehe', 1870–1930* (Bielefeld: transcript, 2011).

19. For a detailed discussion and profound criticism of Laqueur's and Schiebinger's use of sources see Michael Stolberg, 'A Woman Down to Her Bones. The Anatomy of Sexual Difference in the Sixteenth and Early Seventeenth Centuries', *Isis* 94 (2003), pp. 274–99. For a more general criticism of the idea of a one-sex model see the literature discussed in Dror Wahrman, 'Change and the Corporeal in Seventeenth- and Eighteenth-Century Gender History: Or, Can Cultural History be Rigorous', *Gender & History* 20 (2008), pp. 584–602.

20. Elaine Hobby, 'Introduction', in Elaine Hobby (ed.), *The Midwives Book: Or the Whole Art of Midwifry Discovered by Jane Sharp (1671)* (New York: Oxford University Press, 1999), pp. IX–XLIII.

21. Bethan Hindson, 'Attitudes towards Menstruation and Menstrual Blood in Elizabethan England', *Journal of Social History* 43 (2009), pp. 89–114.

22. Thomas Laqueur, 'Orgasm, Generation, and the Politics of Reproductive Biology', in Catherine Gallagher and Thomas Laqueur (eds), *The Making of the Modern Body: Sexuality and Society in the Nineteenth Century* (Berkeley: University of California Press, 1987), pp. 1–41, here p. 1.

23. Carl Mayer, 'Einige Worte über Sterilität, vorgetragen in der Gesellschaft für Geburtshülfe in Berlin am 15 April 1856', *Archiv für pathologische Anatomie und Physiologie* 10, 11 and 12 (1856), pp. 115–43.

24. Reinhold Gerling, *Ursachen und Heilung der Unfruchtbarkeit bei Mann und Frau* (Leipzig: Hans Hedewig's Nachf., c.1929), p. 46. Gerling argued that after orgasm, the uterus worked like a suction pump. For advice for infertile couples and the importance of female orgasm see for example Axel Meyer, *Hygiene der kinderlosen Ehe* (Berlin: Alfred H. Fried & Cie., 1891).

25. When sexologists started to do systematic research on male and female orgasms, they stressed the similarities between male and female capacities for and experiences of orgasm, not the differences. See Putz, *Verordnete Lust*, p. 115.

26. Stolberg, 'A Woman Down to Her Bones', p. 290.

27. For a critique of social essentialism see Ian Hacking, *The Social Construction of What?* (Cambridge: Harvard University Press, 1999). See also Bruno Latour, *Reassembling the Social: An Introduction to Actor-Network-Theory* (Oxford and New York: Oxford University Press, 2005). For an explicit social constructivist approach see for example Ralf Bröer, 'Genitalhypoplasie und Medizin. Über die soziale Konstruktion einer Krankheit', *Zeitschrift für Sexualforschung* 17 (2004), pp. 213–38. The author explains the 'invention' of 'genital hypoplasy' as a reaction of medical experts towards the growing visibility of the 'new woman' and the declining birth rate and as a strategy to expand professional expertise. Changes in medical concepts and ways of diagnosis do not come into the picture, nor do the possibly changing physical conditions of maturing young women.

28. Laqueur, *Making Sex*, p. 21.

29. Ingo Schulz-Schaeffer, Stefan Böschen, Jochen Gläser, Martin Meister and Jörg Strübing, 'Introduction: What Comes after Constructivism in Science and Technology Studies?' *Science, Technology & Innovation Studies*, Special Issue 1 (2006), pp. 1–9, here p. 4. The expression 'joy in repetition' is taken from Michael Guggenheim and Helga Nowotny, 'Joy in Repetition Makes the Future Disappear', in Bernward Joerges and Helga Nowotny (eds), *Looking Back, Ahead – The 2002 Yearbook of the Sociology of the Sciences* (Dordrecht: Kluwer Academic Publishers, 2002), pp. 1–31.

30. Daston, 'Science Studies and the History of Science', p. 812.

31. Laqueur, *Making Sex*, p. 22.

32. Ludmilla Jordanova, 'Gender and the Historiography of Science', *The British Journal for the History of Science* 26 (1993), p. 469–83, here p. 477.

33. Joan Scott, 'Millennial Fantasies: The Future of Gender in the 21st Century', in Claudia Honnegger and Caroline Arni (eds), *Gender – Die Tücken einer Kategorie* (Zürich: Chronos, 2001), pp. 19–38.

34. Ulrike Klöppel, *XX0XY ungelöst. Hermaphroditismus, Sex und Gender in der deutschen Medizin. Eine historische Studie zur Intersexualität* (Bielefeld: transcript Verlag, 2010); Sandra Eder, 'The Volatility of Sex: Intersexuality, Gender and Clinical Practice in the 1950s', *Gender & History* 22 (2010), pp. 692–707.

35. Anne Fausto-Sterling, 'The Bare Bones of Sex: Part 1– Sex and Gender', *Signs: Journal of Women in Culture and Society* 30 (2005), pp. 1491–527, here p. 1495.

36. Anon., 'Unfruchtbarkeit (Sterilität), männliche', *Meyers Konversationslexikon,* 4th edn (Leipzig: Verlag des Bibliographischen Instituts, 1890/91), vol. 18: Jahres-Supplement, 1890–1891.

37. See e.g. James Marion Sims, 'Illustrations of the Value of the Microscope in the Treatment of the Sterile Condition', *The British Medical Journal* (1868), pp. 465–6 and 492–4; Emil Noeggerath, *Die latente Gonorrhoe im weiblichen Geschlecht* (Bonn: Max Cohen & Sohn, 1872); Ferdinand Adoph Kehrer, 'Operationen an der Portio vaginalis', *Archiv für Gynäkologie* 10 (1876), pp. 431–58; R. Ultzmann, 'Ueber männliche Sterilität', *Wiener medizinische Presse* 19 (1878), pp. 5–7 and 76–9; Ferdinand Adolf Kehrer, 'Zur Sterilitätslehre', in Ferdinand Adolf Kehrer (ed.), *Beiträge zur klinischen und experimentellen Geburtskunde und Gynäkologie* (Giessen: Emil Roth, 1879–1880), pp. 76–139; P. Fürbringer, 'Zur Kenntniss der Impotentia generandi', *Deutsche medicinische Wochenschrift* 14 (1888), pp. 557–9.

38. R. Ultzmann, 'Ueber männliche Steriliät'; R. Ultzmann, 'Ueber Potentia generandi und Potentia coeundi', *Wiener Klinik* 11 (1885), pp. 1–32; Hermann Rohleder, *Die krankhaften Samenverluste, die Impotenz und die Sterilität des Mannes, ihre Ursachen und Behandlung. Zum Gebrauch für die ärztliche Praxis* (Leipzig: Verlag des 'Reichs-Medicinal-Anzeigers' B. Konegen, 1895), Josef Steinbach, *Die Sterilität der Ehe. Ihre Ursachen und ihre Behandlung. Mit besonderer Berücksichtigung der neuesten bakteriologischen Forschungsresultate* (Vienna: Braumüller, 1888); K. Brunnenberg, *Ueber die Häufigkeit und Ursachen der Sterilität unter dem Krankenmaterial der kgl. Universitäts-Frauenklinik zu Würzburg von 1889–96* (Würzburg: Scheiner, 1897); Franz Kellerer, *Die Ursachen der Sterilität* (Würzburg: Stürz 1887), pp. 34–7.

39. P. Müller, *Die Sterilität der Ehe. Entwicklungsfehler des Uterus* (Stuttgart: Ferdinand Enke, 1885).

40. E. Heinrich Kisch, *Die Sterilität des Weibes, ihre Ursachen und ihre Behandlung* (Vienna: Urban & Schwarzenberg, 1886).

41. Richard Weber (that is, Jakob Ruhemann), *Das Weib als Gattin und Mutter, seine naturgemäße Bestimmung und seine Pflichten* (Berlin: Hugo Steinitz Verlag, 1889), p. 108.

42. Hope Bridget Adams, *Das Frauenbuch. Ein ärztlicher Ratgeber für die Frau in der Familie und bei Frauenkrankheiten,* (Berlin: Reinhold Schwarz, 1896).

43. Meyer, *Hygiene der kinderlosen Ehe*, p. 10. Such advice was not reserved to literature directly addressed at infertile couples. Kühner's book, *Love*, went through several editions between 1895 and 1903. It had a chapter on 'infertility' in which the author mixed old metaphors (e.g. of seed and land) to explain relative infertility, but in which we also find descriptions of controversies around different methods of artificial insemination. Regarding the treatment of infertility, Kühner had clear ideas about how this should be done. To find out about the causes of childlessness the first step had to be the microscopic analysis of the semen. Like Meyer he cautioned his readers that even in cases of 'seemingly perfectly developed masculinity', sterility of the sperm could prevail. A. Kühner, *Die Liebe. Ihr Wesen und ihre Gesetze vom Standpunkte naturgemäßer Lebensweise. Ärztliche Ratschläge* (Berlin: Möller, 1903), p. 229.

44. M. Rosenthal, 'Über den Einfluss von Nervenkrankheiten auf Zeugung und Sterilität', *Wiener Klinik* 6 (1880), pp. 135–66.

45. On the process by which auscultation and the stethoscope developed into a 'normal' method of diagnosis, and the difficulties in understanding this process not as a logical result of the qualities of the method, see Jens Lachmund, *Der abgehorchte Körper. Zur historischen Soziologie der medizinischen Untersuchung* (Opladen: Westdeutscher Verlag, 1997), p. 22. For a similar approach to the introduction of temperature taking as a diagnostic method see Volker Hess, 'Die Normierung der Eigenwärme. Fiebermessen als kulturelle Praktik', in Volker Hess (ed.), *Normierung der Gesundheit. Messende Verfahren der Medizin als kulturelle Praxis um 1900* (Husum: Matthiesen Verlag, 1997), pp. 169–88.

46. Readers interested in comparing the potential of different approaches could, for instance, look at the new literature on anthrax. For a much acclaimed discourse analysis see Philipp Sarasin, *Anthrax. Bioterror als Phantasma* (Frankfurt a. M.: Suhrkamp Verlag, 2004). For a fascinating study on the way in which nature and culture interact and reshape anthrax see Susan Jones, *Death in a Small Package: A Short History of Anthrax* (Baltimore: Johns Hopkins University Press, 2010).

47. Anon., 'Unfruchtbarkeit', *Allgemeine deutsche Real-Encyclopädie für die gebildeten Stände. Conversations-Lexikon*, eighth edition, vol. 11 (Leipzig: Brockhaus, 1836), p. 484–5; 'Unfruchtbarkeit', in *Allgemeine deutsche Real-Encyklopädie für die gebildeten Stände. Conversations- Lexikon*, 9th edn, vol. 14 (Leipzig: Brockhaus, 1847), p. 489.

48. Helen Berry and Elizabeth Foyster, 'Childless Men in Early Modern England', in Helen Berry and Elizabeth Foyster (eds), *The Family in Early Modern England* (Cambridge: Cambridge University Press, 2007), pp. 158–83.

49. See e.g. Birgit Bublies-Godau (ed.), *'Dass die Frauen bessere Democraten, geborene Democraten seyen . . .'. Henriette Obermüller-Venedey: Tagebücher und Lebenserinnerungen 1817–1871* (Karlsruhe: Badenia Verlag, 1999).

50. It is beyond the scope of this article to elaborate on the difficult process which led to a better understanding of mechanisms of reproduction. For more information see John Farley, *Gametes & Spores: Ideas about Sexual Reproduction, 1750–1914* (Baltimore: Johns Hopkins University Press, 1982). See also Florence Vienne, 'Vom Samentier zur Samenzelle: Die Neudeutung der Zeugung im 19. Jahrhundert', *Berichte zur Wissenschaftsgeschichte* 32 (2009), pp. 215–29.

51. P. Gosselin, 'Nouvelle études sur l'oblitération des voies spermatique et sur stérilité consécutive à l'épididymite bilatérale', *Archives Générales de Médecine* 5 (1847), p. 257–70.

52. Thomas Blizard Curling, 'Observations on Sterility in Man with Cases', *The British and Foreign Medico-chirurgical Review* 33 (1864), pp. 494–508, here p. 495.

53. Rudolf Virchow, *Die Cellularpathologie in ihrer Begründung auf physiologische und pathologische Gewebelehre. Zwanzig Vorlesungen, gehalten während der Monate Februar, März und April 1858 im pathologischen Institute zu Berlin* (Berlin: Verlag von August Hirschwald 1858).

54. Andrew Cunningham and Perry Williams (eds), *The Laboratory Revolution in Medicine* (Cambridge: Cambridge University Press, 1992). Especially in Germany, laboratory methods gained importance quickly.

55. On microscopes and their use in medicine see Helmut Kettenmann, Jörg Zaun and Stefanie Korthals (eds), *Unsichtbar – Sichtbar – Durchschaut. Das Mikroskop als Werkzeug des Lebenswissenschaftlers* (Berlin: Museumspädagogischer Dienst, 2001).

56. On the acceptance of bacteriology in Germany see Silvia Berger, *Bakterien in Krieg und Frieden. Eine Geschichte der medizinischen Bakteriologie in Deutschland 1890–1933* (Göttingen: Wallstein Verlag,

2009), Philipp Sarasin, Silvia Berger, Marianne Hänseler and Myriam Spörri, 'Bakteriologie und Moderne. Eine Einleitung', in Philipp Sarasin, Silvia Berger, Marianne Hänseler and Myriam Spörri (eds), *Bakteriologie und Moderne. Studien zur Biopolitik des Unsichtbaren, 1870–1920* (Frankfurt a. M.: Suhrkamp Verlag, 2007), pp. 8–43; Christoph Gradmann, *Krankheit im Labor. Robert Koch und die medizinische Bakteriologie* (Göttingen: Wallstein Verlag, 2005). There were, of course, important setbacks and even in Germany bacteriology also met with criticism. However, especially during the 1880s the expectations regarding bacteriology were extremely high as new pathogens became identified at very short intervals. For critical views on bacteriology and its limited impact, especially in Britain, see Michael Worboys, 'Was there a Bacteriological Revolution in Late Nineteenth-Century Medicine?' *Studies in History and Philosophy of Biological and Biomedical Sciences* 38 (2007), pp. 20–42.

57. Alexander Peyer, *Atlas der Mikroskopie am Krankenbette*, fourth edition (Stuttgart: Ferdinand Enke, 1897), plate 97, p. 465.

58. Sims, *Illustrations of the Value of the Microscope*, p. 465.

59. Noeggerath related four cases in which he had analysed sperm. All were from 1871. 'I asked for the intercourse to take place at 7 o'clock in the morning using a condom. Together with its contents, this was put into a bottle with a wide neck. The bottle was kept next to the oven until the patient brought it to me for the analysis. She was instructed not to let the glass cool down too much'. Noeggerath, *Die latente Gonorrhoe im weiblichen Geschlecht*, p. 83. See also L. Casper, *Impotentia et sterilitas virilis* (Munich: Jos. Ant. Finsterlin, 1890), p. 162.

60. Müller, *Sterilität der Ehe*, p. 153.

61. Curschmann and Ultzmann avoided the topic in their writings on sterility and impotence. See H. Curschmann, 'Die functionellen Störungen der männlichen Genitalien', in Hugo von Ziemssens (ed.), *Handbuch der speziellen Pathologie und Therapie* (Leipzig: Vogel, 1878), pp. 357–451; Ultzmann, 'Ueber männliche Sterilität'; R. Ultzmann, 'Ueber Potentia generandi und Potentia coeundi', *Wiener Klinik* 11 (1885), pp. 1–32.

62. Putz, *Verordnete Lust*, pp. 24–40.

63. The procedure advocated by Sims and used by Levy and others was later called the Sims-Huhner test. It is still used as an additional part of infertility diagnosis to test for immune factors that might inactivate sperm. Sims was interested in gaining information on the compatibility of sperm and mucus, however, most of the literature analysed for this paper does not even mention this side effect. I am under the impression that most authors wanted to do a sperm test and instrumentalised the female genitals as receptacle – a function later taken on by condoms or small glass containers.

64. Adele E. Clarke, *Disciplining Reproduction: Modernity, American Life Sciences, and 'the Problems of Sex'* (Berkeley: University of California Press, 1998).

65. During the 1920s, health propaganda used figures compiled by Benzler during the 1890s. While Benzler used case records of soldiers who had had gonorrhoea, his statistics on the frequency of sterility among them was not based on sperm tests but on the reproductive histories of their marriages. See Benzler, 'Sterilität und Tripper', *Archiv für Dermatologie und Syphilis* 45 (1898), pp. 33–56. Nor does self-experimentation by physicians seem to have been much of an option. There are rare examples of experiments on the question of whether excessive sexual activities could temporarily lead to azoospermia. See Casper, *Impotentia et sterilitas virilis*.

66. There were some statistics compiled which showed the frequency of azoospermia depending on age and diseases. They were based on autopsies. See A. Busch, 'Über Azoospermie bei gesunden und kranken Menschen, nebst einigen Bemerkungen zur pathologischen Histologie des menschlichen Hodens', *Zeitschrift für Biologie* XVIII (1883); A Schlemmer, 'Beitrag zur Histologie des menschlichen Spermas, nebst einigen forensischen Bemerkungen über Aspermatozie', *Vierteljahrsschrift für gerichtliche Medicin. Neue Folge* 27 (1877), pp. 496–521.

67. Kehrer, 'Zur Sterilitätslehre'.

68. See for example H. Lier and S. Ascher, 'Beiträge zur Sterilitätsfrage', *Zeitschrift für Geburtshilfe und Gynäkologie* 18 (1890), pp. 262–323. The authors analysed the case records of Prochownik who practiced in Hamburg. Originally, they had intended to refute Kehrer's figures but found them reconfirmed.

69. Kehrer, 'Zur Sterilitätslehre', p. 79.

70. Kehrer, 'Zur Sterilitätslehre', p. 96.

71. It is, of course, difficult to estimate how widespread certain forms of treatment really were. In his article 'Operations of the Portio vaginalis', published in 1876, Kehrer summarised a large number of publications which proposed different ways of surgically widening the cervix. Different instruments were developed and Kehrer believed that Sims's method was much used by German gynaecologists. Publishing in 1875, Martin had been able to present 386 cases in which he had incised the cervix.

72. For a more detailed account see Margaret Marsh and Wanda Ronner, *The Empty Cradle: Infertility in America from Colonial Times to the Present* (Baltimore: Johns Hopkins University Press, 1996), pp. 41–74. For a feminist critique of this 'penetration' of the female body see Eva Fleischer, *Die Frau ohne Schatten. Gynäkologische Inszenierungen zur Unfruchtbarkeit,* (Pfaffenweiler: Centaurus, 1993).

73. James Marion Sims, *Klinik der Gebärmutterchirurgie mit besonderer Berücksichtigung der Behandlung der Sterilität. Deutsch herausgegeben von Dr Hermann Beigel,* 2nd edn (Erlangen: Verlag von Ferdinand Enke, 1870), pp. 293–7. In this second edition, published only two years after the first, Beigel included not only a long quote from Sims's article on the 'Value of the Microscope' but also case histories from Beigel's own practice.

74. Sims, 'Illustrations of the Value of the Microscope', p. 466.

75. Kehrer, 'Operationen an der Portio vaginalis', p. 443.

76. Kehrer, 'Operationen an der Portio vaginalis', p. 449.

77. Noeggerath published his cases in 1872, seven years before Neisser managed to isolate the pathogen of gonorrhoea.

78. Emil Noeggerath, 'Latent Gonorrhea, Especially with Regard to its Influence on Fertility in Women', *Transactions of the American Gynecological Society* 1 (1876), pp. 268–300, here p. 286–7.

79. On sex hormones see Oudshoorn, *Beyond the Natural Body*; Christina Ratmoko, *Damit die Chemie stimmt. Die Anfänge der industriellen Herstellung von weiblichen und männlichen Sexualhormonen 1914–1939* (Zürich: Chronos Verlag, 2010).

80. Josef Levy, *Mikroskop und Sterilität* (Munich: Verlag von Jos. Ant. Finsterlin, 1879); see also Levy, 'Die männliche Sterilität', *Frauenarzt* 4 (1889), pp. 1–5; 57–70; 128–34; 182–96; 240–55; 313–27.

81. Thomas Schlich, 'Die Konstruktion der notwendigen Krankheitsursache: Wie die Medizin Krankheit beherrschen will', in Cornelius Borck (ed.), *Anatomien medizinischen Wissens. Medizin – Macht – Moleküle* (Frankfurt: Fischer Verlag, 1996), pp. 201–29.

82. Reconstruction of the case history as presented in Levy, 'Die männliche Sterilität', pp. 250–51.

83. Müller, *Sterilität der Ehe*, p. 145.

84. Evidence of the social origins of the patients is often, but not always, provided when case records are presented. For the 1920s, records from the hospital of the University of Tübingen show that middle-class women were more likely to be treated for infertility although by this time the treatment of working-class women was often covered by their health insurance. This was not the case during the last decades of the nineteenth century.

85. W. Bokelmann, 'Zur Unfruchtbarkeit des Weibes', *Berliner Klinik. Sammlung klinischer Vorträge* 69 (1894), pp. 1–21, here p. 12.

86. In a study on the experience of In-Vitro-Fertilisation (IVF), social anthropologist Sarah Franklin has shown that the women who decided to use IVF did not necessarily expect to become pregnant, but started IVF because they felt that they had to try everything that was in their power. Women often hoped that unsuccessful IVF would at least allow them to let go of their hopes and expectations. As Franklin shows, however, often this hope did not come true. Sarah Franklin, *Embodied Progress: A Cultural Account of Assisted Conception* (London: Routledge, 1997).

87. Kisch, *Die Sterilität des Weibes, ihre Ursachen und ihre Behandlung*, p. 148.

88. Fürbringer, 'Zur Kenntniss der Impotentia generandi', p. 558.

89. Noeggerath, 'Latent Gonorrhea, Especially with Regard to its Influence on Fertility in Women', pp. 293–4.

90. Noeggerath, 'Latent Gonorrhea, Especially with Regard to its Influence on Fertility in Women', p. 290. For similar statements see for example Hermann Beigel, *Pathologische Anatomie der weiblichen Unfruchtbarkeit (Sterilität), deren Mechanik und Behandlung* (Brunswick: Friedrich Vieweg und Sohn, 1878); Ultzmann, 'Ueber männliche Sterilität'.

91. Rohleder, *Die krankhaften Samenverluste, die Impotenz und die Sterilität des Mannes*, p. 109.

92. Paul Fürbringer, 'Sterilität des Mannes', in Albert Eulenburg (ed.), *Real-Encyclopädie der gesamten Heilkunde. Medicinisch-chirurgisches Handwörterbuch für praktische Ärzte* (Berlin and Vienna: Urban & Schwarzenberg, 1900), pp. 313–24, here p. 317.

93. Prochownik, to give an example, claimed that starting from 1883 he did not treat women for infertility before the sperm of their husbands had been tested. Lier and Ascher, 'Beiträge zur Sterilitätsfrage', p. 266.

94. Fürbringer, 'Zur Kenntniss der Impotentia generandi', p. 599.

95. Bokelmann, 'Zur Unfruchtbarkeit des Weibes', p. 21.

96. For a different interpretation regarding the meaning of sperm testing see Vienne, 'Gestörtes Zeugungsvermögen' and Vienne, 'Vom Samentier zur Samenzelle'. Vienne interprets sperm testing as a medicalisation which did not pertain to the male body.

6 'I Just Express My Views & Leave Them to Work': Olive Schreiner as a Feminist Protagonist in a Masculine Political Landscape with Figures

Liz Stanley and *Helen Dampier*

I have written two long letters to my brother. I don't argue with him: I just express my views & leave them to work. That's the best way with him.[1]

Introduction

Gender history as we see it is a multifaceted body of ideas and research held together by recognising disturbances as well as regularities in the gender order, and it includes exploration of challenges to and reworkings of conventional gender hierarchies. An example of such reworking is the focus of discussion here: the political interventions of South African feminist writer and social theorist Olive Schreiner (1855–1920) and the influence of these activities.[2] Schreiner left colonial South Africa for Britain in 1881. When she returned in late 1889 she had become one of the world's most famous women, author of the international best-selling novel *The Story of An African Farm*, followed by publication of allegories on ethical and political topics which captured public attention worldwide.[3] She also started publishing social commentary on political and economic matters, and before returning to Africa had conceived a major project, to investigate South African society and its racial and political divisions in a series of essays to be published pseudonymously as, 'A Returned South African'. When the first essay appeared in 1891, the author's identity became known and Schreiner was quickly established as a major radical social commentator on South African matters. South Africa at the time was on the world stage as the epicentre of imperialist and capitalist expansion and central to the 'scramble for Africa' by the competing imperialist autocracies, one of the reasons Schreiner's commentaries achieved such high profile.

The Schreiner Letters Project has transcribed and published the complete nearly 4,800 surviving Olive Schreiner letters located in archival locations worldwide and is also analysing these in research-based publications.[4] The attention here is on Schreiner's letters to her brother Will (William Philip) Schreiner, Attorney-General and then later

Gender History Across Epistemologies, First Edition. Edited by Donna R. Gabaccia and Mary Jo Maynes.
Chapters © 2013 The Authors. Book compilation © 2013 Blackwell Publishing Ltd.

Prime Minister of the Cape Colony (part of what later became South Africa) at a crucial period of its history; to the so-called Cape liberal politicians John Xavier Merriman and Francois Stephanus Malan, who were Will's close colleagues; and to less close ones such as the Afrikaner Bond leader Jan Hofmeyr.[5] Discussion of these letters is organised around exploration of important epistemological questions. How can Schreiner's political influence within the masculine political landscape of the Cape Colony in the late-nineteenth and early-twentieth centuries be gauged? Did she shape or change any of the tumultuous events which occurred there? Can her letters provide compelling evidence of her political influence on the white masculine political landscape of the Cape? And if so, what import does this have for understanding the gender order more widely? Examined here in relation to Schreiner's presence in a masculine political landscape, such epistemological questions also exercise historiography more generally. With what certainty can knowledge claims about the past be advanced? Can cause and effect be demonstrated between influence being exerted and behaviour or events being changed? And if it can, then what is appropriate and sufficient evidence to convincingly show this?

We explore these questions in the context of feminist historiography's concern with gender, and in particular 'separate spheres'. The idea of separate spheres has importantly influenced how the lives of women and men in late-nineteenth-century Europe and elsewhere have been conceived and how the dynamics of the gender order are understood.[6] They have also proved contentious because of often not readily fitting specific times, places and persons.[7] As Lynn Abrams aptly comments,

> the tension [exists] between the grand narrative of modern European women's history and the micro-study of a particular place and experience. Adopting a perspective far removed from the metropolitan heart of Europe forces one to think differently about the prime motors of change and the chronology of that change ... an alternative history can only emerge from a historical practice which privileges a social memory crafted around narratives of women whose sense of the past included themselves.[8]

We agree with this need for an alternative history conceived away from the 'metropolitan heart', and the particular woman whose narratives we explore in this way is Olive Schreiner. In doing so, we also recognise the complexities of separate spheres in practice in the context we are dealing with, which is the white enclave states of the Cape, Natal, Transvaal and Orange Free State, which later in 1910 united to form the Union of South Africa.

On one level, white enclave South Africa before and during Schreiner's lifetime embodied gendered and raced separate spheres in the many raced and gendered separations which configured its social and political life.[9] On another, the period's racialised social structures and practices were both constituted and dismantled daily in practical ways by black people increasingly being treated in de-humanised ways as labouring 'hands', initially concerning men living and working in diamond and gold mining compounds and later affecting women and men who worked in domestic and related services.[10] For black people, the racial practices that constituted 'separate spheres' formed a harsh disciplining reality, but at the same time these were also routinely and mundanely breached as services and labour were required, organised and carried out on a daily basis. The result was that for whites, gendered separate spheres were in some contexts (particularly among the urban educated elite) maintained in an exaggerated form, enabled through reliance on black labour carrying out activities which white lower-class women would have done elsewhere, while in other contexts (the farm, frontier or widowhood in both) women might take on many 'male' activities and roles. Both the disciplining *and* this complicated breaching have to be acknowledged analytically, and the implications for understanding the interface of gender and racial hierarchies in the context reckoned with in historical scholarship.

In the European and North American context, gender historians have recognised that separate spheres were traversed, if not overturned, in family and kinship contexts and in semi-private ones in civil society, in part because women provided an array of necessary labour for public sphere organisations and activities. That is, in practice gendered separate spheres were modulated and often conjoined, particularly at everyday and familial levels. However, this both translates and does not, in interesting ways, to the South African context. In the white enclave communities of South Africa, from Schreiner's childhood to her middle adulthood, there was an attenuated civil society largely bereft of the many groups and organisations characterising European societies.[11] The colonial political sphere of the Cape (and also of the independent Boer settler states of the Transvaal and Orange Free State and the British colony of Natal) was male, small-scale, sequestered and widely seen as corrupt, with the remit of its government contained and constrained by the British imperial presence via its Governor and the military, legal and bureaucratic apparatus he commanded. The Cape's political sphere was also largely separated from the thriving 'private' sphere centring on family and kinship mapped mainly onto land and agricultural production of various kinds, with later enclave industrial production occurring around mining in diamonds and gold. Of course material complexities coexisted with the simplicities of separate spheres ideology: as noted above, by no means all white women lived entirely confined lives. The circumstances of frontier and farming life militated against this, for women routinely managed significant aspects of agricultural production and trading, and often oversaw large groups of household and other servants.[12]

But at the same time, the bounded character of this breaching is notable. There was only a narrow set of possibilities, largely resulting from the occluded presence of black labour of all kinds. That is, the actual daily presence and labour of black people was combined with notions of separation, for they were routinely involved in carrying out work as nursemaids, herdsmen, field-hands, domestic workers and many more occupations. But also, in spite of these complex daily realities, the impact of ethnic/racial separate spheres thinking both limited the kinds of work seen as appropriate for white women, and relatedly it provided an 'other' which was viewed in ethnic and then increasingly in racial terms as threatening and dangerous and so requiring white women's sequestration from it, which lent a particular flavour to the dynamics and interrelationships of gendered separate spheres in the southern African context.[13]

Schreiner, then, grew up in the complexly configured, highly gendered and raced context of a white colonial enclave which was dependent upon routine servicing from black people's labour. Succinctly, in practice separate spheres overlapped and were interrelated in colonial South Africa and the enclave was actually surrounded, underpinned and supported by the black majority.[14] She left in 1881 to live in Britain and elsewhere in Europe, returning to South Africa in late 1889. In the period away, she published *The Story of an African Farm.*[15] Its immense international success propelled her and her subsequent publications, including many shorter allegorical writings, into the glare of public attention. At this time, her friends and acquaintances included some of the 'great and the good' and the liberal intelligentsia of British political and cultural life, including William Gladstone, his daughter Mary Gladstone Drew, Charles Dilke, Emilia Dilke, Robert Browning, George Moore, Helen Taylor, Oscar Wilde, Keir Hardie, Frank Harris and W. T. Stead, as well as the reformers she is more commonly associated with, including Eleanor Marx, Edward Carpenter and Havelock Ellis, among many others. Schreiner became a much lionised public figure whose ideas and opinions were taken seriously as one of the world's most famous women and she was seen to be on a par with international male public figures such as the imperialist entrepreneur and politician Cecil Rhodes.

When Schreiner first returned to South Africa in late 1889, a sense of palpable shock comes across in her letters concerning the slow pace of life in the white enclave and the narrowness of white people's lives and opinions, describing them as a nation of 'Philistines' with no aristocracy of 'blood or intellect or of muscular labourers'.[16] She immediately started work on her 'A Returned South African' essays.[17] Schreiner had conceived these as a 'project' before she left Britain, writing to the editor and journalist Stead in such terms.[18] She presented them as an epistemological endeavour concerned with what she described in the first essay as two forms of knowledge, of insiders and outsiders, which competed with each other in making claims to know about a country.[19] These essays are concerned with the particular mixture of races and ethnicities characterising South Africa and addressed to a complicated 'home', composed of reading audiences in the imperial metropole, the white enclave populations of colonial South Africa, as well as a wider international audience. Schreiner's writing went hand in hand with her close involvement in the social aspects of Cape white enclave political life, which centred on events around the short parliamentary session in Cape Town. This was quickly followed by her critique of the policies and practices of Rhodes as Cape Prime Minister as well as head of De Beers diamonds and also a major presence in the gold industry, and also her critique of the Cape's liberal politicians and their failure to provide an effective opposition to Rhodes and his followers. She became, as our subtitle states, a feminist protagonist in this highly masculine political landscape, with its background figures being those of other white women and of the black population. Following her 1889 return to the Cape, Schreiner developed allegiances with like-minded South Africans, including women's organisations during the South African War and feminist networks thereafter and also members of the burgeoning black intelligentsia. These alliances lasted through to her departure for Britain at the end of 1913. She then remained in Britain until her final return to Africa in mid-1920, and over this latter period, in addition to her close connections with international feminist and pacifist individuals and groups, Schreiner also established close connections with members of various black delegations which arrived in London to lobby the imperial parliament.[20]

Although Schreiner developed demonstrably friendly links with key black political figures of the time, including John Tengo Jabavu, Solomon Plaatje, John Dube, A. K. Soga, Abdullah Abdurahman and Mohandas Gandhi among others, this cordial relationship paradoxically led to few letters being exchanged between her and them.

This is because, apart from the people Schreiner was personally very close to, her correspondents were people she actively disagreed with and her letters were an important means by which she sought to change their minds and political behaviours. Few Schreiner letters to these black leaders exist as a consequence, because she and they agreed on most political matters. There is in fact just one letter initiating a friendship with Abdurahman and one letter rather sadly reminding Gandhi of his pacifist principles, although the many mentions of an array of black leaders in her letters to other people show contacts with them to have been extensive. This points to just how focused Schreiner's exhortatory letters were on divisive political topics, particularly race matters.[21] And from this follows our attention to her letter writing to the so-called Cape liberal politicians, including her brother, for though there was much disagreement between her and them, Schreiner's letters suggest she hoped she could influence them to behave in accordance with their stated political principles.

Previous political biographers and historians of South Africa amply recognised the influence of Schreiner's political analysis and strategising on Cape politicians and its political life more generally.[22] However, the succeeding generation of scholars rejected the liberal stance of earlier works and instead focused around a Marxist analysis of race and labour in the context of apartheid South Africa.[23] There were many gains; but the loss of knowledge of the earlier period of white radicalism ironically and unintentionally had the effect of reinforcing the distortions of apartheid knowledge making. Under apartheid, much work failed to 'see' both the early rapidly expanding black intelligentsia and bourgeoisie, and also the white radicalism on race matters that our discussion here is concerned with.[24] However, the many rich sources in South African archives and a new generation of historiography engaging with such issues is helping recover this lost knowledge.[25] Olive Schreiner moved in an international and national landscape and wrote many letters. In her case these sources are largely epistolary in character, with her letters located in archives outside, as well as within, the country.[26] Among other things, her letters enable this period of white radicalism and the relationship with black political figures to be seen and its importance for understanding the South African past to be explored.[27] Relatedly, Schreiner's letters analytically interrogate, inquire and argue with ideas concerning feminism, imperialism, capitalism, colonialism, questions of race and racism, the state, labour, the woman question, war and other topics.[28] They also provide considerable information on her practical involvements and related writing projects.[29] They are, then, a crucially important source material.

Letters are sometimes viewed as a disreputable data source because of their lack of direct referentiality and their inscription of dialogical, perspectival, emergent and serial aspects.[30] However, no written sources escape their ontological status as mediated forms and all historical documents have such characteristics, not just letters. Consequently, the issues we raise about reading and interpreting epistolary sources are also relevant to other kinds of archival materials. In addition, letters allow scholars to explore the viewpoints of letter writers and their addressees over time, opening up for scrutiny an epistolary network such as Schreiner's, wherein letter writing was interspersed with other kinds of political activity. Olive Schreiner's letters are a particularly interesting and important resource in this regard: they are written by a key feminist theorist and social commentator; they span an especially momentous period of change between the 1870s and 1920 in terms of technologies of letter writing and major social issues of the time and subsequently; they engage analytically with the social and other changes occurring and consider where these would take society in the future; they were often written and used *as* politics, rather than just being about politics, and they provide tantalising hints about interconnections between white radicals and the black political and intellectual elite.[31] Obviously the existence of political letters as a subgenre of letter writing is well known and has been the focus of some recent interesting discussions, which have considered the ways in which women have deployed letters as a means of circumventing the prohibitions and limitations imposed in more formal political contexts.[32] In general, however, previous scholars have assumed the impact or otherwise of letter writing trends by referring to a range of circumstantial evidence, while our discussion moves beyond contentions of an 'it is likely' character, to explore how cause and effect might be pinned down.

In what follows, we consider in detail Schreiner's 'expressing *my* views and leaving them to work' strategy for gaining political influence, as commented on in the letter providing this article's epigraph. In doing so, we explore a number of instances where her influence is undoubted, but where it is, nonetheless, surprisingly difficult to demonstrate this with certainty, and from this we then consider how a more certain view of influence or its absence might be gained. As well as outside-the-text ways of thinking about exactly how influence can be demonstrated and proven, we shall also discuss ways of doing this which relate to letters themselves, because important textual demonstrations of influence can be found within her letters.

Olive Schreiner's 'characteristic shrewdness' – Walker's case for influence

Olive Schreiner's brother Will (1857–1919) was an important legal and political presence in South African public life, starting in 1887 with his appointment as legal advisor to the Cape Governor, until his death in 1919 while serving as High Commissioner in London. Eric Walker, a leading South African liberal historian who wrote the key political biography of Will Schreiner, treats Olive Schreiner's influence on her brother's political views and practices as a certain fact and provides several in-depth examples.[33] Therefore, we start exploring influence and its proof by examining what Walker saw as certainties and the evidence he provided to substantiate them, because his work provides a strong case for seeing Schreiner as a feminist protagonist who had considerable influence and impact in this masculine political landscape.

Will Schreiner became legal advisor to Rhodes's De Beers Company and then Cape Attorney-General in 1893 when Rhodes became Prime Minister. When Will became Prime Minister in October 1898, he worked to heal the political breaches caused by the Jameson Raid (an 1895–6 plot in which Rhodes attempted to use force to annex the Transvaal – an independent Boer (later Afrikaner) republic). He also tried to thwart Imperial Governor Milner's and British Colonial Secretary Chamberlain's provocation of the South African War of 1899–1902 between Britain and the two Boer Republics of the Transvaal and Orange Free State. Later his thinking moved leftward: he headed the legal defence of the Zulu king, Dinuzulu, against trumped-up charges in 1907–8; he opposed the Union of the four settler states (the Boer republics and the British colonies of the Cape and Natal); he led a 1909 black delegation to Britain to lobby against the draft of the South Africa Act, which unified the four white settler states and from

1910 to 1914 he was a senator with the role of representing black views in the Union parliament's upper house.[34]

Over the period when Olive Schreiner published her political writings, women had no formal presence in South African political life; they were voteless in the settler states and then in the Union of South Africa in 1910.[35] There was a strong local culture of gender conventions governing its formal political life, and within this, with just a few exceptions, the ways women gained informal influence through political salons and similar means in European and US contexts were largely absent.[36] Olive Schreiner commented her brother had little political 'nose', no 'shrewdness', and he agreed.[37] Schreiner had keenly developed and widely recognised, if not always welcomed, political skills, while Will's were minimal. But it was he who had the high profile public political career, while she forced her ideas into the public domain through high circulation writings like 'A Returned South African' and *The Political Situation* essays. Schreiner harnessed this fame to facilitate political connections, using women's proto-feminist networks to put pressure on 'the men' and also through letters which articulated analytical ideas and arguments and sought to influence the political views and behaviours of her addressees, as we explore later. Her letters to Will provide important evidence of her challenging and subverting prevailing separate spheres conventions. Letters by many of her correspondents, including Will Schreiner, John Merriman, F. S. Malan and Jan Smuts, also show that these men accepted her right and ability to dissent, even while often disagreeing with her.

Many passages in Walker's political biography of Will Schreiner emphasise Olive Schreiner's political shrewdness and her influence on her brother at important junctures in his political life. Walker had no doubt about this influence, stating for instance that 'If he went with Rhodes and the Bond, Schreiner knew that Olive would be grieved. And her grief would hurt him, since he had long regarded her as a kind of detached and most eloquent conscience reinforcing the still, small voice he always found so insistent. It was no light matter for him to go against her'.[38] Comments like this very certain statement of Olive Schreiner's influence occur multiply in Walker's book and add up to something very compelling, but what proof is there of such claims?

One instance of Walker claiming her influence concerns the fact that in 1898, following Cape and British investigations of the Jameson Raid, a vote of no confidence in the Rhodes government was moved by Will Schreiner, who expected Jan Hofmeyr, leader of the Afrikaner Bond, to then become Prime Minister. Olive Schreiner, always with an eye on the political future, advised her brother that if a strong liberal bloc was to be formed, Will himself should lead it and that Hofmeyr would 'stand back' for this; Walker concludes '[Will] Schreiner settled accounts with his little demon [the still, small voice of conscience] and decided to go forward'.[39] Then in April 1899, in the run-up to the South African War and as Prime Minister of the Cape Colony, Will had to respond to the political difficulties of the Transvaal Republic, which was trapped between not wanting its political system overrun by uitlanders (outsiders), present largely in gold-mining and finance activities around the Rand gold mines, and British provocation of war by claiming the uitlanders were being denied political rights. Will had little sympathy for the uitlander protests, and Walker comments that 'Olive, with characteristic shrewdness, had noticed this lack in her brother's mental equipment' and advised him to 'deal direct' with the parties involved.[40]

Walker's conclusion is that 'Schreiner did not, indeed, could not go; so to the end he remained without first-hand knowledge', that is, he did not go to the Transvaal himself.[41] However, years after Walker's biography was written, Will Schreiner's papers were donated to what is now the National Library of South Africa in Cape Town, which show that Will *did* deal directly with both sides, using trusted envoys.[42] Walker, then, was incorrect; the Schreiner letters to Will which are now available (i.e. not just those Walker had access to) show the strength of her counsel to her brother and demonstrate that he did a volte-face in his attempts to prevent war, by moving in precisely the direction of her counsel. What does not exist, however, is evidence which *directly* links her counsel to his change, however likely her influence on him is.[43]

The second example concerns the July 1899 recall of General Butler, then commander of Britain's troops in South Africa, because he was too peace-loving. Before leaving, Butler wrote to Will Schreiner, still Prime Minister, to strongly support Will's political tactics of peacemaking. Even though Olive Schreiner was an outspoken, high profile public supporter of the Transvaal, Will sent Butler's letter to her, writing on its back his hope that the Transvaal could avoid being provoked into declaring war, probably a treasonous act were it to be known.[44] As many of Schreiner's letters to Will during September 1899 show, they were fully in each other's political confidence, so sending her Butler's letter clearly demonstrates his trust in her discretion and desire for her counsel.[45] In the larger political landscape, what followed these events was a major increase in political tension and then war, largely because of Milner's intransigence in forcing war on the Transvaal. Then, Walker writes, 'While [Will] was debating thus [about resigning] he received a letter from Olive. "Ultimately", she wrote, "we have nothing to fight the Capitalists with but the guns and forts of the Transvaal . . . If the English government once gains control . . . South Africa may and almost must fall into the hands of the Capitalists . . ." That, for [Will] Schreiner, was decisive'.[46] This provides another instance where Walker sees Olive Schreiner's influence as direct and decisive, but the specifics of why he does so are not detailed.

After the South African War (1899–1902), the question of the political relationship between the white settler states was immediately on the agenda. Regarding this, Walker states that ' . . . just before the ultimatum [starting the war], Olive had written him a letter on the subject [of federation] which had set him thinking, as so many of her shrewd letters did'.[47] He links Will's shift from supporting Union, to supporting a looser federation with internal checks and balances, with this letter, commenting that by 1908, 'It must be federation or nothing, for not only did [Will] share with his sister Olive the belief that small states were . . . . more favourable to liberty . . . but . . . that the federal principle was peculiarly applicable to South Africa . . . In a legislative union . . . the Cape's liberal policy would be in constant danger'.[48] This was, indeed, Olive Schreiner's position, and in a letter to Will she marshals her arguments and wonders 'on what a thoughtful mind like yours bases its desire for Union'.[49] One of her suggestions was 'Stand by the side which is for the moment weakest . . . Our day will come & England will have to honour a cheque endorsed by Justice . . . Always follow your little sister's advice & you'll get to heaven at last'.[50] Will Schreiner did precisely this and resigned office on 13 June 1900, stating the need for a more conciliatory approach to the punishment of Cape Colony men who fought as rebels during the war. Again, Will's change of mind and its timing are highly suggestive, but no more direct evidence than this exists regarding Olive Schreiner's influence on him in this matter, however likely and supported by circumstantial evidence it may be.

Will Schreiner's political views and practices continued to change. His 1908–9 defence of the Zulu king Dinuzulu, and then post-1910 his role as an elected senator representing black people in parliament, signify a more general liberalising of his political views, which eventuated in an invitation from the 1909 black delegation that went to Britain to protest against the draft of the South Africa Act to lead it. Our fourth example concerns the fact that by the end of 1913, Will had also become a public supporter of women's and black suffrage, in one speech emphasising 'the subject we are discussing [women's franchise] and the object we have to serve are indissolubly connected with the abolition of all prejudices, and I class the discrimination on grounds of sex with the fearful discrimination against humanity on the ground of race or colour'.[51] Walker comments that Olive Schreiner and Will's eldest daughter Lyndall were significant figures in the women's suffrage campaign, implying this is why his views changed. However, of more relevance is that Olive Schreiner was a full adult suffragist, and she insisted that no franchise measure should be supported which did not bestow full political rights to black people as well as white women. It seems to have been this adult suffrage position that Will Schreiner was influenced by – his franchise speech was made in the context of the introduction of a Natives Land Act by an increasingly retrogressive Union government and his speech expressed his recoil from it enshrining segregationist and discriminatory principles.[52] This is, again, a major change from his earlier approach to franchise matters, and once more it is a move in the direction of his sister's views and political advice to him. But once more there is no incontrovertible evidence of a causal link.

Over the course of his political life, Will Schreiner became demonstrably more liberal, in particular regarding race matters. His sister's letters to him exhorted, cajoled, persuaded and advised him that he should move politically in the direction that he, in fact, did move in. As Olive commented to her close friend Betty Molteno, 'My dear brother seems becoming much more liberal on the native question. But I never argue with him. Seeds grow quickest under ground'.[53] Walker frequently states that her shrewdness and advice were 'decisive' and led Will to change. However, his political biography is very much of its day in its absence of chapter and verse references to substantiate factual claims and its failure to document the privately held sources and first person knowledge made available to him. Consequently, while Walker's insistence that Schreiner was a 'key influence' on her brother has to be taken seriously, he provides no direct and incontrovertible evidence for this.[54]

We have discussed Walker's case for Olive Schreiner's political influence on Will Schreiner in detail because of Walker's certainty about this. However, looking closely at the four key examples we have taken from Walker, it is not so open and shut as he assumes because, as we have shown, his claims are not backed by precise detail. With the exception of Butler's letter, the epistolary and other evidence which might have demonstrated Olive Schreiner's influence over Will in a more direct and indisputable way is no longer available, or perhaps never existed in writing. Consequently, we shall now move on to consider her influence in a different way. This is by considering the links between her letters and her published work as an author. Schreiner's published writings were internationally renowned, and there is ample evidence in the form of translations, sales figures, new editions, reviews and a host of written comments in letters, autobiographies and memoirs by readers, attesting to their influence. Schreiner's letters to John Merriman provide an interesting example to discuss her influence, for Merriman was both repeatedly generous in his praise of Schreiner's published work, and a determined opponent of one cause she held dear, women's enfranchisement, and also an uncertain supporter of another, the cause for black equal rights.

'If . . . a law were passed, that you, John X. Merriman, were not a fit & proper human being' – influence across Schreiner's letters and her published writings

Merriman was a cabinet minister in various Cape administrations from 1875 onward and became its last Prime Minister in the period immediately before the Union of South Africa, that is, from 1908 to 1910.[55] Merriman parted company from Rhodes after the Jameson Raid and increasingly cooperated with the Afrikaner Bond, to the extent that he became a key protagonist in ensuring Union around a racial – indeed, racist – principle which governed not only the franchise but also denied other rights to black people. A politician through and through in a way that Will Schreiner never was, Merriman, like the other Cape liberals Sauer, Innes and Malan, did not operate on fixed principle but by making deals to ensure himself high political office.[56] For Olive Schreiner, how he and these men conducted themselves seriously weakened the liberal grouping in the Cape parliament. Her letters to Merriman on this and related matters are among her most fascinating, displaying her intellectual prowess and political acumen. Across the period 1896 to 1913, these letters argue with, flatter and persuade Merriman that his voting record and other political behaviours ought to match his proclaimed liberal principles. Examples particularly relevant to the present discussion include Schreiner's lengthy endeavour to persuade Merriman to put his principles regarding the 'native question' and black political rights into practice, and also to convince him that women should be treated equally with men and that he should support (or even just not oppose) women's enfranchisement measures.

Presciently, by the early 1890s Schreiner was convinced that race would become *the* defining issue for South Africa. In one of her many arguments to Merriman, she insists that 'a course of stern unremitting justice is demanded from us towards the native, & that only in as far as we are able to raise him . . . can the future of South Africa be anything but an earthly Hell', and so Merriman and the other liberals should stop supporting retrograde legislation for the sake of short-term political gain.[57] Schreiner perceived the push for Union in these terms, that is, it was at basis concerned with cheap labour and black subjugation. She attended the debates about Union in the Cape parliament and wrote to her brother about the occasion when Union was passed:

> That scene in the house yesterday, was without any exception the most contemptible from the broad human stand-point I have ever seen in my life . . . they squirmed & lied, & each one giving the other away, & all gave away principle . . . Men selling their souls & the future – & fate watching them.[58]

'They' included Malan, and the 'fate watching' in this letter was embodied by Dr Abdullah Abdurahman, leader of the African People's Organisation representing the coloured populations of the Cape and more widely, who had sat next to Schreiner and had also observed the reneging on principle occurring. And just as Schreiner predicted in her letters and in her essay *Closer Union*, once Union was achieved then a succession of racially and politically retrogressive legislation *was* pushed through with full support from the erstwhile Cape liberals, including Malan, who she had hoped would resist this.

At the end of their epistolary friendship, Schreiner wrote to Merriman about the 1913 Natives Land Act, the most notorious of such legislative onslaughts on black rights because it was the founding basis of apartheid legislation after 1948, that 'I thought your speech on the Native Bill very fine, but oh if you could have seen your way to vote against the Bill!'[59] Her 'but oh' and exclamation mark speak volumes – this is the last proper letter Schreiner wrote to him, and she ceased writing because of the way he had voted. As with Malan, Schreiner's argumentative and exhortatory letters to Merriman ended once she concluded he had crossed a line beyond which there could be no persuading him to behave in a more principled way. In Merriman's case, this concerned the Land Act; in Malan's, it was Union and his reneging on promised support for black and women's enfranchisement.

However, whatever the complications of evaluating Merriman's response to Schreiner's political analyses and prognostications in her *letters*, as soon as her *published writing* appeared in the public domain he wrote appreciatively to her regarding its ethical stance and message. That is, it is difficult to evaluate the influence of Schreiner's letters on Merriman, but evident that he greatly respected her published work. Merriman was, in fact, among the few white South Africans to praise her allegorical novella *Trooper Peter Halket of Mashonaland*.[60] This book was highly controversial in condemning massacres carried out by Rhodes's Chartered Company troops in what is now Zimbabwe and naming Rhodes as personally responsible.[61] She wrote to Merriman, 'I am indeed glad of your opinion of Peter Halket',[62] while to Will Schreiner she explained in more detail:

> Dear old John X Merriman   sent me quite a touching little note when he passed here to go up. However we may differ on the woman question . . . I can never forget that he was the one, only, human creature in South Africa . . . who wrote me one word of sympathy when at so much terrible cost to myself I brought out Peter Halket. His letter was not only sympathetic . . . it came straight from the heart, & his letters & view of all things generally come entirely from the head.[63]

This highlights the importance of the links which existed between Schreiner's different genres of writing; and whilst recognising the significance of her letters, it is important not to neglect or downplay the impact of her published work. It also raises the complexity of her response to Merriman – and his to her.

Schreiner's 'we differ' comment in the letter above alludes to what was generally seen as Merriman's highly negative stance regarding women's participation in public and professional life. She was consequently reluctant to debate the woman question with him because it was a subject which, as she put it, 'lies so near to my heart, touches me so deeply that I can hardly dis-cuss it as an indifferent matter'.[64] But she *did* try to explain her position, including encouraging him to put himself in the situation of women:

> If you, John X Merriman were for five years owing to illness, business or absence from home, to abstain from casting your vote it would probably not appreciably affect the country, & not by a little affect your personal health, wealth, happiness or freedom . . . But if a law were passed, that you, John X. Merriman, were not a fit & proper humanbeing to exercise the vote & prohibiting you from doing so, then in a moment the matter would become one of primary importance, worth fighting

over & perhaps even under certain conditions laying down your life for. So small a thing in itself it would yet indicate your place in the society of which you form a part, your relation to your fellow men in a hundred ways, & so be of vital import.[65]

In spite of Merriman's known views, Schreiner's letters to various people in 1911 comment with amazement about a letter he sent her about *Woman and Labour*, published at the start of the year.[66] To her sister Ettie, for instance, she wrote with an atypically large number of exclamation marks:

> You know what a bitter opponent of any emancipation for women old Merriman has always been. I don't know if you remember his speech when the bill was introduced into the house! My book hadn't been six days in Cape Town when I got a long letter from him, saying how much he had enjoyed reading the book . . . the old fellow is always looking up favourable reviews of the book, & wrote yesterday to tell he 'was delighted to find a most sympathetic review in the 'Economist'' . . . – which he was going to send me! It's quite touching if you knew <u>how</u> bitter he was – he couldn't even talk of ˆtheˆ woman's movement without getting in a rage![67]

Why did Merriman write this letter and send her the reviews? It could be argued that Schreiner influenced Merriman in broad ways in her published writing, while her letters expressed political views antithetical to him that he ignored. But it is not as straightforward as this because Olive Schreiner's *writing* and her *letters* are not so easily prised apart: her letters are not separate from her social theorising and they articulate views which also appear in her published work. Schreiner's letters to Merriman discuss, under the banner of 'I can hardly discuss at all', many of the same ideas which appeared in *Woman and Labour* and which were initially expressed in her letters, including in those to Merriman. Would a man militantly opposed to women's rights have responded so positively to *Woman and Labour* if Schreiner's letters had not engaged with him on this over a lengthy period? The common-sense interpretation of the change here is that the views expressed in her letters were persuasive and slowly influenced him, so that when he came across them in her published work he was already predisposed to react more favourably than she had anticipated.

However, in order to find any decisive, less circumstantial evidence of Schreiner's influence on Merriman, an investigation of the entirety of his epistolary and related textual activities, and those of his major correspondents, would be needed to search for documentary proofs. This would be both an enormous task and also might yield no result because he might not have written about this to any of his correspondents. Therefore, we now discuss an example where Olive Schreiner's political influence is fully demonstrated, outline the particular circumstances which produced the document in question and consider the certain proofs it provides of Schreiner's influence.

'Always give your enemies what they don't want!' – marks upon the text

Schreiner's 1899 political essay *An English South African's View of the Situation* warned that a war between Britain and the Boer Republics would be hard fought and devastating on both sides, rather than the British walkover many imagined.[68] The essay originated in the political analysis and strategising in her 'private' letters and also in the open letters she published in a range of newspapers. This particular essay started as an open letter in a newspaper and was expanded to a pamphlet and then a short book, and it achieved high sales and was rapidly translated into many world languages. Schreiner and other political figures, particularly in the Transvaal and Free State, saw it as an important part of the anti-war and pro-Republican campaign, viewing her letter/pamphlet/book *as* politics rather than just *about* this. Schreiner wrote to Jan Hofmeyr about it, that:

> I hope you received the copy of my paper on the Situation which I sent to you. I am going to republish it in pamphlet form . . . Will the Bond care to take any copies, & if so how many, at 3d each. ~~I ha~~ I cannot afford to republish it unless I know a certain number will be taken . . . I am going to have it translated into all the European languages . . . Always give your enemies what they don't want! . . . If you think the Bond would order any of pamphlets, please wire to me Box 406 Johannesburg.[69]

Hofmeyr was not only leader of the Bond but also *the* most influential politician over many years in the Cape, with very strong links with Boer/Afrikaner politicians and organisations elsewhere too. Schreiner's letter makes a number of assumptions, in particular that Hofmeyr would share her view of the importance of her paper, and also that their unnamed 'enemies' would as well. This might seem vainglorious – except for the certainty provided by Hofmeyr's notes to his secretary on the back of the letter, which concern its importance and how it was to be responded to:

> R 7–6-99
> Moloy ordered 100. Send 400 C. P. Schultz & acc to me.
> I appreciate enthusiastic labours our common cause. Your burning words find entrance where nobody else can.
> I think Kruger displayed an unexpectedly liberal spirit at BFT. am sure he could have done a great deal more if he had been encouraged by the other side. This morning wired to a Bloemfontein friend: –
> (Insert wire to Fischer) 'I deplore' &c)
> He replied this afternoon
> (Fischer's wire 7th June) 'I fear my friend does not see that by not making concessions which H Exc did not ask for then Kruger would be playing enemy's game.[70]

Hofmeyr's notes provide a number of instances of actions which were to be taken in direct response to Schreiner's letter. Firstly, two separate orders for copies of her essay were placed, with Hofmeyr and the Bond paying for the largest. Secondly, Hofmeyr replied to her in extremely flattering terms about her 'burning words finding entrance' and in doing so he provided her with highly confidential information about Kruger, President of the Transvaal, during a Bloemfontein conference negotiating with Milner. Thirdly, Hofmeyr instructed the secretary that she should be sent his telegram to Fisher, one of the envoys whom Will Schreiner had sent to the Republics. And fourthly, he also instructed the secretary that Fischer's reply to himself should be sent to her as well. There is nothing circumstantial about discerning the impact of Schreiner's influence here, the proofs are certain.

Finding clear and incontrovertible demonstration of Schreiner's influence as in Hofmeyr's notes and the more complex example of the Butler letter sent to her by her brother is rare. So does this mean that only circumstantial claims can be made about Schreiner's political influence, apart from in such specific instances? So far we have assumed that demonstrating influence requires a directly evidenced change in someone's expressed views or behaviours, as with the Hofmeyr example, of a cause and effect kind. However, there is another way to think about the influence and impact of letter writing, which is to conceive this in epistolary and textually oriented terms which are 'to the letter'. That is, to focus on the specifically epistolary forms that influence and impact might take. We now turn to a consideration of this and how this approach might help forward our epistemological inquiry about Schreiner's influence as a feminist protagonist in the political landscape of the Cape Colony.

Doing things with letters: the performative character of Schreiner's epistolary activities and influence

The idea of an epistolarium has been central to our understanding and analysis of the (extant and the missing and presumed destroyed) letters written by Olive Schreiner and other people who engaged in high-volume letter writing.[71] In the case of Schreiner's letters, conceptualising the shape and concerns of her epistolarium suggests there are characteristic features of it, both overall and with respect to particular correspondents. These characteristics can provide helpful ways of exploring the influence and impact of her letters in ways that do not rely on externalist measures of this. Of particular relevance here is the performative character of many of Schreiner's letters. Here we use 'performative' in the J. L. Austin, technical sense of 'how to do things with words'.[72] That is, the term performative does not mean 'a performance' for Austin but has the more rigorous meaning of words or phrases that actually do the thing they are about: the immediately legally binding character of 'I do' in a marriage ceremony is one example Austin provides. 'I promise to pay the bearer on demand', written on British banknotes and signed by the Bank of England's chief cashier since 1694, is another and reminds us that banknotes originated as handwritten promissory or signed IOU letters.

The first kind of performative letter writing which Schreiner engaged in can be shown by an example where she initiated a political friendship in the context of the Cape Women's Enfranchisement League (WEL), writing to a Mrs Goosen:

> My friend Mrs Haldane Murray has just written to tell me how hard you are working for us at Cathcart. This is just to hold out a hand of friendship to you. I know how difficult it often is to start a new thing in an up-country, but once started, & when our women really understand the the great good, not only to themselves, but to men & all the nation, the freedom of women will bring, I believe our South African women will be even more earnest & successful than others.[73]

This letter *in itself* constitutes 'the hand of friendship' that Schreiner writes of holding out to Mrs Goosen. Metaphorically, it *is* the hand of the WEL; and later in this letter it is also extended to Mrs Goosen's husband as well, by invoking Schreiner's husband and enclosing a political pamphlet by him that was to be given to Mr Goosen. The effect is that her letter does not so much welcome Mrs Goosen to the WEL fold, as confirm that she is already part of it. Schreiner's inclusive phrasing – 'us', 'you', 'our women' and so on – reinforces this effect of producing the friendship within the letter. Performative ways of opening up and confirming friendly relations also have a more general place in how Schreiner's letters achieve influence and impact. Many examples occur from the 1880s on in the context of her feminist friendships, including in letters to Alys Pearsall Smith, Beatrice Potter (later Webb), Mary Sauer, Fred and Emmeline Pethick-Lawrence and others; and later from 1914 to 1918 this occurs in her letters to people in pacifist networks too, including such feminist notables as Jane Addams, Aletta Jacobs and Catherine Marshall.

The second kind of performative letter writing engaged in by Schreiner acts as a closure and is *in itself* the closing that her letter states will happen:

> I can't write to you about public matters. I personally have never wished Gladstone to be recalled, nor did I think your ministry ought to resign. Would he gain anything better by it? But I am opposed to Botha's silly Imperialism when he talks English, & narrow back-velt-ism when he talks Dutch!! Give my love to your wife, & the dear children. I hope the young generation will live to see a nobler broader, less racial spirit than we see in South Africa to-day.[74]

This letter marks the end of the powerful correspondence between Schreiner and Malan. Although her 'I cannot write to you again' statement is followed by three comments on political matters (Herbert Gladstone's recall, Prime Minister Botha's conduct, and racialism), these were in fact the last things Schreiner wrote to Malan. Literally, she *would* not write to him again, and in this example she finalised the correspondence by having three 'last (political) words', the third of which acts as a final comment on Malan himself, one of the older generation with a more racial less noble approach. Schreiner sent a very similar last letter to Merriman, written in the context of retrograde political events which ended Schreiner's hope that his political behaviour might become more actively liberal. In addition, performative last letters which operate a closure have a more general place within Schreiner's political armoury. Important examples, for instance, occur in the context of women's suffrage in South Africa, when erstwhile colleagues adopted a policy of 'on the same terms as men' and therefore supported a racial basis to women's suffrage.[75]

The third kind of performative letter writing by Olive Schreiner assumes and *in itself demonstrates* a favourable view of her political judgement and position which was shared by her and her correspondent. This can be seen particularly clearly in letters acting as a recommendation of a particular person and/or the political cause they were representing. For instance, she provided a number of people with epistolary introductions to the Transvaal politician Jan Smuts and his wife Isie Smuts, to her Dutch feminist friend Aletta Jacobs, and to the British Labour Party leader Keir Hardie, as well as to Will Schreiner. Schreiner sent one such letter directly (rather than to the person concerned) to her brother Will, then Prime Minister of the Cape in wartime, concerning a Reuters journalist who had been sent to head its South African office:

> Yesterday we had a man to lunch with us Collins, Reuter's General Manager in Australia. He is a man of considerable intelligence & much influence in journalistic world. He is on his way to England will see Lord Salisbury &c. We tried to let him into the ?inwardness of affairs here a little . . . He has a letter of introduction to you from ~~the~~ ^an^ Australian Premier . . . Introduce him to Hoffmeyr &c ~~& sh~~ He's rather a good sort, clear & sharp. Could be <u>very useful</u> at home.[76]

While Collins was provided with a letter of introduction from the Australian Prime Minister to present to Will, Schreiner takes it for granted that Will would find her own letter a more trustworthy guide. She also wrote many letters of introduction for women, including to secure access for her much loved nieces to British feminist circles and also to attest to the suitability of women she knew for humanitarian war work over the period 1914 to 1918. The common feature of this kind of letter writing is that tacitly it 'works' because of a shared evaluation on the part of the person making the request, the addressee of the letter and by Schreiner herself, concerning Schreiner's value or reliability in recommending someone.

The character or public persona of 'Olive Schreiner' was clearly pivotal in ensuring the performative character of these letters of introduction; that is, this persona was the guarantor of the intended outcome, which was ensuring someone had an entrée into a new political network. However, that Schreiner had such a character or persona was the result of continued activity, rather than it being an innate quality or attribute. Her published writings were obviously of importance here, but so too was her letter writing, in particular her brokerage letters. This is the fourth kind of Schreiner performative letter writing we want to discuss, and it relies on her public persona being accepted as a guarantor in trading political favours. That is, such letters *in themselves broker political effects* by doing political favours in both directions. An example here involves Schreiner brokering for Adele Chapin.[77] Chapin was in South Africa in 1899 to 1902, acting on behalf of British Colonial Secretary Joseph Chamberlain and Governor Alfred Milner, and she wanted to secure her entrée into Transvaal political circles and political information. Schreiner wrote to Jan Smuts, then State Attorney and a key political figure in the pre-war Transvaal, about this.[78] She commented:

> I am coming over to Pretoria on Friday next with an American friend Mrs Chapin . . . I know you are too busy to spare much time, & Mrs Chapin is very anxious to meet you . . . She is a great friend of ~~unreadable~~ the Governors & in constant correspondence with him; she also knows the Chamberlains with whom she will probably stay on her return to England; ^as she did before she came out here,^ . . . anything said will go straight to Chamberlain – ~~unreadable~~ Milner . . .[79]

Schreiner also wrote to her brother Will on the same matter, clearly realising that Chapin was a kind of unofficial spy for Britain:

> There is an American friend of mine staying at Mount Nelson hotel for some days on her way from Johannesburg to England. ^Mrs Chapin^ She is a great friend of Mrs Chamberlain's & Milners. She was very anxious to meet you. I told her I could not possibly promise that you would call, but that I would ask you to if you have time. She might give you some interesting news about the League in Johannesburg as she knows much. She is sympathetic to our side, but of course all you say may go straight to Chamberlain & Milner.[80]

These letters were written in the run-up to the South African War (1899–1902), with Schreiner's knowledge – conveyed in both of the above letters – that what Adele Chapin heard would most likely go to her political masters. In her letter writing, Schreiner's being in the know and well connected on this matter was demonstrated to both Adele Chapin and Jan Smuts, and thereby increased Schreiner's political status in the eyes of both. It enabled the Transvaal to convey, through a source they would trust because in a sense guaranteed by Schreiner, the political information they wanted Chamberlain and Milner to receive. It would also have had the effect of increasing Chapin's marketability as a successful peddler of to-be-trusted information with both Britain and the Transvaal, again guaranteed by Schreiner's intervention. And Schreiner's related brokerage letter to Will Schreiner indicates how thoroughly her political strategising and brokering was engaged in, working across a range of relationships that transcended any separation between personal and political spheres.

Thinking of Schreiner's letters in their own terms by drawing on Austin's ideas about the performative in the technical sense of a letter doing the very thing it is about, provides a fruitful means of discerning the range of ways in which her letters had direct influence and impact. Doing so makes clear how much influence and political importance Schreiner had and the varied ways in which she secured influence within and across different networks and contexts. While the discussion here has focused on an earlier period, later examples also abound and could have been provided regarding, for instance, her political lobbying around war and pacifism while in Britain from 1914 to 1920 (including for instance demanding and being granted an interview with Lloyd George on the outbreak of the Great War in 1914), and her involvement in helping raise money for the defence of the South African trades unionist Samuel Masabala and other black political causes in 1920. Relatedly, the performative is an important aspect of Schreiner's letters more generally, as our comment that all four of Schreiner's key performative forms of letter writing have more general expression, in addition to the particular examples provided here, will have indicated.

A feminist protagonist in a masculine political landscape: on influence and separate spheres

We have reviewed Olive Schreiner's influence on the political views and behaviour of a number of well-known figures within the political landscape of South Africa, using the examples discussed to raise a general epistemological issue facing all historical scholarship, gender history included: how can impact and influence in the historical past be convincingly demonstrated. In all the examples discussed, there is reasonable certainty that Schreiner *did* have influence, for the weight of circumstantial evidence strongly supports this. But showing such influence in the stronger terms of certainty backed by direct evidence has proved difficult, apart from in the two exceptional instances of Hofmeyr's notes and Butler's letter. However, rethinking notions of influence and cause and effect by focusing on the frequently performative character Schreiner's letters conveys that in a number of ways her letter writing had *direct* effects for the addressees of her letters. Succinctly, these letters in and of themselves changed things. The performative dimensions of letter writing, we suggest, need to be encompassed in thinking about influence and its proofs, rather than these being conceived as always lying outside the text. Texts and words can have powerful effects, not just 'things' in a narrower material sense.

We conclude that Olive Schreiner 'just expressing my views' in her letters *did* in fact have undoubted effects and demonstrable influence in the masculine political landscape, and we hope to have argued this 'to the letter' in ways that readers will find convincing. But where does this take us in responding to the epistemological and ontological questions introduced earlier? An immediate response (we elaborate later in the conclusion) is that matters of ontology or 'being' are at the heart of episte-mological issues about knowing, and this has consequences for how to understand the historical landscape and the gendered relationships and spheres which charac-terise it. That is, earlier we noted Abrams's comment that working from the supposed peripheries rather than the 'metropolitan heart' necessitates (or should) a change of perspective, a shift to a feminist historiography conceived around narratives of women whose sense of the past included their own contexts, as she puts it.[81] This change of perspective is what we have endeavoured to provide here, together with a glimpse of an alternate history of a momentous period in the South African past. We have done this by exploring Schreiner's epistolary perspectives on and interventions in South Africa's masculine political landscape, as one of the keenest minded feminist social theorists of her generation and later. And we hope this approach has also re-stored her to view as a shrewd and effective political strategist who had considerable influence.[82]

Looked at in relation to the historical time period of their writing and the network of correspondents they were written to, Olive Schreiner's letters can be seen as not only hugely important because of their content, but also as ontologically and episte-mologically complex in the sense that their meaning for their addressees and also their influence and impact are not immediately transparent. Working in a referential frame concerning letters as historical documents perceives them as problematic because they are perspectival, tailored 'to the person' who is the addressee and lack direct referential properties – they are part of context, but in a way often deemed by researchers to be somehow faulty. However, it is their perspectival, dialogical, emergent, temporal and serial characteristics that underpin the fascination of letter writing for feminist histori-ography as we practice it. As we have shown, these characteristics are not deficiencies but strengths because they provide an analytical purchase on understanding context and its dynamics. That is, letters do not need to be 'the facts' and nothing but this in order to have impact and influence. Context, then, needs to be thought about in ways which include letter writing, reading and replying and the importance of this in cultural and personal life.

A large collection of letters like Olive Schreiner's has interesting characteristic features, presences and absences and changes in people's letter writing over time can be explored by drawing together things which more conventional scholarship usually keeps separate. In her case, these include her published writing, political practices and social networks as well as her 'private' letters. And as we have shown, by working with the grain of epistolarity rather than against it, and relatedly by exploring the performative in the Austin sense, many examples of the direct influence of Schreiner's letters come into view. There are, we have proposed, appropriate and sufficient ways of showing the influence of Schreiner's letters outside of the narrowly referential. Recognising the performativity of many of her letters throws light on the letter writing itself, and it also connects these letters with 'real-life' as experienced by new members of suffrage campaigns, amateur spies, worried politicians and newspaper men moving jobs, among others. Succinctly, Schreiner's letters, not just her published writings, were influential and had demonstrable impacts in the highly masculine political landscape of South Africa of the time, and they did so in the range of performative ways we have explored. In addition, if her letters had influence like this, then other people's letter writing will have done so too, which opens up for consideration the possible influence of 'others' more generally, and in particular white women and black people and how they too might have made their mark – but alas not mark enough – upon the evolving political context of South Africa.[83]

Using Schreiner's letters as a focus for discussion has, we hope, fleshed out our ear-lier comments about the complexities of separate spheres in the South African context and the intertwining of gender and race in this. A binary way of thinking about sepa-rate spheres is both helpful and unhelpful when thinking from this particular colonial periphery, for the gendered and raced separations strongly marking the white enclaves of South Africa were sometimes super-exaggerated but also frequently traversed and in Schreiner's case at times almost dissolved.[84] Contra the tenor of arguments from Davidoff and Weintraub, we conclude that what is needed in analytically responding to this complexity is *not* to reify fractures of public and private, but instead to adopt a more radical approach and dismantle such binary ways of thinking.[85]

In South Africa over Schreiner's lifetime, separate spheres thinking and its practices were enshrined but also massively undercut by unacknowledged presences, including economically powerful Boer matriarchs, redoubtable frontierswomen, strategising feminists, the omnipresence of black people in 'white' spaces which were entirely dependent on their skills and labour and a rapidly emergent and active black intelligentsia. Coexisting with such complexities were the self-perpetuating white oligarchies which formed the governments of the four settler states and conceived the world using gendered and raced binaries. And so how is the political strategising of Schreiner as a feminist protagonist to be understood against the distinctive and extremely complicated backcloth of this political landscape? Her performative letters took shape and had the influence they did in this framework and their impact certainly cannot be classified or measured by reference to binary notions of public and private, personal and political. Consequently we note with interest some root and branch reconceptualisations of separate spheres thinking, and in particular Peggy Watson's interesting idea of a 'curved space' created by the political actors that it simultaneously creates. For Watson, 'rather than acting "within" political space or being prevented from doing so by virtue of space's lack, [political actors] instead *constitute* as they are constituted by a specific political "curved space"'.[86] This accords with our research on Schreiner's letters and their complex interfaces with social and political life; and in association with recognising the strong heterotopic aspects of letter writing in inscribing a kind of parallel 'other place', such rethinking provides useful tools for feminist historiography working at the assumed margins and peripheries of masculine political landscapes.[87]

Kathleen Canning suggests that '[t]he gender history of the future is one that can confidently admit the possibility of disparate temporalities. Rather than attempting to fit gender back into established chronologies and categories, its more productive outcome may be to allow dissonance within grand narratives'.[88] We have explored such disparate temporalities and narrative dissonances in connection with Olive Schreiner's letters in order to show how this particular feminist protagonist was able to achieve influence in the masculine political landscape of white South African political life. We look forward to a gender history which actively promotes, not just allows, such dissonance within its narratives. Regarding the microhistory of the particular place and experience we have discussed, Schreiner's letters show that in some historical circumstances gender dynamics and separate spheres may be neither so binary nor so impermeable as once supposed, and also, they hint at the existence of alternative motors of change and the fascinating might-have-been of a very different South African future. That 'could have been' future was still a possibility when Olive Schreiner began writing her letters in the 1870s, but not when she came to terminate some of the correspondences considered here.

Notes

The Olive Schreiner Letters Project is funded by the Economic and Social Research Council (ESRC) (RES-062–23-1286); we gratefully acknowledge the ESRC's support. We are grateful also to the organisers of the Minneapolis Workshop on 'Gender History Across Epistemologies', University of Minnesota, 15–16 April 2011, and to Patricia Lorcin, who moderated the session on 'Reading Letters Across Epistemologies' and provided helpful comments. Thanks to Donna Gabaccia and Mary Jo Maynes and the anonymous reviewers for *Gender &*

History for detailed comments on our original article. In addition, Liz Stanley thanks the Sociology Department of the University of Pretoria, where much of the research and thinking for this article occurred as part of a Visiting Professorship.[NB. The access dates for all website references is 6 February 2012]

1. Olive Schreiner to Betty Molteno, 17 June 1900, <http://www.oliveschreiner.org/vre?view=collections& colid=92&letterid=34>. All transcriptions are precisely 'to the letter' and include the omissions, insertions, deletions and mistakes of the originals; ^this^ indicates an insertion, ~~this~~ is a deletion, and this is an underline, in the original letters.

2. See Ruth First and Ann Scott, *Olive Schreiner: A Biography* (London: Andre Deutch, 1980); Joyce Berkman, *The Healing Imagination of Olive Schreiner: Beyond South African Colonialism* (Oxford: Plantin Publishers, 1989); Anne McClintock, *Imperial Leather: Race, Gender and Sexuality in the Colonial Context* (London: Routledge, 1995); Carolyn Burdett, *Olive Schreiner and the Progress of Feminism* (Basingstoke: Palgrave, 2001); Liz Stanley, *Imperialism, Labour and the New Woman: Olive Schreiner's Social Theory* (Durham: Sociology Press, 2002); Liz Stanley, '"Shadows Lying Across Her Pages": Epistolary Aspects of Reading "The Eventful I" in Olive Schreiner's Letters 1889–1913', *Journal of European Studies* 32 (2002), pp. 251–66.

3. Olive Schreiner, *The Story of An African Farm* (London: Chapman & Hall, 1883).

4. In late 1913, as Schreiner prepared to leave South Africa, she destroyed letters sent to her and asked her correspondents to destroy hers to them. Valuing the work people did and seeing 'the life' as incidental to this, she was opposed in principle to 'biographising' and wanted to prevent it happening to her. She also foresaw her letters and those to her being bought and sold in a marketplace, and wanted both to protect her correspondents and to stymie this. For the Olive Schreiner Letters Online, see <http://www.oliveschreiner.org> and for project research publications, go to <www.oliveschreiner.ed.ac.uk/TeamPublications.html>.

5. For an overview of Cape and wider politics of the time, see T. H. R. Davenport and Christopher Saunders, *South Africa: A Modern History* (Basingstoke: Macmillan, 2000), pp.194–299. On key Cape liberals and 'Cape liberalism', see Peter Kallaway, 'F. S. Malan, the Cape Liberal Tradition, and South African Politics 1908–1924', *Journal of African History* 15 (1974), pp. 113–29; Phyllis Lewsen, *John X. Merriman: Paradoxical South African Statesman* (New Haven and London: Yale University Press, 1982); Phyllis Lewsen, 'The Cape Liberal Tradition – Myth or Reality?', *Race* 13 (1971), pp. 65–80; Rodney Davenport, 'The Cape Liberal Tradition to 1910' in Jeffrey Butler, Richard Elphick and David Welsh (eds), *Democratic Liberalism in South Africa* (Middleton, Connecticut: Wesleyan University Press, 1987), pp. 21–34. Some historians reject the idea of liberalism in this context. Although by European standards they by no means fitted the liberal concept, these politicians were 'relatively liberal' and were known as liberals in the South African context explored here. Thus our usage. The Afrikaner Bond was established in the Cape in 1880 to oppose British imperial influence and promote South Africa-wide Boer interests. From the 1880s, it was under the control of Hofmeyr, who had a more conciliatory approach. Until the mid-1890s the Bond exerted political influence chiefly by entering into alliances with politicians who would promote its concerns. It later gained direct political power in the Cape parliament. See Mordechai Tamarkin, *Cecil Rhodes and the Cape Afrikaners: The Imperial Colossus and the Colonial Parish Pump* (London: Cass, 1996).

6. See Barbara Welter, 'The Cult of True Womanhood: 1820–1860', *American Quarterly* 18 (1966), pp. 151–74; Leonore Davidoff and Catherine Hall, *Family Fortunes: Men and Women of the English Middle Class, 1780–1850* (1987; repr. London: Routledge, 2002); Mary Poovey, *Uneven Developments: The Ideological Work of Gender in Mid-Victorian England* (Chicago: University of Chicago Press, 1988); Jane Rendall, 'Women and the Public Sphere', *Gender & History* 11 (1999), pp. 475–88; Joan Landes, 'Further Thoughts on The Public/Private Distinction', *Journal of Women's History* 15 (2003), pp. 28–39; Mary Ryan, 'The Public and the Private Good: Across the Great Divide in Women's History', *Journal of Women's History* 15 (2003), pp. 10–27.

7. See Cameron Macdonald and Karen Hansen, 'Sociability and Gendered Spheres', *Social Science History* 25 (2001), pp. 535–61; Cathy Davidson and Jessamyn Hatcher (eds), *No More Separate Spheres* (Durham: Duke University Press, 2002); Mary Ryan, 'The Public and the Private Good', pp. 10–27; Joan Scott and Debra Keates (eds), *Going Public: Feminism and the Shifting Boundaries of the Private Sphere* (Urbana: University of Illinois Press, 2004); Alison Piepmeier, 'Stepping Out: Rethinking The Public and Private Spheres', *Journal of Women's History* 18 (2006), pp. 128–37; Lynn Abrams, 'The Unseamed Picture: Conflicting Narratives of Women in the Modern European Past', *Gender & History* 20 (2008), pp. 628–43; Jeanne Boydston, 'Gender as A Question Of Historical Analysis', *Gender & History* 20 (2008), pp. 558–83.

8. Abrams, 'The Unseamed Picture', pp. 640–41.

9. For overviews of the changing configurations and dynamics of race in South Africa, see William Beinart and Saul Dubow (eds), *Segregation and Apartheid in Twentieth-Century South Africa* (London: Routledge, 1995) and Paul Maylam, *South Africa's Racial Past: The History and Historiography of Racism, Segregation*

and Apartheid (London: Ashgate, 2001). See also Simon Dagut, 'Gender, Colonial "Women's History" and the Construction of Social Distance: Middle-Class British Women in Later Nineteenth-Century South Africa', *Journal Southern African Studies* 26 (2000), pp. 555–72.

10. Regarding notions of separate spheres, for the early period in South Africa see Kirsten McKenzie, 'Women's Talk and the Colonial State: The Wylde Scandal, 1831–1833', *Gender & History* 11 (1999), pp. 30–53; and in other colonial contexts see Penny Russell, *A Wish of Distinction: Colonial Gentility and Femininity* (Melbourne: Melbourne University Press, 1994).

11. This was a product of the character of white migration to South Africa and the kind of colonial society that resulted. Relatedly, there were few towns, land was generally poor and so farms were huge and isolated, and educational opportunities ranged from absent to limited.

12. As Schreiner pointed out in her 1898 'A Returned South African' essay on 'The Boer Woman', which later posthumously appeared in Olive Schreiner, *Thoughts on South Africa* (London: T. Fisher Unwin, 1923). For a critical discussion of the neglect of frontier and other women in South African historiography, see Helen Bradford, 'Women, Gender and Colonialism: Rethinking the History of the British Cape Colony and its Frontier Zones, c.1806–1970', *Journal of African History* 37 (1996), pp. 351–70.

13. We describe this as 'ethnic/racial' over the time-period of Schreiner's youth and younger womanhood, up to approximately 1910, because racial categorisation did not supplant the importance of ethnic groupings and their very different relationships at local levels with white colonialists until after Union of the settler states and its rapid introduction of racially-retrograde legislation.

14. See Karel Schoeman, *Olive Schreiner: A Woman in South Africa 1855–1881* (Johannesburg: Jonathan Ball Publishers, 1989).

15. Olive Schreiner, *The Story of an African Farm*.

16. Olive Schreiner to Havelock Ellis, 15 April 1890, <http://www.oliveschreiner.org/vre?view=collections& colid=137&letterid=396>.

17. These were linked and intended for later publication in book form as 'Stray Thoughts on South Africa', although a dispute with the intended US publisher and then the South African War (1899–1902) prevented this. With some related essays, they were posthumously published as Olive Schreiner, *Thoughts on South Africa*.

18. Olive Schreiner to W. T. Stead, January–March 1889, <http.www.oliveschreiner.org/vre/T120 (M722): W.T. Stead Papers/1- pages 39-41>.

19. Olive Schreiner, *Thoughts on South Africa*, pp. 27–30.

20. Schreiner's reasons for leaving South Africa in 1913 were complicated and include her deteriorating heart condition and search for better medical treatment, her anger at racially retrograde changes occurring in its political life and the near-breakdown of her marriage over her suspicion that her husband 'Cron' Cronwright-Schreiner was involved with another woman.

21. For a detailed discussion of issues around race concerning Schreiner's letter writing practices, see Liz Stanley and Helen Dampier, '"I Trust that our Brief Acquaintance May Ripen into Sincere Friendship": Networks Across The Race Divide In South Africa In Conceptualising Olive Schreiner's Letters, 1890–1920', *OSLP Working Papers on Letters, Letterness & Epistolary Networks, No. 2* (2010), <http://www.oliveschreinerletters.ed.ac.uk/GiantRaceArticlePDF.pdf>.

22. For useful overviews, see Stanley Trapido, 'South Africa and the Historians', *African Affairs* 71 (1972), pp. 434–58 and Wessel Visser, 'Trends in South African Historiography and the Present State of Historical Research', Unpublished paper presented at the Nordic Africa Institute, Uppsala, Sweden, 23 September 2004. Regarding well-known examples, see Sarah Gertrude Millin, *General Smuts* (London: Faber & Faber, 1935); Eric A. Walker, *W. P. Schreiner: A South African* (Oxford: Oxford University Press, 1937); Lewsen, *John X. Merriman*; Phyllis Lewsen, 'Olive Schreiner's Political Theories and Pamphlets' in Cherry Clayton (ed.), *Olive Schreiner* (Johannesburg: McGraw-Hill, 1983), pp. 212–20.

23. Martin Legassick, 'Legislation, Ideology and Economy in Post-1948 South Africa', *Journal of Southern African Studies* 1 (1974), pp. 5–35; Frederick Johnstone, *Class, Race and Gold. A Study of Class Relations and Racial Discrimination in South Africa* (London: Routledge & Keegan Paul, 1976); Shula Marks and Anthony Atmore (eds), *Economy and Society in Pre-Industrial South Africa* (London: Longman, 1980); Shula Marks and Stanley Trapido (eds), *The Politics of Race, Class and Nationalism in Twentieth-Century South Africa* (Harlow: Longman, 1987); Harold Wolpe, *Race, Class and the Apartheid State* (London: Currey, 1988).

24. Liz Stanley, *Mourning Becomes . . . Post/Memory, Commemoration & the Concentration Camps of the South African War* (Manchester: Manchester University Press, 2006); Liz Stanley and Helen Dampier, 'The Number of the South African War (1899–1902) Concentration Camp Dead: Standard Stories, Superior Stories and a Forgotten Proto-Nationalist Research Investigation,' *Sociological Research Online* 14:5 (2009), <www.socresonline.org.uk/14/5/13.html>.

25. Regarding the intertwining of women's and black history, see Nomboniso Gasa (ed.), *Women In South African History* (Cape Town: Human Sciences Research Council, 2007).

26. At Schreiner's death, around 20,000 of her letters appear to have existed; now there are *c*.4,800 extant, with large numbers having been obtained and then destroyed by her then estranged husband Cronwright-Schreiner after preparing *The Life of Olive Schreiner* and *The Letters of Olive Schreiner*. See S. C. Cronwright-Schreiner, *The Letters of Olive Schreiner* (London: T. Fisher Unwin, 1924) and S. C. Cronwright-Schreiner, *The Life of Olive Schreiner* (London: T. Fisher Unwin, 1924). We are of course aware that the destructions mark what remains; this in largely unknowable ways, except that the evidence suggests they were of entire correspondences rather than targeted at censoring particular letters.

27. For Schreiner's relevant letters on such topics, see <http://www.oliveschreiner.org/vre?page=nativequestion> and <http://www.oliveschreiner.org/vre?page=raceandlabour>. See also Liz Stanley and Helen Dampier, '"She Wrote Peter Halket": Fictive and Factive Devices in Olive Schreiner's Letters and *Trooper Peter Halket of Mashonaland*' in David Robinson et al. (eds), *Narratives and Fiction* (Huddersfield: University of Huddersfield Press, 2008), pp. 85–102; Liz Stanley and Helen Dampier, '"Men Selling their Souls & the Future – and Fate Watching Them": Olive Schreiner on Union', *Quarterly Bulletin of the National Library of South Africa* 64 (2010), pp. 121–36; Stanley and Dampier, 'I Trust that our Brief Acquaintance may Ripen into Sincere Friendship'; Liz Stanley and Helen Dampier, '"The Tone Of Things There I Fear Rather Hopeless" – Olive Schreiner, Will Schreiner, Charles Dilke and the 1909 Protest Against The Draft South Africa Act', *Quarterly Bulletin of the National Library of South Africa* (2012, in progress).

28. For Schreiner's letters on these and also topics, see <http://www.oliveschreiner.org/vre?page=bytopic>.

29. The convention among many scholars of epistolarity is that 'the letter' forms a distinct if complex genre around absence, interiority and self-making. However, Schreiner's letters after 1889 are concerned with the material world and the 'other' of her correspondents and consequently 'the familiar' and 'the personal' are reconfigured within and by them.

30. See Ken Plummer, *Documents of Life 2* (London: Sage, 2001); Brian Roberts, *Biographical Research* (Buckingham: Open University Press, 2001) and for a counter-view of letters, Liz Stanley, 'The Epistolarium: On Theorising Letters and Correspondences', *Auto/Biography* 12 (2004), pp. 216–50.

31. See Stanley, 'Shadows Lying Across Her Pages'; Stanley, 'The Epistolarium'; Liz Stanley, 'On Small and Big Stories of the Quotidian: The Commonplace and the Extraordinary In Narrative Inquiry' in David Robinson et al. (eds), *Narratives and Everyday Life* (Huddersfield: University of Huddersfield Press, 2010), pp. 1–24; Liz Stanley, 'Letters, The Epistolary Gift, The Editorial Thirty-Party, Counter-Epistolaria: Rethinking The Epistolarium', *Life Writing* 8 (2011) pp. 135–52; Stanley and Dampier, 'She wrote Peter Halket'; Liz Stanley and Helen Dampier, 'Towards the Epistolarium: Issues In Researching and Publishing the Olive Schreiner Letters', *African Research & Documentation* 113 (2010), pp. 27–32; Stanley and Dampier, 'Men Selling their Souls & the Future – and Fate Watching Them'; Stanley and Dampier, 'I Trust that our Brief Acquaintance may Ripen into Sincere Friendship'; Liz Stanley, Helen Dampier and Andrea Salter, 'Olive Schreiner Globalising Social Inquiry', *Sociological Review* 58 (2010), pp. 657–80; Liz Stanley and Andrea Salter '"Her Letters Cut are Generally Nothing of Interest": The Heterotopic Persona of Olive Schreiner and The Alterity-Persona Of Cronwright-Schreiner', *English in Africa* 36 (2009), pp. 7–30.

32. For examples see Michael Warner, *The Letters of the Republic* (Cambridge: Harvard University Press, 1990); James How, *Epistolary Spaces* (London: Ashgate, 2003); Caroline Bland and Maire Cross (eds), *Gender and Politics in the Age of Letter-Writing 1750–2000* (London: Ashgate, 2004) and Emma Rothschild, *The Inner Life of Empires* (Princeton: Princeton University Press, 2011).

33. Walker, *W. P. Schreiner*; see also Guy Willoughby, '"Coloured and Native British Subjects of South Africa" and the Act of Union in 1909', *Quarterly Bulletin of the National Library of South Africa* 64 (2010), pp. 108–16. Will Schreiner's political career also figures prominently in biographies and autobiographies of his contemporaries. See Millin, *General Smuts*; F. S. Crafford, *Jan Smuts: A Biography* (Cape Town: Timmins for Allen & Unwin, 1946); James Rose Innes, *James Rose Innes: Chief Justice of South Africa Autobiography* (London: Oxford University Press, 1949); Lewsen, *John X. Merriman*. The major archival collections are: W. P. Schreiner Collection, National Library of South Africa, Cape Town; W. P. Schreiner Collection, University of Cape Town.

34. As this suggests, over time Will Schreiner developed many close links with black, coloured and Indian politicians, journalists and other leading figures; see Stanley and Dampier, 'I Trust that our Brief Acquaintance may Ripen into Sincere Friendship'. There are close parallels here with Olive Schreiner herself and also their other siblings Ettie Stakesby Lewis and Theo Schreiner, with the political base of the latter being Ettie's leading and Theo's supporting role in a Christian fundamentalist temperance context.

35. Olive Schreiner, *Thoughts on South Africa*; Olive Schreiner, *The Political Situation* (London: Unwin, 1896); Olive Schreiner, *Trooper Peter Halket of Mashonaland* (London: Unwin, 1897), Olive Schreiner, *An English South African's View of the Situation* (London: Hodder and Stoughton, 1899); Olive Schreiner, *Closer Union* (London: Fifield, 1909); Olive Schreiner, *Woman and Labour* (London: Unwin, 1911).

36. The handful of South African exceptions in this time period include feminist links between Schreiner and her friends Mary Sauer and Jessie Rose Innes, who were married to prominent Cape Liberal politicians; Marie Koopmans De Wet, who presided over a salon of the Cape Afrikaner elite and Schreiner's older sister Ettie Stakesby Lewis, who was a major figure in the South African Christian Temperance movement.

37. Walker, *W. P. Schreiner*, p. 139.

38. Walker, *W. P. Schreiner*, p. 47.

39. Walker, *W. P. Schreiner*, pp. 111–12.

40. Walker, *W. P. Schreiner*, p. 139.

41. Walker, *W. P. Schreiner*, p. 139.

42. See exchanges of letters over this period in the W. P. Schreiner Collection, National Library of South Africa, Cape Town.

43. This raises the more general historiographical point that often the researcher knows with reasonable certainty from circumstantial evidence that something is so, but lacks the direct evidence that would demonstrate this with incontrovertible certainty.

44. Walker, *W. P. Schreiner*, pp. 177–8.

45. See for example Olive Schreiner to Will Schreiner, 14 September 1899, <http://www.oliveschreiner.org/vre?view=collections&colid=91&letterid=66> and 24 September 1899, <http://www.oliveschreiner.org/vre?view=collections&colid=91&letterid=70>.

46. Walker, *W. P. Schreiner*, pp. 190–91.

47. Walker, *W. P. Schreiner*, p. 216.

48. Walker, *W. P. Schreiner*, p. 306.

49. Olive Schreiner to Will Schreiner, 14 September 1899, <http://oliveschreiner.org/vre?view=collections&colid=91&letterid=66>.

50. Olive Schreiner to Will Schreiner, 20 June 1900, <http://www.oliveschreiner.org/vre?view=collections&archiveid=33&colid=92&letterid=35&arrangeby=reciascdateasc>; Walker, *W. P. Schreiner*, p. 235.

51. Walker, *W. P. Schreiner*, p. 351.

52. Walker, *W. P. Schreiner*, pp. 349–50.

53. Olive Schreiner to Betty Molteno, 18 September 1897, <http://www.oliveschreiner.org/vre?view=collections&colid=89&letterid=17>.

54. Such evidence might have been provided by Will Schreiner's letters to his sister, but these too were routinely destroyed by her.

55. Phyllis Lewson, *Selections From the Merriman Correspondence 1890–1924* (Cape Town: Van Riebeeck, 1960–1969); Lewsen, *John X. Merriman*.

56. As Schreiner wrote to Merriman, 'Under our wretched party system of government, it seems all persons & no principles'. Olive Schreiner to John X. Merriman, 2 August 1907, <http://www.oliveschreiner.org/vre?view=collections&colid=51&letterid=27>.

57. Olive Schreiner to John X. Merriman, 25 May 1896, <http://www.oliveschreiner.org/vre?view=collections&colid=51&letterid=2>.

58. Olive Schreiner to Will Schreiner, 9 April 1909, <http://www.oliveschreiner.org/vre?view=collections&archiveid=33&colid=101&letterid=20&arrangeby=reciascdateasc>.

59. Olive Schreiner to John X. Merriman, June 1913, <http://www.oliveschreiner.org/vre?view=collections&archiveid=28&colid=51&letterid=42&arrangeby=reciascdateasc>.

60. Schreiner, *Trooper Peter Halket of Mashonaland*.

61. His biographer, Phyllis Lewsen, states that 'Olive Schreiner's . . . *Peter Halket of Mashonaland*, impressed him deeply. Its polemical attacks on Rhodes, which Merriman found brave and pertinent, caused a vicious campaign against her . . . a letter from Merriman in late 1896 moved her profoundly and began a remarkable though intermittent correspondence'. (Lewsen, *John X. Merriman*, pp. 183–4). Unfortunately Schreiner's response to his initial letter cannot be traced in the Merriman collection (Merriman Collection, National Library of South Africa, Cape Town).

62. Olive Schreiner to John X. Merriman, 3 April 1897, <http://www.oliveschreiner.org/vre?view=collections&archiveid=28&colid=51&letterid=9&arrangeby=reciascdateasc>.

63. Olive Schreiner to Will Schreiner, 10 May 1908, <http://www.oliveschreiner.org/vre?view=collections&colid=100&letterid=29>.

64. Olive Schreiner to John X. Merriman, Wednesday 1906, <http://www.oliveschreiner.org/vre?view=collections&colid=51&letterid=25>.

65. Olive Schreiner to John X. Merriman, Wednesday 1906, <http://www.oliveschreiner.org/vre?view= collections&colid=51&letterid=25>.

66. Olive Schreiner, *Woman and Labour* (London: Unwin, 1911).

67. Olive Schreiner to Ettie Stakesby-Lewis, 5 May 1911, <http://www.oliveschreiner.org/vre?view= collections&colid=77&letterid=118>.

68. Schreiner, *An English South African's View of the Situation*.

69. Olive Schreiner to Jan Hofmeyr, 3 June 1899, <http://www.oliveschreiner.org/vre?view=collections& colid=141&letterid=15>

70. Jan Hofmeyr notes, written on Olive Schreiner to Jan Hofmeyr, 3 June 1899, <http://www. oliveschreiner.org/vre?view=collections&colid=141&letterid=15>.

71. Stanley, 'The Epistolarium'; Stanley, 'Letters, The Epistolary Gift, The Editorial Thirty-Party, Counter-Epistolaria'.

72. J. L. Austin, *How To Do Things With Words* (Cambridge: Clarendon Press, 1962).

73. Olive Schreiner to Mrs Goosen, 14 May 1909, <http://www.oliveschreiner.org/vre?view=collections& colid=42&letterid=1>.

74. Olive Schreiner to F. S. Malan, 16 October 1913, <http://www.oliveschreiner.org/vre?view= collections&colid=44&letterid=9>.

75. See for example, Schreiner's letters to Julia Solly and to Minnie Murray, <http://www.oliveschreiner.org>.

76. Olive Schreiner to Will Schreiner, 30 April 1899, <http://www.oliveschreiner.org/vre?view= collections&colid=91&letterid=23>.

77. Adele Chapin was married to the US consular agent in Johannesburg, Robert Chapin.

78. A lawyer by training, Smuts was legal advisor to Cecil Rhodes from 1895, but after the Jameson Raid became State Secretary in the Transvaal. He served as a Boer general during the South African War, and was later a key force in South African politics, serving twice as Prime Minister. An international statesman, he was instrumental in setting up the League of Nations. See Millin, *General Smuts*; F. S. Crafford, *Jan Smuts: A Biography* (Cape Town: Timmins for Allen & Unwin, 1946).

79. Olive Schreiner to Jan Smuts, n.d. 1899, <http://www.oliveschreiner.org/vre?view=collections&colid= 70&letterid=7>. In Milner's case, it certainly did. In a 28 March 1899 letter to Adele Chapin, he commented 'Do you see much of Olive Schreiner? She is, to me, the most interesting of S. African humans, and it is bad luck she never comes – perhaps can never come – to this part of the world . . .' Sir Alfred Milner, *The Milner Papers*, vol. 1, *South Africa 1897–1899*, Cecil Headlam (ed.) (London: Cassell & Company, 1931), p. 336.

80. Olive Schreiner to Will Schreiner, 4 June 1899, <http://www.oliveschreiner.org/vre?view=collections& archiveid=33&colid=91&letterid=37&arrangeby=reciascdateasc>.

81. Abrams, 'The Unseamed Picture', pp. 64–41.

82. Rather than as a novelist, as she is mainly remembered today, including in South Africa.

83. For Schreiner's involvements with black leaders and politicians and issues in researching this, see Stanley and Dampier, 'I Trust that our Brief Acquaintance May Ripen into Sincere Friendship'.

84. An interesting example is found in a Schreiner letter to her close friend Mary Sauer: 'It's rather interesting that after the people's congress meeting two old fashioned Africanders, Doppers!! came to me, & asked whether I wasn't going to the Bond congress. I said no, I wasn't a Bond's man, & no women were admitted. They said solemnly, that it didn't matter, that I ought to go to parliament!!!! This was to me very interesting as showing how even the hardshell old Dopper can modify his view, the moment he sees a practical reason for it!!' Olive Schreiner to Mary Sauer, Sunday 1903; <http://www.oliveschreiner.org/vre?view=collections&colid=62&letterid=133>). The Doppers were the most narrow and puritanical of the Dutch Reform Church schisms in South Africa.

85. See Leonore Davidoff, '"Regarding Some "Old Husbands" Tales": Public and Private in Feminist History', in Leonore Davidoff, *Worlds Between: Historical Perspectives On Gender and Class* (Oxford: Polity Press, 1995), pp. 227–76. And also Jeff Weintraub, 'The Theory and Politics of the Public/Private Distinction' in Jeff Weintraub and Krishan Kumar (eds), *Public and Private in Theory and Practice* (Chicago: University of Chicago Press, 1997), pp. 119–224.

86. Peggy Watson, 'Rethinking Transition: Globalism, Gender and Class' in Joan Scott and Debra Keates (eds), *Going Public: Feminism and the Shifting Boundaries of the Private Sphere* (Urbana: Illinois University Press, 2004), pp. 282–304.

87. Liz Stanley, Andrea Salter and Helen Dampier, 'The Epistolary Pact and Letterness in the Schreiner Epistolarium', *a/b: Auto/Biography Studies* (2013, in press).

88. Kathleen Canning, *Gender History in Practice* (Ithaca: Cornell University Press, 2006), p. 61.

7 Gender without Groups: Confession, Resistance and Selfhood in the Colonial Archive

Christopher J. Lee

This article represents an attempt to come to terms with challenges of archival evidence, historical experience and gendered categories of analysis. It argues for the value and importance of individual lives against the conformities of group histories. In 1997, while conducting research at the National Archives of Malawi, I came across a document that described in fine detail a relationship between an African woman named Adaima and an unnamed white man, the author of the document. Written in pencil, this text was a confession in the form of a long letter, although the intended recipient, like the author, remained anonymous. Presumably the recipient was a colonial official, given the legal request the author made. What most surprised me about the document was its sheer existence – a piece of evidence that offered a vivid, first-hand account of an interracial relationship, the general topic of my research. As my time in the archive continued, it became clear that it was indeed a small miracle of description that appeared completely idiosyncratic and isolated. Due to its length and the brevity of my first trip, I made a note of it, but moved on. In 1999, I transcribed it in full, but, given its remote singularity, remained unsure what I could do with a limited if fascinating and unique archival fragment of this kind.

In 2006, I returned once more, bringing a digital camera to photograph it in full. I realised that what was holding me back was not the content of the document, which remained invaluable, but established techniques of social history that demand common patterns of experience through aggregated data, the collection of multiple life histories, and, in sum, the privileging of groups over individuals. While the experience of Adaima and her partner (or lover, or benefactor or abuser?) was not unusual– African-European relationships were quite ordinary as evidenced by the number of 'mixed' race children who were born – this small story of a relationship turned wrong appeared too incidental as a basis from which to construct a social history. I consequently faced a difficult choice. Should I submerge it within a broader colonial history, as one experience among many, or somehow keep the integrity of Adaima's story intact?

In this article, I have chosen to foreground her life, as imperfectly preserved as it is in this fragment, against the backdrop of social history. I position Adaima's

Gender History Across Epistemologies, First Edition. Edited by Donna R. Gabaccia and Mary Jo Maynes.

story somewhere between the genres of biography and social history, since it speaks to broader patterns of historical experience as well as the unique significance of individual lives. This article consequently revisits questions and debates over historical analysis and the categories we use to capture and explain the meanings of past human experience. In this regard, Ranajit Guha's classic essay 'Chandra's Death' (1987) offers an immediate model for reconstructing subaltern lives like Adaima's from sparse documentation.[1] Similar to his examination of the tragic, accidental death of a Bagdi woman in Bengal following a miscalculated abortion procedure, Adaima's story begins with an effort to remedy a social transgression, by retelling it to a colonial authority. This fact explains its eventual placement within a colonial archive as with Chandra's story. But, as witnessed in Guha's account, such incidents raise questions of evidence and method: it is difficult to write histories of subaltern people and communities because their obscurity and, at times, impenetrability reflect enduring conditions of colonial power.

These concerns have also preoccupied historians of women and gender. In her 1991 essay, 'The Evidence of Experience', Joan Scott directed attention to the question of 'evidence' and its representation of 'experience' to interrogate the foundations of historical practice by revisiting the tacit assumptions of these two central methodological elements. She praised recent work on women and subaltern groups that had challenged 'normative history' by reconsidering 'conventional historical understandings of evidence' by drawing from non-state archives and popular culture. Yet she also chided recent scholarship for leaving aside questions of context and power in the reconstruction of such histories. 'The evidence of experience then becomes evidence for the fact of difference', Scott cogently argued, 'rather than a way of exploring how difference is established, how it operates, how and in what ways it constitutes subjects who see and act in the world'.[2]

Despite the passage of two decades, these matters have been recurrent, indicating both the scope and implications of the questions raised. This article is concerned with revisiting this historiographical moment shared by Guha and Scott to identify a separate dimension for rethinking historical method – the idea of 'groups' as an organising principle for the writing of history. It addresses several themes within this special issue of *Gender & History*, particularly definitions of conceptual language, the question of historical narrative and how these matters shape our conditions of knowledge and analysis of the past. A prevalent practice since the rise of social history during the 1960s and 1970s has been an emphasis on thematic categories – of race, class and gender, for example – and the group experiences they represent. Indeed, it is through the very existence of social groups that categories come into being: whether through the power of self-consciousness and self-naming among those groups, the power of states to name and categorise groups, or, more often than not, a combination of the two. Social historians have been keen to historicise the interplay between group formation and the emergence of categorical identities to underscore how identities are neither intrinsic nor 'natural' but instead active, ongoing creations. To paraphrase E. P. Thompson's well-known remark about the English working class, social groups are present at their own making.[3]

But this approach has contained conceptual assumptions and produced empirical costs – specifically, the role and importance of the individual life vis-à-vis social groups and their related categories of analysis. Although the genres of biography and autobiography continue to address and reinscribe the lives of individuals, marginal and otherwise, I contend that the analytic stress and politics of 'group-ness' can overshadow the idiosyncrasies of individual experience – the individual life is granted meaning only when it reflects or represents the experiences of an entire social group or community. A tension between the complexities of personal experience and categories of analysis can therefore emerge. In the pages of this journal, Jeanne Boydston once lamented assumptions of stability and universality imparted by the use of 'categories of analysis', gender and otherwise. Joan Scott touched upon this matter herself in a recent forum in the *American Historical Review* on her influential 1986 discussion of gender as a category for historical analysis, suggesting that gender has been productively used to understand the shaping of social relations and their politics, but less attention 'oddly, or perhaps predictably', has been granted to how 'politics constructs gender'. In her view, historians addressing the history of 'women' have 'worked with a fixed meaning for the category, taking the physical commonality of females as a synonym for a collective entity designated "women"'. This practice has resulted in a paradox, whereby scholars insist that women are discursively constructed, yet they continue to work tacitly with a stable and 'natural' definition of 'women'.[4]

This article is written in the spirit of these observations. It does not recommend that 'groups' as an analytic tool and point of reference should be rendered obsolete. It does not seek to create a false opposition between groups and individuals. Furthermore, it does not intend to recapitulate arguments for social construction. Both groups and individuals alike make claims to identity and possess forms of agency to shape its meaning. Instead, I address the term 'group' to invoke a different order of magnitude – to question how we as historians use evidence to generalise meaning, to think specifically about how the demands of social history require that we accumulate as many individual experiences as possible to draw firm conclusions about the past. In short, this article does not pose 'groups' – women, workers, slaves, religious communities, among many other examples – as a problem within historical practice, but queries how individual experiences may be understood and valued on their own terms, against the quantitative conformities of group histories. Indeed, this line of questioning would not be possible without the contributions and insights of social history, which have identified broad patterns of human experience across geographies and historical time. Moving effortlessly between groups and individuals has been an indispensable feature of historical practice. But if we are to loosen the grip that group categories have for interpretation, to allow for a greater individual subjectivity that poses unique questions of lived experience rather than reinforce categories of analysis, to paraphrase Boydston, then the pervasive role of groups deserves attention.[5] The questions posed here, therefore, seek to return to basic assumptions about what counts as social history with the intention of reviving a degree of critical awareness toward historical approach and method, scales of meaning and the space between social history and auto/biography, issues of representation and the question of rights and ownership to one's individual agency and the private acts that follow from it.

To illustrate these themes, the remainder of this article consists of a text/context analysis drawn from the document mentioned earlier. This confession by an anonymous white settler regarding his relationship with an African woman charts a familiar set of boundaries between public and private realms of evidence and experience. Nevertheless, it is a rare piece of first hand evidence amid state documents and local oral

histories that substantiate the occurrence of such relationships, but often in ways mit-
igated by official discourse or, in the case of personal memory, time. Furthermore, it
provides an opportunity to address the aforementioned questions through a case study
that interrogates the specific historical differences between 'miscegenation' (typically
white men having sexual relationships with African women) and 'black peril' anxieties (African men sexually 'threatening' white women).[6] A fundamental gendered
and racial distinction exists between these two phenomena – the former was far more
common, yet the latter captured dramatic public attention in colonial legal codes, settler newspapers, popular literature and, not least, executions of African men accused
of such violations, even with insubstantial evidence. These moral panics that centred
on community integrity and racial group cohesion proved to be a diversion from more
ordinary occurrences of white men engaging in relationships with African women.

This article, therefore, critically addresses the group politics of colonial white
male entitlement by positioning the life of one African woman against the prevalence
of black peril narratives in defining colonial histories of sexuality. But it also resists
the conclusion that Adaima's story is emblematic of the experiences of other women,
an argument I support based on the individual details of her case. In sum, this minor,
yet remarkable historical drama underscores how individual experiences, even those
contained within fragmentary forms of archival knowledge, can work against claims
of representation by social groups and, by extension, categories of analysis that can
obscure alternative patterns of history. Exploring the uses of contingent forms of
historical knowledge in this fashion not only provides nuance, but enables a critical
reconsideration of the role of collective scale in defining 'the social' in social history.

Between groups and individuals – perils of distraction in southern Africa

Before reprinting the document, it is important to introduce the context in which it
was written. A contemporary political map of southern Africa can obscure the regional
networks and histories that arose during the period of British imperial rule from the
late-nineteenth century until after the Second World War. The region was defined
as such not only by a common imperial sovereign, but equally by patterns of white
settlement, due to favourable attributes of climate, as well as the mobility of African
men and women seeking financial gain and social opportunity introduced by colonial
rule. Mining industries in Southern and Northern Rhodesia (contemporary Zimbabwe
and Zambia, respectively) centred on gold and copper, in addition to market incentives
for cultivating cash crops such as cotton, tobacco and tea in Nyasaland (contemporary
Malawi) created a push-pull dynamic between rural and urban areas across the region.
Colonial states, however provisionally weak in their authority and management abilities,
sought to regulate such prospective pathways, encouraging labour migration for the
benefit of regional economies while also seeking to control the social and political lives
of African workers such that they did not interfere with either economic priorities or
the community life of white settlers. Colonial concerns over interracial intimacy and
sexual threat, particularly by African men, emerged within this context of labour and
mobility.

In October 1908, one such migrant, a man named Singana from Nyasaland, was
accused of attempted rape by a white woman, Janette Falconer, as she walked home
after dinner in the town of Umtali, Southern Rhodesia. Singana, who worked as a house

painter, was taken to trial in Salisbury in November. The first trial ended in a hung jury due to questions about Falconer's testimony, specifically the accuracy of her claim that Singana was her attacker. The subsequent second trial resulted in a guilty verdict with execution recommended under the Criminal Law Amendment Ordinance of 1903. However, doubts soon emerged about Singana's guilt. Officials within the Rhodesian government noted inconsistencies and conducted a separate investigation to discover that Singana could not possibly have been involved, that instead a man named Shikube was her purported assailant, though even he was not guilty of attempted rape. Singana was eventually pardoned. Yet this widely reported episode, as recently recounted by Jock McCulloch, fuelled white apprehension toward African men, a pervasive anxiety that intermittently surfaced as 'black peril' scares. As observed by many scholars, these heightened moments of social fear highlight the relationship between politics, race and sexuality under colonial rule – namely, how colonial power included private life within its realm of jurisdiction, however haphazardly. But what is lost empirically and analytically by resorting to an emphasis on this collective white anxiety? How do the lives of Singana, Shikube and Falconer accrue symbolic meaning that distorts the complexities of their actual lives? To what extent does increasing the scale for measuring meaning to a group level create a reductive picture, one that offers broad insight, but also diminishes the texture and complexity of individual experiences?[7]

Black peril scares in Southern Rhodesia between 1902 and 1916 remain among the most vivid public manifestations of sexual attitudes and biopolitical control during the colonial period in southern Africa. Approximately two hundred African men were imprisoned and twenty executed. These episodes were not necessarily surprising or unforeseen, given the persistent demographic imbalance between white settler communities and African communities throughout the region. Indeed, certain peak years of 1908, 1910 and 1911 have been linked to increases in white immigration, which enhanced anxieties rather than ameliorated them. Yet demographic figures alone cannot explain these episodes. Gender held near equal importance to race. In addition to the Criminal Law Amendment Ordinance of 1903 which carried a death penalty for not only rape, but attempted rape, other measures passed during this period include the Immorality Suppression Ordinance No. 9 of 1903 and its later extension, the Immorality and Indecency Suppression Ordinance No. 1 of 1916, both of which targeted white women specifically, seeking to prevent relations between white women and black men. White men, in contrast, were not held accountable for relationships with African women. In short, early legislation directed itself toward a particular equation of race and gender – one that protected not simply white privilege, but white male entitlement. These panics therefore resulted in a series of laws that sought to restrain white women as well as punish African men. The issue of interracial sex in Southern Rhodesia proved to be a distinctly gendered process of managing social behaviour.[8]

Yet, even if black peril scares were symptomatic of broader sentiments of uncertainty over gendered forms of mobility and racial transgression, these panics had qualities dependent on time and place.[9] Moreover, they were decidedly modern. Although settler-African relationships had existed in southern Africa since at least the seventeenth-century Dutch settlement of the Western Cape – some even acquiring a romantic aura as in the case of 'Eva' (born 'Krotoa'), the wife of Danish explorer Pieter van Meerhoff – emergent strands of scientific racism crucially informed the colonial orders established during the late nineteenth and early twentieth centuries.[10]

Moral panics in the colony of Natal during the 1870s, amid the transition to British control, offer one marker of this broad shift from a permissive frontier context to the establishment of firm racial boundaries. By the early twentieth century, this shift toward aversion appeared complete, with Johannesburg experiencing periodic scares from the 1890s through the 1910s – a time when rapid urbanisation on the Rand brought together people of different racial groups with little social control.[11] By the 1920s and 1930s, such episodes had acquired enough social and moral momentum to step beyond law and politics to enter popular cultural discourse. South African writer Sarah Gertrude Millin provides the most infamous example, reinforcing white anxieties over racial 'contamination' and 'degeneration' in books like *God's Stepchildren* (1924).[12]

But progressive African intellectuals like Solomon Plaatje also addressed the issue of crossing racial boundaries due to the proximity between poor whites and the African working class. In an essay pointedly entitled 'The Mote and the Beam' (1921) after the Biblical maxim warning of hypocritical judgment, Plaatje criticised the paradox of white attitudes, namely that 'one-sided' laws allowed for white men 'to flood the country with illegitimate half-castes' despite public pronouncements against interracial sex.[13] Plaatje's scathing observations affirm what recent scholarship has underscored – that while these perils signalled broad concerns over colonial morality and social control, they equally distracted from lived experience that often contradicted these claims for order. The matter of interracial sex resided within a larger colonial discourse involving attitudes toward polygamy, prostitution and perceived African immorality generally. And while perils themselves coincided with spikes in white immigration and economic downturns, they equally signalled ongoing attempts to manage the place and mobility of social groups – settler and African alike – in nascent political orders when statutory law and the pervasiveness of racism itself failed to establish control and stability. These qualities point to the hazards of collective meaning vis-à-vis individual experience – namely, the potential disjuncture between community concerns and actual lives.[14]

In sum, the occurrence of perils, while intermittent, speaks to one problem of groups introduced at the beginning. Panics generated meaningful social effects that characterised the social and political opportunities of different communities. Yet, as a group phenomenon, they also diverted attention from the realities of many interracial relationships, occluding the individual lives involved. Based on perceived rather than actual threats, they produced social 'noise' that 'camouflaged' actual practices, particularly the frequency of white men having intimate relations with African women.[15] While 'white peril' did emerge as a regional issue during the 1920s, it experienced far quieter treatment than its 'black' counterpart.[16] But addressing it offers a useful and significant counterpoint, indicating how white male behaviour was supervised, how African women could be far more vulnerable than white women and how the more ubiquitous practice of colonial concubinage decentres the black peril phenomenon with its disjointed correspondence between incidents of reported crime and the incitement of social concern. This different research focus moves beyond repeating the functional qualities of black peril scares to shore up white group solidarity – a point well-established now in the historical literature – that leaves aside the circumstances of individual experience.

Adaima's story offers an opportunity to understand what this personal experience was like. While attention to the discursive qualities of group events can provide insight into general patterns of social behaviour and power, such emphasis can overlook their effects and meaning in the individual lives caught at the centre of them, sidelining more concrete evidence of cause and effect. Restoring these marginalised persons to history can be a challenging task, given the lack of first person documentation – whether written or oral – on the intimacies of African-European relationships. Hence, the value of the first person text I reproduce here in its entirety. Although it contains its own limitations – in particular being a monologue in the voice of a European man – it provides an example of how and why writing histories without groups can reveal the texture and complexity of personal experiences, ones that articulate the choices and views of individual people who inhabited such groups, even if they left only fragmentary details in their wake.

Adaima's story – the complete document

Adaima, daughter of Nanseta, formerly residing at Chingwalawalu's village but now removed to Ndenga, came to Zomba about five years ago in guest of custom – one of my houseboys (Hamisi) came across her and brought her to my house. She stayed at my place for about 3 or 4 months and unfortunately became pregnant. While pregnant she left my house and went over to the Camp and took up her abode with a K. A. R. [King's African Rifles] Askari of the name Salima. Out of sentiment I sent for her father (Nanseta) and got him after some difficulty to persuade her to return to my place, pointing out that she was pregnant and that I did not wish the child that was to be born to be left to the mercy of a man who was not its father.

The child was born early in 1914 and is now nearly 4 years old – a boy who goes by the name of 'James'. I have had absolutely no connection with his mother from the time she first became pregnant, but owing to my strong attachment to this child James, I have tolerated the mother's presence here since his birth. The mother noticing my attachment to this child has been blackmailing me for the past 4 years during which period I have paid her considerably over £80 in cash. In addition to this money payment she has helped herself freely to my stores – pots and pans, jugs, basins, soap, tobacco, sugar, rice, chickens, etc. etc.

Her behaviour since the birth of this child has been somewhat as follows: – Every few days or weeks she gets extremely violent, smashing everything in the house she can lay her hands on, tearing down curtains and any of my clothing she can lay her hands on, fighting with my servants who try to restrain her and tearing the clothing off their backs. Four of my servants have left me because of her behaviour and the old servants I now have left me at their wits end to know what to do and implore me to take the action I am now taking. She has repeatedly struck at me with rackets, sticks, etc. but owing to my strong attachment to this child James I have gone on putting up with it. In addition to smashing everything she can lay her hands on she has done away with such things as my boots . . . scissors, pen knives, etc. etc. and no doubt given them to her admirers. Her blackmail lies in this that she has demanded to be paid 50/- a month failing which she has threatened to take this child James to the Resident here so as to make the matter public.

I now come to a very important point. I have already said that I have had no connection with her, ever since she first became pregnant about 5 years ago. But my servant knows she has been cohabiting with others, and the proof of this lies in the fact that she now has another child which she has cunningly handed over to her mother to look after as there was no mistaking its paternity. As a matter of fact I know that the father of this child is one of my servants, Bwanali, whom I discharged some time ago. I suppose that even from the native point of view this fact of her becoming pregnant by another would justify her being sent away by me. And knowing my attachment to James she says she will not go without taking this child James with her. She knows I will not consent to this and she therefore remains in here making a nuisance of herself, smashing things in the house, fighting with my servants and threatening to go to the Resident. This as I say has been going on for the past four years. When I tell her to go away she says she won't go without taking this child James with her. James has been brought up by me with the same care as a white child would receive – clothed,

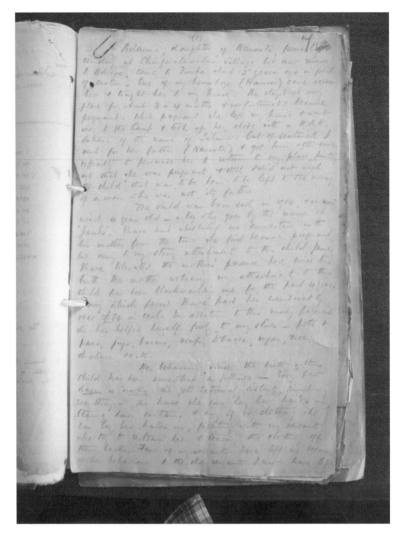

Figure 1: A photograph of the original document by the author from the file
NS 1/35/3 in the National Archives of Malawi.

fed and looked after by a specially paid servant. She has repeatedly been very cruel to this child and
for the past 3 years has done nothing for him.

One of her commonest forms of annoyance is that when I am going anywhere she walks round
the rooms and takes away my razors, brushes, and all the things one needs in . . . and when asked
to . . . then becomes violent and starts smashing and tearing things in the house and fighting the
servants. The whole house bears evidence of her depredations – panes smashed, pictures beaten
down, mosquito curtains and table cloths ripped up with knives, curtains torn down etc. etc. All my
servants and even her brothers and sisters who from time to time have stayed with her will bear out
all I have said if evidence is wanted. She has frequently left the house awake at night, shouting and
yelling, fighting with the servants who try to restrain her, and smashing things right and left.

I don't know what the law will permit I am to do in this case, but as you can understand I want
to be free of this woman. She was not acquired by me in the customary way from her parents, but
as I have said was 'picked up' by one of my houseboys and brought here – her home being in the
Liwonde district. I want this child James to remain with me as I want him properly looked after and

educated. I certainly don't want him to drift to her village and suffer from every form of neglect. The woman can go back to her second child by me of my ex-servant (Bwanali).

This morning, because I did not catch what sum of money she demanded, she broke several things in the house and ripped off two cushion covers.

I don't know what character her Headman Ndenga would give her, but the Principal Headman, Chingwalawalu, says that it is a 'bad family' and that if it were not for the presence of muzungus [whites] he would with his own hands lop off her father's head for his truculent behaviour.[17]

Adaima's story – text, context and ephemeral knowledge

As discussed earlier, this document describes a relationship between an unnamed European man and an African woman named Adaima. It also narrates a custody battle that ensued over their son James, a key dimension that explains the purpose of this testimony and its inclusion in a colonial archive. The document is undated, though it was likely written around 1918, given the age of James described in the document as well as supplementary, though unrelated, papers that surround it within the archival folder labelled 'Native Secretariat (NS) 1/35/3' in the National Archives of Malawi. Indeed, the sense of surprise that attended my discovery of this document was in part due to its archival placement – the only shared connection with the other documents in this file being colonial state concern for 'half-caste' (mixed-race) children, none of which provided remotely similar detail. This confession and the relationship it describes is therefore an example of idiosyncratic incidents haphazardly deposited and preserved in colonial archives. As Ann Laura Stoler has recently argued, archives are replete with contingent documents that regard not the causes or consequences of major events nor even 'events' as such, but instead chart tensions and anxieties materialised through everyday occasions of colonial life.[18] As a consequence, colonial repositories do not always reflect official state views, but can offer 'fugitive traces of subjectivity', in Antoinette Burton's words, that illuminate what it meant to live under certain historical conditions.[19] Such traces constitute ephemeral forms of knowledge often personal in scope that present the historian with a choice to treat such non-events as individual, even eccentric, in scope or whether they are woven – and potentially dissolved – into broader patterns of social experience.[20]

Given these parameters, how might one begin to think about Adaima's story? One initial observation is that there were no black peril scares in Nyasaland, a reflection of its lower density of white settlement that numbered only 1,486 people in a 1921 government census (in comparison to 33,620 people in Southern Rhodesia during the same year).[21] An estimated 1,175,000 Africans lived in Nyasaland at the time. Yet interracial relationships were not uncommon, given the very existence of colonial files on 'half-caste' children. In 1929 the Anglo-African Association of Nyasaland had been founded to provide representation for persons of mixed racial – or, as they preferred, 'Anglo-African' – background. A 1934 government census conducted at the urging of the Association placed their total population at 1,202 persons, a number that was not insignificant given that the European community numbered 1,975 persons in a 1931 census.[22] Indeed, by 1935 the Nyasaland administration began to consider policy on the matter of 'half-caste' children, referring to the 1934 Foggin Commission report of Southern Rhodesia that addressed questions of status and education for such children.[23] The fragmented history of Adaima, James and the author can, therefore, be seen as both unique and ordinary. While it can be contextualised within a broader pattern of domestic life at the time, its evidence of experience remains firmly individual, providing a transcript valuable for its rare private detail, in contrast to the public transcripts of black peril further to the south.

Of primary importance is the fact that this relationship involves a white man and an African woman. Although it consists of a monologue by the unnamed European – it is probable, though not certain, that he is a British settler – the document itself is polyphonic in that Adaima and James both have a clear presence and speak through their actions as described by the narrator. While it is next to impossible to determine who Adaima was, the inclusion of her name, her son's name, her place of origin and the contrasting absence of the narrator's personal information reinforce her authority, agency and historical presence. Furthermore, we can glean some information that can help us imagine her status and life. She was the daughter of Nanseta, suggesting that she may be the daughter of a chief of that name that resided in the tea growing Cholo district of southern Nyasaland.[24] This possibility of status is compromised in part by the narrator's references to other headmen and the concluding comment that, according to another chief, she came from a 'bad family', a judgment of her father's 'truculent behaviour'. Liwonde is also mentioned as her home, indicating that she had resided near Zomba. Perhaps more pertinent is the general sense of mobility on her part throughout the document's account. As the author indicates, she was brought to his household by a servant, coming and going thereafter. Though he did have contact with her father Nanseta after she left his household while pregnant, the relationship between the author and her father does not appear to be close or even a familiar one. Given that concubinage arrangements could be actively orchestrated by family members and customary authorities, these observations tell us both of the informality of the relationship, which the narrator touches upon in passing, and the relative impermanence of domestic working relations more generally.[25]

The biography of the author is equally elusive. He undoubtedly gained wealth of some kind, being able to maintain a household with a number of servants as well as provide payments to Adaima over a period of four years in the amount of £80, a considerable sum. The possibility of owning land and growing profitable cash crops such as tobacco and tea had been an incentive for single men to migrate to the colony since the late nineteenth century. Furthermore, it is clear from the nature of the letter and its audience that the author had personal connections with the government, a status likely accrued through long-term residence. The archival placement of the letter in the Native Secretariat section implies that it reached a high level of attention.[26] But more significant is the threat of scandal, and the intimation that this situation could affect the status of the author, thus explaining his financial payments and endurance over a period of several years. The author seeks a form of separation from Adaima, if not exactly divorce given the relationship's apparent informality, as well as custody over his son James, indicating not only a domestic arrangement but a matter of family. He requests an official audience – a district commissioner or perhaps the native commissioner – while hoping the handling of the matter will be private. The author wants 'to be free of this woman' and have James 'remain with me as I want him properly looked after and educated'.[27] This desire for custody clearly expresses a sense of responsibility and identification with James, who 'has been brought up by me with the same care as a white child would receive – clothed, fed, and looked after by a specially paid servant'.[28]

This aspiration for control is nevertheless informed by broader notions of racial and cultural difference, as reinforced by the disparaging view toward the possibility of James staying with his mother, encapsulated in the author saying 'I certainly don't want him to drift to her village and suffer from every form of neglect'.[29] In short, the letter reveals a complex boundary between public norms and private situations, accepted social discourse and the sentimental bonds of family. This sense of difference and the perceived threat it presents to James in the author's purview raises additional questions and ambiguities about the relationship between Adaima and the narrator. He writes in passing that Adaima was 'picked up' and that she was 'not acquired by me in the customary way from her parents' indicating a situation of contingency.[30] Although the writer describes her violent behaviour, it is entirely plausible she too was a victim of violence or rape by him. Certainly, the ambivalence of the author is among the most striking characteristics of this document, captured with his initial comment that Adaima 'unfortunately became pregnant'. His wording and tone imply that the pregnancy was unexpected, unintended and embarrassing. This perspective is further underscored by the author's attempt to downplay any sexual intimacy, despite the obvious fact it occurred. 'I have had absolutely no connection with his mother from the time she first became pregnant', he writes early on in the letter, 'but owing to my strong attachment to this child James, I have tolerated the mother's presence here since his birth'.[31] He repeats this point later by insisting 'I have had no connection with her ever since she first became pregnant about 5 years ago'.[32] A sense of regret shot through with formality consequently emerges. Coding his relationship with Adaima through euphemistic expressions like 'connection' occludes their sexual intimacy and expresses a latent white anxiety over racial boundaries and their transgression. Yet, the domestic scene the author details through description of possessions, 'houseboys' and so forth provides a vivid sense of the intimate context of this situation and how such private spaces presented an unstable setting for colonial social boundaries on an everyday basis.

The inherent tension expressed through the physically violent behaviour of Adaima exemplifies the pervasiveness of this threat. It is important to re-emphasise that she has no conventional voice in this letter, and this point raises immediate questions of narrative bias. The author seeks custody of James, so portraying her negatively works to his benefit. Indeed, his pejorative characterisation falls into a gendered trope of the irrational, hysterical woman. A litany of descriptive comments of her being 'a nuisance', 'smashing things', 'fighting', 'threatening', 'tearing things' and 'shouting and yelling' to the point where 'the whole house bears evidence of her depredations' proves this attempt at derision.[33] The author recurrently validates this thumbnail psychological portrait by noting its routine – 'Every few days or weeks she gets extremely violent' – as well as the public nature and impact of her alleged behaviour: 'Four of my servants have left me because of her behaviour and the old servants I now have left me at their wits end to know what to do and implore me to take the action I am now taking'.[34] The inclusion of his servants on the matter endeavours to suggest that his view is not an isolated one, informed by racial or cultural difference, but that a purported consensus exists regarding the negative effects of her conduct.

On the other hand, despite the intrinsic limitations of this document, Adaima's actions indicate agency and even emotion, through bold feelings of anger and frustration that can be conjectured and understood in different ways. The letter reveals a material dimension to the relationship, with the theft of items reflecting not only a form of resistance – a standard 'weapon of the weak' – but also suggesting material incentives for their relationship being initiated on her part.[35] Indeed, the author's description that their relationship and his attachment to James have created a situation where she 'has been blackmailing me for the past 4 years during which period I have paid her considerably over £80 in cash' indicates that her actions consist of strategic gain rather than blank hysteria or irrationality – a tactic perhaps encouraged by her father who persuaded her to return after she initially left the narrator's household.[36] This furtive sense of agency extends to other relationships described within the letter. Not only did she have a relationship with the author, but also with a soldier of the King's African Rifles as well as with one of the author's servants.[37] These actions threatened the author's personal authority and consequently his sense of control. The narrator's fear, in the first case, that 'the child that was to be born' could 'be left to the mercy of a man who was not its father' and, in the second instance, the fact of a second pregnancy, which he surmises 'that even from the native point of view' could 'justify her being sent away by me', are both portrayed as events that undermine his power.[38] Yet, despite these displays of resistance and agency on her part, his paternity concerns compelled a course of tolerance in the face of vulnerability, either to 'persuade her to return to my place', as in the first case, or to tolerate her disruptive behaviour, despite his description that she remained 'in here making a nuisance of herself'.[39]

Against this backdrop, this letter can be read not only as a confession by a white man regarding his relationship with an African woman for the purpose of a custody claim, but it can equally be understood as a gendered narrative of one woman's agency and wilful action in the face of one man's sense of authority. Indeed, the emergence of Adaima's power through this narrative rests in how she presented a challenge to his paternal control specifically and his colonial power more generally. An inversion occurs. The author himself expresses this intimidation and the self-consciousness on her part that actively informed it when he writes '*knowing* my attachment to James she says she will not go without taking this child James with her. She *knows* I will not consent to this and she therefore remains in here making a nuisance of herself, smashing things in the house, fighting with my servants, and threatening to go to the Resident'.[40] This active sensibility is finally displayed in her threat of making their sexual relationship and James's existence public knowledge.[41] Adaima clearly understood the social ramifications of their relationship and was willing to use blackmail in order to empower herself, even if her actual motivations remain hidden. Taken as a whole, the type of awareness and self-knowledge described by the author reveals recognition of power, demonstrating a sense of conscious action despite lacking her direct voice in the document itself.

Adaima's agency and resistance are common to many colonial histories and return us to more general questions of interpretation. To what extent is Adaima's story typical? Does placing her against a broader historical backdrop enhance or reduce her individual experience as being one among many? Can we conclude that this is simply one woman's attempt at resistance to keep the custody of her child, or does it speak to a broader history of women under colonial rule, or both? These questions ask the degree to which individual experiences like hers should be scaled up to represent a form of group politics. While they are not intended to produce a conclusion applicable to all historical occasions, they do seek to unsettle assumptions of what constitutes the social in social history as well as the extent of political claims, even when acts of resistance appear transparent. The document reproduced here contains an abundance of detail about a specific situation. But beyond Adaima's relationship with the author, her son and her place of birth, little biographical information comes forth in this narrative fragment. Indeed, what is still unclear about Adaima's life, among many facets, are the ways in which her social position and agency may have been further circumscribed by other men – her father, brothers or maternal uncles, as is common among matrilineal societies in the region – or women – her mother, aunts, sisters – in addition to affective considerations regarding her relationship with James and with her intimate partners, including the narrator.[42] Did she have a strong affection for James? Was her relationship with the narrator initially desired by her, or was it entirely arranged? Was her aggressive behaviour a reaction against a violent form of traumatic, physical disempowerment on his part? Answers to such questions are difficult to substantiate conclusively. But recognising the existence of such unresolved factors illustrates a need to be attentive to the limitations of such evidence and of romanticising her resistance through the concerns and politics of larger social groups that can attempt to speak and answer for such personal histories, eliding the idiosyncratic elements of power, vulnerability and even affection embedded within them.[43]

Conclusions

This article has interrogated claims of evidence and experience to address the differences between individual and group histories. It has juxtaposed the issue of 'black peril' panics in southern Africa against the individual case of one relationship between an unnamed white man and an African woman named Adaima. This approach has highlighted the contrasting histories and perspectives that can emerge, with the general purpose of critiquing black perils as a group-centred distraction from the details of individual experience. While understanding their origins and outcomes is important, black perils concealed far more common situations of 'miscegenation' that could have a profound impact on the individual lives involved. Yet, given the inversion of power presented, I equally hesitate to call this situation emblematic of the experiences of other African women. This article consequently asks what a historian should do with isolated documents of this kind, which possess distinct limitations yet offer insight on the everyday lives of people we might not have otherwise. It would be easy to pass over this archived story, to consider it exceptional and therefore disregard it. On the other hand, Adaima's story could be dissolved into a broader, aggregated social history, albeit at the risk of losing a vivid sense of her personal history.

This article has sought to preserve the power of Adaima's story by reproducing it whole. This tactic disrupts regional group narratives of black peril as well as working against the reductive potential of categories of analysis, as cited by Boydston and Scott. My approach is not simply a restorative gesture, but an attempt at presenting an individual articulation of power along gendered and racial lines. Taking this critical stance is not meant to discount broader patterns of experience nor to argue for the elimination of thematic categories of interpretation. Indeed, what we can piece together about Adaima's life is dependent on both the details of this document as well as what we know about the broader historical context in which she lived. Moreover, as Scott would contend, this document is not merely evidence of certain sets of colonial power relations, but, given its place in the colonial state's archival record, it is a direct effect of them. Still, it does retain a strong personal dimension. This anonymous letter depicts two separate attempts to escape a situation of power and exploitation by both Adaima and the author alike. The fact that this turbulent situation lasted for nearly five years suggests the degree to which resolution was sought beyond state scrutiny. In these ways, this document reveals the personal, not simply the social and public, dimensions of such situations that reflect individual choice and action based on a specific horizon of possible options.

This document, therefore, depicts more textured senses of agency than might be conveyed through categories of analysis or group experience, whether moral panics or other social phenomena. The document republished here resembles earlier studies in African women's history by Shula Marks and Marcia Wright that restored marginalised women and their documents to historical narratives of the region – South Africa and central Africa, respectively – to demonstrate the value of reproducing primary sources as a means of representing the agency and voices of women, as well as the predicaments and challenges of their lives.[44] This case study additionally resonates with dilemmas addressed with some controversy by Gayatri Chakravorty Spivak, who, like Scott, raised issues about restoring the lives of women to history, given how the presence and role of women are structured by conditions of power that inform historical events and the contexts in which they are archived thereafter. Yet I take a critical view toward generalised notions of the subaltern woman as a 'concept-metaphor' that represents a point of orientation for critically engaging social and political relations of power.[45] Should individual experience be conscripted into critical projects to function as a 'concept-metaphor'? What historical idiosyncrasies, social texture and politics are occluded when a group stance is privileged over personal action and meaning?

These broad questions are intended to stir conversation and debate, and I pose them without offering firm answers. I do think that addressing the role of historical groups in addition to categories of analysis – since they are not always the same – deserves critical attention in the shaping of historical interpretation. This approach provides one means for addressing the methodological problems of stability and universality raised at the start by Scott and Boydston. Without question, the situation described in this archival document constitutes an example of the intersectional nature of many historical situations, exhibiting different views, struggles and claims, whether or not this fragmented narrative is tilted toward absolute fact or possibly fictive fantasy. But it is also a tense intersection between individual lives and group identities, ideals and politics. The perspectives and actions found do bear the imprint of group histories and concerns, and historical agency should never be conceived as purely individual. It is always provisional, shaped by the context of power in which it occurs.[46]

Keeping the story personal, however, rather than resorting to group meaning enables one to retain a sense of the individuals involved and their role in shaping and defining thematic experiences like gender and race – or to echo Scott, 'exploring how difference is established, how it operates, how and in what ways it constitutes subjects who see and act in the world' – thus charting a mutually-constitutive terrain between biography and social history.[47] The strength of the biographical genre – namely its focus on the will and value of the individual against the backdrop of history – should not be the exclusive realm of people who leave large personal archives. Insisting upon individual experience, it bears repeating, does not result in the absence or de-emphasis of gendered, racial or cultural themes either. Such issues remain. Rather, thinking without or beyond 'groups' can restore marginal lives to history without prescriptively subsuming them into larger categories of analysis and meaning. Indeed, their lives can indicate the very ways in which such broad thematic experiences of difference and power are articulated. Social groups are not the final, or even the most meaningful, resort. A different option is to reconsider the ways in which individual experiences – even those limited to single documents – can be empirically, conceptually and politically sufficient in and of themselves.

Notes

I thank the editors of this special issue, Donna R. Gabaccia and Mary Jo Maynes, as well as the participants of the 'Gender History across Epistemologies' workshop for their support and comments. I also thank the anonymous peer reviewers for their critical insights. Antoinette Burton and an audience at the African Gender Institute at the University of Cape Town provided early encouragement. Research support came from Stanford University, the Fulbright-Hays program and the Izaak Walton Killam Trust.

1. Ranajit Guha, 'Chandra's Death', in Ranajit Guha (ed.), *Subaltern Studies, Volume V: Writings on South Asian History and Society* (Delhi: Oxford University Press, 1987), pp. 135–65.
2. Joan W. Scott, 'The Evidence of Experience', *Critical Inquiry* 17 (1991), pp. 773–97, here pp. 776–7. This argument for greater methodological self-consciousness proposed by Scott can be viewed as a reflection of a broader turn occurring then, influenced by the work of Judith Butler on performativity and power in the social construction of gender as well as the cultural turn of the 1980s, which Scott's work fundamentally shaped. See Joan W. Scott, 'Gender: A Useful Category of Historical Analysis', *American Historical Review* 91 (1986), pp. 1053–75; Joan W. Scott, *Gender and the Politics of History* (New York: Columbia University Press, 1988); Judith Butler, *Gender Trouble: Feminism and the Subversion of Identity* (New York: Routledge, 1990); Judith Butler, *Bodies that Matter: On the Discursive Limits of 'Sex'* (New York: Routledge, 1993).
3. E. P. Thompson, *The Making of the English Working Class* (New York: Vintage, 1963). My thinking on 'groups' in this section is inspired by Rogers Brubaker, *Ethnicity without Groups* (Cambridge: Harvard University Press, 2004), especially chapters 1 and 2, pp. 7–63.
4. Jeanne Boydston, 'Gender as a Question of Historical Analysis', *Gender and History* 20 (2008), pp. 558–83; Joan W. Scott, 'Unanswered Questions', *American Historical Review* 113 (2008), pp. 1422–9, here p. 1424.
5. Boydston, 'Gender as a Question of Historical Analysis', pp. 578–9.
6. For more on this distinction, see Dane Kennedy, *Islands of White: Settler Society and Culture in Kenya and Southern Rhodesia, 1890–1939* (Durham: Duke University Press, 1987), pp. 174–9.
7. Jock McCulloch, *Black Peril, White Virtue: Sexual Crime in Southern Rhodesia, 1902–1935* (Bloomington: Indiana University Press, 2000), pp. 1–4. For earlier studies, see Kennedy, *Islands of White*, chapter 7, pp. 128–47; John Pape, 'Black and White: The "Perils of Sex" in Colonial Zimbabwe', *Journal of Southern African Studies* 16 (1990), pp. 699–720. For a broader discussion of social 'scares', see Sonya O. Rose, 'Cultural Analysis and Moral Discourses: Episodes, Continuities, and Transformations', in Victoria E. Bonnell and Lynn Hunt (eds), *Beyond the Cultural Turn: New Directions in the Study of Society and Culture* (Berkeley: University of California Press, 1999), pp. 217–38.
8. In fact, the original 1903 legislation grew out of pre-existing legislation, the Criminal Law Amendment Ordinance of 1900, which intended to protect young women from sexual exploitation by brothels and similar means of prostitution. McCulloch, *Black Peril, White Virtue*, pp. 4, 5, 57. For other studies on women and morality generally during this period, see Elizabeth Schmidt, *Peasants, Traders, and Wives: Shona Women in the History of Zimbabwe, 1870–1939* (Portsmouth: Heinemann, 1992); Diana Jeater, *Marriage, Perversion, and Power: The Construction of Moral Discourse in Southern Rhodesia, 1894–1930* (Oxford: Clarendon Press, 1993).
9. Interracial (or intergroup) sex, of course, has been a theme of colonial encounters across the world. See, for example, Ramón A. Gutiérrez, *When Jesus Came the Corn Mothers Went Away: Marriage, Sexuality, and Power in New Mexico, 1500–1846* (Stanford: Stanford University Press, 1991); Martha Hodes (ed.), *Sex, Love, Race: Crossing Boundaries in North American History* (New York: New York University Press, 1999); Owen White, *Children of the French Empire: Miscegenation and Colonial Society in French West*

Africa, 1895–1960 (Oxford: Oxford University Press, 1999); George E. Brooks, *Eurafricans in Western Africa: Contested Arenas of Commerce, Social Status, Gender, and Religious Observance* (Athens: Ohio University Press, 2003); Ann Laura Stoler (ed.), *Haunted By Empire: Geographies of Intimacy in North American History* (Durham: Duke University Press, 2006).

10. Julia C. Wells, 'Eva's Men: Gender and Power in the Establishment of the Cape of Good Hope, 1652–74', *Journal of African History* 39 (1998), pp. 417–37; George M. Fredrickson, *White Supremacy: A Comparative Study in American and South African History* (Oxford: Oxford University Press, 1981), chapter 3, pp. 93–135; Anthony W. Marx, *Making Race and Nation: A Comparison of South Africa, the United States, and Brazil* (New York: Cambridge University Press, 1998), chapter 4, pp. 65–76.

11. On Natal, see Norman Etherington, 'Natal's Black Rape Scare of the 1870s', *Journal of Southern African Studies* 15 (1988), pp. 36–53. On Johannesburg, see Charles van Onselen, *New Babylon, New Ninevah: Everyday Life on the Witwatersrand, 1886–1914* (1982; repr. Johannesburg: Jonathan Ball, 2001), pp. 237–9, 247, 257–74.

12. Sarah Gertrude Millin, *God's Stepchildren* (New York: Boni and Liveright, 1924). For commentary on this issue in South African literature, see J. M. Coetzee, *White Writing: On the Culture of Letters in South Africa* (New Haven: Yale University Press, 1988), chapter 6, pp. 136–62. See also Gareth Cornwell, 'George Webb Hardy's *The Black Peril* and the Social Meaning of "Black Peril" in Early Twentieth-Century South Africa', *Journal of Southern African Studies* 22 (1996), pp. 441–53.

13. Solomon T. Plaatje, 'The Mote and the Beam: An Epic on Sex-Relationship 'Twixt White and Black in British South Africa (1921)', *English in Africa* 3 (1976), pp. 85–92, here p. 87.

14. On issues of morality, see Jeater, *Marriage, Perversion, and Power.* For the broader political context, see Carol Summers, *From Civilization to Segregation: Social Ideals and Social Control in Southern Rhodesia, 1890–1934* (Athens: Ohio University Press, 1994).

15. Nancy Rose Hunt, 'Noise Over Camouflaged Polygamy, Colonial Morality Taxation, and a Woman-Naming Crisis in Belgian Africa', *Journal of African History* 32 (1991), pp. 471–94.

16. For this issue in Southern Rhodesia, see Schmidt, *Peasants, Traders, and Wives*, pp. 174–8; McCulloch, *Black Peril, White Virtue*, p. 73.

17. Note: this transcription is nearly, though not entirely, complete, with the exception of a few sentences where the writing was illegible, as I have indicated with ellipses. Words that are underlined are emphasised in the original. National Archives of Malawi (henceforth NAM), Native Secretariat (NS) 1/35/3, Folio 7, pp. 1–4.

18. Ann Laura Stoler, *Along the Archival Grain: Epistemic Anxieties and Colonial Common Sense* (Princeton: Princeton University Press, 2008), p. 106.

19. Antoinette Burton, 'Introduction: Archive Fever, Archive Stories', in Antoinette Burton (ed.), *Archive Stories: Facts, Fictions, and the Writing of History* (Durham: Duke University Press, 2005), pp. 1–24, here p. 14.

20. Conceptualising archives has been a topic of much attention, to a great extent building upon Michel Foucault's work on the archaeology of knowledge. See, for example, Michel Foucault, *The Archaeology of Knowledge*, tr. A. M. Sheridan Smith (New York: Pantheon Books, 1972); Carolyn Hamilton et al. (eds), *Refiguring the Archive* (Cape Town: David Philip, 2002); Carolyn Steedman, *Dust: The Archive and Cultural History* (New Brunswick: Rutgers University Press, 2002).

21. *Federation of Rhodesia and Nyasaland: Census of Population, 1956* (Salisbury: Central Statistical Office, 1960), p. 3.

22. On the size of the Anglo-African community see NAM, s1/705¹/30, Folio 27, 4 January 1934. On population figures for the European, Indian and African communities, see the *Nyasaland Protectorate Census* (Zomba: Government Printer, 1931).

23. The full title of the report is *Report of the Committee appointed by the Government of Southern Rhodesia to Enquire into Questions Concerning the Education of Coloured and Half-Caste Children in the Colony* (Salisbury: Government Printer, 1934). See NAM s26/2/4/5, Folio 14.

24. My thanks to Joey Power for alerting me to this name reference.

25. Oral histories I collected discussed these arrangements. Interview with Jessica Ascroft and Ann Ascroft, 9 November 1999, Blantyre, Malawi; Interview with Yusuf Ishmael, 17 October 1999, Blantyre, Malawi. On labour mobility in Nyasaland, see, for example, Wiseman Chijere Chirwa, 'Child and Youth Labour on the Nyasaland Plantations, 1890–1953', *Journal of Southern African Studies* 19 (1993), pp. 662–80; Joey Power, '"Eating the Property": Gender Roles and Economic Change in Urban Malawi, Blantyre-Limbe, 1907–1953', *Canadian Journal of African Studies/Revue Canadienne des Études Africaines* 29 (1995), pp. 79–107.

26. On settler life in Nyasaland, see, for example, John McCracken, 'Planters, Peasants and the Colonial State: The Impact of the Native Tobacco Board in the Central Province of Malawi', *Journal of Southern African*

Studies 9 (1983), pp. 172–92; John McCracken, 'Economics and Ethnicity: The Italian Community in Malawi', *Journal of African History* 32 (1991), pp. 313–32.

27. NAM, NS 1/35/3, Folio 7, p. 3.
28. NAM, NS 1/35/3, Folio 7, p. 3.
29. NAM, NS 1/35/3, Folio 7, p. 3.
30. NAM, NS 1/35/3, Folio 7, p. 3.
31. NAM, NS 1/35/3, Folio 7, p. 1.
32. NAM, NS 1/35/3, Folio 7, p. 2.
33. NAM, NS 1/35/3, Folio 7, pp. 1, 2, 3.
34. NAM, NS 1/35/3, Folio 7, pp. 1, 2.
35. James C. Scott, *Weapons of the Weak: Everyday Forms of Peasant Resistance* (New Haven: Yale University Press, 1985).
36. NAM, NS 1/35/3, Folio 7, p. 1.
37. NAM, NS 1/35/3, Folio 7, pp. 1, 2.
38. NAM, NS 1/35/3, Folio 7, pp. 1, 2.
39. NAM, NS 1/35/3, Folio 7, pp. 1, 2, 3.
40. My emphasis. NAM, NS 1/35/3, Folio 7, pp. 2, 3.
41. NAM, NS 1/35/3, Folio 7, p. 2.
42. One uncertainty is whether Adaima came from a matrilineal society or a patrilineal one. The author's insistence on the role of her father suggests the latter, though this could be a misinterpretation on his part.
43. On the issue of female desire under colonialism, see Heidi Gengenbach, '"What My Heart Wanted": Gendered Stories of Early Colonial Encounters in Southern Mozambique', in Jean Allman, Susan Geiger and Nakanyike Musisi (eds), *Women in African Colonial Histories* (Bloomington: Indiana University Press, 2002), pp. 19–47. On the problems with the resistance paradigm, see Lila Abu-Lughod, 'The Romance of Resistance: Tracing Transformations of Power through Bedouin Women', *American Ethnologist* 17 (1990), pp. 41–55; Frederick Cooper, 'Conflict and Connection: Rethinking Colonial African History', *American Historical Review* 99 (1994), pp. 1516–45; Sherry Ortner, 'Resistance and the Problem of Ethnographic Refusal', *Comparative Studies in Society and History* 37 (1995), pp. 173–93.
44. Shula Marks (ed.), *'Not Either an Experimental Doll': The Separate Worlds of Three South African Women* (Bloomington: Indiana University Press, 1987); Marcia Wright, *Strategies of Slaves and Women: Life-Stories from East/Central Africa* (London: James Currey, 1993). On restoring women's history in southern Africa more generally, see Belinda Bozzoli, 'Marxism, Feminism and South African Studies', *Journal of Southern African Studies* 9 (1983), pp. 139–71; Helen Bradford, 'Women, Gender and Colonialism: Rethinking the History of the British Cape Colony and Its Frontier Zones, *c.*1806–70', *Journal of African History* 37 (1996), pp. 351–70; Helen Bradford, 'Peasants, Historians, and Gender: A South African Case Study Revisited, 1850–1886', *History and Theory* 39 (2000), pp. 86–110; Shula Marks, 'Changing History, Changing Histories: Separations and Connections in the Lives of South African Women', *Journal of African Cultural Studies* 13 (2000), pp. 94–106.
45. Gayatri Chakravorty Spivak, 'Subaltern Studies: Deconstructing Historiography', in Ranajit Guha and Gayatri Chakravorty Spivak (eds), *Selected Subaltern Studies* (Oxford: Oxford University Press, 1988), pp. 3–32, here p. 26.
46. My thoughts on agency as being embedded within relations of power not only draw from Joan Scott and Judith Butler cited earlier, but also Talal Asad, *Genealogies of Religion: Discipline and Reasons of Power in Christianity and Islam* (Baltimore: The Johns Hopkins University Press, 1993), pp. 13–17; Saba Mahmood, *Politics of Piety: The Islamic Revival and the Feminist Subject* (Princeton: Princeton University Press, 2005), chapter 1, pp. 1–39.
47. Scott, 'The Evidence of Experience', p. 777.

8 The Power of Renewable Resources: *Orlando*'s Tactical Engagement with the Law of Intestacy

Jamie L. McDaniel

Virginia Woolf's 1928 novel *Orlando: A Biography* famously concerns a sex-changing protagonist and the social dilemmas this change creates for the character across different periods of British history. For the female Orlando, one of these major dilemmas involves the administration of property she had owned as a man. Throughout the novel, the biographer mentions the status of the case in the nineteenth-century High Court of Chancery, which dealt with the administration of estates. This repetition suggests that the lawsuit's resolution will contain some important consequence for Orlando. However, Orlando reacts indifferently to the message that much of her property has been sold to pay for legal expenses. Any surplus property can only be 'tailed and entailed upon the heirs male' of Orlando.[1] 'Entail' has legal ramifications related to property – namely, it is the restricting of property in an inheritance to lineal heirs of a particular class. In this instance, sex defines that class. 'Tail' emphasises the impossibility of another descendant path for the property by suggesting a continuous chain from one male heir to another without end, a strategy that carries on the male family name. With barely a second thought, Orlando neglects to read the remaining 'legal verbiage', swiftly signs the document and sends it back for processing.[2]

Orlando's lack of concern near the end of the novel, however, does not indicate apathy towards property. Rather, as Orlando moves from male to female, she discovers that as a woman she is freed of the constraints of the rules of patrilineal intestate succession and of all the rules of propriety that follow from those strict and static laws of inheritance. She is not only free of these rules; she embraces her ability to own and control personal property, especially the ability to possess the properties (in both senses) of pen and ink. Woolf creates this transformation in Orlando's thinking in ways that parallel the manner in which English property law consisted, on the one hand, of strict operations of patrilineal inheritance and, on the other, of surprising areas of instability.

In addition, Woolf may well have been conscious of certain liberalisations in English property law that had recently come into effect, giving women greater rights of inheritance and possession; her citation of C. P. Sanger's legal treatise in *Orlando*'s

Gender History Across Epistemologies, First Edition. Edited by Donna R. Gabaccia and Mary Jo Maynes.
Chapters © 2013 The Authors. Book compilation © 2013 Blackwell Publishing Ltd.

preface suggests this knowledge. Orlando's casual dismissal of the lawsuits filed against her estate reflects the liberation she gains upon coming out of her confinement as a man and into her own as a (female) writer. In essence, *Orlando* presents a model of feminist tactical engagement with property and property law – a model that uses the rules of the patriarchal legal system to undermine the system. Property, then, provides a central site of Woolf's intervention in women's history through *Orlando*'s linking of property and the creation of a viable biographical narrative for women.

The year 1925 – three years prior to *Orlando*'s publication – was important for laws concerning property in the United Kingdom. In the Introduction to the 'Review of Legislation, 1925' from the 1927 volume of the *Journal of Comparative Legislation and International Law*, F. P. Walton writes, 'Of all the multifarious enactments of the year [of 1925] the group of Acts which have placed the English law of property upon an entirely new footing may well be considered the most important'.[3] Seven acts in 1925 affected the conveyance, inheritance and ownership of property: the Law of Property Act 1925, the Settled Land Act, the Trustee Act, the Land Charges Act, the Land Registration Act, the Universities and Colleges Estates Act and the Administration of Estates Act. In particular, the Administration of Estates Act revised a British legal institution that had been the norm since the feudal system in medieval England: the common law principle of primogeniture. Prior to the 1925 acts, property was primarily seen as an extension of the Royal Family's ownership of all lands in the empire and would, therefore, pass from one monarch to the next. The dissolution of primogeniture, though, revokes the primacy of a male heir's right to land. The six other acts instituted during 1925 call into question the Crown's ability to sustain this all-encompassing position.[4] Britain's land was changing and so was the identity conveyed through its ownership. Thus, conceptions of female identity as related to property ownership were particularly tenuous. The passage of the Administration of Estates Act ended women's long legal battle for individual and equal control of property. This history included the Matrimonial Causes Act of 1857, the Married Women's Property Act of 1870 and the Married Women's Property Act of 1882.[5] This last act finally, according to Dorothy Stetson, 'altered the common law doctrine of coverture to include the wife's right to own, buy, and sell her separate property'.[6] With the addition of laws granting equal voting rights in 1928, this decade proved to be one of exciting changes in the legal treatment of women in the United Kingdom.

Given this historical context, it is not surprising that much of *Orlando*'s previous scholarly criticism focuses on Virginia Woolf's romantic friendship with author Vita Sackville-West, and Sackville-West's loss of her family estate, Knole, due to the family's practice of primogeniture.[7] James Naremore and Frank Baldanza have argued that by dedicating *Orlando* to Sackville-West, Woolf was satirising British property law by symbolically 'giving back' to Vita the house she had lost to a male relative.[8] Another common argument about *Orlando* suggests that the novel describes what it means to be British throughout the centuries depicted in the novel – a kind of biographical sketch of Britain that parallels the biographical connection between Woolf's novel and Sackville-West.[9] For example, Suzanne Raitt argues that, in its reliance on the mode of biography, *Orlando* becomes 'a piecing together of national culture' and national identity. Raitt compares the writing of *Orlando* to *The Dictionary of National Biography* (*DNB*), first published in 1885. Woolf's father Sir Leslie Stephen served as the first principal editor of the *DNB* from 1885 until 1891 and had hoped his daughter would follow in his footsteps.[10] The *DNB*, as does *Orlando*, 'condenses and defines tradition by telling over again the stories of distinguished men and women, and makes national achievement visible by placing it between the covers of many large and impressive volumes'.[11] Raitt's discussion emphasises Woolf's satire of Victorian biography and its use of the Victorian biographical methodology, which demonstrates the techniques of condensation (noting a few stories of a few significant men and women) and repetition (telling those few significant stories over and over). This approach to writing biography consequently creates a Victorian 'grand narrative' of British national achievement and, thus, British national identity. Raitt's analysis likewise suggests that Woolf's novel, in its use of timelessness and placelessness, represents a grand narrative of the history of the British people, of what it means to be British in many times and places. I agree with Raitt's assertion.[12] However, Woolf's grand narrative remains sceptical of biography's ability to represent the whole of British society and consistently points out those persons neglected by predominant accounts of national identity such as the *DNB* – persons marginalised because of their race, ethnicity or, most importantly for Woolf, gender.[13]

In approaching *Orlando*'s contribution to female historiography, I address a common epistemological assumption of qualitative research in the social sciences, namely the relationship between the researcher and the researched, especially as this assumption relates to literary studies. Practitioners of qualitative methods assume that they can learn the most about the object of research by participating in or being immersed in a research situation. I see the topic of this special issue of *Gender and History* – that is, the construction of bridges across methodological divides to help scholars better understand gender history – as an opportunity to reconsider my assumptions as a literary scholar and the value that literary scholarship places on a kind of critical detachment from its objects of inquiry. As a literary scholar, for example, I am trained to be suspicious of authors' remarks and evaluations of their own work; because an author says her work approaches gender using a Jungian perspective does not mean that adopting this perspective is the best way to understand her work. Although authors are often their own worst critics, this critical detachment can prevent literary scholars from full engagement with the text. As an alternative, looking to research models used by other disciplines as well as the epistemologies inherent in the object of analysis – in my case, the approaches Woolf uses in *Orlando* to interrogate and understand Britain's gendered political history of property – leads to a fuller immersion in the research situation and a stronger interaction between the researcher and researched. To this end, I promote an 'epistemological doubling' in this study of gender history as a means of more fully realising the interaction between the researcher and the researched. I blend three ways of knowing – literary analysis, biography (both of the individual citizen and of the British nation) and a gendered legal history of property – because Woolf uses these three epistemologies.

Through this epistemological doubling, I discern, for both Woolf and myself, a preoccupation with looking back, a process through which writers revisit narratives of national and gender identity – narratives that did not account for nor represent particular sections of the British public – for the goal of redefining what, as a result of this absence, was defined as properly 'British' for a woman. By enacting new narratives of identity that challenge the propriety of traditional accounts, contemporary women writers and gender history scholars aim to stake a claim for a place within the

British body politic. Representations of property act as central catalysts in this critique, revealed through epistemological doubling, by showing how property law and shifting cultural definitions of propriety have sought to prevent the creation and viability of an identity narrative for women.

The definition of 'propriety' undergoes three shifts in meaning from its first use in the fifteenth century to its later use in the eighteenth and nineteenth centuries. First, the entry for 'propriety' in the *Oxford English Dictionary Online* notes little distinction between definitions of 'property' and 'propriety' in their original uses in the fifteenth and sixteenth centuries; in many instances, they were used synonymously. Both terms referred to '[t]he fact of being owned by some one, or of being one's own, "ownness"; the fact of owning something, right of possession or use; ownership, proprietorship' or '[s]omething owned, a possession'. The terms, in short, both referred to an object being owned and the right to own it. The second meaning that emerges involves innate and sometimes definitional characteristics particular to an object: '[p]roper or particular character; own nature, disposition, idiosyncrasy; essence, individuality; sometimes, proper state or condition' or '[a] quality or attribute; esp. an essential or distinctive quality; a characteristic, a peculiarity = PROPERTY'. Finally, the third sense of 'propriety' reverses in some ways the second sense's connection with essential definitional characteristics. The first recorded use of 'propriety' to mean '[f]itness, appropriateness, aptitude, suitability; appropriateness to the circumstances or conditions; conformity with requirement, rule, or principle; rightness, correctness, justness, accuracy' or, similarly, '[c]onformity with good manners or polite usage' occurred in Frances Burney's novel *Cecilia* from 1782.[14] While this third sense of the word maintains the definitional connotations of the second sense, the location from which those definitional elements arise has shifted. Instead of innate characteristics, the forces that define a subject or object in this third sense come from without, using culturally constructed rules of 'appropriateness' or 'manners' as criteria for judging the propriety or impropriety of that subject or object.

This shift from internal to external definitional elements enables an understanding of the ways that propriety and property work together to reinforce relationships of male hierarchy and status. In tracing the history of contemporary thought on property and social justice, Carol Rose suggests that current definitions of 'propriety' have never totally subsumed the original lack of difference between 'property' and 'propriety'. In *Property and Persuasion*, Rose discusses the origin and continuing development in the eighteenth, nineteenth and twentieth centuries of the governmental ability to appropriate property for official use – otherwise known as the 'takings' issue.[15] She writes, 'This version of property did *not* envision property as a set of tradable and ultimately interchangeable goods; instead, different kinds of property were associated with different kinds of roles'.[16] The purpose of property through this understanding is to accord to each person that which is 'proper' or 'appropriate' to his or her personal identity, creating a paradigm for the creation of their biographical narrative, of how each life should unfold. 'And what is "proper" or appropriate', Rose continues, 'is that which is needed to keep good order in the commonwealth or body politic'.[17] According to Rose, a person's property consequently fixes his or her identity within the nation, creating a static relationship between the individual and the body politic, between personal biography and national biography.[18] In this light, property ultimately defines a subject's individual identity (woman, for example) within a proper national identity

(Britishness) and that subject's relationship to other national inhabitants. Propriety, then, is an overcoding of property with dominant cultural ideas concerning a person's or group's correct role and contribution to a national identity.

If certain property is meant for certain subjects only, and that property defines identity to a large extent, then the sense of propriety associated with property creates an expectation that only certain 'proper' life events should occur because of owning various kinds of property. Only a particular life narrative can result from owning a particular kind of property, and only a particular life narrative can lead to the owning of a particular kind of property. For the male Orlando, biography becomes inextricably linked to real property (immovable property such as houses and land) because of his ancestry's association with this kind of property. This connection shows how the novel relates real property with the passing on of a familial and abstracted male identity, which excludes identities it deems 'improper'. In *Orlando*, this improper identity is female.

The opening scene of the novel begins a trend that continues throughout Orlando's tenure as a male: establishing male propriety and female impropriety through the association of a familial and static male identity with real property, specifically Orlando's house. The sixteen-year-old Orlando 'would steal away from his mother and the peacocks in the garden and go to his attic room and there lunge and plunge and slice the air with his blade', reliving his ancestors' actions prompted by the green arras in the attic.[19] After seeing the arras, Orlando reflects that his 'fathers had been noble since they had been at all. They all came out of the northern mists wearing coronets on their heads'.[20] The house's rooms become an impetus and a setting for the re-enactment and remembrance of his ancestors' exploits. Noticeably absent from these descriptions is any mention of female ancestors, suggesting the practice of primogeniture. Orlando mentions a female relative only once, as he looks over the valley containing his family's lands and houses. After describing a 'vast mansion like that of Orlando's father', Orlando points out his father's house, his uncle's house and his aunt's 'three great turrets among the trees there'.[21]

In a later example where Orlando discusses his lineage, he defers to the power of the pen rather than the power of real property, an apparent reversal of his initial emphasis on the house as a source of historical and biographical significance. The biographer writes, 'He said (reciting the names and exploits of his ancestors) that Sir Boris had fought and killed the Paynim; Sir Gawain, the Turk; Sir Miles, the Pole; Sir Andrew, the Frank; Sir Richard, the Austrian; Sir Jordan, the Frenchman; and Sir Herbert, the Spaniard'.[22] Orlando's contemplation of his family history gives him a burst of imaginative output with his writing. He even compares the difficulty of writing with those tasks of war performed by his ancestors: Orlando 'soon perceived, however, that the battles which Sir Miles and the rest had waged against armed knights to win a kingdom, were not half so arduous as this which he now undertook to win immortality against the English language'.[23] Writing is the key to immortality for Orlando, unlike his ancestors' military deeds now represented through 'dust and ashes'. However, a closer look at this passage reveals the true source of Orlando's 'divine melody' of words: 'an incantation rising from all parts of the room'.[24] The house and its invocation of historical reflection lie at the centre of Orlando's inspiration and are responsible for his imagination and his writing – not the rigors of the compositional process that Orlando mentions many times.

Similarly, this lack of self-sufficiency through Orlando's words arises during one of his conversations with Sasha, the male Orlando's primary love interest. Orlando describes Sasha in poetic similes, comparing her to a fox, an olive tree, a green hilltop, snow, cream and marble, among other terms.[25] Orlando is met with Sasha's silence after this burst of poetic language. The history of Orlando's family as it relates to his real property, however, promotes conversation between the two lovers, a goal not achieved through poetic language alone. Orlando gives Sasha 'the whole history of his family; how their house was one of the most ancient in Britain; how they had come from Rome with the Caesars and had the right to walk down the Corso (which is the chief street in Rome) under a tasselled palanquin'.[26] For the male Orlando, words, whether poetic or otherwise, have no power without some kind of real property to support them. After relating his family's history, Orlando questions Sasha about her family's real property and the identities it confers upon her relatives: 'Where was her own house? What was her father? Had she brothers? Why was she here alone with her uncle?'[27] Like Orlando's earlier listing of his own relatives, he makes no mention of female relatives, furthering the propriety that the novel has established between male ancestry and real property. In Orlando's eyes, Sasha's identity is defined by the real property that surrounds her, not her 'own house' but the house belonging to the paternal line of her family. In the ensuing weeks after this conversation, Orlando 'thought only . . . of means for making her irrevocably and indissolubly his own'.[28] Although Orlando intends this comment in a romantic sense, the possessive undertones of the words are undeniable. When taken in conjunction with Orlando's questions about Sasha's real property and paternal lineage, the remark implies that Orlando, like many males of the same time period, sees Sasha specifically, and women more generally, as properly his property. The male Orlando views real property as the major way of producing a biographical narrative that will be remembered and respected by his descendants, a continuance of his identity in history.

Tensions about the administration of property, such as those voiced by the male Orlando, became prevalent during the period of Woolf's writing. Indeed, Virginia Woolf acknowledges the importance of property law in the preface to *Orlando*. Woolf writes, 'I am specially indebted to Mr. C. P. Sanger, without whose knowledge of the law of real property this book could never have been written'.[29] Modern readers best know Charles Percy Sanger through his article anthologised in student editions of *Wuthering Heights* (1847) that details the chronology of the events in Emily Brontë's novel and its use of the law of real property; Virginia and Leonard Woolf first published Sanger's essay in 1926.[30] A barrister by profession, Sanger's legal work primarily concerned wills and the law of intestate succession; he edited the third edition of Francis Hawkins's influential work, *A Concise Treatise on the Construction of Wills* (1885), and published his best known legal work, *The Rules of Law and Administration Relating to Wills and Intestacies* in 1914. In this book, Sanger offers a detailed examination of the differences between men's and women's rights to pass down property after death. Property and narrative are inseparable and, to the female Orlando's mind, intolerably so; Sanger's work provides a way to discuss the instability of English property law, and particularly the laws of intestate succession, as well as the opportunity to show how Woolf's novel picks up on that instability and uses it productively in the female Orlando's story through a focus on legal classification, the written word as personal property and the fate of Orlando's long poem 'The Oak Tree'.

While C. P. Sanger discusses both wills and the law of intestate succession, he never offers a clear definition of a 'will'. The closest he comes to a definition is when he states, 'Wills are written documents; the testator's intention is determined by ascertaining what the written words, judicially interpreted, mean'.[31] Sanger's definition offers a specific medium for wills but little in terms of genre or form. He notes a will's primary legal role when he notices that English law 'differs from that of most other countries in the fact that it gives a practically unlimited power of disposition of property by will'.[32] In describing 'intestacy', Sanger states, 'A person dies wholly intestate if he or she has left no will, or if all the dispositions of the will have failed by lapse or otherwise. Partial intestacy occurs where the will does not effectively dispose of all the testator's real and personal estate'.[33] Additionally, wills provide direct language for executors, lawyers, judges and other legal professionals to interpret. *Intention*, then, is the focus for the interpretation of wills: How did the deceased intend the property to be distributed? However, property held in accordance to the law of intestate succession has no clear line of descent indicated by the deceased. Therefore, much of the law of intestacy revolves around *classification*: Who is the heir-at-law, and who is the next of kin? His classification of individuals indicates their rights to the specific property of the deceased.

Another definitional issue arises in the differentiation between real property and personal property in Sanger's section on the law of intestacy. Different laws applied to each kind of property; Sanger writes, 'In English law the rules as to real property are entirely different from those as to personal property, including leaseholds'.[34] Therefore, the method of distribution among heirs-at-law and next of kin depended upon a piece of property's classification as real or personal. Sanger apparently gives a clear definition of each kind of property when he states, 'Broadly, real estate is immoveable, personal estate is moveable property, subject to the important exception that terms of years in real estate (or chattels real, as they are called) are personal property'.[35] However, even the law's ostensibly clear definition of the two types of property in his section on the law of intestacy contains an exception. This exception is the first of many that follow. On the one hand, Sanger discusses how corn and other 'annual crops' are personal property because an intervention by the owner of the land must be employed in order to grow these kinds of crops. On the other hand, this personal property classification 'does not extend to apples and other fruit grown on trees; it applies to a "crop of that species only which ordinarily repays the labour by which it is produced, within the year in which that labour is bestowed, though the crop may, in extraordinary seasons, be delayed beyond that period"'.[36] Because little work or intervention is necessary to grow fruit trees, the fruit from those trees constitute real property, not personal property. Sanger relates a further clarification involving trees later in the same section. He writes, 'Trees form part of the soil unless they are completely severed'.[37] Thus, whether dead or alive, trees in the soil are real property, and trees removed from the soil are personal property. Despite the specific exceptions or clarifications, of which there are many, the importance of his final discussion lies in the inability to clearly differentiate between real and personal property.

In cases of intestacy, a widowed woman had fewer rights than a widowed man. A widowed woman also had more restrictions placed on her appropriation of property, with some districts in England requiring chastity on the woman's part as a condition of inheritance.[38] In general, widows of husbands that did not leave wills were entitled to £500 only, even if the deceased's real and personal estate was more valuable. Additionally, the widow was 'entitled to live in the chief mansion house of her husband for 40 days after his death'. Barristers referred to this period of time as a 'widow's quarantine'.[39] In contrast, widowed husbands were entitled to the full value of both real and personal properties of a deceased wife. Thus, the real and personal property became part of the husband's estate, with one notable exception in terms of personal property. Sanger notes that if personal property is 'held to her separate use', then a husband does not automatically collect that personal property.[40] Sanger states that the cases in which a woman 'has [personal] property not to her separate use are becoming uncommon', with the only exceptions involving a creditor's right to a woman's personal property.[41] No such exemption exists for real property, making personal property a more fluid commodity for inheritance. Sanger also writes that the 'lineal descendants *in infinitum* of any person deceased represent their ancestor, and stand in the same place as their ancestor would have done if living'.[42] The importance of personal property for women, then, is its ability to transfer a representation of their individual identity to future generations without becoming part and parcel of their husband's estate and family identity.[43]

As a type of personal property, writing can exist independent of real property. *Orlando*'s emphasis on writing as a kind of personal property relates to C. P. Sanger's description of personal property and intestacy. As long as writing is held in separate use by women, that personal property does not automatically become the husband's, according to Sanger. For women, the personal property of writing cannot be subsumed under their husbands' potential estates in the event of their death without a will, unlike houses and land. Writing consequently becomes an important part of a woman's legacy.

Orlando suggests that a woman's position in society affords her no more powers or rights than if she were dead, an implicit acknowledgment of the law of intestacy that places emphasis on classification. For example, in the conclusion to the passage describing the three 'charges' against Orlando in the Court of Chancery the biographer writes:

> Thus it was in a highly ambiguous condition, uncertain whether she was alive or dead, man or woman, Duke or nonentity, that she posted down to her country seat, where, pending the legal judgment, she had the Law's permission to reside in a state of incognito or incognita as the case might turn out to be.[44]

Although concerned with Orlando's legal situation, the passage reflects more generally upon an Englishwoman's rights to property as well. The parallel format of the sentence equates life with being a titled male citizen and death with being a female 'nonentity', a person without form or definition and a 'nobody'. 'Nonentity' contributes to this formlessness or immateriality with its ghostly undertones. Orlando is not only a 'nobody' in title and property, but she also has 'no body', no definable or stable biology in the eyes of the law. As a result, in legal situations, male citizens become defined in terms of what they possess, while female citizens are defined in terms of what they lack. The use of 'incognito' and 'incognita' to describe Orlando's situation equally links identity to the possession of property. A lack of property, then, results in an indiscernible identity for both men and women.

Similarly, many characters and the biographer associate death with Orlando's characterisation. For example, at the first mention of Orlando's legal suit, the biographer writes:

The chief charges against her were (1) that she was dead, and therefore could not hold any property whatsoever; (2) that she was a woman, which amounts to much the same thing; (3) that she was an English Duke who had married one Rosina Pepita, a dancer; and had had by her three sons, which sons now declaring that their father was deceased, claimed that all his property descended to them. [45]

This passage demonstrates the concern that the law of intestate succession has with classification. Just as the litigants attempt to classify Orlando as deceased, dame or dad, the biographer also formally classifies the three different accusations. Yet, like the biographer's parallel sentence structure in the description of the three 'charges' in Chancery, these descriptions by the biographer indicate the difficulty in classifying any elements of a system distinctively. Even as the biographer attempts to differentiate among the three 'charges', death necessarily becomes the common bond: through explicitly mentioning Orlando's possible death in the first charge, through equating the state of womanhood with the state of death in the second charge and through the sons' rights to the property because of primogeniture and death in the third charge. The lack of any female offspring highlights the differences between male and female inheritors. In fact, Sanger describes the results of this kind of situation for men and for women. Although all of the property would go to the eldest son of the three, three daughters would have had to share the inheritance equally.[46] Each of the three positions is predicated on the same basis and the same outcome: death results in the loss of real property for women. In other words, real property becomes part of their husbands' estates and identities, leaving women in a state of incognita and exposing the inherent contradictions of classification in estate law.

As the female Orlando tactically engages with moveable personal property, rather than static real property, as a source of biographical narrative creation, she begins to exhibit a dynamism in her behaviour and characterisation. The law of intestacy in the novel, along with Orlando's associations with death, critiques what was seen as the proper legal position of women in British society. Orlando, and thus all British women, might as well be dead in the eyes of British law because of the weaknesses in the property rights for women. The emphasis on death and the law of intestacy may also be a nod toward the 1925 formal legal revocation of primogeniture, a practice that depended upon death for its survival. However, the novel's depiction of property rights does not insinuate a lack of belief in the ability to improve the legal system or a woman's inability to use the current laws to her advantage. Orlando's own transition from associating identity with real property to associating identity with personal property indicates a British woman's ability to use that legal system to her advantage. As the novel unfolds, it presents a counterpoint to the historical continuation of a familial identity that forms the basis of the male Orlando's identification with real property. Instead, the use of personal property by the female Orlando localises her identity, focusing instead upon the passing on of a narrative of discrete female identity, not the biography, name and tradition of a family.

The female Orlando's interactions with the band of gypsies that she travels with soon after her transformation begin to help Orlando understand the possible liabilities of real property. Immediately after Orlando joins the troop of gypsies, she notices the freedom afforded to them. The biographer writes, 'The gipsies followed the grass; when it was grazed down, on they moved again'.[47] This freedom comes from a lack of real property; in the novel, the gypsies depend only upon personal, moveable property for their existence. They view the land of the world as a communally owned property, and any duke who accumulated land 'was nothing but a profiteer or robber who snatched land and money from people who rated these things of little worth'.[48] As the male Orlando had done with Sasha, the female Orlando 'could not help with some pride describing the house where she was born, how it had 365 rooms and had been in the possession of her family for four or five hundred years. Her ancestors were earls, or even dukes, she added'.[49] However, discussing the mansion and the biography it represents does not have the same effect on the gypsies as it has on Sasha. The gypsies are not impressed; in fact, they 'were uneasy'.[50] Neither Rustum (the head gypsy) nor any of the other gypsies sees the point of building 365 bedrooms when one is enough. Orlando finally realises that '[f]our hundred and seventy-six bedrooms mean nothing to them'.[51] They perceive no value in real property, and owning real property does not differentiate the gypsy families from Orlando's family as Orlando had initially thought; the gypsies' 'own families went back at least two or three thousand years'.[52] Because gypsies find themselves in a marginalised position similar to the position of women, the fact that the gypsies' ancestry is based in personal, moveable property shows the female Orlando that biography through property is not restricted to the male sex nor to real property.[53]

Through her experience with the gypsies and their interaction with personal property, the female Orlando learns that biographical narrative and identity are not restricted to real property, as the male Orlando had thought. One of Orlando's concluding thoughts at the end of the text, as she looks out upon the land that was once hers, is a recollection of questions that Rustum asked her: 'What is your antiquity and your race, and your possessions compared with this [natural scene]? What do you need with four hundred bedrooms and silver lids on all your dishes, and housemaids dusting?'[54] Orlando's remembrance of these questions implies that she has come to the same conclusion as Rustum, that real property provides restriction instead of freedom. As Orlando ponders these thoughts, 'the landscape (it must have been some trick of the fading light) shook itself, heaped itself, let all this encumbrance of houses, castles, and woods slide off its tent-shaped sides'.[55] From Orlando's perspective, real property is an 'encumbrance' that prevents the creation of imagery. Orlando acknowledges through this remembrance the importance that the gypsies and their attitude towards real property have played in her development. The action associated with moveable property serves as a reminder of an individualised identity rather than a familial identity.

Orlando has a vision of her house almost immediately after coming to this conclusion about real property, which highlights the dynamic characteristics of her imagination not found in the male Orlando. In earlier discussions of Orlando's house, the dialogue focused on actual depictions of, or interactions with, the mansion and the surrounding land and trees. These earlier references to the house and Orlando's family history create a more static picture of the house, thus suggesting that the identity conferred by its existence and inheritance will continue throughout the ages. During this vision, though, the vast park surrounding Orlando's house 'appeared on the bald mountainside'.[56] After the park appears, with its trees, deer and moving carts, 'there appeared the roofs and belfries and towers and courtyards of her own home'.[57] The park, the activities occurring in the park and Orlando's house all appear from and disappear into the mountain; this vision of property is more organic because it comes from an individual's perception – a figment of Orlando's imagination. The house becomes a constructed image rather than a 'real' piece of property, suggesting that the female Orlando derives identity through the creative power of the imagination rather than from ownership of real property.

As implied in this vision of Orlando's house and land, the female Orlando begins to focus on conveying an individual identity in personal property rather than the continuation of a transcendent familial identity in real property. The most prominent example of Orlando's turn to personal property is her emphasis on ink and paper, materials that she sees as indispensable for writing. The first occurrences of Orlando's wish for ink and paper take place during her time with the gypsies. At this point, Orlando does not credit writer's block with her inability to write – as the male Orlando had earlier – but rather the lack of the required materials for writing. In deciding whether or not to remain with the gypsies, Orlando thinks that it is 'impossible to remain forever where there was neither ink nor writing paper'.[58] At one point, the ink seems to take on the role of educator, blotting out ideas that Orlando had written which run counter to those concerning property that she learned from the gypsies: 'Orlando, who had just dipped her pen in the ink, and was about to indict some reflection upon the eternity of all things, was much annoyed to be impeded by a blot, which spread and meandered round her pen'.[59] At the beginning of chapter six, the biographer describes Orlando's preparations for writing. Orlando does not focus on the property itself but rather the action of writing that occurs in the space. The lists in each of these passages where Orlando or the biographer mentions pen and paper parallel the listings of Orlando's paternal family history that she discusses with Sasha earlier in the novel. The emphasis has moved beyond representations of male identity in real property and instead focuses on putting 'the contents of her mind carefully' onto paper.[60] By replacing the repetition of Orlando's ancestors with the repetition of personal property, the references to ink and paper break with the biographical technique of condensation and repetition discussed by Suzanne Raitt in her examination of *The Dictionary of National Biography* and reject the wordy and euphemistic kind of biographies that the Victorians wrote by showing that discrete marginalised identities, and particularly the identities of women, cannot be remembered by repeating the narrative of ancestors instituted within real property.

Like the male Orlando, the female Orlando visits the tombs of her ancestors and shows how she now uses personal property as a catalyst for self-development. This passage lies in stark contrast to the male Orlando's earlier visit to the catacombs, where his respect for their deeds is evident. She thinks that 'the bones of her ancestors' have 'lost something of their sanctity' since her time with the gypsies.[61] The biographer continues describing Orlando's thoughts, which hold the basis of her shift in perspective:

> Somehow the fact that only three or four hundred years ago these skeletons had been men with their way to make in the world like any modern upstart, and that they had made it by acquiring houses and offices, garters and ribbands, as any other upstart does, while poets, perhaps, and men of great mind and breeding had preferred the quietude of the country, for which choice they paid the penalty by extreme poverty, and now hawked broadsheets in the Strand, or herded sheep in the fields, filled her with remorse.[62]

Her thoughts on the despicable nature of her ancestors' actions reflect the gypsies' idea about the communality of property. Orlando's motivation for respect shifts from accumulation to composition, with the implicit comparison between the ancestor's house and the poet's writing. Orlando sees moving past her male ancestors' emphasis on real property as 'growing up', which she twice repeats, a progression past traditional uses of property to indicate familial identity. [63]

Unlike Sasha, who is the male Orlando's primary love interest, Shelmerdine, who is the female Orlando's primary love interest, does not show much concern for real property. The female Orlando does not subject Shel to the same interrogation about family property, instead focusing on Shel's ability to create narrative. Orlando constantly asks Shelmerdine to tell a story; soon after meeting Shel, Orlando implores him, '"Shel, my darling" she began again, "tell me . . ."'.[64] The ellipsis indicates a type of indifference towards the content of the narrative and a focus instead on the act of narrative creation to fill that ellipsis; the biographer writes that 'they talked for two hours or more, perhaps about Cape Horn, perhaps not . . .'[65] Orlando also asks Shel to describe Cape Horn after learning the results of the case in Chancery. The use of ellipsis, and Shel's repetition of the same Cape Horn narrative, indicate that the content of the narrative does not matter; narrative creation attracts Orlando to Shel.

The importance of writing and narrative creation comes full circle in Orlando's final statement about her house, in which the house becomes a constructed image rather than a 'real' piece of property:

> The house was no longer hers entirely, she sighed. It belonged to time now; to history; was past the touch and control of the living. Never would beer be spilt here any more, she thought . . . or holes burnt in the carpet. Never two hundred servants come running and brawling down the corridors with warming pans and great branches for the great fireplaces. Never would ale be brewed and candles made and saddles fashioned and stone shaped in the workshops outside the house.[66]

Unlike the passage in which the male Orlando presents an encapsulation of British military history in a list of his supposed ancestors and the house serves as the inspiration through an 'incantation' for his 'divine melody' of words, the house in this final mention instead becomes a discursive creation of the female Orlando's narrative. [67] The key to this passage is, indeed, time as related in the verb tenses used to depict the events. Unlike the original image of her house, where readers get only a short, imagistic description of the building proper, the events of the described narrative that could take place in her house in essence 'build' the house for the reader, giving the excerpt a sense of the present and an urgency not shown in previous portrayals of the house. On the other hand, the events that Orlando is thinking about have, in fact, occurred in the house during the course of Orlando's narrative, giving readers a sense of the past that conflicts with the urgency of the present. This indeterminacy traps the house between a narrative of definite past events and a narrative of a possible, conditional future.

Orlando creates a similar conditional narrative in her final experience with her work 'The Oak Tree'. Throughout the novel, an actual oak tree on her property has provided a place of refuge and inspiration. In this final scene, Orlando recounts a narrative about burying a first edition of her now published work under the tree's roots. Although this narrative would seem to symbolise an acknowledgement of the tree's role– and, consequently, real property's role – in writing the work, the narrative, like the final story about her house, is written in a conditional form: '"I bury this as a tribute," she was going to have said, "a return to the land of what the land has given me"'.[68] In playing the role of the author by, in essence, 'taking back' the narrative she has just created – in other words, by refusing to act out the conditional narrative with the burial – Orlando reasserts the power that personal property holds for women. As C. P. Sanger writes in his treatise, 'Trees form part of the soil unless they are completely severed'.[69] While the oak tree on Orlando's land is clearly real property, Orlando's 'The Oak Tree' acts as a kind of metaphorical tree taken from the ground – a word released from the patriarchal power of real property. This reference is a final comment upon the state of women's property rights in Britain. She questions the power of the oak tree, but not 'The Oak Tree': Orlando's ultimate disavowal of her house and lands for the narrative offered through her paper and pen.

Orlando's shifting outlook on property reflects my movement from a more strictly traditional literary approach to the epistemological doubling I highlight at the outset of this essay. Unlike *Orlando*'s depiction of real property, the critical detachment of literary criticism is not gendered masculine. However, this approach is reminiscent of real property's static, propriety-oriented nature. It can be exclusionary, and it relies upon static disciplinary divisions. These divisions dictate that the only proper readings of a text use the proper method directed by tradition or long-held beliefs about a text. For example, Woolf's acknowledgment of C. P. Sanger in *Orlando*'s preface has often been dismissed as an item for serious inquiry because the preface has traditionally been read as parody. In contrast, epistemological doubling uses Woolf's critical methods of literary criticism, biography and legal history as a framework for interpreting the novel. *Orlando* serves as a literary analysis of the biography genre by presenting itself as a non-fictional work. The biographer-narrator offers a series of close readings that satirise the Victorian version of the biographical literary form. I, too, employ the methods of close reading, especially in my examination of the linguistic differences between the descriptions of Orlando as a man and woman. At the same time, as I address the biographical turn in the critical tradition of *Orlando*, which has often neglected other approaches for a strictly biographical one, I demonstrate that the novel provides Woolf with one means of confronting a different kind of biographical baggage, especially her father's legacy as editor of the *DNB*, her own legacy as an author and literary scholar, her relationship with Vita Sackville-West and Sackville-West's loss of Knole. Finally, Woolf and I both grapple with property law: Woolf sought to understand her daily encounters with the laws that prevented women from full personhood and the ways that those laws have affected women in Britain over the course of several centuries; I examine how Woolf contributes to this legal history of British women. As with *Orlando*'s feminist tactical engagement with personal property, a model that uses the rules of the legal system to critique the system, epistemological doubling does not undermine or critique the text but rather helps to develop a fuller immersion in the research situation of many literary scholars and provides a stronger interaction between the researcher and researched, an important element of qualitative research in the social sciences.

The narrative of Orlando's development in her use of personal property depicts an alternative to the kinds of static and familial biographical associations held in real property – a tactical engagement with property that offers the female Orlando a narrative of identity dynamic in its creation. The difficulty in distinguishing between different kinds of property reinforces the inability to classify Orlando's sex or the genre of the novel definitively. Instead, the novel is a series of 'exceptions' and 'buts', like the law of intestacy it borrows from. Following the news that she has lost most of her real property in the legal case, Orlando has realised the fleeting nature of real property, now favouring instead the power of renewable resources: ink, paper and especially writing.

Notes

The author would like to thank Jim Baxter, Mary Grimm, Gary Stonum, Danielle Nielsen, Chalet Seidel, Asdghig Karajayerlian, Nárcisz Fejes, Erika Olbricht, Sarah Gridley, Paul McCallum and especially Kurt Koenigsberger for their helpful commentary on and critical engagement with the issues I raise in this article.

1. Virginia Woolf, *Orlando: A Biography*, ed. Mark Hussey (1928; repr. New York: Harcourt, 2006), p. 187.
2. Woolf, *Orlando*, p. 187.
3. F. P. Walton, 'Review of Legislation, 1925', *Journal of Comparative Legislation and International Law* 9 (1927), pp. xxvii–xxxiii, here p. xxviii.
4. The Law of Property Act 1925 made it easier to transfer property through lease and deed. The Settled Land Act affected the conveyance of property in order to keep that property within a person's family. The Trustee Act changed the way stocks, bonds and other securities were purchased. The Land Charges Act regulated contracts, payments or other factors that limited the title of registered property. The Land Registration Act introduced the system of land registration by title and the Universities and Colleges Estates Act changed the structure through which colleges were funded by the state.
5. Each of these three acts carried importance for women and property in the nineteenth century. The 1857 Matrimonial Causes Act widened the ability to get a divorce and made divorce a civil matter rather than a religious one handled by ecclesiastical courts. The Married Women's Property Act of 1870 provided the right for women to earn money and to inherit property. Finally, the Married Women's Property Act of 1882 gave the same rights that unmarried women had to married women, namely, to own and control property; in other words, married women became legally recognised as individuals apart from their husbands. For more about the status of women in the second half of the nineteenth century, see Mary Lyndon Shanley, *Feminism, Marriage, and the Law in Victorian England, 1850–1895* (Princeton: Princeton University Press, 1989).
6. Dorothy Stetson, *A Woman's Issue: The Politics of Family Law Reform in England* (London: Greenwood, 1982), p. 90.
7. The novel is often marketed as 'the longest and most charming love letter in literature', a well-known remark made by Vita's son Nigel Nicolson. Nicolson also writes that *Orlando* 'turned into something much more than the joke Virginia had first intended', which also suggests that the role of property in the novel and, particularly C. P. Sanger's contribution to that role, deserves further inquiry. Nigel Nicolson, *Portrait of a Marriage: Vita Sackville-West and Harold Nicolson* (New Haven: Yale University Press, 1973), p. 202; Nigel Nicolson, *Virginia Woolf* (New York: Viking, 2000), p. 107.
8. For further information on the connections among the Sackvilles, Knole, Virginia Woolf and *Orlando*, see Frank Baldanza, 'Orlando and the Sackvilles', *PMLA* 70 (1955), pp. 274–9; James Naremore, *The World Without a Self: Virginia Woolf and the Novel* (New Haven: Yale University Press, 1973).
9. Much of *Orlando*'s criticism focuses on questions related to the biography and autobiography genres as well as on Virginia Woolf's relationship with author Vita Sackville-West. Victoria L. Smith notes that the novel 'has been variously described as a *roman à clef*, a künstlerroman, an anti-novel, metafiction, magical realism, an autobiography (and a specifically female one at that) and a biography'. The rationale for these latter two designations is obvious. Many times throughout the novel, the biographer-narrator interrupts the tale to contemplate his or her role as a biographer. The biographer reveals much of the reasoning behind the inclusion or exclusion of events from the narrative and questions the objectivity that he or she holds in relating these events to the reader. In fact, Smith argues that any reading of *Orlando* must take biographical and autobiographical concerns into consideration. She sees the interplay between the fictional plot of the novel and its factual counterpart, between a series of deeply personal real events in Woolf's life and the novelisation of those events in a publicly circulated text, as Woolf's way of considering the post-structuralist difficulty of representation in language, especially for women. Likewise, Jean O. Love argues that *Orlando* is 'peculiarly bound' to Woolf's friendship with Sackville-West. Like Smith, Love makes extensive use of Woolf's letters to Sackville-West and her diary entries about the novel's composition, particularly the diary entries beginning in 1922 when Woolf first met Sackville-West. Love concludes that Orlando's difficulties in gaining a unified view of herself parallels Woolf's own issues with her sexual identity and she suggests that Woolf viewed Sackville-West as most likely experiencing these same concerns. Victoria L. Smith, '"Ransacking the Language": Finding the Missing Goods in Virginia Woolf's *Orlando*', *Journal of Modern*

Literature 29 (2006), pp. 57–75, here pp. 58–60; Jean O. Love, '*Orlando* and Its Genesis: Venturing and Experimenting in Art, Love and Sex', in Ralph Freedman (ed.), *Virginia Woolf: Revaluation and Continuity* (Berkeley: University of California Press, 1980), pp.189–218, here p. 193.

10. Suzanne Raitt, *Vita and Virginia: The Work and Friendship of V. Sackville-West and Virginia Woolf* (Oxford: Clarendon Press, 1993), p. 19.

11. Raitt, *Vita and Virginia*, p. 20.

12. Jane de Gay uses a similar method in her reading of *Orlando*. De Gay compares Leslie Stephen's 'zeitgeist' approach to literary history with Woolf's critique of that approach. In the *DNB* and *English Literature and Society in the Eighteenth Century* (1904), Stephen focuses on the ideological and cultural contributions of 'mainstream and influential writers' and divides 'the century into a series of "schools" gathered under key, male figures'. Woolf offers an alternative vision of literary history in *Orlando* and *A Room of One's Own* through her selection of mostly female individuals, like Orlando and Shakespeare's fictional sister Judith, who try to 'retain artistic integrity in opposition to contemporary trends'. Although representations of property lie outside of de Gay's area of inquiry, they serve much the same purpose as the particular rhetorical strategies that de Gay asserts Woolf employs in her alternative literary history. Jane De Gay, 'Virginia Woolf's Feminist Historiography in *Orlando*', *Critical Survey* 19 (2007), pp. 62–72, here p. 64.

13. For other discussions of genre, biography and *Orlando*, see Beth A. Boehm, 'Fact, Fiction, and Metafiction: Blurred Gen(d)res in *Orlando* and *A Room of One's Own*', *Journal of Narrative Technique* 22 (1992), pp. 191–204; Elizabeth Cooley, 'Revolutionizing Biography: *Orlando*, - The Significance of Constantinople in *Orlando*, *Roger Fry*, and the Tradition', *South Atlantic Review* 55 (1990), pp. 71–83; Rachel Blau Du Plessis, *Writing Beyond the Ending: Narrative Strategies of Twentieth-Century Women Writers* (Bloomington: Indiana University Press, 1985); Mary Jacobus, *Reading Woman: Essays in Feminist Criticism* (New York: Columbia University Press, 1986); Karen R. Lawrence, 'Orlando's Voyage Out', *Modern Fiction Studies* 38 (1992), pp. 253–77; David Roessel, 'The Significance of Constantinople in *Orlando*', *Papers on Language and Literature* 28 (1992), pp. 398–416; J. J. Wilson, 'Why is *Orlando* Difficult?' in Jane Marcus (ed.), *New Feminist Essays on Virginia Woolf* (Lincoln: University of Nebraska Press, 1981), pp. 170–84.

14. 'Propriety', *Oxford English Dictionary Online* (2011), <http://www.oed.com>.

15. For more information on the relationship among property ownership, the takings issue and national identity, see Tom Bethell, *The Noblest Triumph: Property and Prosperity through the Ages* (New York: St. Martin's Press, 1998); Alan Ryan, *Property* (Minneapolis: University of Minnesota Press, 1987).

16. Carol Rose, *Property and Persuasion: Essays on the History, Theory, and Rhetoric of Ownership* (Boulder: Westview Press, 1994), p. 59.

17. Rose, *Property and Persuasion*, p. 58.

18. Rose, *Property and Persuasion*, p. 59.

19. Woolf, *Orlando*, p. 11.

20. Woolf, *Orlando*, p. 12.

21. Woolf, *Orlando*, p. 15.

22. Woolf, *Orlando*, p. 60.

23. Woolf, *Orlando*, pp. 60–61.

24. Woolf, *Orlando*, p. 60.

25. Woolf, *Orlando*, p. 34.

26. Woolf, *Orlando*, p. 35.

27. Woolf, *Orlando*, p. 35.

28. Woolf, *Orlando*, p. 36.

29. Woolf, *Orlando*, p. 6.

30. Despite his mention in the preface to *Orlando* and his long-standing relationship with Woolf, critics have paid little attention to C. P. Sanger's possible contributions to *Orlando*'s composition because the novel and its preface are usually taken as ironic, parodic, comic or, most often, some combination of the three. Caroline Webb's article on listing in *Orlando* and James Joyce's *Ulysses* (1922) focuses on the preface to Woolf's novel as a satirical tool that critiques literary authority through its list of those authors responsible for Woolf's literary 'inheritance'. Webb mentions the acknowledgement of C. P. Sanger as a part of this satire; she writes, 'If C. P. Sanger indeed helped his friend [Woolf] understand the law of real property that governed the inheritance of Knole, she does not accord it the reverence her preface suggests'. However, because of her focus on satire, Webb dismisses the connection between Woolf and Sanger out of hand, particularly given the context of *Orlando*'s focus on property – offering only one paragraph speaking to the topic. In her note about his acknowledgement, Webb suggests that, because *Orlando* is a fictional work, Woolf's mention of Sanger in the Preface is meant to satirise his application of the way law is administrated in reality to the fictional *Wuthering Heights*. Nonetheless, Webb relies upon non-fictional information in

order to support her reading of the novel and many critics have suggested that *Orlando* cannot be understood without an understanding of the real events surrounding its composition. Although my reading does not necessarily preclude a satirical interpretation of the novel, it does build upon and expand *Orlando*'s critical tradition by explaining how property works more generally in the novel and how Sanger's writing may have influenced the novel's representation of property. Caroline Webb, 'Listing to the Right: Authority and Inheritance in *Orlando* and *Ulysses*', *Twentieth-Century Literature* 40 (1994), pp. 190–205, here p. 193.

31. Charles Percy Sanger, *The Rules of Law and Administration Relating to Wills and Intestacies* (London: Sweet and Maxwell, 1914), p. 2.

32. Sanger, *Rules of Law*, p. 1.

33. Sanger, *Rules of Law*, p. 123.

34. Sanger, *Rules of Law*, p. 123.

35. Sanger, *Rules of Law*, p. 164.

36. Sanger, *Rules of Law*, pp. 164–5.

37. Sanger, *Rules of Law*, p. 167.

38. Sanger, *Rules of Law*, p. 135.

39. Sanger, *Rules of Law*, pp. 129–31.

40. Sanger, *Rules of Law*, p. 125.

41. Sanger, *Rules of Law*, p. 125.

42. Sanger, *Rules of Law*, p. 138.

43. Many critics have explored the historical process of maintaining women's exclusion from legitimate and automatic inheritance of property through case law and the role of precedent. Amy Louise Erickson argues that the anonymous male author of *The Lawes Resolutions of Women's Rights: Or, the Lawes Provision for Woemen* (1632), the earliest treatise that explained women's legal rights, uses wit to critique the case law it depicts. She writes, 'This spelling of "women" [from the title] had been used previously to imply that women were the woe of men, but the sardonic comments on the common law's attitude to women made here by the anonymous male author implies rather that the law could be the woe of women'. Erickson also suggests that the manual was intended as both a manual for lawyers and a text meant as a pedagogical tool to educate women on their lack of legal rights. Barbara Kiefer Lewalski connects *The Lawes Resolutions of Womens Rights* specifically to arguments made by Anne Clifford (1589–1676) in her property and inheritance lawsuits. Concerned primarily with the community of women represented as a support network in Clifford's diary, Lewalski argues that the diary 'provides an intriguing insight into their construction of self and world as they contested Jacobean patriarchal ideology, supported on the one hand by a sense of female community and on the other by the firm conviction that God the Divine Patriarch was on their side against the many earthly patriarchs who oppressed them'. Nicky Hallet specifically identifies Clifford, an ancestor of Vita Sackville-West, as a source for Orlando. Both Clifford and Sackville-West 'were dispossessed of their estates by patriarchal legal process'. Despite the fact that the 1925 Administration of Estates Act had revised the common law principle of primogeniture, Sackville family custom continued to follow the practice of primogeniture in its distribution of property when Sackville-West's father died in 1928. Indeed, the tradition continues. Vita Sackville-West's grandson Adam Nicolson inherited Sissinghurst, the house his grandmother purchased after losing Knole, in 2004. In his book on the house, *Sissinghurst, An Unfinished History*, he mentions several times that he has sisters, one of them older, yet he inherited the house when their father died. Each of these instances provides an example of how precedent and case law work together with historical process to strategically exclude women from the continuation of familial and personal identity associated with real and personal property. Amy Louise Erickson, *Women and Property in Early Modern England* (London: Routledge, 1993), p. 21; Barbara Kiefer Lewalski, *Writing Women in Jacobean England* (Cambridge: Harvard University Press, 1993), p. 125; Nicky Hallett, 'Anne Clifford as Orlando: Virginia Woolf's Feminist Historiology and Women's Biography', *Women's History Review* 4 (1995), pp. 505–24, here p. 505; Adam Nicolson, *Sissinghurst, An Unfinished History: The Quest to Restore a Working Farm at Vita Sackville-West's Legendary Garden* (New York: Viking, 2010), pp. 36–7.

44. Woolf, *Orlando*, p. 125.

45. Woolf, *Orlando*, p. 124.

46. Sanger, *Rules of Law*, p. 138.

47. Woolf, *Orlando*, p. 104.

48. Woolf, *Orlando*, p. 109.

49. Woolf, *Orlando*, p. 109.

50. Woolf, *Orlando*, p. 109.

51. Woolf, *Orlando*, p. 110.

52. Woolf, *Orlando*, p. 109.
53. Abby Bardi associates the trope of the gypsy with gender indeterminancy in Virginia Woolf and Charlotte Brontë's works. She writes that 'Woolf finds resonance with the protean quality with which she represents gender; like gender in *Orlando*, gypsies constitute a floating signifier whose signified ... managed to elude' non-Romani observers. Abby Bardi, '"In Company of a Gipsy": The "Gypsy" as Trope in Woolf and Brontë', *Critical Survey* 19 (2007), pp. 40–50, here p. 41.
54. Woolf, *Orlando*, p. 239.
55. Woolf, *Orlando*, p. 239.
56. Woolf, *Orlando*, p. 111.
57. Woolf, *Orlando*, p. 111.
58. Woolf, *Orlando*, p. 110.
59. Woolf, *Orlando*, p. 173.
60. Woolf, *Orlando*, p. 196.
61. Woolf, *Orlando*, p. 128.
62. Woolf, *Orlando*, p. 129.
63. Woolf, *Orlando*, pp. 128–9.
64. Woolf, *Orlando*, p. 185.
65. Woolf, *Orlando*, p. 185.
66. Woolf, *Orlando*, p. 233.
67. Woolf, *Orlando*, pp. 60–61.
68. Woolf, *Orlando*, p. 238.
69. Sanger, *Rules of Law*, p. 167.

9 The Politics of Gender Concepts in Genetics and Hormone Research in Germany, 1900–1940

Helga Satzinger

The history of biological understandings of sex difference and sex determination reveals a surprising variety of conflicting views. In the first half of the twentieth century, notions of a binary and discontinuous sex difference competed with more fluid concepts of a binary order postulating the two poles of male and female connected by a continuum of different stages of 'intersexuality'. Genetic experiments laid the groundwork for new claims that male or female organisms resulted from the combined effects of male and female genetic factors with possible intermediate stages of 'intersexes'. Following a contrasting model in biochemistry, sex hormones were framed in a binary male-female order despite contradictory experimental results. The results of genetics and hormone research, moreover, entered into different political debates and struggles around gender. Around 1900, for example, the supporters of gender equality used the brand new theory of chromosomes' crucial role in inheritance to argue for women's university education. In the 1920s and 1930s genetic concepts of sex determination showed up in the conflicting debates about homosexuality, blurring gender norms, degeneration, racial purity and miscegenation.

The history of these and other conflicting concepts reveals how deeply scientific concepts were informed by political aims and desired or abhorred gender orders. These concepts were never based on purely 'scientific' or experimental results alone. It is not unusual for historians of science to find this sort of influence, as the construction of knowledge is understood as a process of social negotiation in interaction with the 'Eigensinn' (intrinsic logic) of the investigated objects, theories and experimental systems used; it is deeply embedded in historical contingencies.[1]

My account of the politics of gender concepts in the history of genetics and hormone research in Germany between 1900 and 1940 revises existing histories of biological sex determination based on sources in the English language from the second half of the twentieth century. These histories follow a narrative of a binary, masculinist concept of sex determination in the 1950s, evolving into a more balanced concept by the 1990s, a concept which finally transcends the binary. The evolution is seen as being brought about by feminist and queer interventions.[2] Going back to earlier decades of the century and to a different scientific arena, however, reveals a

Gender History Across Epistemologies, First Edition. Edited by Donna R. Gabaccia and Mary Jo Maynes.
Chapters © 2013 The Authors. Book compilation © 2013 Blackwell Publishing Ltd.

more nuanced and contradictory historical process. There is no simple story of linear progress to tell, and the story does not begin with a strictly binary, 'two-sex-model' of difference.[3]

By unravelling the politics of multiple gender concepts in the sciences of the early twentieth century I hope to link the history of the scientific study of sex difference with gender historians' work on multiplicities of genders and their continuous renegotiation.[4] Social history has shown convincingly how various gender orders have been invented, explored and contested. So it should not surprise us that in the sciences as well, there was not one and only one gender order at stake. As a historian of science I investigate scientific concepts of sex difference as resulting from various social – and gendered– processes, in which authority, power, responsibility and relevance are attributed to scientists, scientific concepts and practices, to the choice of objects and explanatory models. Taking my cue from gender history, whereby the meaning of female and male is very malleable, I investigate the gendering of scientific objects or concepts – such as sex difference, hormones, genes, chromosomes and germ cells. I examine how these epistemic objects were shaped by and embodied political debates about the gender order and how they, in turn, influenced them.

Sex/gender, nature/culture and Mother Nature's 'political correctness'

Let me first clarify two points related to the terms 'sex' and 'gender', to prevent possible misunderstanding. The use of the term gender is problematic, especially when talking about biological understandings of sex difference.[5] The German language has one term for sex and gender, "Geschlecht", which does not distinguish between the "natural" and the "cultural". The English distinction between sex and gender, on the other hand, often sets up a 'natural' or biological entity – 'sex'– and leaves its investigation to the sciences.[6] However, feminist science studies showed that there was no gender-free concept of biological 'sex difference' even before Judith Butler pointed out the conceptual flaws of the sex-gender distinction.[7] Writing in English on biological concepts of 'sex difference' creates the problem of how to find a new term for 'sex' to indicate that biologists also 'do gender' when investigating 'sex difference'. With no alternative at hand I will still use the terms 'sex', 'sex difference' and 'sex determination' when I refer to scientists' efforts to deal with what they see as the nature of the difference between humans of different generative potential. I also want to stress the point that we have no adequate terminology yet to describe and account for the materiality of different bodies while avoiding the gendered assumptions of the biological sciences. Even the biological constituents of the body, like 'cells', 'genes', 'hormones' and 'chromosomes' embody gendered concepts, which I hope to show.

The nature/culture and sex/gender conceptual divides create another problem. During the last few decades feminist science studies have shown convincingly how social concepts of gender shape scientific knowledge. Biology is a particularly striking and obvious example as some of its topics deal with sex difference and sex determination, procreation, male or female behaviour and heredity, to name a few areas where gender is an inevitable part of the process of knowledge production and knowledge itself. Biology and medical sciences of the nineteenth and twentieth centuries were crucial tools in the construction of knowledge about women's nature and the legitimation of their subordination.[8] It was, and is, a very important task to deconstruct biological and medical concepts of gender which reiterate all too familiar sexist claims about women's difference from men, be it mathematical ability, orientation in space or reproductive strategies. Based on the critical deconstruction of those gender concepts, several authors in science and gender studies claim that 'better science' would be possible once gender biases were removed. Once feminist perspectives prevail and pose new questions, the argument goes, neglected topics could come to the fore, thus restructuring and innovating knowledge for the better.[9]

However, there is a blind spot in this argument. It is based on a tacit and a very old assumption, already used by women like Mary Wollstonecraft and Olympe de Gouges in the late-eighteenth century: nature does not know a hierarchical gender order.[10] Today we still find the assumption lurking in feminist critiques that once we investigate 'nature' in a gender-neutral way, we will find nature's undistorted and 'true' properties. The natural world is posited as 'politically correct', waiting to be discovered. Historians of science are usually more sceptical with regards to 'scientific facts' of the natural world. For them, the investigative processes by which scientific facts are 'fabricated' are the focus of attention. It is not really important, or at least it should not be important, if those facts themselves meet the expectations of the historian. But, is it really no problem, when 'nature' defies the feminist investigators' political convictions with regard to the appropriate gender order? Usually the discovery of 'gender stereotypes' in scientific concepts – whatever they might be – rings alarm bells, indicating that something might be wrong with these scientific facts. But the opposite case seems to go unnoticed. There is no alarm bell ringing when the scientific fact meets a contemporary feminist norm of gender difference.

Three examples taken from the recent history of biology illustrate that the presumption of a 'politically incorrect nature' is rather unusual in feminist science studies. Scott Gilbert and Karen Rader investigated the substantial participation of women scientists in developmental genetics in the second half of the twentieth century. They concluded that the prominent presence of women in this scientific discipline helped to overcome masculinist assumptions and to come to a better, or more adequate, understanding of embryonic development.[11] In a similar line of thought Sarah Richardson argued that the influence of an outspoken feminist scientist led to investigating the process of sex determination in humans in a new and more appropriate way in the 1990s.[12] This scientific intervention was successful at this particular point in time as the general social atmosphere encouraged the exploration of new gender concepts. According to Richardson, the prevalent focus on male development and the neglect of female development, as well as the belief in the normality of a strict binary order was thus overcome by the end of the 1990s. Finally, in her 1996 paper 'Gender and Genitals', Ruth Hubbard criticised the '[w]estern assumption that there are only two sexes', which 'probably derives from our culture's close linkage between sex and procreation'. In her view, 'this binary concept does not reflect biological reality'.[13] To illustrate this, she referred to various forms of 'intersexes' and societies where these 'intersexes' were regarded as normal human variants. In the Dominican Republic, for example, some girls usually developed into young men during puberty. This transformation was seen as normal by the villagers, whereas western scientists explained it as an effect of a specific and pathological testosterone metabolism in individuals with a 'male' x-y chromosome status, preventing male development before puberty. In conclusion Hubbard asked the medical profession 'to remove their binary spectacles and, rather than explore what it means to be "male" or "female", look into what it means to be neither or both, which is what most of us are'.[14] In Hubbard's approach sex and gender blur; people with all sorts of bodies assign themselves a particular social identity, which is no longer framed in a binary sex/gender system. By doing so, she argued, these people question their pathologisation of sexual indeterminacy by the medical and biological professions. Hubbard's example shows two ways of referring to 'nature'. On the one hand, there are people using the notion of pathology to posit a seemingly natural order in which there are men and women only, with their clear-cut difference defined by their reproductive potential. Variations are pathologies that demand medical intervention. On the other hand, there are people or cultures, including even some scientists, which create and provide social spaces for all individuals who are there, 'naturally', by birth, without superimposing a binary gender order.[15] The ethical foundation of Hubbard's approach follows the conviction that everyone born has the right to exist, and medicine and science should not help to create social discrimination.[16] According to Hubbard nature offers more than two sexes, therefore medicine and the biological sciences should not impose a binary sex/gender order.

But, why should we refer to 'nature' to legitimate anti-discriminatory politics? Can we assume that 'nature' is politically correct and prepared to help us against discrimination? Is it just a matter of getting the sciences on the right political track and then we will discover or 'reinvent' 'nature' as it is out there, happily, perfectly compatible with our political convictions? Even if this were the case, I would argue that we should not base our politics on the sciences.

'Primatology is politics by other means', Donna Haraway claimed provocatively some years ago.[17] Primatology is a contested scientific arena, where concepts of human 'nature' and sex difference are developed. Haraway showed convincingly how the successive intervention of female and feminist anthropologists changed the gendered agenda and concepts of primatology and that they conceptualised more than one gender order. But Haraway also showed that this feminist intervention remained within the conceptual paradigm of sociobiology, and therefore, within the understanding that our nature and 'reproductive strategies' simply reflect investment strategies in a competitive, capitalist society. In a similar line of thought I wish to show how genetics and endocrinology, in dealing with concepts of sex difference and sex determination, developed not one but different gender orders which, in a highly contradictory way, were part of the politics of their times. To support the claim that scientific concepts are politics by other means, I will investigate what exactly was on the political agenda.

Gender politics in the sciences

I identify three arenas for examining the politics of gender concepts at work in genetics and hormone research: the creation of scientific knowledge and its consequences for the dynamics of the respective science, the use of scientific gender concepts in political debates and the gendered organisation of scientific work, where women and men had different tasks, duties and authority.[18] In those three arenas of science, gender orders were invented and negotiated, although we cannot assume a direct causality between the gender order of the workplace, the knowledge produced and the politics supported. The social gender orders did not translate directly into the scientific ones, and vice versa. There was always tension, contradiction and asynchronicity. There were also specific disciplinary traditions, experimental systems and concepts, which incorporated and perpetuated certain gender concepts. These concepts could not be overcome just by changing the social gender order – at least in the short time frame of my study. Moreover, a gender concept could act as liberating in one arena, while stabilising a hierarchical order in another. This will be shown in more detail below.

My case studies come from zoological genetics and biochemical hormone research in Germany, and in particular, from the work of two zoologists and one biochemist and their male and female co-workers.[19] Theodor Boveri (1862–1915), Richard Goldschmidt (1878–1958) and Adolf Butenandt (1903–1990) were all key figures in their scientific fields. Boveri is known even today for his identification of chromosomes as the sites of the inheritable units we now call genes. Goldschmidt was a leading geneticist in the 1920s in Germany, who was both inspirational and controversial. Butenandt became famous for the chemical isolation of 'sex-hormones' from the late 1920s onwards. The three eventually reached the highest possible scientific positions in Germany. Boveri acted in 1913 and 1914 as founding director of the Kaiser Wilhelm Institute (KWI) for Biology; Goldschmidt became head of one of its departments (1914–1935) and Butenandt became director of the KWI for Biochemistry in 1936, all in Berlin. They worked during times of dramatic political change: from the time of the Empire (Boveri and Goldschmidt), to the Weimar Republic and then National Socialism (Goldschmidt and Butenandt). Goldschmidt, who was Jewish, was forced to emigrate in 1935–36 because of Nazi anti-Semitism, whereas Butenandt was able to advance his career by active collaboration with the Nazi regime. He even stayed at the top after 1945, when he became president of the Max Planck Society, and he remained a leading figure in West German biomedical research until the 1970s.[20] The early decades of the twentieth century also saw the feminist struggle for equality, suffrage and economic independence; the decriminalisation of male homosexuality and, confronting these movements, the anti-democratic and anti-feminist efforts of the völkish and Nazi political movement that succeeded in 1933 with the establishment of a totalitarian regime in Germany.

During these same years dramatic achievements occurred in the biological sciences. With the rediscovery of Gregor Mendel's laws of inheritance in 1900, genetics developed as a new discipline. In 1905 Nettie M. Stevens (1861–1912) and Edmund Wilson (1856–1939) proposed a new concept of sex difference as hereditary. It was no longer believed to be nutrition or special circumstances during conception that decided the sex of the offspring.[21] Now genetic factors were seen as responsible for the development of a fertilised egg cell into a male or female organism; observable chromosomal difference could be correlated to sex difference, suggesting a causal connection. In the 1920s hormone research approached the biological riddle of sex difference by isolating and identifying those gonadal substances that could be seen as responsible for the development of adult males or females.[22]

Things turned out to be rather complicated, and the binary either-or logic of sex difference did not account for all the observations and experimental results. 'Intersexes' became part of the evolving theories of sex difference, which could range from minor, irrelevant variations of the normal state to severe pathologies in need of surgical or pharmaceutical intervention.[23] As will be shown in more detail below, gender difference became in a new way a matter of racial difference in the 1920s and a subject of normative practices aimed against Jewish assimilation and Jewish-German marriages. Race and gender were not only analogous in their classifying powers, but also conceptually interwoven. When sex hormones were first investigated, they were classified as male or female, but soon they transcended the scientists' attempts to order them. Female hormones were found in male organisms; male hormones could have feminising effects in experimental settings. Thus, they became 'heterosexual' hormones.[24] The hormonal gender trouble was severe, and the Dutch biochemist John Freud proposed in 1936 to abandon the classification of sex hormones completely and use the name 'growth promoters' instead.[25] However, despite this observed gender unruliness, there is no convincing historiographic explanation of why the concept of male and female sex hormones, with gender inscribed into their very names like oestrogen or prostaglandin, has survived the twentieth century.

Gender at the workplace

Before going into more detail about these scientific developments, I will identify elements of the gender order in the scientific workplace of the three research groups around Boveri, Goldschmidt and Butenandt. All three cases belong to a time when the model of the male breadwinner in heterosexual married couples was normative. Earning their own living was acceptable for women only before marriage or in other exceptional cases. In the first decade of the twentieth century, women were formally admitted to university study in Germany, but a professional career in academia was a rare exception for women; even today they have severe difficulties gaining influential positions equalling those of men.[26]

In the decades covered here, women worked in all the research groups under investigation. Their work was of crucial importance; however, the gender order in their workplaces did not grant them equality. Theodor and Marcella Boveri (née O'Grady, 1863–1950) were a binational married couple, both scientists with equivalent educations. Marcella Boveri stayed in her husband's shadow, collaborating on experiments and publishing only one paper on her own. Marcella came from the US where she had teaching and research positions at Bryn Mawr and Vassar College. She had come to the University of Würzburg to study for her Ph.D. with Theodor Boveri but married him instead. She was the first woman to be admitted to Würzburg to study. The authorities could not reject her as she had previous scientific training.

As Theodore Boveri's wife, she was of importance not only as his collaborator but also as a pioneering woman scientist, helping to open the university doors to German women. Her success was a paradoxical one. She demonstrated that women who had studied at universities did not necessarily compete with men on the job market but potentially improved the career chances of their husbands if they worked in the same field. The Boveris became important mentors and supporters of women's university education; they mentored nearly half of all women who earned a Ph.D. at Würzburg before 1914. In addition, Boveri's institute hosted several women scientists from the US as visiting scholars, providing research opportunities that furthered their careers at colleges in the US. Some of these women contributed substantially to Theodor Boveri's research by solving methodological problems relevant to his approach.[27]

The case of Richard Goldschmidt was different as he was not a professor at a university. He offered opportunities to postdoctoral women scientists at his KWI department in Berlin where they could pursue research, but only one woman, Mathilde Hertz (1891–1975), got a permanent paid position that lasted until her forced emigration in 1935–36.[28] In his later years in the US, when Goldschmidt was older and less powerful, women became his main collaborators.[29] As one of the very few senior geneticists of the 1940s and 1950s, he appreciated the work of maize geneticist, Barbara McClintock (1902–1992), who, in 1983, was to be awarded the Nobel Prize for Physiology or Medicine for her early work on transposable elements in the chromosomes. This work challenged the leading genetic concepts of her time, but was not well received. Both Goldschmidt and McClintock referred positively and supportively to each other's work in the 1950s, at times when he was highly controversial and she found herself rather isolated in the scientific community.[30] In his Berlin years Goldschmidt had mostly relied on the support of women working in subordinate positions at the institute – librarians, multilingual secretaries and technical assistants.[31]

In the early years of the twentieth century, the 'technical assistant' was established as a new profession for women in the sciences and medicine in Germany. Technical assistants had their own specific formal educational requirements and examinations and worked in clinics, research laboratories, industry and governmental institutions. Scientific work had started to require large-scale data production and processing. A division of labour evolved which made an educated support staff necessary in science laboratories. In this situation the new profession of 'technical assistant' met the needs of scientists and of women who did not want to or were unable to invest a lot of money in academic study. An academic education could not promise women secure job prospects. Working as a technical assistant, however, gave women the opportunity to earn a living before marriage or sustain themselves at a very modest level, if they decided to or had to stay single, and they could work in the sciences without having to compete with men for academic positions. Goldschmidt could draw on the work of those women for his large-scale breeding experiments, for example, for the care of the animals and for the collection and evaluation of the experimental data.

The biochemist Adolf Butenandt also needed the skills of female technical assistants for the large-scale animal testing required for his hormone isolation projects. He started his career and first efforts to isolate the female hormone with his later wife, Erika von Ziegner (1906–1990), and several other women working as technical assistants on the physiological tests. In his laboratories, there was a gendered division of labour between male academic chemists and female technical assistants. For Butenandt women clearly had to restrict themselves to supporting men, and there is ample evidence that he could not tolerate independent women scientists.[32]

In all the cases covered, the gender order at the workplace was characterised by the male head of the household and head of the institute or research group. Usually women worked in a supportive position, either as the academically trained wife, the Ph.D. student or the female technical assistant. Single women academics, in highly precarious positions, collaborated with these groups, mostly for a short time. But, basically, women did not become equals in scientific workplaces. The prevalence of technical assistants even suggests that this new profession in German scientific research helped to keep women out of academic training and to reduce the competition between men and women on the academic job market. Despite these limitations, since around 1900 the gender order had gained a certain flexibility with regard to women's education and employment. During the Weimar Republic there was more openness to women's independence and their pursuit of professional careers – one might even say there was evidence of some sort of early gender bending. This limited experimentation ended in 1933. The model of the male breadwinner in a heterosexual couple remained the dominant model for the time investigated and far beyond.

Chromosomes and gender equality

In the late nineteenth century, until his untimely death in 1915, Theodor Boveri and his wife Marcella investigated hereditary processes at the level of cells, which were regarded as the smallest unit of a living organism.[33] At centre stage was the investigation of the paternal and maternal contribution to the next generation. They investigated which cellular material was transmitted and whether it was transmitted equally from each parent. Consequently, cell division, the creation of germ cells, their fusion in fertilisation and the subsequent development of an organism became the objects of study. In the nineteenth century August Weismann (1834–1914) and Ernst Naegeli (1817–1891) had proposed the hypothesis that there must be a minute substance in every cell which contained the plan for the whole organism, and which was transmitted via cell division to the 'daughter cells'.[34] The problem was identifying the hereditary substances coming from the paternal and maternal organisms. The Boveris used microscopy, staining techniques and carefully designed experiments. Their model organisms were sea urchins and the parasitic worm, Ascaris megalocephala. Both species had, in the eyes of the zoologists, male and female forms and could serve as a model for the human case.

Within the cells certain stainable particles could be identified. They became visible during cell division, were transmitted to the daughter cells but then disappeared until the next cycle of cell division started. These particles – chromosomes – were the perfect candidates to be identified as the heredity-bearing substance, as they are still considered today. But careful investigation and experimentation was necessary to prove that in every cell cycle the same number of chromosomes appeared in the same form and that each of them had its own specific and irreplaceable relevance for the normal development of an organism. In the years 1902–1904, shortly after the rediscovery of the Mendelian laws of inheritance, Theodor Boveri identified the chromosomes as the material entity on which Mendelian 'Anlagen' – later called genes – were situated. He saw the chromosomes as the crucial substance of heredity, which always in pairs, were passed on from one cell generation to the next. One set of the pair came from the maternal organism and one from the paternal organism via their egg cell or spermatozoon, respectively, which had fused during fertilisation. Boveri's interpretation was later called the chromosomal theory of heredity and became one of the building blocks of the science of genetics. Chromosomes are today seen as containing the substance DNA, which carries the genes that, by coding for proteins and their regulation, supposedly determine every organism and its function.

A precondition for the identification of the chromosomes as the hereditary material was a new interpretation of fertilisation as the fusion of two morphologically and functionally different germ cells, the 'female' egg cell and 'male' spermatozoon. In 1902 Theodor Boveri described fertilisation with a special focus on the movements and distribution of chromosomes. He could show that the spermatozoon contributed chromosomes only to the next generation.[35] The chromosomes of the paternal and maternal cells joined in pairs, and Boveri initially believed in the complete equality of the two sets of chromosomes in terms of shape, size and function. It was only some years later that new findings on chromosomal sex determination made him change his mind.

Around 1900 evolutionary thought and the view that cell division was the primordial mode of reproduction created a problem: the existence and function of the male spermatozoon was in need of explanation. Theodor Boveri came to a conclusion, which, curiously enough and in one respect only, resembles a rather recent interpretation of the evolutionary position of the y-chromosome, now usually understood as the chromosome characterising male mammals.[36] According to Boveri, in early evolution the primordial cell was characterised by its ability to divide into two 'daughter'-cells. The next step in evolution was the fusion of two cells forming a new organism. Then, those cells that aggregated into colonies or 'families' of sixteen cells differentiated by size and thus formed primordial germ cells, with the smaller one becoming the prototype, so to speak, of the male and the larger one of the female germ cell. From this evolutionary step onwards, the 'male' spermatozoon was in a process of continuous miniaturisation, until it contained only chromosomes. The chromosomes were the only material necessary for the 'male' role in reproduction; they guaranteed the spermatozoon's and the male's further existence in producing the variability of thenext generation. Basically, even until today, the production of variability is seen as the reason why heterosexual reproduction has evolved. Why the primordial 'maternal' cell produced different offspring in the first instance was, however, neither questioned nor explained by Boveri. Evolutionary progress, differentiation and variation of and within species became dependent on the 'invention' of the male and sexual reproduction; with this hypothesis, the spermatozoon (and the male) gained its relevance.

The hereditary process – in the heterosexual model – was conceptualised around the equality of the paternal and maternal contribution: the chromosomes of the germ cells. An array of hypotheses and experimental findings was necessary to stabilise this equality claim. Their behaviour during cell division, germ cell formation, fertilisation and embryonic development made the chromosomes the ideal cellular component to harbour the newly rediscovered hereditary factors, which followed the Mendelian laws. And, the Mendelian laws of inheritance also postulated – per assumption and experimental design – the equal contribution of male and female parent. The gene as the elementary unit of heredity was conceptualised within this framework which excluded a priori a possible maternal inheritance transmitted via the cytoplasm.

But, proving equality was a tricky problem at the level of the gendered germ cells. First there was the undeniable morphological size difference: the spermatozoon contributed only chromosomes to the next generation, whereas the egg cell contributed chromosomes and the cytoplasm, which contained all the substances needed for the cell's function, division and subsequent differentiation. Even more, this female cytoplasm was active – it reorganised the chromosomes during ontogenesis.[37] For the process of cell differentiation during ontogenesis, a mechanism was needed which guaranteed that only certain parts of the hereditary material, that is parts of the chromosomes, were present in different cell lines so that they could differentiate into muscles, nerve or liver cells, etc.[38] According to Boveri's and his female co-workers' findings in the years between the late 1880s and 1910, the cytoplasm reorganised the chromosomes during ontogenesis.[39] In the germ line, however, the chromosomes were not affected by plasmatic activity; here, following Weismann's germ line theory, the hereditary material was transmitted unchanged to the next generation of organisms. This assumption guaranteed that male influence to the next generation equalled the female, and it made the findings about the chromosomes compatible with the new experimental approaches of Mendelian genetics. But, Boveri could not propose a mechanism by which the 'female' cytoplasm stayed inactive in the germ line.

In Boveri's work, the two gendered germ cells were seen as mutually dependent on each other.[40] There was no conflict of different reproductive strategies as current biological thought assumes. Around 1900, the tendency to perform cell division was inhibited in both the egg cell and in the spermatozoon when apart. Both cells needed each other to guarantee procreation, which was regarded as the raison d'être of all life forms. However, there were contemporary observations and experiments on parthenogenesis, according to which the egg cell could start dividing and developing into a full-grown organism, without fusing with a spermatozoon. Due to its lack of cytoplasm, however, the spermatozoon was very unlikely to divide into two cells and start procreation on its own. A gendered difference remained.

Genetic concepts in Boveri's work were thus gendered at several levels: with the help of the gendered germ cells, and the use of heterosexual procreation as the model for all hereditary processes, the cell and its components were ordered by gender. The 'female' egg cell contributed chromosomes and cytoplasm and the 'male' spermatozoon contributed chromosomes to the next generation. Therefore, only the chromosomes could guarantee a paternal contribution to heredity equalling the maternal. Identifying the chromosomes as the definitive hereditary substance ensured gender equality (rather than female preponderance) in the process of inheritance. The paternal contribution matched the maternal only if the cytoplasm was deemed irrelevant in heredity.

The cytoplasm became female and subordinate. Within the cell a gendered hierarchy was established. In Boveri's work the cytoplasm was still powerful and active, but only during the embryonic development of the organism. Here was the realm of female influence, which could be framed in the classic notion of nutrition, care and guidance.[41] The cytoplasm did not contribute hereditary traits to the next generation. Only the chromosomes were seen as the cellular units, which could 'imprint' hereditary properties onto the cell and organism. Symbolically, the chromosomes became male, even though both egg and sperm contained them. For the following decades, this hierarchical gendered order of the cell and hereditary processes created a blind spot for genetics, which focused on the genes in the chromosomes only. Processes of cytoplasmatic organisation of the 'hereditary substance' have since slowly come back into focus under the name of epigenetics. The older concepts of the gene as the only determining physical unit in the DNA can now be questioned in a new way.[42] However, this is not necessarily the consequence of a clandestine feminist revolution brought about by a 'better, gender conscious approach' in genetics. It is simply the result of new capacities to calculate and model complex interactions of molecular components of the chromosomes and cytoplasm of the cell.

Interactive or hierarchical binary?

In Boveri's last publication the chromosomes were not perceived as the all-powerful entities controlling the cell and the organism. There was always collaboration and interdependence between the chromosomes and the cytoplasm, especially during development. But this understanding did not become mainstream in genetic research and thought.[43] The investigation into heredity was reduced to cross-breeding experiments in the search for genes on chromosomes. For this approach Thomas Hunt Morgan's (1866–1945) research group, which started their chromosome mapping project with the fruit fly Drosophila melanogaster in 1911, became particularly important. The model organism Drosophila was not as well-suited to investigating the interaction of chromosomes and cytoplasm, as Boveri's sea urchins were. But, cross-breeding Drosophila allowed for the establishment of a theory of the gene as sites on the chromosome.[44] This new experimental approach was highly productive; it created a dramatic momentum and came to dominate zoological genetics. With genetics evolving, an initially cooperative binary gender order was transformed into a hierarchical and asymmetric one; it was transformed into a classic dualism, where one part of the two – the chromosome (and after 1953, the DNA) – became the active representative of the whole cell or organism, whereas the cytoplasm became the subordinate female and passive other.[45]

There is an irony to this story. The new genetic gender equality, established with the help of the chromosomes to safeguard men's equal contribution to the next generation, was used in other realms such as political efforts to gain women's equality. In the early decades of the twentieth century, female doctors and geneticists, and also male geneticists, even argued in favour of women's admission to universities based on the new results of genetics. Women, they argued, could no longer be seen as inferior; they inherited half of their faculties from their fathers – as did their brothers.[46]

Chromosomes and the binary, inheritable sex difference

The identification of chromosomes as the hereditary material had another effect on biology. The chromosomal theory of heredity became the basis for the new genetic interpretation of sex difference in 1905 by Nettie M. Stevens and Edmund Wilson.[47] Wilson was an old friend of the Boveris, and Stevens had worked in Boveri's laboratory shortly before she proposed the new interpretation. Both had first hand knowledge of the work on chromosomes as hereditary material. In the case of insects, a difference in the number or size of the chromosomes could be correlated with the difference between male and female organisms. Depending on the species chosen for investigation, two types of germ cells could be identified which differed in the amount of chromosomal substance they transmitted; either the size or the number of chromosomes differed between them. In most of the species investigated, two types of spermatozoa were present; in some species two types of egg cells were produced. Male and female offspring were now viewed as the result of an accidental combination of germ cells and their chromosomes during fertilisation. Sex difference became genetically based and binary, an either-or difference.

With this new interpretation men and women could be seen as binary alternatives. Some could see them as equals; for others there was still the possibility to see men as the fully developed version of man and women as the lesser one. But the important novelty was that being a man or a woman could now be seen as the result of a chromosomal lottery with women getting forty-eight and men getting forty-seven chromosomes.[48] The new theory of chromosomal sex determination had another considerable advantage for women in the asymmetric gender order of the time: women could no longer be held responsible if they gave birth to girls only. Now they could claim that 'boy or girl' depended on the actual chromosomal constitution of the 'male' spermatozoon, which took part in fertilisation. The father 'decided' on the sex of the child.

The new binary concept of chromosomal sex difference became crucial for Morgan's above-mentioned gene mapping project, which produced the first theory of the gene as a discrete unit in a linear arrangement on the chromosomes. In this respect the concept was highly productive, while it also helped to stabilise the binary gender order within the cell. But, it also created a new problem for biology as older embryological concepts of sex difference could not be incorporated into genetics. Embryology was based on studies in comparative anatomy in the nineteenth century that saw sex difference as the result of development from a primordial, bisexual embryo. In this older view, all organisms had a bisexual potential, whereas the new genetic model based on chromosomal difference postulated a binary either-or sex difference from the moment of fertilisation.

'Intersexes' – reconciling sex difference in embryology and genetics

Richard Goldschmidt, a member of the same German research community as Boveri, was successful in developing a genetic interpretation of sex determination compatible with embryological concepts.[49] In 1913 he started cross-breeding experiments to investigate the new heredity of sex difference. He used various geographic populations– or 'races' in the terminology of taxonomists – of the gypsy moth *Lymantria dispar* prevalent in Europe and Japan. Certain combinations of different populations resulted in offspring which no longer showed clear signs of being male or female, such as wing pigmentation or size and morphology of the antennae. Goldschmidt termed these specimen 'intersexes'. He claimed that he could produce all stages of intersexes between male and female by choosing the appropriate populations for his experiments. He postulated the existence of male and female genetic factors, which were responsible for sex determination within one organism. Male and female organisms would have both male and female genetic factors situated on the chromosomes and in the cytoplasm. Their mixture, strength and the timing of activity determined male or female or intersexed identity.[50] Goldschmidt refined his model in the 1920s and succeeded in reconciling the newer genetic and older embryologic concepts of sex determination. According to his interpretation every individual organism and even each of its cells had the potential to develop in the male or female direction, with all intermediate stages possible. In Goldschmidt's model, masculinity and femininity were not two exclusive binary possibilities, but rather admixtures.[51] There was no pure masculinity or femininity: each 'Geschlecht' (sex), according to Goldschmidt, was a mixture of both 'Geschlechter' (sexes), with one of the two prevailing.

Goldschmidt started to refer to his findings in the context of political debates about male homosexuality and hermaphroditism during the First World War. Joining his colleagues from sexology, such as Magnus Hirschfeld (1868–1935), he argued in favour of the decriminalisation of homosexuality as one of many natural ways of being. Hermaphrodites should not be assigned one of two sexes, as they simply did not fit into those categories. Goldschmidt's genetic model of sex determination allowed him to formulate this novel view. However, even this argument still had the potential to pathologise extreme forms of intersexuality, and it could still incorporate a claim of male dominance. The crucial, and at his time highly controversial point was that there was no femininity-free masculinity: each sex contained elements of the other.

Goldschmidt's right-wing and völkish colleagues found ways to use his scientific work for completely different political ends in the 1920s. They took his results from the cross-breeding experiments as scientific foundation for their antisemitic and anti-feminist political agenda by arguing for the preservation of the racial purity of the Nordic race and of a strictly binary gender order. The racial hygienist Fritz Lenz (1887–1976) was one of the key figures in this process. He later became a leading human geneticist of the Nazi era, when he was appointed head of department for eugenics at the Kaiser-Wilhelm Institute for Anthropology, Human Heredity and Racial Hygiene in Berlin. After 1945 he was appointed the first professor of human genetics in West Germany.

Lenz was an ambitious young medical doctor and dedicated to the project of racial hygiene. He started his career in 1912 with a Ph.D. about the sex-linked inheritance of diseases in men and sex determination. Subsequently he worked within the theoretical paradigm Goldschmidt had established. He even cross-bred specimens of the moth *Lymantria dispar* to investigate sex determination and the creation of intersexed animals.[52]

For Lenz and his völkish colleagues, the Nordics or Aryans were the most highly developed race. They were characterised by the most pronounced physical and mental difference between men and women, which was marked politically by their difference in their legal status. Lenz saw the blurring of a clear binary human gender order, as it unfolded in the years of the Weimar Republic, as a dangerous sign of racial degeneration. Using the results of Goldschmidt's cross-breeding experiments, Lenz claimed that miscegenation ('Rassenmischung' or even 'Rassenschande') was the genetic cause for this process. As Germany no longer had colonies after 1919, miscegenation was mainly seen as occurring in the marriages between so-called Aryans and people of Jewish descent. During the later years of the German Empire, the idea had circulated already that German-Jewish marriages caused degeneration by effeminising men and masculinising women, thus leading to the decline in birth rate and weakening the State. This trope had become a key element of antisemitic, anti-democratic and anti-feminist political thought before the First World War.[53] In the 1920s, science, and especially genetics, could be used to support it. According to Lenz and his allies, the highly visible New Woman of the Weimar republic, female suffrage and the efforts to invent new gender orders beyond the heterosexual matrix of strict binaries could be understood as a genetic process of degeneration. Marriage bans were argued to be the necessary consequences; they were first put in place with the Nuremberg laws in 1935. This was the point at which Goldschmidt found himself legally classified as Jewish, deprived of his German citizenship; his children faced marriage bans.

Goldschmidt's genetic concept of sex determination and its experimental foundation were used for opposite political agendas: in favour of diversity in gender and sexual orientation and in support for racist and anti-feminist efforts. For genetic research, the case was different. Lenz did not use Goldschmidt's gene concept, which was based on the study of the inheritance of sex difference. In Goldschmidt's view genes did not necessarily cause the same phenotype under all circumstances. Like the genetic factors for masculinity and femininity, all genetic factors had to be conceptualised as differing in 'strength'; they were not stable and independent of their context.

This concept of the gene was unacceptable for Lenz and his colleagues who aimed at a new genetics-based racial anthropology. They needed a gene concept where the gene was reliable and always produced the same effect. Otherwise racial traits would not necessarily reappear in following generations; racial difference would blur like sex difference, especially in a case of 'miscegenation'. Goldschmidt's genes not only made the two sexes rather fluid and connected by a continuum of intersexes, they were also not suitable to guarantee thestable inheritance of racial characters. Consequently, Lenz rejected Goldschmidt's gene concept, but he used some results of Goldschmidt's experiments for the scientific foundation of his political concepts of a social order, which demanded clear distinctions and hierarchies between men and women or people classified as members of different races.

Sex hormones and the binary again

A third experimental and conceptual approach to the problem of sex determination was the search for 'sex hormones' and their function in the organism of vertebrates.[54] The German biochemist Adolf Butenandt started the search for sex hormones in mammals and humans in the mid-1920s in collaboration with his future wife and technical assistant, Erika von Ziegner. At that time he was a young biochemist at the University of Göttingen whose work was supported by the Berlin pharmaceutical company, Schering-Kahlbaum.[55] Contemporary endocrinologists and biochemists used a binary model of sex difference; male hormones were seen as antagonists of the female hormones.[56] This model was based on the assumption that the male or female gonads produced the respective hormones that determined the sex of the organism. Castration experiments had shown that without gonads the sex characters of the organism disappeared. Substituting for lost gonads by implanting gonads or injecting gonadal extracts could reconstitute these sexual characters. Testes were seen as the production site of male hormones, and ovaries as the origin for female hormones. Many disciplines competed in the research on these substances, which promised to become powerful tools as drugs, once they could be chemically isolated and identified. Biochemists, physiologists, gynaecologists, embryologists and others used gonadal extracts or urine for their experiments, which led to controversial results and once again challenged the initial assumption of a binary order of female and male hormones.[57] Male organisms could produce female hormones and male hormones could be transformed into female hormones and vice versa in the biochemical laboratory. As soon as synthetic hormones could be produced in large quantities in the mid-1930s, experiments proved the feminising effects of supposedly male hormones and the masculinising effects of supposedly female hormones.[58] The seemingly simple categorisation of these hormones into male and female had become questionable.

Butenandt is especially interesting to investigate in this context because we can see clearly how he preserved the initial hormonal gender order, leaving it unchanged in the face of contradictory experimental evidence. Starting with the assumption of a binary order of the hormones, he isolated a 'female' hormone (named Progynon) in the late 1920s, and in collaboration with his assistant Ulrich Westphal, a corpus lutem hormone responsible for pregnancy in the early 1930s (Progesterone); he completed the hormonal set with the isolation of a hormone identified as male (Androsterone). In 1939 he was awarded 'the Nobel prize in Chemistry for the work on the sex hormones'.[59]

To identify the chemically isolated hormones as male or female and to identify their efficacy, specially designed animal tests were needed. These animals were transformed into instruments of measurement. They received injections of hormonal extracts, and then the effects on certain tissues helped to identify the extract containing the most effective hormone. Female hormones could be seen by their effect on the vaginal tissue of castrated mice, whereas the comb growth of capons, measured in millimetres, indicated the effects of the male hormone.[60] Butenandt was not interested in the physiology of the hormones; his experimental approach was not suited to understanding their role in sex determination during development. He was in search of a drug and focused on the identification and isolation of substances. He pursued the crystallisation of male and female hormones as those substances that proved to be the most effective in his experimental settings. By design, the experiments merely confirmed the existence of male or female hormones as expected. The isolated and later synthesised substances were to be sold as medication – to compensate for gendered frailties, be it weakening physical or mental features of masculinity or femininity.

With hormones available in pure form and larger quantities, new experiments showed the paradoxical effects of the supposedly male or female hormones even in Butenandt's laboratory. Despite his own and other scientists' results he continued to identify all sex-related hormones as male, female or pregnancy hormones, even as late as the 1950s. His perseverance is even more striking, as he could have used Richard Goldschmidt's model of sex determination according to which a mixture of male and female sex-determining substances, in combination and respective balance, determines the organism's male and female physical features. Indeed, Goldschmidt had integrated the new biochemical findings on the sex hormones (by Butenandt and others) into his model of sex determination by the late 1920s, but Butenandt did not refer to Goldschmidt's model.[61] In 1936 Butenandt nearly became the colleague of Goldschmidt, when he took up the position as the Director of the Kaiser Wilhelm Institute for Biochemistry in Berlin, whose former Jewish director Carl Neuberg (1877–1956) had been sent into forced retirement.[62] In the same year Goldschmidt was himself forced to emigrate, and he lost his citizenship and the position as head of department at the Kaiser Wilhelm Institute of Biology. Both institutes were neighbours in the Berlin suburb Dahlem; Butenandt and Goldschmidt belonged to the same prestigious scientific community, which had, however, excluded its Jewish members by 1936.

It is apparent that there were political reasons why Butenandt did not accept Goldschmidt's model. The model of every higher organism being a mixture of male and female characters had ultimately become branded a 'Jewish model'. By the mid 1930s it was mostly Jewish scientists, now in emigration, who developed and used it. The model was not compatible with Butenandt's right-wing, völkish concept of masculinity, which had to be pure and not 'contaminated' by feminine features. Butenandt persisted with his concept; there was no more scientific opposition to fear, and in the political situation of the time, his model was deemed politically correct.

But, even without these political motives, it would have been difficult for Butenandt to give up his model and change his experimental approach. Such a change would have meant giving up the leading role as a biochemist, crystallising and identifying organic substances, and handing scientific leadership over to physiology or embryology where the development of sex difference in organisms could be studied with different methods and concepts. He did not do this. Instead, his solution was to give up research on hormones by the mid 1930s and look for a new epistemic object. He continued with his experimental approach, which henceforward aimed at the identification and crystallisation of other 'active principles' as chemical agents. He and his research group focussed on genes and viruses and other highly powerful substances and tried to identify them chemically.[63]

Conclusion

The Butenandt case clearly shows how political reasons encouraged the acceptance and rejection of a particular scientific model of sex differences. It also shows that there were constraints within particular disciplinary traditions and experimental systems, which made a change of approach extremely difficult for the scientists involved. The blunt pressure of politics increased Butenandt's power within the scientific community and also shielded him from criticism. The combination of all these factors added to the stabilisation within German science of a concept of sex difference and sex determination, which could have been challenged by a different disciplinary approach existing in principle at the time. But virtually no powerful research group with the appropriate support or funding existed.

In the works of Boveri and Goldschmidt, experimental settings and commitments to disciplinary traditions also set the stage for the gender concepts possible in genetics. This material and practical framework is important in explaining why certain concepts were developed and applied. These concepts sometimes moved in opposite directions: an equality claim at the level of germ cells' chromosomes stabilised a gendered hierarchy within the cell and the gendered agenda of genetics. The new chromosomally determined sex difference had the same effect, and it disconnected genetics from embryology at a key point. If we include among explanatory factors the political salience of the different models, things become even more complicated: the equality claim at the level of the chromosomes helped to support a new notion of male equality in reproduction, which countered a perceived superiority of women. However, in politics this new genetic equality could be used to argue in favour of women, who had not reached political, social, legal and economic equality with men. Research on chromosomal sex determination could be called upon to protect women from blame when they gave birth to a child of the wrong gender, but it also supported the notion of a binary, discontinuous sex difference. The concept of a sex difference as proposed by Goldschmidt defined intermediate stages between male and female as natural and reconnected embryology and genetics. The political uses of these findings again encompassed opposite tendencies – liberalisation on the gender/sexuality front and support for racist, antisemitic and anti-feminist politics.

Is there a personal component to this political pattern? Do the individual scientists matter when certain experimental systems and disciplinary traditions of thought have their own dynamics, when scientific work determines which (scientific) gender concepts can be developed and used? Do scientists' personal gender-political convictions count at all? The era in question here saw political debates on gender difference, moves toward political and educational equality, challenges to a binary, hierarchical gender order and also efforts to reinstall it. At the social level there was no hegemony of gender concepts; nevertheless, the general framework of male dominance was not fundamentally transformed. However, I think it makes sense to assume that the choice of scientific questions and experimental approaches is not arbitrary. Scientific fields are fields where authority, respect and power are distributed in rather uneven ways. Therefore gender orders are part of this field as well. The choice of a particular disciplinary field and approach by a particular person may well depend on the tolerance and freedom offered by the members of this field with regards to possible gender orders. This may contribute to the connections between the social gender order at the scientific workplace and the scientific gender orders developed in this place – it is a loose, contradictory and very dynamic relationship, and not a simple causal one.

Notes

1. See for example the different approaches of Ludwik Fleck, *Genesis and Development of a Scientific Fact* (1935; repr. Chicago: University of Chicago Press, 1979); Karin Knorr-Cetina, *The Manufacture of Knowledge: An Essay on the Constructivist and Contextual Nature of Science* (Oxford: Pergamon Press, 1984); Bruno Latour and Steve Woolgar, *Laboratory Life: The Construction of Scientific Facts* (Princeton: Princeton University Press, 1979); Hans-Jörg Rheinberger, *Toward a History of Epistemic Things: Synthesizing Proteins in the Test Tube* (Stanford: Stanford University Press, 1997).
2. Sarah S. Richardson, 'When Gender Criticism Becomes Standard Scientific Practice: The Case of Sex Determination Genetics', in Londa Schiebinger (ed.), *Gendered Innovations in Science and Engineering* (Stanford: Stanford University Press, 2008), pp. 22–42.
3. Here I differ from Thomas Laqueur, *Making Sex: Body and Gender from the Greeks to Freud* (Harvard: Harvard University Press, 1990). The one-sex-model was not dead in the 20th century.
4. See for example: Jeanne Boydston, 'Gender as a Question of Historical Analysis', *Gender & History* 20 (2008), pp. 558–83.
5. To make things even more confusing we can find the phrase 'gender is engrained in our genes' in popular parlance, which is exactly the opposite of what was intended with the use of the term 'gender'. On the trivialisation of 'gender' see Joan Scott, 'Gender: Still a Useful Category of Analysis?', *Diogenes* 225 (2010), pp. 1–5.
6. It was not feminist scholarship which invented the distinction. In 1955 psychologists at the Johns Hopkins Hospital in Baltimore introduced the term 'gender' to distinguish between the body and the psychosexual development of children with ambiguous genitals, which were surgically changed to a female or male 'normality'. This approach was part of a long term – and finally strongly criticised – medical experiment which should show the malleability of social or psychological gender identities and their relative independence from the body. See: Ulrike Klöppel, *ungelöst. Hermaphroditismus, Sex und Gender in der deutschen Medizin* (Bielefeld: transcript, 2010), pp. 307–36.
7. Just to mention some classics: Ruth Hubbard (ed.), *Women Look at Biology Looking at Women: A Collection of Feminist Critiques* (Boston: Hall, 1979); Fischer-Homberger, *Krankheit Frau und andere Arbeiten zur Medizingeschichte der Frau* (Bern: Huber, 1979); Ruth Bleier, *Science and Gender: A Critique of Biology and its Theories on Women* (New York: Pergamon, 1985); Donna Haraway, *Primate Visions: Gender, Race, and Nature in the World of Modern Science* (New York: Routledge, 1989); Emily Martin, 'The Egg and Sperm: How Science has Constructed a Romance Based on Stereotypical Male-Female Roles', in Evelyn Fox Keller and Helen E. Longino (eds), *Feminism and Science* (Oxford, New York: Oxford University Press, 1996), pp. 103–17; Anne Fausto-Sterling, 'The Bare Bones of Sex: Part 1 – Sex and Gender', *Signs* 30 (2005), pp. 1491–527; Judith Butler, *Gender Trouble: Feminism and the Subversion of Identity* (New York: Routledge, 1990).
8. For example: Claudia Honegger, *Die Ordnung der Geschlechter. Die Wissenschaften vom Menschen und das Weib, 1750–1850* (Frankfurt: Campus, 1991).
9. Most prominent: Londa Schiebinger, *Gendered Innovations in Science and Engineering* (Stanford: Stanford University Press, 2008); Londa Schiebinger, *Has Feminism Changed Science?* (Cambridge, London: Harvard University Press, 1999).
10. Marcellina's aria 'Il capro e la capretta' in Mozart's *Le Nozze di Figaro* (1786) reflects this conviction of feminist Enlightenment thought.
11. Scott F. Gilbert and Karen A. Rader, 'Revisiting Women and Feminism in Developmental Biology', in Angela Creager, Elizabeth Lunbeck and Londa Schiebinger (eds), *Feminism in Twentieth-Century Science:*

Technology, and Medicine (Chicago: University of Chicago Press, 2001), pp. 73–97. See also Evelyn Fox Keller, 'Developmental Biology as a Feminist Cause?' in Sally Gregory Kohlstedt and Helen E. Longino (eds), 'Women, Gender, and Science. New Directions', *Osiris* 12 (1997), pp. 16–28.

12. Richardson, 'Gender Criticism'.

13. Ruth Hubbard, 'Gender and Genitals: Constructs of Sex and Gender', in Andrew Ross (ed.), *Science Wars* (Duke University Press, 1996), pp. 168–79.

14. Hubbard, 'Gender', p. 178.

15. On the medical history of the creation of a binary sex/gender order, including current debates on intersexed people, see Klöppel.

16. See also Hubbard's outspoken anti-racist work. Ruth Hubbard, 'Race & Genes', Social Sciences Research Council (2006), <http://raceandgenomics.ssrc.org/Hubbard>.

17. Donna Harraway, 'Primatology is Politics by Other Means', *Proceedings of the Biennial Meeting of the Philosophy of Science Association*, (1984), pp. 489–524; Donna Haraway, 'Investment Strategies for the Evolving Portfolio of Primate Females' in Mary Jacobus, Evelyn Fox Keller and Sally Shuttleworth (eds), *Body/Politics: Women and the Discourse of Science* (New York: Routledge, 1990), pp. 139–62.

18. See for example: Theresa Wobbe (ed.), *Frauen in Akademie und Wissenschaft. Arbeitsorte und Forschungspraktiken 1700–2000* (Berlin: Akademie Verlag, 2002); Karin Hausen, 'Wirtschaften mit der Geschlechterordnung. Ein Essay', in Theresa Wobbe (ed.), *Zwischen Vorderbühne und Hinterbühne. Beiträge zum Wandel der Geschlechterbeziehungen in der Wissenschaft vom 17. Jahrhundert bis zur Gegenwart* (Bielefeld: transcript, 2003), pp. 83–107; Margaret W. Rossiter, 'Which Science? Which Women?', in Sally Gregory Kohlstedt and Helen E. Longino (eds), 'Women, Gender and Science. New Directions', *OSIRIS* 12 (1997), pp. 169–85.

19. For a more detailed account see Helga Satzinger, *Differenz und Vererbung. Geschlechterordnungen in der Genetik und Hormonforschung, 1890–1950* (Cologne, Weimar, Vienna: Böhlau, 2009). See also: Helga Satzinger, 'The Chromosomal Theory of Heredity and the Problem of Gender Equality in the Work of Theodor and Marcella Boveri', in *Conference: A Cultural History of Heredity III: 19th and Early 20th Centuries*. Prepring 294, Max Planck Institut für Wissenschaftsgeschichte, Berlin (2005), pp. 102–14; Helga Satzinger, 'Theodor and Marcella Boveri: Chromosomes and Cytoplasm in Heredity and Development', *Nature Reviews Genetics* 9 (2008), pp. 231–8; Helga Satzinger, 'Racial Purity, Stable Genes, and Sex Difference: Gender in the Making of Genetic Concepts by Richard Goldschmidt and Fritz Lenz, 1916 to 1936', in Susanne Heim, Carola Sachse and Mark Walker (eds), *The Kaiser Wilhelm Society for the Advancement of Science under National Socialism* (Cambridge: Cambridge University Press, 2009), pp. 145–70.

20. On Butenandt's career in Nazi Germany see: Walter Schieder and Achim Trunk (eds), *Adolf Butenandt und die Kaiser-Wilhelm-Gesellschaft. Wissenschaft, Industrie und Politik im 'Dritten Reich'* (Göttingen: Wallstein, 2004).

21. Marilyn Bailey Ogilvie and Clifford J. Choquette, 'Nettie Maria Stevens (1861–1912): Her Life and Contributions to Cytogenetics', *Proceedings of the American Philosophical Society* 125 (1981), pp. 292–311; Stephen G. Brush, 'Nettie M. Stevens and the Discovery of Sex Determination by Chromosomes', *ISIS* 69 (1978), pp. 162–72.

22. Anne Fausto-Sterling, *Sexing the Body: Gender Politics and the Construction of Sexuality* (New York: Basic Books, 2000); Nelly Oudshoorn, 'On Measuring Sex Hormones: The Role of Biological Assays in Sexualising Chemical Substances', *Bulletin of the History of Medicine* 64 (1990), pp. 243–61; Nelly Oudshoorn, 'Endocrinologists and the Conceptualisation of Sex, 1920–1940', *Journal of the History of Biology* 23 (1990), pp. 163–86; Nelly Oudshoorn, *Beyond the Natural Body: An Archeology of Sex Hormones* (New York: Routledge, 1994); Chandak Sengoopta, 'Glandular Politics: Experimental Biology, Clinical Medicine, and Homosexual Emancipation in Fin-de-Siècle Central Europe', *ISIS* 89 (1998), pp. 445–73; Chandak Sengoopta, 'The Modern Ovary: Constructions, Meanings, Uses', *History of Science* 38 (2000), pp. 425–88; Chandak Sengoopta, *The Most Secret Qintessence of Life: Sex, Glands, and Hormones, 1850–1950* (Chicago: University of Chicago Press, 2006).

23. See especially the work of Magnus Hirschfeld and 'The First Institute for Sexual Science (1919–1933)' on the website of the Magnus-Hirschfeld-Gesellschaft, <http://www.hirschfeld.in-berlin.de>.

24. Oudshoorn, *Archaeology*; Oudshoorn, 'Endocrinologists'.

25. Fausto-Sterling, *Sexing*, p. 193.

26. Patricia M. Mazón, *Gender and the Modern Research University: The Admission of Women to German Higher Education, 1865–1914* (Stanford: Stanford University Press, 2003); Johanna Bleker (ed.), *Der Eintritt der Frauen in die Gelehrtenrepublik: Zur Geschlechterfrage im akademischen Selbstverständnis*

und in der wissenschaftlichen Praxis am Anfang des 20. Jahrhunderts (Husum: Mattiesen, 1998); Annette Vogt, *Vom Hintereingang zum Hauptportal. Lise Meitner und ihre Kolleginnen an der Berliner Universität und in der Kaiser-Wilhelm-Gesellschaft* (Stuttgart: Franz Steiner Verlag, 2007); Hiltrud Häntzschel and Hadumod Bußmann (eds), *Bedrohlich gescheit. Ein Jahrhundert Frauen und Wissenschaft in Bayern* (Munich: C. H. Beck,1997).

27. Satzinger, *Differenz*, pp. 51–84.
28. Satzinger, *Differenz*, pp. 213–16 on Mathilde Hertz in Berlin; pp. 228–35 on Käte Pariser and Anne-Marie du Bois; pp. 235–7, 238–46 on the general situation of women.
29. Satzinger, *Differenz*, pp. 243–6 on Aloha Hannah Alava and Leonie Kellen Piternick.
30. Satzinger, *Differenz*, pp. 239–43, 246. On McClintock see Evelyn Fox Keller, *A Feeling for the Organism: The Life and Work of Barbara McClintock* (New York: Freeman 1983) and Nathaniel Comfort, *The Tangled Field: Barbara McClintock's Search for Patterns of Genetic Control* (Cambridge: Cambridge University Press, 2001). Both interpret Goldschmidt's support for McClintock as disadvantageous for her standing in the scientific community. On the Nobel Prize see: 'The Nobel Prize in Physiology or Medicine 1983', <http://www.nobelprize.org/nobel_prizes/medicine/laureates/1983/>.
31. Satzinger, *Differenz*, pp. 203–09.
32. Satzinger, *Differenz*, pp. 299–338, 350–72.
33. For further detail please consult Satzinger, *Differenz*, pp. 85–141; Satzinger, 'Chromosomal Theory'; Satzinger, 'Theodor and Marcella Boveri'.
34. I do not go further into the more than obvious metaphoric gendering of those cellular processes where mother cells divide into daughter cells. Giving birth was the model for cellular procreation, and germ cells became male and female. For the modelling of molecular genetics on heterosexual procreation; see: Angela N. H. Creager, 'Mapping Genes in Microorganisms', in Jean Paul Gaudillière and Hans-Jörg Rheinberger (eds), *From Molecular Genetics to Genomics: The Mapping Cultures of Twentieth-Century Genetics* (London, New York: Routledge, 2004), pp. 9–41; Roberta Bivins, 'Sex Cells: Gender and the Language of Bacterial Genetics', *Journal of the History of Biology* 33 (2000), pp. 113–39.
35. There were some exceptions, though. In some species the spermatozoon also contributed a particle called centrosome, which was necessary for the cellular apparatus that distributed the chromosomes into the daughter cells during cell division. However, there was never cytoplasm in the spermatozoon.
36. On the recent miniaturisation of y-chromosomes: Richardson, 'Gender Criticism'.
37. This active role has been overlooked so far in recent gender and science studies; see Evelyn Fox Keller, *Refiguring Life: Metaphors of Twentieth-Century Biology* (New York: Columbia University Press, 1995); Bonnie B. Spanier, *Im/partial Science: Gender Ideology in Molecular Biology* (Bloomington: Indiana University Press, 1995).
38. Today this process is explained by gene regulation while the chromsomes and the DNA in the chromosomes are not changed structurally.
39. Those were the American women scientists, working as visiting scholars at the laboratory of Boveri: Nettie M. Stevens, Alice M. Boring, Florence Peebles and Mary J. Hogue.
40. Boveri's description is obviously analogous to a bourgeois married couple of his time. For a comparison, see the 'romance' of egg cell and spermatozoon in more recent biology textbooks as analysed by Emily Martin, 'Egg and Sperm'. Today's sociobiologists see conflicting reproductive strategies of egg and sperm at work, there is no longer cooperation.
41. The framework of the egg as the female nutritional contribution has been used for a long time. See Esther Fischer-Homberger, *Harvey's Troubles with the Egg* (Sheffield: European Association for the History of Medicine and Health Publications, 2001). See also Keller, *Refiguring Life*; and Spanier, *Science*.
42. Evelyn Fox Keller, *The Century of the Gene* (Cambridge, London: Harvard University Press, 2000).
43. In the German context of the 1920s the cytoplasm-nucleus interaction remained relevant for geneticists. Jonathan Harwood, *Styles of Scientific Thought: The German Genetics Community 1900–1993* (Chicago, London: University of Chicago Press, 1993). With Lysenkoism starting to dominate Russian genetics after the War, scientific questions concerning the cytoplasm in genetics became more or less a taboo in the West.
44. Robert E. Kohler, *Lords of the Fly: Drosophila Genetics and the Experimental Life* (Chicago: University of Chicago Press, 1994); Hans-Jörg Rheinberger, Jean Paul Gaudillière (eds), *Classical Genetic Research and its Legacy: The Mapping Cultures of Twentieth-Century Genetics* (London, New York: Routledge, 2004).
45. On the philosophical context of this classic hierarchical binary, Cornelia Klinger, 'Feministische Theorie zwischen Lektüre und Kritik des philosophischen Kanons', in Hadumod Bußmann and Renate Hof (eds), *Genus. Gender Studies in den Kultur- und Sozialwissenschaften. Ein Handbuch*, (Stuttgart: Kröner Verlag, 2005), pp. 328–64.

46. Satzinger, *Differenz*, p. 42. Thus far, I have found the geneticist Agnes Bluhm (1862–1943); the physicist Hope Adams-Lehmann (1855–1916); the zoologists Oscar Hertwig (1849–1922) and Wulf Emmo Ankel (1897–1983) and the Norwegian geneticist Otto Mohr.

47. Brush, 'Stevens'; Ogilvie and Choquette, 'Stevens'.

48. It was not until the 1950s that scientists identified the number of human chromosomes as forty-six in men and women: with men having one smaller 'sex chromosome', called the y-chromosome.

49. For a more detailed and referenced account, see Satzinger, 'Racial Purity'; Satzinger, *Differenz*, pp. 154–292.

50. See Richardson, 'Gender Criticism' for a comparison with the most recent model.

51. Goldschmidt's concept was not the only one of his time to question a binary, discontinuous sex difference. His colleague at the KWI for Biology, Max Hartmann (1876–1962), saw various stages of intersexuality in the mating behaviour of single cell organisms and developed his theory of 'sexuality' including intersexual forms. The differences with Goldschmidt's theory lay in the explanation of the causes of sex development. See Heng-an Chen, *Die Sexualitätstheorie und 'Theoretische Biologie' von Max Hartmann in der ersten Hälfte des zwanzigsten Jahrhunderts* (Wiesbaden: Franz Steiner Verlag, 2003).

52. Fritz Lenz, *Über die krankhaften Erbanlagen des Mannes und die Bestimmung des Geschlechts beim Menschen. Untersuchungen über somatische und idioplasmatische Korrelation zwischen Geschlecht und pathologischer Anlage mit besonderer Berücksichtigung der Hämophilie* (Jena: Gustav Fischer Verlag, 1912); Fritz Lenz, 'Erfahrungen und Entartung bei Schmetterlingen', *Archiv für Rassen- und Gesellschaftsbiologie* 14 (1922), pp. 249–301.

53. Ute Planert, 'Reaktionäre Modernisten. Zum Verhältnis von Antisemitismus und Antifeminismus in der völkischen Bewegung', *Jahrbuch für Antisemitismusforschung* 11 (2002), pp. 31–51.

54. For detailed accounts of this research, see endnote 22.

55. Satzinger, *Differenz*, pp. 293–338, 373–400.

56. Oudshoorn, *Natural Body*, pp. 22–30; Fausto-Sterling, *Sexing*, pp. 158–94. The most prominent representative of this approach was Eugen Steinach (1861–1944) who, with the help of Schering-Kahlbaum's gonadal extracts performed experiments with animals.

57. Oudshoorn, 'Natural Body', pp. 25–30; Sengoupta, *Quintessence*, pp. 136–9; Fausto-Sterling, *Sexing*, pp. 170–94.

58. For these contradictory findings in Butenandt's laboratory see Satzinger, *Differenz*, pp. 385–93.

59. See the website of the Nobel Foundation <http://www.nobelprize.org/nobel_prizes/chemistry/laureates/ 1939/press.html>. Due to the political circumstances, the German authorities did not allow him to accept the prize. Butenandt shared the prize with the Swiss biochemist Leopold Ruzicka.

60. This is a rather crude simplification of the process. For more details on Butenandt's approach, see Satzinger, *Differenz*, pp. 317–18, 320–25, 327.

61. Satzinger, *Differenz*, pp. 373–400.

62. Satzinger, *Differenz*, pp. 333–6.

63. Satzinger, *Differenz*, pp. 401–23.

10 The Language of Gender in Lovers' Correspondence, 1946–1949

Sonia Cancian

My Unforgettable Nietta,
it's cold in this new room of mine, a room that offers me nothing but a gloomy silence, yet I need this space to find a reaction in my heart. It's a silence that inspires a voice; a silence that echoes the beat of my heart.
'All is still, and yet all to the heart speaks to me . . .
This peace away from here where can I find it?
You are lovely, season of springtime,
Renew flowers and love'[1]
Of your memory, I embrace my every thought,
Of your love, I crown my every sorrow
It's easy to speak when the heart dictates, it's easy to remember when every single thing takes you there, there to your homeland, to your home, to your heart. Oh yes, my little Tetina, there is no greater memory than the one in my heart on this day, there is no recollection, more invincible that the memory has carved in my soul about this day two years ago. But all of this furiously passes by in the same way that the doubts of not loving each other enough pass [2]

Correspondence, literary scholars note, rarely entails only innocent and spontaneous expressions; it is more frequently about searches into the self, undertaken through the prism of the writer's readerly memory and in the context of the author's own developing literary awareness.[3] I begin this essay with the poetic words written by a young lover to his fiancée in Montreal in 1949. The main scope of the article is grounded in a gender analysis of language that imbues a large corpus of lovers' correspondence. Moreover, I make explicit the interconnections between gender and the epistolary source. By using gender as a category of analysis, I mean 'not simply social roles for women and men but the articulation in specific contexts of social understandings of sexual difference', and in using language, 'not simply words in their literal usage but the creation of meaning through differentiation'.[4] In examining gender dynamics and language in the letters, my argument dovetails with Joan Scott's point that 'if we attend to the ways in which "language" constructs meaning we will also be in a position to find gender'.[5] In the first part of the article, I show how these letters are, from an epistemological viewpoint, a valuable source that illuminates the diverse ways in which the language in romantic correspondence makes evident gender attitudes and norms that are otherwise difficult to observe and interpret in sources of a less personal nature. In the second section, I examine the diverse ways in which language is used in lovers' correspondence to express expected gender ideologies and the myriad ways in which the writers push these ideologies in one way or another.

Gender History Across Epistemologies, First Edition. Edited by Donna R. Gabaccia and Mary Jo Maynes.

Love letters combine, as Bernard Bray notes, feelings, narratives, descriptions, autobiographical fragments and ornamentation.[6] The Antonietta Petris-Loris Palma letter collection analysed in this article elucidates the ways in which gender works in romantic love correspondence between two young people living in mid-twentieth century Italy and Canada. The lyrics quoted above, part of the renowned 'Cherry Duet' in Pietro Mascagni's Opera, *L'Amico Fritz* (The Friend Fritz), that are drawn from a letter written to Antonietta Petris serve as a window onto some of the ways in which young lovers mobilised a metaphorical world to pledge reassurances concerning their loyalties, longings and affections to their long-distance lovers. From an epistemological viewpoint, the intimate letter is a source that makes visible the invisible – that is, it allows us to see things we, as outside readers, could not normally access. As part of my main argument, I discuss the ways in which writing letters amplified the affection between correspondents who were already attracted to each other before beginning their correspondence, and transformed desire into 'something understood as love'.[7]

The collection

One week after they had shared their first embrace and declared their affections for one another in Ampezzo Carnico, Antonietta Petris and Loris Palma began to exchange letters. It was August 1946. Loris, a young electrical technician, had returned home to Venice, where he lived with his family and worked in an electrical firm. Antonietta returned to her life in Ampezzo Carnico, a small town nestled in the Friulian Alps near the Italian-Austrian border. Eighteen-year-old Antonietta lived in an extended family household with her mother, grandparents and her uncle. Her father, who had left for the French islands, Saint Pierre and Miquelon – a few miles south of Newfoundland in Canada – when she was barely six months old, resumed communication with his wife and family in Italy once the war was over. In December 1947, after nearly a twenty-year absence, Vittorio Petris returned to his family in Ampezzo Carnico. With his return home came the proposition that Antonietta and her mother should join him in Montreal. Antonietta was completing her apprenticeship to become a seamstress, like her mother.

One summer evening in 1946, Antonietta was introduced to Loris Palma at one of Ampezzo's many outdoor dance halls. From that first meeting, he decided she was the love he sought. Antonietta was not as immediately convinced. It was only after talking with her friends, and going dancing and hiking with Loris and friends that she began to take a liking to him. Following Loris's departure from Ampezzo Carnico, a flurry of letters ensued between them on a daily basis. The over 460 letters they exchanged from 1946 to 1949 between Venice and Ampezzo Carnico, at first, and later between Venice and Montreal – where Antonietta immigrated in September 1948 – brought both of them unanticipated discoveries about themselves, their love and a life together in Canada.[8]

Migrant letters

The Petris-Palma letter collection was partly written in Italy and partly in Canada. While the collection is arguably a lovers' correspondence, the letters also qualify as migrant letters. As recent scholarly studies show, migrant letters underscore the first hand experiences, thoughts, preoccupations, gender ideologies, class dynamics and personal subjectivities of migrants and the non-migrants with whom they corresponded.[9] They offer valuable insights into diverse subjects of importance to migrants and non-migrants, ranging from news about kin, community and work life, financial woes and (un)employment, dreams and nostalgia. Prior to the mass distribution of telephones, affordable international calling rates in the 1970s and 1980s and current digital technologies, letter writing constituted the most prevalent form of communication used by family members and other loved ones living long distances apart. Migrant letters provided literate, newly literate and semi-literate individuals with a medium through which they could convey news about their family and surroundings, provide advice, reassure loved ones and exchange thoughts about their preoccupations. Much like other kinds of letters, migrant letters were usually written in the moment, and they usually sought 'to capture and convey the concern of their writer, what was paramount in her mind right then'.[10] There is no question that letters written in contexts of migration and separation are as diverse as their writers. The process of migration – with its dramatic tensions between resignation and restlessness, satisfaction and longing, experienced in contexts that can include political oppression, religious persecution and economic deprivation – 'creates a need for someone to tell a story, to have his or her life heard, to make life sensible and significant'.[11] Migrant and non-migrant letters record and give expression to such tensions and exigencies.[12] The practice of writing letters created an opportunity and a need for a person 'to construct, articulate and deliberate their knowledge of the world'.[13] For millions of individuals who migrated outside their homelands and their family members who remained behind, intimate face-to-face conversations and ordinary, world-making discourse were no longer possible.[14] As Gerber notes, 'writing – an even less accustomed practice for many than reading – had to suffice to accomplish the goal of achieving continuity'.[15]

Gender and the epistolary source

To write and exchange intimate letters usually permitted correspondents to seek solace and 'spiritual communion' in a separate space in which the outside world was excluded. In fact, writing letters offered correspondents a space in which they could choose to elaborate, deny, mediate or underscore their most pressing thoughts.[16] Because the Petris-Palma letters were accessible to the lovers alone, we can observe the ways in which the writers helped to sustain their long-distance relationship despite the myriad of challenges they faced. In examining the familiar letter of the eighteenth century, Bruce Redford writes that letter writing created 'a distinctive world at once internally consistent, vital, and self-supporting'.[17] For Loris and Antonietta writing between 1946 and 1949, the effects of letter writing were no different: writing letters gave them a world of their own in which they could articulate, mediate and share their thoughts, their desires, their longings and their affections in ways that they alone could understand of each other. The letters of Antonietta and Loris illustrate this point in the excerpts below. In one case, for instance, Antonietta confides to Loris that others around her view her as 'happy and without worries; they admire my personality, but they don't know how much I suffer for one thing or another'.[18] Loris too, with the exception of Antonietta as his confident, felt he had 'no one who can understand me, except my own words and my prayers'.[19] In both cases, the writers exchanged letters indicating they were each other's intimate confidents – the only persons (they implied) with whom they shared a world that was separate from the one they shared with others.

Letter writing further served as a catalyst for sustaining and expanding desires and affections between lovers. In his analysis of love, lust and literacy, Jack Goody writes that 'Expression on paper has important repercussions on people's emotions, not simply expressing already existing feelings but in creating or expanding those sentiments through a process of reflexivity'.[20] This reflexivity is commonly identified in the practice of writing to a beloved across distances.[21]

Separation and idealisation were often integral to letter writing.[22] In the letters of Antonietta, idealisation of her beloved Loris, and an enhanced feeling of their mutual love are frequently underscored. For instance, in the first weeks following their initial separation in 1946, Antonietta wrote:

> Tonight I think of you, you whom I cannot see. I reread your letter from Venice, an affectionate letter as usual, I can honestly say, like you, that the distance does not make us forget our love and affection. Instead, love grows (as you say) through distance. Yes, I feel that I love you more.[23]

Similarly, in a letter written two years later, Loris described how their relationship by correspondence had evolved, thus underscoring that separation for him also created time for reflection on the relationship and himself. On 16 December 1948, he wrote:

> from last year until now, our love has changed, it has doubled and multiplied. The three years of our engagement have allowed me to know you, even though we were far apart from each other, and despite some sour difficulties. Perhaps it is because of this that I was able to know you, because you supported and encouraged me.[24]

His conviction in their love is also evident in a letter written one month later, in which he described the anticipation of finally seeing Antonietta again as, 'the greatest joy in my life'.[25] This much longed for reunion between them implied much more than marriage; it signified a change that would take Loris to another continent, to another world.[26]

Antonietta's departure for Canada on 21 September 1948, two years after their continuous correspondence and occasional meetings, had an enormous impact on Loris's physical and mental well-being. Writing to Antonietta, however, provided some solace and comfort. Moreover, it inspired him to confide his deepest feelings in writing. Acquainted with Italian opera since childhood, in his letters Loris not infrequently mirrored the dramatic tone identified in opera narratives. For instance, in a letter written just hours following Antonietta's departure, Loris manages to convey self-reflection and control interwoven with physical and emotional dark despair:

> That day an abyss opened under my feet, and I had to pay careful attention not to plunge inside, yes, my spirit and my heart were [?], my body had never before felt a similar fatigue, my legs did not hold me steady, rather they were there to vacillate my body back and forth, every part of me felt the symptoms of a general exhaustion, and I remained standing there more out of courage, than out of willpower and strength [. . .] I had already prepared myself for the separation, but I was not saved from the worst part of it all in those final moments.[27]

Gender and language

The gender ideologies that Loris Palma and Antonietta Petris discussed through the language they used in their letters are characteristic of mid-twentieth-century Italian society. At the same time, their intimate letters illustrate ways in which young lovers accepted, negotiated and challenged expected gender norms and ideologies in their relationship both within Italian society and transnationally, within Canadian society. Since the mid-1970s, feminist scholars have analysed gender in language systems employed verbally and in writing.[28] 'Language', as Judith Lorber asserts, 'reflects and creates the culture's "unconscious"'.[29] The Petris-Palma collection provides a window into how gender and language intersect with romantic love. In this second part of the article, I examine ways in which gender identities were created, resisted and challenged in long-distance intimate relationships. Separation between individuals who were intensely involved in a relationship required them to mediate their intimacy. In order to do so, lovers would frequently discuss gender expectations both explicitly and implicitly in their vision of their relationship.

In the household gendered division of labour, norms were replicated, yet also resisted and challenged. Once Loris's father was laid off work, the responsibility was placed on Loris to continue working and provide for his parents and two sisters at home in Venice. Loris viewed his love for Antonietta, coupled with his seriousness in attending to his familial duties, as proof of his future breadwinning capacities. In several letters to her, he underscored the point that by fulfilling his duties with his immediate family (and writing to her about it), he assured her that he would be a dependable provider-husband when their life together began:

> In these past few days or rather months, life has reserved for me several surprises. Although it was inevitable, they have made me more understanding, more reasonable, and more responsible. All of these are privileges for my personal experience, which you will be able to sing about your friend, who is conscious of familial consequences, and because he is more than a friend, he will love you more.[30]

As the family crisis persisted over several months, Loris grew increasingly fatigued. The weight of family responsibility was overwhelming, to the point he stopped frequenting his favourite bar and attending the games of his favourite soccer team. With the beginning of the New Year, and his increasing loneliness, Loris became more committed to his emigration to Canada, despite the tensions this would cause to his immediate family. While he fulfilled his duty by economically supporting his family, he also dreamed (with increased intensity) about leaving them to be reunited with Antonietta. On 10 January 1949, he wrote that he was:

> conscious more than ever of my responsibilities as a son toward my family. Yesterday, Sunday on the 9th of this month, I worked all day until late into the evening; exhausted and wiped out. I closed the day with my loved ones, and soon I was in bed. [. . .] Begin to process the necessary documents [. . .] I am absolutely (tired and frustrated as we say in Venetian [dialect]) to continue to live like this, without you at this point, my life is void of meaning and scope, except to be appreciated and loved by you.[31]

For Antonietta, her relationship with Loris signified that they would marry and have children one day. Within a few weeks of their first declarations of love, she already viewed motherhood as an important evolution in their romantic relationship:

> Now I only live for our future! What will be our tomorrow? I only see that it will be rosy! Life will smile at us, we'll have our little nest, a beautiful baby, our little child! I'll educate him and would be happy if he's like you, especially in goodness. We will be so happy![32]

Having children was important to Loris as well, as he wrote on 1 January 1949: 'A child will be our joy, a child will be another step, his presence will be proof of how far we have come'. However, motherhood signified also that Antonietta would provide him with a motherly nurturance and solace. In the following line, Loris equates her goodness as a woman with her capacity to be a mother to him: 'You are a good woman because you love me, you are a good woman because you nurture me like a mother, and I can firmly appreciate your virtues and your attributes'.[33]

In the correspondence, the language of gender in traditional divisions of labour was further underscored in future projections of roles. For instance, in her description of a weekend with her parents and their friends spent in the Laurentian Mountains, north of Montreal, Antonietta related to Loris that she had gone hunting. The following excerpt underscores the seriousness with which she described hunting as a man's activity, an activity that was embraced by both her father and his male friend and business partner; and the humour that she used to describe her own participation in the activity. Antonietta used humour to challenge Loris's gendered expectations of her role as wife and mother:

> The next day, I went hunting with my father, and two other friends of his, and they had some serious luck. I didn't. I did absolutely nothing, I had a small rifle with no cartridges (don't laugh); this is the way it was, my father wanted to load the rifle, but I said something that still makes him laugh ('don't load it for me' in Italian).[34]

The next lines point to Antonietta's recurring humour on the subject of hunting. This time she paraphrased to Loris her conversation with Mrs Chinelli (the wife of her father's business partner) about keeping him home with her on Sundays. In recalling the conversation with a light tone, she was gingerly making him aware of her desire to spend Sundays with him – and that he not join the men, just in case he was thinking of it.

> In this season, everyone here goes hunting, but they often return empty-handed. They're already talking about turning you into a hunter . . . of crabapples!? As Signora Chinelli, [. . .] the wife of my father's partner repeats to me, 'When your Lorenzo will be here, I urge you not to let him go with these two rascals (alluding to her husband and my father), keep him home, make sure he stays with you, and that he doesn't go hunting on Sundays.[35]

Loris's letters to Antonietta were infused with patriarchal language to show, perhaps unintentionally, characteristics of self-control and self-restraint, his breadwinning capacities and his protective abilities as a man. In comparison to Antonietta's language, Loris's tone was often more instructional and serious, and at times, more convoluted. By contrast, Antonietta's language was more characteristically feminine: nurturing, sensitive to others, spontaneous and dynamic. In her writing she sought support but she also offered reassurance and showed resilience. Moreover, she exhibited an inherent awareness of herself and life in general; she offered advice without being instructional.

Upon reflecting on their first romantic encounters, Loris described himself as an honest and virtuous man, a man who possessed sound judgment and enough willpower and inner strength to overcome his own sexual desires. In doing so, he portrayed himself as trustworthy, in control of himself and his environment:

> Memories! What beautiful memories run through my mind as my heart quickens its beats at the recollection. With much regret you describe the thoughts, recommendations, the doubts that you

harboured in light of my departure. Your doubts were fleeting ones without concrete realisations because I understood my duty and my responsibility towards you. I don't mean to praise myself, but if I were not truly an honest man, dignified of my actions, I would have certainly behaved in another way. You understand, of course![36]

Once Antonietta's father returned to Ampezzo Carnico in December 1947, after a nearly twenty-year absence, he urged Antonietta and her mother to join him in Montreal. While both his wife and daughter were not initially enthusiastic about leaving their home and their family in Italy, Loris's reaction to the news helped to convince them to emigrate to Canada. He assured them that he would join them in Montreal as soon as he could, following his military duty and completion of the required documentation for his immigration. Loris's desire to begin a new life in Canada appeased Antonietta's worries about leaving him behind.[37] However, on 21 September 1948, the day of Antonietta's departure, Loris was forced to face unfamiliar emotions. Reflecting on their final farewell at Rome's airport, he expressed the tensions he experienced that day:

> I wanted to be strong, I wanted to give you the impression that I was a strong man, but those moments were too much to bear, too forceful was the separation [...] None too soon I had before me the sorrows I had felt many times at our former goodbyes, already my heart was swelling, and my throat was tightening from the tears I was trying to repress, until I saw the tears in your eyes.[38]

Antonietta's response to his first letter demonstrates both her desperation and resourcefulness. Antonietta's response matched the intensity in Loris's letter; however, it also evidenced how well she knew herself and her acceptance and resistance to the challenges they faced in their long-distance relationship:

> I started to read it, of course the first time, I didn't read it, I devoured it, I understood just a few of the words – the most beautiful ones which gave me so much sorrow – and I cried, I cried so hard until tears rolled down and my chest heaved in desperate sighs. That cry, however, brought me serenity, it melted the knot that constantly tightened at my throat, and when I got up from bed to go into the kitchen, I was smiling [...] It's useless to despair, you need to be strong, they say, but that's in theory, sure we can be strong, but when the heart is overflowing [...] nothing keeps you silent, no one knows how to diminish your pain [...] all will pass, I will know how to accept and wait with patience [...] always with the hope that fate will smile upon us.[39]

This reflection reveals her 'resistant centre', but also, and perhaps more poignantly, how she had learned and appropriated female roles, among other places, at the opera.[40] This observation leads me to my final point about the ways that operatic motifs informed the letters and the gendered identities of their authors.

In addition to letter writers' understandings of gender, made evident in their discussions of divisions of labour and in their use of symbolic language, in this section, I examine ways in which we 'see' gender at work in the interpretation of the cultural production of Italian opera. The opera lyrics of Verdi, Puccini, Mascagni and others, which punctuate the Petris-Palma collection, provide a rare gateway into understanding the reception and appropriation of the music, characters and lyrics by this rather ordinary Italian couple. Musicologists agree that opera, 'with its unique power to "represent" in an inimitably charged register that combines several arts, is capable not only of reinforcing social hierarchies, but of destabilizing and even of contesting them'.[41] Moral codes, values and normative behaviour of the nineteenth-century bourgeoisie, feminist musicologist Susan McClary remarks, were developed and disseminated through operatic representations.[42] While neither Loris's nor Antonietta's families belonged to the bourgeoisie, this did not preclude Loris or Antonietta from frequenting or being attuned to the music of opera. As a child, Loris frequently accompanied his grandfather to the opera house where he was employed as the theatre's carpenter. Thus, Loris would have been regularly exposed to the music, narratives and nightly performances of Italian operas at the Fenice Theatre in Venice. In many of his letters to Antonietta, he references Puccini's and Verdi's arias, as well as the lyrics of other Italian operas.

Antoniette had already been deeply moved by the arias she had heard as a young woman in her home town, the more so when she attended opera performances with Loris at Venice's magical Fenice Theatre. Loris's enthusiasm for opera had found its match. Antonietta too would make references to Italian opera arias in her correspondence with Loris. In doing so, she appropriated, identified and differentiated her own experiences as a woman in love. For both Loris and Antonietta, Italian opera was a lens through which they each identified as a man or a woman in love. One letter, for instance, illustrates how Antonietta closely identified with and differentiated her story from *Madama Butterfly's* young Japanese heroine. In this letter, she draws a comparison between her relationship with Loris and Cio-Cio-San's relationship with the young American lieutenant, B. F. Pinkerton. She then contrasts the tragic turn of events for Cio-Cio-San (as a woman who waits for her man in vain) with her own experience:

> As I write to you my thoughts transport me to the stupendous Fenice Theatre, I recall the moving story of the young Japanese woman, Cio-Cio-San and the marvellous romantic music, 'One fine day we'll see'.[43] This is the way she waited, with constancy and faith, he was required to return home, where the young girl waited for him, and wished to hear him sing, oh my 'tiny little wife, perfume of verbena'.[44] But alas! Poor her, how deceived she was! Yes, she found him but he was not alone, another woman was by his side. My story is completely different. Only in her waiting can I identify with her, a waiting that is, however, much less painful. As I wait for you now, I will have to draw inspiration from her, to live for you and with you – to wait for you and be certain that you will return one day, and call me 'My little Nietta'.[45]

Citations of opera lyrics also provided Loris with a language of poetry and drama through which he declared his love and devotion to his beloved, much as the character, Radames in Giuseppe Verdi's *Aïda*, declares his everlasting love and devotion to his beloved Aïda:

> If that warrior I were!
> If (only) my dream came true! . . .
> An army of brave men by me led . . .
> And victory . . . and the acclaim of Memphis all!
> And to you my sweet Aïda, return with laurels crowned . . .
> To tell you: for you I've fought, for you I've won!
> Heavenly Aïda, form divine, mystic wreath
> Of light and flowers,
> Of my thoughts you are queen,
> You of my life are the splendour.
> Your lovely sky I would wish to give you again.
> The sweet breezes of the native soil;
> Raise for you a throne near the sun.[46]

In citing Radames's monologue to Aïda, Loris appropriated the role of Radames – a character that embodies masculinity and honour.[47] With a twist of his own creativity, he began the citation with his words, 'let this pledge assure you', before proceeding with the aria's lyrics. Loris then concluded Radames's aria with his own literary invention: 'A throne near the willow'. With the words, 'Now more than ever I kiss you with my every passion, and you are, like always, close to me, as you are especially in this, I believe, well-deserved rest. Kisses, your Loris', Loris closed the letter.[48] As I show in the above section, letters of this nature are useful material that allows us to 'see' subjects under construction, and the cultural productions upon which they draw.

Conclusion

To conclude briefly, this article shows insightful ways in which lovers' correspondence provides a close-up view of the gendered, intimate worlds of letter writers intensely involved in long-distance love relationships. Epistemologically, lovers' correspondence (between migrants and non-migrants) is a valuable source that provides historians and other scholars the tools to examine intimate relationships, gender dynamics, subjectivities, language and a constellation of other elements using various categories of analysis. From a gender perspective, these letters demonstrate the degree to which normative ideologies were accepted, resisted and challenged in a long-distance romantic relationship in Italy and Canada during the post-war period. They bring to light, moreover, the myriad of unconscious ways that letter writers recreated identities of the self in their use of language, and in the case of the Petris-Palma letter collection, in their references to the cultural production of opera.

Notes

For their helpful comments on earlier versions of this article, I thank Ursula Lehmkuhl, Patricia Lorcin and the participants of the 'Gender History across Epistemologies' Workshop held 15–16 April 2011 at the University of Minnesota. I also thank the anonymous reviewers from *Gender & History* for their very insightful and constructive comments and suggestions. For her excellent copy-editing skills, I thank Melanie Huska. A special thank you is extended to the editors of this special issue, Donna Gabaccia and Mary Jo Maynes. For their interest and perennial encouragement, I am very grateful to them. Finally, I thank Mrs. Antonietta Petris for lending me her letters and granting me permission to draw from them. Most especially, I thank Antonietta for her friendship.

All translations of the letter excerpts and other citations are mine.

1. Pietro Mascagni, *L'Amico Fritz,* Act 2, Libretto by P. Suardon, in Nico Castel, *Italian Verismo Opera Libretti*, Scott Jackson Wiley ed., vol. 1 (Mt. Morris, New York: Leyerle Publications, 2000), p. 688.
2. Letter from Loris Palma to Antonietta Petris, 1 January 1949. Private collection.
3. Suellen Diaconoff, review of Marie-France Silver and Marie-Laure Girou Swiderski (eds), *Femmes en toutes lettres. Les épistolières du XVIIIe siècle*, *Diderot Studies* 29 (2003), pp. 205–07, here p. 205.
4. Joan W. Scott, *Gender and the Politics of History* (New York: Columbia University Press, 1999), p. 55.
5. Scott, *Gender and the Politics of History*, p. 55.
6. Bernard Bray, 'Treize propos sur la Lettre d'Amour', in Mireille Bossis and Charles Porter (eds), *L'Epistolarité à Travers les Siècles: Geste de communication et/ou d'écriture* (Stuttgart: Franz Steiner Verlag, 1990), pp. 40–47, here pp. 40–41.
7. Hsu-Ming Teo, 'Love Writes: Gender and Romantic Love in Australian Love Letters, 1860–1960', *Australian Feminist Studies* 20 (2005), pp. 343–61, here p. 344. Furthermore, as Bernard Bray suggests: 'the love letter – even if, as we know, is about love – doesn't merely speak of love, but accompanies it, surpasses it, claims it, comments on it, regrets it. An impure genre, the love letter combines in the analysis and in the observation of feelings, also narratives, descriptions, autobiographical fragments, ornamentation that constitute as many personality projections'. Bray, 'Treize Propos sur la Lettre d'Amour', pp. 40–41.
8. Seventy letters from the complete collection exchanged between Antonietta Petris and Loris Palma were sent between Italy and Canada. In addition, the collection holds numerous letters written by Antonietta's and Loris's immediate and extended families in Ampezzo Carnico, Venice and Montreal. Much of the

correspondence is divided fairly equally between the two letter writers with many of the letters written in response to each other. Most letters were written in pen – with much of the ink bleeding through the wafer-thin paper used especially for international mail between Italy and Canada; some letters were written in pencil to facilitate their being read on the both sides of the paper. Many of the letters have been preserved with their corresponding envelopes. This complete private collection is written entirely in Italian. A note on the translation of the opera lyrics in the letter excerpts: The translations into English of the opera scores are drawn from the literal translations provided in Nico Castel's volumes cited in the article. I first identified a small selection of letters from the collection in 1998 when I initially contacted Loris Palma, then director of a Venetian cultural association in Montreal. In 2003, for subsequent doctoral research, I began a more in-depth search for Italian migrant letters written between Canada and Italy during the post-war years. Mr Palma provided me with approximately twenty additional letters that he had exchanged with his wife, Antonietta Petris. Excerpts of these letters were included in my book, *Families, Lovers, and their Letters: Italian Postwar Migration to Canada* (Winnipeg: University of Manitoba Press, 2010). In the months that followed Mr Palma's passing in August of 2007, I met with Mrs Antonietta Petris and her two daughters, and I later learned of the hundreds of love letters that Mrs Petris had kept, which she generously agreed to lend me. Once the book project was conceived, meetings with Antonietta Petris were held on a regular basis. The further we delved into the letters and reread them, the more Mrs Petris became increasingly pleased (at times, even jubilant!) reminiscing details of her relationship with Loris. Over time, the reflective and tactile experience of revisiting the correspondence has led Mrs Petris to experience newfound joys, satisfactions and a deeper sense of purpose in her life as a recent widow.

9. Consider for instance: Charlotte Erickson, *Invisible Immigrants: The Adaptation of English and Scottish Immigrants in Nineteenth-Century America* (Coral Gables: University of Miami Press, 1972); Samuel Baily and Franco Ramella, *One Family, Two Worlds: An Italian Family's Correspondence across the Atlantic, 1901–1922* (New Brunswick: Rutgers, 1988); Wolfgang Helbich, Walter A. Kamphoefner and Ulrike Sommer (eds), *News from the Land of Freedom: German Immigrants Write Home* (Ithaca: Cornell University Press, 1991); David Fitzpatrick, *Oceans of Consolation: Personal Accounts of Irish Migration to Australia* (Ithaca: Cornell University Press, 1994); Dirk Hoerder, *Creating Societies: Immigrant Lives in Canada* (Montreal-Kingston: McGill-Queen's University Press, 1999), Suzanne Sinke, *Dutch Immigrant Women in the United States, 1880–1920* (Champaign: University of Illinois Press, 2002), Haiming Liu, *The Transnational History of a Chinese Family: Immigrant Letters, Family Business, and Reverse Migration* (New Brunswick: Rutgers University Press, 2005), David A. Gerber, *Authors of their Lives: The Personal Correspondence of British Immigrants to North America in the Nineteenth Century* (New York: New York University Press, 2006); Cancian, *Families, Lovers, and their Letters*; Kathleen A. DeHaan, 'Negotiating the Transnational Moment: Immigrant Letters as Performance of a Diasporic Identity', *National Identities* 12 (2010), pp. 107–31.
10. Nicky Hallett, 'Introduction 2. "Anxiously yours": the Epistolary Self and the Culture of Concern', *Journal of European Studies* 32 (2002), pp. 107–18, here p. 108.
11. DeHaan, 'Negotiating the Transnational Moment', p. 107.
12. DeHaan, 'Negotiating the Transnational Moment', p. 107.
13. DeHaan, 'Negotiating the Transnational Moment', p. 108.
14. Gerber, *Authors of their Lives*, p. 57.
15. Gerber, *Authors of their Lives*, p. 57.
16. Gerber, *Authors of their Lives*, p. 286.
17. Bruce Redford, *The Converse of the Pen: Acts of Intimacy in the Eighteenth-Century Familiar Letter* (Chicago: University of Chicago Press, 1986), p. 9.
18. Letter from Antonietta Petris to Loris Palma, 3 January 1949. Private collection.
19. Letter from Loris Palma to Antonietta Petris, 24 January 1949. Private collection.
20. Jack Goody, *Food and Love: A Cultural History of East and West* (London and New York: Verso, 1998), p. 107.
21. Goody, *Food and Love*, p. 110.
22. Goody, *Food and Love*, p. 111.
23. Letter from Antonietta Petris to Loris Palma, 6 September 1946. Private collection.
24. Letter from Loris Palma to Antonietta Petris, 16 December 1948. Private collection.
25. Letter from Loris Palma to Antonietta Petris, 16 January 1949. Private collection.
26. The awareness that love, distance and writing can create more intense feelings of affection became even more evident when over sixty-five years after first receiving this letter, Antonietta reread it and exclaimed, 'My God, we fell in love via correspondence!' Personal Communication with Antonietta Petris, 15 February

2011. As Hsu-Ming Teo points out in reference to Australian love letters, 'these letter writers write because they are in love; but perhaps they also love because they write'. Teo, 'Love Writes', p. 344.

27. Letter from Loris Palma to Antonietta Petris, 23 September 1948. Private collection.
28. Robin T. Lakoff, *Language and Woman's Place* (New York: Harper & Row, 1975); Barrie Thorne and Nancy Henley (eds), *Language and Sex: Difference and Dominance* (Rowley: Newbury House, 1975); Jennifer Coates (ed.), *Language and Gender: A Reader* (Oxford: Blackwell, 1998); Deborah Cameron, *The Feminist Critique of Language: A Reader* (London: Routledge, 1990); Deborah Tannen, *You Just Don't Understand: Women and Men in Conversation* (New York: Morrow, 1990); Kira Hall and M. Bucholtz, *Gender Articulated: Language and the Socially Constructed Self* (New York: Routledge, 1995).
29. Judith Lorber, *Paradoxes of Gender* (New Haven: Yale University Press, 1994), p. 100.
30. Letter from Loris Palma to Antonietta Petris, 23 January 1949. Private collection.
31. Letter from Loris Palma to Antonietta Petris, 10 January 1949. Private collection.
32. Letter from Antonietta Petris to Loris Palma, 3 September 1946. Private collection.
33. Letter from Loris Palma to Antonietta Petris, 16 January 1949. Private collection.
34. Letter from Antonietta Petris to Loris Palma, 29 November 1948. Private collection.
35. Letter from Antonietta Petris to Loris Palma, 29 November 1948. Private collection.
36. Letter from Loris Palma to Antonietta Petris, 11 November 1946. Private collection.
37. Letter from Loris Palma to Antonietta Petris, 16 February 1949. Private collection.
38. Letter from Loris Palma to Antonietta Petris, 23 September 1948. Private collection.
39. Letter from Antonietta Petris to Loris Palma, 30 September 1948. Private collection.
40. Catherine Clément, *Opera, or the Undoing of Women,* tr. Betsey Wing (Minneapolis: University of Minnesota Press, 1988), p. 180.
41. Jane F. Fulcher, 'Introduction to Part I', in Victoria Johnson, Jane F. Fulcher and Thomas Ertman (eds), *Opera and Society in Italy and France from Monteverdi to Bourdieu* (Cambridge: Cambridge University Press, 2007), pp. 29–33, here p. 33.
42. Susan McClary, 'Foreword: The Undoing of Opera: Toward a Feminist Criticism of Music', in Clément, *Opera, or the Undoing of Women*, pp. ix-xviii, here p. xviii.
43. Giacomo Puccini, 'Madama Butterfly', Libretto by Giuseppe Giacosa and Luigi Illica, in Nico Castel, *The Complete Puccini Libretti*, Marcie Stapp ed., vols. 1 and 2, 2nd edn, revised (Mt. Morris, New York: Leyerle Publications, 2002), p. 333
44. Puccini, 'Madama Butterfly', p. 334.
45. Letter from Antonietta Petris to Loris Palma, 31 March 1947. Private collection.
46. Giuseppe Verdi, 'Aïda'. Libretto by Giuseppe Ghislanzoni, in Nico Castel, *The Complete Verdi Libretti*, vol. 1 (Geneseo, New York: Leyerle Publications, 1994), pp. 6–7.
47. P. J. Smith, 'O "Patria Mia": Female Homosociality and the Gendered Nation in Bellini's *Norma* and Verdi's *Aida*', in Richard Dellamora and Daniel Fischlin (eds), *The Work of Opera: Genre, Nationhood, and Sexual Difference* (New York: Columbia University Press, 1997), pp. 93–114, here p. 106.
48. Letter from Loris Palma to Antonietta Petris, 19 November 1946. Private collection.

11 Gender-Bending in El Teatro Campesino (1968–1980): A *Mestiza* Epistemology of Performance

Meredith Heller

El Teatro Campesino began with a small leaflet distributed to grape pickers in Delano, California. Neat rows of typewriter print announced the inception of a 'bi-lingual community farm workers' theatre project' and directed those interested to gather at 8.30 pm on 2 November 1965 to contribute talents such as 'simple narrative', singing and instrument playing.[1] What was printed at the bottom of the flier would become Teatro Campesino's enduring and unifying message: 'If you can sing, dance, walk, march, hold a picket sign, play a guitar or harmonica or any other instrument, you can participate! No acting experience required'.[2] From 1965 to 1967, El Teatro Campesino (the farm workers' theatre) performed their political skits on stages made from flatbed trucks, on street corners, at the edges of vegetable fields and in union halls.[3] Growing quickly from this grassroots start, Teatro Campesino became one of the most visible artistic forums in the 1970s for promoting El Movimiento (the Chicano civil rights movement) and expressing cultural pride. Incorporating Chicano and Mexican *carpa* (tent show) performance traditions, historical iconography and Mayan, Aztec and Catholic spirituality, Teatro Campesino confronted the dominant American structure of power by privileging Spanish language, Chicano culture and *indigenismo*.[4]

In academia, Teatro Campesino has become the model for a theatre project that can both reflect social injustice and also effect social change. Likewise, Teatro Campesino figurehead Luis Valdez has been positioned within a 'great-man conceptual framework' as the father of Chicano theatre in the United States. Teatro Campesino and Luis Valdez have also been criticised in academic circles, albeit much less frequently, for replicating and perpetuating gender and sexual oppressions. Like other political rights organisations in the 1960s and the 1970s, Teatro Campesino maintained unity by promulgating their shared identity of difference. Yet Diana Taylor and Margaret Rose assert that a prevailing emphasis on cultural, ethnic or class solidarity within contemporary civil rights movements can deprioritise internal inequalities that lead to gender or sexual discrimination.[5] The type of organisational framework that prioritises these overriding imperatives makes it 'much easier for the community to recognise the racism directed at them than the sexism that exists both outside and within its boundaries'.[6] Taylor suggests that subsuming individuals' diverse identities into a singular,

Gender History Across Epistemologies, First Edition. Edited by Donna R. Gabaccia and Mary Jo Maynes.
Chapters © 2013 The Authors. Book compilation © 2013 Blackwell Publishing Ltd.

united front will eventually lead to internal stratification and oppression. Some feminist scholars believe that the predominant historical account of Teatro Campesino and Luis Valdez likewise replicates this matrix by making the work of its Chicana performers peripheral, marginal or invisible.[7]

In the 1980s, Yvonne Yarbro-Bejarano and Yolanda Broyles-González offered alternate historiographic accounts of several Chicano Teatro Nacional de Aztlán (TENAZ) troupes.[8] By integrating oral testimony ethnographies into their interdisciplinary studies, these scholars hoped to avoid the canonical 'chronological and text centered' analysis they felt had marginalised or downplayed Chicanas.[9] During an eighteen month research residency with El Teatro Campesino in the early 1980s, Broyles-González was allowed unrestricted access to rehearsals, performances, archives and troupe members. Through a laborious collection of personal interviews and unpublished archival material, Broyles-González crafted a 'whole new history' of Teatro Campesino, one that highlighted the *teatristas*' experiences, documented instances of their exclusion and revealed areas of their occlusion.[10] Broyles-González promoted her new historiography at the 1982 University of Arizona's Renato Rosaldo lecture series and the National Association for Chicano Studies conference in 1984. She asserts that both lecture papers were prevented from publication by powerful male academic opponents of her 're-vision'. She says that Luis Valdez 'went as far as to contact my publishers and threaten them' if he was not allowed editorial control over her work.[11] But it was not just her use of unconventional ethnographic methods that triggered this professional hostility; Broyles-González used oral testimony to reveal *teatristas*' contributions and also to support her own scathing analysis of misogyny woven into the history and historiography of Teatro Campesino. She believed these women were relegated to marginal positions within the troupe because of 'well-worn stereotypes of gender roles' functioning simultaneously with race and class assumptions about the Chicana woman as primarily a 'wife/mother/lover'.[12] By mapping her argument over the words of Teatro Campesino's *teatristas*, Broyles-González not only credited their unwritten history but also irrefutably justified her own critical stance that an oppressive matrix of race, ethnicity, class and gender was imposed on the bodies and identities of Chicana women. The *teatristas*' stories became the academic means to define their subjectivity, a subjectivity that was wholly shaped by racist and misogynistic cultural practices.

This article explores what I term '*mestiza* performance practices': choices and techniques that allowed *teatristas* to embody their intersecting identities of sex, gender and ethnicity and also navigate away from pejorative positions of singularity, separatism and oppression. Teatro Campesino *teatrista* Diane Rodriguez has analogised her relationship with the troupe to a traditional western marriage. While not totally egalitarian, 'it's not like someone is dictating to us that we must be here … Rather, we all have our own input and we all want to be here because we can contribute'.[13] By comparing herself to a wife, Rodriguez acknowledges the constraints created by her so-called 'biological roles' and also expresses feelings of active dedication and willing contribution.[14] This dual consciousness is further emphasised when she explains that she and the other *teatristas* 'could have walked away, but we stayed because we believed we were moving a community to self-empowerment through art'.[15] While Rodriguez's work may have been downplayed or marginalised in Teatro Campesino, in El Movimiento and in academia, she believes that embracing her culturally-specific gender role did not prevent her from actively participating and meaningfully contributing.

While it is important to reveal how Chicanas have been marginalised in the history and academic historisation of Teatro Campesino, feminist scholars must also examine ways in which these women actively engaged with, altered or pluralised their subject positions. In illuminating the creation, implementation and evolution of several gender-bending performances, this article asserts that performance practices were both a creative outlet for artistic expression and also a means for *teatristas* to shape and control their own multilayered identities. Unlike theories of a universal, singular identity of difference, multiracial feminism allows for multiple identities to simultaneously and complementarily exist in one body. Chela Sandoval proposes a differential consciousness where women of colour should not be encapsulated by their gender, class or race alone but instead move actively among these various power bases and ideological positions.[16] Emma Pérez creates a space for the 'decolonial imaginary' in which women of colour can experience and theorise about their own specificity, history and legacy in non-western and therefore non-opposing ways.[17] By 'queering mestizaje', Alicia Arrizón is able to theorise about Chicanas in a way that allows racial hybridity and transculturation to be empowering and positive rather than contradictory.[18] In these theories, the subjectivity of women of colour is constructed not from one but, as Yarbro-Bejarano surmises, 'multiple determinants – gender, class, sexuality and contradictory membership in competing cultures and racial identities'.[19]

In the influential text *Borderlands/La Frontera*, Gloria Anzaldúa presents the '*mestiza* consciousness' as a framework for how Chicanas can embody legacies of location, ethnicity and gender and also exist in a way that is not oppressively confined by these identities.[20] The *mestiza* is a Chicana woman who combines Spanish, American Indian and Mexican ancestry and therefore potentially embodies multiple and/or contradictory racial, cultural, sexual, colonised, class, gender and border identities. This *mestiza* woman does not reject or abandon these aspects of her identity or history but rather integrates these factors into her contemporary self to create a grounded yet flexible dual consciousness. Cherríe Moraga speculates that this type of consciousness is achieved by embodying and enacting 'a theory in the flesh'.[21] For both Moraga and Anzaldúa, embodied theory is accomplished through the writings of radical women of colour. It is my position that Teatro Campesino's *teatristas* were able to both identify with Chicana gender roles and also create flexibility in these borders by performing their 'theory in the flesh' with gender-bending parts.

Using photographs, scripts, fliers, programmes and media from the recently reopened Teatro Campesino archives, this article illustrates instances of male/female, non-female, androgynous, sexless and otherworldly gender-bending performance by Chicanas.[22] Staged gender-bending, also referred to as cross-casting or drag, is canonically defined as an individual of one dimorphic sex category performing opposing gender displays for an audience who is aware of his or her underlying 'authentic' sex and gender. For example, Steven Schacht and Lisa Underwood define drag queens as 'individuals who publicly perform being women in front of an audience that knows they are "men" regardless of how compellingly female – "real" – they might appear otherwise'.[23] By consciously employing the term 'gender-bending', I seek to expand this definition to include stage acts that may replicate but can also complicate, layer, deemphasise, multiply, blur or otherwise shake up normative conceptions of identity.

I argue that the *teatristas* were able to coexist and grow within Teatro Campesino and El Movimiento because gender-bending roles allowed them to embody a plural subjectivity. A core member of Teatro Campesino from 1973 to 1980, Diane Rodriguez frequently played what she called 'androgynous' or 'non-female' characters such as La Muerte (Death) and Satanás (Satan).[24] Core member Socorro Valdez was known for performing 'male' or 'sexless' roles such as *pachucos* (thugs) and *calaveras* (skeletons).[25] Core members Yolanda Parra and Olivia Chumacero played the mythical angel character San Miguel (St Michael). Angela Cruz played Satanás. Stephanie Buswell and Vicki Oswald played *diablos* (devils). I assert that these non-normative performances of gender and sex – these acts of gender-bending – allowed *teatristas* to 'transform or rewrite [their] environment, to continually augment [their] powers and capacities' and to reconfigure static, binary or singular definitions of Chicanahood.[26] I argue that the *teatristas*' efforts to create and perform gender-bending characters demonstrate their active embodiment and mobilisation of a *mestiza* consciousness.

Historiography of the *teatrista*: shifting analysis from script to stage

While expressions of *Chicanismo* and *indigenismo* were exploding in 1970s and 1980s arts movements, western academia was also going through an epistemological change. Scholars in humanities and social sciences were publicly questioning canonical texts and actively engaging with cross-disciplinary theories and methods to map the untold stories of marginalised individuals. For example, feminist performance studies scholar Sue-Ellen Case confronted the established notion that Greek scripts and acting theories were foundational to contemporary theatre practice. She argued that none of these canonical texts were written by or portrayed Greek women accurately and that they in fact perpetuated (and are perpetuating) socially pejorative beliefs about women's weak, passive or biologically-ruled natures.[27] This type of gender-focused critique of canonical texts was also initially used to point out instances of stereotyping and essentialising in Chicano TENAZ theatre productions. For example, Yarbro-Bejarano's study on Teatro de la Esperanza, largely based on textual critique, concluded that when Chicanas are perpetually depicted in familial roles, they 'propagate the notion that women's power to change society is limited to influencing their husbands'.[28] While beginning to integrate ethnographic methods into their work, feminist scholars still relied on familiar text-centred script analyses to add legitimacy to arguments.

Broyles-Gonzales, who had access to a multitude of unpublished play scripts during her research residency with Teatro Campesino in San Juan Bautista, asserted that scripted protagonists were never female and therefore all female parts were stereotypical, auxiliary roles. Using the type of feminist critique that Case applied to Greek playscripts, Broyles-González argued that Teatro Campesino plays perpetuated a Chicana subjectivity defined by biological or age relationship to men. Satellite identities such as *la madre, la abuela, la hermana, y la esposa/novia* (the mother, the grandmother, the sister and the wife/girlfriend) were then further essentialised into one of two reductive categories: *La Virgen* (the innocent) or *La Malinche* (the fallen woman). Defined by a 'handful of visible female traits' such as biological sex relation, gender role as homemaker and caretaker, sexual availability and ethnicity/colour, Chicana characters represented a 'single dimension' of social powerlessness and cultural victimisation.[29]

These claims can indeed be supported by examples from the small collection of Teatro Campesino plays published in 1971 as well as the many scripts now publicly available in the Teatro Campesino archives.[30] For example, in one of Teatro Campesino's earliest plays, *Las Dos Caras del Patroncito* (The Two Faces of the Farm Boss) (1966), the only female character is the silent, unnamed, fur bikini-clad wife of the white farm boss, a status symbol that the *esquirol* (scab) 'acquires' when he takes over the role of *patroncito*. In *La Pastorela* (The Shepherd's Play) (1976), Gila, the only female character, is forced into marriage by her father but then spurned by her would-be husband when she does not spend enough time preparing food. Later, when a *hermitanio* (hermit) attempts to sexually molest her, her family justifies his actions as a product of 'spells' and not lechery. Broyles-González believed that these fragmented, non-threatening and controllable female types 'consistently demonstrated stagnation in [Teatro Campesino's] treatment of women'.[31]

In focusing on the creation and perpetuation of pejoratively gendered character types, early feminist scholars were not necessarily addressing the actual Chicanas who embodied these roles and otherwise participated in *teatro*. So while Broyles-Gonzalez's original gender critique was grounded in the script, her final conclusions about Teatro Campesino were also carefully supported by primary statements from the *teatristas*. For example, when interviewed about the canon of female parts, Diane Rodriguez explained 'there have been very few roles in Teatro Campesino that I have thoroughly enjoyed. Because of what they're saying and who they are'.[32] Her statement implies that these essentialised Chicana characters did directly affect the enjoyment, satisfaction and perhaps even the subjectivity of the *teatristas* who constantly embodied them. Using oral testimony to support her arguments, Broyles-González used women's 'own words' to not only highlight their contributions and debunk the 'great man' myth of Luis Valdez but also to support her larger analysis that the *teatristas* themselves were essentialised within the troupe.[33]

Broyles-González made it no secret that her methods and conclusions contributed to a substantial delay in her scholarship. Although her research residency was conducted in the early 1980s, her book on El Teatro Campesino was not published until 1994. By then, the use of oral testimony collection and post-structural analysis was common practice in many humanities and social sciences fields.[34] *Theatre Journal* reviewer Laura D. Nielsen wrote a glowing review of the book, commenting that Broyles-Gonzalez's exemplary work on Chicano historiography and performativity 'writes against the grain' of previous publications on the subject.[35] José Muñoz wrote in *The Drama Review* that 'her methodology ... in direct opposition to conventional modes of theatre history' was successful in revealing the social processes behind women's overlooked contributions.[36] And in the feminist studies journal *Signs*, Mary Pat Brady praised Broyles-González for writing 'against the grain of Teatro' and focusing on 'the collective work of the ensemble'.[37] But while Brady appreciated the use of feminist methods of analysis in the book, she added that Broyles-Gonzalez's conclusions focused too much on the patriarchal organisation of the troupe and the book 'would have been complemented by greater attention to the story of Chicanas' developing roles within the ensemble'.[38]

While Broyles-González uses *teatristas*' words to highlight their experiences, her larger critique of Teatro Campesino and El Movimiento constantly shifts the focus away from their accomplishments. The oral statements she chose to publish do not focus on the *teatristas* as much as they support her overarching conclusions about gendered cultural misogyny. And while Broyles-González writes that these interviews were in fact the nucleus of her book, there is only one short chapter devoted to this original research. In a manuscript draft of this chapter, Broyles-González has penned into the margin a note explaining that, instead of elaborating farther, she has decided to continue her discussion of the *teatristas* in a future book.[39] This projected book on the innovations of El Teatro Campesino's *teatristas* was never completed.

By focusing on the limitations of the *teatristas* within hegemonic cultural beliefs and practices, Broyles-González does not allow these women enough credit for their own acts of agency. Sandoval theorises that women of colour should pursue a 'tactical subjectivity' that precludes entrapment in a singular and unitary definition of self and allows them actively to negotiate their multiple and often contradictory locations and allegiances, systematically to deconstruct simple binarisms and build coalitions.[40] Like Pérez's space of the decolonial imaginary, Sandoval's differential consciousness is a 'theoretical tool for uncovering the hidden voices of Chicanas' and also allowing those voices to enact agency.[41] While pejorative or sexist casting practices and organisational structures need to be identified as a counterpoint to the scholarly literature on Teatro Campesino, feminist analysis must also seek out places where *teatristas'* activity mobilised and altered definitions of themselves as marginalised victims.

In the early Delano, California days of El Teatro Campesino, simple and straightforward performances were disruptive, subversive and powerful. The power of these *actos* (skits) was in their appeal as a visual act of transmission, 'a learning experience with no formal prerequisites' of reading or writing.[42] The physical body's ability to act as a conduit for basic human truths and complex social issues is one of the core epistemologies of performance theory. I suggest that when Moraga's 'theory in the flesh' is theatrically performed, static categories of gender, ethnicity and sexuality can potentially blur, shift and hybridise. In the words of Anzaldúa, this paradigm must be produced through 'continual creative motion that keeps breaking down the unitary aspect' of identity.[43] *Teatristas* such as Diana Rodriguez, Olivia Chumacero and Socorro Valdez continually reiterate:

> I think my most favorite roles have been the roles that are neither man nor woman. The androgynous roles, like the Muerte and like Satanás. Those are the most fun. What's happened with playing, um, female roles . . . they were always somehow victimised because that's how it was seen in the society, do you know what I'm saying? So they weren't that much fun to play. You know, they're very supportive. They weren't very fun . . . So I have always liked to play the roles that are neither man nor woman. They're the most fun.[44]

These 'fun' roles, the roles the *teatristas* chose to perform time and time again, were not the one-dimensional Chicana characters that Broyles-González discussed. In shifting analysis away from playscripts and towards performance practices, it becomes clear that while *teatristas* may have been dissatisfied with scripted parts, they also actively pursued opportunities to enact complex, hybrid characters.

I assert that gender-bending performance practices were direct methods of reworking the bounded subjectivities imposed on Chicanas by Teatro Campesino, El Movimiento and American society. The *teatristas* eagerly performed 'fun' roles such as Diablo, Satanás and Calavera with strength, physicality, tenacity and gusto. Yarbro-Bejarano mentions in a 1986 *Theatre Journal* article that Broyles-Gonzalez's work on Teatro Campesino will call 'attention to [the *teatristas'*] imaginative strategies for dealing with these limitations'.[45] While Yarbro-Bejarano hints towards a discussion of gender-bending practices, only one paragraph of Broyles-Gonzalez's book actually addresses these performance innovations. The physical embodiment of a category of characters that could not be entirely bounded by a reductive or singular identity is an extremely significant part of Teatro Campesino, and the transformative nature of these performances has yet to be sufficiently addressed. I propose that gender-bending performances were direct and active methods for *teatristas* to rework singular subjectivity and embody an actively plural *mestiza* consciousness. Using my own feminist method of close-reading performance tactics, the following sections explore the *teatristas'* gender-bending performances. This analysis will both document the evolution of these role-types as well as provide examples of resistant and complex performance strategies.

Bending the gender roles of the *teatristas:* Socorro Valdez's masculine *calavera*

Evidence of *teatristas* gender-bending as masculine, androgynous and sexless mythical characters is stamped into the history of Teatro Campesino. I have discovered numerous photographs in the newly public Teatro Campesino archives of actors with breasts and hips performing in head to toe *calavera* costumes, masks and skullcaps. I have found an image of a *teatrista* blowing dense smoke out of her nostrils and down over her sinister goatee as the frightening Luzbel (Lucifer). I have examined stills of Socorro Valdez standing aggressively as a *machismo*-dripping *pachuco*. And on her hands and knees with tongue wagging out as a dog-like *calavera*, Valdez is virtually unidentifiable.[46] According to Diane Rodriguez, these types of roles were referred to as 'the androgynous roles' or 'the roles that are neither man nor woman'.[47] 'Androgyny' is a type of gender-bending performance that confuses dimorphic gender categories by combining masculine and feminine traits on a single performing body. Androgyny also refers to performances that are absent of gender displays and which confront the invisible and assumed connection of sexed bodies to gender. Maria Marrero writes that this latter type of performance, 'not as the encompassment of all genders but as an erasure of visible gender or sexual markers, was the significant representational possibility' for *teatristas*.[48] Mythical or otherworldly characters began as unsexed, ungendered and unraced 'universal beings' so, when bringing them to life, *teatristas* had a range of possibilities for character development that included shifting, mixing or otherwise bending standard identity categories.[49]

Several unpublished photos in the Teatro Campesino archives elaborate on Socorro Valdez's characterisation of the *calavera* character, Huesos (bones), for the 1980 Californian and European tour of *El Fin del Mundo* (The End of the World).[50] As this masculine *pachuco* character demonstrates, *calaveras* began as neutral figures but could potentially to take on gendered and raced characteristics. Valdez's basic costume is a light-coloured sleeveless leotard covered by a full-size painted image of a skeleton.[51] Her face and neck are sharply defined in contrasting white and black makeup lines that mimic a human skull; while her face is painted white, her eyes and nose are filled in with large black circles and huge teeth envelop her mouth and jaw. The general indicators of her skeletal leotard and makeup communicate the universal and inhuman look of a *calavera*. But over this skeletal frame she wears zoot suit style trousers held up with wide suspenders and a pack of cigarettes tucked under one of the straps.[52] Her short hair or wig is formed into a large pompadour. Directly below her coiffure, Valdez has pulled a wide bandana down over her eyebrows and ears, and stippled-on muttonchop sideburns jut from underneath this bandana. The layering of these ethnically and masculinely distinct displays over the neutral *calavera* form creates an eerie hybrid effect: a subject that no longer lives yet still retains distinct aspects of his former human identity.

I have not found a video recording of this production, but many of Valdez's acting techniques for producing gender and race are identifiable through a close reading of performance photographs. In one photo Valdez is thrusting her hands into her pockets while simultaneously pushing them forward, creating tension in her upper arms, shoulders and chest. Her shoulders remain hunched as she pushes out her lower chest and pelvis.[53] Combined with an unbalanced stance, this body positioning replicates the look of upper body strength as well as core-centred propulsion. This very masculine *pachuco* stance has been iconically characterised by Edward James Olmos in the stage and film versions of Teatro Campesino's *Zoot Suit*. In other photo stills, Valdez's Huesos is in mid-interaction with protagonist Reymundo Mata and several other *calaveras*. As she talks and gestures to them, Valdez thrusts her chest and shoulders forward and pulls her hips back, creating an aggressive and confrontational body tableau. Although covered in black and white makeup, her eyes peeking below her bandana are perceptibly tensed and fixed on her subject.[54] Holding tension in her jaw and jutting it towards her scene partners, Valdez successfully replicates a recognisable gender display of *machismo*. Although *calaveras* begin as universal beings, Valdez's clothing, carriage and body language effectively communicate a physical power and aggressive energy that is culturally identifiable as masculine.

Although Valdez's performance of Huesos oozes *machismo*, these photos clearly show that her short and thin body is unevenly matched to her larger-than-life *pachuco*. Performing next to Marco Rodriguez, the biologically male actor playing Reymundo, Valdez barely reaches to the bottom of his chin (although her pompadour does give her a few extra inches).[55] Her tight leotard does not disguise her physical form and her slumped stance outlines the curves of her waist, bottom and breasts. In historical examples of women who passed as men, secondary sex characteristics such as breasts, hips and waists were effectively concealed or downplayed by loose or androcentric clothing choices or by binding and padding undergarments. But Valdez's costume does not obliterate or even fully conceal the shape of her body. Indeed, it is not necessary that she or her character be understood as either biologically male or female because, although Huesos acts in a masculine manner, he is neither male nor female. As a *calavera*, he does not have an 'essential' sex identity because, underneath the pompadour and muttonchops, the zoot suit trousers and the bandana, Huesos is nothing but an *esqueleto*, a collection of bones.

After examining archival photos from this production, it was evident to me that Huesos was played by a female actor. Valdez is small and curvy and possesses many biological markers that are culturally associated with femininity. Yet after having watched Valdez perform in this very production of *El Fin Del Mundo*, Broyles-González writes 'how astonished I was to discover backstage after the performance that the extraordinary Huesos was played by a woman'.[56] I suggest that Valdez's performance as a *calavera pachuco* was so convincing because the role itself did not rely on or emphasise her own identity in any meaningful way. In more traditional gender-bending performances such as male impersonation and drag queening, the act is presented as an 'illusion' which is revealed when the performer's 'authentic' identity is disclosed; a removal of a wig or hat validates the audience's suspicions as to how the actor's body is fundamentally different from that of the performance. In the case of *calavera* characters, the acting body is not meant to contrast, support or otherwise inform the quality of the act or the character.

Reflecting on her willingness to take on and perform such roles, Valdez explains it was a method of 'aborting the fact that I was female and only female'.[57] This quote is reproduced in Broyles-Gonzalez's work to support claims that *teatristas* felt their 'female' Chicana identity constricted them. But equally important is the context in which this statement was made: in order to 'abort' a singular identity, Valdez actively pursued a performance in which her body could simultaneously characterise traditional and non-traditional categories of sex, gender and ethnicity. In doing so, Valdez created a space 'among' and also 'between them' where her subjectivity as 'female and only female' blended and hybridised with her character's, at once possessing biological and racial specificity and also eschewing such simple classifications of self.[58] In performing 'theory in the flesh' as Huesos, Valdez's acting body becomes undefined by cultural borders of identity and 'she can move across them, refusing to be contained by them'.[59] Although Valdez herself is always visually available for audiences to identify and classify, it is her embodiment of the *calavera* character that makes her performance both striking and effective.

Bending the gender roles of the *teatristas*: gender-neutral *calaveras*

In a 1976 talk show interview, Teatro Campesino core member Phil Esperanza explains 'each and every one of us has a *calavera* inside. And so when you reach that point, skin color, nationality, it doesn't make any difference because we are all *calaveras* inside'.[60] While mythical characters could take on binary signifiers or a mixture of signifiers, they all begin with this 'common denominator'.[61] Characters such as these offered *teatristas* a blank slate on which to build their final performance, one that could or could not conform to specific gendered, sexed or raced identities. While *teatristas* did perform some mythical characters in distinctly gendered and raced ways, nonsignified characters were just as common. *Teatristas* performed as ungendered *calaveras* in *La Carpa de Los Rasquachis* (1976 and 1978) and *El Fin Del Mundo* (1980), the gender indistinct Satanás and *diablos* in *La Pastorela* (1977 and 1980), as La Muerte in *La Carpa de Los Rasquachis* (1976 and 1978) and as Diablo in *Corridos* (1970s). The *teatristas* performed these androgynously 'unsexed' roles without inhibition of movement, body language or voice, which reflected the audience's lack of authority to position them or their characters based on preconceived notions of gender and cultural role.[62]

In addition to her masculinised Huesos character, Socorro Valdez performed as Calavera, the ungendered skeleton companion to Diablo in the 1978 European tour of *La Carpa de los Rasquachis*.[63] Every villain in the play (and there are many) is enacted either by Diablo or Calavera. Calavera morphs into various personas when directly interacting with protagonist Jesus Pelado Rasquachi and then back into original form as an inhuman skeleton creature. Valdez's base costume for this role is a black long-sleeved leotard, black stockings and ballet flats. As with her Huesos character, a crude skeletal structure is printed down the front. The top half of her head and face is concealed in a smooth, skull-shaped headpiece that extends from the base of her skull over the top of her head to her upper lip. A black cloth covers her neck while the exposed skin in the mask's eye holes is filled in with black makeup. Free from the mask, the bottom half of her face and mouth is painted black and highlighted with long white teeth.

In one photo, Valdez is animalistically posed on her knees, hands flopping in the air and head tilted quizzically to the side.[64] In this particular scene, Jesus Rasquachi has been employed as a dog walker and Calavera has morphed into 'Babushka', the dog of a wealthy Russian woman. While the mask Valdez wears as Calavera does not allow for much expression around her eyes, forehead, cheeks and nose, her slightly smiling mouth and exposed tongue supports her inhuman characterisation. On her right, Diane Rodriguez plays an elaborately made-up Russian woman dressed in a feathered hat, cat-eye glasses and long fur coat. She strikes a snooty yet demure pose as she holds a delicate chain on the tip of her extended index finger: the leash of her babushka. To the left, Jesus Rasquachi is sporting a thick black moustache and dressed in the *campesino* uniform of a flannel shirt and trucker hat. Kneeling in-between the upper-class Russian woman and the male *campesino*, Calavera appears to lack their distinct gendered, sexed and raced identities. In this photo tableau, the body of Valdez is transmitting only in terms of her characterisation of the *calavera* creature; Valdez's own body and identity does not influence or augment her portrayal as it does for the actors who flank her. In fact, Calavera is purposefully posed on the floor, head cocked to the side and tongue out, in contrast to the more traditional representations of flexing *machismo* and delicate femininity that surround it. The most human thing this *calavera* character does is speak to Jesus Rasquachi. Of course, Calavera is a villain, so it is only to berate him.

In other photographs from this production, Calavera has morphed out of its villain persona and is elaborately bowing to its 'partner in crime' Diablo. As Calavera, Valdez extends her hands in the air and, while one leg is pointed towards the audience, her other leg is bent down to facilitate a deep and sweeping bow.[65] In another photo, Valdez is tensed and crouching with knees bent and hands poised to strike. She faces the audience, the black hollows around her eyes creating a striking contrast to her white mask and fully open mouth.[66] In these photos, Valdez freely uses the full range of her body: she crouches, points her legs, shapes her body into an 'S', extends her arms and thrusts her chin forward. Her *calavera* leotard does not conceal her physical form, which is 'marked' with secondary sex characteristics.[67] While performing these elaborate full body movements, Valdez's costume in no way hides her bottom and hips, her short but curving figure and her breasts. But if her *calavera* costume were loose fitting or accompanied by a heavy cloak so that the shape of her body was less evident, she would not be able to create such elaborate characterisations.

And even if audiences could not visually identify her by shape, they certainly had other means to identify and classify Valdez. By 1978, Valdez was known as a prominent and skilled player in Teatro Campesino productions; at least some individuals would be familiar with her work and repertoire of characters. Hand bills, posters and programmes with her name would also serve to identify her as a Chicana woman. Although Valdez is enacting a character that has no specific gender, sex or ethnicity, her own signification would be readily available to audience members. But Valdez did not need to conceal herself in order to legitimise her performance or attract audiences. *Calavera* characters were a continual part of the Teatro Campesino repertoire specifically because they were such familiar and beloved symbols. As Rodriguez explains, the *calavera* 'is a very universal symbol … It's a symbol that is very strong, and that our race is not afraid of'.[68] Therefore, in her characterisation, the embodied identity of Valdez is only relevant in terms of her physical ability to enact the *calavera* creature. While Valdez's distinct body and cultural identity never truly disappears, the universal neutrality of the character itself negates any need for her to be classified, represented or otherwise implicated in the act. These gender-bending roles allowed performers to enact gender or racial displays if they wished but also allowed them the leeway to create and enact a character apart from hegemonic cultural definitions.

Bending the gender roles of the *teatristas*: '*en unas pocas centurias*, the future will belong to the *mestiza*'[69]

In *Borderlands/La Frontera*, Anzaldúa explains that in order to achieve *mestiza* consciousness, Chicanas must 'break down the subject-object duality that keeps [them] prisoner' and create space for polymorphic movement.[70] *Mestiza* consciousness therefore depends on an awareness of subject positions as well as the ability to mobilise those positions as a 'necessary prelude to political change'.[71] Evidence in the Teatro Campesino archives demonstrates how *teatristas* achieved mestiza consciousness not only by enacting gender-bending characters but also by actively reworking the characters themselves. Broyles-Gonzalez's short discussion of gender-bending critiques the stifling and racially-masking nature of the costumes.[72] During a *Nine AM Morning Show* interview with Lillian Rojas, *teatrista* Olivia Chumacero models the style of *calavera* costume that was being used in the 1980 production of *El Fin Del Mundo*: a light-coloured leotard with a cartoonish skeleton shape painted down the front. Several archival snapshots show Chumacero in this costume during and after a European run of this production. Unlike her interview appearance, Chumacero is in full makeup in these photos. She sports black-rimmed eyes, white and black defined features and two rows of long skeletal teeth surrounding her mouth painted in a style similar to that of Valdez's Calavera in *La Carpa de los Rasquachis*.[73] But the significant difference between Chumacero's costume for this production and Valdez's costume for *La Carpa* is that Chumacero does not wear the half-mask over her face and head that Valdez did.

The half-mask worn by Valdez in *La Carpa* undoubtedly stifled her ability to act with her entire face. But during the *Nine AM Morning Show* interview, Chumacero holds one of these *calavera* half-masks in her hand and explains,

> But now we don't use the mask; we have makeup. And it's very interesting because you can use your entire face for your expressions. It's really interesting. Before we went from half-mask, half *calavera* mask, and the lower part was makeup. And now we do the entire face and it's just great.

Her interviewer, Lillian Rojas, exclaims 'now you get to use the whole body'.[74] While still portraying a sex-, gender- and race-neutral figure, the transition from mask to makeup allowed *teatristas* more flexibility in how they could enact these characters.

I assert that the *teatristas* contributed to and perhaps even instigated this shift in how *calavera* characters were costumed. It is obvious from archival records that *teatristas* took on many technical production roles in Teatro Campesino; programmes and fliers list *teatristas* as directors, assistant directors, choreographers, lighting designers, technical directors, music designers, musicians and costume designers. In fact, almost every programme from 1977 to 1980 lists Diane Rodriguez as a costumer or costume designer. In the second segment of the *Nine AM Morning Show*, Chumacero explains that 'we have a costume lady in our company. Her name's Diane Rodriguez and usually she's the one that gets everything together and makes it'.[75] It is a fair assumption that Rodriguez – herself a performer of these *calavera* roles – had influence in the decision to shift *calavera* costumes from half-masks in 1978 to makeup in 1980. This costume choice not only allowed *teatristas* more physical performance flexibility, it also exemplifies their active pursuit of performance flexibility.

Discussing her own *calavera* character on the *Nine AM Morning Show*, Chumacero notes that many of the *calavera* characters in this production have distinct personality characteristics. Chumacero announces that her character is named La Flaca because the skeletal bones on her costume are painted thinly. Used as a title or name rather than an adjective, La Flaca employs a gendered article and noun to indicate a feminine or female person.[76] But *calaveras* were actualised through the actor's own creativity and improvisation; as Broyles-González explains, 'to play a role or character … meant literally to create a character by improvising it to life, bringing it to life virtually from scratch'.[77] Therefore, the most accurate information as to what type of *calavera* La Flaca is must come from Chumacero's own interpretation and performance. During the interview, Chumacero herself translates her character's title from Spanish into English not as 'the thin woman' but gender-neutrally as 'the thin one'.[78] Because these parts were creatively built and performed by the individual actor, Chumacero's verbal interpretation best represents the character's signification. And while several *calaveras* in *El Fin Del Mundo* do perform gender and race (like Valdez's Huesos), neither Chumacero's translation of her character nor her costume can be singularly or distinctly categorised. Although she could enact this character in an identifiable way, Chumacero's explanation makes it clear that she has chosen for herself how this character will be performed.

Moving toward a *mestiza* discourse on Teatro Campesino's *teatristas*

The bodies of the Teatro Campesino *teatristas* are at once sites of gendered, sexed and raced specificity and also their means of mobilising these boundaries and inhabiting a new consciousness. El Movimiento established a powerful front of solidarity by perpetuating an identity of difference. Removed from pejorative or marginalised connotations of race or class, *Chicanismo* projects proudly invoked history, culture and *indigenismo* 'in the construction of an exclusionary, singular Chicano identity'.[79] But while this separatist consciousness has been framed as subsuming Chicana experience, I argue that even within the borders of Teatro Campesino, 'the construction of an inclusive multiple' Chicana consciousness is evident.[80] More than simply an alternative performance option, gender-bending was *the* performance option for Chicanas to traverse a pejorative, exclusionary or otherwise singular subjectivity and inhabit a plural identity.

By working toward *la causa* through established Chicano TENAZ artistic outlets, *teatristas* likely did find their voices and contributions marginalised or subsumed under the banner of solidarity. And a relational theory of difference must acknowledge the inherent essentialism in Chicanas' gendered and raced heritage, cultural roles and social positions. But I assert that the gender-bending work of the *teatristas* demonstrates their awareness of and embodiment of these identity borders as well as their active production of a plural identity, and further their tolerance for this position of ambiguity and duality. To re-quote Rodriguez, 'we could have walked away, but we stayed because we believed we were moving a community to self-empowerment through art'.[81] While the sexist organisational structures and scripted roles in Teatro Campesino and El Movimiento are an important part of the story, so are the ways *teatristas* both embodied and mobilised those structures. *Teatristas* had the tools actively to complicate and expand their singular positions in the troupe: gender-bending characters. These roles represented a significant opportunity for them both within the troupe repertoire and also as 'agents of action and radical change' within El Movimiento.[82] By actively taking on and evolving gender-bending parts, the women of Teatro Campesino created a more flexible position for themselves as Chicanas, as members of *teatro* arts and as La Raza (the race).

By approaching the study of Teatro Campesino's *teatristas* through multiracial feminist analysis, my goal has been to uncover acts of *mestiza* consciousness in a performance methodology that combined liminality with plurality. As Anzaldúa writes, it is 'only by remaining flexible [that the *mestiza*] is able to stretch the psyche horizontally and vertically'.[83] While audiences may have been aware that Socorro Valdez, Diane Rodriguez, Olivia Chumacero or the other *teatristas* were Chicanas, when these women played gender-bending roles their acting bodies were unconstrained by such definitional borders. But rather than losing their subjectivity in these performances, they became blended or hybrid figures, at once possessing biological and cultural specificity and also inhabiting a space of difference. By focusing on the gender-bending performances of the *teatristas* as well as their active evolution of these characters, a clearer picture of these women and their specific contributions can be introduced into the historiography of Teatro Campesino.

Notes

I wish to thank Ariel Schindewolf, Karen Lunsford, Christina McMahon, Carlos Morton, Rose Elfman, Maxine Heller and the anonymous referees for their help and advice. Versions of this article were presented at the *Necessary Theatre* conference at the University of California, Santa Barbara, the *Anxieties of Overexposure* conference at the University of California, Los Angeles and the Latino Focus Group at the Association for Theatre in Higher Education.

1. El Teatro Campesino, *El Teatro Campesino: The Evolution of America's First Chicano Theatre Company 1965–1985* (San Juan Bautista: El Teatro Campesino Inc, 1985), p. 7.
2. El Teatro Campesino, *El Teatro Campesino*, p. 7.
3. The translation of El Teatro Campesino as 'the farm worker's theatre' is generally accepted in academia and the public press. However, the word *campesino* is literally translated as rural person or country peasant.
4. Expressions of *Chicanismo* and *indigenismo* in the United States are generally artistic (visual or literary) and focus on the connection to Chicano or Mexican religious and historical legacies as well as promote pride in contemporary cultural practices.
5. See Diana Taylor's introduction in Diana Taylor and Juan Villegas (eds), *Negotiating Performance: Gender, Sexuality and Theatricality in Latin/o Theatre* (Durham: Duke University Press, 1994), pp. 1–16;

Margaret Rose, 'Traditional and Nontraditional Patterns of Female Activism in the United Farm Workers of America, 1962 to 1980', *Frontiers* 11 (1990), pp. 26–32.

6. Taylor, *Negotiating Performance*, p. 5.
7. See Yvonne Yarbro-Bejarano, 'Chicanas Experience in Collective Theatre: Ideology and Form', *Women & Performance: A Journal of Feminist Theory* 2, 2 (1985), pp. 45–58; 'The Female Subject in Chicano Theatre: Sexuality, "Race", and Class', *Theatre Journal* 38 (1986), pp. 389–407. Yolanda Broyles-González, 'Women in El Teatro Campesino: 'Apoco estaba molacha La Virgen de Guadalupe?', in Teresa Cordova et al. (eds), *Chicana Voices: Intersections of Class Race and Gender* (Austin: CMAS Publications, 1986), pp. 162–87; Yolanda Broyles-González, 'Toward a Re-Vision of Chicano Theatre History: The Women of El Teatro Campesino', in Lynda Hart et al. (eds), *Making a Spectacle: Feminist Essays on Contemporary Women's Theatre* (Ann Arbor: University of Michigan Press, 1989), pp. 209–37; Yolanda Broyles-González, 'The Living Legacy of Chicana Performers: Preserving History through Oral Testimony', *Frontiers* 11 (1990), pp. 46–52; Yolanda Broyles-González, forward to Laura E. Garcia, Sandra M. Gutierrez, and Felicitas Nuñez (eds), *Teatro Chicana: A Collective Memoir and Selected Plays* (Austin: University of Texas Press, 2008), pp. x–xviii.
8. Teatro Nacional de Aztlán (hereafter TENAZ) was the umbrella term for many Chicano theatre troupes operating in the United States during the 1960s and the 1970s.
9. Yolanda Broyles-Gonzlez, *El Teatro Campesino: Theater in the Chicano Movement* (Austin: University of Texas Press, 1994), p. 132.
10. Broyles-González, 'The Living Legacy of Chicana Performers', p. 47. Broyles-González uses *teatrista* specifically to refer to female performers in Teatro Campesino. While she interviewed both female and male troupe members, only *teatristas*' accounts appear in her published work. She explains that the *teateros* did not talk about gender issues enough to make their testimonial useful to her project. *El Teatro Campesino*, p. 134.
11. Yolanda Broyles-González, 'The Powers of Women's Words: Oral Tradition and Performance Art', in Juan Flores and Renato Rosaldo (eds), *A Companion to Latina/o Studies* (Malden: Blackwell Pub, 2007), pp. 116–25, here p. 120. After being specifically commissioned for the Renato Rosaldo lecture series, Broyles-González's talk was not published in its yearly monograph and does not appear in archival lists. The conflict between Broyles-González and Valdez serves as just one example of the larger pattern of contention between male and female Chicano studies scholars in the 1980s and early 1990s.
12. Broyles-González, *El Teatro Campesino*, pp. 140, 144.
13. Diane Rodriguez, interview with Broyles-González, 'The Living Legacy of Chicana Performers', p. 51.
14. Broyles-González, *El Teatro Campesino*, p. 144.
15. Diane Rodriguez, correspondence with Maria Teresa Marrero, 'Out of the Fringe? Out of the Closet', *The Drama Review* 44, no. 3 (2000), pp. 121–53, here p. 134.
16. Chela Sandoval, *Methodology of the Oppressed* (Minneapolis: University of Minnesota Press, 2000).
17. Emma Pérez, *The Decolonial Imaginary: Writing Chicanas into History* (Bloomington: Indiana University Press, 1999), p. xvi.
18. Alicia Arrizón, *Queering Mestizaje: Transculturation and Performance* (Ann Arbor: University of Michigan Press, 2006), p. 3.
19. Yvonne Yarbro-Bejarano, 'Gloria Anzaldúa's *Borderlands/La Frontera*: Cultural Studies, "Difference", and the Non-Unitary Subject', *Cultural Critique* 28 (1994), pp. 5–28, here p. 11.
20. Gloria Anzaldúa, *Borderlands/La Frontera: The New Mestiza* (San Francisco: Aunt Lute Books, 1987), p. 77.
21. Cherríe L. Moraga, 'Entering the Lives of Others: Theory in the Flesh' in Cherríe L. Moraga and Gloria Anzaldúa (eds), *This Bridge Called My Back: Writings by Radical Women of Color* (Berkeley: Third Woman Press, 2002), pp. 21–2, here p. 21.
22. Housed by the California Ethnic and Multicultural Archives (hereafter CEMA) at the University of California, Santa Barbara's (UCSB) Davidson Library, the El Teatro Campesino archives (1964–1988) contain personal, performance and publicity photographs, audio and video, unpublished scripts with handwritten notes, graphic art and designs, newspaper clippings, programmes, posters and internal paperwork. Closed after Broyles-González's research residency, the archives were transferred to UCSB in the late 1980s. In 1985, archivist Andres V. Gutierrez wrote that 'the formal relationship we are establishing with the University will provide for the preservation of the Archives and the increased availability of the collection for *legitimate scholarly research*' (italics mine). In late 2009, these archives became accessible for 'general scholarly research'. El Teatro Campesino, *El Teatro Campesino*, p. 44.
23. Steven P. Schacht and Lisa Underwood, 'The Absolutely Flawless but Flawlessly Customary World of Drag Queens and Female Impersonators', in Steven P. Schacht and Lisa Underwood (eds), *The Drag Queen Anthology* (New York: Harrington Park Press, 2004), pp. 1–18, here p. 4.

24. Diane Rodriguez, interview by Broyles-González, 'The Living Legacy of Chicana Performers', p. 50.

25. Socorro Valdez, interview by Broyles-González, *El Teatro Campesino*, p. 149. *Pachuco* does not have a direct English equivalent but might be historically generalised as a male youth who participated in urban street gangs. *Calavera* is technically translated as 'skull' but the word for skeleton, *esqueleto*, is far less commonly used. Many examples from the Teatro Campesino archives and scholarly writing translate this word as 'skeleton'.

26. Elizabeth Grosz, *Volatile Bodies: Toward a Corporeal Feminism* (Bloomington: Indiana University Press, 1994), p. 188.

27. Sue-Ellen Case, 'Classic Drag: The Greek Creation of Female Parts', *Theatre Journal* 37 (1985), pp. 317–27.

28. Yolanda Yarbro-Bejarano, 'The Image of the Chicana in Teatro', in Jo Cochran, J. T. Stewart and Mayumi Tsutakawa (eds), *Gathering Ground: New Writing and Art by Northwest Women of Color* (Seattle: The Seal Press, 1984), pp. 90–96, here p. 94.

29. Broyles-González, *El Teatro Campesino*, pp. 135–6.

30. Luis Valdez and El Teatro Campesino, *Actos* (San Juan Bautista: Cucaracha Publications, 1971).

31. Broyles-González, *El Teatro Campesino*, p. 140.

32. Broyles-González, *El Teatro Campesino*, p. 140.

33. Broyles-González, *El Teatro Campesino*, p. 134.

34. Charlotte Canning, 'Constructing Experience: Theorizing Feminist Theatre History', *Theatre Journal* 45 (1993), pp. 529–40, here p. 534.

35. Laura D. Nielsen, review of *El Teatro Campesino: Theater in the Chicano Movement*, by Yolanda Broyles-González, *Theatre Journal* 48 (1996), p. 388.

36. José Esteban Muñoz, review of *El Teatro Campesino: Theater in the Chicano Movement*, by Yolanda Broyles-González, *The Drama Review* 41, no. 1 (1997), pp. 155–8, here p. 156.

37. Mary Pat Brady, review of *El Teatro Campesino: Theater in the Chicano Movement*, by Yolanda Broyles-González, *Signs* 23 (1998), pp. 1090–93, here pp. 1091, 1092.

38. Brady, review, p. 1092.

39. Manuscript of chapter three, Yolanda Broyles-González, *El Teatro Campesino: Four Cardinal Points*, 8 October 1990, p. 62. CEMA 97, Box 1.

40. Sandoval, *Methodology of the Oppressed*, p. 58.

41. Pérez, *The Decolonial Imaginary*, p. xvi.

42. El Teatro Campesino, *El Teatro Campesino*, p. 4.

43. Anzaldúa, *Borderlands/La Frontera*, p. 80.

44. Diane Rodriguez, interview by UCLA librarian Paulina Sahagun, San Juan Bautista, 1983. CEMA 5, Series 9.

45. Yarbro-Bejarano, 'The Female Subject in Chicano Theatre', p. 389.

46. Socorro Valdez is the younger sister of Teatro Campesino figurehead Luis Valdez. For the purposes of this article, I refer to her by last name only and Luis Valdez by first and last name.

47. Diane Rodriguez interview. CEMA 5, Series 9.

48. Marrero, 'Out of the Fringe?', p. 134.

49. Phil Esperanza, interview by Leticia Ponce, *Catch 2: Los Vendidos*, Denver, KWGN, ch. 2, 1976. CEMA 5, Series 5.

50. Prevalent in Mexican mythos and culture, *calaveras* are skeletal apparitions that symbolise a spiritual connection between the world of the living and that of the dead or the unknown. *Calaveras* are important elements in Día de los Muertos (Day of the Dead) celebrations and appear frequently in the artwork of Mexican illustrator José Guadalupe Posada.

51. While human skeletal structures are medically classified as male or female based on pelvic shape and size, the bones painted on *calaveras* costumes are too simplistic to indicate biological sex.

52. *Tramos* (peg leg) trousers are part of the zoot suit look popular among young male Chicanos in Los Angeles during the 1930s and the 1940s. This reference is from a costume sketch by Peter J. Hall in a playbill for a Los Angeles production of *Zoot Suit*. CEMA 5 Series 14, Box 9, Folder 6.

53. Photograph of Socorro Valdez in *El Fin del Mundo* European tour, 1980. CEMA 5, Series 6, Box 8, Folder 5, photograph # 59.

54. Photograph of Socorro Valdez in *El Fin del Mundo* European tour, 1980. CEMA 5, Series 6, Box 8, Folder 6, photograph #70A and Box 9, Folder 1, photograph #75.

55. Photograph of Socorro Valdez in *El Fin del Mundo* European tour, 1980. CEMA 5, Series 6, Box 8, Folder 5, photograph #59.

56. Broyles-González, *El Teatro Campesino*, p. 129.

57. Socorro Valdez interview, *El Teatro Campesino*, p. 150.
58. Gloria E. Anzaldúa, 'La Prieta' in Moraga and Anzaldúa, *This Bridge Called My Back*, pp. 220–33, here p. 232.
59. Moya Lloyd, *Beyond Identity Politics: Feminism, Power and Politics* (London: Sage Publications, 2005), p. 48.
60. Phil Esperanza interview. CEMA 5, Series 5.
61. Phil Esperanza interview. CEMA 5, Series 5.
62. Socorro Valdez interview, *El Teatro Campesino*, p. 149.
63. The title *La Carpa de los Rasquachis* cannot be translated in a direct way. *Carpa* means tent but I believe the title refers to *carpa* performances popular in the Southwestern United States and Mexico. In a 1973 script, *Rasquachis* is translated as the lifestyle of the oppressed: run-down, dirty, poor, crude and short. CEMA 5, Series 1, Box 13, Folder 5.
64. Photograph of Socorro Valdez in *La Carpa de Los Rasquachis*, 1976. CEMA 5, Series 6, Box 12, Folder 4, photograph #18.
65. Photograph of Socorro Valdez in *La Carpa de Los Rasquachis*, 1976. CEMA 5, Series 6, Box 12, Folder 3, photographs #5 and #10.
66. Photograph of Socorro Valdez in *La Carpa de Los Rasquachis*, 1976. CEMA 5, Series 6, Box 12, Folder 3, photograph #15.
67. Peggy Phelan, *Unmarked: The Politics of Performance* (London: Routledge, 1993).
68. Diane Rodriguez, interview by Leticia Ponce, *Catch 2: Los Vendidos*, Denver, KWGN, ch. 2, 1976. CEMA 5, Series 5.
69. Anzaldúa, *Borderlands/La Frontera*, p. 80.
70. Anzaldúa, *Borderlands/La Frontera*, p. 81.
71. Yarbro-Bejarano, 'Gloria Anzaldua's *Borderlands/La Frontera*', p. 13.
72. Broyles-González, *El Teatro Campesino*, p. 152.
73. Photograph of Olivia Chumacero in *El Fin Del Mundo*, European tour, 1980. CEMA 5, Series 6, Box 8, Folder 3, photographs #2 and #7.
74. Olivia Chumacero, interview with Lillian Rojas, *Nine AM Morning Show: Part II*, Monterey, KMST, ch.46. 27 March 1980. CEMA 5, Series 5.
75. Olivia Chumacero interview, *Nine AM Morning Show*. CEMA 5, Series 5.
76. The translation of this term has been discussed with Ariel Schindewolf, a doctoral candidate in Hispanic Linguistics at UCSB. Ariel Schindewolf, personal interview, 2 June 2011.
77. Broyles-González, *El Teatro Campesino*, p. 150.
78. Olivia Chumacero, interview, *Nine AM Morning Show*. CEMA 5, Series 5.
79. Yarbro-Bejarano, 'Gloria Anzaldua's *Borderlands/La Frontera*', p. 12.
80. Yarbro-Bejarano, 'Gloria Anzaldua's *Borderlands/La Frontera*', p. 12.
81. Marrero, 'Out of the Fringe?', p. 134.
82. Kirsten F. Nigro, 'Inventions and Transgressions: a Fractured Narrative on Feminist Theatre in Mexico', in Taylor and Villegas, *Negotiating Performance*, pp. 137–58, p. 138.
83. Anzaldúa, *Borderlands/La Frontera*, p. 79.

12 Changing Paradigms in Migration Studies: From Men to Women to Gender

Nancy L. Green

Over the last four decades, research has moved from the 'discovery' of immigration as a topic of the new social history to another discovery. Initially conceptualised as a story of largely male workers, whose mobility formed and forms an integral part of modern capitalism, migration history then 'found' female migrants. Consideration of their productive and reproductive work and closer attention to the gender composition of migration streams have thus become increasingly important aspects of migration studies, a veritable 'tidal wave'.[1] From Michael Piore's *Birds of Passage* in 1979 to Mirjana Morokvasic's forceful reminder that 'Birds of Passage are Also Women' in 1984 to Katharine Donato et al.'s recent evaluation of the field, migration studies have evolved substantially since the 1980s.[2] Using the United States and France, two major historical sites of labour immigration, I aim to push our thinking further, asking questions of both one and a half centuries of immigration history and of four decades of historiography in order to explore the ways in which states, societies, individuals, groups and researchers have conceptualised mobility along gendered lines. Migration studies may be seen as an example of how different epistemologies – themselves changing over time – have brought new ways of understanding mobility.

Both the United States and France were major countries of immigration from the nineteenth century onward. Both provide similar stories of immigration, albeit with somewhat different timelines of installation, integration and oscillating periods of welcome and rejection. The point of this article is not to compare and contrast the two countries (which I have done elsewhere) but to use examples from their relatively similar histories of immigration to further question our ways of 'knowing' migration patterns and experiences.[3] The choice of other historic countries of immigration (Canada or Australia, Argentina or Brazil) would undoubtedly inflect the analysis differently, but the reliance on the US and French historiographies is merely meant to raise questions about our ways of understanding migration which can then be compared to other cases. In both countries, with the development of migration studies in the last forty years, the first level of knowledge came with a focus on male migrants and their labour markets. A second series of historiographic studies questioned that vision and focused on immigrant women as another way of understanding migration. As I will further argue, it is the

Gender History Across Epistemologies, First Edition. Edited by Donna R. Gabaccia and Mary Jo Maynes.
Chapters © 2013 The Authors. Book compilation © 2013 Blackwell Publishing Ltd.

changing epistemologies of gender studies which today bring yet newer questions – and answers – to the field. These are as much the result of our shifting ways of knowing than of anything inherent in the subject itself.

Histories and historiographies of immigration

The history and historiography of migration each have their own distinct temporalities. The general histories of immigration both to the United States and to France are now well known.[4] From the perspective of the United States alone, mid-nineteenth century rural homesteading and railroad expansion brought northern European immigrants to the country via eastern seaports and Chinese immigrants via western seaports, while the industrialisation and urbanisation of the country later in the century drew eastern and southern Europeans across the Atlantic. From the perspective of the sending countries, population pressures and social and religious discontent 'sent' millions overseas. Yet as labour needs were fulfilled in the United States, first Chinese workers were barred from entry (Chinese Exclusion Act of 1882), and then the arrival of eastern and southern Europeans was drastically limited with the quota legislation of the 1920s that halted mass immigration for decades to come. Changing laws and changing origins of immigrants subsequently transformed the American population: after the 1965 Immigration and Nationality Act significantly altered the rules for entry, the last part of the twentieth century saw a significant renewal of the United States population through immigration from Latin America and Asia.

France, in the meantime, became a precocious European importer (instead of exporter) of labour from the late nineteenth century on. It first attracted its immediate northern neighbours – Germans and Belgians – in the second half of the nineteenth century. It then began actively recruiting other European immigrants, especially from Italy and Poland, to work in mining and metallurgy both before and especially after the First World War. As the United States closed its borders in the early 1920s, France's doors remained open until the Depression. After the Second World War, the thirty years of post-war prosperity was largely fuelled by workers from Spain and Portugal and from the French colonies, especially in North Africa. Although labour immigration was halted in the mid-1970s, refugees and labourers from China, Turkey and sub-Saharan Africa have since diversified France's immigration population, constituting a melange of European, colonial and more distant origins.

The general history of immigration to the United States and France has been more similar over the long run than is usually recognised. Both countries have repeatedly engaged in heated debates about 'old' and 'new' immigrants, hailing past groups' long-term assimilation while forgetting the xenophobia that initially greeted even Catholic immigrants (Poles and Italians) in Catholic France. France's colonial past and its implications for colonial and postcolonial immigration may be seen as fundamentally different from the American immigration experience, yet there are also striking similarities in the treatment, perception and experiences of Mexican immigrants to the United States and North African immigrants to France.[5]

The questions we ask guide our research and writing. All three (questions, research, writing) change over time. There are epistemological trends. In migration studies, charting assimilation in the 1950s and 1960s gave way to a search for ethnicity in the 1970s and 1980s and an emphasis on transnationalism since the 1990s. The shift of language and focus from 'immigration' to 'migration' has drawn more attention to the ways in which people move back and forth across borders, joining borderland studies in emphasising the possibilities of multiple identities.[6] At the same time, scholarly approaches over the last four decades have shifted decisively from an unacknowledged focus on men to a forceful foregrounding of women to an emphasis on gender construction and relations. Each way of knowing has, furthermore, produced different knowledge about states, labour markets, communities and individuals. How, then, have all of the waves of newcomers to the United States and to France been accounted for, and in what ways have the explanations themselves been gendered?

In both countries macro-explanations for immigration have most often been closely linked to industrialisation. The male factory worker was, and often still is, the first image that comes to mind when the historic 'immigrant worker' is evoked either in the United States or France. Even though foreign homesteaders (in the United States) preceded him and immigrant service workers (in the United States and France) have succeeded him, the immigrant factory worker was central to the understanding of the new social history of immigration that took off in the 1970s in the United States and a decade later in France. The field emerged out of labour history in both countries with a longer commitment to gender-blind class analyses in France, and the 'discovery' of immigrant workers was a way of looking at diversity within the working class and within the nation state itself.

But at the same time, another branch of the new social history was asking different questions about social relations: what about women? While immigration history was pointing to ethnic diversity within the working class, women's history, especially in the United States, was pointing to gendered divisions across the board. Both historiographies sought explicitly to question a monolithic vision of 'the working class' and to make visible the invisible. In the case of immigrant women, the timing of historiography and history most clearly diverged in the United States. Women had been a majority of the immigration streams since the 1930s in the United States, but they were not 'discovered' until feminist historians started looking for and found them.[7] In France, the feminisation of immigration waves was later historically. It occurred in the 1970s, largely due to the halt of – male – labour migration while family reunification was still allowed. It was thus largely concomitant with both the feminist movement in France and sociologists there asking new questions.[8] The immigrant woman thus became a subject of study in her own right from the 1970s on, although more precociously in the United States than in France. 'Adding' women to the migration story was partly a function of studying community formation. Yet it also led to new knowledge about different labour markets (such as textiles, garments and domestic work), different forms of oppression and different forms of agency. Whereas Hasia Diner's early work on Irish domestics in the United States was a first boost to the historical study of immigrant women in the US, the history of domestic work in France was, for years, tied to a different paradigm, that of the 'rural exodus' of provincial women migrating to the city. Only recently have dissertations been undertaken in France to study the history of foreign – Luxembourgeois or Swiss – domestics there.[9]

The different timing of the development of both women's and gender studies in the United States and in France has been a source of discussion in its own right, linked to different political and institutional cultures, reflecting longer emphasis on class analyses and a much more splintered feminism in France. However, even with the French 'lag' (a comparative notion) recognised and oft-lamented, I would argue that generally speaking, over the last forty years, scholars of immigration history in both the United States and France have moved from male-dominated tales of the first wave of historiography to a more female focused second wave of knowing migration, to a current framework of gender. The differences in historiographic timing – French historiography, due to its 'lag' may, in fact, have largely skipped over the second stage – show how epistemologies may be ignored or resisted from one setting to another, but also can themselves migrate. French scholars long debated and sometimes contested the importation of American gender models and methods, but in migration history the general, if slower, shift from men to women to gender has taken place as well, while in both countries immigrant women's history and gendered histories of migration continue to coexist.[10]

Gender

Although Simone de Beauvoir launched the gender question with her famous statement that one is not born a woman but becomes one, it was arguably Joan Scott's influential 1986 article, 'Gender: A Useful Category of Historical Analysis', that became the compelling late twentieth-century reference for the new gender studies among historians, launching an epistemological tidal wave.[11] As applied to migration history, a gendered approach has thus raised new questions. Whereas earlier queries were grounded in a more structuralist epistemology questioning class, capitalism and the labour market, more recent questions seek to understand the gendered constructions and interactions of the migration phenomenon both at the state and individual levels, and show how gender too can be a shifting category of difference. We may ask not only how men and women have experienced immigration with different expectations and strategies, but also how lawmakers, border officials and employers have imagined and defined a normative immigrant worker at the gates. Furthermore, historians themselves have at times implicitly construed migration as male and at other times as female. I would argue that gender studies are not and should not be seen in competition with women's history. A new history of gender and migration that takes into account who came, when and why is men's history, women's history and gender history at the same time. It is a question of social history, of representations and relationships and of individuals' lives across space and in movement that can help us better understand the history of migration itself. 'Gender and migration' has become a conference catchword in the United States (even if sometimes only masking the foregrounding of women's roles and experiences). Donato et al. have emphasised the need to push the concept of gender forward as a more encompassing way of knowing the immigrant experience. In France (De Beauvoir notwithstanding), the new gender studies have come perhaps more belatedly to the academy, but there too they are making their way as a new focus of immigration research.[12]

The term 'gender' has itself often come to be used in a variety of ways within migration history and in other fields. It is sometimes simply a misnomered shorthand for telling the story of women. Joan Scott herself has lamented the overly dispersed use of the term.[13] More theoretically, the term is used to analyse the social construction of the categories women or men, but 'gender' may also refer to the social interactions between men and women. Rather than foreswear the many uses of the term, this multiplicity of meanings may be applied to immigration history, using French and American examples, in order to ask four sets of questions that can produce different types of knowledge about migration.

First of all, numbers count in either a 'men's' or 'women's' history of migration. Indeed, they help complicate either history. How many women and men migrated? A sense of the numbers is important because the sex ratios help explain not only who migrates. They also reveal gendered ratios; that is, we can use the figures to help understand how migration has been conceptualised by state and society. The second question thus has to do with the representations of migrants and migration. We can ask, for example, to what extent xenophobic fears are gendered, imagining and targeting male and female immigrants differently. The subsequent questions deal with the before and after of the migration process itself. How has gender had an impact on migration, on who leaves and who does not? And, fourth, how does migration have an impact on gender relations? How do periods of absence and shifting labour roles affect families or construct new identities for solo migrants? It is the researchers' agenda as much as the activities of the immigrants themselves that have shaped our ways of knowing mobility patterns. By moving from immigration as a male story to highlighting the women who have migrated, to studying the gendered representations and relationships that cause and accompany migration, I would argue that all three epistemologies are necessary in order to continue to deepen our understanding of the category 'immigrant'.

The figures

Counting is not everything, but it is an important start for knowledge about migration patterns. Numbers have been used to chart general migration streams, largely according to nationality. Sex ratios have most often been used to point to the more or less familial make up of different national communities. However, we can go further in order to use sex ratios as important indicators that reveal certain gendered aspects of the meaning of migration itself – the reasons for or the constraints on movement and settling.[14] The numbers of men and women who have left one country for another are a first indication of the ways in which migration is not a uniform act. The figures do not necessarily explain how, or the circumstances and choices of leaving, but breaking down the migration phenomenon demographically allows greater insight into the experience itself. Women may have migrated as daughters or as wives, alone or with their families, simultaneously with the men or in a follow-up migration stream after taking care of selling off the family farm or business. We cannot always know who made the decision to leave. Was it women urging men to go forth, men seeking to better family circumstances or collective decisions based on a family economy? What about female adventurers or single women seeking jobs or mates? If it is difficult to be sure of motives, we can identify who left, or at least those who arrived.

What is striking are the myriad ways of interpreting the data. The data first of all show the obvious: men and women do not leave in the same proportions. The corollary is that migration skews gender ratios both at home and among those same populations at the point of destination. The second most frequent observation until recently was that men migrate more than women, although early migration analyst E. G. Ravenstein observed that it depended on destination: distance matters.[15] Women may move a lot, but over shorter spaces. Here, a Franco-American comparison is telling.

Only one-quarter of the Italian immigrant population in the United States was female in 1929, whereas in France, much closer geographically to Italy, there were, at that time, 42 per cent women among Italians.[16] Yet a consequence of the preponderance of male migrants in the nineteenth-century transatlantic migrations was that historians at first ignored female migrants – even though they could represent up to 30 or 40 per cent of many migration streams, hefty numbers under any circumstances. Third, and most recently, however, the interpretive focus has shifted to charting the moment of 'feminisation' of the migration streams, the period(s) when women immigrants become more numerous than men. The shift in composition of global migration figures over time is telling. As mentioned above, the number of women arriving in the United States exceeded the number of men arriving as of the 1930s; in France this occurred in the 1970s.[17] Two factors seem to explain this: labour markets and state policy.

Recognising that women too have been immigrant workers has, in both the United States and France, fundamentally shifted the very image of immigrants and immigrant work. Fields and factories have been peopled by foreign-born women too, ever since the nineteenth century. The textile factories in the northeast United States and northern France are but the most well-known examples. The migration streams in and of themselves reflect larger shifts in work patterns in both countries. Nineteenth-century male migrants moved towards male-defined jobs in mining, heavy industry or agricultural work, while late twentieth-century female immigrants help us understand not just the 'feminisation' of migration but the service-sectorisation of the west's economies as well.

Attention to general patterns of change over time may, however, mask more specific migration patterns by national origin or occupation. The sex ratios of the Irish in the United States in the nineteenth century or the German and Luxembourgeois in France in the late-nineteenth and early-twentieth centuries were strikingly female predominant well before the 'feminisation' of other groups' migration flows. As sex ratios they describe men and women, as gender ratios they help explain shifting categories of difference in migration and labour patterns. Domestic service has always attracted single women, and single – or married – women have sought such opportunities abroad. In France, provincial women from Brittany and other areas had migrated to the cities as part of nineteenth-century internal migration practices. In the northern United States (before the 'Great Migration' brought southern Blacks to the north), foreign women from the mid-nineteenth century on quickly filled this role.[18] Domestic workers are perhaps the female equivalent of foreign factory workers in that they have played an archetypical role in representing the image of their gender's 'migrant worker' for public authorities and for many historians alike. Male factory workers and female domestics, as categories, speak to the gendered construction of labour markets as much as to the migration flows themselves.

Yet gender ratios are analytic categories rather than simply fixed binaries of demographic sex ratios. And they are as much a result of state policy as of labour markets. If we return to the global figures, the reasons for the 'feminisation' of immigration in the United States after the 1930s and in France after the 1970s, were not only tied to the textile industry's or bourgeois women's need for help. It was also a secondary effect of state policies. The closing of borders (the United States Quota Laws of 1921 and 1924; the French suspension of labour immigration in 1974) affected the gendered makeup of subsequent immigration flows. It seems clear in hindsight that the

immigration restrictions were, among other things, a largely gendered process. By limiting the arrival of (male) workers while (grudgingly?) allowing family reunification,
the 'closure' policies in fact resulted in an increase in the percentage of women arriving
in the succeeding years. Whether this was explicitly anticipated by the legislators or not
needs more research. Dominique Daniel has argued, in effect, that United States legislators were anthropologically challenged; they did not understand the family structures
of the especially Asian and Hispanic populations that were allowed greater entry after
the 1965 law. It seems that in France as well, there was little discussion of a foreseeable
feminisation of immigration.[19] Just as employer policies of recruitment may construct
gender ratios, state policies barring immigrants have inflected the ratios in other ways.
When the United States Bracero Program recruited men only as guest workers, it made
family reunification very difficult. When immigration officials interpreted the Chinese
Exclusion Act, they especially excluded women. When French recruiters went to North
Africa to seek workers for their plants in the 1950s, it was men they sought, not women,
and the dormitories they built for them in France were male only. The shanty towns
that subsequently sprouted up were as much a result of lack of proper housing as due
to the gender imbalance of the initial recruitment and informal family reunification.[20]
State immigration and private employers' policies may thus be explicitly or implicitly
gendered; the result is visible in the figures of arrivals, but only if we ask the right
questions.

Representations

While an empirical approach to migration streams remains important, the last twenty
years of historiography have clearly shown the importance of combining it with a
cultural/constructivist approach to understanding historical phenomena. Just as a new
interpretation of gender ratios as analytic rather than static categories can lead to new
insights into the *results* of labour market mechanisms and state policies, an important
corollary question has to do with the ways in which immigrants have been *perceived*,
regardless of the numbers. The gendered imaginaries of immigration by the state are
particularly important to understand due to its power to set policy. Much has been written
about the creation of racial hierarchies of the desirable and the undesirable in the United
States and France. The early nationality quotas in the United States, in particular, were
based on the explicit undesirability of certain categories. The initial racialisation and
then the whitening of the European immigrants in the United States have been largely
explored.[21] Fears of miscegenation – whether between whites and blacks, whites and
Chinese, not to mention between Lithuanian Jews and Galizianer Jews – by state,
society or the immigrants themselves often underlay early twentieth-century notions
about immigration. In France, the long-term consequences of colonisation and colonial
and postcolonial migration to the metropole have been hotly debated, with a belated
and contested recognition of the racialisation of colonial workers. Although French
law never instituted national quotas, theorists and doctrinaires there also worried about
the 'races' most amenable to assimilation, and scholars have shown the inegalitarian
rationales behind specific measures and the hierarchies of favouritism by which to
state hoped to whiten the immigration streams in demographically challenged France.
Colonial and postcolonial immigration to France ('the empire strikes back') both loom

large in contemporary visions of immigration and are but a part of the complex 150-year history of immigration to France.[22]

Yet, in addition to racial or xenophobic differentiation, how have receiving states and societies imagined and constructed gendered scenarios of immigration and, importantly, how have these shifted over time? And how do sending states imagine (and worry about) the departure of male or female citizens?[23] The questions themselves help deepen our understanding of the history of migration (and of the labour force). The American and French need for an industrial workforce was clearly gendered in favour of men: male immigrants were recruited insofar as those jobs were designated 'male' jobs. The notable exceptions were recruitment to the textile factories that were defined as appropriate for and thus populated by women. The need for care service workers today genders work force and immigration needs in favour of women. In both cases, the gendered categories themselves have been socially constructed, with assumptions about inherent male or female characteristics linked to specific jobs. Yet gender stereotyping can change: there is nothing inherently stable in the definitions. Garment work can be considered 'female' until male immigrant garment workers arrive or metallurgy jobs can be defined as 'male' before they become deskilled and redefined as 'female'. Similarly, immigration streams can be represented as male or female depending on the period. But, at any given moment, employers and policy makers may join forces in their representations of who is needed and therefore who is welcome – or not welcome. Certain categories of women (or men) may strike fear in the wary eyes of immigration officials. In the nineteenth and early-twentieth centuries, at Ellis Island and other United States entry points, women travelling alone were seen with suspicion. New fears today in France focus on other types of women. Veiled North African women or under-dressed Eastern European women have become stigmatised symbols for fears of polygamy and prostitution, the imaginings of worst-case scenarios which have at times widened the circle of suspicion against women as a whole.[24] A gendered analysis of such representations is important in order to understand the constructed nature of the stereotypes.

By exploring gendered representations of migration and the ways in which they can change over time, three images (which hardly exhaust the possibilities) may summarise the ways in which the gender of migration has been constructed at different junctures through: (1) praise of manliness; (2) fear of sexuality in general, and of female sexuality or homosexuality in particular and (3) musings on marriage and migrating families. First, for most of the nineteenth and twentieth centuries, open door policies in both France and the United States seem to have been constructed largely in praise of the male immigrant, linked to the idea of the male worker coming forth to jobs, whether in field or factory. This would shift dramatically by the end of the twentieth century as de-industrialisation and the rise of the service sector redefined needs and henceforth favoured immigration streams of nurses and caregivers, which have been largely defined as female jobs. Second, one could argue that a corollary to the early masculine construction of labour market needs and the interpretation of the laws by immigration officials was suspicion about sex and the single woman. Yet fear of the female immigrant (whether representing prostitution in the United States, polygamy in France or miscegenation in both places) and praise of the male immigrant could also be reversed when migration was contemplated, third, as a familial project. A classic look at gender ratios links higher percentages of women to higher rates of family migration and thus to higher rates of staying on and lower rates of remigration – an assimilatory tale read through demographic statistics. Recent studies in the United States have looked at the ways in which homosexuality was barred at the United States borders. Margot Canaday has explored the sexuality of citizenship; Eithne Luibhéid and Erica Rand have argued convincingly that the classic immigrant image was resolutely heterosexual and familial, as is apparent in the iconic Ellis Island imagery.[25] In France, interwar immigration analyst Georges Mauco was explicit in hailing women as a stabilising force, and other contemporary observers went so far as to argue that it was a 'natural right' of men to have their families join them. For Mauco and others writing in early 1930s France, foreign women and families could aid in the assimilation of immigrant workers, helping attach them to the rural areas in which they first found work (rather than escaping to industrial jobs), not to mention helping redress France's long-standing demographic imbalance. For the Algerian War period, Todd Shepard has shown how immigration to France was also imagined within a heterosexual norm.[26]

Yet attention to a gendered epistemology of representation necessarily highlights the contradictory and changing images of immigrant women and immigrant families. Welcomed as a way of settling an otherwise too footloose male population, immigrant families have also been stigmatised at times. Both in France and the United States, the immigrant family has been seen as reinforcing traditional values and preventing assimilation. More work needs to be done in understanding the ways in which categories such as 'assimilation', 'modernisation' or 'tradition' have been gendered by legislators, polemicists, immigrants and historians alike. Assimilation, modernisation and participation in the labour force seem to have been largely constructed as male, while tradition has been construed as female – unless, on the contrary, family values are seen as a stabilising force ultimately aiding assimilation itself.[27]

All of these questions may be asked from another perspective as well, that of the sending countries. They too may have had gendered ways of envisioning those who leave, albeit often by constructing binary images of migration flows. Most nineteenth-century European countries that worried about the loss of potential soldiers or skilled workers largely imagined the emigrant as a man. But later and elsewhere, as women joined the flow, the maternalist dictatorships of Italy, Spain or Portugal worried about losing mothers, seen as literal reproducers of national identity.[28] The French and Italians fought over women discursively and with concrete incentives; the Italian government encouraged Italian women to stay at home or at least to return to Italy to have their babies (paying for the round trip), while French observers complained that Italian emigration policies were discouraging women from joining their husbands in France.[29]

Receiving or sending state policies, along with immigrants' own practices are thus embedded in a social construction of gender in which certain forms of behaviour are considered appropriate and others not. Migrating, taking leave of country and family, may be seen by home countries or individual families as being a traitor to home, hearth and country, or it may be seen as economically necessary and a welcome adventure, depending on who is doing it and in what context. Beyond state policies, we need to ask how emigrants have made their choices; with gendered expectations, or not? The assumption long prevalent that men move and women wait has been shown to be deeply flawed.[30] As a gender analysis of representations must show, migrants have often been imbedded in images that do not quite fit.

The turn to a gender analysis of migration thus asks new questions of mobility, labour markets and state policies that complement – rather than replace in my view – our knowledge of male factory workers and female domestic servants. While the stories of men and women immigrants remain valuable building blocks of knowledge that are themselves situated in important questions about class and community formation, new attention to gender ratios and representations of migrants complement class and race as ways of understanding mobility.

The impact of gender on migration

My last two questions address a different understanding of migration, the before and the after. First of all, how have gender relations in the countries of emigration affected the decision to depart? The importance of the family economy and family strategies as inducements to emigration have been well studied. Paid and unpaid economic roles for women, who have often been both wives and workers, but also the presence of 'house husbands' in the past, as today, have complicated our notions of a simple division of roles within the family. Gender history has in certain ways revisited family history, going beyond the complex description of multiple roles in order to question how decisions within families have been constructed, and with perhaps more attention to tensions within families as 'hierarchies of power' 'come to life within households'.[31] We can postulate that the forces encouraging leave-taking are themselves gendered, and that we need to return to the sending societies to understand the ways in which gender relations at home and not just receiving society policies or labour markets may encourage or discourage emigration. The French sociologist Abdelmalek Sayad argued early on for the importance of understanding emigration in order to understand immigration.[32] One of the major epistemological problems of migration history – or all of historical research for that matter – is that we only know about it after it happens. We infer causality from the perspective of hindsight. Scholars have examined the demographics, the economics and the social conditions of departure. But how have these factors been construed or constructed along gender lines? Primogeniture and inheritance laws in the nineteenth century, declining rural jobs in a time of agricultural concentration, proto-industrialisation or the colonised status of the sending countries have all had uneven impacts on differential labour opportunities and thus on the push to leave. Similarly, the gendered norms of 'traditional' societies clearly had an effect on the possibilities of departures. However, we must be careful not to exaggerate the meaning of 'traditional'. Different societies have encouraged or discouraged husbands, fathers, mothers or wives from leave-taking then and now. Who is sent away or who chooses to migrate, for labour, cultural or even matrimonial reasons?

'Matrimonial migration' is perhaps the most explicit example of the ways in which gender relations may cause mobility, although marriage may be either the cause or the result of migration. Beyond the affairs of the heart, marriage migration may be the best way to redress the demographic imbalances of migration in both the sending and receiving countries. Women may migrate to seek mates, as many Irish women did in the nineteenth century; as Irish men left en masse for industrial jobs in England, Irish women headed alone to the United States where there were more jobs for them and more men. But while single Irish women went to the United States looking (among other things) for spouses, some Eastern European Jewish men (among others) apparently went to the United States to escape theirs, as the missing husbands' notices in both the New York and Warsaw Yiddish newspapers attested.[33] Arranged marriages within organised transnational marriage markets may be a way of combining marriage and migration to get around legal immigration strictures and/or fostering group preservation while satisfying the needs of lonely immigrants and aspiring emigrants still at home. People can marry in order to migrate; state policies of family reunification inadvertently encourage it. The Japanese picture brides in the United States are the best known women who migrated in order to marry within a transnational but ethnically homogeneous marriage market, but the practice has existed within other groups as well. When Armenian women who survived the genocide were matched with Armenian men in Canada, the migration of those picture brides was meant to redress demographic imbalance both in the homeland and in the immigrant communities abroad. More women had been left behind after genocide and emigration, and there was a surplus of men overseas. Arranged marriages, for them and others, have been a way of ensuring the survival of the group.[34] Emigration to France from Italy, Poland, Spain or Algeria has similarly been anchored not only in the rhythms of work opportunities there but also in matrimonial markets at home that need more study. Whereas Algerian immigrant men's marriages to women from their home villages have been seen in France as a result of, among other things, state policy of family reunification (lauded by liberals, decried by the far right), it can also be seen as partaking in a long history of matrimonial migration redressing gender imbalances at home and abroad subsequent to labour market migration.

The impact of migration on gender

And what about the gendered effects of migration?[35] How does migration affect gender roles and the interactions between men and women? The effects may be varied. I once argued that emigration meant emancipation for Eastern European Jewish immigrant women who went to study in France. Yet what for some women may have been a form of freedom, may have also led to a triple discrimination for others, due to class, origin and sex. A gendered analysis of the effects of migration goes well beyond the classic question of whether emigration is good for the receiving or sending countries. It is a question about individuals as well and their desires or abilities to redefine roles. The jury is still out on the debate over oppression on the one hand and agency on the other.

Beyond the issue of a differential impact of migration on each sex, how does migration affect relations between the sexes and in itself construct or reconstruct gendered identities? One of the great understudied topics of migration history has to do with the initial period of separation and the difficulties of reunion. The very first pages of Henry Roth's novel about a Jewish immigrant child on the Lower East Side of New York City, *Call it Sleep*, are a masterful account of the nervous woman arriving at Ellis Island after a long sea journey, clutching her son's hand, fearful that her husband won't recognise her, only to reunite with a grumpy husband who is in turn embarrassed by his wife's old-world style. One could undoubtedly write a similar late twentieth-century story located on the docks in Marseilles as Algerian men greet or accompany their new wives to metropolitan France. To this day, separations and reunions constitute gendered rhythms of mobility. How do couples negotiate their time apart, and how does migration put strains on men, women and families, creating new expectations and norms on the part of those who leave first and those who follow?[36] Above all, how do readjustments occur as economic roles and breadwinners change places or as some learn language skills more quickly than others? Gendered roles and sexuality may shift. Notions of motherhood and fatherhood like patterns of courtship and family roles may change as a result of moving abroad, where working in factories rather than fields and access to new forms of urban leisure have an impact on childbearing and family size. As the recent volume *Intimacy and Italian Migration* well shows, the 'Italian mother' is not an unchanging constant throughout emigration sites, even if she and the Italian family have become a trope of national identity.[37] Whereas settlement has been studied largely in cultural terms – assimilation or retention of ethnicity – what about its differential impact on men and women and on the relations between the two? Migration not only affects gender ratios; it affects gender relations.

Gendered categories of understanding

Only by asking these questions can we capture new ways of understanding how individuals, groups and states have imagined, constructed and lived im/emigration in different ways. Race and class continue to matter, but so do the constraints and construction of gender roles. Men and women may leave home for different reasons. Not all men migrate to work. Not all women migrate to marry. In addition to the by now classic understandings of emigration waves through the lens of national and cultural origins and labour market opportunities, asking about the different ways in which men and women chose to leave and how gendered choices affect migration patterns and vice-versa means shifting the focus again. Immigration history has been a way of understanding labour markets and the state. Gender adds an important level of complexity to both, while studying migration through the lens of gender yields new ways of understanding the mobility itself.

Last, but hardly least, we may return to the historiography and to the major paradigms of migration history as studied over the last forty years to ask how gender as an epistemology can inflect ways of understanding assimilation, ethnicity and transnationalism. As assumptions about assimilation (through the 1960s in the United States, through the 1970s in France) gave way to enquiries about ethnicity in the United States and the '*droit à la différence*' (the right to be different) in France, researchers asked few questions about the gendered meanings of those terms. One could argue that, in the first stage, assimilation was coded as masculine. Assimilation meant becoming 'modern', a concept largely linked to labour force participation, with immigrant women seen as staying at home as bearers and perpetuators of tradition and thus laggards in the assimilation teleology. Besides the fact that concomitant immigration research showed how women also engaged in paid labour outside the home, the implicit and often explicit linking of women to tradition began to shift in other ways. As research interests and the understanding of immigration shifted to greater emphasis on ethnic diversity and the recognition of cultural retention, one could argue that historians elevated tradition itself to a more positive value. Clubs, churches, associations and neighbourhoods, privileged sites of female participation, instead of factories and fields, became the focus of ethnic studies. Curiously, however, it seems that for many researchers ethnicity still remained 'male'. The highly touted ethnic entrepreneur certainly was, although the immigrant women garment entrepreneurs in the Paris region studied by Mirjana Morokvasic were a notable early exception.[38] The study of community organisations qua organisations engendered a somewhat different if still largely male-centred study, around male community leaders, although the organisations were often a site of women's activity and women were never far from sight.[39]

The general point here is that the researcher's shift of focus from work to home, from labour to culture and to ethnicity as a form of immigrant history research has rarely been questioned explicitly in gendered terms. Perhaps the positive re-evaluation and the institutionalisation of ethnicity took 'tradition' away from the sole province of female immigrants. More recent questions about transnationalism seem to have taken two, contradictory, turns. On the one hand, there has been a heralding of the citizen of the world, who is more often than not a male figure (the businessman with multiple passports) rather than a female one. On the other hand, transnationalism has also become a sort of reinforced ethnicity, stressing ties to home which may be female-centred around piety or family or male-centred, focusing on investments in business, sports or infrastructure. The point is to question how researchers have themselves perhaps participated in constructing 'male' or 'female' tales of assimilation, ethnicity or transnationalism.

A research framework along the above lines raises more questions than it can answer, from gender ratios to the social construction of male and female migration *imaginaries* to the gendered impetus to migration and the gendered effects of mobility. I remain stubbornly ecumenical about the construction and limits of our knowledge, ever-changing through new questions. The construction of knowledge is the historian's burden. The suggestions based on a reading of four decades of historiography on one-and-a-half centuries of history of immigration to the United States and France may surely be extended with regard to other immigration societies. Three things, however, will always make even our gendered understandings of migration continually more complex. First of all, expectations and fears about the gendered composition of migration change over time. Just as the demographic mix of migration changes over time, so do representations about the desirability and undesirability of different categories of immigrants, whether by race, national or religious origin or sex. Secondly, immigrant behaviour and attitudes about immigrants are also a function of class. We have largely focused above on working-class immigrants, but many of the same questions may be asked about middle-class or elite immigrants, with possibly different results. The men and women of the upper classes may themselves at different times be desired or feared, seen as welcomed newcomers or dangerous competitors. Third, immigrants themselves are resourceful individuals, and their own decision-making, caught in a web of gendered, class and ethnic expectations, may go with the flow or strike out into uncharted waters. People make their decisions as individuals or within family strategies, but they do so within the scope of opportunities constructed both at home and abroad. What is important, however, is to recognise and analyse the often asymmetrically gendered understanding of migration in order to integrate emigrants and immigrants as gendered actors into the complex history of mobility.

Notes

1. Katharine M. Donato, Donna R. Gabaccia, Jennifer Holdaway, Martin Manalansan IV and Patricia R. Pessar, 'A Glass Half Full? Gender in Migration Studies', *International Migration Review* 40 (2006), pp. 3–26.
2. Michael J. Piore, *Birds of Passage, Migrant Labor and Industrial Societies* (Cambridge: Cambridge University Press, 1979); Mirjana Morokvasic, 'The Overview: Birds of Passage are also Women',

International Migration Review 18 (1984), pp. 886–907; Donato et al., 'A Glass Half Full?' See also Donna R. Gabaccia's earlier concerns about the fragmentation of immigrant women's history, 'Immigrant Women: Nowhere at Home?' *Journal of American Ethnic History* 10 (1991), pp. 61–87 and her own synthesis for the United States, Donna R. Gabaccia, *From the Other Side: Women, Gender, and Immigrant Life in the U.S. 1820–1990* (Bloomington: Indiana University Press, 1994).

3.   On the similarities and dissimilarities in French and American histories of immigration, see Nancy L. Green, 'The Comparative Method and Poststructural Structuralism – New Perspectives for Migration Studies', *Journal of American Ethnic Studies* 13 (1994), pp. 3–22; Nancy L. Green, *Repenser les migrations* (Paris: Presses Universitaires de France, 2002).

4.   For useful introductions to United States and French immigration history, see for example, Thomas Archdeacon, *Becoming American: An Ethnic History* (New York: The Free Press, 1983); Roger Daniels, *Coming to America: A History of Immigration and Ethnicity in American Life* (1990; repr. New York: Perennial, 2005); Aristide R. Zolberg, *A Nation by Design: Immigration Policy in the Fashioning of America* (New York: Russell Sage Foundation; Cambridge: Harvard University Press, 2006); Dorothee Schneider, *Crossing Borders: Migration and Citizenship in the Twentieth-Century United States* (Cambridge: Harvard University Press, 2011); Gérard Noiriel, *Le creuset français: Histoire de l'immigration XIXe-XXe siècles* (Paris: Seuil, 1988); Ralph Schor, *Histoire de l'immigration en France de la fin du XIXe siècle à nos jours* (Paris: Armand Colin, 1996); Marie-Claude Blanc-Chaléard, *Histoire de l'immigration* (Paris: La Découverte, coll. Repères, 2001).

5.   E.g., Marissa Ellis, 'Migrer, Demeurer, Ecrire: La culture migratoire de l'espace dans les littératures beure et chicano', Diplôme d'études approfondies (unpublished master's thesis, École des Hautes Études en Sciences Sociales, 2004).

6.   Nina Glick Schiller, Linda Basch and Cristina Blanc-Szanton (eds), *Towards a Transnational Perspective on Migration: Race, Class, Ethnicity, and Nationalism Reconsidered* (New York: New York Academy of Sciences, 1992); Pierre-Yves Saunier, 'Transnationalism', in Akira Iriye and Pierre-Yves Saunier (eds), *The Palgrave Dictionary of Transnational History* (Basingstoke: Palgrave Macmillan, 2009), pp. 1047–55; Patricia Pessar and Sarah J. Mahler, 'Transnational Migration: Bringing Gender In', *International Migration Review* 37 (2003), pp. 812–46. But see also the earlier work of Mary C. Waters, *Ethnic Options: Choosing Identities in America* (Berkeley: University of California Press, 1990).

7.   See, in particular, the important article of Marion F. Houstoun, Roger G. Kramer and Joan M. Barrett, 'Female Predominance of Immigration to the United States Since 1930, A First Look', *International Migration Review* 18 (1984), pp. 908–63 and Donna R. Gabaccia, 'Women of the Mass Migrations: From Minority to Majority, 1820–1930', in Dirk Hoerder and Leslie Page Moch (eds), *European Migrants, Global and Local Perspectives* (Boston: Northeastern University Press, 1996), pp. 90–111. Other early work includes Maxine Schwartz Seller (ed.), *Immigrant Women* (Philadelphia: Temple University Press, 1981). See also Christiane Harzig (ed.), *Peasant Maids, City Women: From the European Countryside to Urban America* (Ithaca: Cornell University Press, 1997).

8.   Isabel Taboada Leonetti and Florence Lévy, *Femmes et immigrées, L'insertion des femmes immigrées en France* (Paris: La Documentation Française, 1978); Louis Taravella, *Les femmes migrantes, bibliographie analytique internationale (1965–1983)* (Paris: Harmattan, 1984) and, for a more recent treatment, see Nacira Guénif Souilamas, *Des beurettes aux descendantes d'immigrants nord-africains* (Paris: Grasset/Le Monde, 1999) and Laurence Roulleau-Berger, *Migrer au féminin* (Paris: Presses Universitaires de France, 2010).

9.   Hasia R. Diner, *Erin's Daughters in America: Irish Immigrant Women in the Nineteenth Century* (Baltimore: Johns Hopkins University Press, 1983); Rhacel Salazar Parreñas, *Servants of Globalization: Women, Migration, and Domestic Work* (Stanford: Stanford University Press, 2001). For France, see Anne Martin-Fugier, *La place des bonnes. La domesticité féminine à Paris en 1900* (Paris: Grasset, 1979) and current work being done by doctoral students, Christine Muller on Luxembourgeois women; Anne Rothenbühler on Swiss domestics in Paris and Blanca Ceceña who is doing a comparative study of Mexican women in the United States and Spanish domestics in France (1950s to 1970s). See also Mareike König, 'Itinéraires de domestiques allemandes à Paris vers 1900: Sources, méthodes et interprétations', *Sextant* no. 21–22 (2004), pp. 83–115.

10. See the series of volumes (of somewhat uneven quality) that were produced from a stimulating conference organised by Philippe Rygiel, et al. in 2006: Philippe Rygiel and Natacha Lillo (eds), *Rapports sociaux de sexe et immigration, Mondes atlantiques XIXᵉ-XXᵉ siècles* (Paris: Publibook, 2006); Nicole Fouché and Serge Weber (eds), 'Construction des sexualités et migration', special issue, *Migrance* 27 (2006), pp. 5–98; Natacha Lillo and Philippe Rygiel (eds), *Images et représentations du genre en migration: mondes atlantiques XIXe-XXe siècles* (Paris: Publibook, 2007); Philippe Rygiel (ed.), 'Réfugié(e)s', special

issue, *Le Mouvement Social* 225 (2008), pp. 3–97; Manuela Martini and Philippe Rygiel (eds), *Genre et travail migrant: mondes atlantiques, XIXe-XXe siècles* (Paris: Publibook, 2009); Manuela Martini and Philippe Rygiel (eds), 'Genre, filières migratoires et marché du travail', special issue, *Migrations Société* 22:127 (January-February 2010), pp. 45–161. Unfortunately, there is no French synthesis equivalent to Gabaccia's *From the Other Side*.

11.   Joan W. Scott, 'Gender: A Useful Category of Historical Analysis', *American Historical Review* 91 (1986), pp. 1053–75.

12.   Donato et al., 'A Glass Half Full?'; Rygiel and Lillo, *Rapports sociaux de sexe et immigration*, but note that many contributions in this series really deal with the history of women rather than gender and many of the contributions are not about France.

13.   Joan W. Scott, 'Unanswered Questions', contribution to AHR Forum 'Revisiting "Gender: A Useful Category of Historical Analysis"', *American Historical Review* 113 (2008), pp. 1422–30. For another critique of the separation of these historiographies, see Laura Lee Downs, *Writing Gender History* (London: Hodder Arnold, 2004).

14.   I was greatly inspired in this respect by the gender ratios workshop organised by Donna R. Gabaccia, 'Gender and Migration' at the Immigration History Research Center, University of Minnesota, Minneapolis, 2 November 2006, as part of the Interdisciplinary Pilot Research Project 'Gender Ratios and Global Migration' of the Immigration History Research Center and the Minnesota Population Center. The first results of the project have recently been published in Katharine M. Donato, Joseph T. Alexander, Donna R. Gabaccia and Johanna Leinonen, 'Variations in the Gender Composition of Immigrant Populations: How They Matter', *International Migration Review* 45 (2011), pp. 495–526; Donna R. Gabaccia and Elizabeth Zanoni, 'Transitions in Gender Ratios among International Migrants', *Social Science History* 36 (2012), pp. 197–221.

15.   E. G. Ravenstein, 'The Laws of Migration', *Journal of the Royal Statistical Society* 48 (1885), pp. 167–235; E. G. Ravenstein, 'The Laws of Migration', *Journal of the Royal Statistical Society* 52 (1889), pp. 241–305.

16.   For the United States, Archdeacon, *Becoming American*, p. 139; for France (1926), Georges Mauco, *Les étrangers en France* (Paris: Armand Colin, 1932), p. 175.

17.   Donato et al., 'Variations'. As the authors point out, breakdown by nationality of origin can be even more telling. Indeed, foreign-born women in France seem to have 'only' increased from 43% in 1962 to (a hefty) 48% in 1999, yet they comprised 53% of Moroccans in France in 1999. Donato et al., 'Variations', pp. 512, 514.

18.   E.g., Leslie Page Moch, *The Pariahs of Yesterday: Bretons in Paris* (Durham: Duke University Press, 2012); Leslie Page Moch, *Moving Europeans, Migration in Western Europe since 1650* (Bloomington: Indiana University Press, 2nd edn., 2003); plus, see note 9 above.

19.   Dominique Daniel, *L'immigration aux États-Unis, 1965–1995: Le poids de la réunification familiale* (Paris: L'Harmattan, 1996) ; Patrick Weil, *Qu'est-ce qu'un Français ? Histoire de la nationalité française depuis la Révolution* (Paris: Grasset, 2002); Patrick Weil, 'Histoire et mémoire des discriminations en matière de nationalité française', *Vingtième siècle* 84 (2004), pp. 5–22.

20.   Erika Lee, 'Exclusion Acts: Chinese Women During the Chinese Exclusion Era, 1882–1943', in Shirley Hune and Gail M. Nomura (eds), *Asia/Pacific Islander American Women: A Historical Anthology* (New York: New York University Press, 2003), pp. 77–89; Deborah Cohen, *Braceros: Migrant Citizens and Transnational Subjects in the Postwar United States and Mexico* (Chapel Hill: University of North Carolina Press, 2011); Alec G. Hargreaves, *Immigration, 'Race' and Ethnicity in Contemporary France* (London: Routledge, 1995).

21.   For literature on 'whiteness' and a critique, see David R. Roediger, *The Wages of Whiteness: Race and the Making of the American Working Class* (London, New York: Verso, 1991) and Eric Arnesen, 'Whiteness and the Historian's Imagination', *International Labor and Working-Class History* 60 (2001), pp. 3–32. On gender and whiteness, see Ruth Frankenberg, *White Women, Race Matters: The Social Construction of Whiteness* (Minneapolis: University of Minnesota Press, 1993).

22.   Mauco, *Les étrangers en France*; Pap Ndiaye, *La condition noire: essai sur une minorité française* (Paris: Calmann-Lévy, 2008); Didier Fassin and Eric Fassin (eds), *De la question sociale à la question raciale? Représenter la société française* (Paris: La Découverte, 2006); Sue Peabody and Tyler Stovall (eds), *The Color of Liberty: Histories of Race in France* (Durham: Duke University Press, 2003); Herrick Chapman and Laura Frader (eds), *Race in France: Interdisciplinary Perspectives on the Politics of Difference* (New York: Berghahn Books, 2004); Mary Lewis, *The Boundaries of the Republic: Migrant Rights and the Limits of Universalism in France, 1918–1940* (Stanford: Stanford University Press, 2007); Elisa Camiscioli, *Reproducing the French Race: Immigration, Intimacy, and Embodiment in the Early Twentieth*

Century (Durham: Duke University Press, 2009); Hargreaves, *Immigration, 'Race' and Ethnicity*; Herman Lebovics, *Bringing the Empire Back Home: France in the Global Age* (Durham: Duke University Press, 2004).

23. Nancy L. Green, 'The Politics of Exit: Reversing the Immigration Paradigm', *Journal of Modern History* 77 (2005), pp. 263–89; Nancy L. Green and François Weil (eds), *Citizenship and Those Who Leave* (Urbana: University of Illinois Press, 2007), although gender was not the focus of this volume.

24. Lee, 'Exclusion Acts'; Marie-Elisabeth Handman and Janine Mossuz-Lavau (eds), *La prostitution à Paris* (Paris: La Martinière, 2005).

25. Margot Canaday, *The Straight State: Sexuality and Citizenship in Twentieth-Century America* (Princeton: Princeton University Press, 2009); Eithne Luibhéid, *Entry Denied: Controlling Sexuality at the Border* (Minneapolis: University of Minnesota Press, 2002); Erica Rand, *The Ellis Island Snow Globe* (Durham: Duke University Press, 2005); Horacio N. Roque Ramírez, (ed.), 'Introduction: Homoerotic, Lesbian, and Gay Ethnic and Immigrant Histories', *Journal of American Ethnic History* 29, special issue (2010), pp. 5–106; Lionel Cantú Jr, ed. by Nancy A. Naples and Salvador Vidal-Ortiz, *The Sexuality of Migration: Border Crossings and Mexican Immigrant Men* (New York: New York University Press, 2009).

26. Mauco, *Les étrangers en France*; Linda Guerry, '(S')exclure et (s')intégrer. Le genre de l'immigration et de la naturalisation. L'exemple de Marseille (1918–1940)' (unpublished doctoral thesis, Université d'Avignon, 2008). On Mauco's troubling career, see Elisabeth Rudinesco, 'Georges Mauco (1899–1988): Un psychanalyste au service de Vichy. De l'antisémitisme à la psycho-pédagogie', *L'Infini* 51 (1995), pp. 69–84; Todd Shepard, 'Hommes, femmes, familles et identité française lors de l'exode d'Algérie', in Nancy L. Green and Marie Poinsot (eds), *Histoire de l'immigration et question coloniale en France* (Paris: La documentation française, 2008), pp. 91–8.

27. For a good overview of French family policies (on *'familles rejoignantes'* and the *'genre de l'assimilation'*) as seen in the Bouches-du-Rhône department of France, see Guerry, '(S')exclure et (s')intégrer', pp. 86–9, 97–100, 251–60. On Italian state policies, see Victoria de Grazia, *How Fascism Ruled Women: Italy, 1922–1945* (Berkeley: University of California Press, 1992) and Caroline Douki, 'The Liberal Italian State and Mass Emigration, 1860–1914', in Green and Weil (eds), *Citizenship and Those Who Leave*, pp. 91–113.

28. Maria José Fernández Vicente, 'Émigrer sous Franco: Politiques publiques et stratégies individuelles dans l'émigration espagnole vers l'Argentine et vers la France (1945–1965)' (unpublished doctoral thesis, Université de Paris 7, 2004); Victor Pereira, 'L'État portugais et les Portugais en France de 1957 à 1974' (unpublished doctoral thesis, Institut d'Études Politiques de Paris, 2007).

29. Guerry, '(S')exclure et (s')intégrer', pp. 86–9.

30. Yet see the interesting work by Caroline B. Brettell, *Men Who Migrate, Women Who Wait: Population and History in a Portuguese Parish* (Princeton: Princeton University Press, 1986) and Linda Reeder, *Widows in White: Migration and the Transformation of Rural Italian Women, Sicily, 1880–1920* (Toronto: University of Toronto Press, 2002).

31. Pierrette Hondagneu-Sotelo, *Gendered Transitions: Mexican Experiences of Immigration* (Berkeley: University of California Press, 1994), p. 187; Sherri Grasmuk and Patricia R. Pessar, *Between Two Islands: Dominican International Migration* (Berkeley: University of California Press, 1991); Claude Meillassoux, *Femmes, greniers et capitaux* (Paris: F. Maspero, 1975).

32. Abdelmalek Sayad, *La double absence: des illusions de l'émigré aux souffrances de l'immigré* (Paris: Seuil, 1999).

33. Suzanne M. Sinke, 'The International Marriage Market: Theoretical and Historical Perspectives', in Dirk Hoerder and Jorg Nagler (eds), *People in Transit: German Migrations in Comparative Perspective, 1820–1930* (Cambridge: Cambridge University Press, 1995), pp. 227–48; Diner, *Erin's Daughters;* Irving Howe, *World of our Fathers* (New York: Harcourt Brace Jovanovich, 1976).

34. Unless it was not: e.g., Florence Mae Waldron, 'I've Never Dreamed it was Necessary to *Marry!*: Women and Work in New England French Canadian Communities, 1870–1930', *Journal of American Ethnic History* 24 (2005), pp. 34–64. On picture brides: Isabel Kaprielian-Churchill, 'Armenian Refugee Women: The Picture Brides', *Journal of American Ethnic History* 12 (1993), pp. 3–29; Eiichiro Azuma, *Between Two Empires: Race, History and Transnationalism in Japanese America* (New York: Oxford University Press, 2005), pp. 53–5.

35. Here too, Grasmuck and Pessar, *Between Two Islands*, were pioneering.

36. Henry Roth, *Call it Sleep* (New York: R. O. Ballou, 1934). On separation and reunion, see Sonia Cancian, *Families, Lovers, and their Letters: Italian Postwar Migration to Canada* (Winnipeg: University of Manitoba Press, 2011).

37. Loretta Baldassar and Donna R. Gabaccia, *Intimacy and Italian Migration: Gender and Domestic Lives in a Mobile World* (New York: Fordham University Press, 2011). See also Vicki L. Ruíz and Virginia Sánchez Korrol, *Latina Legacies: Identity, Biography, and Community* (New York: Oxford University Press, 2005) and Gloria González-López, *Erotic Journeys: Mexican Immigrants and Their Sex Lives* (Berkeley: University of California Press, 2005).
38. Mirjana Morokvasic, 'Garment Production in a Metropole of Fashion: Small Entreprise, Immigrants and Immigrant Entrepreneurs', *Economic and Industrial Democracy* 9 (1988), pp. 83–97.
39. Ruíz and Sánchez Korrol. *Latina Legacies*; Charlotte Baum, Paula Hyman and Sonya Michel, *The Jewish Woman in America* (New York: Dial Press, 1976).

13 Reconsidering Categories of Analysis: Possibilities for Feminist Studies of Conflict

Shirin Saeidi

Debates regarding feminist uses of gender and sexuality as categories of analysis have once again been rekindled within feminist studies. In her 2006 essay entitled 'Beyond the Americas: Are Gender and Sexuality Useful Categories of Historical Analysis?'[1] Afsaneh Najmabadi, a historian of modern Iran, chronicles her struggles with surpassing gender and sexual binaries while using them as categories of analysis in her pathbreaking book *Women with Moustaches, Men without Beards.*[2] Najmabadi asks, 'How can we bring out as many possible directions of meaning to see the complex node at which notions of gender and sexuality are worked out, without seeking a singular logical underpinning?'[3] A methodological concern with assumptions of singularity that conceal the historical specificities and multiplicities of genders and sexualities as categories of analysis was also at the forefront of US historian Jeanne Boydston's thought-provoking 2008 article, 'Gender as a Question of Historical Analysis'.[4] Boydston similarly questions the usefulness of gender as a category of analysis when the historical processes of gender that we are so adamant to emphasise as feminist scholars are often explored uniformly and with binary associations that efface understandings of non-linear interrelationships between multiple forms of the social.

This discussion has also been initiated by feminist scholars of conflict studies, and this variant of the debate is the focus of my article. Jill Vickers, for instance, argues that because Western feminists have systematically relied on specific approaches to studying gender and the nation, their scholarship is currently unable to capture the complexities of this association in different contexts as it lacks contextually appropriate theories and methods.[5] Jean Bethke Elshtain has also joined this conversation, voicing her dissatisfaction with the routine application of gender as a category of analysis in feminist studies of war. She too laments that we have lost sight of the analytical variations which can be noted if closer attention is paid to historical contexts, suggesting that citizenship and identity formation are processes that may generate more nuanced feminist analyses of conflict.[6]

However, despite these cautionary notes, mainstream feminist studies of conflict serve as salient examples of the continued uncritical deployment of gender and sexuality as categories of analysis. I heed the above concerns regarding a lack of focus on the

Gender History Across Epistemologies, First Edition. Edited by Donna R. Gabaccia and Mary Jo Maynes.

particularities of case studies in some feminist investigations of conflict. These scholars' critiques make a persuasive case for arguing that the use of sexuality and gender as imported categories of investigation can impede the production of knowledge in studies of the global South and North when one particular categorical routine becomes 'common sense for our work'.[7] The first section of this article relates a brief trajectory of the ways that gender, sexuality and the nation-building process have been examined in the context of political violence and intervenes in the theoretical underpinning that upholds this formulation. It illustrates the use of the two main approaches in the deployment of gender and sexuality as categories of analysis in feminist studies of conflict. This section argues that the assumptions which underpin the nexus between gender, sexuality and political violence are usually explored by scholars through the nation state in confined and confining terms. Next, the interrelationship between the emotive context and epistemology is offered as one site where the limitations imposed through one's use of categories can be flagged and attended to by researchers, through shifts in positionality and adjustments in consciousness.

Finally, I present an analysis of archival and ethnographic research on gendered subjectivities and the nation-building process in the Islamic Republic of Iran, from 1980–88. This encompasses the Iran-Iraq war and was a period in which there were local violent contentions between Islamists and leftist political organisations for control of institutional power following the 1979 revolution which brought an end to the Pahlavi Dynasty in Iran (1925–79). In September 1980, with the support of the international system, Iraq invaded Iran and what would be an eight-year war began. It is estimated that this conflict resulted in the death of between 188,000 and 213,000 people on the warfront, and approximately 16,000 were martyred in city bombings and attacks.[8] The war and the revolution brought large numbers of women into the workforce, notably in the nursing profession.[9] At the same time, between 1980 and 1983 a civil war broke out between supporters of an Islamic Republic in Iran and various oppositional organisations, the most popular being the People's Mojahedin Organisation, and the Fadaiyan Majority and Fadaiyan Minority factions.[10] The Mojahedin and Fadaiyan Minority shared similarities with guerrilla movements in Latin America, but were unable to compete politically with the Islamic Republic Party, which was able to mobilise popular support through mosques and under the undisputed leadership of Ayatollah Ruhollah Khomeini. These organisations and other guerrilla groups sought to intervene violently in the construction of an Islamic Republic in Iran.[11] This conflict continued at fluctuating levels following initial clashes in 1980. In 1981, for instance, the Mojahedin retaliated against the consolidation of power by the Islamic Republic Party by killing over 1,000 influential clerics and laymen in bombing attacks.[12] From 1980 to the present day, one local NGO in Iran estimates that the Mojahedin has killed close to 17,000 armed and unarmed Iranians, with most of the killings having taken place between 1980 and 1988.[13] In turn, the Islamic Republic, relying significantly on a suspect's affiliation with oppositional political organisations, carried out mass arrests and executions. The number of these arrests and executions remains uncertain to this day.

My exploration of gendered subjectivities in various spaces in Iran, including warfronts, hospitals and prisons, at this particularly bloody juncture in Iranian history, reveals a less hierarchical and patriarchal association between gender, sexuality and nation-building during conflict than has been typically highlighted in mainstream feminist studies of conflict. I acknowledge that nationalist projects have been strongly justified and inspired by conventional gender discourses of the nation.[14] Concurrently, I will suggest in this article that perhaps, in particular contexts, a state can be constructed through both feminist and state-guided nationalist characteristics when we listen carefully to women's 'own appropriations of their female and nationalist identities' and the ways in which they renegotiate the official nation-state-building enterprise.[15] Furthermore, by refusing to enter studies of conflict with a predetermined understanding of women's and men's gendered subjectivities, or assuming that Western theorisations hold universal truths, we may discover more about identity-making processes and additional narratives of nationhood that flourish during a particular conflict and for a specific group.

Current feminist approaches to studying conflict

Feminist studies of war focus largely on the gendered effects of, and/or the gendered and sexual constructions propelled by, conflict.[16] These two approaches are more interrelated than distinct, as both presume gender and sexuality as functionally hierarchal, binary and oppositional social constructs. This is because violence during wartime is understood not to create, but rather to accentuate the various forms of sexual discrimination and gender hierarchies which exist during times of 'peace'.[17] This contention rests, in part, on the argument that the state is exclusively imagined and enacted as a 'masculine' structure.[18]

These are essentially abstract notions, but they nevertheless shape significant portions of feminist studies of conflict as if they became activated consistently across space and time. In the first trajectory, investigations of warfare demonstrate the gendered construct or gendered effects of sexual violence, occupation, nationalism, imperialism, the state's security regime and revolution, to name just a few sites of analysis.[19] These studies have drawn attention to how people are affected or defined by political violence enacted through patriarchal state-societal forces, as well as people's agencies in surviving daily life in conflict zones. In the second approach to using gender and sexuality as categories of analysis, studies concentrate on describing the heteronormative imaginings and enactments of nationhood during nationalistic moments of violent conflict.[20] These studies are primarily interested in depicting how the stereotypical construction of masculinities and femininities are produced during wars to engender the fictive imaginings of nationhood and the gender-specific political actions of its citizens.

An unrefined emphasis on identity/difference politics has meant that there is insufficient engagement with feminist works which dispute mainstream feminist understandings but may help construct more compelling analyses that draw from people's wartime experiences. For instance, some feminist studies have highlighted that feminist theorisations of the state ceased long ago.[21] They have also suggested that more rigorous investigations of political dynamics in local sites may show us the ways in which the public/private divide can be destabilised through 'social practices' and spatial contentions.[22] Feminist scholars have illustrated that if gender and sexual binaries become less definitive in studies, hidden social processes, such as men and women's unexpected governance of local sites during conflict, may also be detected.[23] Feminist studies have problematised the construction of gender and sexual hierarchies through identity binaries and public-private boundaries that essentialise differences between warfront/homefront, man/woman and war/peace.[24] It has been illustrated that conventional associations between gender, sexuality and the nation pay scant attention to the contingent and fluid nature of gender and sexual identities, as well as the possibility that state-endorsed nationalisms may fail.[25] The literature has demonstrated that nationalism during conflict does not necessarily clash with feminist aspirations in the global South when we historicise women's local activism.[26] Put simply, due to its social nature and historical constructedness, we know that interconnections between gender, sexuality and the nation during wartime can take a multitude of forms through people's real-time and imaginative reproductions of self and space.[27]

Disrupting categorical boundaries: positionality, affect and understanding

Boydston suggests that by letting go of categories we may begin to respond to less scripted questions on gender and sexuality which emerge from the specificities of our studies.[28] However, gender and sexuality can simultaneously be categories, questions and tools. This complexity makes it methodologically impractical to prioritise or de-prioritise gender as a category. More importantly, I am unsure as to how we can make gender less central to our perceptions in contexts where feminist consciousness – multiple visions of social reality that account for various forms of inequalities, discriminations and imaginations – undergirds investigation.[29] I believe that using gender and sexuality as categories of analysis is not intrinsically, and need not be functionally, restrictive. If we are paying attention, then, in unpredictable moments during the research process, these categories can transform into conceptual tools for analysing and revising interconnected epistemologies that ultimately develop whole projects. More specifically, this section demonstrates that by analytically engaging with the affective questions that the research process generates, gender and sexuality as categories of analysis can gradually account for greater theoretical and empirical variance by interrogating positionalities and demanding adjustments in the researcher's feminist consciousness for the duration of a specific project. Whilst feminist scholars of conflict readily address their positionalities and emotional relationships to their projects, rarely is affect connected to methodological frameworks.[30] The transformations that emotional labour engenders in the researcher's own subjectivity could reveal associations and evidences that remain invisible without an awareness of one's own positionalities.

Methodological concerns over the limits that assumptions pose for researching politics have been voiced by scholars of both conflict and Middle East studies. In a recently published article, Tarak Barkawi and Shane Brighton illustrate that within the social sciences, war is primarily believed to be a destructive force, and this 'anti-militarist' stance has historically limited domains of enquiry.[31] From a different angle that also speaks of the importance of recognising the emotional labours of research for methodological purposes, Cyrus Schayegh asserts that the complexities of state-societal relations during the Pahlavi Monarchy, which ruled over Iran prior to the 1979 revolution, have yet to be adequately addressed in Iranian studies. Schayegh argues that this is because 'in the West, many historians of Iran are Iranians, for whom monarchy and revolution were deeply personal experiences'.[32] Similarly, Houchang Chehabi postulates the following, concerning studies of Iran's Pahlavi Monarchy: 'the upheavals of the post-revolutionary years have preoccupied scholars so much that the detailed and dispassionate analysis of Iran under its last dynasty is still in its infancy'.[33] Methodologically accounting for our priorities, questions and patterns by repositioning ourselves and allowing for shifts in our consciousness when necessary, permits submerged perspectives to infiltrate investigations and develop more robust empirical analyses and theoretical prisms.

What follows illustrates how evidence gathered through personal narratives in case studies can develop into theoretical propositions when we analyse encounters with emotions as evidence and remain open to shifting our positionality and consciousness through this knowledge. I demonstrate this by showing how gender and sexuality can also be tools for deciphering narratives and that there also exists an 'epistemology arising from ontology', when researchers are prepared to rethink their categories and at times even let go of their embedded explanations.[34] From 2007–2010, I conducted extensive archival and ethnographic work in Iran, Sweden, Germany and the UK. Broadly, I was interested in understanding women and men's gendered subjectivities in everyday life during the period between 1980 and 1988. As stated earlier, this was during the Iran-Iraq war and following the 1979 revolution. It is understood as a particularly violent and isolated time in contemporary Iranian history because of intersections between local and international violence due to the revolution's unexpected outcomes. My study focused on a range of different spaces and the following social groups were interviewed: former Islamist volunteers of the Iran-Iraq war, nurses employed during the war and leftist political prisoners.

My research practices included participant observation, narrative analysis and in-depth interviews using the snowball sampling method and, when possible, the interviews were recorded. Interview data was analysed thematically, and I linked emergent themes with individual narrations of experience.[35] I also relied considerably on my field notes, including recordings, scribbles, commentaries, questions and analyses, which were used to reflect, regroup and prepare for further interviews and archival research.[36] These interpretations were vital for gaining insight into my own positionality during the interviews and archival work, and shifting my consciousness when it circumscribed the horizons respondents' narratives assembled.[37] I relied on my field notes analytically in and out of the field.

At the time when this project began, I had already been living as an anti-racist feminist of colour for close to a decade, and intellectually I was familiar with the relevance of power relations in the production of knowledge. I had not, however, thought extensively about the visceral dimensions of this understanding. During my fieldwork, interviews revealed my unconscious perspectives, as respondents demanded recognition of their emotional positionality towards me. The questions this process generated subsequently became material knowledge and informed my use of categories of analysis. For example, while meeting with Parvin H., a former political prisoner and her teenage son, going without sexual intimacy whilst in prison came up during our discussion. Without intending to, I said 'But that must not have been a problem for you', to which my interviewee quickly and sharply responded, 'Yes, it was actually'.[38] As an Iranian American woman from the diaspora, my nostalgic perspective lay behind this categorical assumption and was at play in my method of interviewing and analysis. Subconsciously, I imagined 'real Iranians', the ones raised in Iran, had more self-control than those living in non-Muslim societies. Apparently, I was uncomfortable talking about sex in front of her son and assumed that she felt the same way. As a younger woman, it was also difficult for me to envision that a woman from her generation wished to follow through with her sexual desires. In another instance, the daughter of a war martyr, Sahar A., was discussing her dedication to modest clothing, and again I unconsciously interrupted by saying, 'But that's easy for you', to which she retorted, 'It is the hardest of all sacrifices Islam requires'.[39] My assumption about an uncomplicated set of negotiations for Muslim women who practice their faith was shaded by a simplified understanding of Islam as simply someone's way of life and not possibly a constant struggle within the self for maintaining one's piety. By being reminded of my bodily unconsciousness through these affectively charged retorts from respondents, I strengthened a feminist consciousness which was suspicious of claims regarding the omnipresence of silences, as well as my own impulse to respond in place of other people, to 'find' their voice.[40] The responsibility and necessity to listen with curiosity, without taking refuge in the boundaries that gendered points of reference constructed, was integrated into my categorical universe and interviewing methods.

Together, the unexpected responses above called for attention to the specificities of my case studies. Interlocutors wanted me to begin moving towards them through an intimacy that I had not previously shared with strangers. However, I quickly learned that this repositioning, created by breaking down the emotive boundaries between participants and myself, was not without structure. Field notes indicate that interviewees contested my emotional engagements during the interview process, which included not only a series of suppressed assumptions that prevented sympathetic listening, but also a lot of crying on my behalf over the losses women endured due to political violence; their 'victimhood'. In short, my life and living 'at the intersection of individual and social dynamics' while carrying out the field research was believed by respondents to prevent me from sufficiently appreciating the complexities surrounding their histories.[41] The following comments are a sample of what I was told. Maryam Nouri, a former political prisoner, mother and author stated, 'I will never forgive you if you misrepresent my criticisms of other prisoners', as I left her home after a week-long stay which included interviews with other former political prisoners to whom she had introduced me.[42] Laleh Z., a war veteran, housewife and mother made the following statement at the end of our interview: 'I hope that you will share your work with all of us that have participated in these interviews. I hope that you write what we have told you'.[43] Halimeh E., a Bakhtiari (an Iranian tribe) mother of three war martyrs stated the following as I was leaving her home in Ahvaz (a city in southern Iran), '[T]hey were like pieces of my body and soul [her sons]. I gave them [to the war]; that's okay, view them as your brothers, there is no difference'.[44]

The symbols, metaphors and timing used to address intersections between my position as a researcher and interviewees' accounts of individual experiences suggest that they wanted me to express solidarity in a sympathetic manner as a 'feeling-with'.[45] This strikes a balance between losing oneself in other people's stories and leaving sufficient distance to acknowledge the individuated nature of their pasts. While they welcomed me into their homes, showed me the physical marks of torture which lingered on their bodies, shared photos and stories of dead loved ones and embraced my identities and affection, interviewees finalised our encounter by reclaiming their love, survival and loss as uniquely their own. For example, as her concluding words,

Halimeh E. chose to identify her sons as pieces of her 'body and soul', but projected a considerably more distant relationship, that of sister, onto me. In Iranian culture, some mothers have a particularly closer relationship to their sons than other women in the family, including even the son's wife. Recognition of narrators' frustration with my emoting over their experiences of political violence posited gender and sexuality as context-specific categories that form through the intersubjective relationship between individual participants and myself, and not my systemised lens for analysis.[46]

Interview dynamics brought to the surface the methodological significance of the conscious and unconscious assumptions I held, forcing my feminist consciousness to work its way through verbal and visual narratives without 'preconceived conceptual schema'.[47] Simultaneous repositionings, in light of interviewees' responses, felt like blindness. I relied on my standpoint politics for motivation while navigating rapid movements as my perception readjusted to analysis without the security of familiarity in sight and sense. I had to stop analysing discourses through my own preferences. During this light but intense journey, the underpinnings of my 'categorical vision' were also fragmented.[48] This is because I could no longer recognise as significant solely the rhetoric that captured my attention the fastest, reached my core the quickest or the binary frameworks I felt most at home with as an Iranian American student of gender, race and sexuality studies. I became accustomed to continually moving between people, feelings, claims and ideas during interviews and archival work until the specific complexities at issue became apparent – not depictions of gender and sexual categories as I understood them through my own history, solidarities and education. Repeated and strategic totalising statements in the written text or during interviews, such as frustration towards the West for supporting Iraq in the war, also informed my analysis. For instance, the relevance of Iran's international isolation during the war and its connection to local political interventions initially emerged through these discourses. However, I did not allow the most well established discourses nor the most articulate individuals to distract me from noticing anomalies, additional logics within narratives or overlaps between social processes, where they emerged. After all, isolation was not only caused by US and regional policies towards Iran, but also developed out of a radical remaking of cultural and social norms within a state that was in transition to becoming an Islamic Republic. However, interviewees were less forthcoming about this information due to their concerns regarding privacy and security. In contrast, when asked specifically about everyday processes such as education, marriage, mourning and child rearing, narrators' elaborated on the manifestation of emotions that traversed through them in a post-revolutionary state at war.

I began noting respondents' interventions that at a first glance may be overshadowed by the storyline's larger claim to 'coherence and common understanding'.[49] Put somewhat differently, I learned to navigate the architecture of narratives that cement past experiences with desires for current action through the standard story plot of beginning, middle and end. How stories of sexual violence and harassment during the war were told serves as an instructive example of the ways in which personal narratives were developed, first into arguments and then supported a reconsideration of mainstream theorisations of citizenship and nationalism. In the summer of 2008, I had two interviews with Somayeh R., a former veteran of war from southern Iran who was an active member of the women's Basij, a paramilitary force. She told me that the popular claim made by the Revolutionary Guards and Basij that a group of Iranian Arab women and girls were raped and murdered by Iraqis in Susangerd (a city in southern Iran) was publicised and memorialised before an official investigation could take place.[50] I also had another revealing interview with Ali Q., a former male member of Basij. Ali informed me that some Iranian female members of the Mojahedin, who had participated in the 1988 operation 'Eternal Light', were raped by Iranian soldiers.[51] Another interlocutor, Habibeh R., recalled how some Iranian men sexually harassed women on the streets of Khorramshahr (a city in southern Iran) at the onset of the Iraqi invasion, though she was adamant that this was not common.[52]

We remember in the present. It is very probable that these narratives were performances used to express interviewees' disapproval of, or allegiance to, reformist or conservative political movements in Iran. At the same time, and perhaps outside of their intentions, they were also displaying how state-sponsored associations between gender, sexuality and the nation during war might be acted upon on the ground. I found the multiple interventions that were being made within recurring discussions of sexual harassment and rape, such as disruptions of the male hero image, or depictions of silent females standing by male soldiers, to hold deeper narrative insight than the claim of wartime sex crimes alone.

When reading memoirs and other archival literature, the process of repositioning myself and questioning my 'categorical vision' was slightly more complicated, simply because there was not another physical human agent present to question my thinking and perspective. I was aware of how important this process was due to my previous experiences with interviewing. During archival research, scholars often feel that their subjectivity destabilises through engagement with the written word. This experience may not, however, occur so readily for everyone. Some might lose sight of the urgency in monitoring their relation to the written text. Similarly to when conducting interviews, when reading memoirs and other literature we can create methods out of our affective engagements with books to move towards the specificities at issue, and away from unjustified simplifications engendered by our egos.

I slowly learned that close readings of texts offered the best protection against making unfair general claims. However, I needed methods for performing this task in isolation. I, therefore, began to write immediate summaries of the literature I was reading (particularly for the war and prison memoirs), which I shared with my supervisor over email. Because of the trust that had developed between us, and the speed with which my analyses were being seen by him via email, the actual act of this exchange made me feel *responsible* to the written word. This is a responsibility that I would otherwise not feel as strongly while undertaking archival work; there is no one else present while we look through libraries across the globe in search of data for our projects, and it is very easy to simply select data that fits our categorical and other assumptions. I would re-read my emails to him that same day, or the next day, and question my analysis and reposition myself accordingly. He never responded to these emails. My interpretations were also not readjusted in accordance to his judgement or preferences and neither of us would have allowed or wanted such a methodology. Rather, this self-reflection in front of another person forced me to acknowledge my own unfair readings, and often, I would go back and re-read memoirs, or at least sections, once again. My own re-readings of the emails, in front of an audience that I had now created through my supervisor, made me feel *accountable* to my readers. A method for holding ourselves both responsible and accountable, and for shifting our positionality, is needed if we are to read and analyse sensibly. Our colleagues, mentors and faculties can facilitate this emotive process by engaging unassumingly with our claims in various ways and during unexpected moments.

With careful attention to narrative themes and structures, popular gender interventions into the state's war propaganda could also be detected through the analysis of memoirs published in Iran. Memoirs on the Iran-Iraq war are currently being authored and narrated in Iran.[53] Although memoirs on the Iran-Iraq war undergo some official state censorship, the Iranian people have skilfully mastered the art of disclosing suppressed histories. For example, in her memoir *Khabarnegar-e Jangi* (Wartime Journalist), Maryam Kazamzadeh writes in the prelude that the men she encountered during her time in different warfronts can be 'role models' for 'all generations' in search of exemplary figures to emulate.[54] The Islamic Republic continues to manipulate the identities of war martyrs to impose its narrative of heroic youth, and Kazamzadeh's introductory sentence converges with such an agenda. However, throughout the memoir, she also narrates how male soldiers and journalists dismissed her, refused to collaborate with her and deliberately scared her, and it was only through the radical support of a few key individuals, such as Mostafa Chamran, Chief Commander of the Revolutionary Guards during the early days of the Iran-Iraq war, that she was able to carry out her professional duty and personal desire to work as a female journalist reporting from the warfront.[55] Despite state interference in publishing, readers were given a sophisticated description of her struggles and eventual success in creating a space for herself in an unwelcoming atmosphere. As such, readers can formulate a specific understanding of her historical experiences as a female journalist in post-revolutionary Iran, one that runs counter to the state's broader war agenda and gender politics enacted both at the time and today. Based on the evidence I gathered during interviews and from memoirs, I began to suspect what in the later stages of my work would become more detailed: that through their spatial and rhetorical disruption of, and at times compliance with, the state's wartime propaganda system, it was also possible for people, including state elites, to destabilise the conventional gender and sexual associations which upheld state-promoted nationalisms and citizenship in the first place.

However, this finding also meant that the ways I understood intersections between the state, nation and citizen had to be rethought, a process that I delve into further in the remainder of this study. I was hearing provocative histories; meetings and interviews continually posed new questions for me. This meant that more interviews were conducted than was originally planned, resulting in approximately 200 in-depth interviews by the conclusion of the project. Where I had further questions regarding my field notes, I contacted respondents once again. I had continued my conversations with several interviewees after the end of my fieldwork. When still uncertain, I shared my analyses with former interviewees in order to obtain their comments. Chiefly constructing arguments through a terrain of ambiguities, I also sought feedback from a colleague who had directly experienced Iran's prisons during the period of 1980–88. Today she is a social scientist and university professor in the US, who has also had extensive conversations with political prisoners and families involved in the Iran-Iraq war, and she commented on significant portions of my analysis. Another colleague, who lost her father in the Iran-Iraq war, also read and commented on my work. Additionally, analyses of in-depth interviews and informal exchanges were entwined with other documents to capture the range of meanings and implications that interpretations offered. Because of the emotional labour of many individuals, I became comfortable with changing my positionality and consciousness and was able to collect and connect pieces of an uncultivated story through multiple feelings, languages, spaces and discourses.

Sensibilities and political acts: Iran's activist citizens from 1980 to 1988

By scrutinising the workings of narratives, additional tools for analysis that give meaning to the 'complex fabric of processes and meanings that constitute a social or cultural history' may be identified in studies that use gender and sexuality as categories of analysis.[56] The various violent conflicts that Iranians experienced between 1980 and 1988, including the war with Iraq and the state's execution and imprisonment of opponents, resulted in sociopolitical separations between families, friends and partners. This was coupled with the internal cultural changes that the establishment of an Islamic state produced. Interviewees frequently located their struggles for survival within the broader context of isolation, loneliness or 'darkness'.[57] Brian Massumi describes these *intensities* or affects as 'autonomous' from feelings which develop within individual bodies.[58] On the other hand, helping us to imagine intersubjectivities within discussions of affect, Franz Fanon, Audre Lorde and Sara Ahmed have all asserted that depending on the racial and gendered position one has in society, affective contexts speak to people's individual and collective histories to generate feelings about the self and one's communities.[59] Affect may be an emotive backdrop, or that 'feeling in the air' that we sense, but it also interfaces with emotive connections between people.[60]

  Building on the work of critical race theorists among others, I shall suggest that if, as scholars of affect, we want to stress the importance of the body to social experience, we must remain cognisant of the interplay between affective contexts and an individual's emotive connections to others.[61] When we study human agents who embody the capacity to act as individuals, it is vital to account for emotions. This is because subject-positionings are informed by self-reflection. A person's location within multiple communities and identities is in constant interplay with the affective environment in which she lives.[62] As such, one's engagement with the affective context is embedded in the identity formation process; an event which is at once profoundly intimate yet always intersubjective.[63] It is this interplay between the collective and individual in subject formation that makes it difficult to overlook individuated emotive histories during wartime. The specifics of Iranians' gendered subjectivities suggest that affect and emotions, however distinct, can overlap during violent conflict. These included suffering, anger, desire, compassion, love and other intimate feelings that overlapped with one another and the affective experience of isolation.[64]

  As the above begins to suggest, women's and men's gendered and affective subjectivities in this case study indicate that not only did affect and emotions amalgamate, but that they also drove some Iranians to act and create ethically committed ways of belonging and reconstituting the self during a time of conflict. From a cultural and historical standpoint, a love of justice and the duty to fight against oppression (*zulm*) is one of the pillars of the Shi'i Muslim faith, to which over ninety-five per cent of Iranians adhere and which is imbued within Persian culture.[65] The struggle for social and political justice was also vital to engendering the 1979 revolution and the post-revolutionary state.[66] Given the affective and participatory realms of the Iranian people's gendered subjectivities, employing critical citizenship as a conceptual tool is potentially useful. There are also strong associations between individual activism and curtailment of the state's capacity to enforce its preferences in the contemporary Middle East.[67] More specifically, I link the above interlacing of affect and emotions to Engin Isin's notion of an activist citizen, to better contextualise its historical significance to the post-1979 Iranian state.[68] Enlivening the activist citizen may capture specificities about women's subjective experiences that the classic liberal paradigm of citizenship misses due to decontextualised notions of the nation state, polity and personhood.[69]

I draw on this slightly revised notion of activist citizenship to explore the following questions in the remainder of the article. How does the way that activist citizens remade polities during conflict, their nation-building efforts that is, interfere with what feminist scholars have rightly identified as the heteronormativity embedded in the official state-building agenda at wartime? What ramifications does this contention hold for feminist assumptions of a 'masculinist' state?

The Islamic Republic of Iran at war: nation-building, heteronormativity and war tactics

The imagery that the state uses to delineate identities during conflict has implications for 'who belongs,' and who can be understood as a citizen of the nation state.[70] At the same time, women have been shown to be human agents during conflict, and as such we should not falsely assume them to be solely its victims, even though this is how they are often represented by states during wartime.[71] Activist citizenship in post-revolutionary Iran began to develop between 1980 and 1988, while Islamists were solidifying their grip over institutions and national culture and as the state was in a process of political transition and involved in an international war. Recoding citizenship and maintaining popular support for the war were entangled enterprises in the Islamic Republic's state-building efforts. These long- and short-term endeavours were pursued through the formation of an Islamist public sphere. More specifically, the state enforced its social regulations through the Quranic verse *amr-e be ma'ruf va nahy-e az monkar* ('commanding what is just and forbidding what is wrong').[72] This civic nationalistic legislation intended to distinguish post-revolutionary citizens through the extent to which they propagated state-sponsored morality, identities, rituals and cultural revisions. Obedience to wartime ethics and implementation of the state's citizenship ideals were vital to engendering this emergent 'political creed' of governance in post-1979 Iran.[73] At the same time, the state endorsed its version of ethnic nationalism. The Islamic Republic officially described Saddam Hussein and the West, not the Iraqi people, as perpetuators of the war. However, state and societal forces also viewed Iraqi soldiers as cowards and the Iranian soldier as a historically recognised Persian warrior. In some instances, the use of two different moralities in this formulation worked to distinguish the cultural boundaries between the Iranian nation and the Iraqi nation.

Furthermore, the delineation of space which upholds both state-endorsed citizenship and nationalism propels heteronormativity within the nation state: the spatial monitoring of bodies through the so-called natural grounds and attributes through which men and women are supposed to interact, and also via institutionalised forms of public and intimate culture. I understand heteronormativity to be the structures, social organisations, cultures and ways of thinking that give heterosexuality a dominant and privileged status in everyday life. Thus, I imagine heterosexuality to be about more than sexuality or the erotic.[74] I conceptualise gender and sexuality as interconnected yet distinct dynamics that are negotiated between people. It is through this vibrant engagement that heterosexuality is experienced. Importantly, different formulations of gender and sexuality as social categories can result in destabilising heteronormativity.[75]

Because of this agenda for nation state building and its diffused heteronormative underpinnings, the Islamic Republic attempted to define the uses of various spaces and demarcate social distinctions based on subjection of its citizenry and nationalist constructs.[76] This resulted in its deployment of an array of wartime tactics on the local terrain for creating normative individual and collective subjecthoods. In order to interrogate the state's wartime tactics, a struggle central to living autonomously in a conflict zone, Iran's activist citizens used their bodies to galvanise polities that supported their individual aspirations. While the body has been central to Western feminist thought, the body's flesh and material capacities have commonly been sidestepped for its metaphorical usages, and this trend exists in feminist studies of conflict and citizenship as well.[77] Women's embodied subjectivities as activist citizens, either intentionally or unintentionally undermined the heteronormativity of state-endorsed citizenship and nationalism. Importantly, this process hinged on Iranians self-mediating the state's segregation and gendering of the public and private spheres in daily life.[78] The non-linear operation of feelings, time and space in this physical form of community making by the activist citizen falls outside of the state's citizenry and nationalist systems of regulation, all of which relied on the making of polities based on bounded, hierarchal and temporally systematised notions of self and other.

I would like to offer a caveat here. I am not arguing that state-sponsored citizenship and nationalism failed to resonate with the population or that they were necessarily distinct from populist views during this time in Iran. As the discussion below suggests, I also do not assume post-revolutionary Iranian state officials as separated and elevated from the social contexts in which they live. Rather, I begin by first demonstrating how activist citizens utilised their bodies to construct additional forms of connectivities during wartime that helped them sustain their autonomy through moral calculations. Next, I delve more specifically into how the state's enforcement of wartime masculinities and femininities within polities were undermined through the activist citizen's physical presence. Separately and together, these sections illustrate that the creative role of the individual in forging the collective destabilised the heteronormativity which upheld the Islamic Republic's endorsements of citizenship and nationalism. In turn, this finding also suggests that national governance in 1980–88 was not as rigid and authoritarian as we previously had assumed it to be during this period of the Islamic Republic.

The body and polity formation: physically contesting state and societal nation-building projects

Similar to European and North American experiences during the Second World War, the fiscal demands of the Iran-Iraq war created conditions which undermined the segregation of the spheres.[79] At the same time, the cultural norms that governed society and the family still placed women in the private realm, causing a significant decline in women's employment during this period.[80] The state continued to depict motherhood as women's most important contribution as citizens to the country during wartime.[81] Often colleagues, supervisors, husbands and fathers were less than supportive when women joined the workforce.[82] Some non-elite women, nevertheless, followed the impetus of the wartime demands and built polities that were receptive to their controversial location in the nation's post-revolutionary economy.

Some nurses established an imaginary repertoire with the heteronormative pace of life while at work. I understand their relations to the spatial and temporal dimensions of heterosexuality to be imaginative because these women were unable and unwilling to fulfil their gendered responsibilities as Iranian culture at the time dictated. They instead blended the spheres to support the construction of communities that recognised them as female participants in the labour market. Pari Y., a nurse and mother of four from Ahvaz remembers all the patients as her 'children' while her own small offspring were sent to nearby Masjid-e Soleiman (a historical city in southern Iran) and stayed with family due to her husband's refusal to help.[83] She immediately goes on to state: 'My nation was being attacked, I worked as many hours a day as my body would allow . . . I felt successful because I had entered the workforce. I was very proud of myself; no one was allowed to take this away from me. I wanted to have my own income'.[84] By quickly remembering that her body not only had the capacity to produce children, but to save the nation, her presence in the workplace was legitimised to lessen the effect of her husband's disapproval and lack of support. Contrary to some feminists' assumption that motherhood is always a barrier for women's citizenship, for this nurse self-reflecting on her identity as a mother reconfirmed her physical strength to stand in the face of oppression, identified in this instance through a remembrance of the war. In turn, we can envisage that this process of reconstituting her identity strengthened her ability to achieve two interrelated personal projects: economic independence for herself and national independence for her country.

Farzaneh G., another nurse from Ahvaz recalls a memory that similarly made her body crucial to the construction of an additional polity and one that sustained her despite her husband's lack of support. She remembered how her children played with injured soldiers scattered around the hospital, as she worked around the clock. She elaborated: 'My milk would run as I attended to the injured, and I watched my son from a distance passed around in the arms of waiting patients, and this energised me; I never got tired'.[85] Because her milk was flowing as she simultaneously nursed the wounded and watched her child from a distance, it materialised her body's malleability. The extension of her body through her flowing milk connects these two different social groups by mediating the public and private spheres to construct a space for her in the workforce. Perhaps most importantly, the sensations that this imagery generated throughout her body and mind revived her resolve to continue working. As activist citizens who self-mediated the state's segregation of the public and private spheres, women used their bodies to imagine associations which recognised virtue in their dual identities as mothers and professionals taking part in the formal economy. In the process of re-imagining the national culture of employment, these nurses built polities which undermined the heteronormativity of state-endorsed citizenship and civic nationalism that discouraged women from participating in the labour market.

Self-mediating the experience of motherhood was also central to the formation of polities for political prisoners, for whom imprisonment often meant that their political identities were pinned against their other desires as young women. Nazli P., a former prisoner recalls her longing to have at least one child; spending close to nine years behind bars, she would take up hours of the day discussing motherhood with prisoners who had already experienced it.[86] Nazli remembers that prison officials monitored conversations between prisoners through *tavvabs* who were also political prisoners, but who had repented and now collaborated with the state against other political prisoners. Reports from *tavvabs* to prison officials often resulted in lashings or separation of prisoners who had become friends. These conversations cultivated 'outlawed emotions' of togetherness and joy amongst prisoners, in a place where they were supposed to be isolated and submit to state power.[87] However, discussions of motherhood also dismissed the state's material control over their reproductive rights as enemy citizens of a state at war. I therefore interpret these deviant talks, which established new connectivities between women, as a blurring of the boundaries between the state's segregation of the spheres. Female political prisoners' conversations regarding children and fantasies of motherhood were acts of citizenship which did not just physically fuse a community together, but recreated spaces to undermine the state's monopoly over the reproductive rights of enemy citizens.

According to the Iranian feminist lawyer Shadi Sadr, the imprisonment of children with their mothers was a gendered tactic that the state used for transforming female leftist political prisoners into proper citizens of the Islamic Republic.[88] Maryam Nouri describes the workings of this tactic and the ways in which her body supported its confrontation. As she exited the birthing inn without her family or husband nearby, she sensed her nation's solidarity as people shouted at the Revolutionary Guardsmen who had forced her to carry her own luggage and newborn child only a few hours after giving birth. The visual display of solidarity from strangers gave her the strength and inspiration to transcend the isolation of prison life and to resist the establishment of an Islamic Republic in Iran from behind bars as a *sar mozeh*. *Sar mozeh* was an individual who continued overtly to oppose the Islamic Republic's prison tactics while imprisoned.[89]

Shortly after having her son and returning to prison, officials offered Maryam's son baby food, but suddenly discontinued serving meals especially made for all other children in the ward. Cherishing the solidarity she felt from her nation months earlier, she refused food for her baby, arguing 'either all the babies get food, or mine will not have any either'.[90] By envisaging the authoritarian nature of the Islamic Republic and its effects on Iranian society, she could sacrifice her child in exchange for an alternative political order. Multiple extensions of her body across spheres took place for this decision to be formulated. The reconceiving of her positionality within an imagined polity meant that the state could not manipulate her identity as a mother to construct a subject for its rule.

At times, the presence of children in prison challenged the state's nationalist discourses that sought to unify the nation against the invading enemy. Leftist political prisoners were accused of being collaborators with Iraq's Baath Party due to their opposition to the establishment of an Islamic Republic. Monireh Baradaran remembers being in prison with an Iraqi woman and her baby. The Iraqi woman was arrested along with her husband on charges related to spying. Monireh remembers young Iranian prisoners shouting, '[L]ook everyone, here comes our enemy!' when the little girl started walking.[91] By visualising the state's discourses of a national enemy through the body of an Iraqi child, these women identified the inconsistencies which were embedded in the abstract narrative ethnic nationalism imposes. As such, for at least a few moments, these Iranian prisoners welcomed Iraqis into their national body.

Iranian nurses remembered their professional and intimate identities to physically connect with Iraqis despite a similar nationalistic discourse. Soheila Farjamfar was employed in numerous hospitals in Khuzestan during the war. In her memoir, *Kafsh-ha-ye Sargardan* (Wandering Shoes) and during our conversations, she described a scene where an ambulance arrived containing the bodies of dead Iraqi soldiers. While male doctors and medical assistants cheered and celebrated, Farjamfar and the other female nurses could only think of the Iraqi women who had become widows that night.[92] Holding back tears, one of the nurses, Roya, stated: 'Tonight the light in the home of an Iraqi woman has been turned off'.[93] In her memoir and during our discussion, Farjamfar immediately followed this scene by reminiscing about how as a child from Khuzestan she viewed Iraqis as her neighbours 'across the water'.[94] She reconnected with her childhood memory of watching Iraqis wave and smile at her as she stood near the Shatt al-Arab waterway with her binoculars. With this memory relived, Farjamfar was able to stand in solidarity with Iraqi women during this moment despite the nationalist pressures exerted by male colleagues.

As Iranians self-determined their positionality in relation to the specific wartime tactics they encountered in daily life, they disrupted the heteronormativities which upheld state-endorsed citizenship and nationalism. Due to the socio-political context of isolation, these women used their bodies to physically rebuild polities by oscillating between the spheres. Through this complex process they delineated their autonomy during a period when both state and society enforced austere conformity.

Politics of local masculinities: unmaking the protector identity of the male warrior

The Islamic Republic's gendered depictions of ideal citizens during the Iran-Iraq war were quite similar to other states in wartime. The Islamic Republic depicted the ideal male citizen as a warrior and the ideal female citizen as a wife or a mother who willingly sent her loved one to battlefields.[95] Iranian women were officially not permitted to be at warfronts or in cities that had turned into warzones if the possibility of rape existed.[96] The allegory of the male warrior as the protector of the nation was interrogated through the presence of local women in Khuzestan who refused to leave their cities when Iraqi forces invaded.[97] However, their contributions at warfronts were not simply another case of militant women taking on symbolised masculinities to wrest new gender rights for themselves. Furthermore, as Tami Amanda Jacoby has argued, women's collaborations within an Islamic framework should not be dismissed as simply co-option.[98] There was a tension between how state and societal forces wanted these women to function in this public site and the ways that they wanted to participate at warfronts.[99] More specifically, by physically engaging with this tension, the local Islamist women of Khuzestan unsettled the oppositional subjectivity of the genders which underpins this fictive construct in which the male warrior is protector of the nation.[100] Through their acts of citizenship, the heteronormativity which undergirded the official state-building agenda during the war was further destabilised.

Women from Khuzestan objected to the wartime tactic of conflating man, warfront and protection and placing it in opposition to women's subjectivities by highlighting its inability to withstand realities on the local terrain. They made this point by challenging the decisions of the state's highest officials. Prior to the 1982 liberation of Khorramshahr, a female war volunteer, Zahra Hosseini decided to speak directly to military commanders.[101] Once she was finally given permission to do so, she informed them that it was in fact President Abulhassan BaniSadr's decisions regarding the movement of supplies and forces that was preventing Iranians from reclaiming occupied Khorramshahr from Iraqis. Before an intimidating audience of male soldiers and officials, she then accused her president and 'many other leading officials around him' of treason (calling them *khaen*).[102] Through her brave analysis, Zahra Hosseini posited female civilians as equals to male warriors in their capacity to create and dismiss war plans.

In another scene she describes in her memoir, as Zahra was delivering food to fighters she was told by a male colleague to move back due to the possibility of rape as Iraqis were dispersed throughout the area. She responded with the following: 'I am here until the end . . . if there is danger, it is for everyone, not only me'.[103] She dismissed her male colleague's attempt to place her under his protection. Indeed, she claims his protection to be a myth, and rape as a mutual concern. Her intervention suggests that there was little difference between their circumstances and options as individuals who had decided to stay and defend their city. Some men supported women's interventions in the state's wartime tactics. During our conversations in June 2008, Zahra recalled that a local religious leader, Sheikh Sharif, negotiated with the Revolutionary Guards for women to stay in Khorramshahr after their evacuation had been formally announced by the Revolutionary Guards.[104] Throughout these conversations, Zahra Hosseini never disassociated from her identity as a female civilian. Simultaneously, she dismantled the gender binaries that legitimised the allegory of men as protectors of the nation, going as far as resituating her subjectivity in light of even military defence strategising.

For Iranians at the time, it was not acceptable for women to live away from their parents prior to marriage. Saham Taghati stayed and volunteered in hospitals despite the fact that her family had left Khorramshahr. Once Khorramshahr was liberated in 1982, she decided to live in Ahvaz, a city which was still under attack, to complete her high school diploma. When her father asked her to stay at a family friend's home in Ahvaz she refused. Her father finally accepted her decision, stating: 'Stay wherever you like, just make sure you continue your education'.[105] She rented a home with a few girlfriends and achieved her high school diploma in Ahvaz while her parents lived in Qom. For a female high school student to have this level of independence in Iran during the 1980s is astonishing. With the male protector absent both from her warfront and adolescent experiences during the war, an underlying belief in gender equality on behalf of father and daughter seeps through this story. It suggests that the oppositional construct of the genders was unsettled as young girls and women decided to take part in defending their city. The unconventional collaboration seen on the part of Saham's father illustrates that the male protector discourse became less compelling for Khuzestani families whose female relatives were active in the war.

Islamist women complicated the conceptualisation of their heroism within Shi'i-Persian culture through acts of citizenship at warfronts, which included death during combat. Nevertheless, for Shi'i Iranians, martyrdom is generally a status associated with men.[106] Shahnaz Haji-Shah, a teen who was part of a first aid unit at a hospital in Khorramshahr, lost her life in 1980 as she tried to rescue potential survivors following an air raid. Her mother remembers her in the following way: 'The first person to reach martyrdom in our family was Shahnaz. She went and opened the path of martyrdom for her two brothers Hossein and Nasser'.[107] In this narrative of her death, Shahnaz is recognised as both an individual martyr and a relative of male martyrs.[108] This undermines the oppositional subjectivities of men and women in understandings of martyrdom for Shi'i Iranians, where women are recognised mostly through familial connections to martyrs. Similar to male martyrs, with her death she creates a path or a background, so her identity was not domesticated through appropriations of the female body. Gender, thus far, does not emerge as a particularly significant category in comparisons of male and female Iranian war martyrs. However, her mother goes on to say:

> She had an awareness of issues that was beyond her age. She understood better than others. She was ahead of her time . . . . At the time of the revolution, saying one's prayers on time was not that common in our society. However, Shahnaz was always very particular about saying her prayers on time.[109]

As this second narrative shows, her life and living are depicted through a discourse of symbolised masculinities that connect her to male martyrs through characteristics such as extraordinary levels of insight and piety. These symbolised masculinities are equally imposed onto male martyrs. Nevertheless, it was her death, not her life, that made her an equal to the male martyr. The legacy of her death leads one to question the gender inequalities which existed in her life. The potential outcomes of this scrutiny are so threatening that in Iran only a few streets are named after female martyrs, whereas the names of male martyrs have been used since the early days of the 1979 revolution to name public spaces.[110] There have been debates within the country as to why the state has made this differentiation.[111] As such, in their death, Iran's female martyrs disrupt the oppositional subjectivities of the genders which reinforce popular imaginings of the male protector during their lifetimes.

Through their activist presence at warfronts, women confronted a specific symbolised masculinity: the male warrior as protector of the nation. Importantly, as activist citizens they did this by fragmenting the oppositional constructs of gender subjectivities that propagated discrimination and prejudice against women. With this physical engagement, they either consciously or subconsciously publicised equality between the genders. Their male colleagues, at times, supported them in this endeavour. These Islamist women and men harvested a new Muslim feminist culture for gender equality in post-revolutionary Iran.[112] State-sponsored citizenship and nationalism, and the heteronormativity which underpinned them, were destabilised through the recognition of gender equality on the local terrain.

Politics of local femininities: nationhood, gender and eroticism

The heteronormative state-endorsed connections between women, the private and the erotic, employed in other contexts, were also enforced in Iran during this time through the regulation of some women's behaviour during periods of public mourning.[113] Wives of martyrs were under more public scrutiny during funerals than other grieving women might have been, due to their symbolic and material associations with the nation state in post-1979 Iran. Many interviewees remember sensing social pressure to withhold from mourning in public, for as wives of martyrs they were expected to uphold wartime morale more acutely than others. Nevertheless, wives of martyrs interrogated this wartime tactic by expressing their emotions at funerals and other periods of emotional distress. These women confronted this state-building strategy, which identified them as the 'beloved' and spatially pushed them into the private realm to further locate sexuality within the domains of state control.

Not only was this wartime tactic challenged, but here once again we see that at times it was male representatives of the state that supported women's confrontations. Habibeh R., who was a veteran of war herself, and whose first husband was killed in the war, depicted this surprising association. She described the liberation she felt during her husband's funeral because of the support from another member of the Revolutionary Guards:

> During my husband's burial, I don't know why – I am usually very reserved and modest – but I stated aloud 'I want to kiss him', and my brother yelled at me and told me to stop, but *shahid's* (referring to martyred husband) friend, who was later martyred, stated 'kiss him, kiss him, do whatever you like . . . there is nothing wrong with this'.

She then proceeded to explain: 'So I kissed him and told him how much I loved him right there in front of men from the Revolutionary Guard, my family and his. I still can't believe I did that'.[114]

I should also add that solidarities were not only expressed between women and men outside of their immediate family, but they were also a social practice that flourished between women. For example, the chemical victims unit became a personal beauty salon for Golnaz T., the wife of a dying soldier, as her sister shaped her eyebrows and the two women shared a moment of humour and affection before hospital staff.[115] Through the activist citizen's repeated interrogations of state and societal efforts at preventing her from displaying affections in public sites, it became difficult to envision the erotic linked solely to the nation through male longings to 'save' Iran as a virginal mother or daughter. Rather, some women undermined the entire association by expressing their own command over spaces and investment in bodies and desires in front of crowds.

In *An Su-ye Devar-e Del* (The Other Side of the Heart), a woman describes her control over, and intimate yearning for, her husband's body while she stood alone, newly widowed at his funeral:

> I closed Asghar's eyes and hands with a white band. I did not allow nurses or his friends from the warfront to touch him. When we were putting his body in the coffin, his friends were hysterical. I told them to be quiet. My effort in calming them was fruitless, they continued. When his corpse was placed in an ambulance, I jumped into the front seat. While washing Asghar's face, I kissed him. I washed his forehead, head and face myself. When they prepared him for burial, I wrote verses from the Quran on his shroud. When everyone gathered around Asghar's grave, I was worried. My heart desired to bury him myself. But a walkway opened. How, I don't know. I only saw that a path opened. I went forward. I took off my shoes. I entered the grave, and was handed the rocks one by one by his friends, and I placed them on his corpse.[116]

In this narrative, the male warrior's incapacity creates an opportunity for this wife of a martyr to renegotiate the state's segregation of the spheres and mourn publicly as she pleased. With an equal amount of longing, Habibeh R., recalled to me and a journalist present in her home, the last day with her husband before his death:

> I just watched him sleep; I moved my hands slowly through his hair [*navazesh-esh me kardam*]–
> this always eased his migraines – I asked him to unbutton his shirt so I could feel his presence
> by seeing his body. There was a heat which came from him, not because of the weather, but
> because of his internal worries. There was also a glow; this was not the same body I had seen
> before.[117]

The sensuality with which Habibeh describes her husband's final living day undermined the social norms through which wives of martyrs are meant to discuss their marital experiences in public. Ghadeh Jaber also challenged the appropriate place and way a woman was to show affection for her martyred husband. She forced Mostafa Chamran's family and the state to bring his body into a mosque the night before his burial, placed her head on his chest and spoke to him until the morning.[118] Typically, the body would be kept in a mortuary until the day of the funeral. During her husband's funeral, another interviewee, Leila P., broke tradition through her insistence that she be allowed to ride in the vehicle carrying his body so that her children could sense up close that their father was gone and have an opportunity to say a final goodbye.[119] Golnar W., from Ahvaz, who did not have a chance to see her husband's body prior to burial, stated 'I wanted to kiss his forehead and place him on my heart'.[120] Some women made their presence felt as female lovers in the public sphere. For other female activist citizens, a display of love and physical connection took place in hospitals. For instance, during the last few minutes of his life, as Manouchehr Moddeq lay dying in a hospital bed from injuries sustained from chemical weapons, Fereshteh Malaki proceeded to kiss her husband 'from head to toe'.[121] Some women expressed their love in public sites and undermined the state's actual and metaphorical control over sexuality during the war.

It was not only families of war martyrs that made this intervention. In the summer of 1988, the Islamic Republic executed many political prisoners. Most of the executed were members of the Mojahedin. A human rights organisation in the West estimates that up to 1,000 prisoners in Tehran's Evin prison, and many more in Karaj's Gohardasht prison, were executed.[122] For families whose loved ones were executed in late July 1988, public mourning of their deaths was strictly banned. Nevertheless, the wife of one executed prisoner remembers that she dug through the mass graves of the Khavaran cemetery with her bare hands. She explains: 'The stench of the corpses was appalling but I started digging with my hands because it was important for me and my two little children that I locate my husband's grave'.[123] Later, when the authorities began referring to the cemetery as *Kaferestan*, the 'land of the unbelievers', and *Lanatabad*, the 'land of the damned', families of the executed renamed the final resting location of their loved ones *Golzar-e Khaveran*, 'Eastern flower fields'.[124] The place where mostly male leftists were buried was reclaimed as a flower palace, and it was women who dug their way through the land and laboured to identify their loved ones' graves. In the most immediate sense, state-endorsed femininity and its conflation with the private sphere was spatially dislocated through the erotics of forbidden and public mourning. Families of the executed associated a terrain of 'soil', silence and flowers with martyred husbands, while the physical and public work of 'bringing into existence' their bodies was left to the hands of women that yearned for them the most.[125] During particular moments of activist citizenship, the land was no longer symbolic of a woman in need of protection, nor was it a male terrain for enacting this struggle.[126]

Concluding thoughts

Feminist studies of conflict have illustrated the gendered effects and nature of war, as well as the heteronormative imagery which link women and men to the nation state in a stereotypical manner. This article has argued that there can be a variety of ways to understand the associations between peoples and nation states at a time of war. It is neither gender and sexuality as categories of analysis nor the politics of a feminist standpoint that have produced uniformity in research designs and findings. Rather, this impasse might be due to a researcher's rigid positionality and fixed consciousnesses. In particular, this article illustrates that by remaining affectively attuned during different phases of the research process, gender and sexuality as categories of analysis may create new spaces for theorising social, historical and political processes.

In order to elaborate on the possible outcomes of using this technique, the Iranian people's nation-building efforts during the period 1980–88, and their confrontation with the state's wartime tactics for concentrating power, was revisited. By moving away from predetermined schemas for understanding women's wartime experiences, new narratives were collected and I argued that the atmosphere of isolation intersected with personal emotive histories to enliven the activist citizen who forged an autonomous sense of belonging alongside the Islamic Republic's state-building agenda. These citizens self-mediated and renegotiated the state's segregation of the public and private spheres, and the circulation of masculinities and femininities within them, to construct polities that interrogated the state's wartime tactics at the local level. Highlighting how the activist citizens' constructions of polities and identities simultaneously challenged the heteronormativity embedded in the official state-building agenda, the tentative conclusions in this article suggest that the 1980–88 Iranian state was entwined with feminist and state-endorsed nationalist characteristics. Ultimately, local reconfigurations of citizenship and nationhood by some Iranians may have unsettled the mainstream feminist understanding of the state as utterly 'masculine' or patriarchal. Women and men's gendered subjectivities also suggest that when we discuss Iranian citizenship from 1980 to 1988, we may not necessarily, and exclusively, be talking about liberal citizenship. The conceptualisation of the activist citizen as a morally and ethically committed person in search of social justice challenges liberal notions of citizenship that rely on abstract personhood and contexts. While further ethnographic investigations of the 1980–88 period are sorely needed, and I consider my work as only having begun this endeavour, the idea that local governance was more negotiable than most studies of the first decade of the Islamic Republic have thus far assumed, is a promising finding.[127] More generally, the empirical and theoretical findings offered in this paper invite us to consider states, including Islamic ones, as having a multiplicity of characteristics contingent on the historical context of subjectivities, affects, emotions, temporalities and spaces. However, we need to first reposition ourselves as researchers before we can begin to understand the transformations that are taking place in the contemporary Middle East.

Notes

I would like to thank the editors of this Special Issue and two anonymous reviewers of this journal for posing challenging questions and providing me with the opportunity needed to develop my ideas. Many thanks go to the Bureau for the Literature and Art of Resistance in Tehran for introducing me to women who had participated in the Iran-Iraq war. Interviewees generously shared their time with me and I thank them all. My 2010 doctoral fellowship at The Centre for Gender Excellence at Linkoping University in Sweden significantly helped with initial revisions, and I was particularly guided by Kasia Gawlicz and Rana Jaleel's sharp criticisms and thoughtful suggestions. Mohammad Mohseni Aref, Peter Nyers, Tamara Lea Spira, Leila Mouri, Catherine Sameh, Kristin Soraya Batmanghelichi, Matt Neal, Ilan Pappe, Roja Fazaeli, Shahla Talebi, Sian Lazar, Haleh Afshar and Heather M. Turcotte also offered critical readings of earlier drafts. I will always be grateful to Glen Rangwala and Cambridge University for helping me create the spaces and emotions I needed to write my own history. Experiencing these sites and sensations was a desire and terror, that I, like many before me, finally negotiated by submitting a PhD thesis. It could have been otherwise. So thank you for remembering this wish.

1. Afsaneh Najmabadi, 'Beyond the Americas: Are Gender and Sexuality Useful Categories of Historical Analysis?', *Journal of Women's History* 18 (2006), pp. 11–21.
2. Afsaneh Najmabadi, *Women with Moustaches and Men without Beards: Gender and Sexual Anxieties of Iranian Modernity* (Berkeley: University of California Press, 2005).
3. Najmabadi, 'Beyond the Americas', p. 18.
4. Jeanne Boydston, 'Gender as a Question of Historical Analysis', *Gender & History* 20 (2008), pp. 558–83.
5. Jill Vickers, 'Bringing Nations In: Some Methodological and Conceptual Issues in Connecting Feminisms with Nationhood and Nationalisms', *International Feminist Journal of Politics* 8 (2006), pp. 84–109. See also Anila Daulatzai, 'The Discursive Occupation of Afghanistan', *British Journal of Middle Eastern Studies* 35 (2008), pp. 419–35.
6. Jean Bethke Elshtain, 'Women, the State, and War', *International Relations* 23 (2009), pp. 289–303. See also Haleh Afshar, 'Women, Wars, Citizenship, Migration, and Identity: Some Illustrations from the Middle East', *Journal of Development Studies* 43 (2007), pp. 237–44.
7. Boydston, 'Gender as a Question of Historical Analysis', p. 561.
8. Website of Sepah Pasdaran (Revolutionary Guards), Iran, <http://alborz.sajed.ir/index.php?option=com_content&view = article&id = 401&Itemid = 30>.
9. Maryam Poya, *Women, Work & Islamism: Ideology and Resistance in Iran* (New York: Zed Books, 1999).
10. The Mojahedin was an Iranian Islamist-Marxist organisation whose political activism was vital to engendering the 1979 Iranian revolution, but which later became involved in a violent power struggle with the leaders of the Islamic Republic. During the Iran-Iraq war members were given refuge in Iraq. After the 1979 revolution, the Organisation of Iranian People's Fadaiyan Guerrillas split into the Fadaiyan Majority and the Fadaiyan Minority. Similar to the Mojahedin, the minority faction believed in armed resistance.
11. Shaul Bakhash, *The Reign of the Ayatollahs: Iran and the Islamic Revolution* (London: I. B. Tauris, 1985).
12. 'Deadly Fatwa: Iran's 1988 Prison Massacre', Iran Human Rights Documentation Center, New Haven, Conneticut (2009). <http://www.iranhrdc.org/english/publications/reports/3158-deadly-fatwa-iran-s-1988-prison-massacre.html>.
13. Ahmed Shaheed, *Report of the Special Rapporteur on the Situation of Human Rights in the Islamic Republic of Iran*, United Nation's Human Rights Council HRC/19/66 (2012), p. 13. For more on these killings, see the website for Habilian, a local NGO in Iran, which has documented the names of victims and locations of their death: Habilian, Iran, accessed in 2012, <http://www.habilian.ir/en/>.
14. Nira Yuval-Davis, *Gender & Nation* (London: Sage, 1997).
15. Rosemary Sayigh, 'Gender, Sexuality, and Class in National Narrations: Palestinian Camp Women Tell Their Lives', *Frontiers: A Journal of Women Studies* 19 (1998), pp. 166–85, at p. 169.
16. Laura Sjoberg and Sandra Via (eds), *Gender, War, and Militarism: Feminist Perspectives* (Oxford: Praeger, 2010); Ann Tickner, *Gendering World Politics* (New York: Columbia University Press, 2001); Marysia Zalewski, 'Well, What is the Feminist Perspective on Bosnia?', *International Affairs* 71 (1995), pp. 339–56.
17. Chris J. Cuomo, 'War is not Just an Event: Reflections on the Significance of Everyday Violence', *Hypatia* 11 (1996), pp. 30–45; Terrell Carver, 'Being a Man', *Government & Opposition* 41 (2006), pp. 450–68.
18. Jan J. Pettman, 'Nationalism and After', *Review of International Studies* 24 (1998), pp. 149–64. It is important to remember that other realms of feminist political analysis have viewed the state as more than

simply a 'masculine' construct. See for example, feminist studies of the welfare state: Helga Maria Hernes, *Welfare State and Woman Power: Essays in State Feminism* (London: Norwegian University Press, 1987); Drude Dahlerup, 'Confusing Concepts – Confusing Reality: A Theoretical Discussion of the Patriarchal State', in Anne Showstack Sassoon (ed.), *Women and the State: The Shifting Boundaries of Public and Private* (London: Unwin Hyman, 1987), pp. 93–127; Frances Fox Piven, 'Ideology and the State: Women, Power, and the Welfare State', in Linda Gordon (ed.), *Women, the State, and Welfare* (Madison: University of Wisconsin Press, 1990), pp. 250–64.

19. Sarah C. Soh, *The Comfort Women: Sexual Violence and Postcolonial Memory in Korea and Japan* (Chicago: University of Chicago Press, 2008); Nadje Al-Ali and Nicola Pratt, *What Kind of Liberation? Women and the Occupation of Iraq* (Los Angeles: University of California Press, 2009); V. Spike Peterson, 'Gendered Nationalism: Reproducing "Us" Versus "Them"', in Lois A. Lorentzen and Jennifer Turpin (eds), *The Women and War Reader* (New York and London: New York University Press, 1998), pp. 41–9; Chandre T. Mohanty, 'US Empire and the Project of Women's Studies: Stories of Citizenship, Complicity and Dissent', *Gender, Place & Culture* 13 (2006), pp. 7–20; Roberta Micallef, 'Incarcerated Women, Honorable Women', in Laleh Khalili and Jilian Schwedler (eds), *Policing and Prisons in the Middle East: Formations of Coercion* (London: Hurst & Company, 2010), pp. 207–21; Hamideh Sedghi, *Women and Politics in Iran: Veiling, Unveiling, and Reveiling* (Cambridge: Cambridge University Press, 2007).

20. Dominic D. Alessio, 'Domesticating "the Heart of the Wild": Female Personifications of the Colonies, 1886–1940', *Women's History Review* 6 (1997), pp. 239–70; Samar Kanafani, 'Leaving Mother-Land: The Anti-Feminine in Fida'i Narratives', *Identities* 15 (2008), pp. 297–316.

21. Johanna Kantola, *Feminists Theorize the State* (New York: Palgrave, 2006).

22. Gillian Youngs, 'Breaking Patriarchal Bonds: Demythologizing the Public/Private', in Marrianne H. Marchand and Anne Sisson Runyan (eds), *Gender and Global Restructuring: Sightings, Sites, and Resistances* (London and New York: Routledge, 2000) pp. 44–58.

23. Gisela Geisler, *Women and the Remaking of Politics in Southern Africa: Negotiating Autonomy, Incorporation and Representation* (Uppsala: Nordiska Afrikainstitutet, 2004); Caroline O. N. Moser and Fiona C. Clark (eds), *Victims, Perpetrators or Actors? Gender, Armed Conflict and Political Violence* (London and New York: Zed Books, 2001).

24. Miriam Cooke and Angela Woollacott (eds), *Gendering War Talk* (Princeton: Princeton University Press, 1993).

25. Thembisa Waetjen, 'The Limits of Gender Rhetoric for Nationalism: A Case Study from Southern Africa', *Theory and Society* 30 (2001), pp. 121–52.

26. Nahla Abdo, 'Nationalism and Feminism: Palestinian Women and the *Intifada* – Not Going Back?', in Valentine M. Moghadam (ed.), *Gender and National Identity: Women and Politics in Muslim Societies* (London and New Jersey: Zed Books, 1994), pp. 148–70; Kumari Jayawardena, *Feminism and Nationalism in the Third World* (New Delhi: Kali for Women; London: Zed Books, 1986); Lois A. West, 'Introduction: Feminism Constructs Nationalism', in Lois A. West (ed.), *Feminist Nationalism* (London and New York: Routledge, 1997), pp. xi–xxxvi.

27. Sita Ranchod-Nilsson and Mary Ann Tetreault (eds), *Women, States, and Nationalism: At Home in the Nation?* (London: Routledge, 2000).

28. Boydston, 'Gender as a Question of Historical Analysis'.

29. Liz Stanley and Sue Wise, *Breaking Out Again: Feminist Ontology and Epistemology* (London and New York: Routledge, 1993).

30. Margot Weiss argues that even when we address our positionality and the situated nature of knowledge creation, we may still be evading aspects of our knowledge production journey. Margot Weiss, 'The Epistemology of Ethnography: Method in Queer Anthropology', *GLQ: A Journal of Lesbian and Gay Studies* 17 (2011), pp. 649–64.

31. Tarak Barkawi and Shane Brighton, 'Powers of War: Fighting, Knowledge, and Critique', *International Political Sociology* 5 (2011), pp. 126–43.

32. Cyrus Schayegh, 'Seeing Like a State', *International Journal of Middle East Studies* 42 (2010), pp. 37–61, here p. 47.

33. Houchang Chehabi, 'The Pahlavi Period', *Iranian Studies* 31 (1998), pp. 495–502, quote from p. 495.

34. Maithree Wickramasinghe, *Feminist Research Methodology* (New York: Routledge, 2010).

35. I have used the full names of interviewees who gave me permission to do so, and pseudonyms in other cases.

36. Gregory F. Barz, 'Confronting the Field(Note) In and Out of the Field', in Gregory F. Barz and Timothy J. Cooley (eds), *Shadows in the Field: New Perspectives for Fieldwork in Ethnomusicology* (New York: Oxford University Press, 1997), pp. 45–62.

37. Other feminist scholars of the Middle East who have offered us pioneering research remember a similar journey. See Soraya Altorki and Camillia Fawzi El-Solh, *Arab Women in the Field: Studying Your Own Society* (Syracuse: Syracuse University Press, 1988).

38. Personal interview, Cologne, Germany, April 2008.

39. Personal interview, Tehran, Iran, May 2008.

40. Shaun Gallagher, 'Body Schema and Intentionality', in José L. Bermdez, Anthony Marcel and Naomi Eilan (eds), *The Body and Self* (London: MIT Press, 1995), pp. 225–44.

41. Mary Jo Maynes, Jennifer L. Pierce and Barbara Laslett, *Telling Stories: The Use of Personal Narratives in the Social Sciences and History* (London and Ithaca: Cornell University Press, 2008), p. 43.

42. Personal interview, Cologne, Germany, April 2008.

43. Personal interview, Shiraz, Iran, July 2008.

44. Personal interview, Ahvaz, Iran, July 2008.

45. Sandra L. Bartky, *Sympathy and Solidarity* (New York: Rowman & Littlefield, 2002), p. 81.

46. Maynes, Pierce, and Laslett, *Telling Stories*.

47. Maynes, Pierce, and Laslett, *Telling Stories*, p. 116.

48. Boydston, 'Gender as a Question of Historical Analysis', p. 561.

49. Joan Scott, *Gender and the Politics of History* (New York: Columbia University Press, 1988), p. 38.

50. Personal interview, Tehran, Iran, June 2008.

51. Operation 'Eternal Light' took place in 1988 after Iran accepted the ceasefire. Male and female members of the organisation invaded Iranian territory from neighbouring Iraq. Personal interview, London, UK, September 2010.

52. Personal interview, Tehran, Iran, June 2008.

53. There are currently over 200 memoirs written or narrated by Iranian women regarding their experiences as nurses, fighters or relatives of war martyrs during the Iran-Iraq war. Memoirs written by political prisoners during this same period are also flourishing in the Iranian diaspora.

54. Reza Raissi, *Khabarnegar-e Jangi: Khaterat-e Maryam Kazamzadeh* [Wartime Journalist: Memories of Maryam Kazamzadeh] (Tehran: Yad banu, *1383*/2003). Date in italics is the year according to Iran's Islamic calendar.

55. See for example, Raissi, *Khabarnegar-e Jangi,* pp. 27, 28, 59, 70, 71.

56. Paul Atkinson and Sara Delamont, 'Rescuing Narrative from Qualitative Research', *Narrative Inquiry* 16 (2006), pp. 164–72; Boydston, 'Gender as a Question of Historical Analysis', p. 576.

57. Isolation is also noted as central to Iranian women's experiences during this period in other studies. See Gholamreza Jamshidi and Nafiseh Hamidi, 'Tajrobeh-ye Zanan dar Jang [Women's Experiences during War]', *Pajuhesh Zanan* 5 (*1386*/2007), pp. 81–108. See especially pp. 93–6.

58. Brian Massumi, *Parables for the Virtual: Movement, Affect, Sensation* (Durham: Duke University Press, 2002), p. 35. See also, Gilles Deleuze, *Essays Critical and Clinical* (London: Verso, 1998).

59. Frantz Fanon, 'The Fact of Blackness', in Frantz Fanon, *Black Skin, White Masks* (London: Paladin, 1970), pp. 77–99; Audre Lorde, 'Eye to Eye: Black Women, Hatred, and Anger', *Sister Outsider: Essays and Speeches* (Berkeley: The Crossing Press, 2007), pp. 145–75; Sara Ahmed, *The Cultural Politics of Emotion* (New York: Routledge, 2004).

60. For more on affect and emotions as interconnected see, Eve Sedgwick, *Touching Feeling: Affect, Pedagogy, Performativity* (Durham: Duke University Press, 2003), pp. 17–19. See also Silvan Tomkins, *Affect, Imagery, Consciousness*, vol. 2, *The Negative Affects* (New York: Springer Publishing, 2008), pp. 289–614. For more on the interplay between the body and affect see Teresa Brennan, *The Transmission of Affect* (Ithaca and London: Cornell University Press, 2004).

61. See for instance, Clare Hemmings, 'Invoking Affect: Cultural Theory and the Ontological Turn', *Cultural Studies* 19 (2005), pp. 548–67.

62. Wimal Dissanayake, 'Introduction/Agency and Cultural Understanding: Some Preliminary Remarks', in Wimal Dissanayake (ed.), *Narratives of Agency: Self-Making in China, India, and Japan* (Minneapolis: University of Minnesota Press, 1996), pp. ix–xxi.

63. Monica Mookherjee, 'Affective Citizenship: Feminism, Postcolonialism and the Politics of Recognition', *Critical Review of International Social and Political Philosophy* 8 (2005), pp. 3–50.

64. Suad Joseph has demonstrated that in the Middle Eastern context, desire may work itself through communities and social networks, making liberal citizenry practices less likely. Suad Joseph, 'Learning Desire:

Relational Pedagogies and the Desiring Female Subject in Lebanon', *Journal of Middle East Women's Studies* 1 (2005), pp. 79–109.

65. On Shi'ism and justice in Persian culture see Roy Mottahedeh, *The Mantle of the Prophet: Religion and Politics in Iran* (Oxford: One World, 2000); Moojan Momen, *An Introduction to Shi'i Islam: The History and Doctrines of Twelver Shi'ism* (New Haven: Yale University Press, 1985).

66. Vanessa Martin, *Creating an Islamic State: Khomeini and the Making of a New Iran* (London: I.B. Tauris, 2003).

67. Shirin Saeidi, 'Creating the Islamic Republic of Iran: Wives and Daughters of Martyrs, and Acts of Citizenship', *Citizenship Studies* 14 (2010), pp. 113–26; Asef Bayat, *Life as Politics: How Ordinary People Change the Middle East* (Stanford: Stanford University Press, 2010).

68. Engin F. Isin, 'Theorizing Acts of Citizenship', in Engin F. Isin and Greg M. Nielsen (eds), *Acts of Citizenship* (London and New York: Zed Books, 2008), pp. 14–43. For Isin, it is only if an act makes a deliberate or unintentional claim for rights or restitutions against some form of injustice or inequality that qualifies it as an act of citizenship which creates the activist citizen. The interplay between creativity and the pursuit of justice in this process is vital. Agency or action in this formulation escape the self and enter the social terrain through *acts* that help us historicise non-elite political interventions through emergent yet peripheral domains.

69. Suad Joseph has also argued that liberal notions of citizenship cannot fully capture women's gendered subjectivities in the Middle Eastern context. See Suad Joseph, 'Gender and Citizenship in Middle Eastern States', *Merip* 198 (1996), pp. 4–10.

70. Joyce P. Kaufman and Kristen P. Williams, 'Who Belongs? Women, Marriage and Citizenship', *International Feminist Journal of Politics* 6 (2004), pp. 416–35.

71. Farhana Ali, 'Rocking the Cradle to Rocking the World: The Role of Muslim Female Fighters', *Journal of International Women's Studies* 8 (2006), pp. 21–35.

72. Azam Khatam, 'Struggles Over Defining the Moral City: The Problem Called "Youth" in Urban Iran', in Linda Herrera and Asef Bayat (eds), *Being Young and Muslim: New Cultural Politics in the Global South and North* (Oxford: Oxford University Press, 2010), pp. 207–21.

73. Michael Ignatieff, *Blood & Belonging: Journeys into the New Nationalism* (London: Vintage, 1994), p. 3.

74. Lauren Berlant and Michael Warner, 'Sex in Public', *Critical Inquiry* 24 (1998), pp. 547–66.

75. Stevi Jackson, 'Gender, Sexuality and Heterosexuality: The Complexity (and Limits) of Heteronormativity', *Feminist Theory* 7 (2006), pp. 105–21.

76. Minoo Moallem, *Between Warrior Brother and Veiled Sister: Islamic Fundamentalism and the Politics of Patriarchy in Iran* (Berkeley: University of California Press, 2005).

77. See Kathy Davis, 'Embody-ing Theory: Beyond Modernist and Postmodernist Readings of the Body', in Kathy Davis (ed.), *Embodied Practices: Feminist Perspectives on the Body* (London: Sage, 1997), pp. 1–23; on citizenship and the body see, Chris Beasley and Carol Bacchi, 'Citizen Bodies: Embodying Citizens – A Feminist Analysis', *International Feminist Journal of Politics* 2 (2000), pp. 337–58.

78. On the state's segregation of spaces during this time see Parvin Paidar, *Women and the Political Process in Twentieth-Century Iran* (Cambridge: Cambridge University Press, 1995). On the methodological importance of exploring how the public and private spheres are locally mediated see Gillian Youngs, *International Relations in a Global Age: A Conceptual Challenge* (Cambridge: Polity Press, 1999). For more on the fluidity which has existed between the public and private spheres in Muslim societies see Asma Afsaruddin (ed.), *Hermeneutics and Honor: Negotiating Female 'Public' Space in Islamic/ate Societies* (Cambridge: Harvard Center for Middle Eastern Studies, 1999).

79. Roksana Bahramitash and Hadi Salehi Esfahani, 'Modernization, Revolution, and Islamism: Political Economy of Women's Employment', in Roksana Bahramitash and Hadi Salehi Esfahani (eds), *Veiled Employment: Islamism and the Political Economy of Women's Employment in Iran* (Syracuse: Syracuse University Press, 2011), pp. 53–82.

80. Pooya Alaedini and Mohamad R. Razavi, 'Women's Participation and Employment in Iran: A Critical Examination', *Critique: Critical Middle East Studies* 14 (2005), pp. 57–73.

81. Parvin Paidar, *Women and the Political Process in Twentieth-Century Iran* (Cambridge: Cambridge University Press, 1995).

82. Soheila Farjamfar, a nurse during the war, recounts how one husband divorced his wife who was working long hours as a nurse. Another woman's husband took a second wife. Soheila Farjamfar, *Kafsh-ha-ye Sargardan: Khaterat-e Soheila Farjamfar* [Wandering Shoes: Memories of Soheila Farjamfar] (Tehran: Sourah Mehr, *1381*/2002). However, it should be noted that it is not always the case that husbands are less than supportive of their wives roles in the workforce in post-1979 Iran. See for example Homa Hoodfar's study of female medical volunteers. Homa Hoodfar, 'Volunteer Health Workers in Iran as Social Activists:

Can "Governmental Non-governmental Organizations" Be Agents of Democratisation?', Occasional Paper no.10 (Women Living Under Muslim Laws, 1998), <http://www.wluml.org/node/450>.

83. Personal interview, Tehran, Iran, May 2008. Child care has been a central issue in the lives of working women during other wars as well. See, for example, Penny Summerfield, *Women Workers in the Second World War: Production and Patriarchy in Conflict* (London: Croom Helm, 1984).

84. Personal interview, Tehran, Iran, May 2008.

85. Personal interview, Tehran, Iran, June 2008.

86. Personal interview, Malmo, Sweden, March 2009.

87. Alison M Jaggar, 'Love and Knowledge: Emotions in the Feminist Epistemology', in Alison Jaggar and Susan R. Bordo (eds), *Gender/Body/Knowledge* (New Brunswick: Rutgers University Press, 1989), pp. 145–71.

88. Shadi Sadr, 'Shekanje va Khoshunat-e Jensi Alayhe Zendaneyan-e Siaysi-ye Zan dar Jomhuri-ye Islami' [Torture and Sexual Abuse of Female Political Prisoners in the Islamic Republic], *Edalat baray-e Iran* [Justice for Iran] (Justice for Iran, 2011). In this report Sadr also argues that rape was common during the 1980–88 period in Iran's prisons. However, during my interviews with fifty former political prisoners now living in Germany and Sweden between 2008 and 2009, interviewees firmly stressed that rape was not widespread during this time.

89. Personal interview, Cologne, Germany, April 2008.

90. Personal interview, Cologne, Germany, April 2008.

91. Personal interview, Frankfurt, Germany, April 2008.

92. Personal interview, Tehran, Iran, May 2008. See also Farjamfar, *Kafsh-ha-ye Sargardan*. Nurses have deviated from the state's war agenda in other contexts too. See for example Margaret R. Higonnet (ed.), *Nurses at the Front: Writing the Wounds of the Great War* (Boston: North Eastern University Press, 2001).

93. Farjamfar, *Kafsh-ha-ye Sargardan*, p. 103.

94. Personal interview, Tehran, Iran, May 2008; Farjamfar, *Kafsh-ha-ye Sargardan*, p. 104.

95. Moallem, *Between Warrior Brother and Veiled Sister.*

96. Morteza Sarhangi, *Banu-ye Mah (6): Goft-o Gu ba Parvin Daepour Hamsar Sardar Shahid Hossein Baghari* [Lady of the Moon: A Conversation with Parvin Daepour the Wife of Commander Shahid Hossein Baghari] (Tehran: Kaman, *1385*/2006), pp. 13–14.

97. Batool Kazruneyan, *Ruzgaran (13): Ketab-e Zanan-e Khorramshahr* [The Book of the Women of Khorramshahr] (Tehran: Ravayat-e Fath, *1382*/2003).

98. Tami Amanda Jacoby, 'Feminism, Nationalism and Difference: Reflections on the Palestinian Woman's Movement', *Women's Studies International Forum* 22 (1999), pp. 511–23.

99. For instance, in her memoir *Paeez-e 59*, when male soldiers suggested that women stay behind and cook instead of participating in the warfront, Zohreh Sotodeh states the following: 'The suggestion that we should sit in the house and cook (even for the selfless, such as the youth of Khorramshahr) was an insult. Worst than that was the arrogant tone with which the boys said this!' See Seyedeh Azam Hosseini and Nahid Soleimani, *Paeez-e 59* [The Fall of 1359] (Tehran: Sourah Mehr, *1387*/2007), here p. 79.

100. Barlas argues that Islam opposes a binary association of the genders. See Asma Barlas, *'Believing Women' in Islam: Unreading Patriarchal Interpretations of the Qur'an* (Austin: University of Texas Press, 2002).

101. Seyedeh Azam Hosseini, *Daa* [Mother] (Tehran: Sourah Mehr, *1388*/2008).

102. Hosseini, *Daa*, p. 437.

103. Hosseini, *Daa*, p. 425.

104. Personal Interview, Tehran, Iran, June 2008.

105. Nahid Soleimani, *Gol-e Simin* (Tehran: Sourah Mehr, *1381*/2001), p. 101.

106. Shahin Gerami, 'Mullahs, Martyrs, and Men: Conceptualizing Masculinity in the Islamic Republic of Iran', *Men and Masculinities* 5 (2003), pp. 257–74.

107. Mohammad Hossein Valadi, *Aflakian-e Zamin* [Angels on Earth] (Tehran: Nashr Shahid, *1386*/2007), p. 11.

108. The recognition of women as both martyrs and relatives of male martyrs is also made here: Alireza Kamari, *Nameh-ha-ye Fahimeh* [Fahimeh's Letters] (Tehran: Daftar-e Adabiyat va Hon-ar-e Moqavemat, *1385*/2006).

109. Valadi, *Aflakian-e Zamin*, pp. 2, 7.

110. Moallem, *Between Warrior Brother and Veiled Sister*, p. 109.

111. Shirin Saeidi, 'Only Five Female Martyrs on Streets of Tehran' tr. from Farsi, *Iranian.com*, (2008) <http://www.iranian.com/main/blog/shirin-saeidi/only-5-female-martyrs-streets-tehran>.

112. The idea of Muslim feminism was first written about in the Iranian context in 1982. See Nahid Yeganeh, 'Women's Struggles in the Islamic Republic of Iran', in Azar Tabari and Nahid Yeganeh (eds), *In the*

Shadow of Islam: Women's Movement in Iran (London: Zed Press, 1982), pp. 26–74. For more on Iranian women's gendered subjectivities during the Iran-Iraq war see Shirin Saeidi, 'Hero of Her Own Story: Gender and State Formation in Contemporary Iran' (unpublished doctoral thesis, Cambridge University, 2012).

113. Paidar, *Women and the Political Process in Twentieth-Century Iran*, p. 340.
114. Personal Interview, Tehran, Iran, June 2008.
115. Personal interview, Tehran, Iran, June 2008.
116. Maryam Zaghyan, *An Su-ye Devar-e Del* [The Other Side of the Heart] (Tehran: bonyad-e hafz-e Asar va Arzesh-ha-ye Defa-e Moghaddas, *1386*/2007), pp. 112–13.
117. Personal interview, Tehran, Iran, June 2008.
118. Habibeh Jafarian, *Niemey-e Penhan-e Mah (1)* [The Moon's Hidden Half] (Tehran: Ravayat-e Fath, *1386*/2007), p. 50.
119. Personal interview, Tehran, Iran, June 2008.
120. Personal interview, Ahvaz, Iran, July 2008.
121. Maryam Baradaran, *Enak Shokaran (1)* [Now Poisoned], 6th edn (Tehran: Ravayat-e Fath, *1386*/2007), p. 76.
122. Geoffrey Robertson, *The Massacre of Political Prisoners in Iran, 1988* (Abdorrahman Boroumand Foundation, 2011), p. 5. Available at: <http://www.iranrights.org/english/document-1380.php>.
123. Anonymous, *Iran: Violations of Human Rights 1987–1990* (Amnesty International, 1990), p. 12.
124. Ervand Abrahamian, *Tortured Confessions: Prisons and Public Recantations in Modern Iran* (London and Berkeley: University of California Press, 1999), p. 217.
125. Carol L. Delaney, *The Seed and the Soil: Gender and Cosmology in Turkish Village Society* (Berkeley and Los Angeles: University of California Press, 1991), p. 12.
126. For more on gendered constructs of the nation and its relation to land see, Sheila Hannah Katz, 'Adam and Adama, '*Ird* and *Ard*: En-gendering Political Conflict and Identity in Early Jewish and Palestinian Nationalisms', in Deniz Kandiyoti (ed.), *Gendering the Middle East* (New York: Syracuse University Press, 1996), pp. 85–105.
127. Forthcoming doctoral theses include the following: Narges Bajoghli, 'The Revolutionary Guards, the Basij, and the Contested Legacies of War in Iran', New York University; Shirin Shafaie, 'Contemporary Iranian War Narratives: A Dialectical Discourse Analysis', School of Oriental and African Studies, University of London.

14 An Epistemology of Collusion: *Hijras*, *Kothis* and the Historical (Dis)continuity of Gender/Sexual Identities in Eastern India

Aniruddha Dutta

In many postcolonial societies, the relation between contemporary gender/sexual identities and historical precursors of gender variance and same-sex desire has been a fraught and controversial question.[1] While right wing nationalist discourses have often attacked such identities as western influences, LGBT (lesbian, gay, bisexual and transgender) activists have traced homoeroticism and gender variance, and even LGBT identities, back through revisionist readings of pre-colonial history.[2] Scholarly accounts usually repudiate the conservative denunciation of homosexuality, but the historicity of gender/sexual identities and their relation to postcolonial modernity remains a debated question across several world regions. For example, Joseph Massad critiques western advocates of LGBT rights in the Arab world for propagating a neocolonial discourse of identity that 'produces homosexuals ... where they do not exist', seeing gay/lesbian identities as modern western constructs that might repress non-identitarian histories of same-sex desire in the non-west.[3] In contrast, Peter Jackson links the emergence of LGBT identities in Southeast Asian nations to their distinctive trajectories of nationalism and capitalism, which are not reducible to western influence, and argues that LGBT identities evidence non-western variants that need not derive their logic or justification from pre-colonial histories of gender/sexual variance.[4]

In India, scholarly and activist debates on the historicity or emergence of gender/sexual identities are thrown into sharp relief in the case of the *kothi* (or *koti*), a category for socioeconomically marginalised gender variant or 'feminine' same-sex desiring males that gained visibility within the emerging institutional movement for LGBT rights in the late 1990s. Some activists advocated *kothi* as a more culturally authentic identity than the putatively westernised 'gay' used by elite English-speaking Indians.[5] Several scholars critique this indigenist argument and link the emergence of the *kothi* to the rise of Indian activism for the sexual health and human rights of sexual minorities, situated within the interlinked globalising expansion of sexual rights activism and HIV-AIDS prevention funding.[6] Lawrence

Gender History Across Epistemologies, First Edition. Edited by Donna R. Gabaccia and Mary Jo Maynes.
Chapters © 2013 The Authors. Book compilation © 2013 Blackwell Publishing Ltd.

Cohen argues that kothis 'emerged in cities like Mumbai as a new social fact', distinct from previous usages of the term, parallel to the rise of funded non-governmental organisations (NGOs) and associated communities.[7] Paul Boyce and Akshay Khanna emphasise the role of state- and donor-funded interventions for HIV-AIDS prevention in constructing the *kothi* as a culturally authentic and vulnerable Indian subgroup within the globalising category of MSM (men who have sex with men) used in transnational HIV-AIDS prevention discourse.[8] As Khanna states, the '*kothi* . . . is in some sense a creation of the [HIV-AIDS] industry itself'.[9]

In contrast, the *hijra*, a better-known term for transvestite communities described in colonial accounts as 'eunuchs', has been studied as an identity with a more historically continuous trajectory, with pre-colonial records stretching back to at least the seventeenth century.[10] While the indigeneity of the *kothi* is contested, the *hijra* has functioned as a quintessential marker of Indic gender/sexual difference. The colonial regime defined the *hijra* as the Indian equivalent of the broader pejorative category of 'eunuchs' and attempted to describe, classify and control them, echoing British attitudes to other gender/sexual practices like widow-burning and child marriage that were made to stand for the debased nature of Indian society.[11] As colonial depictions were superseded in the twentieth century, the *hijra* was reclaimed as a prominent non-western 'third gender' or transgender group resisting the western schema of sexual dimorphism.[12] Recent ethnographies by Lawrence Cohen and Gayatri Reddy critique earlier pathologising or essentialising constructions of the *hijra*, describing the *hijra* as a complex identity of marginalised male-born (or rarely intersex) transvestites who combine kinship-based social organisation with Islamic and Hindu religious practices.[13] *Hijras* may undergo castration and penectomy, which confers higher status within intra-community hierarchies, and claim auspiciousness to undertake ritual blessing for money and gifts during occasions such as childbirth in middle-class families.[14] The ethnographies of Kira Hall and Gayatri Reddy situate the *kothi*, too, within this more historically continuous (sub)cultural formation as a same-sex desiring gender variant community related to *hijras*, though not organised into hierarchised clans like them – in contrast to the emphasis on the institutionally-mediated emergence of the *kothi* in Cohen, Boyce and Khanna.[15]

This article will study the historicity of *hijra* and *kothi* as prominent vernacular categories of Indic gender/sexual difference with reference to broader debates on identity, (post)colonialism and modernity in postcolonial and South Asian historiography.[16] I will suggest that the apparent contrast between the historical continuity of the *hijra* and the contemporary institutional construction of the *kothi* masks deeper similarities in how both identities have emerged through collusions between subcultural processes of community formation and governmental power.[17] The focus on the involvement of postcolonial institutional networks (NGOs, donors and the state) in the emergence of the *kothi* as an identity of same-sex desiring males in Cohen, Boyce and Khanna's ethnographies recalls Foucault's widely influential theorisation of the historical emergence of identity-based conceptions of sexuality within modern regimes of power and knowledge.[18] In contrast, the aforementioned ethnographies by Hall and Reddy study the cultural dynamics of *kothi* identification in relation to *hijras*, suggesting a greater historical continuity in its formation. Thus, differing epistemological priorities and sites of inquiry result in diverging suggestions about the historical ontology of Indian gender/sexual identities.

These differences may be located within broader debates in postcolonial and subaltern studies on the historical continuity or rupture of identity formations in South Asia due to the governmental institutions of colonial and postcolonial modernity.[19] Drawing upon Benedict Anderson's influential theorisation of the role of print capitalism and colonial institutions such as the census in forging national and ethnic identities, scholars like Sudipta Kaviraj and Arjun Appadurai postulate a sharp transition from ambiguously bounded forms of social difference to more rigidly defined identities through colonial and postcolonial institutions of power.[20] Kaviraj has argued that premodern collectivities were 'not enumerated' and had 'fuzzy boundaries', while, as Appadurai states, '[colonial] enumerative strategies helped to ignite communitarian and nationalist identities'.[21] Nicholas Dirks argues that colonial administration systematised 'India's diverse forms of social identity' into the overarching framework of caste.[22] Others like C. A. Bayly and Sumit Guha argue for a more continuous trajectory of identity formation from pre-colonial to modern collectivities that was not radically ruptured by (post)colonial institutions.[23] Sumit Guha critiques Anderson, Appadurai and Kaviraj for overemphasising the role of (post)colonial governmental power and neglecting to study how seemingly 'traditional' collectivities such as religious communities dynamically reproduce themselves from pre-colonial to modern periods.[24] He argues that communities demonstrate historical agency and evolve without direct input from (post)colonial governmental technologies.[25] However, this overview is not to reduce this complex literature to a static dichotomy between historical continuity and postcolonial rupture. Kaviraj's later work theorises how pre-colonial conditions influence postcolonial social formations, although he does not demonstrate this for specific identities.[26] Partha Chatterjee's recent work charts mutual interactions between communitarian or kinship-based collectives and postcolonial governmental institutions.[27] While arguing that 'classificatory criteria used by colonial governmental regimes have continued into the postcolonial era' and shape the 'dominant criteria for identifying communities', Chatterjee also notes the historical agency of communities that use putatively 'traditional' logics of kinship to represent themselves to governmental power.[28]

Reading Guha and Bayly in conjunction with, rather than in opposition to, Kaviraj and Chatterjee, I will explore the interaction between the self-reproduction of communities and postcolonial institutions in the case of gender/sexual identities, and trace how continuities between historical logics of community formation and postcolonial governmental processes might underlie profound shifts in identity formation for both *hijra* and *kothi* categories. Drawing upon colonial ethnology, contemporary ethnographies and my own ethnographic fieldwork in India, I demonstrate that there have been locally variegated, yet translocally connected, subcultural formations of gender/sexual variance with different degrees of distinction or overlap between *hijra* and lesser-known categories such as *kothi*. I describe how this variegated terrain of gender/sexual variance might be increasingly consolidated into a more standardised identitarian rubric through collusions between the self-representation of subcultural networks or communities and (post)colonial cartographies of identity. These range from colonial ethnological compendia to contemporary media representations and surveys by NGOs. Such structural collusions between institutional and (sub)cultural processes of identity formation result in the attempted standardisation of the distinction between *hijra* and other identities across a range of locations, constructing emergent normative identity-based divisions that might circumscribe lived practices. The translocal consolidation of these

identities creates significant temporal discontinuities between older forms of gen-
der/sexual variance and emerging identitarian formations in India, but this rupture
itself might be instituted in collusion with older communities and subcultures.

Thus, I suggest that both *hijra* and *kothi* may be evolving through interrelated and
active epistemological projects of naming, describing and classifying gender/sexual
identities, through which their definitional boundaries are becoming more standardised
in relation to each other. As I will describe, *hijra* becomes defined in terms of gender
variance as a transgender identity while *kothi* is defined with reference to (homo)sexual
behaviour as a subsection of MSM, constructing an increasing separation between gender and sexual identities that, as noted by scholars like Jackson, is a distinctive feature
of modern discourses of gender/sexuality.[29] However, the emergence of *hijra* and *kothi*
as seemingly consolidated, bounded and distinct identities demonstrates not only the
role of postcolonial epistemologies and cartographies of identity but also the standardisation of pre-existing subcultural demarcations, necessitating an epistemological
practice that bridges multiple methods and sites of enquiry to illuminate the collusion of multiple governmental and subcultural processes of identity formation. To that
end, this article will bridge archival study, oral histories and ethnography, particularly
focused on eastern India where I have conducted participation observation with several community-based organisations, NGOs and associated community networks since
2007.[30] The first section of the article examines British colonial censuses and ethnology
as an early attempt to consolidate the *hijra* translocally as a 'eunuch' group. Subsequent sections focus on the contemporary period, examining constructions of the *hijra*
and *kothi* in relation to institutional projects of gender/sexual rights and HIV-AIDS
prevention. More broadly, the article suggests that the analysis of collusions between
vernacular subcultural formations and governmental discourses of identity helps to illuminate the complex imbrications of historical continuity and postcolonial emergence
in modern South Asia, and to explain the historical involvement of non-elite communities in the emergence of normative rubrics of gender/sexual identity in postcolonial
societies where such identities evidence historical precursors.

Colonial ethnology: investigating the truth of the eunuch

As noted by Lawrence Preston, British observations of groups they called 'eunuchs' began roughly in the late eighteenth century, and are scattered within the correspondence
from contingents of the British East India Company in the early phase of mercan-
tile colonialism.[31] Most accounts describe 'eunuchs' as malformed and repulsive.[32]
Preston chronicles British interactions with the community known as *hijra* (or *hijda*)
in western India as one of the first colonial encounters with 'eunuchs'. The *hijras* of
western India enjoyed hereditary rights such as revenue shares under the indigenous
Maratha regime. As the British gradually took over Maratha territories from 1817 onward, these rights were curtailed, and this community was increasingly forced into the
expanding urban underworld of low caste workers, prostitutes and beggars.[33] 'Eunuchs'
were subsequently criminalised under the Criminal Tribes Act of 1871, a law that was
revoked in 1952 after independence.[34] In the original act, 'eunuch' could refer both
to any person 'dressed or ornamented like a woman' and anyone who upon medical
inspection 'appeared to be impotent', encompassing both gendered performance and
physiology.[35]

British administrators and officers started compiling ethnological compendia on different regions of British India after the inauguration of monarchical rule in 1858. The first census was undertaken between 1868 and 1872, and thereafter at ten-year intervals. In this literature, one notices several diverging names and descriptions for groups described as 'eunuchs', including differences in physiological characteristics and group initiation rites. While the colonial literature seems to have discovered '*hijra*' as one of the first known Indian terms for 'eunuch', it references other regional names and fails to suggest a uniform community across the diverse systems of rule in early colonial India. *Hijra* appears as a distinct caste in the first detailed list of castes and tribes compiled by Kitts in 1885, based on the census of 1881.[36] Subsequent compendia list different names – *khoja, pavaya, khasua, mukhanas* – but they are often listed as synonymous with or redirected from '*hijra*', thus helping to establish *hijra* as the consolidated label for groups that appear to be regionally diverse, notwithstanding their similarities.[37] *Hijra* seems to be a word in Hindi and Urdu, languages that assumed national character through the colonial period as opposed to more 'regional' languages like Marathi, Tamil or Bengali, which might explain its use as the most common signifier for 'eunuchs' in the colonial archive.[38]

The ethnological compendia following the censuses of 1881, 1891, 1901 and 1911 are commonly concerned with investigating the physiological characteristics of eunuchs but diverge in their descriptions. As Reddy notes, there is an overarching epistemological concern with discovering the physiological truth of eunuch bodies.[39] Some reports make the membership of eunuch groups contingent upon congenital deformation, some upon 'natural' impotence and others upon ritualistic initiation through castration and penectomy.[40] Moreover, several reports distinguish between 'natural' eunuchs and those 'artificially' made into eunuchs through castration, designated by different names. For example, in Thurston's *Castes and Tribes of Southern India* (1909), the entry marked *hijra* is redirected to an entry on the *khoja*, which includes a description of the *hijra*. *Khojas* are described as 'artificial' castrated eunuchs employed by wealthy nobility, whereas *hijras* are 'natural' eunuchs who are born impotent, forming their own groups with specific religious practices.[41] Contradictorily, in Russell's *The Tribes and Castes of the Central Provinces of India* (1916), *khasuas* are deemed to be 'natural' eunuchs with congenital deformation, whereas *hijras* are 'artificial', 'reduced to the like condition by amputation'.[42]

Thus, the precise relation between different vernacular terms is already a point of contention. As Hall states, 'Although the term *koti* is largely absent . . . a significant number of colonialist texts mention groups that resemble today's *kotis* as a point of contrast [to] the supposedly "more authentic" *hijra* community. A tension between the real eunuch and its artificial shadow thus governs the colonialist record'.[43] However, I will note that significantly, *hijras* were not always named as the 'more authentic' community, as seen in Russell above. Rather, the ethnological literature was contradictory in its terminological classification, unable to fix a true eunuch body or coherent 'authentic' category such as *hijra*.

As the census stopped enumerating castes altogether after independence, it does not appear that the postcolonial state attempted to standardise these contradictory definitions of the *hijra*. However, the colonial ethnological literature did seem to standardise the usage of *hijra* (rather than *khoja, khasua,* etc.) as the most common name for 'eunuch' groups in subsequent literature. The question of who exactly constituted these groups remained a point of contention in some twentieth century ethnographic literature. As noted by Cohen, an exchange between the anthropologists George Carstairs and Morris Opler in *American Anthropologist* between 1957 and 1960 agreed that *hijras* were castrated males, but debated whether they were prostitutes, or blessed newborn children in their role as ritual devotees of a mother goddess, Bahuchara Mata.[44] Here, the point of contention was not physiology but rather the real occupation of *hijras*.

Postcolonial ethnography: an intersectional epistemology of *hijras*

Recent ethnography critiques older epistemological concerns with the physiological essence or true occupation of *hijras*, counteracting essentialising moves to locate 'real' or 'natural' eunuchs. Rather, scholars have focused on the intersection of social, religious and kinship practices through which *hijras* constitute themselves, including religious rituals (Islam and goddess-worship) and kinship structures such as hierarchised lineages comprising tiered ranks of *gurus* (heads) and *chelas* (disciples). Based on his ethnographic research in the north Indian city of Varanasi, Cohen constructs a working definition of the *hijra*, including community membership within hierarchised lineages, comprising the *hijra guru* and her initiated disciples as its smallest unit: '*hijras* are organised into households with a *hijra* guru as head, into territories delimiting where each household can dance and demand money from merchants, and into larger regional and supraregional associations or *pancayats* linking them to other cities across South Asia'.[45] Reddy's ethnography on *hijra* groups in the southern city of Hyderabad corroborates this description and further specifies that 'there are seven hijra houses or "lineages" in India', to which all individual households belong.[46] Thus, in Reddy's ethnography, while the community in Hyderabad identifies through the term *kojja* when speaking in the regional language of Telegu, they also represent themselves as part of the larger *hijra* community as members of *hijra* lineages that are spread nationwide.

While describing *hijra* communities, Reddy and Cohen counteract essentialised definitions of *hijras*, noting that members of *hijra* households may or may not be castrated and pursue a variety of occupations including ritual blessing and sex work.[47] However, while describing occasional transitions or overlaps between *hijra* and other categories, even this intersectional epistemology of the *hijra* has largely focused on household- or lineage-based *hijras* as evidenced in the cited excerpts from Cohen and Reddy, potentially leading to an inadvertently restrictive description that emphasises lineage-based kinship.

Moreover, while counteracting essentialised hierarchies between 'true'/'natural' and 'artificial' eunuchs, this literature evidences significant differences on the relation between the *hijra* category and other vernacular terms for male-born gender variance, among which the *kothi* has emerged since the late 1990s as the most salient 'sexual minority'. In Reddy's ethnography, *kothi* is a generic label for non-masculine males used by *hijras* in Hyderabad, encompassing both *hijra* and non-*hijra* sections, with an internal cartography separating *hijras* (*catla kothis*) with other *kothi* subgroups like *kada-catla kothis* (*kothis* in male attire).[48] On the other hand, *kothi* does not occur as an umbrella category in Hall's ethnography in Delhi, but signifies a non-*hijra* transgender group who may parody *hijra* practices but do not self-identify as *hijra*, though some transition to being *hijra*.[49] In Cohen's 1995 ethnography in Varanasi, *hijras* are compared to groups called *jankhas*, with household affiliation and castration being important to the 'full adoption of *hijra* identity'.[50] Cohen argues that *jankhas* are not 'inauthentic' or 'incomplete' *hijras* but a distinct group linked more to low-caste burlesque than *hijra* occupations, though some may also occasionally self-identify as *hijra*.[51] Later revisiting this work, Cohen notes that *kothi* was only marginally known as a term in Varanasi.[52]

Translocal consolidations: relating *hijra* and *kothi* emergence

Building upon the implications of colonial ethnology as well as postcolonial ethnography, the following sections will develop an argument that is implied but not ethnographically elaborated in the existing literature: there are locally varied vernacular cartographies evidencing varying degrees of overlap or distinction between *hijra* and other categories. I will suggest that the translocal consolidation of *kothi* and *hijra* as increasingly standardised and distinct identities are *interrelated* processes, both connected to postcolonial governmentality, although the collusion of *hijra* identification with governmental power has not been emphasised in the literature.

In contrast to the focus on *hijras* within lineages (or *gharanas*) in the literature, I will explore non-*gharana* claims to *hijra* identity, showing how some of the most occupationally visible *hijras* are not 'authentic' by the norms of lineage-based kinship, and evidence both transition from and overlap with other categories. Such categorical overlaps seem to have an indefinite historical provenance, and might be a structural feature of the uneven territorial control of *hijra gharanas*. But over the last two decades, *gharana*-based *hijras* have actively undertaken to define 'real' or 'authentic' *hijras* as a minority in collusion with NGOs and the media, around the same time when NGOs started defining MSM and *kothi* as vulnerable groups. This attempted construction of the *hijra* as a bounded lineage-based group increasingly separates *hijra* from non-*hijra* (*kothi*, MSM) identities in NGO, state and media discourses in a way that colonial ethnology was unable to standardise, such that who can identify as *hijra* becomes more circumscribed at the level of official discourse, and potentially, lived reality. Meanwhile, various subcultural terms for gender variance related to *hijra*, like *dhurani* and *dhunuri* in eastern India, are increasingly translocally consolidated as *kothi*, which becomes a distinct non-*hijra* identity under the MSM rubric. In the subsequent sections, I will describe the institutional-subcultural collusions underlying the translocal standardisation of *hijra* and *kothi* categories with reference to field notes and oral histories that I have gathered as a participant observer with communities and organisations at multiple sites within the eastern Indian state of West Bengal. The state has seen a growing movement for the civil rights and sexual health of 'sexual minorities' since the early 1990s, led by non-governmental and community-based organisations (NGOs and CBOs). As these organisations bridge metropolitan and non-metropolitan areas, the state provides an appropriate site to study the interactions of lower class non-metropolitan communities with NGOs/CBOs and the consolidation of *hijra* and *kothi* through such interactions.

Dhurani, dhunuri, hijra: translocal subcultures in West Bengal

As per the documented history of the movement for gender/sexual rights in Eastern India, early groups like Fun Club (1990) emerged within upper-middle-class circles in the capital city of Kolkata around a nascent 'gay' identity.[53] While early social groups were short-lived, the first successful mobilisations were Counsel Club (1993) and the Naz Foundation's Calcutta project (initiated 1993–94), which subsequently facilitated the formation of CBOs in smaller towns. This expansion was aided by increasing HIV-AIDS funding for 'sexual minorities' from the Indian state and foreign donors from the early 2000s.[54] Sarswata, an activist associated with Counsel Club in Kolkata, helped found two CBOs whose members I have become acquainted with: Dum Dum Swikriti Society in the northern Kolkata suburbs and the adjacent Nadia district, and further north, Madhya Banglar Sangram in the district of Murshidabad (henceforth, Swikriti and Sangram). Such CBOs have served to bridge city-based activists with lower class and non-metropolitan communities or networks of gender/sexually variant people. As Sarswata described in one of our conversations, a few Kolkata activists had informal contacts with lower-class communities, which were subsequently bolstered through institutional expansion: 'In the mid-90s, some people joined Counsel Club through whom it could extend its reach to underprivileged communities'.

Hijra gharanas, or hierarchised lineages, seem to have been the most organised of these communities. In my conversations with *hijras*, as well as NGO activists, I was told that there are three main *gharanas* in West Bengal – Shyambajari, Mechhua and Gunghoria or Gunghor – putatively descended from a single lineage. Each of these lineages is organised into tiered ranks of *guru-ma* (mother *gurus*) and *chelas* (disciples) and divided into households. Senior *gurus* serve as heads of independent households with their *chelas*, who might serve as second-tier *gurus* to *natichelas* (*chelas* of *chelas*) and so on. Each household has its designated territory where *chelas* undertake *hijra* occupations. Typically, junior *chelas* or *nati-chelas* undertake the ritualised occupation of *badhai* in their territory – proffering blessings in return for money and gifts at houses with newborn children, and sometimes, visiting local shops for donations as well. Some *chelas* also participate in the more secretive occupation of sex work with mainstream men, which is seen as more disreputable by *gharana* norms relative to the asexual religiosity of *badhai*.[55] While *hijre* and *hijra* are the commonly used terms for such transvestites in the Bengali language, *chhibri* (literally, castrated) is also used synonymously in intra-community contexts, though many junior *chelas* are *akua* (not castrated). There are also lower-class networks of diverse gender/sexually marginalised people outside *gharana* households, who evidence varying degrees of public visibility and complex relations of overlap or distinction with the *hijra/chhibri* category – such as people who sexually network (cruise) in public spaces, male sex workers and cross-dressed beggars in trains.

One of the members of Counsel Club who played a major role in the formation of non-metropolitan CBOs was Ranajay, himself from a small town north of Kolkata. Ranajay's story provides an entry point into the aforementioned networks. In a long interview, he described to me how he discovered networks of male-born gender variant persons when he went to cruise and socialise in the south Kolkata lake area around 1989–90.[56] There, he learnt intra-community codes used within these subcultural networks, including terms of gender/sexual difference unknown in mainstream Bengali, such as *dhurani*, signifying 'feminine' males who often desire relatively 'masculine' men. *Dhurani* could also refer more specifically to sex workers, being connected to the verb *dhurano* (to have sex) within the subcultural code. Yet, it did not seem to be a consolidated gender/sexual identity in the way that *kothi* or *hijra* increasingly became, as is evidenced in Ranajay's narrative:

> One evening, I heard someone call out, 'hey, this boy is a *dhurani*!' . . . I went back and asked, 'what did you call me? What is *dhurani*?' 'Oh, those who take it in the mouth or the butt'. 'But I don't do that!' I replied. 'Well, you know, those who walk in a feminine way, are a bit girlish, like us'. 'But I am not like that, I don't do that either!' So finally this person told me, 'Well, anyone who loves to keep our company is *dhurani*!'

This exchange indicates the process of interpellation into the network and the concurrent mapping of insiders and outsiders – but not in the form of rigid identitarian boundaries. Despite his 'masculine' behaviour and disavowal of sexual penetrability, Ranajay gained acceptance within this network of 'feminine' persons by learning their subcultural code – which they called *khaurir bhasha*, the language of trickery or play.[57] One day, he heard this 'language' being spoken by a self-identified *hijra* who visited the lakes, and remarked, 'oh, you are speaking our language as well!' The *hijra* took offense and replied, 'it's you people who have taken our language from us!' Other *hijras* he later met similarly distinguished themselves as a community distinct from these looser networks, with a greater claim on the 'language'. However, the nature and extent of this distinction seems to have been locally variegated.

To chart the translocal span as well as local variations of these subcultural networks and their 'language', it is insightful to compare and connect contrasting sites – Kolkata, the metropolitan capital, with Berhampore in the Murshidabad district, a regionally important town and the administrative headquarters, which like other similar towns has served as a node of organisational expansion. The exact genealogy of the subcultural networks in Berhampore prior to institutionalisation and their relation to *hijra gharanas* is undocumented. However, in 2009 I met an older participant in these circles, Govinda, who provided me with an account of the years of his youth during the 1980s, long before the local CBO Sangram was established in 2006. He particularly dwelt on abuse and stigma; young males who visibly differed from norms of masculinity would often be targeted in public through terms of abuse like *meyeli*, *chhuri* (girlish) or *moga* (roughly, 'fag' or 'sissy'). However, in response to such demarcation, there also seemed to be a converse process in which older gender variant males would pick out more newly visible persons through their perceived behaviour, establishing a loose network of trusted peers.

Govinda fondly narrated his initiation into this network in a way that closely echoed Ranajay's story. One day while bathing at the river Ganges, someone called out to him – '*Ayi chhuri, tor nang achhey*?' (Roughly, 'Hey girl, you got any husbands?') Initially startled, he soon identified the person who called him out as 'someone like me'. Jaydip, his new friend, thus read and interpellated Govinda as non-masculine, even appropriating a term of abuse (*chhuri*) as the recognition of their commonality. As in Ranajay's narrative, we see the process of hailing insiders into the network through a reading of perceived non-masculine behaviour. 'After that day, I started going around town with Jaydip and our friends', Govinda reminisced. While this peer group or network developed through such responses to social stigma, they also seemed to have an inherited intra-community code similar to Kolkata networks: 'We picked up our language from the older ones among us'. Govinda's narrative presented a range of terms to describe their gender/sexual variance – *dhunuri*, *moga*, *chhuri* – some referring to (homo)sexual behaviour like *moga*, some to effeminacy like *chhuri*, and some to both, like *dhunuri*, signifying 'feminine' males who have sex with men. Only one or two among Govinda's circle had heard the term *kothi*, which gained linguistic prevalence among a younger generation after the formation of Sangram. Govinda called their language itself *dhunuri bhasha* and described it as '*amader bhasha*', 'our language'. Since *dhunuri* seems to correspond linguistically to *dhurani* used in the Kolkata cruising areas, this suggests the translocal span of the networks through which such terms were disseminated.

Similar to the South Kolkata lakes, there were also focal points of cruising and socialising such as a 'square field' in central Berhampore. 'We used to come here and to other such public spaces long before Sangram was established', Ram, a frequent visitor and part of Govinda's circle, told me. No one could remember when socialising had begun around the field, though it was hardly spontaneous and required active defence against potentially hostile reactions from the police. These dangers necessitated the *thek* or the *khol* – houses of trusted peers where people gathered to gossip, discuss news, even bring in sexual partners. These partners were usually more 'masculine' men called *parikh* in the subcultural code, who seemed to be on the fringes of the network and did not usually pick up the subcultural language. But this boundary between a feminised inner circle and masculine outsiders was also diffuse, as seen previously in Ranajay's case. For instance, sex within *dhunuri* inner circles where one of them took on a 'masculine' penetrative role was also prevalent, though somewhat taboo – possibly drawing from *hijra* restrictions against intra-community sex.[58] Somewhat hesitantly and shyly, Govinda admitted to having had penetrative sex with some of his *dhunuri* friends.

However, despite using several inherited terms for gender/sexual variance, Govinda and his peers like Ram did not use any of these intra-community labels for representation to the mainstream as a separate community, though their gender variance was hardly invisible. Ram and Govinda lived with their families and dressed as men, and though they had not married, some others in their circle were married men. In socio-economic terms, most of Govinda's and Ram's close friends ranged from lower middle class to lower class and pursued relatively mainstream occupations.[59] Govinda and Ram had small businesses in wholesale spices and handicrafts respectively. Thus, for them, the sartorial and occupational distinction from *hijras* seemed clear even though their 'language' evidences many overlaps with that of *hijras* situated within *gharanas*. Govinda asserted that he 'did not know any *hijras*', implying his avoidance of the more marginal *hijras* based on his relatively mainstream position and respectability.

However, Ram's friends include Annapurna, who had been initially a part of this peer group but subsequently joined a *hijra gharana*. At present, Annapurna leads one of the two *gharana*-affiliated *hijra* households in Murshidabad, which undertake the ritual blessing of newborn children within their respective territories. Ram had known Annapurna as one of their *dhunuri* peers, but she differed from them in that she began cross-dressing in public, left her family, took initiation under the older leader of the *hijra gharana* in the area and underwent castration. In both Ram's and Annapurna's narration of this story, there is a transition from *dhunuri* to *chhibri* or *hijra*, but also a clear distinction between *dhunuris* like Govinda and *hijras* like Annapurna, though they had participated in the same extended network in their youth.

But this distinction between *dhunuri* and *hijra* is less clear for many people lower down the socio-economic strata relative to Ram and Govinda. This particularly applies to people who cross-dress while performing sex work (*khajra*) or while blessing people for money in commuter trains (*chhalla*), when they may be publicly perceived as *hijra*. But they may also otherwise dress as males or live with their families, blurring the categorical distinction between *hijra* and *dhunuri*. Although sometimes called *hijra* and *chhibri* by Berhampore *dhunuris* like Ram, they are usually neither literally *chhibri* (castrated), nor formally initiated under a *hijra guru*, given that *gharana* leaders often disparage public sex work and *chhalla* as disreputable. As Annapurna told me, these cross-dressers were not really *hijras*: 'those ones sometimes call themselves *hijras*, sometimes *dhuranis* . . . as suits their purpose'.

However, this need not imply a uniformly hostile relation between *gharanas* and these 'other' *hijras*. While there have been occasional media reports of 'real eunuchs' assaulting 'fake' ones, the quotidian relations between non-*gharana* and *gharana hijras* in Bengal seems to be a more delicate practice of tolerance, premised on the maintenance of the territorial rights of the *gharana hijras* in a particular locality.[60]

About halfway on the rail link between Kolkata and Berhampore, there is a small town called Ranaghat in the district of Nadia, which has over the years become the third site of my fieldwork. One evening in 2010, I accompanied Avijit and Arghya, two members of the CBO Swikriti, on a bicycle trip to 'field areas' where they undertake community outreach to increase HIV-AIDS awareness. Avijit and Arghya used both *dhurani* and *kothi* to talk about themselves, but their sense of distinction from *hijras* was less marked than for Govinda. Biking along the narrow lanes of Kanchrapara, a town near Ranaghat, they pointed out an apparently abandoned old house where a group of young *dhuranis* lived together separately from their families. 'Like a *hijra* household?' I asked. 'Yes'. 'But not a formal *hijra* group?' I prodded further. 'No, but they do *chhalla* in trains'. Avijit described how they were indistinguishable from castrated *hijras* when cross-dressed – clearly, becoming *hijra* as a livelihood required neither castration nor *gharana* affiliation. I asked whether the *gharana hijras* of the area disliked or censured this. 'No, demanding *chhalla* in trains is fine', Avijit said, 'Even we do it sometimes!' The *chhallawalis*, as Avijit described them, would even visit local *hijra* households to maintain pleasant relations and would acknowledge *hijra gurus* as seniors without undergoing full initiation. Avijit was friends with one of these *chhallawalis*, Moloy, who would be usually in *chhibripon* ('in *chhibri* mode', i.e. cross-dressed) without being *gharana*-affiliated. One evening, we met Moloy on a train near Ranaghat. I reproduce a section of our conversation:

Avijit: Hey, are you going to get castrated?

Moloy [claps loudly]: No, I am a *tonna* [man]! If I can't do well as *chhibri* I will cut my hair and become *tonna*! [clapping is a gesture associated with *hijras*]

Avijit: So who is your *guru* now? Sometimes you say Chandramukhi [a *hijra guru*], sometimes you say Puchki [another *chhallawali*].

Moloy: There is no certainty to who my *guru* is! . . . I became the disciple of Chandramukhi, but when they asked me to get castrated I quarreled and came home . . . then I started doing *chhalla*, and took Puchki as my *guru*.

Moloy, therefore, had lived both inside and outside *hijra gharanas* and performed *chhalla* cross-dressed while living with her natal family, appropriating *chhibri* ('castrated') as a metaphor even while claiming to be *tonna* (man). This overlap with social masculinity, and resistance to actual castration, earned her *guru* Chandramukhi's disfavour, recalling hierarchies based on respectability among *hijras* who disparaged gender shifting in Reddy's ethnography.[61] Even so, such overlap seemed permissible for those who did *chhalla*.

Badhai – the ritual blessing of newborn children – was a different matter. 'For that, you need to take the *anchal* [full initiation] of the *hijra guru* who controls that particular area', Avijit told me. It appeared that the territoriality of *gharana hijras* in Nadia was exercised through strict control on the practice of *badhai* in their area, but cross-dressed *chhalla* did not impinge upon territorial rights enough to attract active censure. But how far could non-*gharana* claimants to public *hijra* visibility stretch such concessions from *gharana* territoriality?

At Ranaghat, I also heard the story of Shyamoli-*ma* (mother Shyamoli), variously described as a *hijra* or *dhurani* who had gathered many *chelas* who pursued occupations like *khajra* (sex work) and *chhalla*. She had died of AIDS-related causes in 2007 before I commenced my fieldwork, and while I never met her in person, the Ranaghat branch of Swikriti includes several of her *chelas* or *nati-chelas* (*chelas* of *chelas*). One afternoon in the CBO office, I had the following conversation with one such *nati-chela*, Subhash, along with some other community members:

> Me: Did she ever become a *gharana*-based *hijra* or do *badhai*?
>
> Subhash: No, she lived with her family. I never saw a *dhol* [drum used for *badhai*] in her house. But she would have many *chelas* who would visit or even stay with her. She would select the beautiful ones and send them to dance at weddings in Bihar [a neighbouring state; cross-dressed dancing boys, called *laundas*, are reputedly a common feature of social occasions in Bihar]. She would take commissions for this; it was her business.
>
> Me: Was she regarded as a *hijra*?
>
> Subhash: No . . . within the town many knew her as a feminine male, she had grown up nearby and lived with her parents, and was *akua* [non-castrated] . . . But outside, I cannot tell if she was. She was not really a *hijra*.
>
> Sumeet [another community member]: How can you say that? Her identity was up to her, no one can say you're not a *hijra* if you say you're one. Also, didn't she do *badhai* elsewhere, outside Ranaghat?
>
> Subhash: Maybe, I don't know. She had some *chelas* who had . . . joined *hijra* households in Bihar. But they would still respect her as their *guru-ma* (mother *guru*) . . . whenever they visited Ranaghat.
>
> Me: What was her relation with the *gharana hijras* of the Ranaghat area?
>
> Subhash: They would tolerate but avoid each other . . . She also did not do *badhai* in the area like these *hijras*, even if she did it elsewhere.

Back in Murshidabad after this conversation, I spoke with one of the two senior *hijra gurus* of the district, Annapurna-*mashi* (Aunt Annapurna) of the Mechhua *gharana*, on the relation of *hijra gharanas* with these liminal yet widespread *hijra* figures outside formal lineages, of which Shyamoli-*ma* seemed to be an exceptionally successful example. In her explanation, Annapurna-*mashi* expanded on the workings of *hijra* territoriality. *Hijra* households divided their local region into distinct territories, such that one may not encroach into another's area. However, there might be small areas that were bypassed by these designated territories, or that *hijras* could not cover adequately.

It was this uneven and ruptured territoriality that created the possibility of *hijra* figures outside *gharana*-affiliated households:

> Suppose in a village where *hijras* do not go, there is a *dhurani* who has taken to cross-dressing in public. Maybe over the years, she starts posing as *hijra* . . . Some people of the area regard her as a *hijra*, some people still regard her as male, and call her *moga* [sissy]. Maybe she buys a *dhol*, and starts doing *badhai* for money. Now, at some point the actual *hijra* household of the area comes to know this . . . So they go there, create trouble and ask the *dhurani* to stop [acting as *hijra*]. But maybe she is already too powerful, has local *chelas*, and resists the *hijras*. So they visit her again, but this time, offer her a position in the *gharana* hierarchy. After all, you have to give her credit . . . she took a wild uncultivated area, where *hijras* did not go, and cultivated it, made it suitable for us!

Thus, faced with the inevitable unevenness and incompleteness of their territoriality in practice, the *gharanas* try to regain territorial control by either preventing external *hijras* from pursuing characteristic *hijra* occupations (especially *badhai*), and failing that, by attempting to assimilate renegade *hijras* as members and re-establish the consolidated kinship network. However, not all challenges to *gharana* territoriality merit equal attention. Asked about the *chhallawalis* in trains, Annapurna replied dismissively, 'oh, those ones sometimes call themselves *hijras*, sometimes *dhuranis* or *kothi*, as suits their purpose', disparaging their shifting identifications without seeking to actively censure them. But Shyamoli-*ma*, with her own kinship structure of *chelas* and her thriving business of dancing boys, mattered more. According to Annapurna-*mashi*, Shyamoli-*ma* had also been approached by *gharana hijras*, and while powerful enough to resist them, ultimately did join the *gharana* hierarchy: 'in later years she came into our system'. Even if this is true, the community in Ranaghat remembers her as an institution unto herself, distinct from the *gharana hijras* of the area.

Gharanas go public: consolidating the *hijra*

While Annapurna, like the *hijras* in Ranaghat, tolerated *chhallawalis* even as she privately disparaged them, recently some *gharanas* in West Bengal have made increasingly public attempts to assert *hijra* authenticity, in collusion with non-governmental organisations and the media. One person who has acted as a *gharana* representative in this capacity is Ranjana, who works with a large NGO in Kolkata and is a prominent *hijra* activist. While I had previously known her as transgender-identified, in early 2010 she identified herself at a public event as a *hijra* under the Shyambajari *gharana* of Bengal. As an NGO official overseeing HIV-prevention projects, Ranjana did not pursue any typical *hijra* occupation and belonged to a higher economic stratum than both *chhallawalis* and *gharana hijras*, except perhaps senior *hijra gurus*. Thus, her identification as a *hijra* struck me as both atypical and significant, given her public stature as an activist.

In the course of an extended conversation, Ranjana recounted that she had decided to join a *hijra* group formally while retaining her NGO job and independent living arrangement and argued that these occupational and residential choices were not the determinants of actual *hijra* identity:

> Many people may call themselves *hijras*, does that mean that they become *hijras*? The real criteria for becoming a *hijra* is not cutting off one's genitals or taking up the *dhol* [drum] to demand money for blessings . . . If you have gone through the *rit* [initiation] and been given the *anchal* [ceremonial

blessing] by a senior *hijra* in a *gharana*, then only you are a *hijra*, and then it doesn't matter what else you do!

Ranjana described her initiation as a new trend in which *gharanas* were opening up to newer forms of recruitment to keep up with changing times when *hijra* occupations were harder to sustain, and to establish good relations with the emerging NGO-based movement for gender/sexual rights. While on one hand this broadens *hijra* identification by downplaying occupation and castration, it insists on formal discipleship under a senior *hijra* leader within a lineage or *gharana* as the ultimate criteria of *hijra* legitimacy, in the absence of other markers of *hijra* belonging.

As Ranjana was well aware, this leaves out people who might both self-identify as *hijra* (or *chhibri*) and be perceived as such in public, without being strictly *gharana*-affiliated. Ranjana stressed that 'begging in trains' (*chhalla*) is forbidden to *chelas* in all three *gharanas* of West Bengal, and those who do *chhalla* are not actually *hijras* even if they have loose associations with *hijra* households (as the *chhallawali* Moloy had). Ironically, cross-dressed beggars in trains are among the most common representatives of the group recognised as '*hijra*' by the mainstream public in Bengal. To go by *gharana* affiliation, then, some of the most visible *hijras* in everyday life are not legitimate *hijras* at all!

During a 2011 interview on a television talk show in which Ranjana was called as a *hijra* activist, she decided to clarify this point:

> See, my *gharana* is an authentic ['authentic' in English] *hijra gharana*. [But] many people think that any man dressed in a *saree* [Indian feminine garment] or clapping their hands in trains is a *hijra* . . . but they are not! *Hijra* is a tradition . . . transmitted through a *guru-chela* system. The ones who beg or extort money in trains, they too are a kind of *hijra*, but they are not a part of *hijra* society.
>
> Interviewer: But how are the common people supposed to understand this? The whole blame is being shifted to your community!
>
> Ranjana: The matter is . . . a few people have utilised it [the *hijra* identity] wrongly . . . [but] the whole blame has fallen on our shoulders.[62]

In this process of a *gharana*-based legitimisation of *hijra* identity, the train *chhallawalis* appear both as inauthentic *hijras* who are cross-dressed men and disreputable beggars spoiling the public reputation of the legitimate '*hijra* society'. Though they remain 'a kind of *hijra*', they are not 'a part of *hijra* society' – an inauthentic yet hypervisible category of illegitimate *hijras*.

From these examples, one could argue that the *gharanas* are a system of spatial consolidation, expanding a hierarchical kinship structure and associated norms of respectability and gendered authenticity over locally diverse practices and subject-positions that might claim visibility as *hijra*, and seeking to establish a normative territoriality over uneven spaces. In the process, the *gharana*-based kinship structure has to be strategically flexible, accommodating exceptional figures like Ranjana and Shyamoli-*ma* as required. Even as *hijra* occupations might be pursued by non-*gharana* *hijras* and forms of *hijra* kinship – such as the *guru-chela* relation – may be selectively replicated outside *gharanas*, the *hijra* gharanas contingently expand to include some outsiders, sometimes even permitting non-traditional professions. Overall, the desired effect is a consolidation of the *hijra* category through kinship, extending its incomplete discursive consolidation in colonial ethnology through postcolonial media and activist representations. Cohen notes how *hijra* leaders have actively represented themselves to the national media as a 'sexually underprivileged' minority since at least the 1980s, appealing to the governmental function of the modern state to demand special concessions.[63] As Reddy notes, this transforms the public representation of the *hijra* from the asexual religiosity of ritual blessing to a gender/sexual minority.[64] But during this process, *gharana*-affiliated *hijras* have sometimes forwarded the claims of 'real' *hijras* and exposed 'fake' ones, seeking to establish the boundaries of this minority identity based on *gharana* norms of authenticity and respectability, over and above local distinctions or overlaps.[65] For example, Ranjana's representation of 'authentic' *gharana hijras* distinguishes them from inauthentic cross-dressed men – the *chhallawalis* who are disparaged for their gender shifting and overlap with masculinity by *gharana* leaders such as Annapurna and Chandramukhi. Such ongoing processes of *hijra* representation have also been formalised in national AIDS policy, where *hijras* are defined as a distinct transvestite 'socio-religious group' organised 'under seven main *gharanas*' and 'covered under the term "transgender"', distinct from *kothis* who become grouped as feminine MSM (men who have sex with men), a construction that I describe in the next section.[66]

As an ongoing process of consolidation across subcultural and institutional registers, *hijra* identity formation speaks to debates about the historical continuity or postcolonial emergence of South Asian identities. While Kaviraj argues that South Asian communities have had 'fuzzy' and overlapping boundaries, it appears that *hijra* and non-*hijra* distinctions have not been uniformly 'fuzzy', but rather, locally variegated.[67] For Kaviraj, modern governmental instruments such as maps and censuses have a determinant influence in the rise of territorially bounded and enumerated identities.[68] However, as argued above, the contradictory ethnological discourse on eunuchs produced via colonial censuses failed to create a coherent *hijra* category: it is rather the seemingly traditional *gharana* kinship system that actively undertakes the ongoing process of consolidation more effectively. This seems to corroborate Guha's argument that 'the warm fuzzy continuum of pre-modern collective life was not ... arbitrarily sliced up by colonial modernity', but rather, as Bayly contends, an indigenous 'critical public' was already in place from the pre-colonial period, and has actively participated in constituting various identities.[69] However, as Chatterjee argues, the interaction of communities and (post)colonial institutions brings about profound changes such as a 'deepening of the web of governmentality ... as practices of everyday life among rural people', extending the reach of governmental institutions and discourses outside metropolitan centers.[70] The collusion between *gharana* kinship and media, NGO and state discourses to construct a bounded 'authentic' subject of governmental welfare affects a historical rupture in identity formations that elides and potentially circumscribes the lived practices and self-representations of various marginal subjects.

The rise of the *kothi*

Kothi does not seem to have been used widely before the late 1990s in West Bengal, nor (as Lawrence Cohen notes) in North Indian cities like Varanasi.[71] It was not commonplace among the older generation of the Berhampore network, while some of Shyamoli-*ma*'s disciples in Ranaghat had known but rarely used the term. But since the late 1990s, *kothi* gained extensive usage within NGOs, CBOs and community networks, alongside terms like *dhurani, dhunuri* or *moga* for older community members and often replacing these terms for the younger generation.

In the late 1990s, *kothi* became prominent with NGO usage, and in the mid-2000s entered the AIDS-control policy of the Indian state as a subgroup of MSM (men who have sex with men), a 'high risk group' (HRG) for HIV infection. The emerging definition of the *kothi* in HIV-AIDS discourse is summarised in the guidelines for the third phase of the National AIDS Control Policy (NACP-III, 2007–2012): *kothis* are males showing 'varying degrees of femininity' and 'involved mainly . . . in receptive anal/oral sex with men', called *parikh* in West Bengal and *panthi* elsewhere in India.[72] Defined as feminine MSM, *kothis* are distinct from *hijras* who are described as lineage-based '"transgenders" or TG', though the guidelines concede in passing that 'self-identified hijras may also identify . . . as kothis' (but not vice versa).[73] These official distinctions thus override overlapping identifications like the aforementioned *chhallawalis* who might switch between *dhurani, kothi* and *hijra/chhibri*.

Boyce argues that the reification of the *kothi* as 'a culturally indigenous category with self-evident meanings' excludes more 'complex understandings of sexual subjectivity', and Cohen critiques the creation of *kothi* as a 'black box' concept, an unquestioned cultural category for same-sex desire in the HIV-AIDS discourse.[74] Countering its indigenist usages, Cohen argues that *kothi* communities often grew around NGOs, though he notes that *hijra* networks could have also aided its dissemination.[75] While these critiques are germane to understanding how *kothi* emerged as an institutional category, they also focus on a top-down history of identity formation, emphasising the involvement of big-city NGOs in constructing this minority identity. This epistemological focus on metropolitan institutional agency has tended to downplay how NGOs have relied on non-metropolitan subcultures.

The following sections chart how institutional activism for gender/sexual rights and sexual health depended on the aforementioned subcultural networks of lower-class gender variant males with varying extents of distinction from *hijra gharanas*. The increasing usage of *kothi* in West Bengal has relied on its correspondences with older subcultural terms used in non-metropolitan networks, such as *dhurani, dhunuri* and *moga*. Even as the *hijra* becomes a more bounded term, the *kothi* emerges through attempts to standardise notions of same-sex desire, as well as the distinction from *hijras*, across these subcultural networks, thus paralleling the consolidation of the *hijra*.

From informal to institutional networks

Of the early Kolkata collectives, both Counsel Club and the Naz Calcutta Project were initiated by middle-class Kolkata activists in 1993.[76] They were loosely affiliated with two larger organisations that pioneered HIV/AIDS-prevention and activism in India: the Counsel Club with the Humsafar Trust and Naz Calcutta with the Naz Foundation International (NFI). The Humsafar Trust and the NFI were associated respectively with rival activists Ashok Row Kavi and Shivananda Khan, leading national activists who built connections with transnational HIV-AIDS and LGBT activism during the 1990s.[77] Parallel to this process of gender/sexual globalisation, the reach of the Kolkata groups expanded into non-metropolitan areas. In 1995, an article entitled 'Magazine about homosexuality being sold openly' ran in the Bengali newspaper *Anandabazar Patrika* and reached small-town readers.[78] Sarswata, from a small northern suburb and a pioneer in small-town organising, narrated his discovery of this article to me as a moment of political initiation.

The recruitment of activists from outside Kolkata proved crucial to the state-wide expansion of NGOs and CBOs. Institutional expansion rapidly increased in the 2000s, which has been attributed to metropolitan organisations like Counsel Club that established 'satellite groups' in districts of West Bengal.[79] However, this emphasis on metropolitan institutions that ostensibly drive gender/sexual globalisation misses the role of translocal *dhurani-dhunuri-hijra* subcultural networks, which facilitated non-metropolitan institutionalisation. After Counsel Club disbanded in the early 2000s, the activist Ranajay became associated with Dum Dum Swikriti Society, established under Sarswata's leadership in Kolkata's northern suburbs. Ranajay helped expand its reach to towns like Ranaghat through contacts with cruising and *hijra* networks. Meanwhile, a participant in the Berhampore network heard about Kolkata CBOs through the Bengali media, and started visiting Swikriti meetings. Gradually gaining familiarity with the Berhampore circle, Sarswata helped establish the CBO Madhya Banglar Sangram there in 2006. Several such small-town CBOs joined an organisational network named MANAS Bangla, with its administrative hub in Kolkata.[80]

This shift from informal to institutional networking was fostered by the increasing availability of funding for HIV-AIDS prevention from western and multilateral funders during the 1990s, and later the Indian state. Transnational meetings such as the International AIDS Conferences evidenced a growing global awareness of the AIDS epidemic and donors like the UK's DFID (Department for International Development) began to provide funds for mapping vulnerable groups and community outreach through larger NGOs and the state.[81] 'Around the late 90s, we started doing the needs-assessment surveys', Sarswata told me; 'there were two such surveys, one in 1996 and one around 1999–2000'. The first survey in Kolkata was by the Naz Calcutta project, which generated the report 'STD/HIV outreach among sexual networks of men who have sex with men in Calcutta', presented at the International AIDS Conference in 1996.[82] This was followed by a survey by Integration Society, an activist group that grew out of Counsel Club.[83]

Through these surveys, activists like Sarswata were introduced to lower- and lower-middle-class spaces in and around Kolkata, identifying vulnerable populations for HIV-AIDS prevention. As surveys extended beyond middle-class gay-identified circles, the Naz Calcutta report adopted the term 'men who have sex with men' (MSM) as a broad non-identitarian, behaviour-based label that would be intelligible to international audiences.[84] MSM, as Tom Boellstorff notes, had arisen in western HIV-AIDS discourse as a term for participants in same-sex behaviour who did not identify as 'gay'.[85] MSM was also adopted by 'baseline surveys' of the Humsafar Trust in Mumbai and subsequently entered the Indian state AIDS-control discourse.[86] While its adoption marked a bid to acknowledge 'cross-cultural variation in . . . sexual identity', ironically, its increasing official usage made it into a hegemonic form of representation.[87] As Sarswata narrated, 'Around 1999, a senior activist told us to use MSM instead of "gay" or "homosexual", so that we would get government projects'.

At the same time, surveyors also picked up subcultural language; as Sarswata narrated, 'we learnt words like *dhurani* through these field visits'. However, the category that gained national circulation among NGOs was not *dhurani*, but *kothi*. As

Cohen describes, *kothi* was discovered as a term during surveys on male sex workers in South India.[88] The Naz Calcutta survey had already noted the term in Kolkata in 1996, suggesting its prior subcultural dissemination (though it was not widespread in its usage). Based on these surveys, Naz Foundation International propagated the term *kothi*, defined as feminised males who desired masculine men (variously called *panthi, parikh* and *giriya*), as an indigenous category that was less elite than 'gay', while the rival Humsafar Trust contested the gendered *kothi-panthi* model as the putatively dominant indigenous structure of male same-sex desire.[89] Despite the differing attitude to *kothi*, Humsafar, like NFI, began mapping *kothis* as a vulnerable subgroup within MSM.[90] Thus, institutional appropriations of (and differences over) subcultural language were subsumed within an emerging lingua franca of HIV-AIDS control, where MSM, as Boellstorff notes, increasingly shifted from denoting non-identified behaviour to designating vulnerable 'populations', including identity-based communities at risk of HIV-AIDS.[91]

Meanwhile, in response to NGO advocacy, the Indian state and its National AIDS Control Organisation (NACO) gradually acknowledged high rates of HIV transmission among groups designated as MSM.[92] National AIDS control policy mapped MSM subgroups according to relative sexual risk for HIV transmission. Given the symbolic position of the *kothi* as a non-elite sexual minority, it entered national AIDS policy as a core 'high-risk group' under the MSM rubric, combining sexual risk with gendered marginality.[93]

The translocal standardisation of subcultural language

On one hand, the institutionalisation of the *kothi* evidences a biopolitical project in the Foucauldian sense, where vulnerable target populations are constructed as 'domains and objects of knowledge' through governmental technologies of HIV-AIDS intervention.[94] But the other side of this story is subcultural collusion in mapping and constructing identities. The project of mapping 'high risk' populations in West Bengal relied on the subcultural cartography of terms like *dhurani* and *dhunuri* that marked loosely bounded gender variant circles. As CBOs like Sangram were established, non-metropolitan groups began interacting with Kolkata circles through a combination of institutional forums like AIDS-awareness workshops and older cruising networks. This forged an increasing standardisation of subcultural usages, evident in Berhampore in the shift from the older generation of Govinda and Ram, to a newer crop of Sangram members. Akhtar, one such member, told me, 'we heard the people in Kolkata speak, and picked up new words like *kothi*'. A common name for the subcultural code or language itself, *ulti*, has increasingly replaced its diverse designations (*dhunuri bhasha* in Berhampore, *khaurir bhasha* in the Kolkata lake areas), and Kolkata *dhurani* and Berhampore *dhunuri* circles are bridged under the emergent consolidated term *kothi*. As Govinda narrated, 'now they all say *kothi*; before, we would say *dhunuri, moga*'. The process of interpellating outsiders on the basis of perceived behaviour, through which Govinda was introduced to the Berhampore network, has continued, but newer members are now commonly hailed as *kothi*. However, the rise of a common vocabulary cannot entirely overshadow local variations: in Ranaghat, while *kothi* is now commonplace, *dhurani* persists due to the influence of Shyamoli-*ma*'s disciples.

The combination of institutional and informal mapping, within the larger process of linguistic standardisation, has consolidated a common *kothi* identity in two senses: normative ideas of sexual behaviour and distinction from *hijras*. While metropolitan activists undertook early surveys, the mapping of 'high risk groups' and cruising areas, integral to HIV-prevention work, is increasingly carried out through local community members, who must be 'recruited to conduct mapping' and provide services as per national AIDS policy.[95] While such work relies heavily on an intimate knowledge of local spaces, this labour is severely undervalued in current funding regimes – the salary for low-tier CBO workers is usually less than Rs. 2000 (about $50) per month.[96] In the process, the loose cartography of *dhurani/dhunuri* and *parikh* – evidencing considerable behavioural diversity within *dhurani/dhunuri* circles, like the masculine Ranajay and the sexually versatile Govinda – are gradually understood as bounded populations differentiated in terms of sexual behaviour. Categories laid out in national AIDS policy documents are propagated through institutional spaces. As Ranajay explained during an NGO meeting in Kolkata in 2010, 'we now map MSM into the following subsections: *kothi*, feminine males, *parikh*, the husbands [*sic*] of *kothi*s and *dupli*, versatile males'. This cartography is enabled through the translocally standardised subcultural language of *ulti*, where *kothi* becomes a more consolidated identity opposed to *parikh* than terms like *dhunuri* or *dhurani* had been.

In the summer of 2009, I accompanied Bijoy, a friend from the Berhampore circle, to a nearby village to help him record a survey. At the house of his friend Rahim, Bijoy proceeded to ask the questions, one of which inquired about sexual roles (options: penetrating, penetrated, versatile). Rahim hesitated – 'what would I do in sex? I would take, I suppose?' Bijoy chimed in, 'Of course you would take, aren't you *kothi*?' At this, Rahim looked embarrassed, replying, 'yes, of course, what else!' While Rahim had been unsure how to map his sexual behaviour vis-à-vis his gender-variance, *kothi* (vs. the masculine, penetrating *parikh*) provided a neat grid of identification – of course, 'feminine' males would also be penetrated. During the survey, a few identified as *dupli* – an emerging usage for 'versatile' – but were also relatively excluded from the inner circle of *kothi* bonding and sisterhood.

These consolidations of identity translate between the translocal language of gender/sexual variance and the risk-based cartography of MSM subsections in transnational HIV-prevention discourse, where penetrated persons are at 'higher risk'.[97] Playing the part of a good peer educator, Bijoy advised Rahim: 'Sister, be careful, always make them (the *parikh*) wear condoms'. Wearing condoms becomes the naturalised function of the masculine, mainstream *parikh*, while gendered marginality, sexual vulnerability and anal penetrability are conflated in the marginalised *kothi*. Thus, the *kothi* serves to standardise locally variegated vernacular categories such that the diffuse boundary between insiders and outsiders in older networks becomes more marked, translating subcultural cartographies of gender variance into the transnational risk-based cartography of HIV-prevention. However, this consolidation is incomplete; both in Berhampore and Ranaghat, newer formulations like *dupli kothi* (*kothi*s who like to fuck) transgress these cartographic boundaries. Such constructions may be regarded pejoratively at the intra-community level, and have not entered state or national official cartographies as separate categories.

As *kothi*s become organised into community-based organisations led by middle-class leaders and funded via city-based NGOs, *kothi* also becomes increasingly distinct from *hijra* or *chhibri*. Sarswata, a salaried activist who has alternated between gay/*samakami* and *kothi* identifications, is the 'mother' to the younger Berhampore circle. Even as this alludes to *hijra* kinship, it further cements the class and gender-based distinction with *hijras* that had been already evident for older *dhunuris* like Govinda and Ram. Sangram's magazine has featured ethnographic accounts of *hijras* as a 'traditional' Indian group, even as CBO members attend pride walks in Kolkata and are interpreted as a sign of globalising 'gay' visibility in media reports.[98] For others with less access to metropolitan networking such as the cross-dressed train beggars (*chhallawalis*), the overlap with *hijra* persists, though not recognised in the official cartography of MSM and *kothi*. Meanwhile, the focus on same-sex behaviour also distances MSM projects from *gharana*-affiliated *hijras*, whose involvement in sex work is less public. Annapurna-*mashi* initially regarded Sangram's condom-promotion activities with suspicion, although her *chelas* have subsequently availed themselves of Sangram's services.

I will close this ethnographic account on an intentionally inconclusive note, since the aforementioned cartographic consolidations of identity are ongoing and unfinished. As noted above, the existing official cartography classifies *kothis* as feminine MSM and *hijras* as lineage-based transgenders. However, in 2011, the West Bengal State AIDS Prevention and Control Society increased funding for CBOs catering to transgender groups, spurring intra-community debates regarding which *kothis* might be considered authentically and consistently 'feminine' enough to be included within 'transgender' CBOs alongside *hijras*, as opposed to same-sex desiring males.[99] While the transnational history of 'transgender' as a category is beyond the scope of this article, emerging trends in West Bengal indicate that *hijra* constructions of gendered authenticity might also inform concerns about *transgender* authenticity, restricting who can enter this newly funded category. This potentially leads to further cartographic distinctions and identitarian strictures, extending the transgender-MSM division between *hijras* and *kothis* into a divide between more and less authentically feminine *kothis*.[100]

Conclusion: collusion and (dis)continuity

To conclude, I will return to questions about historical continuity and postcolonial emergence with reference to these processes of identity formation. I have attempted to demonstrate how both *hijra* and *kothi*, while evidencing distinct histories of construction, emerge as (seemingly) coherent identities through the collusion of multiple subcultural and governmental processes. An epistemology of these collusions must necessarily bridge multiple sites of enquiry – in the case of *hijra*, ranging from colonial censuses and ethnology to contemporary media representations and the kinship system of the *gharanas*, all of which have contributed to consolidate the identity in official discourses. The *kothi*, on the other hand, evidences the collusion of subcultural networks that are less structured than *gharanas* with governmental technologies of HIV-AIDS control. Locally variegated subjects, like the *dhurani* of Kolkata and *dhunuri* of Berhampore, are translocally consolidated into an MSM sub-category, constructing 'domains and objects of knowledge' for the funder-state-NGO nexus.[101] Simultaneously, institutional cartography colludes with subcultural language and vernacular categories, creating hegemonic identities at the community level – witness Rahim's initiation into being properly *kothi*, fitting both into the target group of HIV-prevention and the peer circle. The consolidation of these networks into a translocal *kothi* identity increasingly standardises the distinction between *hijra* and non-*hijra*, and potentially elides locally variegated distinctions and overlaps. On the whole, *hijra* becomes defined in terms of socio-religious and kinship norms that regulate its boundaries as a 'transgender' identity, whereas *kothis* become conceptualised in terms of their passive/receptive role within male same-sex behaviour (MSM), though *kothi* femininity may cross over to the 'transgender' category as well. Both cases evidence the attempted construction of bounded identities amid the deepening web of governmentality that marks the postcolonial period for Chatterjee.[102] But as Sumit Guha argues, governmental constructions of identity evidence complicities and continuities with pre-existent logics of community formation, in this case *gharana*-based kinship and *dhurani/dhunuri* networks.[103]

The ongoing consolidation of *hijra*, *kothi* and MSM potentially delegitimises subject-positions that cannot be easily assimilated into coherent identities – 'inauthentic' *hijras* outside *gharanas* who cross-dress in trains for their living; *kothis* with ambiguous gender/sexual behaviours that breach the institutional cartography of MSM subgroups. Clearly, these processes of identity formation have material consequences of inclusion or exclusion vis-à-vis emergent minority identities. Moreover, they elide histories of categorical fluidity, boundary crossing and the tolerance of ambiguity, evidenced in the stories of *hijras* outside *gharanas* like *Shyamoli*-ma or masculine *dhuranis* like Ranajay. Through such elisions, forms of collusion and continuity between subcultural and governmental processes of identity formation might constitute profound discontinuities in how gender/sexual variance is imagined and lived on the margins.

Notes

I would like to express my gratitude to the community members and staff associated with Madhya Banglar Sangram and Dum Dum Swikriti Society for facilitating the research for this article. My fieldwork in West Bengal was made possible by grants from the Interdisciplinary Center for the Study of Global Change, University of Minnesota and the Graduate Research Partnership Program, University of Minnesota. I am thankful to the editors of this Special Issue of *Gender & History* and the anonymous peer reviewers for their incisive comments and helpful suggestions in the course of editing this article for publication.

1. I use the phrase 'gender/sexual identity' broadly to include varied configurations of gendered and sexualised subject-positions without presuming a strict separation between gender identity and sexual orientation.
2. For critical discussions of nationalist denunciations of homosexuality, see Deborah P. Amory, '"Homosexuality" in Africa: Issues and Debates', *Issue: A Journal of Opinion* 25 (1997), pp. 5–10, here p. 5; Ratna Kapur, 'A Love Song to Our Mongrel Selves: Hybridity, Sexuality and the Law', *Social and Legal Studies* 8 (1999), pp. 343–58; for examples of LGBT readings of pre-colonial history, see Giti Thadani, *Sakhiyani: Lesbian Desire in Ancient and Modern India* (London: Cassell, 1996); Ruth Vanita and Saleem Kidwai (eds), *Same-Sex Love in India: Readings from Literature and History* (New York: Palgrave Macmillan, 2001).
3. Joseph Massad, 'Re-orienting Desire: The Gay International and the Arab World', *Public Culture* 14 (2002), pp. 361–85, here p. 363.
4. Peter Jackson, 'Capitalism and Global Queering: National Markets, Parallels among Sexual Cultures, and Multiple Queer Modernities', *GLQ: A Journal of Lesbian and Gay Studies* 15 (2009), pp. 357–95, see esp. pp. 360–61.
5. Shivananda Khan, 'Males Who Have Sex With Males in South Asia: A Kothi Framework', *Pukaar* 31 (2000), pp. 3–5.

6. For example, see Lawrence Cohen, 'The Kothi Wars: AIDS Cosmopolitanism and the Morality of Clas-sification', in Vincenne Adams and Stacy L. Pigg (eds), *Sex in Development: Science, Sexuality, and Morality in Global Perspective* (Durham: Duke University Press, 2005), pp. 269–303.
7. Cohen, 'The Kothi Wars', p. 293.
8. Paul Boyce, 'Conceiving Kothis: Men Who Have Sex with Men in India and the Cultural Subject of HIV Prevention', *Medical Anthropology* 26 (2007), pp. 175–203, see esp. pp. 181–2; Akshay Khanna, 'Taming of the Shrewd Meyeli Chhele: A Political Economy of Development's Sexual Subject', *Development* 52 (2009), pp. 43–51, see esp. pp. 49–50.
9. Khanna, 'Taming of the Shrewd Meyeli Chhele', p. 49.
10. Gayatri Reddy, *With Respect to Sex: Negotiating Hijra Identity in South India* (Chicago: University of Chicago Press, 2005), p. 9.
11. For an overview of colonial attitudes to the *hijra*, see Lawrence W. Preston, 'A Right to Exist: Eunuchs and the State in Nineteenth-Century India', *Modern Asian Studies* 21 (1987), pp. 371–87.
12. For *hijras* as a 'third sex' or 'third gender', see Serena Nanda, *Neither Man nor Woman: The Hijras of India* (Belmont: Wadsworth Publishing, 1990); Gil Herdt, *Third Sex, Third Gender* (New York: Zone Books, 1994).
13. Lawrence Cohen, 'The Pleasures of Castration: The Postoperative Status of Hijras, Jankhas and Academics', in Paul R. Abramson and Steven D. Pinkerton (eds), *Sexual Nature, Sexual Culture* (Chicago: University of Chicago Press, 1995), pp. 276–304; Reddy, *With Respect to Sex*, pp. 2–16.
14. Reddy, *With Respect to Sex*, p. 2.
15. Kira Hall, 'Intertextual Sexuality: Parodies of Class, Identity, and Desire in Liminal Delhi', *Journal of Linguistic Anthropology* 15 (2005), pp. 125–44; Reddy, *With Respect to Sex*, pp. 45–6.
16. There has been a lack of comparably prominent vernacular categories for female-born persons in activist and academic literatures, perhaps owing to the greater visibility and focus on male-born queer subjects in activism and the public sphere, a problem that deserves separate treatment beyond the scope of this article.
17. I refer here to the Foucauldian concept of governmentality and the 'art of government'; see Michel Foucault, 'Governmentality' in Graham Burchell, Colin Gordon and Peter Miller (eds), *The Foucault Effect: Studies in Governmentality* (Chicago: University of Chicago Press, 1991), pp. 87–104.
18. Michel Foucault, *The History of Sexuality*, vol. 1: *An Introduction*, tr. Robert Hurley (New York: Vintage Books, 1990), pp. 68–70.
19. In Foucault's theorisation, modern state institutions are situated within a 'general technology of power' that he terms 'governmentality'; it is in this sense I use the phrase 'governmental institutions' here. I use 'governmental power' as a shorthand for both specific institutions and the wider 'technology of power' within which they are placed. See Michel Foucault (auth.), M. Senellart, F. Ewald, A. Fontata and A. I. Davidson (eds), *Security, Territory, Population: Lectures at the College de France, 1977– 78*, tr. G. Burchell, (London: Palgrave Macmillan, 2007), p. 120.
20. For such arguments see Sudipta Kaviraj, 'The Imaginary Institution of India', in Partha Chatterjee and Gyanendra Pandey (eds), *Subaltern Studies: Writings on South Asian History and Society*, vol. 7 (Delhi: Oxford University Press, 1992), pp. 1–39; Arjun Appadurai, 'Number in the Colonial Imagination', in Peter van der Veer and Carol Breckenridge (eds), *Orientalism and the Post-colonial Predicament: Perspectives on South Asia* (Philadelphia: University of Pennsylvania Press, 1993), pp. 314–39; Dipesh Chakrabarty, 'Modernity and Ethnicity in India: A History for the Present', *Economic and Political Weekly* 30 (1995), pp. 3373–80; Bernard Cohn, *An Anthropologist among the Historians and Other Essays* (Oxford: Oxford University Press, 1998); Nicholas B. Dirks, *Castes of Mind: Colonialism and the Making of Modern India* (Princeton: Princeton University Press, 2001); Partha Chatterjee, 'Community in the East', *Economic & Political Weekly* 33 (1998), pp. 277–82.
21. Kaviraj, 'The Imaginary Institution of India', p. 26; Appadurai, 'Number in the Colonial Imagination', p. 315.
22. Dirks, *Castes of Mind*, p. 26.
23. See C. A. Bayly, 'Returning the British to South Asian History: The Limits of Colonial Hegemony', *South Asia* 27 (1994), pp. 1–25; Sumit Guha, 'The Politics of Identity and Enumeration in India *c.*1600–1990', *Comparative Studies in Society and History* 45 (2003), pp. 148–67; Sumit Guha and Michael Anderson (eds), *Changing Concepts of Rights and Justice in South Asia* (New Delhi: Oxford University Press, 1998); Radhika Singha, 'Civil Authority and Due Process: Colonial Criminal Justice in the Banaras Zamindari, 1781–1795', in Michael Anderson and Sumit Guha (eds), *Changing Concepts of Rights and Justice in South Asia* (New Delhi: Oxford University Press, 1998), pp. 30–81.
24. Guha, 'The Politics of Identity', pp. 149–50.

25. Guha, 'The Politics of Identity', pp. 149–50.

26. Sudipto Kaviraj, 'Outline of a Revisionist Theory of Modernity', *Journal of European Sociology* 46 (2005), pp. 497–526.

27. Partha Chatterjee, *Lineages of Political Society: Studies in Postcolonial Democracy* (New York: Columbia University Press, 2011).

28. Chatterjee, *Lineages of Political Society*, pp. 199–203.

29. Jackson, 'Capitalism and Global Queering', p. 360.

30. In 2007, I conducted participant observation with the community-based organisation (CBO), Madhya Banglar Sangram. Between 2009 and 2012, I continued working with several CBOs across Kolkata, Nadia and Murshidabad in West Bengal, particularly Dum Dum Swikriti Society and Madhya Banglar Sangram. All personal names mentioned in the context of my fieldwork are changed to protect the confidentiality of my interviewees and interlocutors. As surnames suggest a public identity (often including religion and caste position in the Indian context) they have been omitted. All translations of quoted material from the original Bengali and explicatory parentheses included within quotes are mine.

31. Lawrence Preston, 'A Right to Exist: Eunuchs and the State in Nineteenth-Century India', *Modern Asian Studies* 21 (1987), pp. 371–87.

32. For example, see John Forbes, *Oriental Memoirs* (London: Richard Bentley, 1834), pp. 359–60; John Warden, 'On the Customs of Gosawees or Gosaeens', Appendix B to Arthur Steele, *Summary of the Law and Custom of Hindoo Castes within the Dekhun Provinces Subject to the Presidency of Bombay* (Bombay: Government of Bombay, 1827), pp. 67–8.

33. Preston, 'A Right to Exist', pp. 385–7.

34. Reddy, *With Respect to Sex*, p. 27.

35. Reddy, *With Respect to Sex*, p. 26.

36. E. J. Kitts, *A Compendium of the Castes and Tribes Found in India* (Bombay: Education Society Press, 1885).

37. For ethnological compendia with entries on '*hijra*', see W. Crooke, *The Tribes and Castes of the North-Western Provinces and Oudh*, vol. 2 (Calcutta: Government of India, 1896), pp. 495–6; R. Risley, *The Tribes and Castes of Bengal*, vol. 2 (Calcutta: Government of India, 1891), pp. 319–20; Edgar Thurston, *Castes and Tribes of Southern India*, vol. 3 (Madras: Government of Madras, 1909), pp. 288–9; R. V. Russell, *The Tribes and Castes of the Central Provinces of India*, vol. 3 (London: Macmillan, 1916), p. 206–07; R. E. Enthoven, *The Tribes and Castes of Bombay*, vol. 3 (Bombay: Government of India, 1922), p. 226–7.

38. Reddy, *With Respect to Sex*, p. 21.

39. Reddy, *With Respect to Sex*, p. 26.

40. On eunuchs as congenitally deformed, see Crooke, *The Tribes and Castes of the North-Western Provinces and Oudh*, p. 495; on eunuchs as impotent, see Thurston, *Castes and Tribes of Southern India*, p. 292; Enthoven, *The Tribes and Castes of Bombay*, p. 226; for descriptions of their ritualistic initiation, see Russell, *The Tribes and Castes of the Central Provinces of India*, pp. 206–07; Enthoven, *The Tribes and Castes of Bombay*, p. 226.

41. Thurston, *Castes and Tribes of Southern India*, pp. 288–90.

42. Russell, *The Tribes and Castes of the Central Provinces of India*, p. 206.

43. Hall, 'Intertextual Sexuality', p. 128.

44. Cohen, 'The Pleasures of Castration', p. 284.

45. Cohen, 'The Pleasures of Castration', p. 276.

46. Reddy, *With Respect to Sex*, p. 9.

47. Reddy, *With Respect to Sex*, pp. 45–56; Cohen, 'The Pleasures of Castration', p. 284.

48. Reddy, *With Respect to Sex*, p. 52.

49. Hall, 'Intertextual Sexuality', p. 129.

50. Cohen, 'The Pleasures of Castration', p. 283.

51. Cohen, 'The Pleasures of Castration', pp. 277, 287.

52. Cohen, 'The *Kothi* Wars', p. 274.

53. Sherry Joseph, *Social Work Practice and Men Who Have Sex with Men* (New Delhi: Sage, 2005), p. 99.

54. Joseph, *Social Work Practice*, p. 100.

55. On such hierarchies of respectability, also see Reddy, *With Respect to Sex*, p. 56.

56. While Bengali lacks gendered pronouns like 'he' or 'she', I compromise by using male-gendered pronouns for those socially identifying as male, however 'feminine', and female-gendered pronouns for those identifying as *hijra* or transgender/transsexual. These identifications may be situational and changeable.

57. On similar languages/codes called *Farsi*, see Hall, 'Intertextual Sexuality', p. 129.
58. On this restriction, see Reddy, *With Respect to Sex*, pp. 45–7.
59. As I noted during conversations, members of this peer group would use Bengali phrases like *nimno moddhobitto* (lower-middle class) in their self-description.
60. 'Real eunuchs beat fake ones', *Hindustan Times*, 30 June 2005, p. 3; 'Eunuchs show all for truth's sake', *Hindustan Times*, 20 July 2005, p. 5.
61. On intra-community hierarchies among *hijras* and *kothis* based on respectability (or *izzat*), see Reddy, *With Respect to Sex*, pp. 44, 60.
62. '*Bhalo Achhi Bhalo Theko*', *Tara Muzik*, 10 July 2011.
63. Cohen, 'The Pleasures of Castration', p. 297.
64. Gayatri Reddy, 'Geographies of Contagion: *Hijras, Kothis*, and the Politics of Sexual Marginality in Hyderabad', *Anthropology & Medicine* 12 (2005), pp. 255–70, here p. 262.
65. 'Real eunuchs beat fake ones', *Hindustan Times*, 30 June 2005; Hall, 'Intertextual Sexuality', p. 126.
66. National AIDS Control Organisation (NACO), *Targeted Interventions under NACP III: Operational Guidelines*, vol. 1: *Core High Risk Groups* (New Delhi: Government of India, 2007), p. 12.
67. Kaviraj, 'The Imaginary Institution of India', pp. 21–6.
68. Kaviraj, 'The Imaginary Institution of India', p. 27.
69. Guha, 'The Politics of Identity', p. 162; Bayly, 'Returning the British to South Asian History', p. 9.
70. Chatterjee, *Lineages of Political Society*, p. 92.
71. Cohen, 'The Kothi Wars', p. 272.
72. NACO, *Targeted Interventions under NACP III: Operational Guidelines*, vol. 1: p. 12.
73. NACO, *Targeted Interventions under NACP III: Operational Guidelines*, vol. 1: p. 12.
74. Boyce, 'Conceiving Kothis', p. 178; Cohen, 'The Kothi Wars', p. 285.
75. Cohen, 'The Kothi Wars', pp. 278, 285, 293.
76. Joseph, *Social Work Practice*, p. 100.
77. Cohen, 'The Kothi Wars', p. 270.
78. '*Prokashye Bikri Hochchhe Samakami Patrika*', *Anandabazar Patrika*, 10 June 1995.
79. Joseph, *Social Work Practice*, p. 100.
80. Subsequently, Manas Bangla has been decentralised into several zones.
81. Joseph, *Social Work Practice*, p. 100.
82. 'STD/HIV Outreach among Sexual Networks of Men Who Have Sex With Men in Calcutta', Naz (Calcutta) Project, Kolkata (1996), <http://www.aegis.org/DisplayContent/download.aspx?type=pdf&sectionID=299635>.
83. Joseph, *Social Work Practice*, p. 100.
84. 'STD/HIV Outreach among Sexual Networks of Men Who Have Sex With Men in Calcutta', Naz (Calcutta) Project, Kolkata (1996).
85. Tom Boellstorff, 'But Do Not Identify as Gay: A Proleptic Genealogy of the MSM Category', *Cultural Anthropology* 26 (2011), pp. 287–312, here p. 291.
86. '1st Baseline Study', The Humsafar Trust, Mumbai (2000), <http://www.humsafar.org/research_papers.htm>
87. Reddy, 'Geographies of Contagion', p. 262.
88. Cohen, 'The Kothi Wars', p. 284.
89. Cohen, 'The Kothi Wars', p. 271.
90. '4th Baseline Study', The Humsafar Trust, Mumbai (2005), <http://www.humsafar.org/research_papers.htm>
91. Boellstorff, 'But Do Not Identify as Gay', p. 298.
92. Ashok Row Kavi, 'Criminalizing high-risk groups such as MSM', *Infochange Agenda* (2008), <http://infochangeindia.org/agenda/hiv/aids-big-questions/criminalising-high-risk-groups-such-as-msm.html>
93. NACO, *Targeted Interventions under NACP III: Operational Guidelines*, vol. 1: p. 12.
94. Foucault, *Security, Territory, Population*, p. 118.
95. NACO, *Targeted Interventions under NACP III: Operational Guidelines*, vol. 1: p. 26.
96. For a critique of funding structures and priorities, see 'Chasing Numbers, Betraying People: Relooking at HIV Related Services in Karnataka', Aneka and Karnataka Sexual Minorities Forum, Bangalore (2012), <http://www.awid.org/News-Analysis/New-Resources2/A-New-Resource-Aneka-and-Karnataka-Sexual-Minorities-Forum-KSMF-Chasing-Numbers-Betraying-People-Relooking-at-HIV-Related-Services-in-Karnataka>
97. NACO, *Targeted Interventions under NACP III: Operational Guidelines*, vol. 1: p. 13.

98. Arunavo Nath, 'Noorjahan', *Padakshep* 1 (2008), pp. 15–16; 'Rural gays dominate rally', *The Asian Age*, 30 June 2003, p. 3.

99. West Bengal State AIDS Prevention & Control Society, *Advertisement for Inviting Applications from CBOs for Empanelment* (Calcutta: Government of West Bengal, 2011).

100. On the emergence of 'transgender' as a distinct category from 'gay', see David Valentine, *Imagining Transgender: The Ethnography of a Category* (Durham: Duke University Press, 2007).

101. Michel Foucault, *Security, Territory, Population*, p. 118.

102. Chatterjee, *Lineages of Political Society*, p. 199.

103. Guha, 'The Politics of Identity', p. 161.

INDEX

Note: Page numbers in *italics* refer to Figures or Tables.

Abdurahman, Abdullah   166–7
Abramenko, Andrik   25
Abrams, Lynn   158, 173
activist citizens, Iran   288–90, 298
Actor-Network-Theory (ANT)   127–8, 136, 148–9
Adaima   181–2, 184, 186–95
Adams, Hope Bridget   134
Administration of Estates Act, UK   199
Africa   91
   gender historiography   82, 91–2
agency   194
Ahmed, Sara   288
Ahudi   88
Akhtar   322
Alaba Ida   80–85, 90–91
   as a colonial intermediary   82–5
   as a public mother   84–5
   as a royal wife   82–4
Alákétu Onyegen   80, 84
Anderson, Benedict   307
androgyny   252
Annapurna   314, 317, 319
Annapurna-*mashi*   316–17, 324
antisemitism   219–20, 227
Anzaldúa, Gloria   248, 251
Appadurai, Arjun   307
archives   15–17, 189
   archival silences   15
   Bodichon, Barbara   63–4
   digital archive   101
Arghya   315
arranged marriages, migration and   271–2
Arrizón, Alicia   248
Asiwaju, A. I.   84
assaultive gaze   39–40, 52

Austin, J. L.   170
autobiographical performativity   64–5, 76
Avijit   315
azoospermia   134, 139, 145. *See also* male infertility

Baldanza, Frank   199
Bambara, Toni Cade   87
banquet, Roman   29–30, 41–2
Baradaran, Monireh   292–3
Barkawi, Tarak   282
Bayly, C. A.   307, 319
Beauvoir, Simone de   89, 265
Beigel, Hermann   141
Bek, Lisa   41
Bergmann, Bettina   36
Berry, Helen   137
Bijoy   323
binary model, *see* two-sex model
biographical methodology   200
black peril   184–5, 189, 193
Bodichon, Barbara Leigh Smith   61–77
   archive   63–4
   letters   61–2, 76–8
      to Bessie Parkes   66–8
      to Marian Evans   69–70, *73–4*, 75
      to William Allingham   73–4
   paintings   61–4, 76–8
      Sisters Working in our Fields   71–4, *71*
      Ye Newe Generation   68–9, *69*
   self-presentation as a female artist   62–3, 65–77
      professional status   68–70
   stance for women's right to a professional identity   63, 68–70, 74–5
   unresolved artistic self   76–7

Gender History Across Epistemologies, First Edition. Edited by Donna R. Gabaccia and Mary Jo Maynes.
Chapters © 2013 The Authors. Book compilation © 2013 Blackwell Publishing Ltd.

body, historical studies   133
Boellstorff, Tom   321
border crossing   8–13. *See also* migration
Borderlands/La Frontera, Teatro Campesino
        248, 256
boundary crossing   13–14
    categorical boundaries   282–8
    gender-bending performances, Teatro
        Campesino   248–9, 251–8
    gender-crossing
        hijra and *kothi*, India   305–25
        House of the Vettii wall paintings
            46–51
    gender historians   3–4
    interracial relationships   181, 183–7.
        See also migration
Boveri, Marcella   220, 222
Boveri, Theodor   219–20, 222, 230
Boyce, Paul   306, 320
Boydston, Jeanne   51, 80, 91, 183, 279,
        282
Bradley, Keith   26
Brady, Mary Pat   250
Bray, Bernard   236
Brighton, Shane   282
Brilliant, Richard   34
Broyles-González, Yolanda   247, 249,
        250–51, 253–4, 257
Burton, Antoinette   189
Butenandt, Adolf   219, 221, 228–30
Butler, General   164
Butler, Judith   62, 64, 216

calavera role, Teatro Campesino   252–7
Cameron Prinsep, Valentine   1
Canaday, Margot   270
Canning, Kathleen   175
Cape Women's Enfranchisement League
        (WEL)   170
case studies   136
Case, Sue-Ellen   249
categories
    disrupting boundaries   282–8
    gender as a category   279–80, 282
    'woman'   2
cervical incision, female infertility treatment
        141–2
Chamran, Mostafa   287, 297
channel maintainers   121
Chapin, Adele   172
chattels, *see* property

Chatterjee, Partha   307, 319
Chehabi, Houchang   282–3
Cherry, Deborah   62, 64, 70, 72
Chicana performers, *see* Teatro Campesino
childbirth, *see also* motherhood; mothers,
        status of
    medicalisation of   90
    symbolism of   82
    Chinese Exclusion Act (1882), United
        States   263, 268
chromosomes   215, 222–6
    gender equality and   222–5
    heredity theory   222
    sex determination   222–3, 225–8,
        230
    y-chromosome   223
Chumacero, Olivia   251, 256–7
cinema studies
    early Hollywood films   20–21, 52
    horror films   22, 40–41, 50
Clarke, Adele   139
Clarke, John   25, 28, 30, 33–4, 44
Clark, Joanna   87–8
Claxton, Ruth   1
Clover, Carol   22, 40–41, 50, 52
Cohen, Lawrence   305–6, 310–11, 319–20,
        322
Collins, Patricia Hill   87
conception, female orgasm relationship
        131. *See also* infertility
concordance lines   112–13, *112–13*,
        119–23, *121*
condoms
    HIV/AIDS prevention, India   323–4
    use in sperm collection   139
conflict studies   279–80
    feminist approaches   281–2, 298
    Iran   280–98
        behaviour during public mourning
            295–8
        disrupting categorical boundaries
            282–8
        gendered subjectivities   288–9
        male protector identity   293–5
        memoirs   287
        nation-building   289–90
        political prisoners   291–3
        wartime tactics   290
        women in employment   290–91
convivium   41–2
Cooper, Anna Julia   82, 85–7

corpus 100–102
  LOUGH corpus 103–5, *104–5*
  lovers' correspondence 235
corpus linguistics 6, 100
  concordance lines 112–13, *112–13,*
    119–23, 121
  emigrant letters analysis 100, 103–24
  gender differences in language 99–100
  Lough family correspondence 103–24
  n-grams 116, *117*
  type/token ratio 105–7, *106, 108*
  word clusters 116, *118*
  word frequencies 107–14
Corpus of Nineteenth-Century Scottish
    Correspondence 98
correspondence, *see* letters
Corridos, Teatro Campesino 254
Counsel Club, India 312, 320–21
Cowie, Elizabeth 62
Curling, J. B. 137–8
curved space concept 175

Dahomey 80
Dampier, Helen 62, 67
Daniel, Dominique 268
D'Arms, John 41–2
Daston, Lorraine 132
de Vos, Arnold 23–4
de Vos, Mariette 23–4
dhunuris, West Bengal 312–17, 322–3
Dictionary of National Biography, The
    (*DNB*) 199–200
digital archive 101
Diner, Hasia 264
dining room, Roman 41–2
Dinuzulu, Zulu king 162, 165
Dirks, Nicholas 307
discourse analysis 2
Donato, Katharine 262
Dossena, Marina 98–9
drag, *see* Teatro Campesino
Dum Dum Swikriti Society, India 312, 315,
    321
Dunbabin, Katharine 41
Dunne, Edward 102

El Fin Del Mundo, Teatro Campesino
    254
El Movimiento 246, 250, 257
Elshtain, Jean Bethke 279
Elspass, Stephan 98

El Teatro Campesino, *see* Teatro Campesino
embryology 226
emigrants, *see also* migration
  German 99
  Irish 97, 102–24, 271
  letter collections 97–100
    corpus linguistics 100, 103–24
    lovers' correspondence 236–7
    quantitative analysis 99–100, 124
  Scottish 98
English Woman's Journal, The 63
epigenetics 224
epistemological critiques 1
epistemological doubling 200–201, 210
Erickson, Charlotte 97
Esperanza, Phil 254
estate law, *see* property
eunuchs, India 306–25
  colonial ethnology 308–10
  institutional networks 320–22
  postcolonial ethnography 310–11
  rise of the *kothi* 319–20
  translocal consolidations 311, 317–19
  translocal subcultures 311–17
experience
  group experiences 182–3
  individual experience 182–4, 194–5
  representation of 182

Falconer, Janette 184–5
Fanon, Franz 288
Farjamfar, Soheila 293
female infertility 140–42
  early treatment 141–2
female orgasm, conception relationship
    131
fertilisation 222
fetishistic scopophilia 29, 39, 46–7
film studies
  early Hollywood films 20–21, 52
  horror films 22, 40–41, 50
  rape-revenge films 50
Finley, Moses 40
Foyster, Elizabeth 137
France, immigration to 262–5
  female immigrants 264–5
    as workers 267, 269–71
  gendered representations 269–71
  gender ratios 267
  racial aspects 268–9
  restrictions 267–8

Frederick, David 20–21, 29, 51–2
freedmen
  House of the Vettii owners 25
  status issues 28
  stereotype 27
  transition to 26–7
Freud, John 220
Friedan, Betty 86–7
Fun Club, India 311

gender 216, 265–6. *See also* gender
    history
  ambiguous nature, House of the Vettii wall
      paintings 29–31, 47–51
  as a category 279–80, 282
  assumed primaryness of 51–2
  concepts of 216–17
  hierarchies 132–3, 157
  issues in German scientific research
      218–22
  linguistic differences in meaning 12
  property rights and 198–211
  stereotypes 217
  gender crossing 50
  gender-bending performances, Teatro
      Campesino 248–9, 251–8
    calavera role 252–7
  gender/sexual identities, India 305–25.
      See also hijra, India; *kothi*, India
  intersexes 217, 219, 226–8
gendered language 6, 99–100, 123–4
  corpus studies 99–124
  lovers' correspondence 238–43
gender history 1–2, 127, 157
  as an alternative to 'women's history' 2
  boundary crossing 3–4
  discourse analysis 2
  epistemological disputes 2–3
  global dimensions 8
  quantitative data 3
  social constructivism 129
generation process 137
genes 223, 225, 227–8
genetics research, Germany 218–19
  chromosomes 222–6
  workplace gender issues 218–22
    technical assistants 221
Gerber, David 97–8, 237
germ cells 222
  gendered difference 222, 224–5
germ line theory 223–4

Germany
  genetics and hormone research
      218–20
    gender issues 220–22
    technical assistant 221
  German emigrants 99
gharanas, West Bengal 317–19
Gilbert, Scott 217
Girton College, Cambridge 63
Goldschmidt, Richard 219–21, 226–30
gonorrhoea, infertility relationship 134–5,
      142, 145
Goody, Jack 238
Goosen, Mrs 170–71
Gouges, Olympe de 217
Govinda 313–14, 322–3
group experiences 182–3
Guha, Ranajit 182
Guha, Sumit 307, 325
gynaecology 130
  sperm analysis relationships 140–43,
      146–7

Haji-Shah, Shalnaz 295
Hales, Shelley 28
Halliday, Michael 114
Hall, Kira 306, 309
Haraway, Donna 218
Hawkins, Francis 203
Helbich, Wolfgang 97
heredity 223
  chromosomal theory 222
  germline theory 223–4
  Mendelian laws of inheritance 223
Hermaphroditus, House of the Vettii wall
      paintings 47–51, *48–9*
Hertz, Mathilde 221
heteronormativity 289–90
heterosexuality 289–90
Higginbotham, Evelyn Brooks 89–90
hijra, India 306–9, 324–5
  colonial ethnology 308–9
  gharanas 312, 317–19
  language 313–14, 322–4
  postcolonial ethnography 310–11
  translocal consolidations 311, 317–19
  translocal subcultures 311–17
Hindson, Bethan 131
Hirschfield, Magnus 226
Hirsch, Pam 66, 69
historiographical knowledge 8

HIV-AIDs prevention, India 305–6,
       320–5
Hofmeyr, Jan 158, 168–70
Hollywood film studies 20–21, 52
homosexuality 226, 270, 305
   India 305–25. *See also hijra*, India; *kothi*,
       India
Honegger, Claudia 129
hormone research, Germany 218–20
   gender issues 218–22
   sex hormones 220, 228–30
   technical assistants 221
horror film studies 22, 40–41, 50
Hosseini, Zahra 294
House of the Vettii, Pompeii 20–52
   house arrangement 23–5, *24*
   lararium (shrine) 44–5
   owners 25–6, 46
   previous scholarly studies 27–31
   service areas 24–5, 43–4, *43*
   wall paintings 28–52
       arrangement 37–8, *38–9*
       gender-crossing 47–51
       gender focus 28–31, *30*, 44–6
       masochism 46–51
       master gaze 22, 35–46
       punishment theme 31–5, *32–9*, 36–42
       sexual themes 31–5, 38–40, 43–6, *43*
       slavery focus 21–2, 28, 31–46
       suffering 22
Hubbard, Ruth 217–18
Humsafar Trust 320, 322
Hunston, Susan 101
Hunt, Nancy Rose 89–90

immigration 262. *See also* France,
       immigration to; migration; United
       States, immigration to
   gendered aspects 269–71, 273–4
   gender ratios 266–8
   histories 263–5, 273–4
   restrictions 267–8
   women as workers 267
   India, gender/sexual identities 305–25
   colonial ethnology 308–10
   institutional networks 320–22
   postcolonial ethnography 310–11
   rise of the *kothi* 319–20
   translocal consolidations 311
   translocal subcultures 311–17
individual experience 182–4, 194–5

infertility 134
   female 140–42
       early treatment 141–2
   male 127, 134–5, 139–40, 142–3, 147–8
       sperm analysis 127, 135–40, 142–3,
           146–7
   patients' perspective 143–7
inheritance, genetic, *see* heredity
inheritance laws 198, 203
   intestate succession 203–6
institutional activism, West Bengal 320
interracial relationships 181, 183–7
   Adaima's story 181–2, 184, 186–95
   black peril 184–5, 189, 193
   white peril 186
intersexes 217–19, 226–8
intestate succession 203–6
   partial intestacy 204
Iran 280–81
   conflict studies 280–98
       behaviour during public mourning
           295–8
       disrupting categorical boundaries
           282–8
       gendered subjectivities 288–9
       male protector identity 293–5
       memoirs 287
       nation-building 289–90
       political prisoners 291–3
       wartime tactics 290
       women in employment 290–91
Irish emigrants 97, 102–3, 271
   Lough family correspondence analysis
       102–24

Jaber, Ghadeh 297
Jackson, Peter 305
Jacoby, Tami Amanda 293
Jameson Raid 162–3
Japanese picture brides 272
Jordanova, Ludmilla 133
Joshel, Sandra 25, 27–8

Kamphoefner, Walter 97
Kaplan, Temma 89
Kaviraj, Sudipta 307, 319
Kazamzadeh, Maryam 287
Kehrer, Ferdinand Adolph 139–42, 146
Kétu, Yoruba 80–81
Khanna, Akshay 306
Khomeini, Ayatollah Ruhollah 280

Kisch, Enoch Heinrich   134
Koloski-Ostrow, Ann Olga   20–21, 30–31,
		51
kothi, India   305–8, 322–5
	postcolonial ethnography 310–11
	rise of 319–20
	translocal consolidations 311

La Carpa de Los Rasquachis, Teatro
		Campesino 254
language   6, 239. *See also* letters; writing
	corpus 100–102
	corpus linguistics 6, 100–124
	emigrant letters 97–100
		quantitative studies 99–100, 124
	gender differences 99–100, 123–4
	linguistic differences 12
	lovers' correspondence 235
	sexual identity, India 313–14, 322–4
La Pastorela, Teatro Campesino   250
Laqueur, Thomas   41, 127, 129–32
Las Dos Caras del Patroncito, Teatro
		Campesino 250
Latour, Bruno   136, 149
laws of inheritance   198, 203
	intestate succession 203–6
	Mendelian, *see* heredity
Leach, Eleanor Windsor   28
Lenz, Fritz   227–8
lesbian, gay, bisexual and transgender
		(LGBT) identities 305. *See also*
		eunuchs, India; homosexuality
letters   5–7, 10–11, 161, 174
	as autobiographical acts 62–5
	Barbara Bodichon 61–2, 64–5
		historical knowledge gathered from
			76–7
		to Bessie Parkes 66–8
		to Marian Evans 69–70, *73–4*, 75
		to William Allingham 73–4
	lovers' correspondence study 235–43
		characteristics of love letters 237
		gender and language 238–43
	migrant letters 97–100, 236–7
		corpus linguistics 100, 103–24
		Lough family correspondence
			102–24
	Olive Schreiner 160–68, 173–5
		performative character 170–73, 175
		to brother Will Schreiner 162–6,
			171–2

	to Jan Hofmeyr 168–70
	to John X. Merriman 166–8
	political letters 162
	quantitative analysis 99–100, 124
Levy, Dr Josef   144
Lorber, Judith   239
Lorde, Audre   288
Lorenz, Katharina   20, 28, 36
Lough family   102–3
	correspondence, corpus linguistics
		103–24
love letters, analysis of   235–43
	characteristics of love letters 237–8
	gender and language 238–43
Luibhéid, Eithne   270

Madhya Banglar Sangram, India   312, 314,
		322, 324
Malan, Francois Stephanus   158, 166–7
male gaze, twentieth-century cinema   20
male infertility   127, 134–5, 139–40, 142–3,
		147–8
	sperm analysis 127, 135–40, 142–3,
		149–50
		collection methods 138–9
		patients' perspective 143–7
Mama, Amina   91
Marks, Shula   194
Marrero, Maria   252
Married Women's Property Act (1870), UK
		199
martyrdom, Iran   294–5
	behaviour of wives of martyrs 295–8
masochism, House of the Vettii wall
		paintings 46–52
masochistic aesthetic   22
Massad, Joseph   305
Massumi, Brian   288
master gaze, House of the Vettii wall
		paintings 22, 35–46
masturbation, use in sperm collection   139
maternalism   88–9
Matrimonial Causes Act (1857), UK   199
matrimonial migration   271–2
Matthiessen, Christian   114
Mau, August   23
Mauco, Georges   270
McClary, Susan   241–2
McClintock, Barbara   221
McCulloch, Jock   185
McLelland, Nicola   98–100, 108, 118, 124

medical history   4, 135. *See also* infertility
  social constructivism   129, 132–3
  medicalisation
  childbirth   90
  female body   130
  male body   127, 130–31, 150
Mendelian laws of inheritance   223
men who have sex with men (MSM), India
      321–5
Merriman, John Xavier   158, 166–8
mestiza performances, Teatro Campesino
      247–8, 256–8
migration   8–10, 237, 262. *See also*
      emigrants; immigration
  gender and   265–6
    figures   266–8
      gender impact on migration   271–2
      migration impact on gender   272–3
      representations   268–71
      women as workers   267, 269–71
    matrimonial migration   271–2
    migrant letters   236–7
Miller, Kerby   97, 102
Millin, Sarah Gertrude   186
Mohanty, Chandra   80
Moloy   315–16
Moraga, Cherríe   248, 251
Morokvasic, Mirjana   262
motherhood   85–90. *See also* childbirth
  Iran   290–92
  public motherhood   81–2, 84–5
  racial influences   85–7
mothers, status of   81–2, 85–6. *See also*
      public motherhood
  versus wives   81–2
Mouritsen, Henrik   25–6
Müller, Paul   134
Mulvey, Laura   20, 27–9, 31, 46–7, 52
Muñoz, José   250
Murnaghan, Sheila   28
Muth, Susanne   36

Naegeli, Ernst   222
Najmabadi, Afsaneh   279
Naremore, James   199
National AIDS Control Organisation
      (NACO), India   322
national historiographies   8
nation-building, Iran   280–81, 289–90,
      298
Natives Land Act 1913, South Africa   167

nature   216–18
Naz Foundation International (NFI)   320,
      322
  Calcutta project   312, 320–22
n-grams   116, *117*
Nielsen, Laura D.   250
Nigeria, 1929 Women's War   88–9
Nnaemeka, Obioma   92
Noeggerath, Emil   142, 145
Nouri, Maryam   292
Nurmi, Arja   98, 108, 118
Nye, Robert   130

Ogundipe-Leslie, Molara   92
Ogunwemi, Chikwenye   81
Oliensis, Ellen   40
Olmos, Edward James   253
O'Mahony, Canice   102
O'Mahony, Eilish   102
one-sex model   41, 130, 132
opera   241–2
Orlando, Virginia Woolf   198–200, 202–11
Ostrow, Steven   25
othermothers   87
Oudshoorn, Nelly   128
Oyĕwùmí, Oyèrónké   81

Pahlavi Monarchy, Iran   280, 282–3
pain for pleasure theme   50
  House of the Vettii wall paintings
      38–40
paintings   7. *See also* House of the Vettii,
      Pompeii
  as autobiographical acts   62–3, 65
  Barbara Bodichon   61–5
    historical knowledge gathered from
      76–7
    Sisters Working in our Fields   71–4, *71*
    Ye Newe Generation   68–9, *69*
Palander-Collin, Minna   98, 108, 118
Palma, Loris   235–43
Parker, Holt   40
Parkes, Bessie Rayner   62, 66, 69
Park, Katherine   130
parthenogenesis   224
partial intestacy   204
Pérez, Emma   248
performativity concept   62–3
  autobiographical performativity   64–5,
      76
  performative letters   170–3, 175

personal property   204–5, 208. *See also*
        property
Petersen, Lauren Hackworth   27
Peters, Willem   23
Petris, Antonietta   235–43
Petronius   27
Peyer, Alexander   138
Piore, Michael   262
Plaatje, Solomon   186
political letters   162. *See also* letters;
        Schreiner, Olive
political prisoners, Iran   291–3, 297–8
Pompeii   23, *23*. *See also* House of the
        Vettii, Pompeii
Portman Hall infant school, London
        63
positionality   282–8
Postcard (At the Golden Gate) 2009   1
power relationships   31, 42, 52. *See also*
        status issues
    sexuality and   40–41
Preston, Lawrence   308
primatology   218
primogeniture   199, 202
professional status. *See also* women's
        suffrage campaign
    Barbara Bodichon   68–70
    Iranian women   290–91
    scientific research, Germany   220–22
        women's right to   63, 68–70, 74–5
property   201–2
    intestate succession   203–6
    lack of   205
    personal property   204–5, 208
    real property   203–11
        as an encumbrance   206–7
    rights   198–211
proposals   114, *116*
propositions   114, *116*
propriety   201–2
psychoanalytic theory   31, 50
public motherhood   81–2, 84–5. *See also*
        mothers, status of
punishment
    House of the Vettii wall paintings   31–9,
        32–9
        eroticised nature   38–42, 52
    slavery relationship   36–41

quantitative data   3
    emigrant letters   99–100, 124

racial issues   85–90
    antisemitism   219–20, 227
    immigration, France and United States
        268–9
    interracial relationships   181, 183–7
    motherhood   85–7
    racial hygiene   227
    South Africa   158–60, 166–7
Rader, Karen   217
Rahim   323
Raitt, Suzanne   199–200, 208
Ram   314–15, 322
Ranaghat, West Bengal   315–6
Ranajay   312–13, 321, 323
Rand, Erica   270
Ranjana   317–18
rape
    conflict studies, Iran   286, 294
    penalties, Rhodesia   185
rape-revenge films   50
Ravenstein, E. G.   266
reactive gaze   39
real property   203–11. *See also* property
    as an encumbrance   206–7
Reddy, Gayatri   306, 309–10, 319
Redford, Bruce   237
reflexivity   238
Rhodes, Cecil   160, 162, 167
Rhodesia   184–5
Richardson, Sarah   217
Rodriguez, Diane   247–52, 255, 257
Rodriguez, Marco   253
Roman slavery, *see* slavery
Rose, Carol   201
Rose, Margaret   246
Rossetti, William   65–6
Rostovtzeff, Michael   27
Roth, Henry   272
royal wives, status issues   82–4. *See also*
        wives, status of

Sackville-West, Vita   199, 210
sadistic voyeurism   29, 46–7
Sadr, Shadi   292
Saller, Richard   26, 38
Sandoval, Chela   248, 251
Sanger, Charles Percy   198–9, 203–5, 210
Sarswata   312, 321, 324
Sayad, Abdelmalek   271
Scagliarini, Daniela Corlàita   28
Schacht, Steven   248

Schayegh, Cyrus   282
Schefold, Karl   34
Schmidt, Frau   141
Schreiner Letters Project   157–8
Schreiner, Olive   157–8
  letters   160–68, 173–5
    performative character   170–73, 175
  political influence   160–62, 173–5
    over brother Will Schreiner   162–6
    over Jan Hofmeyr   168–70
    over John X. Merriman   166–8
  published writings   157, 160, 163, 165–6
Schreiner, Will   157–8, 162–6
Schrier, Arnold   102
science   4
  genetics and hormone research, Germany
      218–19
    gender issues   218–22
    technical assistants   221
Scottish emigrants   98–9
Scott, Joan   2, 31, 91, 133, 182–3, 265
Scott, Mike   121
separate spheres   158–60, 174–5
  South Africa   174–5
sex   216
sex determination   215–16
  genetics and hormone research   218–19
    chromosomal sex determination
        222–3, 225–8, 230
      sex hormones   228–30
  historical studies   217–19
sex difference   2, 129, 216
  genetics and hormone research   218–19
    chromosomal basis   225–6
    sex hormones   228–30
  hereditary nature   219
sex hormones   220, 228–30
sexuality
  House of the Vettii wall paintings   31–5,
      38–40, 43–6, *43*
  power relationships   40–41
  slavery relationships   40–41, 43–4
Sharif, Sheikh   294
Shepard, Todd   270
Shikube   185
Shyamoli-*ma*   316, 322
Siddall, Elizabeth   62
sign 'woman'   62
Sims, James Marion   138–9, 141
Singana   184–5
Skinner, Marilyn   29, 40

slavery   26–7
  as focus of House of the Vettii wall
      paintings   21–2, 28, 31–46
  enslaved black women   86
  punishment relationship   36–41
  sexuality relationships   40–41, 43–4
  status issues   26, 42–3
  transition to freedom   26–7
Smith, Paul   65
Smith, Sidonie   64–5
Smuts, Jan   172
social constructivism   128–33
  in gender studies   129
  in history of medicine   129, 132–3
social essentialism   127
Sogliano, Antonio   23
Sommer, Ulrike   97
South Africa   157–61. *See also* Schreiner,
      Olive
  racial structure   158–60, 166–7
  separate spheres   174–5
  women's suffrage campaign   165, 167–8,
      171
South African War 1899–1902   162, 164,
      172
sperm analysis   127, 135–50
  case study   144
  collection methods   138–9
  gender significance in introduction of
      sperm testing   149–50
  patients' perspective   143–7
spermatozoa   137, 222–3
Spivak, Gayatri Chakravorty   194
Stanley, Liz   62, 67
status issues, *see also* power relationships
  banquet as social status display   41
  freedmen   28
  gender hierarchies   132–3, 157
  sexuality relationships   40–41
  slaves   26, 42–3
  wives   81–2
    royal wives   82–4
    subordination   81–2
    versus mothers   81–2
Stephen, Sir Leslie   199–200
stereotypes
  eastern females   1
  freedmen   27
  gender   217
    Teatro Campesino productions   247
sterility, *see* infertility

Stetson, Dorothy   199
Stevens, Nettie M.   219, 225
stiwanism   92
Stolberg, Michael   132
Stoler, Ann Laura   189
Subhash   316
suffering theme, House of the Vettii wall
     paintings   22

Taghati, Saham   294
Taylor, Diana   246
Teatro Campesino   246–58
   gender-bending performances   248–9,
     251–8
     calavera role   252–7
   history   249–52
   mestiza performances   247–8, 256–8
   stereotypes of gender roles   247
technical assistants, German scientific
     research   221
Thomas, William I.   97
Thompson, Mary Lee   33–4, 36
Toolan, Michael   107
torture, *see* punishment
travellers   75
Tribble, Chris   121
Trimalchio vision   27
two-sex model   130, 132, 216. *See also*
     intersexes
   chromosomes and   225–8
   criticisms   217–18
   sex hormones and   228–30
Tynan, Kate   102
type/token ratio   105–7, *106*, *108*

Underwood, Lisa   248
United States, immigration to   262–5
   female immigrants   264–5
     as workers   267, 269–71
   gendered representations   269–71
   gender ratios   267
   racial aspects   268
   restrictions   267–8
     Chinese Exclusion Act, 1882   263, 268

Valdez, Luis   246–7
Valdez, Socorro   251–6
Vettius Conviva, A.   25, 42, 52
   status as freedman   25
Vettius Restituti, A.   25, 52
   status as freedman   25–6

Vickers, Jill   279
Virchow, Rudolf   138

Walker, Eric   162–6
Wallace-Hadrill, Andrew   28, 30, 43
Walton, F. P.   199
war, *see* conflict studies
Watson, Julia   64–5
Watson, Peggy   175
ways of knowing   2–3
Weismann, August   222–4
West Bengal
   gender/sexual identity subcultures
     311–17
   hijra consolidation   317–19
   institutional networks   320–22
   rise of the *kothi*   319–20
white peril   186
widow's quarantine   205
Wilson, Edmund   219, 225
Wirth, Theo   34–7
wives, status of   81–2
   royal wives   82–4
   versus mothers   81–2
Wollstonecraft, Mary   217
'woman'
   category of   2
   sign   62
women's suffrage campaign, South Africa
     165, 167–8, 171
Women's War, Nigeria (1929)   88–9
Woolf, Virginia   198–9, 203, 210
   Orlando   198–200, 202–11
words as performances   5
Wright, Marcia   194
writing   202. *See also* letters
   as personal property   205, 208–9
   Olive Schreiner   157, 160, 163,
     165–6
Wyke, Maria   29

y-chromosome   223
Yarbro-Bejarano, Yvonne   247–9, 251–2
Yá Shegén   80, 83–5
Yooung, Tim   75
Yoruba   81

Zanker, Paul   42
Ziegner, Erika von   221, 228
Znaniecki, Florian   97
Zulu king Dinuzulu   162, 165